ZAPS: The Norton Psychology Labs give students a firm understanding

of fundamental concepts by allowing them to experience psychological phenomena firsthand, taking the role of either subject or researcher in engaging, diverse experiments and demonstrations. Ideal for cognitive psychology courses, these groundbreaking online labs are a fun and unique way for students to learn core principles.

A total of 60 ZAPS labs are available for student use, with the following three new experiments recently added:

- **Depth of Processing:** Students learn that the way information is processed influences how well it is remembered.
- **Dual-Coding Theory:** Students participate in an experiment that explores the differences between visual and verbal representations of information.
- **Object-Based Attention:** Students test their ability to keep their attention focused on specific objects.

A **class results** feature allows instructors to collect ZAPS data for the experiments performed by the students in their courses.

The ZAPS Norton Psychology Labs are also closely integrated into the *Cognition*, Fourth Edition, **Student StudySpace**: wwnorton.com/studyspace.

Additional Package Option:

The **ZAPS Workbook** gives students detailed instructions for completing each experiment, explanations of the psychological phenomenon that each experiment explores, and a worksheet of critical-thinking questions to be filled in and handed to the instructor.

See ZAPS in action

Consistent Four-Part Pedagogy

The four-part pedagogy of ZAPS clarifies the concepts behind each experiment:

An **Introduction** helps students connect each experiment to a concrete, real-world example.

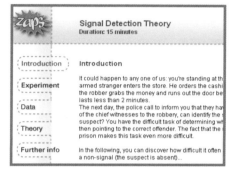

An **Experiment** allows students to experience psychological phenomena in the role of subject or researcher. Where appropriate, a Data section with a detailed breakdown of results follows the experiment. Instructors can collect aggregate class data.

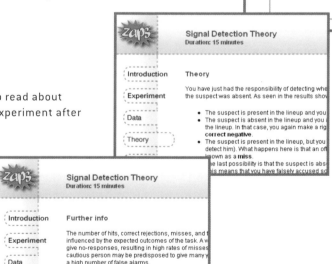

A **Theory** section allows students to read about the theoretical basis behind each experiment after completion.

A **Further Info** section offers students additional real-world examples or discussion of similar phenomena.

See more at wwnorton.com/zaps.

COGNITION

FOURTH EDITION

COGNITION
Exploring the Science of the Mind

Daniel Reisberg
Reed College

W. W. Norton & Company
New York • London

W. W. Norton & Company has been independent since its founding in 1923, when William Warder Norton and Mary D. Herter Norton first published lectures delivered at the People's Institute, the adult education division of New York City's Cooper Union. The firm soon expanded its program beyond the Institute, publishing books by celebrated academics from America and abroad. By midcentury, the two major pillars of Norton's publishing program—trade books and college texts—were firmly established. In the 1950s, the Norton family transferred control of the company to its employees, and today—with a staff of four hundred and a comparable number of trade, college, and professional titles published each year—W. W. Norton & Company stands as the largest and oldest publishing house owned wholly by its employees.

Copyright © 2010, 2006, 2001, 1997 by W. W. Norton & Company, Inc.

Editor: Sheri L. Snavely
Editorial Assistant: Wamiq Jawaid
Ancillaries Editors: Rachel Comerford and Matthew Freeman
Project Editor: Rebecca A. Homiski
Copyeditor: Alice Vigliani
Art Directors: Rubina Yeh and Hope Miller Goodell
Book Design: Lisa Buckley
Composition and Layout: Matrix Publishing Services
Manufacturing: The Courier Companies—Westford, MA
Senior Production Manager, College: Benjamin Reynolds

Library of Congress Cataloging-in-Publication Data
Reisberg, Daniel.
  Cognition: exploring the science of the mind / Daniel Reisberg—4th ed.
    p. cm.
  Includes bibliographical references and index.
  ISBN: 978-0-393-93048-1 (hardcover)
  1. Cognitive psychology. I. Title.
  BF201.R45   2010
  153—dc22

                                                    2009015568

W. W. Norton & Company, Inc., 500 Fifth Avenue, New York, N.Y. 10110
www.wwnorton.com
W. W. Norton & Company Ltd., Castle House, 75/76 Wells Street, London W1T 3QT

  4567890

For Friderike

Contents

Preface

I was a college sophomore when I took my first course in cognitive psychology. I was excited about the course then, and I've been excited about the field ever since. Why? First, cognitive psychologists are asking terrific questions. Some of the questions concern broad issues that have intrigued humanity for thousands of years. Why do we think the things we think? Why do we believe the things we believe? What is "knowledge," and how *secure* (how complete, how accurate) is our knowledge of the world around us?

Other questions asked by cognitive psychologists are of a more immediate, personal, concern: How can I help myself to remember more of the material that I'm studying in my classes? Is there some better way to solve the problems I encounter? Why is it that my roommate can study with the radio on, but I can't?

And sometimes the questions have important consequences for our social or political institutions: If an eyewitness reports what he saw at a crime, should we trust him? If a newspaper raises questions about a candidate's integrity, how will voters react?

Of course, we want more than interesting questions—we also want *answers* to these questions, and this is the second reason I find cognitive psychology so exciting. In the last half-century, the field has made extraordinary progress on many fronts, providing us with a rich understanding of the nature of memory, the processes of thought, and the content of knowledge. There are many things still to be discovered—that's part of the fun. Even so, we already have something to say about all of the questions just posed and many more as well. We can speak to the specific questions and to the general, to the theoretical issues and to the practical. Our research has uncovered principles useful for improving the process of education and we have made discoveries of considerable importance for the courts. What I've learned as a cognitive psychologist has changed how I think about my own memory; it's changed how I make decisions; it's changed how I draw conclusions when I'm thinking about events in my life.

On top of all this, I'm excited about the connections that cognitive psychology makes possible. In the modern academic world, intellectual disciplines are often isolated from each other, sometimes working on closely related problems without even realizing it. In the last decades, though, cognitive psychology has forged rich connections with its neighboring disciplines, and in this book we will touch on topics in philosophy, economics, biology, linguistics, politics, computer science, and medicine. These connections bring obvious benefits, since insights and information can be traded back and forth between the domains. In addition, these connections highlight the importance of the material we will be examining, since these connections make it clear that the issues before us are of interest to a wide range of scholars. This provides a strong signal that we are working on questions of considerable power and scope.

I have tried in this text to convey all this excitement. I've done my best to describe the questions being asked within my field, and the substantial answers we can provide for these questions, and finally, some indications of how cognitive psychology is (and has to be) interwoven with other intellectual endeavors.

I also had other goals in writing this text. In my own teaching, I try to maintain a balance among many different elements: the nuts and bolts of how our science proceeds, the data provided by the science, the practical implications of our findings, and the theoretical framework that holds all of these pieces together. I've tried to find the same balance in this text.

In addition, I try throughout this book to "tell a good story," one that conveys how the various pieces of our field fit together into a coherent package. As part of this effort, I've emphasized the flow of ideas—how new theories lead to new experiments, and how those experiments can lead to new theory. I've also emphasized the ways in which different forms of evidence weave together—so that, for example, the coverage of neuroscience is not just used to tell students which brain areas seem associated with which function; instead, the neuroscience is used to address the psychological questions that have long been of interest to the field.

The notion of telling a "good story" also emerges in another way: I've always been impressed by the ways in which the different parts of cognitive psychology are interlocked. Our claims about attention, for example, have immediate implications for how we can theorize about memory; our theories of object recognition are linked to our proposals for how knowledge is stored in the mind. Linkages like these are intellectually satisfying, because they ensure that the pieces of the puzzle really do fit together. But, in addition, these linkages make the material within cognitive psychology easier to learn, and easier to remember. Indeed, if I were to emphasize one crucial fact about memory, it would be that memory is best when the memorizer perceives the organization and interconnections within the material being learned. (We'll discuss this point further in Chapter 5.) With an eye on this point, I've therefore made sure to highlight the interconnections among various topics, so that students can appreciate the beauty of our field, and can also be helped, in their learning, by the orderly nature of our theorizing.

I've also worked hard to help students in two other ways. First, I've tried throughout the book to make sure the prose is approachable. I want students to gain a sophisticated understanding of the material in this text, but I certainly don't want students to struggle with the ideas. Therefore, I've kept the presentation as straightforward as possible, and have attempted to keep the presentation focused for students by highlighting the main themes that bind our field together. This edition is streamlined for increased clarity, and we've also added more illustrations to facilitate student understanding.

Second, I have, in this edition, taken several steps to form a stronger "alliance" with readers. My strategy here grows out of the fact that, like most teachers, I value the questions I receive from students, and the discussions I have with them. In the classroom, this allows a two-way flow of information, which unmistakably improves the educational process. Of course, this two-way flow is not possible in a textbook, but I've offered what I think is a good approximation: Often, the questions I hear from students, and the discussions I have with them, focus on the relevance of the material we're covering—relevance to students' own lives, or relevance to the world outside of academics. In this edition, I've tried to present my answers to these student questions, and to re-create the discussions, in *The Cognition Workbook* (and I'll say more about the *Workbook* in a moment). I hope in this way to make sure that students see that the material is relevant to their lives—and perhaps also as exciting for them as it is for me.

Have I met all of these goals? You, the readers, will need to be the judge of this. I would love to hear from you about what I have done well in the book, and what I could have done better; what I've covered (but should have omitted) and what I've left out. I'll do my best to respond to every comment. You can reach me via regular mail (at Reed College) or via e-mail (reisberg@reed.edu).

The book's fifteen chapters are designed to cover the major topics within cognitive psychology. The first section of this book lays the foundation. Chapter 1 provides the conceptual and historical background for the subsequent chapters. In addition, this chapter seeks to convey the extraordinary scope of this field and why, therefore, research on cognition is so important. This chapter also highlights the relationship between theory and evidence in cognitive psychology, and discusses the logic on which this field is built.

Chapter 2 then offers a brief introduction to the study of the brain. Most of cognitive psychology is concerned with the functions that our brains make possible, and not the brain itself. Nonetheless, our understanding of cognition has certainly been enhanced by the study of the brain, and, throughout this book, we will use biological evidence as one means of evaluating our theories. (Indeed, one of the trends across this book's various editions has been an increased presentation of the relevant neuroscience.) Chapter 2 is designed to make this evidence fully accessible to the reader—by providing a quick survey of the research tools used in studying the brain, an overview of the brain's anatomy, and also an example of how we can use brain evidence as a source of insight into cognitive phenomena.

In the second section of the book, we consider the problems of object recognition, and then the problem of attention. Chapter 3 discusses how we recognize the objects that surround us. This seems a straightforward matter—what could be easier than recognizing a telephone, or a coffee cup, or the letter *Q*? As we will see, however, recognition is surprisingly complex. Chapter 4 then considers what it means to "pay attention." The first half of the chapter is concerned largely with selective attention, in which one seeks to focus on a target while ignoring distractors. The second half of the chapter is concerned with divided attention, in which one seeks to focus on more than one target, or more than one task, at the same time. Here, too, we will see that seemingly simple processes often turn out to be more complicated than one might suppose.

The third section turns to the broad problem of memory. Chapters 5, 6, and 7 start with a discussion of how information is "entered" into long-term storage, but then turn to the complex interdependence between how information is first learned and how that same information is subsequently retrieved. A recurrent theme in this section is that learning that is effective for one sort of task, one sort of use, may be quite ineffective for other uses. This theme is examined in several contexts, and leads to a discussion of current research on unconscious memories—so-called "memory without awareness." These chapters also offer a broad assessment of human memory: How accurate are our memories? How complete? How long-lasting? These issues are pursued both with regard to theoretical treatments of memory, and also the practical consequences of memory research, including the application of this research to the assessment, in the courtroom, of eyewitness testimony.

The book's fourth section is about knowledge. Earlier chapters showed over and over that humans are, in many ways, guided in their thinking and experiences by what they already know—i.e., the broad pattern of knowledge they bring into each new experience. This invites the questions posed by Chapters 8, 9, 10, and 11: What is knowledge? How is it represented in the mind? Chapter 8 examines the idea that knowledge can be represented via a complex network, and includes a discussion of associative networks in general and connectionist modeling in particular. Chapter 9 turns to the question of how "concepts," the building blocks of our knowledge, are represented in the mind. Chapters 10 and 11 focus on two special types of knowledge. Chapter 10 examines our knowledge about language, with discussion both of *linguistic competence* and *linguistic performance*. Chapter 11 considers *visual knowledge* and examines what is known about mental imagery.

The chapters in the fifth section are concerned with the topic of thinking. Chapter 12 examines how each of us draws conclusions from evidence—including cases in which we are trying to be careful and deliberate in our judgments, and also cases of informal judgments of the sort we often make in our everyday lives. Chapter 13 turns to the question of how we reason from our beliefs—how we check on whether our beliefs are correct, and how we draw conclusions, based on things we already believe. Both of these chapters examine the strategies that guide our thinking, and some of the ways that these strategies can, on occasion, lead to error. The chapters then turn to the pragmatic issue of how these errors can be diminished through education. Chapter 13 also discusses how we make decisions and choices, with a special focus first on "economic" theories of decision-making, and then on some of the seeming "irrationality" in human decision-making. Next, Chapter 14 considers how we solve problems. The first half of the chapter discusses problem-solving strategies of a general sort, useful for all problems; the chapter then turns to more specialized strategies, and with this, the topic of expertise. The chapter concludes with a discussion of the role of creativity and insight within problem solving.

The final chapter in the book does double service. First, it pulls together many of the strands of contemporary research relevant to the topic of consciousness—what consciousness is, and what consciousness is for. In addition, most students will reach this chapter at the end of a full semester's work, a point at which students are well served by a review of the topics already covered, and also a point at which students are ill served by the introduction of much new material. Therefore, this chapter draws most of its themes and evidence from previous chapters, and in that fashion serves as a review for many points that appear earlier in the book. By the same token, Chapter 15 highlights the fact that we are using these materials to approach some of the greatest questions ever asked about the mind, and, in that way, this chapter should help to convey some of the power of the material we have been discussing throughout the book.

This basic structure of the book is the same as it was in the previous editions. But much has changed in this edition. I have, of course, updated all chapters, to include important new research. In particular, I've expanded the neuroscience coverage in many areas. As just one example, I've now said much more about the neuroimaging data that help us understand the contrast between *familiarity* and *source memory*. (These two forms of memory are established by different mechanisms, each served by its own brain sites; and then are used via different processes, each involving its own sites.) Other examples are scattered throughout the entire text.

Also new for this edition is an element already mentioned: *The Cognition Workbook*. It's common these days for textbooks to come with supplementary materials, and, in most cases, these are written by people other than the book's author. For my book, however, I wanted supplements that were fully integrated with the text, truly emphasizing themes that were already in the book, but also carefully picking up on points that the text hadn't covered. In addition, any textbook is, in a way, a very personal endeavor—it is a particular author's view of the field—and I've always found it jarring when a text's supplementary materials took a perspective, or offered a view, that didn't line up well with the emphasis of the text itself.

It's for all of these reasons that I wanted to write the workbook myself, to make sure that you, the reader, got the best ancillary materials I could arrange, and also to make sure that you got ancillary materials that were completely in tune with the goals, themes, and emphases of the main text. The workbook includes two types of materials: First, in my own classroom, I include many demonstrations—usually miniature versions of experimental procedures—so that students can see for themselves what these experiments involve, and can also see just how powerful many of our effects are. The workbook contains adaptations of these classroom demonstrations, designed so that they can be used in whatever fashion an instructor (or the reader) wishes: Readers who want to run the demos for themselves, as they read along, certainly can. Instructors who want to run the demos within their classrooms (as I do) are certainly encouraged to do so. Instructors who want to use the demonstrations in discussion sections, aside from the main course, can do that as well. In truth, I suspect that some demos will work better in one of these venues, and that other demos will work better in others, but, in all cases, I hope the demos help bring the material to life—putting students directly in contact both with our experimental methods and our experimental results.

Second, in my own course, I often want to go beyond the information in the text itself. Part of this "going beyond" involves an emphasis on research methods, and so I've included, in the workbook, an essay for each chapter that explores key principles involved in our research. One essay, for example, works through the question of what a "testable hypothesis" is, and why this is so important; another essay works through the power of random assignment; another discusses how we deal with confounds. In all cases, my hope is that these essays will guide students toward a sophisticated understanding of why our research is as it is, and why, therefore, our research is so persuasive. In addition, each of the essays ends with a discussion question, so that students can think about, and *apply*, the issues being considered. (For instructors' and teaching assistants' use, I've also written guidelines for how a class might explore these discussion questions. This material is included with the online Test Bank.)

My own students are also eager to know how the material we're studying *matters*— for their own lives, or for the broader world. To help them think about this issue, I often draw on my own experience in working with law enforcement and the criminal justice system. In my work, I'm sometimes called on to help juries understand how an eyewitness might be certain in his recollection, but *mistaken*. I also sometimes work with police officers, to help them determine how to draw as much information from a witness as possible, without leading the witness in any way. Based on this experience, each chapter of the workbook also includes an essay that discusses how the material in that chapter might be useful for the legal system. This essay will, I hope, be immediately interesting for students, and will persuade them that the material they're studying has important real-world consequences. In turn, it's my hope that this will make it obvious to students why it's crucial that the science be done carefully and well—so that we bring only high-quality information into the legal system. And for these essays, too, I've written discussion questions (for students', instructors', *or* TAs' use), to help students think about these materials, and to explore the implications of what they're studying.

In addition, my students often seek "take-home messages" from the material that will, in a direct way, benefit them. We are, after all, talking about memory, and students obviously are engaged in an endeavor of putting lots of new information—information they're learning in their courses—into their memories! We're talking about attention, and students often struggle with the chore of keeping themselves "on task" and "on target." In light of these points of contact, I've written an essay for each chapter designed to build the bridge between the course materials and the concerns that often fill students' lives. This will, I hope, make the material more useful for students, and also make it clear just how important an enterprise cognitive psychology is!

Finally, let me turn to the happiest of chores—thanking all of those who have contributed to this book. I begin with those who helped with the previous editions: Bob Crowder (Yale University) and Bob Logie (University of Aberdeen) both read the entire text of the first edition, and the book was unmistakably improved by their insights. Other colleagues read, and helped me enormously with, specific chapters: Enriqueta Canseco-Gonzalez (Reed College); Rich Carlson (Pennsylvania State University); Henry Gleitman (University of Pennsylvania); Lila Gleitman (University of Pennsylvania); Peter Graf (University of British Columbia); John Henderson (Michigan State University); Jim Hoffman (University of Delaware); Frank Keil (Cornell University); Mike McCloskey (John Hopkins University); Hal Pashler (UCSD); Steve Pinker (MIT); and Paul Rozin (University of Pennsylvania).

The second edition was markedly strengthened by the input and commentary provided by these colleagues: Martin Conway (University of Bristol); Kathleen Eberhard (Notre Dame University); Howard Egeth (Johns Hopkins University); Bill Gehring (University of Michigan); Steve Palmer (University of California, Berkeley); Henry Roediger (Washington University); and Eldar Shafir (Princeton University).

In the third edition, I was again fortunate to have the advice, criticism, and insights provided by a number of colleagues who, together, have made the book better than it otherwise could have been, and I'd like to thank: Rich Carlson (Penn State); Richard Catrambone (Georgia Tech); Randall Engle (Georgia Tech); Bill Gehring and Ellen Hamilton (University of Michigan); Nancy Kim (Rochester Institute of Technology); Steve Luck (University of Iowa); Michael Miller (University of California, Santa Barbara); Evan Palmer, Melinda Kunar, and Jeremy Wolfe (Harvard University); Chris Shunn (University of Pittsburgh); and Daniel Simons (University of Illinois).

A number of colleagues also provided their insights and counsel for the fourth edition—either for the textbook itself or for *The Cognition Workbook*. I'm therefore delighted to thank: Ed Awh (University of Oregon); Glen Bodner (University of Calgary); William Gehring (University of Michigan); Katherine Gibbs (University of California, Davis); Eliot Hazeltine (University of Iowa); William Hockley (Wilfrid Laurier University); James Hoffman (University of Delaware); Helene Intraub (University of Delaware); Vikram Jaswal (University of Virginia); Karsten Loepelmann (University of Alberta); Penny Pexman (University of Calgary); and Christy Porter (College of William and Mary).

I also want to thank the people at Norton. Jon Durbin and I worked together for a dozen years, on many books, and built a bond of trust, respect, and good will that was an enormous resource for me. Jon has now moved to another corner of Norton's operations, and he'll be missed. I'm delighted, though, to be working with Jon's replacement, Sheri Snavely, whose energy and activity as an editor, even in the earliest stages of our collaboration, have already been of immense value. Also Rebecca Homiski, Ben Reynolds, and Wamiq Jawaid have done a fabulous job of keeping the production on track, on schedule, and of the highest quality. And Alice Vigliani continues to be a wonderful copyeditor, and I hope her peonies flourish forever.

Finally, it is Jacob, Solomon, and Friderike who make this all worthwhile. They forgive me the endless hours at the computer, but also (thank heavens) tug me away from the computer at the right moments. They remind me of what is important, and also keep my life on track. I couldn't do any of this without them.

Daniel Reisberg
Portland, Oregon

FOURTH EDITION

COGNITION

PART 1

The Foundations of Cognitive Psychology

What is cognitive psychology and what does it study? In Chapter 1, we define this discipline and offer an early sketch of what this field can teach us—through its theories and through its practical applications. We also provide a brief history, in order to explain why cognitive psychology takes the form that it does.

Chapter 2 has a different focus. In the last decade or two, cognitive psychology has formed a productive partnership with the field of *cognitive neuroscience*—the effort toward understanding our mental functioning by close study of the brain and nervous system. In this book, our emphasis will be on psychology, not neuroscience, but even so, we'll rely on neuroscience evidence at many points in our discussion. To make sure this evidence is useful, we need to provide some background, and that is the main purpose of Chapter 2. In that chapter, we provide a rough mapping of what's where in the brain, and we describe the functioning of many of the brain's parts. We also discuss the broad issue of *what it means* to describe the functioning of this or that brain region, because, as we will see, each of the brain's parts is enormously specialized in what it does. As a result, mental achievements like reading or remembering or deciding depend on the coordinated functioning of many different brain regions, with each region contributing its own small bit to the overall achievement.

The Science of the Mind

This is a book about our broad intellectual functioning. What's at stake, though, is far more than "intellectual functioning," because, as we will see, virtually everything that we do, and everything that we feel or say, depends on our *cognition*— what we know, what we remember, and how we think.

As one example, we will, in just a few pages, consider the way in which someone's ability to cope with grief depends on how memory functions. We will also discuss the role of memory in shaping someone's self-image—and hence their self-esteem. As a more basic example, we will also discuss a case in which your understanding of a simple story depends on the background knowledge that you supply. Similar claims can be made for virtually every conversation you participate in, and every social interaction you witness: In each of these settings, your ability to understand your world depends critically on knowledge you bring to the situation. Examples like these make it clear that cognition matters in an extraordinary range of circumstances, and it is on this basis, then, that our focus in this book is, in a real sense, on the intellectual foundations of almost every aspect of human experience.

Across the next fifteen chapters, we will ask how humans recognize objects in the world around them, and how they manage to pay attention to certain aspects of the world without being overwhelmed by the flood of other inputs available. We will ask how people place new information into their memories, and then how they draw this information out of memory and use it later on. We will ask how people solve problems, draw conclusions, and make decisions. In all of these cases, the immediate target of our discussion will be on the specifics of these cognitive processes. Our broader goal, however, is an understanding of the full range of events that *depend on* these processes—and that range turns out to include almost every bit of our behavior, our emotions, and our achievements!

3

■ This chapter begins with a sketch of the scope of cognitive psychology. The domain of this field includes activities that are obviously "intellectual" (like remembering, or attending, or making judgments), and also a much broader range of activities that *depend on* these intellectual achievements.

■ A brief review of the history of cognitive psychology highlights two essential themes. One is the idea that we cannot study the mental world by means of direct observation. The second theme is that we *must* study the mental world if we are to understand behavior; this

is because our behavior depends in crucial ways on how we *perceive* and *understand* the world around us.

■ Combining these themes, we are led to the view that we must study the mental world *indirectly*, but as we will see, the (inferential) method for doing this is the same method used by other sciences, including physics.

■ Finally, we consider an example of research in cognitive psychology, to illustrate the types of data that psychologists consider and the logic they use in testing their theories.

The Scope of Cognitive Psychology

When the field of cognitive psychology was first launched, it was generally understood as the *scientific study of knowledge*, and this conception of the field led immediately to a series of questions: How is knowledge acquired? How is knowledge retained so that it's available when needed? How is knowledge used—as a basis for action, or as a basis for generating further knowledge?

There are many reasons to seek answers to these questions, including a range of circumstances in which the answers might be quite useful. For example, imagine that you are studying for next Wednesday's exam, but for some reason the material just won't "stick" in your memory. You find yourself wishing, therefore, for a better strategy to use in studying and memorizing. What would that strategy be? Is it possible to have a "better memory"?

As a different case, let's say that while you're studying your friend is moving around in the room, and you find this to be quite distracting. Why can't you just shut out your friend's motion? Why don't you have better control over your attention and your ability to concentrate?

Here's one more example: You pick up the morning newspaper and are horrified to learn how many people have decided to vote for candidate X. How do people decide whom to vote for? For that matter, how do people decide what college to attend, or which car to buy, or even what to have for dinner? What forces drive our decisions?

Before we are through, we will consider evidence pertinent to all of these questions. Let's note, though, that in most of these cases, things aren't going as you might have wished: You fail to remember; you are unable to ignore a distraction; the voters make a choice you don't like. But what about the other side of things? What about the remarkable intellectual feats that humans achieve—brilliant deductions or creative solutions to complex problems? In this text, we will also have a lot to say about these cases, and thus how it is that we accomplish the great things we do.

Clearly, then, there is an important set of issues in play here, but even so, the questions just catalogued risk a misunderstanding, because they make it sound like cognitive psychology is concerned only with our functioning as intellectuals. As we said at the very start, though, the relevance of cognitive psychology is far broader than this—thanks to the fact that a huge range of our actions, thoughts, and feelings all depend on *knowledge*. To illustrate this point, let's look at the study of *memory* and ask: When we investigate how memory functions, what exactly is it that we are investigating? Or, to turn this around, what tasks rely on memory?

When you are taking an exam, you obviously rely on memory—memory for what you have learned during the term. Likewise, you rely on memory when you are at the supermarket and trying to remember the cheesecake recipe so you can buy the ingredients. You rely on memory when you are reminiscing about childhood. But what else draws on memory?

Consider this simple story (adapted from Charniak, 1972):

> Betsy wanted to bring Jacob a present. She shook her piggy bank. It made no sound. She went to look for her mother.

This four-sentence tale is easy to understand, but only because you provided some important bits of background yourself. For example, you weren't at all puzzled, as you read the story, about why Betsy was interested in her piggy bank; you weren't puzzled, specifically, about why the story's first sentence led naturally to the second. This is because you already knew (a) that the things one gives as presents are often things bought for the occasion (rather than things already owned), (b) that buying things requires money, and (c) that money is stored in piggy banks. Without these facts, you would have been bewildered about why a desire to give a gift would lead someone to her piggy bank. (Surely you did not think she intended to give the piggy bank itself as the present!) Likewise, you immediately understood why Betsy *shook* her piggy bank. You didn't suppose that she was shaking it in frustration or trying to find out if it would make a good percussion instrument. Instead, you understood that she was trying to determine its contents. But you knew this only because you already knew (d) that children don't keep track of how much money is in their bank, and (e) that one cannot simply look into the bank to learn its contents. Without these facts, Betsy's shaking of the bank would make no sense. Similarly, you understood what it meant that the bank made no sound. That's because you know (f) that it's usually coins (not bills) that are kept in piggy banks, and (g) that coins make noise when they are shaken. If you didn't know these facts, you might have interpreted the bank's silence, when it was shaken, as good news, indicating perhaps that the bank was jammed full of $20 bills—an inference that would have led you to a very different expectation for how the story would unfold from there.

Of course, there's nothing special about the "Betsy and Jacob" story, and so it seems likely that we'll encounter a similar reliance on background knowledge in many other settings. This clearly suggests that, in general, our understanding of stories or ordinary conversations depends on memory—depends on our drawing key bits of information from our storehouse of knowledge. Indeed, if we didn't supply this information, then anyone telling the "Betsy and Jacob" story would need to spell out all the connections and all the assumptions. That is, the story would have to include all the background facts that, *with* memory, are supplied by you. As a result, the story would have to be many times longer than it currently is, and the telling of it much slower. The same would be true for every story we hear, every conversation we participate in. Memory is thus crucial for each of these activities.

Here is a different sort of example: In Chapter 6, we will consider various cases of clinical amnesia—cases in which someone, because of brain damage, has lost the ability to remember certain materials. These cases are fascinating at many levels, including the fact that they provide us with key insights into what memory is for: Without memory, what is disrupted?

One well-studied amnesia patient was a man identified as H.M.; his memory loss was the unanticipated by-product of brain surgery intended to control his epilepsy, and the loss was quite profound. H.M. had no trouble remembering events prior to the surgery, but he seemed completely unable to recall any event that occurred after his operation. If asked who the president is, or about recent events, he reported facts and events that were current at the time of the surgery. If asked questions about last week, or even an hour ago, he recalled nothing.

The memory loss, of course, had massive consequences for H.M.'s life, and some of the consequences are perhaps surprising. For example, he had an uncle of whom he was very fond, and H.M. often asked about his uncle: How is he? What's he doing these days? Unfortunately, the uncle died sometime after H.M.'s surgery, and H.M. was told this sad news. The information came as a horrible shock, triggering enormous grief, but because of his amnesia, H.M. soon forgot about it.

Sometime later, H.M. again asked about his uncle and was once more told of the uncle's death. With no memory of having heard this news before, H.M. was again hearing it "for the first time," with the shock and grief every bit as strong as it was initially. Indeed, each time he heard this news, he was hearing it "for the first time." With no memory, he had no opportunity to live with the news, to adjust to it. Hence his grief could not subside. Without memory, H.M. had no way to come to terms with his uncle's death.

A different glimpse of memory function comes from H.M.'s poignant comments about his state and about "who he is." Each of us has a conception of who we are, of what sort of person we are. That conception is supported by numerous memories: We know whether we're deserving of praise for our good deeds or blame for our transgressions because we remember our good deeds and our transgressions. We know whether we've kept our promises or achieved our goals because, again, we have the relevant memories. None of this is true for people who suffer from amnesia, and H.M. sometimes commented on the fact that in important ways, he didn't know who he was. He didn't know if he should be proud of his accomplishments or ashamed of his crimes; he didn't know if he'd been clever or stupid, honorable or dishonest, industrious or lazy. In a sense, then, it would seem that without a memory, there is no self. (For broader discussion, see Hilts, 1995; M. Conway & Pleydell-Pearce, 2000.)

What, then, is the scope of cognitive psychology? As we mentioned earlier, this field is sometimes defined as the scientific study of the acquisition, retention, and use of knowledge. We have now seen, though, that these topics are relevant to an extraordinarily broad range of concerns. Our self-concept, it seems, depends on our knowledge (and, in particular, on our episodic knowledge). Our emotional adjustments to the world, as we have seen, rely on our memories. Or, to take much more ordinary cases, our ability to understand a story we've read, or a conversation, or, presumably, any of our experiences, depends on our supplementing that experience with some knowledge.

In short, cognitive psychology may help us understand capacities that are relevant to virtually every waking moment of our lives. Activities that don't, on the surface, appear intellectual would nonetheless collapse without the support of our cognitive functioning. This is true whether we're considering our actions, our social lives, our emotions, or almost any other domain. This is the scope of cognitive psychology and, in a real sense, the scope of this book.

A Brief History

In its modern form, cognitive psychology is roughly 50 years old. Despite this relative youth, cognitive psychology has had an enormous impact—so much so that many speak of the "cognitive revolution" within psychology. This "revolution," which took place across the 1950s and 1960s, represented a striking change in the style of research and theorizing employed by most psychologists. The new style was intended initially for studying problems we have already met: problems of memory, decision-making, and so on. But these new styles were soon exported to other domains and have provided important insights in these domains. In important ways, then, the cognitive revolution changed the intellectual map of our field.

The Years of Introspection

To understand all of this, we need some historical context. In the late 19th century, scholars—notably Wilhelm Wundt (1832–1920) and his student Edward Bradford Titchener (1867–1927)—launched the new enterprise of research psychology, defining their field for the first time as an endeavor separate from philosophy or biology.

In Wundt's and Titchener's view, psychology needed to be concerned largely with the study of conscious mental events—our feelings, thoughts, perceptions, and recollections. But how should these events be studied? The early researchers started with the obvious fact that there is no way for you to experience my thoughts, or I yours. The only person who can experience or observe your thoughts is you. They concluded, therefore, that the only way to study thoughts is for each of us to **introspect**, or "look within," to observe and record the content of our own mental lives and the sequence of our own experiences.

Wundt and Titchener insisted, though, that the introspection could not be casual. Instead, introspectors had to be meticulously trained: They were given a vocabulary to describe what they observed; they were trained to be as careful and as complete as possible; and above all, they were trained simply to report on their experiences, with a minimum of interpretation.

This style of research was enormously influential for several years, but psychologists gradually became disenchanted with it and it is easy to see why. As one concern, these early investigators were soon forced to acknowledge that some thoughts are *un*conscious, and this meant that introspection was inevitably limited as a research tool. This follows from the fact that introspection, by its nature, is the study of conscious experiences, and so can tell us nothing about unconscious events.

Indeed, we now know that unconscious thought plays a huge part in our mental lives. For example, what is your phone number? It's likely that the moment you read this question, the number "popped" into your thoughts without any effort, noticeable steps, or strategies on your part. But, in fact, there's good reason to think that this simple bit of remembering requires a complex series of steps (see, for example, Chapter 8). These steps take place outside your awareness, and so, if we rely on introspection as our means of studying mental events, then we have no way of examining these processes.

But there are also other problems with introspection: In order for any science to proceed, there must be some way of testing its claims; otherwise, we have no way of separating correct assertions from false ones, accurate descriptions of the world from fictions. Hand in hand with this requirement, science needs some way of resolving disagreements: If you claim that Earth has one moon, and I insist that it has two, we need some way of determining who is right. Otherwise, we have no way of locating the fact of the matter, and so our "science" will become a matter of opinion, not fact.

With introspection, though, this testability of claims is often unattainable. To see why, let's imagine that I insist my headaches are worse than yours. How could we ever test my claim? It might be true that I describe my headaches in extreme terms: I talk about my "unbelievable, agonizing, excruciating" headaches. But that might simply mean that I am inclined toward extravagant descriptions; it might reflect my verbal style, not my headaches. Similarly, it might be true that I need bed rest whenever one of my headaches strikes. Does that mean my headaches are truly intolerable? It might mean instead that I am self-indulgent and rest even in the face of mild pain. Perhaps our headaches are identical, but you're stoic about yours and I'm not.

How, therefore, should we test my claim about my headaches? What we need is some means of directly comparing my headaches to yours, and that would require transplanting one of my headaches into your experience, or vice versa. Then one of us could make the appropriate comparison. But there is no way to do this, leaving us, in the end, truly unable to determine if my headache reports are exaggerated or not, distorted or accurate. We're left, in other words, with no access to the objective facts. Our only information about my headaches is what comes to us through the filter of my description, and we have no way to know how (or whether) that filter is coloring the evidence.

For purposes of science, this is not acceptable. For science, we need objective observations, observations that we can count on. We need observations that aren't dependent on a particular point of view or a particular descriptive style. It is not enough to consider "the world as one person sees it." Instead, we want to consider the world as it objectively is. In scientific discourse, we usually achieve this objectivity by making sure all the facts are out in plain view, so that you can inspect my evidence, and I yours. In that way, we can be certain that neither of us is distorting or misreporting or exaggerating the facts. And that is precisely what we cannot do with introspection.

The Years of Behaviorism

The concerns just raised led many psychologists, particularly those in the United States, to abandon introspection as a research method. Psychology could not be a science, they argued, if it relied on introspective data. Instead, psychology needed objective data, and that meant we needed to focus on data that were out in the open, for all to observe.

What sorts of data does this allow us? First, an organism's *behaviors* are observable in the right way: You can watch my actions, and so can anyone else who is appropriately positioned. Therefore, data concerned with behavior are objective data, and so grist for the scientific mill. Likewise, *stimuli* in the world are in the same "objective" category: These are measurable, recordable, physical events.

In addition, you can arrange to record the stimuli I experience day after day after day and also the behaviors I produce each day. This means that you can record how the pattern of behaviors changes with the passage of time and with the accumulation of experience. Thus, my *learning history* can also be objectively recorded and scientifically studied.

In contrast, my *beliefs*, *wishes*, *goals*, and *expectations* are all things that cannot be directly observed, cannot be objectively recorded. Thus, we need to rule out any discussion of these "mentalistic" notions. These can be studied only via introspection (or so it was claimed), and introspection, we have suggested, is worthless as a scientific tool. Hence, a scientific psychology needs to avoid these invisible internal processes or events.

It was this perspective that led researchers to the **behaviorist** movement, a movement that dominated psychology in America for roughly the first half of the 20th century. This movement was in many ways a success and uncovered a range of broad principles concerned with how our behavior changes in response to different configurations of stimuli (including those stimuli we call "rewards" and "punishments"). Many of these principles remain in place within contemporary psychology and provide the base for an important enterprise called "learning theory," as well as a wide range of practical applications. (For a description of these principles, see Schwartz, Wasserman, & Robbins, 2002.)

By the late 1950s, however, psychologists were convinced that a great deal of our behavior could not be explained in the ways that behaviorists claimed—that is, could not be explained only with reference to objective, overt events (such as stimuli and responses). The reason, to put it plainly, is that we can easily show that the way people act, and the things that they say, and the way that they feel, are guided not by the objective situation itself, but by how they *understand* or *interpret* the situation. Therefore, if we follow the behaviorists' instruction and focus only on the objective situation, we will regularly misunderstand why people are acting as they are and make the wrong predictions about how they will behave in the future. To put this point another way, the behaviorists' perspective demands that we not talk about mental entities like beliefs, memories, and so on, because there is no way to study these entities directly, and so no way to study them scientifically. Yet it seems that these subjective entities play a pivotal role in guiding behavior, and so we *must* consider these entities if we want to understand behavior!

Evidence pertinent to these assertions is threaded throughout the chapters of this book. Over and over, we will find it necessary to mention people's perceptions and strategies and understanding, as we strive to explain why (and how) they perform various tasks and accomplish various goals. Indeed, we've already seen an example of this pattern: Imagine that we present the "Betsy and Jacob" story to people and then ask them various questions about the story: Why did Betsy shake her piggy bank? Why did she go to look for her mother? Their responses will surely reflect their understanding of the story, which in turn depends on far more than the physical stimulus—that is, the 29 syllables of the story itself. If we wanted to predict their responses, therefore, we would need to refer to the stimulus (the story itself) *and also* to the persons' knowledge and understanding of, and contribution to, this stimulus.

Here's a different example that makes the same general point: There you sit in the dining hall. A friend produces this physical stimulus: "Pass the salt, please." You immediately produce a bit of salt-passing behavior. In this exchange, there is a physical stimulus (the words that your friend uttered) and an easily defined response (your passing of the salt), and so this simple event seems fine from the behaviorists' perspective: The elements are out in the open, for all to observe, and can easily be objectively recorded. But let's note that things would have proceeded in the same way if your friend had offered a different stimulus. "Could I have the salt?" would have done the trick. Ditto for "Salt, please!" or "Hmm, this sure needs salt!" If your friend is both loquacious and obnoxious, the utterance might have been, "Excuse me, but after briefly contemplating the gustatory qualities of these comestibles, I have discerned that their sensory qualities would be enhanced by the addition of a number of sodium and chloride ions, delivered in roughly equal proportions and in crystalline form; could you aid me in this endeavor?" You might giggle (or snarl) at your friend, but you would still pass the salt.

Now let's work on the science of salt-passing behavior. When is this behavior produced? Since we've just observed that the behavior is evoked by all of these different stimuli, we would surely want to ask: What do these stimuli have in common? If we can answer that question, we're well on our way to understanding why all of these stimuli have the same effect.

If we focus entirely on the observable, objective aspects of these stimuli, they actually have little in common. After all, the actual sounds being produced are rather different in that long utterance about sodium and chloride ions and the utterance, "Salt, please!" And in many circumstances, *similar* sounds would not lead to salt-passing behavior. Imagine that your friend says, "Salt the pass," or "Sass the palt." These are acoustically similar to "Pass the salt" but wouldn't have the same impact. Or imagine that your friend says, "She has only a small part in the play. All she gets to say is, 'Pass the salt, please.'" In this case, exactly the right syllables were uttered, but you wouldn't pass the salt in response.

It seems, then, that our science of salt-passing won't get very far if we insist on talking only about the physical stimulus. Stimuli that are physically different from each other ("Salt, please" and the bit about the ions) have similar effects. Stimuli that are physically similar to each other ("Pass the salt" and "Sass the palt") have different effects. Physical similarity, therefore, is plainly not what unites the various stimuli that evoke salt-passing.

It is clear, though, that the various stimuli that evoke salt-passing do have something in common with each other: *They all mean the same thing*. Sometimes this meaning derives easily from the words themselves ("Please pass the salt"). In other cases, the meaning depends on certain pragmatic rules. (For example, we pragmatically understand that the question "Could you pass the salt?" is not a question about arm strength, although, interpreted literally, it might be understood that way.) In all cases, it seems plain that to predict your behavior in the dining hall, we need to ask what these stimuli *mean to you*. This seems an extraordinarily simple point, but it is a point, echoed over and over by countless other examples, that indicates the impossibility of a complete behaviorist psychology.[1]

---

[1]We should note that the behaviorists themselves quickly realized this point. Hence, modern behaviorism has abandoned the radical rejection of mentalistic terms; indeed, it's hard to draw a line between modern behaviorism and a field called "animal cognition," a field that often employs mentalistic language! The behaviorism being criticized here is a historically defined behaviorism, and it's this perspective that, in large measure, gave birth to modern cognitive psychology.

The Roots of the Cognitive Revolution

We seem to be nearing an impasse: If we wish to explain or predict behavior, we need to make reference to the mental world—the world of perceptions, understandings, and intentions. This is because how people act is shaped by how they *perceive* the situation, how they *understand* the stimuli, and so on. But how should we study the mental world? We can't employ introspection, because we've argued that introspective data are (at best) problematic. It would seem, then, that we're caught in a trap: We need to talk about the mental world if we hope to explain behavior. But the only direct means for studying the mental world turns out to be unworkable.

The solution to this impasse was actually suggested many years ago, by the philosopher Immanuel Kant (1724–1804). To use Kant's **transcendental method**, one begins with the observable facts and then works backward from these observations. In essence, one asks: How could these observations have come about? What must the underlying *causes* be that led to these *effects*?

This method, sometimes called "inference to best explanation," is at the heart of most modern science. Physicists, for example, routinely use this method to study objects or events that cannot be observed directly. To take just one case, no physicist has ever observed an electron, but this has not stopped physicists from learning a great deal about electrons. How do they proceed? Even though electrons themselves are not observable, their presence often leads to observable results—in essence, *visible effects* from an *invisible cause*. Thus, among other things, electrons cause observable tracks in cloud chambers, and they produce momentary fluctuations in a magnetic field. Physicists can then use these observations the same way a police detective uses clues—asking what the "crime" must have been like if it left this and that clue. (A size 11 footprint? That probably tells us what size feet the criminal has, even though no one observed his feet. A smell of tobacco smoke? That suggests the criminal was a smoker. And so on.) In the same fashion, physicists observe the clues that electrons leave behind, and from this information they form hypotheses about what exactly electrons must be like, in order to have produced these specific effects.

Of course, physicists (and other scientists) have a huge advantage over a police detective; indeed, this is crucial for the distinction between science and police work: If a police detective has insufficient evidence, she can't arrange for the crime to happen again, so that more evidence will be produced. But scientists do have this option; they can arrange for new experiments, with new measures. Better still, they can set the stage in advance, to maximize the likelihood that the "culprit" (in our example, the electron) will leave useful clues behind. They can, for example, add new measuring devices to the situation, or they can place various obstacles in the electron's path. In this way, the scientist can gather more and more data, including data that are crucial for testing the specific predictions of a particular theory. This prospect—of reproducing experiments and varying the experiments to test hypotheses—is what gives science its power. It's what allows scientists to assert that their hypotheses have been rigorously tested, and it's what gives scientists assurance that their theories are correct.

Psychologists work in the same fashion. We know that we need to study mental processes; that's what we learned from the limitations of behaviorism. But we also know that mental processes cannot be observed directly; we learned that from the downfall of introspection. Our path forward, therefore, is to study mental processes *indirectly*, relying on the fact that these processes, themselves invisible, have visible consequences: measurable delays in producing a response, performances that can be assessed for accuracy, errors that can be scrutinized and categorized, and so on. By examining these and other effects produced by mental processes, we can develop—and then *test*—hypotheses about what the mental processes must have been. In this fashion, we use Kant's method, just as physicists do, to develop a science that does not rest on direct observation.

Research in Cognitive Psychology: An Example

In case after case, cognitive psychologists have applied the Kantian logic to explain how we remember, how we make decisions, how we pay attention or solve problems. In each case, we begin with a particular performance—say, on a memory task—and then hypothesize a series of unseen mental events that made the performance possible. But, crucially, we don't stop there. We also ask whether some other, perhaps simpler, sequence of events might explain the data, or whether some other sequence might explain both these data and some other findings. In this fashion, we do more than ask how the data came about; we also seek the *best* way to think about the data.

For some data, the sequence of events we hypothesize resembles the processing steps that a computer might use. (For classic examples of this approach, see Broadbent, 1958; Miller, Galanter, & Pribram, 1960.) For other data, we might cast our hypotheses in terms of the strategies a person is using or the inferences she is making. No matter what the form of the hypothesis, though, the next step is crucial: The hypothesis is tested by collecting more data. Specifically, we seek to derive new predictions based on our hypothesis: "If this is the mechanism behind the original findings, then things should work differently in this circumstance or that one." If these predictions are tested and confirmed, this is a strong argument that the proposed hypothesis was correct. If the predictions are not confirmed, then a new hypothesis is needed.

How does this method work in practice? Let's explore this point with a concrete example. We will return to this example in Chapters 4 and 5, and there put it into a richer theoretical context. For now, though, our focus is on the method, rather than on the theory itself.

Working Memory: Some Initial Observations

Many of the sentences in this book—including the present one, which consists of 19 words—are rather long. In many of these sentences, words that must be understood together (such as "sentences . . . are . . . long") are widely separated (note the 12 words interposed between "sentences" and "are"). Yet you have no trouble understanding these sentences.

We begin, therefore, with a simple fact—that you are able to read, even though ordinary reading requires you to integrate words that are widely separated on the page. How should we explain this fact? What is the (unseen) cause that leads to this (easily observed) fact? The obvious suggestion is that you're relying on some form of *memory*, which allows you to remember the early words in the sentence as you forge ahead. Then, once you have read enough, you can integrate what you have decoded so far. In this section's very first sentence, you needed to remember the first seven words ("Many of the sentences in this book") while you read the interposed phrase ("including . . . 19 words"). Then you had to bring those first seven words back into play, to integrate them with the sentence's end ("are rather long").

The form of memory proposed here is generally called **working memory**, to emphasize that this is the memory you use for information that you are actively working on. Working memory holds information in an easily accessible form, so that the information is, so to speak, at your fingertips, instantly available when you need it. Thus, having decoded the first part of a sentence, you store its semantic content in working memory so that it is ready at hand a moment later, when you are all set to integrate this content with the sentence's end.

How can we ensure that working memory's contents will be instantly available, always ready when you need them? In part, the answer lies in working memory's *size:* Working memory is hypothesized to have only a small capacity, and so, with only a few items held in this store, there will never be a problem locating just the item you want. (If you have only two keys on your key ring, it's easy to find the one that unlocks your door. If you had a hundred keys on the ring, the situation would be rather different.)

Can we test this proposal? One way to measure working memory's capacity is via a **span test**. In this test, we read to someone a list of, say, four items, perhaps four letters ("A D G W"). The person has to report these back, immediately, in sequence. If she succeeds, we try it again with five letters ("Q D W U F"). If she can repeat these back correctly, we try six letters, and so on, until we find a list that the person cannot report back accurately. Generally, people start making errors with sequences of seven or eight letters. Most people's letter span, therefore, is about seven or eight. This not only confirms our hypothesis that working memory is limited in size but, just as important, also provides a simple example of how we can learn about this memory's properties by seeing how this (unseen) memory influences observable performance.

Working Memory: A Proposal

If we measure people's memory span, we find that they often make errors—reporting letters that they hadn't heard at all—and these errors follow a simple pattern: When people make mistakes in this task, they generally substitute one letter for another with a similar sound. Having heard "S," they'll report back "F"; or having heard "V," they'll report back "B." The problem is not in hearing the letters in the first place: We get similar sound-alike confusions if the letters are presented visually. Thus, having *seen* "F," people are likely to report back "S"; they are not likely, in this situation, to report back the similar-looking "E."

This finding provides another "clue" about working memory's nature, and Baddeley and Hitch (1974) proposed a model to explain both this finding and many other results as well. Their model starts by stipulating that working memory is not a single entity. Instead, working memory has several different parts, and so they prefer to speak of a **working-memory system**. At the heart of the system is the **central executive**. This is the part that runs the show and does the real work.

We'll say more about the executive in upcoming chapters; this turns out by itself to be an intriguing and complex topic. For now, though, let's focus on the fact that the executive is helped out by a number of low-level "assistants." These assistants are not at all sophisticated; they are useful for mere storage of information and not much more. If any work needs to be done on the information—interpretation or analysis—the assistants can't do it; the executive is needed. Nonetheless, these assistants are highly useful: Information that will soon be needed, but isn't needed right now, can be sent off to the assistants for temporary storage. Therefore, the executive isn't burdened by the mere storage of this information and is freed up to do other tasks.

In effect, the assistants serve the same function as a piece of scratch paper on your desk. When you're going to need some bit of information soon (a phone number, perhaps), you write it down on the scratch paper. Of course, the scratch paper has no mind of its own, and so it can't do anything with the "stored" information; all it does is hold on to the information. But that's helpful enough: With the scratch paper "preserving" this information, you can cease thinking about it with no risk that the information will be lost. This in turn allows you to focus your attention more productively on other, more complex chores. Then, when you are ready for the stored information (perhaps just a moment later) you glance at your notes, and there the information is.

Working memory's assistants provide the same benefit, and one of the most important assistants is the **articulatory rehearsal loop**. To see how this works, try reading the next few sentences while holding on to this list of numbers: "1, 4, 6, 4, 9." Got them? Now read on. You are probably repeating the numbers over and over to yourself, rehearsing them with your inner voice. But this turns out to require very little effort, so you can continue reading while doing this rehearsal. Nonetheless, the

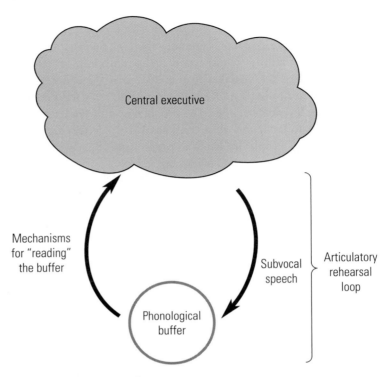

FIGURE 1.1 The Working-Memory System
Working memory's central executive is supported by a number of low-level assistants. One assistant, the articulatory rehearsal loop, involves two components—subvocal speech (the "inner voice") and a phonological buffer (the "inner ear"). Items are rehearsed by using subvocalization to "load" the buffer. While this is going on, the executive is free to work on other matters. However, the executive is needed to "read" the contents of the buffer before they decay; the executive can then pronounce the items again, launching another cycle through the loop.

moment you need to recall the numbers (what were they?), they are available to you. How did you do this? The numbers were maintained by working memory's rehearsal loop; with the numbers thus out of the way, the central executive was free to continue reading. And that is the advantage of this system: With mere storage handled by the helpers, the executive is available for other, more demanding tasks.

How does the rehearsal loop function (Figure 1.1)? To manage the task of storing numbers while reading, working memory's central executive must first identify the numbers (i.e., read them off the page). With that done, the executive needs to shuffle these numbers off to storage, so that it's not burdened with them. That way, the executive will be free to work on other things (such as reading the rest of the page). For this purpose, the executive relies on the process of **subvocalization** to pronounce the numbers. In essence, you silently say the numbers to yourself. Of course, the activity of speaking is immensely well practiced, and so there's no need for the executive to monitor or supervise this activity. Thus, once the executive has initiated the speech, it can turn to other matters, and that is exactly what we want: The chore of holding on to the numbers is now carried by the "inner voice," not the executive.

Subvocalization, in turn, produces a representation of these numbers in the **phonological buffer**. In other words, an auditory image is created in the "inner ear." This image will fade away after a second or two, and before it does, the executive is needed once again: The executive "reads" the contents of the buffer, as if listening to the "echo" in order to remind itself what the numbers were. Then the executive initiates the next pronunciation by the inner voice, to begin another cycle, and at that point it can go back to its other business.

Note, then, that the executive is needed once per cycle: to launch the next round of subvocalization. For the remainder of the cycle, though, the numbers are maintained by the rehearsal loop, not the executive, leaving the executive free to focus on other activities, and this is, of course, the advantage of using this system.

Evidence for the Working-Memory System

Baddeley and Hitch proposed this model as an explanation for the available evidence; it was, in their view, the best way to explain the facts collected so far. Specifically, people make "sound-alike" errors in a span task because they're relying on the rehearsal loop, and this loop literally involves one mechanism (the "inner voice") that is ordinarily used for overt speech, and one (the "inner ear") ordinarily used for actual hearing. In essence, then, the memory items are briefly stored as (internal representations of) sounds, and so it's no surprise that errors, when they occur, are shaped by this mode of storage.

All of this provides the first step of the Kantian logic we have described—generating a hypothesis about unseen mechanisms (e.g., the operation of the rehearsal loop) in order to explain visible data (e.g., the pattern of the errors). Crucially, though, this model also leads to many new predictions, and these allow us to test the model's accuracy. This is the step that turns a "mere" hypothesis into solid scientific knowledge.

For example, imagine that we ask people to take the span test while simultaneously saying "Tah-Tah-Tah" over and over, out loud. This **concurrent articulation** task obviously requires the mechanisms for speech production. Therefore, these mechanisms are not available for other use, including subvocalization. This is because, simply, you can't use muscles in two different ways at the same time, and so you cannot subvocalize one sequence while overtly vocalizing something else (see Figure 1.2).

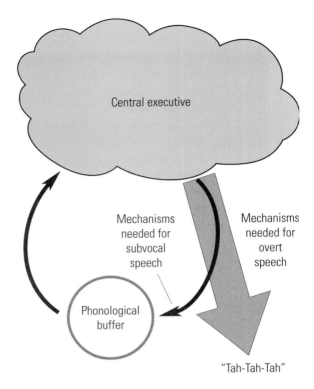

FIGURE 1.2 The Effects of Concurrent Articulation
The mechanisms needed for subvocal speech (the "inner voice") overlap heavily with those needed for overt speech. Therefore, if these mechanisms are in use for actual speech, they are not available for subvocal rehearsal. Hence, many experiments block rehearsal by requiring participants to say "Tah-Tah-Tah" out loud.

According to the model, how will this constraint matter? First, note that our original span test measured the combined capacities of the central executive and the loop. That is, when people take a span test, they store some of the to-be-remembered items in the loop, and other items via the central executive. With concurrent articulation, though, the loop isn't available for use, and so we are now measuring the capacity of working memory without the rehearsal loop. We should predict, therefore, that concurrent articulation, even though it's extremely easy, should cut memory span drastically. This prediction turns out to be correct. Span is ordinarily about seven items; with concurrent articulation, it drops to three or four.

Second, with visually presented items, concurrent articulation should eliminate the sound-alike errors. Saying "Tah-Tah-Tah" over and over blocks use of the articulatory loop, and it is in this loop, we've proposed, that the sound-alike errors arise. This prediction, too, is correct: With concurrent articulation, sound-alike errors are largely eliminated.

Third, we can also test people's memory spans by using complex visual shapes. People are shown these shapes and then must echo the sequence back by drawing what they have just seen. If we choose shapes that are not easily named, then the shapes cannot be rehearsed via the inner-voice/inner-ear combination. (What would one subvocalize to rehearse these?) With such stimuli, there should be no effect of concurrent articulation: If people aren't using the rehearsal loop, there should be no cost attached to denying them use of the loop. This prediction is also correct.

Finally, here is a different sort of prediction. We have claimed that the rehearsal loop is required only for storage; this loop (like all of working memory's assistants) is incapable of any more sophisticated operations. Therefore, these other operations should not be compromised if the loop is unavailable. This, too, turns out to be correct: Concurrent articulation blocks use of the loop but has no effect on someone's ability to read brief sentences, to do logic problems, and so on. Likewise, we can present people with a string of three or four letters and ask them to remember these while solving a simple problem. After they've solved the problem, they report back the original letters. It turns out that half-filling working memory in this fashion has virtually no impact on problem-solving; performance is just as fast and just as accurate under these circumstances as it is without the memory load. The reason is that this memory load is accommodated within the rehearsal loop, placing no burden on the executive. And it is the executive, not the loop, that is needed for problem-solving, again in accord with the overall model.

The Nature of the Working-Memory Evidence

No one has ever seen the "inner voice" or "inner ear" directly. Nonetheless, we're confident that these entities exist, because they are essential parts of our explanation for the data and there seems to be no other way to explain the data. Moreover, our claims about the inner voice and inner ear have consistently led us to new predictions that have been confirmed by further testing. It's in this way that we can use the observable evidence to reconstruct what the unobserved structures and processes must be.

Let's note also that in supporting our account, we have many forms of data available to us. We can manipulate research participants' activities, as we did with concurrent articulation, and look at how this manipulation changes their performance (i.e., the size of the measured memory span). We can also manipulate the stimuli themselves, as we did in testing memory for visual shapes, and see how this changes things. We can also look in detail at the nature of the performance, asking not just about the overall level of performance, but also about the specific errors (sound-alike vs. look-alike). We can also measure the speed of participants' performance and ask how this is influenced by various manipulations. We did this, for example, in asking whether problem-solving is compromised by a concurrent memory load. The assumption here is that mental processes are very quick but nonetheless do take a measurable amount of time. By timing how quickly participants answer various questions or perform various tasks, we can ask what factors speed up mental processes and what factors slow them down.

"I Can't Hear Myself Think in Here!"
Many tasks draw on working memory, and working memory (in turn) often relies on the articulatory rehearsal loop. However, this loop is difficult to use in a noisy environment: The noise occupies the auditory "buffer," and so the buffer can't be used as part of the loop. This can drastically impede any sort of mental work in a noisy environment!

We can also gather data from a very different source: So far, we have been concerned with people's *performance* in our tasks—for example, how much or how well they remember. However, we can gain further insights into working memory by considering the biological mechanisms that make this performance possible. That is, we can draw evidence from the realm of **cognitive neuroscience**—the study of the biological basis for cognitive functioning.

For example, what exactly is the nature of subvocalization? Does it literally involve covert speech and thus movements (perhaps tiny movements) of the tongue, the vocal cords, and so on? One way to find out would be to paralyze these various muscles. Would this disrupt use of the rehearsal loop? As it turns out, we don't have to perform this experiment; nature has performed it for us. Because of specific forms of neurological damage, some individuals have no ability to move these various muscles and so are unable to speak. These individuals suffer from **anarthria**—that is, they cannot produce speech. Data indicate, however, that these individuals show sound-alike confusions in their data, just as ordinary participants do. This observation suggests that actual muscle movements are not needed for subvocalization.

Instead, "inner speech" probably relies on the brain areas responsible for *planning* the muscle movements of speech. This is by itself an interesting fact, but for present purposes, note the use of yet another type of data: observations from **neuropsychology**, concerned with how various forms of brain dysfunction influence observed performance.

We can pursue similar questions by examining the brain activity of people without any brain damage. Recent developments in brain-imaging technology tell us that when a participant is engaged in working-memory rehearsal, considerable activity is observed in brain areas that we know (from other evidence) are crucially involved in the production of spoken language, as well as in areas that play an important role in the perception and understanding of spoken language. These findings suggest that claims about the "inner voice" and "inner ear" are more than casual metaphors; instead, the "inner voice" literally uses mechanisms that are ordinarily used for overt speech, and the "inner ear" uses mechanisms ordinarily used for actual hearing (cf. Jonides, Lacey, & Nee, 2005; for more on the neuroscience of working memory, see Jonides et al., 2008).

We can also gain insights by comparing diverse populations—for example, by comparing people with normal hearing to people who have been deaf since birth and who communicate via sign language. It turns out that the deaf rely on a different assistant for working memory: They use an inner hand (and covert sign language) rather than an inner voice (and covert speech). As a result, they are disrupted if we have them wiggle their fingers during a memory task (akin to a hearing person saying "Tah-Tah-Tah"), and they also tend to make "same-hand-shape" errors in working memory (analogous to the sound-alike errors made by the hearing population). These results speak not only to the generality of the claims made here, but also to the need to fine-tune these claims when we consider other groups of people.

Finally, it is important that we have built our argument with *multiple lines* of evidence. That's because, in most cases, no single line of evidence is by itself decisive. There are, after all, probably other ways to explain our initial observations about span, if those results were all we had to go on. There are also other ways to explain the other individual findings we have mentioned, if these likewise were considered in isolation. It's only when we take the results as a package that we can make headway, and if we have done our work well, there will be just one theoretical account that fits with the entire data pattern. At that point, with no other way to explain the data, we will conclude that we have understood the evidence and that we have correctly reconstructed what is going on in the mind, invisibly, never directly observed.

We might also mention that there's no reason right now for you, as a reader, to memorize this catalogue of different types of evidence. This is because we will encounter each of these forms of data again and again in this text. Our point for now, therefore, is not to create an intimidating memory load for the readers, but instead to highlight—and, indeed, to celebrate—the fact that we need multiple tools to test, and eventually to confirm, our claims.

Working Memory in a Broader Context

Having made all of these methodological points, let us round out this section with one final comment. Why should we care about the structure of working memory? Why is working memory interesting? The memory-span task itself seems quite unnatural: How often do we need to memorize a set of unrelated numbers or letters? For that matter, how often do we need to work on a problem while simultaneously saying "Tah-Tah-Tah" over and over? In short, what does this task, or this procedure, have to do with things we care about?

The answer to these questions allows us to replay an issue we have already discussed: We rely on working memory in a vast number of circumstances, and so, if we understand working memory, we move toward an understanding of this far broader set of problems and issues. For example, bear in mind our initial comments about the role of working memory in reading or in any other task in which you must store early "products," keeping them ready for integration with later "products." One might imagine that many tasks have this character; reading, reasoning, and problem-solving are a few. If you make effective use of working memory, therefore, you will have an advantage in all of these domains. Indeed, some scholars have suggested that "intelligence" in many domains amounts to nothing more than excess capacity in working memory. (See, for example, Kyllonen & Cristal, 1990.)

In a similar vein, the use of articulatory rehearsal seems a simple trick—a trick you use spontaneously, a trick in which you take no special pride. But it is a trick you had to learn, and young children, for example, often seem not to know the trick. There is some indication that this can be a problem for these children in learning to read: Without the option of relying on articulatory rehearsal, reading becomes much more difficult. It also appears that the rehearsal loop plays an important role when someone is learning new vocabulary, including vocabulary in a new language (Baddeley, Gathercole, & Papagno, 1998; Gathercole, Service, Hitch, Adams, & Martin, 1999). So here, too, is an important function of the working-memory system.

These examples can easily be multiplied, but by now the point should be clear: Working memory and articulatory rehearsal are relevant to a wide range of mental activities in adults and in children. Understanding working memory, therefore, may give us insight into a broad range of tasks. Similar claims can be made about many other cognitive resources: By understanding what it means to pay attention, we move toward an understanding of all the contexts in which attention plays a role. By understanding how we comprehend text, or how we use our knowledge to supplement our perceptions, we move toward an understanding of all the contexts in which these play a part. And in each case, the number of such contexts is vast.

We end this chapter, therefore, by echoing a comment we have already made: The machinery of cognition is essential to virtually all of our waking activities (and perhaps some of our sleeping activities as well). The scope of cognitive psychology is broad indeed, and the relevance of our research is wide.

Chapter Summary

- Cognitive psychology is concerned with how people remember, pay attention, and think. The importance of all these issues arises in part from the fact that most of what we do, think, and feel is guided by things we already know. One example is the comprehension of a simple story, which turns out to be heavily influenced by the knowledge we supply.

- Cognitive psychology emerged as a separate discipline in the late 1950s, and its powerful impact on the wider field of psychology has led many to speak of this emergence as the cognitive revolution. One predecessor of cognitive psychology was the 19th-century movement that emphasized introspection as the main research tool for psychology. Psychologists soon became disenchanted with this movement, however, for several reasons: Introspection cannot inform us about unconscious mental events; even with conscious events, claims rooted in introspection are often untestable, because there is no way for an independent observer to check on the accuracy or completeness of an introspective report.

- The behaviorist movement rejected introspection as a method, insisting instead that psychology speak only of mechanisms and processes that were objective and out in the open for all to observe. However, evidence suggests that our thinking, behavior, and feelings are often shaped by our perception or understanding of the events we experience. This is problematic for the behaviorists: Perception and understanding are exactly the sorts of mental processes that the behaviorists regarded as subjective and not open to scientific study.

- In order to study mental events, psychologists have turned to a method in which one focuses on observable events but then asks what (invisible) events must have taken place in order to make these (visible) effects possible.

- Research in working memory provides an example of how cognitive psychologists use evidence. One theory of working memory proposes that this memory consists of a central executive and a small number of low-level assistants, including the articulatory rehearsal loop, which stores material by means of covert speech. Many forms of evidence are used in supporting this account: measures of working memory's holding capacity in various circumstances, the nature of errors people make when using working memory, the speed of performance in working-memory tasks, evidence drawn from the study of people with brain damage, and evidence drawn from brain-imaging technology.

The Workbook Connection

See the *Cognition Workbook* for further exploration of the science of the mind:

- Demonstration 1.1: The Articulatory Rehearsal Loop
- Research Methods: Testable Hypotheses
- Cognitive Psychology and Education: Enhancing Classroom Learning
- Cognitive Psychology and the Law: Improving the Criminal Justice System

The Neural Basis for Cognition

As discussed in Chapter 1, cognitive psychologists rely on many sorts of findings, including response times, error rates, and questionnaire responses. No one source of data is more important than the others; all contribute to the broad fabric of evidence that allows us to test our theories. Indeed, we have discussed the fact that a reliance on many pieces of evidence, and *diverse* pieces of evidence, is an important aspect of research on cognition; this is crucial for the "inference to best explanation" that is at the methodological core of our field.

One form of evidence, however, does need its own presentation: evidence concerning the brain functioning that makes cognition possible. We will encounter this biologically rooted evidence throughout this book, woven together with other sorts of data, as we develop and test our theories. But first we need to lay the appropriate foundation—some background information about the brain and the methods used to study the brain.

We will begin with an example that involves some of the bizarre symptoms that can result from brain damage; we will use this example to illustrate what we can learn about the mind by studying the brain, and what we can learn about the brain by studying the mind. This example will, in addition, highlight the fact that each part of the brain has its own specialized function, so that our behaviors, thoughts, and feelings almost invariably depend on the coordinated action of many brain regions. To explore this point, we will need to consider some basic brain anatomy, and also look at some of the methods used to study the functioning of the brain's various parts. Then, with this broad framework in place, we will zoom in for a closer look at one part of the brain—the tissue that allows us to see, and to understand, the visual world that surrounds us.

- We explore the example of *Capgras syndrome* to illustrate how seemingly simple achievements actually depend on many parts of the brain; we also highlight the ways that the study of the brain, and brain damage, can illuminate questions about the mind.

- We then survey the brain's anatomy, emphasizing the function carried out by each region. The identification of these functions is supported by neuroimaging data,

which can assess the activity levels in different areas, and also by studies of the effects of brain damage.

- We consider the *visual system* as an illustration of what we can learn from closer scrutiny of brain function. Here we see that the analysis of the visual input begins the moment visual information enters the nervous system, and depends on many highly specialized brain areas, all working in parallel with the others.

Capgras Syndrome: An Initial Example

The human brain is an extraordinarily complex organ in which the functioning of the whole is dependent on many interconnected systems. As a result, damage virtually anywhere in the brain will produce specific—and sometimes highly disruptive—symptoms. These symptoms are often tragic for the afflicted persons and their families, but they can also be a rich source of insight into how the brain functions.

Consider, for example, a remarkable disorder known as **Capgras syndrome** (Capgras & Reboul-Lachaux, 1923). This disorder is rare on its own, but it seems to be one of the accompaniments to Alzheimer's syndrome, and so is sometimes observed among the elderly (Harwood, Barker, Ownby, & Duara, 1999). More directly, though, the disorder can result from various injuries to the brain (Ellis & De Pauw, 1994).

Someone with Capgras syndrome is fully able to recognize the people in her world—her husband, her parents, her friends—but she is utterly convinced that these people are not who they appear to be. The real husband or the real son, the afflicted person insists, has been kidnapped (or worse). The person now on the scene, therefore, isn't the genuine article; instead, he or she must be a well-trained, well-disguised impostor.

Imagine what it is like to have this disorder. You turn to someone you know extremely well—perhaps your father—and say, "You look like my father, sound like him, and act like him. But I can tell that you're not my father. *WHO ARE YOU?*"

Often a person with Capgras syndrome insists that there are slight differences between the impostor and the person he has replaced—subtle changes in personality or tiny changes in appearance. Of course, no one else detects these (nonexistent) differences, compounding the bewilderment experienced by the Capgras sufferer. These feelings spiral upward, with the patient developing all sorts of paranoid suspicions about why a loved one has been replaced and why no one seems to acknowledge this replacement. In the extreme, the Capgras sufferer may be led to desperate steps, in some instances murdering the supposed impostor in an attempt to end the charade and relocate the "genuine" character. In one case, a Capgras patient was convinced his father had been replaced by a robot and so decapitated him in order to look for the batteries and microfilm in his head (Blount, 1986).

What is going on here? The answer, according to some researchers, lies in the fact that facial recognition involves two separate systems in the brain, one of which leads to a cognitive appraisal ("I know what my father looks like, and I can perceive that you closely resemble him"), and the other to a more global, somewhat emotional appraisal ("You look familiar to me and also trigger a warm response in me"). The concordance of these two appraisals then leads to the certainty of recognition ("You obviously are my father"). In Capgras syndrome, though, the latter (emotional) processing is disrupted, leading to the intellectual identification without the familiarity response (Ellis & Lewis, 2001; Ellis & Young, 1990; Ramachandran & Blakeslee, 1998): "You resemble my father but trigger no sense of familiarity, so you must be someone else."

The Neural Basis for Capgras Syndrome

A crucial step in examining this hypothesis about Capgras syndrome is to examine the brains of people with this disorder. This examination is made possible by **neuroimaging techniques**, developed in the last few decades, that allow researchers to take high-quality, three-dimensional "pictures" of living brains, without in any way disturbing the brains' owners. We will have more to say about neuroimaging later, but first, what do these techniques tell us about Capgras syndrome?

One form of neuroimaging data comes from PET scans, and these tell a great deal about the structure of the brain—including abnormalities in the brain tissue (PET will be described in more detail later in this chapter). These scans suggest a link between Capgras syndrome and abnormalities in several brain areas (Edelstyn & Oyebode, 1999; also see O'Connor, Walbridge, Sandson, & Alexander, 1996; see color insert, Figure 1). One site of damage is in the temporal lobe, particularly on the right side of the head. This damage probably disrupts circuits involving the **amygdala**, an almond-shaped structure that—in the intact brain—seems to serve as an "emotional evaluator," helping an organism to detect stimuli associated with threat or danger. The amygdala is also important for detecting *positive* stimuli—indicators of safety or indicators of available rewards. It seems likely, then, that the amygdala, the "evaluator," is essential for making the judgment of "you look familiar to me and trigger a warm emotional feeling"—one half of our two-systems hypothesis.

Patients with Capgras syndrome also have brain abnormalities in the frontal lobe, specifically in the right **prefrontal cortex**. What is this area's normal function? To find out, we turn to a different neuroimaging technique, fMRI, which allows us to track moment-by-moment activity levels in different sites in a living brain. (We'll say more about fMRI in a later section.) This allows us to answer such questions as: When a person is reading, which brain regions are particularly active? How about

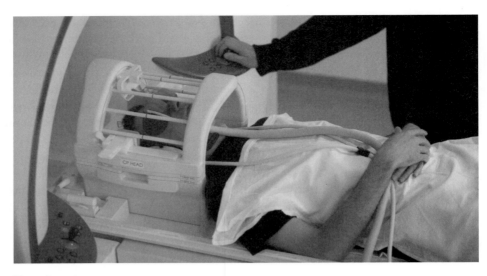

Neuroimaging

Scanners like this one are used both for MRI and fMRI scans. MRI scans tell us about the *structure* of the brain; fMRI scans tell us which portions of the brain are especially active during the scan. fMRI scans usually result in color images, with each hue indicating a particular activity level. For examples of MRI scans, see Figure 4 in the color insert; for examples of fMRI scans, see Figure 5 and Figure 14 in the color insert.

when a person is listening to music? With data like these, we can ask which tasks make heavy use of a brain area, and from that base we can draw conclusions about what the brain area's function is.

An important hint about Capgras syndrome comes from fMRI scans of patients suffering from an entirely different problem: schizophrenia (Silbersweig et al., 1995). Neuroimaging reveals diminished activity in the patients' frontal lobes whenever they are experiencing hallucinations. One plausible interpretation is that the diminished activity reflects a decreased ability to distinguish internal events (thoughts) from external ones (voices), or to distinguish imagined events from real ones. (Cf. Glisky, Polster, & Routhieaux, 1995.)

How is this relevant to Capgras syndrome? With damage to the frontal lobe, Capgras patients may be less able to keep track of what is real and what is not, what is plausible and what is not. As a result, weird beliefs can emerge unchecked, including delusions (about robots and the like) that you or I would find utterly bizarre.

What Do We Learn From Capgras Syndrome?

As it turns out, several lines of evidence support this account of Capgras syndrome (e.g., Ellis & Lewis, 2001; Ramachandran & Blakeslee, 1998). Some of the evidence comes from the psychology laboratory and confirms the suggestion that recognition ordinarily has two separate parts—one that hinges on factual knowledge, and one that's more "emotional" and tied to the warm sense of familiarity (see Chapter 6). In addition, we have mentioned some of the neuroscience evidence—evidence that tells us, first, where the brain damage is located in Capgras patients, and second, the likely functions of these brain sites when they're *not* damaged. This evidence fits well with our hypothesis: The damage to the amygdala is likely to be the reason why Capgras patients experience no sense of familiarity when they look at faces they know quite well. The damage to the prefrontal cortex, in turn, helps us understand why Capgras patients, when they experience this lack of familiarity, offer such crazy hypotheses about their skewed perception.

Obviously, then, our understanding of Capgras syndrome depends on a combination of evidence drawn from cognitive psychology and from cognitive neuroscience; we use both perspectives to test (and, ultimately, to confirm) the hypothesis we've offered. In addition, just as both perspectives can illuminate Capgras syndrome, both can be *illuminated by* the syndrome. That is, we can use Capgras syndrome (and other biological evidence) to illuminate broader issues about the nature of the brain and of the mind.

For example, Capgras syndrome suggests that the amygdala plays a crucial role in supporting the feeling of familiarity. Other biological evidence suggests that the amygdala also plays a central part in helping people remember the emotional events of their lives (e.g., Buchanan & Adolphs, 2004). Still other evidence indicates that the amygdala plays a role in decision-making (e.g., Bechara, Damasio, & Damasio, 2003), especially for decisions that rest on emotional evaluations of one's options. Facts like these tell us a lot about the various functions that make cognition possible and, in this case, tell us that our theorizing needs to include a broadly useful "emotional evaluator," involved in many cognitive processes. Moreover, Capgras syndrome tells us that this emotional evaluator works in a fashion separate from our evaluation of factual information, providing us a way to think about the occasions in which someone's evaluation of the facts points toward one conclusion, while an emotional evaluation points toward a different conclusion. These are clues of great value as we seek to understand the processes that support ordinary remembering or decision-making.

Cases like Capgras syndrome are just as valuable in helping us understand how the brain functions in normal people—that is, when all the neural systems are intact. For example, consider what this syndrome teaches us about how the parts of the brain work together for even the simplest achievement. In order to recognize your father, for example, one part of the brain needs to store the factual memory of what your father looks like. Another part of the brain is responsible for analyzing the visual input you receive when looking at a face. Yet another brain area has the job of comparing this now-analyzed input to the factual information provided from memory, to determine if there's a match or not. Another site provides the emotional evaluation of the input. A different site presumably assembles the data from all these other sites, and so registers the fact that the face being inspected does match the factual recollection of your father's face and also produces a warm sense of familiarity. Ordinarily, all of these brain areas work together, allowing the recognition of your father's face to go smoothly forward. If they don't work together—that is, if the coordination among these areas is disrupted—yet another area works to make sure you offer plausible hypotheses about this, and not zany ones. (And so, if your father looks less familiar to you on some occasion, you're likely to explain this by saying, "I guess he must have gotten new glasses" rather than "I bet he's been replaced by a robot.")

Unmistakably, then, this apparently easy task—seeing one's own father and recognizing who he is—requires multiple brain areas. The same is true of most tasks, and in this way, Capgras syndrome illustrates this crucial aspect of brain function.

The Principal Structures of the Brain

In order to discuss Capgras syndrome, we needed to refer to different brain areas; we also had to rely on several different research techniques. Thus, the syndrome also illustrates another point—namely, that this is a domain in which we need some technical foundations before we can develop our theories. Let's start building those foundations.

The human brain weighs between 3 and 4 pounds; it's roughly the size of a small melon. Yet this structure has been estimated to contain a trillion nerve cells (that's 10^{12}), each of which is connected to 10,000 or so others—for a total of roughly 10 million billion connections. How should we begin our study of this densely packed, incredibly complex organ?

One place to start is with a simple fact that we've already met—namely, that different parts of the brain perform different jobs. We've known this fact about the brain for many years, thanks to clinical evidence showing that the symptoms produced by brain damage depend heavily on the location of the damage. In 1848, for example, a horrible construction accident caused Phineas Gage to suffer damage in the frontmost part of his brain; this damage led to severe personality and emotional problems. In 1861, physician Paul Broca noted that damage in a different location, on the left side of the brain, led to a disruption of language skills. In 1911, Édouard Claparède (1911/1951) reported his observations with patients who suffered from profound memory loss, a loss produced by damage in still another part of the brain.

Clearly, therefore, we need to understand brain functioning with reference to brain anatomy. Where was the damage that Gage suffered? Where exactly was the damage in Broca's patients, or Claparède's? In this section, we fill in some basics of brain anatomy.

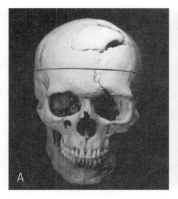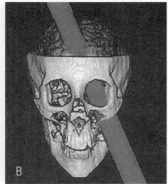

Phineas Gage's Skull

Phineas Gage was working as a construction foreman when some blasting powder misfired and launched a piece of iron into his cheek and through the front part of his brain. Remarkably, Gage survived and continued to live a more-or-less normal life, but his pattern of intellectual and emotional impairments provide valuable cues about the function of the brain's frontal lobes.

Hindbrain, Midbrain, Forebrain

The human brain is divided into three main structures: the hindbrain, the midbrain, and the forebrain. The **hindbrain** sits directly atop the spinal cord and includes several structures crucial for controlling key life functions. It's here, for example, that the rhythm of heartbeats and the rhythm of breathing are controlled. The hindbrain also plays an essential role in maintaining the body's overall tone; specifically, the hindbrain helps maintain the body's posture and balance, and it helps regulate the brain's level of alertness.

The largest area of the hindbrain is the **cerebellum**. For many years, investigators believed the cerebellum's main role was in the coordination of our bodily movements and balance. Recent studies, however, suggest that the cerebellum also plays a diverse set of other roles, and damage to this organ can cause problems in spatial reasoning, in discriminating sounds, and in integrating the input received from various sensory systems (J. M. Bower & Parsons, 2003).

The **midbrain** also has several roles. It plays an important part in coordinating our movements, including the skilled, precise movements of our eyes as we explore the visual world. Also in the midbrain are circuits that relay auditory information from the ears to the areas in the forebrain where this information is processed and interpreted. Still other structures in the midbrain help to regulate our experience of pain.

For our purposes, though, the most interesting brain region (and, in humans, the largest region) is the **forebrain**. Drawings of the brain show little other than the forebrain, because this structure surrounds (and hides from view) the entire midbrain and most of the hindbrain. Of course, it is only the outer surface of the forebrain that is visible in such pictures; this is the **cortex** (from the Latin word for "tree bark").

The cortex is just a thin covering on the outer surface of the brain; on average, it is a mere 3 mm thick. Nonetheless, there is a great deal of cortical tissue; by some estimates, the cortex constitutes 80% of the human brain. This considerable volume is made possible by the fact that the cortex, thin as it is, consists of a very large sheet of tissue; if stretched out flat, it would cover more than 2 square feet. But the cortex isn't stretched flat; instead, it is all crumpled up and jammed into the limited space inside the skull. It's this crumpling that produces the brain's most obvious visual feature— the wrinkles, or **convolutions**, that cover the brain's outer surface (Figure 2.1).

Some of the "valleys" in between the wrinkles are actually deep grooves that anatomically divide the brain into different sections. The deepest groove is the **longitudinal fissure**, running from the front of the brain to the back, and separating the left **cerebral hemisphere** from the right. Other fissures divide the cortex in each hemisphere into four lobes (see color insert, Figure 1), and these are named after the bones that cover them—bones that, as a group, make up the skull. The **frontal lobes** form the front of the brain—right behind the forehead. The **central fissure** divides the frontal lobes on each side of the brain from the **parietal lobes,** the brain's topmost part. The bottom edge of the frontal lobes is marked by the **lateral fissure**, and below this are the **temporal lobes**. Finally, at the very back of the brain, connected to the parietal and temporal lobes, are the **occipital lobes**.

Subcortical Structures

Hidden from view, underneath the cortex, are the **subcortical** parts of the forebrain. One of these is the **thalamus**, a brain region that acts as a relay station for nearly all the sensory information going to the cortex. Directly underneath the thalamus is the **hypothalamus**, a structure that plays a crucial role in the control of motivated behaviors such as eating, drinking, and sexual activity.

Surrounding the thalamus and hypothalamus is another set of interconnected structures that together form the **limbic system** (see color insert, Figure 2). Included here is the **amygdala**, and close by is the **hippocampus**, both located underneath the cortex in the temporal lobe. These structures are essential for learning and memory, and for emotional processing. The patient H.M., discussed in Chapter 1, developed his profound amnesia after surgeons removed these structures—a strong confirmation of their role in the formation of new memories.

Like most parts of the brain, the subcortical structures come in pairs, and so there is a hippocampus on the left side of the brain and another on the right, a left-side amygdala and a right one. Of course, the same is true for the cortex itself: There is a temporal cortex (i.e., a cortex of the temporal lobe) in the left hemisphere and another in the right, a left occipital cortex and a right one, and so on. In all cases, cortical and subcortical, the left and right structures in each pair have roughly the same shape, the same position in their respective sides of the brain, and the same pattern of connections to other brain areas. Even so, there are differences in function between the left-side and right-side structures, with the left-hemisphere structure playing a somewhat different role from the corresponding right-hemisphere structure.

Let's bear in mind, though, that the two halves of the brain work together; the functioning of one side is closely integrated with that of the other side. This integration is made possible by the **commissures**, thick bundles of fibers that carry information back and forth between the two hemispheres. The largest commissure is the **corpus callosum**, but several other structures also ensure that the two brain halves work together as partners in virtually all mental tasks.

Neuroimaging Techniques

As we have noted, the symptoms that result from brain damage depend heavily on the site of the damage. A **lesion** (a specific area of damage) on the hippocampus produces memory problems but not language disorders; a lesion on the occipital cortex produces problems in vision but spares the other sensory modalities. The consequences of brain lesions also depend on which hemisphere is damaged: Damage to the left side of the frontal lobe, for example, is likely to produce a disruption of language use; damage to the right side of the frontal lobe doesn't

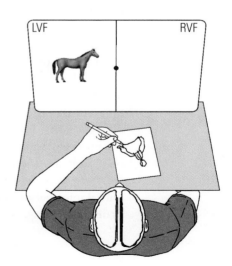

Patients with Split Brains

The two brain hemispheres have distinct functions, and this can plainly be seen in the so-called split-brain patients. These patients have undergone a surgery (rarely used in recent years) that severed their corpus callosum, disrupting communication between the hemispheres. What happens, therefore, if we present a picture in the patient's left visual field? If *asked* what the picture was, the person can give no response—because the visual information has not reached brain sites in the left hemisphere that control speech. If the patient is asked to *sketch* something in response to the picture, the patient offers an appropriate drawing.

The experimenter asks: "What goes on this?"
The split-brain patient responds: "I don't know."
(*but then goes ahead and draws the saddle*)

have this effect. These facts confirm that different brain areas perform different functions.

A similar conclusion follows from **neuroimaging** data. As we mentioned earlier, neuroimaging allows us to take precise three-dimensional pictures of the brain. Several such techniques are available, including **computerized axial tomography**, or CT scans, and **positron emission tomography**, or PET scans. CT scans use X-rays to study the brain's anatomy. PET scans provide a precise assessment of how blood is flowing through each region of the brain; they are used to study the brain's functioning. (This method rests on the fact that when a particular brain area is more active it needs—and receives—a greater blood flow; see color insert, Figure 3.)

Both of these techniques rely on a bank of detectors surrounding the head—a bank of X-ray detectors for CT scans, a bank of photon detectors for PET scans. A computer then compares the signals received by each of the detectors and uses this information to pinpoint the source of each signal. In this way, the computer can reconstruct a three-dimensional map (or image) of the brain—a map, in CT scans, that tells us what *structures* are where, or, in PET scans, that tells us about *activity levels* and, specifically, what regions are particularly active or inactive at any point in time.

In recent years, investigators have relied more on two newer techniques. **Magnetic resonance imaging** (MRI) relies on the magnetic properties of the atoms that make up the brain tissue, and it yields fabulously detailed pictures of the brain (see color insert, Figure 4). A closely related technique, **functional magnetic resonance imaging** (fMRI), measures the oxygen content in the blood flowing through each region of the brain; this turns out to be an accurate index of the level of neural activity in that region. In this way, fMRI scans provide an incredibly precise picture of the brain's moment-by-moment activities.

The results of a CT or MRI scan are relatively stable, changing only if the person's brain structure changes (because of an injury, perhaps, or the growth of a tumor). The results of PET or fMRI scans, in contrast, are highly variable, because the results depend heavily on what task the person is performing. This confirms the fundamental point that different brain areas perform different functions and are involved in different tasks. More ambitiously, though, we can use the neuroimaging procedures as a means of exploring brain function—using fMRI scans, for example, to ask which brain sites are especially activated when someone is listening to Mozart or when they are engaged in memory rehearsal. In this fashion, the neuroimaging data can provide crucial information about how these complex activities are made possible by specific brain functioning.

Neuroimaging: An Example

As an example of the power of neuroimaging techniques, consider a study by Tong, Nakayama, Vaughan, and Kanwisher (1998). In one condition of their study, participants were looking at pictures of *faces* while their brains were scanned; the data showed high levels of activation in an area called the **fusiform face area** (FFA), an area that seems highly responsive to faces and much less responsive to other visual stimuli (see color insert, Figure 5A). In a second condition, participants were looking at pictures of houses while their brains were scanned; now the data showed high levels of activity in a different region: the **parahippocampal place area** (PPA), a brain site that seems to respond actively whenever pictures of *places* are in view (see color insert, Figure 5B). Data like these make it clear that different areas of the brain are specialized not just for vision but for specific types of visual targets.

The most interesting condition of the Tong et al. study, however, was one in which a picture of a face was put in front of one of the participant's eyes while a picture of a house was put in front of the other eye. This is a situation known to produce **binocular rivalry**: The visual system is unable to handle both stimuli at once, or to fuse the stimuli into a single complex perception. Instead, the visual system seems to flip-flop between the stimuli, so that for a while the person is aware only of the face; then for a while aware of only the house; and so on.

In the Tong et al. study, participants pressed buttons to indicate, at each moment in time, whether they were aware of seeing the house or aware of seeing the face. At the same time, the researchers used an fMRI scan to keep track of the activity levels in the FFA (again, normally responsive to faces) and the PPA (normally responsive to places).

What should we expect here? If these brain areas respond simply to the stimuli that are available, then the activity levels would not have varied as the experiment progressed. The stimuli, after all, were never changed. But if these brain areas reflect the participants' conscious perception, then activity should fluctuate, with a change in brain activity occurring each time the binocular rivalry produces a new perception.

To analyze the data, the researchers relied on the **BOLD** signal (for *blood oxygenation level dependent*). This signal measures how much oxygen the blood's hemoglobin is carrying in each part of the brain, and this provides a quantitative basis for comparing activity levels in different brain areas.

Figure 5c in the color insert shows the key result. At moments in which the participant reported a conscious switch from seeing the face to seeing the house, activity in the PPA went up and activity in the FFA went down. At moments in which the participant reported the reverse switch, the activity levels in these two brain areas showed the opposite pattern.

Note, then, the power of these techniques. We can use brain scanning, first, to figure out the special function of different brain regions, and thus to learn (for example) which brain regions are crucial for the perception of faces, and which for the perception of other stimuli. Second, we can use measurements like the BOLD signal to track activity levels across time and to ask how the brain activity changes in response to new stimuli or new thoughts. Third, we can ask what exactly a brain state corresponds to: Does activity of the FFA, to put it crudely, tell us only what stimuli are present, sending their images to the nervous system? Or does activity of the FFA tell us what the person is consciously perceiving? The Tong et al. data favor the second option, with the striking suggestion that we can use brain scans as a means of studying some of the bases for conscious awareness. (For more on consciousness, see Chapter 15; for other examples of just how much we can learn from neuroimaging, see Jonides, Nee, & Berman, 2006; Norman, Polyn, Detre, & Haxby, 2006. For some *reservations* about neuroimaging, see, among others, Dumit, 2004; Uttal, 2001; Wade, 2006.)

Correlation Versus Causation

Neuroimaging data strongly suggest that different jobs are carried out by different bits of the brain, inviting us to ask questions like these: What job does the occipital cortex do? What work does the temporal lobe do? Answering these questions is referred to as the **localization of function**.

There is, however, a limitation to the neuroimaging data. We have already seen, for example, that activity levels increase in the FFA when a face is being perceived, but does this mean the FFA is needed for face perception? Perhaps the FFA activation is just a by-product of face perception and does not play a crucial role. As an analogy, think about the fact that a car's speedometer becomes "more activated" (i.e., shows a higher value) whenever the car goes faster. That doesn't mean that the speedometer *causes* the speed or *is necessary* for the speed. Indeed, the car would go just as fast and would, for many purposes, perform just as well if the speedometer were removed. The speedometer's state, in other words, is *correlated* with the car's speed, but in no sense causes (or promotes, or is needed for) the car's speed.

In the same way, neuroimaging data tell us whether a brain area's activity is *correlated* with a particular function, but we need other data to ask whether those brain sites play a role in *causing* (or supporting, or allowing) that function. In many cases, those other data come from the study of brain lesions: If damage to a brain site disrupts a function, that's an indication that the site does play some role in supporting that function.

Also helpful here is a technique called **transcranial magnetic stimulation** (TMS). This technique creates a series of strong magnetic pulses at a specific location on the scalp, causing a (temporary!) disruption in the small brain region directly underneath this scalp area (Helmuth, 2001). In this way, we can ask, in an otherwise normal brain, what functions are compromised when a particular bit of brain tissue is temporarily "turned off." As a result, we can ask, in a normal brain, whether that brain tissue plays a causal role in supporting the appropriate brain function.

Primary Motor Projection Areas

The combination of neuroimaging, lesion studies, and TMS has taught us a great deal about how different functions are localized in the brain. Let's look at (some of) what we've learned.

Certain areas of the brain seem to be the arrival points for information coming from the eyes, ears, and other sense organs. Other areas are the departure points for signals leaving the forebrain and controlling muscle movement. In both cases, these areas are called **primary projection areas**, with the arrival points known as the **primary sensory projection areas** and the departure points contained in regions known as the **primary motor projection area**.

Evidence for the motor projection area comes from studies in which investigators apply mild electrical current to this area in anesthetized animals. This stimulation often produces specific movements, so that current applied to one site causes a movement of the left front leg, while current applied to a different site causes the ears to perk up. These movements show a pattern of **contralateral control**, with stimulation to the left hemisphere leading to movements on the right side of the body, and vice versa.

The sites stimulated in these studies—and thus the primary motor projection area—are in a strip of tissue located toward the rear of the frontal lobe (see Figure 2.1). The term "projection" is borrowed from geography because this area seems to form a "map" of the body, with particular positions on the cortex corresponding to particular parts of the body.

Investigators have been able to draw these maps in some detail, and Figure 2.2 shows one representation of the result. In the figure, a drawing of a person has been overlaid on a depiction of the brain, with each part of the little person positioned on top of the area of the brain that controls its movement. As the figure shows, areas of

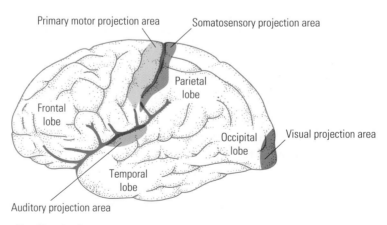

FIGURE 2.1 The Forebrain

The primary *motor* projection area, located toward the rear of the frontal lobe, sends out the signals that ultimately result in muscle movement. This drawing also shows the primary *sensory* projection areas. Information arriving from the skin senses is projected to a region in the parietal lobe (the somatosensory projection area). Information arriving from the eyes is projected to the occipital lobe; information from the ears, to the temporal lobe.

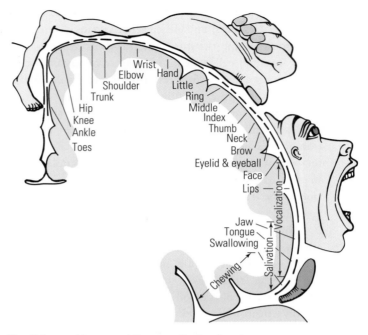

FIGURE 2.2 The Primary Motor and Sensory Projection Areas
This drawing shows which parts of the body are controlled by different parts of the projection area; clearly, more cortical space is devoted to the body parts that we can move with greatest precision.

the body that we can move with great precision (e.g., fingers and lips) have a lot of cortical area devoted to them; areas of the body over which we have less control (e.g., the shoulder and the back) receive less cortical coverage.

Primary Sensory Projection Areas

Information arriving from the skin senses (your sense of touch or your sense of temperature) is projected to a region in the parietal lobe, just behind the motor projection area; this is labeled the "somatosensory" area in Figure 2.1. If a patient's brain is stimulated in this region (with electrical current or touch), the patient will typically report a tingling sensation in a specific part of the body. Figure 2.1 also shows the region in the temporal lobes that functions as the primary projection area for hearing (the "auditory" area). If directly stimulated here, patients hear clicks, buzzes, and hums. An area in the occipital lobes is the primary projection area for vision; stimulation here produces the experience of seeing flashes of light or visual patterns.

These sensory projection areas differ from each other in important ways, but they also have features in common, and they're features that parallel the attributes of the motor projection area. First, each of these areas provides a map of the sensory environment. In the somatosensory area, each part of the body's surface is represented by its own region on the cortex; areas of the body that are near to each other are typically represented by similarly nearby areas in the brain. In the visual area, each region of visual space has its own cortical representation, and again, adjacent areas of space are usually represented by adjacent brain sites. In the auditory projection area, different frequencies of sound each have their own cortical sites, and adjacent brain sites are responsive to adjacent frequencies.

Second, in each of these maps the assignment of cortical space is governed by function, not by anatomical proportions. In the parietal lobes, parts of the body that are not very discriminating with regard to touch, even if they're physically large, get relatively little cortical area. Other, more sensitive areas of the body (the lips, tongue, and fingers) get far more space. In the occipital lobes, more cortical surface is devoted to the fovea, the part of the eyeball that is most sensitive to detail.

Finally, we also find evidence here of contralateral connections: The left parietal lobe receives its main input from the right side of the body, for example; the right receives its input from the left side of the body. Likewise for the visual projection areas, although here the projection is not contralateral with regard to body parts; instead, it's contralateral with regard to physical space. Specifically, the visual projection area in the right hemisphere receives information from both the left eye and the right, but the information it receives corresponds to the left half of visual space (i.e., all of the things you see toward the left when you are looking straight ahead). The reverse is true for the left cerebral hemisphere: It receives information from both eyes, but from only the right half of visual space.

Association Areas

The projection areas described so far—both motor and sensory—make up only a small part of the human cortex—roughly 25%. The remaining cortical areas are traditionally referred to as the **association cortex**, on the idea that this section of the brain performs the task of associating simple ideas and sensations in order to form more complex thoughts and behaviors.

This terminology, however, is falling out of use, in part because this large volume of brain tissue can be subdivided further on both functional and anatomical grounds. These subdivisions are perhaps best revealed by the diversity of symptoms that result if the cortex is damaged in one or another specific location. For example, some lesions in the frontal lobe produce **apraxias**, disturbances in the initiation or organization of voluntary action. Other lesions (generally in the occipital cortex, or in the rearmost part of the parietal lobe) lead to **agnosias**, disruptions in a person's ability to identify familiar objects. Agnosias usually affect one modality only, so a patient with visual agnosia, for example, can recognize a fork by touching it but not by looking at it. A patient with auditory agnosia, by contrast, might be unable to identify familiar voices but might still recognize the face of the person speaking.

Still other lesions (usually in the parietal lobe) produce **neglect syndrome**, in which the individual seems to ignore half of the visual world. A patient afflicted with this syndrome will shave only half of his face and eat food from only half of his plate. If asked to read the word "pigpen," he will read "pen," and so on.

Damage in other areas causes still other symptoms. We mentioned earlier that lesions in the left frontal lobe, usually at sites just above the lateral fissure, can result in disruption to language capacities, a problem referred to as **aphasia**.

Finally, damage to the frontmost part of the frontal lobe, the **prefrontal area**, causes a variety of problems. In many cases, these are problems of planning and implementing strategies. In other cases, patients with damage here show problems in inhibiting their own behaviors, relying on habit even in situations for which habit is inappropriate. Frontal lobe damage can also (as we mentioned in our discussion of Capgras syndrome) lead to a variety of confusions, such as whether a remembered episode actually happened or was simply imagined.

We will have more to say about many of these diagnostic categories—aphasia, agnosia, neglect, and more—in upcoming chapters. There we'll be able to consider these disorders in the context of other things we know about object recognition, attention, and so on; this will allow us to draw important lessons from these clinical data. Our point for the moment, though, is a simple one: These various clinical patterns make it clear that the so-called association cortex contains many subregions, each specialized for a particular function, but with all of the subregions working together in virtually all aspects of our daily lives.

The Visual System

This brief tour has mentioned just a few of the brain's parts, and it has also focused only on large-scale structures. For many purposes, though, we need to take a closer look at the brain to see how the brain's functions are actually carried out. In this section, we'll illustrate this sort of closer look by considering the brain systems that allow us to see—and to recognize the objects that we see. We take the visual system as our example for two reasons. First, it is a modality through which humans acquire a huge amount of information, whether by reading or simply by viewing the objects and events that surround us. If we understand vision, therefore, we understand the processes that bring us much of our knowledge. Second, investigators in this area have made enormous progress, providing us with a rich portrait of how the visual system operates, and so the study of vision provides an excellent illustration of how the close study of the brain can proceed and what it can teach us.

The Photoreceptors

You look around the world, and instantly, effortlessly, you recognize the objects that surround you—words on this page, objects in the room in which you're sitting, things you can view out the window. You know the identities of these objects, and you also perceive that each has a particular size, position, color, and texture.

What makes all of this possible? The sequence of events begins, of course, with the eye.

Light is produced by many objects in our surroundings—the sun, lamps, candles—and this light then reflects off of most other objects. It is usually this reflected light—reflected from this book page, or from a friend's face—that launches the processes of vision. Some of this light hits the front surface of the eyeball, passes through the **cornea** and the **lens**, and then hits the **retina**, the light-sensitive tissue that lines the back of the eyeball (see Figure 2.3). The cornea and lens focus the incoming light, just as a camera lens might, so that a sharp image is cast onto the retina. The cornea is fixed in its shape, but the shape of the lens can be adjusted by a band of muscle that surrounds it. When the muscle tightens, the lens bulges somewhat, creating the proper shape for focusing images cast by nearby objects; when the muscle relaxes, the lens returns to a flatter shape, allowing the proper focus for objects farther away.

On the retina, there are two types of **photoreceptors**, cells that respond directly to the incoming light. The **rods** are sensitive to much lower levels of light and so play an essential role whenever we're moving around in semidarkness, or whenever we're trying to view a fairly dim stimulus. But the rods are also color-blind: They distinguish among different intensities of light (and so contribute to our perception of brightness), but they provide no means of discriminating one hue from another.

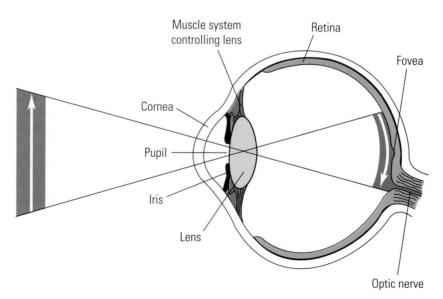

FIGURE 2.3 The Human Eye
Light enters the eye through the pupil and is focused by the cornea and the lens so that a sharp image is projected onto the light-sensitive retina. The fovea is the region of the retina with the greatest sensitivity to detail.

Cones, in contrast, are much less sensitive than rods and so need more incoming light to operate at all. But cones are sensitive to color differences. More precisely, there are three different types of cones, each having its own pattern of sensitivities to different wavelengths. We perceive color, therefore, by comparing the outputs from these three cone types. Strong firing from only the cones that prefer short wavelengths, for example, accompanied by weak (or no) firing from the other cone types, signals purple. Blue is signaled by equally strong firing from the cones that prefer short wavelengths and those that prefer medium wavelengths, with only modest firing by cones that prefer long wavelengths. And so on.

Cones also have another crucial function: They allow us to discern fine detail. The ability to see detail is referred to as **acuity**, and acuity is much higher for the cones than it is for the rods. This explains why we point our eyes toward a target whenever we wish to perceive it in detail. What we are actually doing is positioning our eyes so that the image of the target falls onto the **fovea**, the very center of the retina. Here cones far outnumber rods (and, in fact, the center of the fovea has no rods at all). As a result, this is the region of the retina with the greatest acuity.

As one moves away from the fovea and into the visual periphery, the rods predominate; well out into the periphery, there are no cones. This is why we're better able to see very dim lights out of the corner of our eyes. Sailors and astronomers have known this for years; when looking at a barely visible star, they know that it's best not to look directly at the star's location. By looking slightly away from the star, they ensure that the star's image will fall outside of the fovea, and onto a region of the retina dense with the more light-sensitive rods.

Lateral Inhibition

Rods and cones do not report directly to the brain. Instead, the photoreceptors stimulate **bipolar cells**, which in turn excite **ganglion cells**. The ganglion cells collect information from all over the retina and then gather together to form the bundle of nerve fibers that we call the **optic nerve**. The optic nerve leaves the eyeball and carries information to various sites in the brain. Most of the fibers go first to an important way station in the thalamus called the **lateral geniculate nucleus**, or LGN; from there, information is transmitted to the primary projection area for vision, in the occipital lobe.

Let's be clear, though, that the optic nerve is far more than a mere cable that conducts signals from one site to another. Instead, the cells that link retina to brain are already engaged in the task of analyzing the visual input. One example of this lies in the phenomenon of **lateral inhibition**, a pattern in which cells, when stimulated, inhibit the activity of neighboring cells. To see why this is important, consider two cells, each receiving stimulation from a brightly lit area (see Figure 2.4). One cell (Cell B in the figure) is receiving its stimulation from the middle of the lit area. It is intensely stimulated, but so are its neighbors, and so all of the cells in this area are

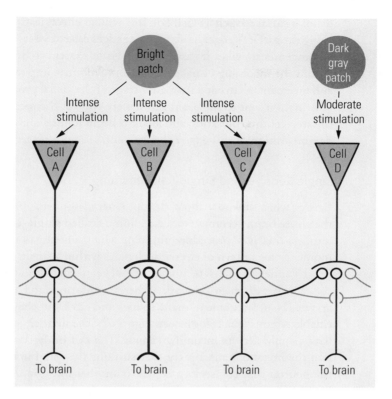

FIGURE 2.4 Lateral Inhibition and Edge Enhancement
Cell B is intensely stimulated by the bright patch but receives lateral inhibition from both of its (strongly activated) neighbors, A and C. As a result, Cell B sends a diminished signal to the brain. Cell C initially receives the same input as B but ends up sending a stronger signal to the brain. This is because C receives lateral inhibition from only one of its neighbors. (Its other neighbor, Cell D, is only moderately stimulated and so is sending out only a small amount of inhibition.) In this fashion, lateral inhibition creates a pattern in which cells receiving input from the edge of a surface send out stronger signals.

inhibiting each other. As a result, the activity level of Cell B is *increased* by the stimulation but *decreased* by the lateral inhibition it is receiving. This combination leads to only a moderate level of activity overall.

In contrast, another cell (Cell C in the figure) is receiving its stimulation from the edge of the lit area. It is intensely stimulated, and so are its neighbors *on one side*. Therefore, this cell will receive inhibition from one side but not from the other, and so it will be less inhibited than Cell B (which is receiving inhibition from all sides). So, in short, cells B and C initially receive the same input, but C is less inhibited than B and will therefore end up firing more strongly than B.

The pattern of lateral inhibition, then, actually leads to stronger responses from cells detecting the edge of a surface (such as Cell C) than from cells detecting the middle of a surface (such as Cell B). This will, in effect, lead to an exaggerated response along the surface's edges, making those edges easier to detect. This process, called **edge enhancement**, makes it easier for the visual system to discern the shapes contained within the incoming visual information. And it is important to note that this edge enhancement occurs at a very early stage of the visual processing. In other words, the information sent to the brain isn't a mere copy of the incoming stimulation; instead, the steps of interpretation and analysis begin immediately, in the eyeball. (For a clear demonstration of this edge enhancement, see color insert, Figure 6.)

Single Neurons and Single-Cell Recording

Part of what we know about the optic nerve—indeed, part of what we know about the entire brain—comes from a technique called **single-cell recording**. As the name implies, this is a procedure through which investigators can record, moment by moment, the pattern of electrical changes within a single neuron.

To understand this technique, it will be useful to know a bit more about **neurons**, the cells that do the main work of carrying information back and forth in the nervous system. Neurons come in many shapes and sizes, but they generally have three identifiable regions (see color insert, Figure 7): The **dendrites** are the part of the neuron that usually detects incoming signals. The **cell body** contains the neuron's nucleus and the metabolic machinery that sustains the cell. Finally, the **axon** is the part of the neuron that transmits a signal to another location. Axons vary considerably in length. The axons of the retinal ganglion cells, for example, stretch from the retina to the LGN, a distance of a couple of inches. In contrast, the axons that send command signals from the spinal cord to the legs can be more than a full meter in length.

The axon often has several branches that terminate on other neurons. They do not touch these other neurons directly; instead, there is a small gap between the adjacent neurons. Communication across this gap is generally done via chemical signals: **Neurotransmitters** are released through the membrane at the end of the axon; these chemicals drift across the gap and stimulate the next neuron. This site—the end of the axon, plus the gap, plus the receiving membrane of the next neuron—is called a **synapse**. The axon's end is therefore called the **presynaptic membrane**; the receiving membrane (typically on the next neuron's dendrites) is the **postsynaptic membrane**.

When the neurotransmitters arrive at the postsynaptic membrane, they cause changes in the membrane that allow certain ions to flow into and out of the postsynaptic cell. If these ionic flows are relatively small, then the postsynaptic cell quickly recovers and nothing more happens. But if the ionic flows are large enough, this triggers a response from the postsynaptic cell. In formal terms, if the incoming signal reaches the postsynaptic cell's **threshold**, then the cell **fires**; that is, it produces an **action potential**—a signal that moves down its axon, which in turn causes the release of neurotransmitters at that neuron's synapse, potentially causing the next cell to fire.

Notice, therefore, that the postsynaptic neuron's initial response can vary in size; the incoming signal can cause a small ionic flow or a large one. The magnitude of this response depends on several factors: How much neurotransmitter did the presynaptic cell release? How sensitive is the postsynaptic cell at this site? Both of these measures can vary from one neuron to the next and also can be altered with experience; this alteration is likely to be the neural basis for much of what we call "learning." In addition, the presynaptic cell may fire many times in succession; these separate firings can have a cumulative effect so that, together, they eventually produce a response in the postsynaptic cell. Likewise, the postsynaptic cell is likely to be receiving inputs from many other cells; these inputs, too, can accumulate, leading to a response.

Crucially, though, once these inputs reach the postsynaptic neuron's firing threshold, the signal that is produced does not vary in size. Either a signal is sent down the axon or it is not; if the signal is sent, it is always of the same magnitude, a fact referred to as the **all-or-none law**. If the cell is stimulated strongly, it may fire more frequently or it may keep firing for a longer time, but the size of the signal that is sent along the axon never changes.

When investigators record the activity of a single neuron, therefore, what they are recording is the cell's firing—in particular, its firing rate. This rate can then be examined in conjunction with a scrutiny of the circumstances in order to figure out what event—either in the external world or elsewhere in the nervous system—triggered the firing. In this way, we can figure out roughly what job the neuron does within the broad context of the entire nervous system.

The technique of single-cell recording has been used with enormous success in the study of vision. In a typical study, the animal being studied is first immobilized. Then electrodes are placed just outside a neuron in the animal's optic nerve or brain. Next a computer screen is placed in front of the animal's eyes, and various patterns are flashed on the screen: circles, lines at various angles, or squares of various sizes at various positions. Researchers can then ask: Which patterns cause that neuron to fire? To what visual inputs does that cell respond?

By analogy, we know that a smoke detector is a smoke detector because it "fires" (makes noise) when smoke is on the scene. We know that a motion detector is a motion detector because it "fires" when something moves nearby. But what kind of detector is a given neuron? Is it responsive to any light in any position within the field of view? In that case, we might call it a "light detector." Or is it perhaps responsive only to certain shapes at certain positions (and therefore is a "shape detector")? With this logic, we can map out precisely what it is that the cell responds to; this is referred to as the cell's **receptive field**—that is, the size and shape of the area in the visual world to which that cell responds. With that, we learn what kind of detector the cell is.

Multiple Types of Receptive Fields

Classic data from single-cell recording come from studies by David Hubel and Torsten Wiesel (1959, 1968), who were awarded the Nobel Prize for their work. Hubel and Wiesel documented the existence of several types of neurons within the visual system, each of which has a different kind of visual trigger, a different type of receptive field. Some neurons in the visual system seem to function as "dot detectors." These cells fire at their maximum rate when light is presented in a small, roughly circular area, in a specific position within the field of view. Presentations of light just outside of this area cause the cell to fire at *less* than its usual "resting" rate, so the input must be precisely positioned to make this cell fire. Figure 2.5 depicts such a receptive field.

Such cells are often called **center–surround cells**, to mark the fact that light presented to the central region of the receptive field has one influence, whereas light presented to the surrounding ring has the opposite influence. If both the center and the surround are strongly stimulated, the cell will fire neither more nor

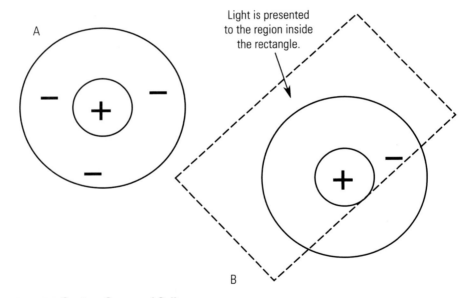

FIGURE 2.5 Center–Surround Cells

Some neurons have receptive fields with a center–surround organization. If light shines onto the central region, the cell increases its firing rate; this is why the center is marked "+". If light shines onto the peripheral region, the cell decreases its firing. If both regions are illuminated, the cell will not change its firing rate in either direction. Stimuli presented outside the periphery have no effect on the cell. If we present a stimulus as shown in Panel B, the entire center is stimulated, but only a portion of the surround. Therefore, the positive signal outweighs the negative, and so the cell's firing rate will increase somewhat.

less than usual; for this cell, a strong uniform stimulus is equivalent to no stimulus at all.

Other cells fire at their maximum only when a stimulus containing an edge of just the right orientation appears within their receptive fields. These cells, therefore, can be thought of as "edge detectors." Some cells prefer vertical edges, some prefer horizontal, some prefer orientations in between. If a cell's preference is, say, for horizontal edges, then nearly horizontal edges will evoke some response from the cell, but the response will be less than that for the cell's favored orientation. Edges sharply different from the cell's preferred orientation (say, a vertical edge for a cell that prefers horizontal) will elicit no response (see Figure 2.6).

Other cells, elsewhere in the visual cortex, fire maximally only if an angle of a particular size appears in their receptive fields; others fire maximally in response to corners and notches. Still other cells appear to be "movement detectors" and will fire strongly if a stimulus moves, say, from right to left across the cell's receptive field. Other cells favor left-to-right movement, and so on through the various possible directions of movement.

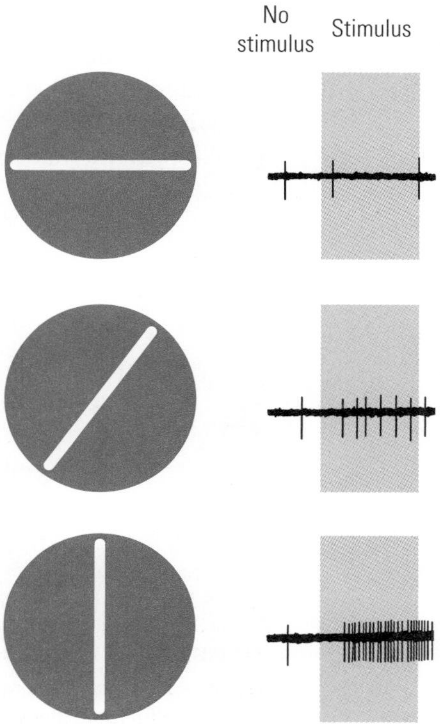

FIGURE 2.6 Orientation-Specific Visual Fields

Some cells in the visual system fire only when the input contains a line segment at the proper orientation. For example, one cell might fire very little in response to a horizontal line, fire only occasionally in response to a diagonal, and fire at its maximum rate only when a vertical line is present. In this figure, the circles show the stimulus that was presented. The right side shows records of neural firing. Each vertical stroke represents a firing by the cell; the left–right position reflects the passage of time. (After Hubel, 1963)

Parallel Processing in the Visual System

This proliferation of cell types suggests that the visual system relies on a "divide and conquer" strategy, with different types of cells, located in slightly different areas of the cortex, each specializing in a particular kind of analysis. This pattern is plainly evident in **Area V1**, the site on the occipital lobe where axons from the LGN first reach the cortex (see Figure 2.7). In this brain area, different cells have different receptive fields, so that each cell serves as a specific type of "detector," responding maximally to its own "preferred" input. The pattern of specialization becomes all the more evident as we consider other brain areas. Figure 2.8, for example, reflects one recent summary of the brain areas known (on the basis of single-cell recording) to be involved in vision. Some of these areas (V1, V2, V3, V4, PO, and MT) are in the occipital cortex; other areas are in the parietal cortex; others are in the inferotemporal cortex (we'll have more to say in a moment about these areas outside of the occipital cortex). Each area seems to have its own function. Neurons in Area MT, for example, are acutely sensitive to direction and speed of movement. Cells in Area V4 fire most strongly when the input is of a certain color and a certain shape.

This pattern of specialization makes it clear that the visual system relies on **parallel processing**—a system in which many different steps (in this case, many different kinds of analysis) are going on at the same time. (Parallel processing is usually contrasted with **serial processing**, in which steps are carried out one at a time—that is, in a series.) One advantage of this simultaneous processing is speed: Brain areas trying to discern the shape of the incoming stimulus don't need to wait until the motion analysis or the color analysis is complete. Instead, all of the analyses go forward in parallel, with no waiting time.

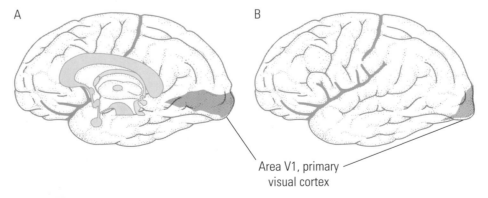

FIGURE 2.7 Area V1 in the Brain

Area V1 is the site on the occipital lobe where axons from the LGN first reach the cortex. Panel A shows the brain as if sliced down the middle; Panel B shows the brain viewed from the side. As the two panels show, most of Area V1 is located on the cortical surface between the two cerebral hemispheres.

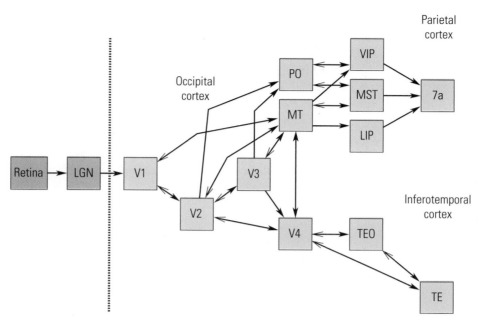

FIGURE 2.8 The Visual Processing Pathways
The visual system relies heavily on parallel processing, with different brain areas engaged in their own specific analyses. Information from the LGN is sent primarily to Area V1, but from there information is sent along several different pathways. (Adapted from art by Steven Luck)

Another advantage of parallel processing is the possibility of mutual influence among multiple systems. To see why this is important, consider the fact that sometimes our interpretation of an object's motion depends on our understanding of the object's three-dimensional shape. This suggests that it might be best if the perception of shape happened first. That way, we could use the results of this processing step as a guide to later analyses. In other cases, though, it turns out that the relationship between shape and motion is reversed: In these cases, our interpretation of an object's three-dimensional shape depends on our understanding of its motion. To allow for this possibility, it might be best if the perception of motion happened first, so that it could guide the subsequent analysis of shape.

How do we deal with these conflicting demands? The visual system has evolved a pattern in which both sorts of analysis go on simultaneously, so that each type of analysis can be enriched and informed by the other. Put differently, neither the shape-analyzing system nor the motion-analyzing system gets priority. Instead, the two systems work concurrently and "negotiate" a solution that satisfies both systems (Van Essen & DeYoe, 1995).

Parallel processing is evident in virtually every aspect of the visual system. Within the optic nerve itself, there are two different types of cells, **P cells** and **M cells**, and these provide the main inputs for the corresponding types of cells in the LGN: P cells provide input for the LGN's **parvocellular cells**; M cells, for the LGN's **magnocellular cells**. (The terms refer to the relative sizes of these cells; *parvo* derives from the Latin word for "small," and *magno* from the word for "large.") P cells and M cells are different in several ways: P cells have smaller receptive fields than do M cells, and they also have a different pattern of firing. P cells continue to fire if a stimulus remains unchanged; M cells fire when the stimulus appears and then again when it disappears, but not in between.

What purpose is served by this specialization? The P cells in the optic nerve and the parvocellular cells in the LGN appear to be specialized for spatial analysis and the detailed analysis of form. The M cells in the optic nerve and the magnocellular cells in the LGN are probably specialized for the detection of motion and the perception of depth.[1]

Evidence for parallel processing continues as we move beyond the occipital cortex. As Figure 2.9 indicates, some of the information is transmitted from the occipital lobe to the cortex of the temporal lobe. This pathway, often called the ***what* system**, plays a major role in the identification of visual objects, telling us whether the object is a cat, an apple, or whatever. A second pathway, which carries information to the parietal cortex, is often called the ***where* system** and seems to perform the function of guiding our action, based on our perception of where an object is located—above or below us, to our right or to our left (Goodale & Milner, 2004; Ungerleider & Haxby, 1994; Ungerleider & Mishkin, 1982).

The contrasting roles of these two systems can be revealed in many ways, including studies of brain damage. Patients with lesions in the occipital-temporal pathway show visual agnosia—an inability to recognize visually presented objects, including such common things as a cup or a pencil. However, these patients show little disorder in recognizing visual orientation or in reaching. The reverse pattern is observed with patients who have suffered lesions in the occipital-parietal pathway: difficulty in reaching, but no problem in object identification (Damasio, Tranel, & Damasio, 1989; Farah, 1990; Goodale, 1995; F. Newcombe, Ratcliff, & Damasio, 1987).

Other clinical data echo this broad theme of parallel processing among separate systems. For example, we noted earlier that different brain areas are critical for the perception of color, motion, and form. If this is right, then someone who has suffered damage in just one of these areas should show problems in the perception of color but not the perception of motion or form, or problems in the perception of motion but not the perception of form or color. These predictions are correct: Some patients do suffer a specific loss of color vision through damage to the central nervous system, even though their perception of form and motion remains normal (Gazzaniga, Ivry, & Mangun, 1998; Meadows, 1974). To them, the entire world is clothed only in

---

[1]Many students find it useful to think of the P cells as specialized roughly for the perception of *pattern*, and M cells as specialized for the perception of *motion*. These descriptions are crude, but they're easy to remember.

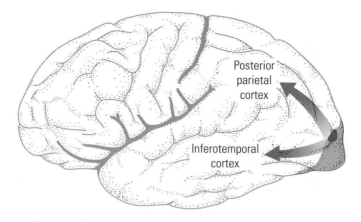

FIGURE 2.9 The *What* and *Where* Pathways

Information from the primary visual cortex (located at the back of the head) is transmitted both to the inferotemporal cortex (the so-called *what* system) and to the posterior parietal cortex (the *where* system).

"dirty shades of gray."[2] Other patients suffer damage to the motion system and so develop a disorder dubbed "akinetopsia" (Zihl, Von Cramon, & Mai, 1983). For such patients, the world is described as a succession of static photographs. They're unable to report the speed or direction of a moving object; as one patient put it, "When I'm looking at the car first, it seems far away. But then when I want to cross the road, suddenly the car is very near." Cases like these provide dramatic confirmation of the separateness of our visual system's various elements, and the ways in which the visual system is vulnerable to very specific forms of damage. (For further evidence with neurologically intact participants, see Bundesen, Kyllingsbaek, & Larsen, 2003.)

Putting the Pieces Back Together

It should be clear, then, that our intellectual achievements depend on an array of different brain areas working together. This was evident in our consideration of Capgras syndrome, and the same pattern emerged in our description of the visual system. Here, too, many brain areas must work together: the *what* system and the *where* system, areas specialized for the detection of movement and areas specialized for the identification of simple forms.

We have identified certain advantages that derive from this cerebral division of labor and the parallel processing it allows. But the division of labor also creates a problem: If multiple brain areas contribute to an overall task, how is their function-

---

[2]This is different from ordinary color blindness, which is usually present from birth and results from abnormalities that are outside the brain itself—for example, abnormalities in the photoreceptors.

ing coordinated? When we see a ballet dancer in a graceful leap, the leap itself is registered by motion-sensitive neurons, but the recognition of the ballet dancer depends on shape-sensitive neurons. How are the pieces put back together? When we reach for a coffee cup but stop midway because we see that the cup is empty, the reach itself is guided by the *where* system; the fact that the cup is empty is registered by the *what* system. How are these two streams of processing coordinated?

Investigators refer to this broad issue as the **binding problem**—the task of reuniting the various elements of a scene, elements that are initially dealt with by different systems in different parts of the brain. And obviously this problem is solved: What we perceive is not an unordered catalogue of sensory elements. Instead, we perceive a coherent, integrated perceptual world. Apparently, then, this is a case in which the various pieces of Humpty Dumpty are reassembled to form an organized whole.

Visual Maps and Firing Synchrony

Look around you. Your visual system registers whiteness and blueness and brownness; it also registers a small cylindrical shape (your coffee cup), a medium-sized rectangle (this book page), and a much larger rectangle (your desk). How do you put these pieces together so that you see that it's the coffee cup, and not the book page, that's blue; the desktop, and not the cup, that's brown?

There is still debate about how the visual system solves this problem, but we can identify three elements that certainly contribute to the solution. One element is *spatial position*. The part of the brain registering the cup's shape is separate from the parts registering its color or its motion; nonetheless, these various brain areas all have something in common: They each keep track of where the target is—where the cylindrical shape was located, and where the blueness was; where the motion was detected, and where things were still. Thus, the reassembling of these pieces can be done with reference to spatial position. In essence, you can overlay the map of *which forms are where* on top of the map of *which colors are where* to get the right colors with the right forms, and likewise for the map showing *which motion patterns are where*.

Information about spatial position is important for its own sake: You have an obvious reason to care whether the tiger is close to you or far away, or whether the bus is on your side of the street or the other. But in addition, location information apparently provides a frame of reference used to solve the binding problem. Given this double function, we shouldn't be surprised that spatial position is a major organizing theme within all the various brain areas concerned with vision, with each area seeming to provide its own map of the visual world.

These maps can be documented via single-cell recording, which confirms that adjacent cells within a bit of brain tissue are usually responsive to adjacent positions within the visual field—so that the cells' receptive fields really do form a map of visual space. Moreover, we can document one such map among the cells responsive to color, another among the cells responsive to motion, and so on. Indeed, more than 30 such maps have been documented (Gazzaniga, Ivry, & Mangun, 2002).

However, spatial position, as important as it is, is not the whole story. Evidence is accumulating that the brain also uses a special *rhythm* to identify which sensory elements belong with which. Imagine two groups of neurons in the visual cortex. One group of neurons fires maximally whenever a vertical line is in view; another group fires maximally whenever a stimulus is in view moving from left to right. Let's also imagine that right now a vertical line is presented, and it is moving in the right way, and so, as a result, both groups of neurons are firing strongly. How does the brain encode the fact that these attributes are bound together, different aspects of a single object? The visual system seems to mark this fact by means of **neural synchrony**. If the neurons detecting a vertical line are firing in synchrony with those signaling movement, then these attributes are registered as belonging to the same object. If they are not in synchrony, the features are not bound together (Buzsáki & Draguhn, 2004; Csibra, Davis, Spratling, & Johnson, 2000; Elliott & Müller, 2000; Fries, Reynolds, Rorie, & Desimone, 2001).

What causes this synchrony? How do the neurons become synchronized in the first place? Here another factor appears to be crucial: *attention*. We will have more to say about attention in Chapter 4, but for now let's just note that attention plays a key role in binding together the separate features of a stimulus. (For a classic statement of this argument, see Treisman & Gelade, 1980; Treisman, Sykes, & Gelade, 1977. For a more recent and more complex view, see Quinlan, 2003, and also Chapter 4.)

Evidence for attention's role comes from many sources, including the fact that when we overload someone's attention, she is likely to make **conjunction errors**— correctly detecting the features present in a visual display, but making mistakes about how the features are bound together (or *conjoined*). Thus, someone shown a blue *H* and a red *T* might report seeing a blue *T* and a red *H*—an error in binding. Similarly, individuals who suffer from severe attention deficits (because of brain damage in the parietal cortex) are particularly impaired in tasks that require them to judge how features are conjoined to form complex objects (e.g., Robertson, Treisman, Friedman-Hill, & Grabowecky, 1997). Finally, studies suggest that synchronized neural firing is observed in an animal's brain when the animal is attending to a specific stimulus, but is not observed in neurons activated by an unattended stimulus (e.g., Buschman & Miller, 2007; Saalman, Pigarev, & Vidyasagar, 2007; Womelsdorf et al., 2007). Results like these argue both that attention is crucial for the binding problem and that attention is linked to the neural synchrony that seems to unite a stimulus's features.

Once again, therefore, we see that seemingly simple mental achievements depend on multiple brain areas and, crucially, the coordination of action across these areas. In addition, these factors, helping to "bind" together different elements of the stimulus, remind us that information is represented in the brain in several different ways: in terms of *which* cells are firing, *how often* they are firing, and also, it seems, the *rhythm* in which they are firing. Finally, note that our account of vision requires discussion of "lower level" activities (such as what happens just one or two synapses into the brain) and also "higher level" activities (including the influence of attention on neural activity). In a sense, then, our account of brain functioning will need to depend on an understanding of cognition at the same time that our account of cognition will rely heavily on what is known about the brain.

Chapter Summary

■ The brain is divided into several different structures, but of particular importance for cognitive psychology is the forebrain. In the forebrain, each cerebral hemisphere is divided into the frontal lobe, parietal lobe, temporal lobe, and occipital lobe. In understanding these brain areas, one important source of evidence comes from studies of brain damage, enabling us to examine what sorts of symptoms result from lesions in specific brain locations. This has allowed a localization of function, an effort that is also supported by neuroimaging research, which shows that the pattern of activation in the brain depends heavily on the particular task being performed.

■ Different parts of the brain perform different jobs, but for virtually any mental process, different brain areas must work together in a closely integrated fashion. When this integration is lost (as it is, for example, in Capgras syndrome), bizarre symptoms can result.

■ The primary motor projection areas are the departure point for nerve cells that initiate muscle movement. The primary sensory projection areas are the main points of arrival for information from the eyes, ears, and other sense organs. Almost all of these projection areas show the pattern of contralateral control, with tissue in the left hemisphere sending or receiving its main signals from the right side of the body, and vice versa. Each projection area provides a map of the environment or the relevant body part, but the assignment of space in this map is governed by function, not by anatomical proportions.

■ Most of the forebrain's cortex has traditionally been referred to as the association cortex, but this area is itself subdivided into specialized regions. This subdivision is reflected in the varying consequences of brain damage, with lesions in the occipital lobe leading to visual agnosia, damage in the temporal lobes leading to aphasia, and so on. Damage to the prefrontal area causes many different problems, but these are generally problems in the forming and implementing of strategies.

■ One brain area that has been mapped in considerable detail is the visual system. This system takes its main input from the rods and cones on the retina. Then, information is sent via the optic nerve to the brain. An important point is that cells in the optic nerve do much more than transmit information; they also begin the analysis of the visual input. This is reflected in the phenomenon of lateral inhibition, which leads to edge enhancement.

■ Part of what we know about the brain comes from single-cell recording, which can record the electrical activity of an individual neuron. In the visual system, this recording has allowed researchers to map the receptive fields for many cells, and this mapping has provided evidence for a high degree of specialization among the various parts of the visual system, with some parts specialized for the perception of motion, others for the perception of color, and so on. These various areas function in parallel, and this parallel processing allows great speed; it also allows mutual influence among multiple systems.

■ Parallel processing begins in the optic nerve and continues throughout the visual system. For example, the *what* system (in the temporal lobe) appears to be specialized for the identification of visual objects; the *where* system (in the parietal lobe) seems to tell us where an object is located.

■ The reliance on parallel processing creates a problem of reuniting the various elements of a scene so that these elements are perceived in an integrated fashion. This is called the binding problem. One key in solving this problem, though, lies in the fact that different brain systems are organized in terms of maps, so that spatial position can be used as a framework for reuniting the separately analyzed aspects of the visual scene.

The Workbook Connection

See the *Cognition Workbook* for further exploration of the neural basis for cognition:

■ Demonstration 2.1: Foveation
■ Demonstration 2.2: The Blind Spot and the Active Nature of Vision
■ Demonstration 2.3: A Brightness Illusion
■ Research Methods: Control Groups
■ Cognitive Psychology and Education: Using Biology to Improve Memory
■ Cognitive Psychology and the Law: Detecting Lies

PART 2

Learning About the World Around Us

In the previous section, we described some of the early steps involved in vision, but we emphasize that these are only the early steps. We begin Chapter 3, therefore, with a discussion of the various ways in which the perceiver analyzes, organizes, and interprets the visual input. We then turn to the broad issue of how we recognize the various objects that surround us in the world, starting with a description of how we recognize printed letters, and then turning to the recognition of more complex (three-dimensional) objects. In both cases, we will discuss the ways in which object recognition is influenced by expectations and prior knowledge. We'll describe how a mechanism made up of very simple components can be sensitive to this knowledge, and that will lead us into a discussion of how complex knowledge can be "distributed" across an entire system.

Chapter 4 then turns to the study of attention. As we'll see, paying attention is a complex achievement involving many different elements. Some of the steps needed for attention will be the same no matter what a person is paying attention to; other steps will depend on the particular task. In either case, paying attention requires that one commit some mental resources, and in the absence of those resources, performance drops off markedly. In addition, these resources are available only in limited quantities, and this constraint may set boundaries on human performance. Part of what's at stake in Chapter 4, therefore, is a discussion of what people can or cannot accomplish, and whether there may be ways to escape the apparent limits on attention.

Recognizing Objects

As we saw in Chapter 2, information about the visual world is picked up by a large array of neural detectors, with each detector tuned to a particular aspect of the stimulus information. Some detectors specialize in horizontal line segments; others detect vertical lines or diagonals. Still others pick out specific patterns of movement or fire only when certain angles or notches are in view. For that matter, there are even neurons (in the monkey's brain) that fire only when a monkey's hand is in view (whether the fingers are stretched out or clenched in a fist) or only when another monkey's face is in view!

However, visual perception involves far more than a simple detection of the stimulus input's properties. As one consideration, we have already mentioned that the input's various attributes are detected by separate brain systems, and so a further step is required to reunite these various attributes so that we recognize that it is the squirrel that is brown and moving and the leaves that are green and still, rather than some other combination of these features. But the complexities of perception do not stop there. In this chapter, we consider some of the other steps involved in perceiving the visual world, and with that, we discuss just how large a role the perceiver plays—not just as a detector of incoming information, but as an active interpreter of that information.

In this text, we'll hold to the side the intriguing question of how you perceive movement or how you figure out how far away from you a stimulus is. These (and other) issues are covered in detail in courses on visual perception. We will focus instead on the critical problem of how we manage to recognize the objects we encounter every day in the world around us. As we will see, this step of recognizing objects is both far more important and far more complex than one might initially guess!

- In important ways, perception goes "beyond the information given" in interpreting a stimulus. Various points of organization are imposed by the perceiver, and they determine what a stimulus looks like and what the stimulus is seen to resemble.

- Recognition of visual inputs begins with features, but how easily we recognize a pattern depends on several factors: We have an easier time recognizing frequently or recently viewed patterns, and also patterns that are well formed (such as letter sequences with "normal" spelling patterns). We explain these findings in terms of a feature net—a network of detectors, each of which is "primed" according to how often or how recently it

has fired. The network relies on distributed knowledge to make inferences, and this process gives up some accuracy in order to gain efficiency.

- The feature net can be extended to other domains, including the recognition of three-dimensional objects. However, the recognition of faces requires a different sort of model, sensitive to configurations rather than to parts.

- Finally, we consider top-down influences on recognition. The existence of these influences tells us that object recognition is not a self-contained process; instead, knowledge external to object recognition is imported into and clearly shapes the process.

Visual Perception

We receive information about the world through various sensory modalities: We hear the sound of the approaching train, we smell the chocolate cake almost ready to come out of the oven, we feel the tap on our shoulder. There is no question, though, that for humans vision is the dominant sense. This is reflected in how much brain area is devoted to vision compared to how much is devoted to any of the other senses. It is also reflected in many aspects of our behavior. For example, if visual information conflicts with information received from other senses, we usually place our trust in vision. This is the basis for ventriloquism, in which we see the dummy's mouth moving while the sounds themselves are coming from the dummy's master. Vision wins out in this contest, and so we experience the illusion that the voice is coming from the dummy.

But how does vision operate? You open your eyes, and you see a world filled with familiar objects—chairs and desks, windows and walls, telephones and pencils. As you read this page, you can see the individual letters printed here, and they are letters that you know and can identify. The letters form words, which you also can recognize; you could say them out loud if requested, and you know the meaning of the words, so that you easily understand these sentences.

How is any of this possible? How do you manage to perceive, and then recognize, the objects you see every day? This is the problem, first, of **form perception**, the process through which you manage to see what the basic shape and size of an object are. Next is the problem of **object recognition**, the process through which you identify what the object is.

Why Is Object Recognition Crucial?

Virtually all knowledge and all use of knowledge depend on form perception and object recognition. To see this, think about a physician who might know how to treat measles, but who doesn't know how to recognize a case of this illness when she encounters one. In this case, the physician's knowledge about treatment becomes useless, because the physician doesn't know when (or with which patients) to use the treatment. Likewise, you know a great deal about telephones, and you use that knowledge in many ways. But you could not do this if you couldn't recognize a telephone when you saw one. Without recognition, you cannot bring your knowledge to bear on the world.

In a similar fashion, object recognition is also crucial for learning. In virtually all learning, one must combine new information with information learned previously. But for this to happen, one must categorize things properly. Today you learn something about Solomon. Yesterday you learned something about Solomon. If you are to integrate the new knowledge with the old, you need to realize that the person before you today is the same person as the one you met yesterday. Without proper categorization, there is no way to combine and integrate information.

Thus, object recognition may not be a glamorous skill, but it is crucial for virtually all of our commerce with the world. Moreover, it is the essential base for learning and memory. For our purposes, therefore, we will start our inquiry where much of knowledge starts: with the recognition and identification of objects in the world.

Beyond the Information Given

In Chapter 2, we saw how the process of object recognition begins: with the detection of simple visual features. But we've known for many years that there is more to the process than this. Early in the 20th century, a group of psychologists called the "Gestalt psychologists" noted that our perception of the visual world is organized in ways that the stimulus input is not.[1] They argued, therefore, that the organization must be contributed by the perceiver; this is why, they claimed, the perceptual whole is often different from the sum of its parts. Some years later, Jerome Bruner voiced similar claims and coined the phrase "beyond the information given" to describe some of the ways that our perception of a stimulus differs from (and goes beyond) the stimulus itself (Bruner, 1973).

---

[1]*Gestalt* is the German word for "shape" or "form." The Gestalt psychology movement was, overall, committed to the view that our theories need to emphasize the organization of the entire shape, and not just focus on the shape's parts.

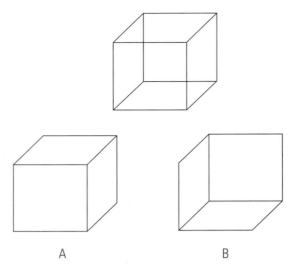

FIGURE 3.1 The Necker Cube

The top cube can be perceived as if viewed from above (in which case it is a transparent version of Cube A) or as if viewed from below (i.e., a transparent version of Cube B).

Consider the form shown in the top of Figure 3.1: the **Necker cube**. This drawing is called an "ambiguous figure" because there is more than one way to perceive it. As one option, it can be perceived as a cube viewed from above (in which case it is similar to the cube marked "A" in the figure); alternatively, it can be perceived as a cube viewed from below (in which case it is similar to the cube marked "B"). Both perceptions fit perfectly well with the information received by your eyes, and so the drawing itself is fully compatible with either of these perceptions. Put differently, the lines on the page are neutral with regard to the shape's configuration in depth; the lines on the page don't specify which is the "proper" interpretation.

Your perception of the cube, however, is not neutral. Instead, you perceive the cube as having one configuration or the other—similar either to Cube A or to Cube B. Your perception, in other words, goes beyond the information given in the drawing, by specifying an arrangement in depth.

The same point can be made for many other stimuli. Consider Figure 3.2, for example. This figure can be perceived as a vase centered in the picture, or it can be perceived equally well as two profiles facing each other. The drawing by itself, it seems, is fully compatible with either of these perceptions, and so, once again, the drawing is neutral with regard to perceptual organization. In particular, it is neutral with regard to **figure/ground organization**, the determination of what is the figure (the depicted object, displayed against a background) and what is the ground. Your perception of this figure, however, is not neutral about this point. Instead, your per-

FIGURE 3.2 The Ambiguous Vase/Profiles Figure
This figure can be perceived either as a white vase against a black background or as two black profiles against a white background.

ception somehow specifies that you are looking at the vase and not at the profiles, or that you are looking at the profiles and not at the vase.

In both of these examples, your perception contains information—about how the form is arranged in depth, or about which part of the form is figure and which is ground—that is not contained within the stimulus itself. Apparently, then, this is information contributed by you, the perceiver.

Organization and "Features"

One might suppose that our perception of the world proceeds in two broad steps. First, we collect information about the stimulus, so that we know (for example) what corners or angle or curves are contained in the input. Second, we interpret this information, and presumably it would be in this second step that we "go beyond the information given"—deciding how the form is laid out in depth (as in Figure 3.1), deciding what is figure and what is ground (Figure 3.2), and so on.

However, this view is *wrong*. As one concern, we mentioned in Chapter 2 that we do not just "pick up" the information in the stimulus, the way a camera might record the light energies reaching it. This is evident, for example, in the phenomenon of lateral inhibition, in which the visual system manages to emphasize some aspects of the input (the edges) and de-emphasize others (regions of uniform brightness) from the very beginning.

In addition, a number of observations suggest that our interpretation, our organization of the input, happens *before* we start cataloguing the input's basic features, and not after, as a secondary "interpretive" step. For example, consider the pattern shown in Figure 3.3. Initially, these black shapes seem to have no meaning, but after a moment, most people discover the word "hidden" in the figure. That is, people find a way to reorganize the figure so that the familiar letters come into view. But let's be clear about what this means. At the start, the form seems not to contain the features

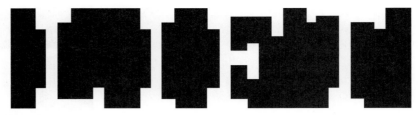

FIGURE 3.3 A Hidden Figure

Initially, these dark shapes have no meaning, but after a moment, the hidden figure becomes clearly visible. Notice, therefore, that at the start, the figure seems not to contain the features needed to identify the various letters. Once the figure is reorganized, however, with the white parts the figure and not the dark parts, the features are easily detected. Apparently, therefore, the analysis of features depends on a prior step, in which the figure is first organized by the viewer.

needed to identify the L, the I, and so on. Once the form is reorganized, though, it does contain these features and the letters are immediately recognized. Apparently, then, the cataloguing of the input's features depends on a prior step in which the form is organized by the viewer: With one organization, the key features are absent; with another, they're plainly present. In essence, then, the features are as much "in the eye of the beholder" as they are in the figure itself.

As a different example, you probably have no difficulty reading the word printed in Figure 3.4, although, in truth, most of the features needed for this recognition are absent from the figure. You easily "provide" the missing features, though, thanks to the fact that you interpret the black marks in the figure as shadows cast by letters hovering just above the page. Given this interpretation and the extrapolation it entails, you can, with no trouble, "fill in" the missing features, and in this way read the word despite the scanty information provided by the stimulus.

These demonstrations create a potential paradox. On one side, our perception of any form must start with the stimulus and must be governed by what is in that stimulus. After all, no matter how you try to interpret Figure 3.4, it will not look to you like a photograph of Queen Elizabeth—the basic features of the queen are just not present. This suggests that the features must be in place before an interpretation is offered, because the features govern the interpretation. But, on the other side, Figures

PERCEPTION

FIGURE 3.4 Missing Features

People have no trouble reading this word, despite the fact that most of the features needed for recognition are absent from the stimulus. However, people easily "supply" the missing features, emphasizing once again that the analysis of features depends on a prior step, in which the overall figure is first organized by the viewer.

3.3 and 3.4 suggest that the opposite is also the case: that the features one finds in an input depend on how the figure is interpreted. Therefore, it is the interpretation, not the features, that must be first.

The solution to this puzzle, though, is straightforward, and it hinges on the fact that the brain relies on parallel processing. In other words, the brain areas analyzing a pattern's basic features do their work at the same time as the brain areas analyzing the pattern's large-scale configuration. Moreover, these two brain areas constantly interact, so that the perception that is achieved is one that makes sense at both the large-scale and fine-grained levels.

The Logic of Perception

Overall, then, the stimulus by itself does not tell you which elements of the input are figure and which are ground, or how the form is arranged in three dimensions. Instead, these crucial organizing themes must be imposed on the stimulus by the perceiver, so that, in effect, the organization is "in the eye of the beholder" and not in the stimulus itself. (For further illustrations of the eye's active role, see color insert, Figure 8.) In addition, these steps of organization are not "add-ons" late in the process of perception. Instead, these organizing steps proceed in parallel with—and so can influence and be influenced by—the very earliest "pick-up" of information from the stimulus.

We should also emphasize that these steps of perceptual organization matter for us in many ways. For one, the organization determines our most immediate impressions of the stimulus. The stimulus we "see," in other words, as well as what the stimulus appears to resemble, are all determined not just by the pattern in front of our eyes, but by the pattern as we have interpreted it—the pattern with the organizing themes we've added.

The perceptual organization also plays a powerful role in deciding whether a form will be recognized as familiar or not. Imagine that we show a series of forms to participants, and Figure 3.2 is presented as part of the series. Via instructions, we manage to suggest to the participants that this figure shows a vase. Later in the series, we again show Figure 3.2, but this time we suggest that it shows two profiles. In this setting, it's likely that participants will not realize they've seen this figure before, will not realize the form is familiar. Apparently, what matters for familiarity is not the objective stimulus, not the pattern of pixels that literally hits the eye. Instead, what matters for familiarity is the figure as *perceived*—the figure *plus* the specifications added by the perceiver—and if these specifications change, the familiarity is lost.

But how does this perceptual interpretation happen? What are the processes through which the interpretation is generated? Investigators do not yet have a full account, although they are making impressive progress in understanding how these processes unfold. Some of the progress involves detailing the relevant brain mechanisms, and this work connects well with the materials described in Chapter 2. Other lines of research focus more on the "logic" of the processes, rather than the biological steps implementing this logic (e.g., Rock, 1983).

In what sense is perception "logical"? Let's note, first, that the interpretation achieved by the perceptual system—the organization of figure and ground, and so on—must fit with all the incoming stimulus information. Just like a good scientist, your perceptual apparatus requires a hypothesis that fits with all the data. Second, the perceptual system seems to prefer the simplest explanation of the stimulus. Here, too, the perceptual system acts just like a scientist—avoiding overly elaborate explanations of the "data" if a simpler explanation will do. Third, the perceptual system seems to avoid interpretations that involve coincidences. As an example, consider Figure 3.5. Most people immediately perceive this form as two lines crossing, but notice that other perceptions are possible: The form could, for example, be perceived as two *V* shapes, one on the top and one on the bottom. However, this interpretation would depend on the two *V* shapes being in exactly the right positions—just touching, with no overlap. In any other position, the combined *V*s would look quite different. Therefore, interpreting Figure 3.5 as two *V*s would rely on a coincidence—that the forms just happen to be in exactly the right positions—and this is why other interpretations of the form seem to be preferred.

Let's be clear, though, that we are not proposing that there really is a little scientist inside your brain, generating hypotheses about the input, calculating the likelihood of this or that coincidence. The perceptual system does work as if it were generating hypotheses and the like, but the key phrase here is "as if." Neural mechanisms somehow function in a way that leaves us, overall, with a process that seems quite logical and seems to analyze and interpret the evidence just as a scientist might. We do not know yet what all those neural mechanisms are, but in the meantime, these logical principles can help us make sense of a great deal of evidence concerning how people

FIGURE 3.5 Avoiding Coincidences
This form could be perceived as two *V* shapes, one on the top and one on the bottom. Or it could be perceived as two *V* shapes with one on the left and one on the right. The visual system seems to avoid these interpretations, however, because they involve an element of coincidence: This is what two *V*s would look like if they just happened to be positioned perfectly—touching and aligned, but with no overlap.

interpret the visual forms they encounter. (For more on the logic of perception, see color insert, Figure 9.)

Object Recognition

In Chapter 2, we saw how the nervous system begins its analysis of the visual input, with a large set of detectors operating in parallel, each detecting a specific attribute of an image. Next, these various attributes are somehow bound together, so that (for example) the perceiver knows that the greenness he detected was a property of the horizontal line and not the vertical one. The processes of perception then have to organize this information: Were the horizontal and vertical lines part of the same object or parts of different objects? Which aspects of the input belong to the figure (and so are crucial) and which to the ground (and can perhaps be ignored)?

Then, with the form organized in this fashion, we are ready (at last) to take the next steps toward identifying what the form actually is—a truck, a tree, or a character in a video game. Let's turn, therefore, to these steps. Our goal in this chapter is to describe how we recognize the huge variety of objects we encounter in our day-to-day world. We'll start, though, with a narrower focus: examining how we recognize the letters and words that make up printed language. Later in the chapter, we'll return to a discussion of visual targets other than print.

Recognition: Some Early Considerations

You are obviously able to recognize a huge number of different patterns—different objects (cows, trees, hats), various actions (running, jumping, falling), and different sorts of situations (crises, comedies). And not only do you recognize all these things, you can also recognize many variations of each. You recognize cats standing up and cats sitting down, cats running and cats asleep. And the same is true for your recognition of pigs, chairs, and any other object in your recognition repertoire.

You also recognize objects even when your information is partial. For example, you can still recognize a cat if only its head and one paw are visible behind a tree. You recognize a chair even when someone is sitting on it, despite the fact that the person blocks much of the chair from view.

All of this is true for print as well: You can recognize tens of thousands of different words, and you can recognize them whether the words are printed in large type or small, italics or straight letters, upper case or lower. You can even recognize handwritten words, for which the variation from one to the next is huge.

In addition, your recognition of various objects, whether print or otherwise, is influenced in important ways by the *context* in which the objects are encountered. For example, consider Figure 3.6. The middle character is the same in both words, but the character looks more like an *H* in the left word and more like an *A* in the right.

With this, you unhesitatingly read the left word as "THE" and not "TAE," and the right word as "CAT" and not "CHT."

How should we think about all this? What mechanism underlies all of these effects? In the next sections, we will develop a proposal for such a mechanism.

Features

One plausible suggestion is that many objects are recognized by virtue of their parts. You recognize an elephant because you see the trunk, the thick legs, the large body. You know a lollipop is a lollipop because you can see the circle shape on top of the straight stick. But how do you recognize the parts themselves? How, for example, do you recognize the circle in the lollipop? Perhaps you do so by virtue of its parts—the constituent arcs, for example.

To put this more generally, recognition might begin with the identification of **features** in the input pattern—features such as vertical lines, curves, or diagonals. With these features appropriately catalogued, you can start assembling the larger units: If you detect a horizontal together with a vertical, you know you're looking at a right angle; if you've detected four right angles, you know you're looking at a square.

Notice, though, that the features that are relevant here are not the features of the raw input. Instead, the features that we use are the ones in our organized perception of the input. That was the point of Figures 3.3 and 3.4, and it is also evident in Figure 3.7. We recognize all the forms in that figure as triangles—even though the essential features (three lines, three angles) are present in only one of them. The features are, however, present in our *organized perception* of the forms, and this returns us to our proposal: We recognize objects by detecting the presence of the relevant features.

Some of the advantages of a feature-based system are obvious immediately. First, features such as line segments and curves could serve as general-purpose building blocks. Not only would these features serve as the basis for recognizing letters, but they could also serve as the basis for recognizing other, more complex visual patterns (chairs, jackets, pickup trucks), opening the possibility of a single object-recognition system able to deal with a wide variety of targets.

Second, we have noted that people can recognize many variations on the objects they encounter—cats in different positions, *A*s in different fonts or different handwritings. But although the various *A*s are different from each other in overall shape, they

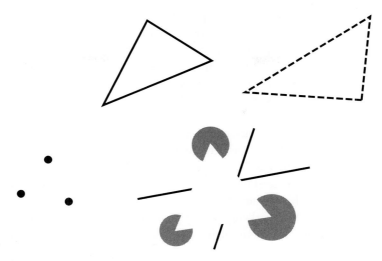

FIGURE 3.7 What Is a Triangle?
The features that we use in object recognition are not the features of the raw input. Instead, the features that we use are the ones in our organized perception of the input. This is evident in the fact that we recognize all of these forms as triangles—even though the essential features (three lines, three angles) are present in only one of them. The features are present, however, in our *organized perception* of the forms.

do have a great deal in common: two inwardly sloping lines and a horizontal crossbar. Focusing on features might allow us to concentrate on what is common to the various *A*s, and so might allow us to recognize *A*s despite their apparent diversity.

Third, several lines of data indicate that features do have priority in our perception of the world. For example, in a **visual search task**, participants have to indicate whether a certain target is or is not present in a display. If the target is defined in terms of a single prominent feature (e.g., searching for an angular shape hidden in a group of circles), this task is absurdly easy; in fact, participants can locate the target if it's hidden among a dozen circles almost as quickly as they can locate it sandwiched between just two circles. This suggests that the visual system does not have to inspect each of the figures to determine whether it has the relevant properties. (If it did, the larger number of figures would require more time.) Instead, the difference between angles and curves jumps out immediately. The same holds for differences in color, orientation, and many other simple features (Treisman & Gelade, 1980; Treisman & Souther, 1985; for a broad review, see Wolfe, 2003).

Fourth, other results suggest that the detection of features is a separate (and presumably early) step in object recognition, followed by subsequent steps in which the features are assembled into more complex wholes. Some of the evidence for this claim comes from people who suffer from a disorder known as **integrative agnosia**, caused by damage to the parietal cortex. These people appear relatively normal in tasks requiring them simply to detect whether particular features are present or absent in a display, but they are markedly impaired in tasks that require them to judge how the features are bound together to form complex objects (e.g., Behrmann, Peterson, Moscovitch, & Suzuki, 2006; Robertson, Treisman, Friedman-Hill, & Grabowecky, 1997).

Similar results have been obtained in studies in which *transcranial magnetic stimulation* (TMS) was used to disrupt portions of the brain in healthy individuals. (For more on TMS, see Chapter 2.) Ashbridge, Walsh, and Cowey (1997) found that disruption of the parietal lobe had no impact on performance when participants were searching a display for targets defined by a single feature (e.g., "Find the red shape"). However, the TMS markedly slowed performance when participants were searching for a target defined by a conjunction of features ("Find the shape that is red and round").

Word Recognition

It seems likely, therefore, that object recognition begins with the detection of simple features. Once this detection is done, separate brain mechanisms are needed to put the features together, assembling them into complete objects. But how does this assembly proceed, so that we end up seeing not just the features but whole words, for example, or Chihuahuas or fire hydrants? Before we tackle this question, let's fill in some more facts that we can use as a guide to our theory-building.

Factors Influencing Recognition

In many studies, participants have been shown stimuli for just a brief duration—perhaps 20 or 30 ms (milliseconds). Older research did this by means of a **tachistoscope**, a device specifically designed to present stimuli for precisely controlled amounts of time. More modern research uses computers for this purpose, but the brief displays are still called "tachistoscopic presentations."

Each stimulus is followed by a post-stimulus **mask**—often just a random jumble of letters, such as "XJDKEL." The mask serves to interrupt any continued processing that participants might try to do for the stimulus just presented, and this allows researchers to be certain that a stimulus presented for (say) 20 ms is visible for exactly 20 ms and no longer.

Can people recognize these briefly visible stimuli? The answer depends on many factors, including how *familiar* the stimulus is. If the stimulus is a word, for example, we can measure familiarity by literally counting how often that word appears in print, and these counts are an excellent predictor of tachistoscopic recognition. In one experiment, Jacoby and Dallas (1981) showed their participants words that were either very frequent (appearing at least 50 times in every million printed words) or infrequent (occurring only 1 to 5 times per million words of print). Participants viewed these words for 35 ms, followed by a mask; under these circumstances, they recognized 65% of the frequent words but only 33% of the infrequent words—demonstrating a clear advantage for frequent words.

Another factor influencing recognition is recency of view. If participants view a word and then, a little later, view it again, they will recognize the word much more readily the second time around. The first exposure **primes** the participant for the second exposure; more specifically, this is a case of **repetition priming**.

As an example, participants in one study read a list of words aloud. The participants were then shown a series of words in a tachistoscope. Some of the tachistoscopic words were from the earlier list and so had been primed; others were unprimed. For words that were high in frequency, 68% of the unprimed words were recognized, compared to 84% of the primed words. For words low in frequency, 37% of the unprimed words were recognized, compared to 73% of the primed words (Jacoby & Dallas, 1981, Exp. 3).

The Word-Superiority Effect

Words frequently viewed are easier to perceive, as are words viewed recently. It also turns out that words themselves are easier to perceive, as compared to isolated letters. This finding is referred to as the **word-superiority effect**.

This effect is usually demonstrated with a "two-alternative, forced-choice" procedure. Thus, in some trials, we might present a single letter—let's say *K*—followed by a post-stimulus mask, and follow that with a question: "Was there an *E* or a *K* in the display?" In other trials, we present a word—let's say "DARK"—followed by a mask, followed by a question: "Was there an *E* or a *K* in the display?"

Notice that a participant has a 50-50 chance of guessing correctly in either of these situations, and so any contribution from guessing is the same for the letters as it is for the words. Note in addition that for the word stimulus, both of the letters we've asked about are plausible endings for the stimulus; either ending would create a common word ("DARE" or "DARK"). Therefore, a participant who saw only part of the display (perhaps "DAR") couldn't use his knowledge of the language to figure out what the display's final letter was. In order to choose between *E* and *K*, the participant really needs to have seen the relevant letter—and that, of course, is exactly what we want.

The results from this procedure are clear: Accuracy rates are higher in the word condition, and so, apparently, recognizing words is easier than recognizing isolated letters. To put this more precisely, participants are more accurate in identifying letters if those letters appear within a word, as opposed to appearing all by themselves (Reicher, 1969; Rumelhart & Siple, 1974; Wheeler, 1970).

Degrees of Well-Formedness

It seems, then, that it's easier to recognize an *E*, say, if the letter appears in context (e.g., in the word "CASE") than if the letter appears on its own. But will any context produce this effect? It turns out that it is also easier to recognize an *E* if it appears within the string "FIKE" than it is if the *E* appears in isolation. Apparently, having a context is helpful even if the context is neither familiar nor meaningful. However, not all contexts provide an advantage. Recognition of the letter *H* (for example) is helped very little if it appears in a context such as "HGFD" or "HZYX."

As a related point, a letter string like "JPSRW" is very difficult to recognize when presented briefly. With exposures of 20 or 30 ms, participants will identify one or two letters from a string like this, but no more. In contrast, a letter strike like "GLAKE" is far easier to recognize, even though it's no more familiar than "JPSRW."

In short, then, the sheer familiarity of a letter string is not the key to tachistoscopic recognition. Instead, what matters is whether the string, familiar or not, is well formed according to the rules of the language. If the string *is* well formed, then it will be easier to recognize *and* will produce a word-superiority effect. Moreover, "following the rules" is a matter of degree, and so a letter string that follows the rules closely will produce a stronger word-superiority effect, and will be easier to recognize, than one that only roughly matches the standard patterns. This is a well-documented pattern that has been known for a long time (Cattell, 1885).

How do we assess "resemblance to English"? One way is via pronounceability (e.g., "GLAKE" is easy to say; "JPSRW" is not); in general, pronounceable strings are more easily recognized with tachistoscopic presentations than are unpronounceable strings. Alternatively, one can assess resemblance to English in statistical terms. One can count up, in English, how often the letter *P* follows the letter *J*, how often the letter *S* follows the letter *P*, and so forth. In this way, one can ask which letter combinations are likely and which are rare. With this done, one can then evaluate any new string in terms of how likely its letter combinations are. Well-formedness measured in this way is also a good predictor of tachistoscopic performance (Gibson, Bishop, Schiff, & Smith, 1964; G. A. Miller, Bruner, & Postman, 1954).

Making Errors

Apparently, then, our perception of words is influenced by spelling patterns, and so we have an easier time recognizing sequences that use common letter combinations, a harder time with sequences that involve unusual combinations. The influence of spelling patterns also emerges in another way: in the mistakes we make. With tachistoscopic exposures, word recognition is good but not perfect, and the errors that occur are quite systematic: There is a strong tendency to misread less-common letter sequences as if they were more-common patterns; irregular patterns are misread as if they were regular patterns. Thus, for example, "TPUM" is likely to be misread as

"TRUM" or even "DRUM." But the reverse errors are rare: "DRUM" is unlikely to be misread as "TRUM" or "TPUM."

These errors can sometimes be quite large—so that someone shown "TPUM" might instead perceive "TRUMPET." But, large or small, the errors show the pattern described: Misspelled words, partial words, or nonwords are read in a way that brings them into line with normal spelling. In effect, people perceive the input as being more regular than it actually is, and so these errors are referred to as **over-regularization errors**. This phenomenon suggests once again that our recognition is guided by (or, in this case, misguided by) some knowledge of spelling patterns.

Feature Nets and Word Recognition

How can we explain this broad pattern of evidence? One explanation begins with a theory of pattern recognition first published 50 years ago (Selfridge, 1959).

The Design of a Feature Net

Imagine that we want to design a system that will recognize the word "CLOCK" whenever it is presented. How might a "CLOCK" **detector** work? Perhaps the detector is "wired" to a C-detector, an L-detector, an O-detector, and so on. Whenever these letter detectors are all activated, this activates the word detector. But what activates the letter detectors? Perhaps the L-detector is "wired" to a horizontal-line detector, and also a vertical-line detector, and maybe also a corner detector, as shown in Figure 3.8. When all of these feature detectors are activated as a group, this activates the letter detector.

The idea, then, is that there is a network of detectors, organized in layers, with each subsequent layer concerned with more complex, larger-scale objects. The "bottom" layer is concerned with features, and that is why networks of this sort are often referred to as **feature nets**.

At any point in time, each detector in the network would have a particular **activation level**, which reflects how activated the detector is at just that moment. When a detector receives some input, its activation level increases. A strong input will increase the activation level by a lot, and so will a series of weaker inputs. In either case, the activation level will eventually reach the detector's **response threshold**, and at that point the detector will **fire**—that is, send its signal to the other detectors to which it is connected.

These points parallel our description of neurons in Chapter 2, and that is no accident. If the feature net is to be a serious candidate for how humans recognize patterns, then the net has to employ the same sorts of building blocks that the brain does. However, let's be careful not to overstate this point: No one is suggesting that detectors are neurons, or even large groups of neurons. Instead, detectors would pre-

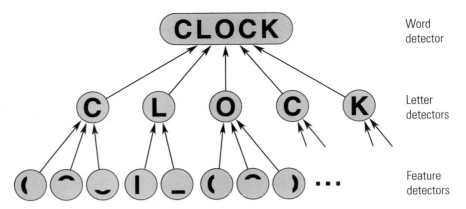

FIGURE 3.8 Networks of Detectors

Word detectors might be triggered by letter detectors, so that the word detector would fire whenever the appropriate letters were presented. The letter detectors in turn might be triggered by feature detectors, so the letter detectors would fire whenever the features were on the scene.

sumably involve much more complex assemblies of neural tissue. Nonetheless, it's plainly attractive that the hypothesized detectors, within the feature net, function in a way that's biologically sensible.

Within the net, some detectors will be easier to activate than others—that is, some detectors require a strong input to make them fire, while other detectors will fire even with a weak input. This readiness to fire is determined in part by how activated the detector was to begin with. If the detector was moderately activated at the start, then only a little input is needed to raise the activation level to threshold, and so it will be easy to make this detector fire. If the detector was not at all activated at the start, then a strong input is needed to bring the detector to threshold, and so it will be more difficult to make this detector fire.

What determines a detector's starting activation level? A number of factors contribute, but among them, detectors that have fired recently will have a higher activation level (think of it as a "warm-up" effect). Detectors that have fired frequently in the past will also have a higher activation level (think of it as an "exercise" effect). Thus, the activation level is dependent on principles of recency and frequency.

We now can put this mechanism to work. Why are frequent words in the language easier to recognize than rare words? Frequent words have, by definition, appeared often in the things you read. Therefore, the detectors needed for recognizing these words have been frequently used, and so they have relatively high levels of activation. Thus, even a weak signal (e.g., a very brief presentation of the word) will bring these detectors to their response threshold and so will be enough to make these detectors fire. Thus, the word will be recognized even with a weak or degraded input.

Repetition priming is explained in similar terms. Presenting a word once will cause the relevant detectors to fire. Once they have fired, activation levels will be temporarily lifted because of recency of use. Therefore, only a weak signal will be needed to make the detectors fire again. As a result, the word will be more easily recognized the second time around.

The Feature Net and Well-Formedness

The net we've described so far cannot explain all of the data. Consider the effects of well-formedness—for instance, the fact that people are able to read letter strings like "PIRT" or "HICE," when they're presented tachistoscopically, but not strings like "ITPR" or "HCEI." This difference can't be explained in terms of letter detectors, since, as it turns out, the same letters are used in "PIRT" and "ITPR," yet one is easy to recognize and one is not. Likewise for "HICE" and "HCEI." The difference also can't be explained in terms of word detectors: None of these letter sequences is a word, and so word detectors would play no role in the recognition of these strings.

How, therefore, should we accommodate these results? One option is to add another layer to the net, a layer filled with detectors for letter combinations. In Figure 3.9, we have added a layer of **bigram** detectors—detectors of letter pairs. These detectors, like all the rest, will be triggered by lower-level detectors and send their output to higher-level detectors. And just like any other detector, each bigram detector will start out with a certain activation level, influenced by the frequency with which the detector has fired in the past, and also the recency with which it has fired.

This turns out to be all the theory we need. Why are English-like nonwords more easily recognized than strings not resembling English ("RSFK" or "IUBE")? Well-formed words involve familiar letter combinations. You have never seen the sequence "HICE" before, but you have seen the letter pair *HI* (in "HIT," "HIGH," or "HILL") and the pair *CE* ("FACE," "MICE," "JUICE"). The detectors for these letter groups, therefore, have high activation levels at the start, and so they don't need much additional input to reach their threshold. As a result, these detectors will fire with only weak input. That will make the corresponding letter combinations easy to recognize, facilitating the recognition of strings like "HICE." None of this is true for "RSFK." Because none of these letter combinations is familiar, this string will receive no benefits from priming. A strong input will therefore be needed to bring the relevant detectors to threshold, and so the string will be recognized only with difficulty. (For more on bigram detectors and how they work, see Grainger, Rey, & Dufau, 2008; Grainger & Whitney, 2004; Whitney, 2001.)

Recovery From Confusion

Imagine that we present the word "CORN" for 20 ms. With this brief presentation, the quantity of incoming information is small, and so some of the word's features may not be detected. Figure 3.10 shows how this might play out. The fast presentation of the *O* wasn't enough to trigger all of the feature detectors appropriate for the

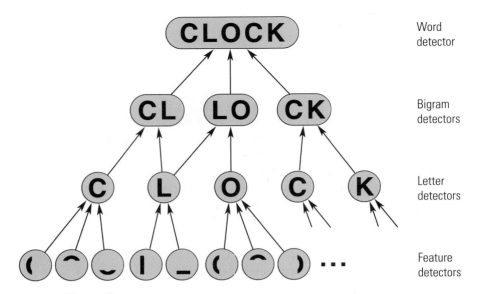

Word
detector

Bigram
detectors

Letter
detectors

Feature
detectors

FIGURE 3.9 Bigram Detectors
It seems plausible that a layer of bigram detectors is interposed between letter detectors and word detectors.

O. In fact, only the bottom-curve detector is firing. Therefore, the *O*-detector will receive input from just one of its features, and so will be only weakly activated. But the same is true for the *U*-detector, the *Q*-detector, and the *S*-detector: These, too, are responsive to the bottom-curve feature detector, and so with this detector firing, they also will be weakly activated.

But now consider what happens at the next level. The *C*-detector is strongly activated, because the *C* was clearly visible. The detectors for *O*, *U*, *Q*, and *S* are all weakly activated, because only one of their feature detectors is firing. As a result, the bigram detectors for *CO*, *CU*, *CQ*, and *CS* are all receiving the same input: a strong signal from one of their letters, and a weak signal from the second letter. Despite this equivalence in the input, though, these bigram detectors won't all respond in the same way. The *CO*-detector is well primed (because this is a frequent pattern), and so the input probably will be enough to fire this detector. The *CU*-detector is less primed (because this is a less frequent pattern); the *CQ*- or *CS*-detectors, if these even exist, are not primed at all. The input will therefore not be enough to activate these detectors.

Thus, at the letter level, there was confusion about the input letter's identity: Several detectors were firing, and all were firing equally. At the bigram level, only one detector responds, and so the confusion has been sorted out and an error has been avoided.

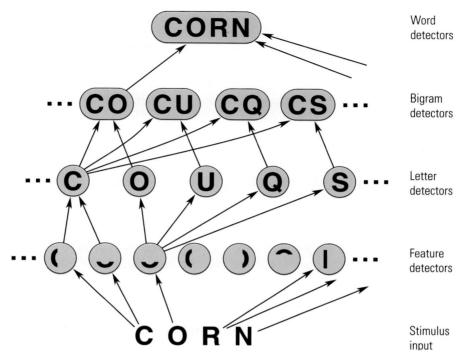

FIGURE 3.10 Recovery From Confusion

If "CORN" is presented briefly, not all of its features will be detected. Imagine, for example, that only the bottom curve of the *O* is detected, and not the *O*'s top or sides. This will (weakly) activate the *O*-detector, but it will also activate the detectors of various other letters having a bottom curve, including *U*, *Q*, and *S*. This will, in turn, send weak activation to the appropriate bigram detectors. The *CO*-detector, however, is well primed and so is likely to respond even though it is receiving only a weak input. The other bigram detectors (for *CQ* or *CS*) are less well primed and so will not respond to this weak input. Therefore, "CORN" will be correctly perceived, despite the confusion at the letter level caused by the weak signal.

Ambiguous Inputs

The mechanism just described also helps in explaining some other evidence. Look again at Figure 3.6 (p. 68). The second character shown is exactly the same as the fifth, but the left-hand string is perceived as "THE" (and the character is identified as an *H*), and the right-hand string is perceived as "CAT" (and the character as an *A*).

This observation is now easily explained. When the ambiguous character is in view, it will trigger some of the features normally associated with an *A* and some normally associated with an *H*. This will cause the *A*-detector to fire, but only weakly (because only some of the *A*'s features are present), and likewise for the *H*-detector. At the letter level, therefore, there is uncertainty about what the incoming character is.

The uncertainty is resolved at subsequent levels. With the *T*-detector firing well and the *A*- and *H*-detectors firing weakly, there will be a moderate signal sent to both the *TH*- and the *TA*-detectors, and likewise to the *THE*- and *TAE*-detectors. But the *TH*-detector is enormously well primed; so is the *THE*-detector. If there were a *TAE*-detector, it would be barely primed, since this is a string rarely encountered. Thus, the *THE*- and *TAE*-detectors might be receiving similar input, but this input is sufficient only for the well-primed *THE*-detector, and so only it will respond. In this way, the net will recognize the ambiguous pattern as "THE," not "TAE." The same is true for the ambiguous pattern on the right, perceived as "CAT," not "CHT."

A similar explanation will handle the word-superiority effect (see, for example, Rumelhart & Siple, 1974). To take a simple case, imagine that we present the letter *A* in the context "AT." If the presentation is brief enough, participants may see very little of the *A*, perhaps just the horizontal crossbar. This would not be enough to distinguish among *A*, *F*, or *H*, and so all these letter detectors would fire weakly. If this were all the information the participants had, they'd be stuck. But let us imagine that the participants did perceive the second letter in the display, the *T*. It seems likely that the *AT* bigram is far better primed than the *FT* or *HT* bigrams. (That is because you often encounter words like "CAT" or "BOAT"; words like "SOFT" or "HEFT" are used less frequently.) Thus, the weak firing of the *A*-detector would be enough to fire the *AT* bigram detector, while the weak firing for the *F* and *H* might not trigger their bigram detectors. In this way, a "choice" would be made at the bigram level that the input was "AT" and not something else. Once this bigram has been detected, answering the question "Was there an *A* or an *F* in the display?" is easy. In this manner, the letter will be better detected in context than in isolation. This is not because context allows you to see more; instead, context allows you to make better use of what you see.

Recognition Errors

There is, however, a downside to all this. Imagine that we present the string "CQRN" to participants. If the presentation is brief enough, study participants will register only a subset of the string's features. Let's imagine, in line with an earlier example, that they register only the bottom bit of the string's second letter. This detection of the bottom curve will weakly activate the *Q*-detector, and also the *U*-detector and the *O*-detector. The resulting pattern of network activation is shown in Figure 3.11, which, as you can see, is nearly identical to Figure 3.10.

We have already argued that the pattern of priming within the network will lead to a "CORN" response in the situation shown in Figure 3.10. But the "grist" for the network is exactly the same in Figure 3.11: The same feature detectors are firing. Therefore, this input, too, will lead to "CORN." Hence, in the first case (when the stimulus actually is "CORN"), the dynamic built into the net aids performance, allowing the network to recover from its initial confusion. In the second case (with

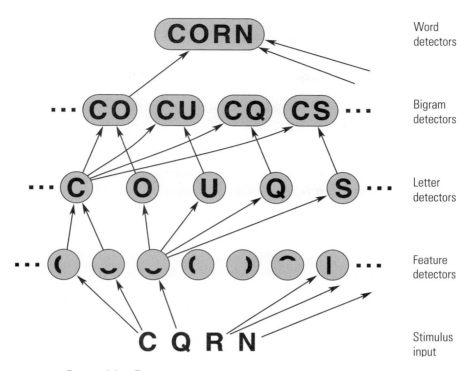

Word detectors

Bigram detectors

Letter detectors

Feature detectors

Stimulus input

FIGURE 3.11 Recognition Errors

If "CQRN" is presented briefly, not all of its features will be detected. Perhaps only the bottom curve of the *Q* is detected, and this will (weakly) activate various other letters having a bottom curve, including *O*, *U*, and *S*. However, this is the same situation that would result from a brief presentation of "CORN" (as shown in Figure 3.10); therefore, by the logic we have already discussed, this stimulus is likely to be misperceived as "CORN."

"CQRN" as the stimulus), the same dynamic causes the network to misread the stimulus.

This example illustrates how over-regularization errors come about. In essence, the network is biased, always favoring frequent letter combinations over infrequent ones. This bias facilitates perception if the input is, in fact, a frequent word. But the bias will pull the network toward errors if the input has an unusual spelling pattern, and the errors will always be of the same sort, turning irregular spelling into more frequent combinations.

These errors are usually unproblematic. Low-frequency words are, as we've just discussed, likely to be misperceived, but (by definition) low-frequency words aren't encountered that often. The network's bias promotes the perception of frequent words, and these (by definition) are the words you encounter most of the time. Hence, the network's bias aids recognition in the more frequent cases and hurts recognition only in the rare cases. Necessarily, then, the network's bias helps perception more often than it hurts.

Distributed Knowledge

We've now considered several indications that, somehow, knowledge of spelling patterns is "built into" the network. For example, the network "knows" that CO is a common bigram in English, while CF is not, and as a result, the network is better prepared for one of these patterns than for the other. One might say that the network "expects" one of these patterns to appear more often, and is therefore ready for that pattern when it does appear. Likewise, when in doubt (if, for example, the input is barely seen), the system is more likely to "infer" a CO is present than a CF. And so on.

However, the sense in which the net "knows" these facts about spelling, or the sense in which it "expects" things or "makes inferences," is worth emphasizing, since we will return to this idea in later chapters. This bit of knowledge is not explicitly stored anywhere. Nowhere within the net is there a sentence like "CO is a common bigram in English; CF is not." Instead, this memory (if we even want to call it that) is manifest only in the fact that the CO-detector happens to be more primed than the CF-detector. The CO-detector doesn't "know" anything about this advantage, nor does the CF-detector know anything about its disadvantage. Each simply does its job, and in the course of doing their jobs, occasions will arise that involve a "competition" between these detectors. (This sort of competition was illustrated in Figures 3.10 and 3.11.) When these competitions occur, they'll be "decided," in a straightforward way, by activation levels: The better-primed detector will be more likely to respond, and so that detector will be more likely to influence subsequent events. That's the entire mechanism through which these "knowledge effects" arise. That's how "expectations" or "inferences" emerge—as a direct consequence of the activation levels.

To put this into technical terms, the network's "knowledge" is not **locally represented** anywhere; it is not stored in a particular location or built into a specific process. Thus, we cannot look just at the level of priming in the CO-detector and conclude that this detector represents a frequent bigram, nor can we look at the CF-detector to conclude that it represents a rare bigram. Instead, we need to look at the *relationship* between their levels of priming, and we also need to look at how this relationship will lead to one detector being more influential than the other. The knowledge about bigram frequencies, in other words, is **distributed knowledge**—that is, it is represented in a fashion that's distributed across the network, and detectable only if we consider how the entire network functions.

What is perhaps most remarkable about the feature net, then, lies in how much can be accomplished with a distributed representation, and thus with simple, mechanical elements correctly connected to one another. The net appears to make inferences and to know the rules of English spelling. But the actual mechanics of the net involve neither inferences nor knowledge (at least, not in any conventional sense). You and I can see how the inferences unfold by taking a bird's-eye view and considering how all the detectors work together as a system. But nothing in the net's functioning depends on the bird's-eye view. Instead, the activity of each detector is locally determined—influenced by just those detectors feeding into it. When all of these detectors work together, though, the result is a process that acts as if it knows the rules. But the rules themselves play no role in guiding the network's moment-by-moment activities.

Efficiency Versus Accuracy

One other crucial fact about the network is that it does make mistakes, misreading some inputs and misinterpreting some patterns. But, as we've seen, these mistakes are produced by exactly the same mechanisms that are responsible for the network's main advantages—its ability to deal with ambiguous inputs, for example, or to recover from its own errors.

Perhaps, therefore, we should view the errors as simply the price one pays in order to gain the benefits associated with the net: If one wants a mechanism that's able to deal with unclear, or partial, inputs, one simply has to live with the fact that sometimes the mechanism will make mistakes. But this invites a question: Do we really need to pay this price? After all, outside of the lab we're unlikely to encounter tachistoscopic inputs. Instead, we see stimuli that are out in view for long periods of time, stimuli that we can inspect at our leisure. Why, therefore, don't we take the moment to scrutinize these inputs so that we can rely on fewer inferences and assumptions, and in that fashion gain a higher level of accuracy in recognizing the objects we encounter?

The answer to this question is straightforward. To maximize accuracy, we could, in principle, scrutinize every character on the page. That way, if a character were missing or misprinted, we would be sure to detect it. But the cost associated with this strategy would be insufferable: Reading would be unspeakably slow (in part because the speed with which we move our eyes is relatively slow—no more than four or five eye movements per second). In contrast, one can make inferences about a page with remarkable speed, and this leads readers to adopt the obvious strategy: They read some of the letters and make inferences about the rest. And for the most part, those inferences are safe—thanks to the simple fact that our language (like most aspects of our world) contains some redundncies, so that one doesn't need every lettr to identify what a wrd is; oftn the missng letter is perfctly predctable from the contxt, virtually guaranteeing that inferences will be correct.

Thus, the efficient reader is not being careless, or hasty, or lazy. Given the redundancy of text, and given the slowness of letter-by-letter reading, the inferential strategy is the only strategy that makes sense.

Descendants of the Feature Net

As we mentioned early on, we have been focusing on one of the simpler versions of the feature net. This has allowed us to bring a number of important themes into view—such as the trade-off between efficiency and accuracy, and the notion of distributed knowledge built into a network's functioning. However, it should be said that many variations on the feature-net idea are possible, each differing somewhat from the specific proposal we have discussed, and each with its own advantages and disadvantages. In this section, we consider some important variations on the network idea.

The McClelland and Rumelhart Model

An influential model of word recognition was proposed by McClelland and Rumelhart (1981); a portion of their model is illustrated in Figure 3.12. Once again, there is a feature base and a network of connections, as various detectors serve to influence one another. This net, like the one we have been discussing, is better able to identify well-formed strings than irregular strings; this net is also more efficient in identifying characters in context as opposed to characters in isolation. However, several attributes of this net make it possible to accomplish all this without bigram detectors.

In the network proposal we have considered so far, activation of one detector serves to activate other detectors. These **excitatory connections** are shown in Figure 3.12 with arrows; for example, detection of a T serves to "excite" the "TRIP" detector. In the McClelland and Rumelhart model, however, detectors can also inhibit each other, so that detection of a G, for example, inhibits the "TRIP" detector. These **inhibitory connections** are shown in the figure with dots. In addition, this model allows for more complicated signaling than we have employed so far. In our discussion, we have assumed that lower-level detectors trigger upper-level detectors, but not the reverse. The flow of information, it seemed, was a one-way street. In the McClelland and Rumelhart model, though, higher-level detectors (word detectors) can influence the lower-level detectors, and detectors at any level can also influence the other detectors at the same level (e.g., letter detectors inhibit other letter detectors; word detectors inhibit other word detectors).

To see how this would work, let's say that the word "TRIP" is briefly shown, allowing a viewer to see enough features to identify, say, only the *R*, *I*, and *P*. Detectors for these letters will therefore fire, in turn activating the detector for "TRIP." Activation of this word detector will inhibit the firing of all the other word detectors (e.g., detectors for "TRAP" or "TAKE"), so that, in a sense, these other words are less likely to arise as distractions or competitors with the target word. At the same time, activation of the "TRIP" detector will excite the detectors for its component letters—that is, detectors for *T*, *R*, *I*, and *P*. The *R*-, *I*-, and *P*-detectors, we've

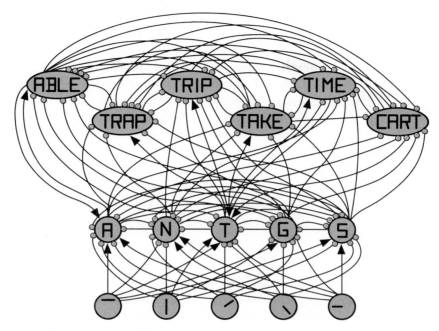

FIGURE 3.12 Alternative Conceptions of the Feature Network
The McClelland and Rumelhart (1981) pattern-recognition model includes both excitatory connections (indicated by arrows) and inhibitory connections (indicated by connections with dots). Connections within a specific level are also possible—so that, for example, activation of the "TRIP" detector will inhibit the detectors for "TRAP," "TAKE," or "TIME."

assumed, were already firing, so this extra activation "from above" has little impact. But the T-detector, we've supposed, was not firing before. The relevant features were on the scene but in a degraded form (thanks to the brief presentation); this weak input was insufficient to trigger an unprimed detector. However, once the excitation from the "TRIP" detector primes the T-detector, it is more likely to fire, even with a weak input.

In effect, then, activation of the word detector for "TRIP" implies that this is a context in which a T is quite likely. The network therefore responds to this suggestion by "preparing itself" for a T. Once the network is suitably prepared (by the appropriate priming), detection of this letter is facilitated. In this way, the detection of a letter sequence (the word "TRIP") makes the network more sensitive to elements that are likely to occur within that sequence. That is exactly what we need for the network to be responsive to the regularities of spelling patterns. And, of course, we've seen that there is ample evidence that humans are sensitive to (and exploit) these regularities.

There are several reasons one might prefer this kind of net over the kind considered earlier. As one consideration, there is evidence that higher-level detectors can activate lower-level detectors, just as the McClelland and Rumelhart model proposes. We will return to these "top-down" effects in a few pages, and we will discuss similar effects in Chapter 4. Second, we can also find biological evidence for this sort of two-way communication in the nervous system: Neurons in the eyeballs send activation to the brain but also receive activation from the brain; neurons in the LGN send activation to the visual cortex but also receive activation from the cortex. These facts make it clear that visual processing is not a one-way process, with information flowing simply from the eyes toward the brain. Instead, signaling occurs in both an ascending (toward the brain) and a descending (away from the brain) direction, just as the McClelland and Rumelhart model claims.

Recognition by Components

We have now said an enormous amount about how people recognize *printed language*. This has allowed us to explore a number of principles and to describe a model that seems able to recognize print. But, of course, we recognize many other objects other than print, including the three-dimensional objects that fill our world—chairs and lamps and cars and trees and your pet cat, Sasha. Can these objects also be recognized by a feature network? The answer turns out to be yes.

Hummel and Biederman (1992; also Hummel & Stankiewicz, 1998) have offered a network theory dubbed the **recognition by components** (or RBC) **model**. The crucial innovation in this model, though, is an intermediate level of detectors, sensitive to **geons** (short for "geometric ions"). Hummel and Biederman's proposal is that geons serve as the basic building blocks of all the objects we recognize; geons are, in essence, the alphabet from which all objects are constructed. Geons are simple shapes, such as cylinders, cones, and blocks (see Figure 3.13a). And only a small set of these shapes is needed: According to Biederman (1987, 1990), we need (at most) three dozen different geons to describe every object in the world, just as 26 letters are all that are needed to produce all the words of English. These geons can then be combined in various ways—in a top-of relation, or a side-connected relation, and so on—to create all the objects we perceive (see Figure 3.13b).

The RBC model, like the network we have been discussing, uses a hierarchy of detectors. The lowest-level detectors are feature detectors, which respond to edges, curves, vertices, and so on. These detectors in turn activate the geon detectors. Higher levels of detectors are then sensitive to combinations of geons. More precisely, geons are assembled into more complex arrangements called "geon assemblies," which explicitly represent the *relations* between geons (such as top-of or side-connected). These assemblies, finally, activate the *object model*, a representation of the complete, recognized object.

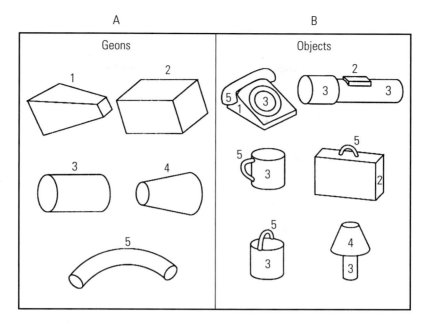

FIGURE 3.13 Geons

Panel A shows five different geons; Panel B shows how these geons can be assembled into objects. The numbers in Panel B identify the specific geons; for example, a bucket contains Geon 5 top-connected to Geon 3.

The presence of the geon and geon-assembly levels, within this hierarchy, buys us several advantages. For one, geons can be identified from virtually any angle of view, and so recognition based on geons is **viewpoint-independent**. Thus, no matter what your position is relative to a cat, you'll be able to identify its geons and thus identify the cat. Moreover, it seems that most objects can be recognized from just a few geons (in the appropriate configuration). As a consequence, geon-based models like RBC can recognize an object even if many of the object's geons are hidden from view.

In addition, several lines of evidence seem to confirm that geons do play a role in recognition. For example, recognition of simple objects is relatively easy if the geons are easy to discern; recognition is more difficult if the geons are hard to identify (Biederman, 1985). As an illustration, consider the objects shown in Figure 3.14. In Columns B and C, about two thirds of the contour has been deleted from each drawing. In Column B, this deletion has been carefully done so that the geons can still be identified; as you can see, these objects can be recognized without much difficulty. In Column C, however, the deletion has been done in a fashion that obscures geon identity; now object recognition is much harder. Thus, it does seem that the geons capture something crucial for identification of these objects. (For other evidence, see Behrmann et al., 2006.)

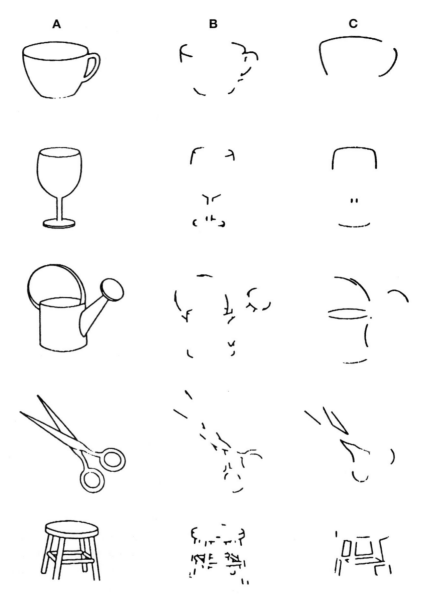

FIGURE 3.14 Recognizing Degraded Pictures

In Column B, one can still identify the objects' geons, and so the forms are easily recognized. In Column C, it is difficult to identify the geons and correspondingly difficult to identify the objects. This evidence adds strength to the claim that geon identification plays an important role in object recognition.

Recognition via Multiple Views

A number of researchers, prominently including Michael Tarr (1995; also Hayward & Williams, 2000; Tarr & Bülthoff, 1998; Vuong & Tarr, 2004; Wallis & Bülthoff, 1999), have offered a different approach to object recognition. They propose that people have stored in memory a number of different views of each object they can recognize: an image of what the cat looks like when viewed head-on, a view of what it looks like from the left, and so on. To recognize the object, therefore, one must match the current view of the object with one of these views in memory. However, the number of views in memory is limited—perhaps a half dozen or so—and so, in many cases, the current view won't line up with any of the available images. In that case, one needs a time-consuming process of "rotating" the remembered view into alignment with the current view. As a result, ease of recognition will be faster from some viewpoints than from others, and so, in this fashion, recognition will be **viewpoint-dependent**.

A growing body of data suggests that recognition actually is viewpoint-dependent in this way. To be sure, we can recognize objects from many different angles, but our recognition is faster from some angles than others, in a fashion consistent with this multiple-views proposal.

How, according to this perspective, does recognition proceed? One proposal involves processes very much like those in the networks we've been discussing (Riesenhuber & Poggio, 1999, 2002; Tarr, 1999). In this model, there is a hierarchy of detectors, with each successive layer within the network concerned with more complex aspects of the whole. Thus, low-level detectors respond to lines at certain orientations; higher-level detectors respond to corners and notches. At the top of the hierarchy are detectors that respond to the sight of whole objects. It is important, though, that these detectors each represent what the object looks like from a particular vantage point, and so the detectors fire when there is a match to one of these view-tuned representations.

A number of proposals have been offered for how this model might be implemented in the nervous system. For example, the view-tuned representations are probably supported by tissue in the inferotemporal cortex, near the terminus of the *what* pathway. Recording from cells in this brain area has shown that many neurons here seem object-specific—that is, they fire preferentially when a certain type of object is on the scene. Crucially, most of these neurons are view-tuned: They fire most strongly to a particular view of the target object. This is just what one might expect with the multiple-views proposal (Peissig & Tarr, 2007).

We should emphasize, though, that there continues to be debate between advocates of the RBC approach (with its claim that recognition is largely viewpoint-independent) and the multiple-views approach (with its argument that recognition is viewpoint-dependent). At the same time, still other approaches to object recognition are also being explored (e.g., Ullman, 2007). Obviously, further data are needed to help us choose among these proposals (for a summary of the state of the art, though, see Peissig & Tarr, 2007). In the meantime, let's be clear that all of the available proposals involve the sort of hierarchical network we've been discussing. In other words, no matter how the debate about object recognition turns out, it looks like we're going to need a network model along the lines we've considered.

Different Objects, Different Recognition Systems?

We have now shifted our focus away from print: A network can also be designed, it seems, to recognize three-dimensional objects. But how far can we travel on this path? Can other sorts of recognition—recognition of sounds, of faces, of smells—be approached in the same way?

The evidence suggests a mixed answer. As it turns out, many domains rather distant from print do show effects similar to the ones we have reviewed, suggesting that similar mechanisms are in play. For example, in recognizing the speech that we hear, or in perceiving complex visual patterns, it turns out that more frequently encountered patterns are easier to recognize. Likewise, repetition priming can be demonstrated with many different kinds of stimuli. It is also true in general that regular

Line in isolation:

Line in an orderly context:

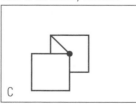 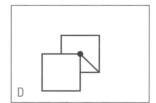

The Object-Superiority Effect
In the word-superiority effect, letters are perceived more accurately if they appear in an orderly context. In the *object*-superiority effect, *lines* are perceived more accurately if they appear in a context. Thus, with a fast presentation, it's easier to distinguish Patterns C and D then it is to tell apart Patterns A and B. Of course, the difference is the same within each pair—the position of just one line. But this line's position is easier to see—and so the distinction within the pair is more visible—if the line appears as part of an orderly shape.

or well-formed patterns are easier to recognize than ill-formed patterns. And when recognition errors occur, they are, overall, in the direction of regularizing the input, just as in the case of print. All of this invites the conclusion that a uniform theoretical treatment will be possible across diverse domains.

However, one category of input does seem to require a different sort of recognition system: faces. As we will see, several pieces of evidence support the claim that face recognition is served by specialized structures and mechanisms, and proceeds according to principles different from the ones we have described so far.

Faces

As we have discussed, damage to the visual system can produce a disorder known as *agnosia*—an inability to recognize certain stimuli. There are actually several subtypes of agnosia, one of which is called **prosopagnosia**. People with this disorder lose their ability to recognize faces, even though their other visual abilities seem to be intact. This seems to imply the existence of a special neural structure involved almost exclusively in the recognition and discrimination of faces (Berhman & Avidan, 2005; Burton, Young, Bruce, Johnston, & Ellis, 1991; Damasio, Tranel, & Damasio, 1990; De Renzi, Faglioni, Grossi, & Nichelli, 1991).

In addition, face recognition also seems distinctive in its very strong dependence on orientation. We've mentioned that there is debate about whether the recognition of houses, or teacups, or automobiles, is viewpoint-dependent, but there can be no question about this for faces. In one study, four categories of stimuli were considered—right-side-up faces, upside-down faces, right-side-up pictures of common objects other than faces, and upside-down pictures of common objects. As can be seen in Figure 3.15, performance suffered for all of the upside-down stimuli. However, this effect was much larger for faces than it is for other kinds of stimuli (Yin, 1969).

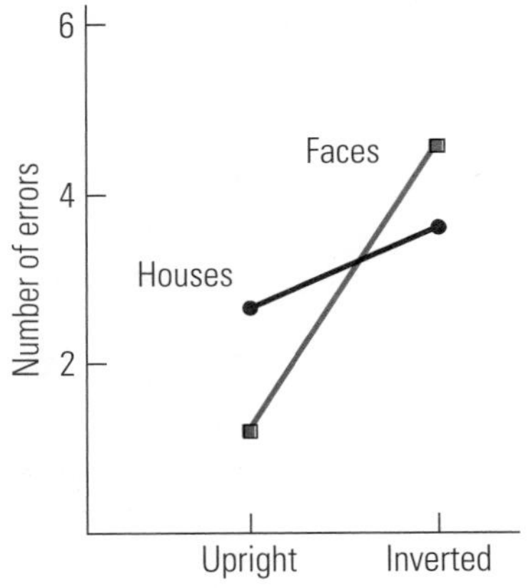

FIGURE 3.15 Memory for Faces Presented Upright or Upside-Down
People's memory for faces is quite good, compared with memory for other pictures (in this case, pictures of houses). However, performance is very much disrupted when the pictures of faces are inverted. Performance with houses is also worse with inverted pictures, but the effect of inversion is far smaller. (After Yin, 1969)

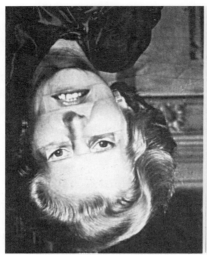

FIGURE 3.16 Perception of Upside-Down Faces

The left-hand picture looks somewhat odd, but the two pictures still look relatively similar to each other. Now try turning the book upside down (so that the faces are upright). In this position, the left-hand face (now on the right) looks ghoulish, and the two pictures look very different from each other. Perception of upside-down faces is apparently quite different from our perception of upright faces. (From Thompson, 1980)

The same point can be made informally. Figure 3.16 shows two upside-down photographs of former British prime minister Margaret Thatcher (from P. Thompson, 1980). You can probably detect that something is odd about them, but now try turning the book upside down so that the faces are right side up. As you can see, the difference between these faces is immense, and yet this fiendish contrast is largely lost when the faces are upside down. Once again, it seems that the perception of faces is strikingly different when we view the faces upside down. (Also see Rhodes, Brake, & Atkinson, 1993; Valentine, 1988.)

All of this seems to imply that face recognition is different from recognition of other sorts—served by its own neural apparatus and particularly dependent on orientation. However, we need to fine-tune this claim a bit because other stimuli, and not just faces, also rely on this special recognition system.

Consider first the evidence of prosopagnosia. In one case, a prosopagnosic bird-watcher has not only lost the ability to recognize faces, he also has lost the ability to distinguish the different types of warblers (Bornstein, 1963; Bornstein, Sroka, & Munitz, 1969). Another patient with prosopagnosia has lost the ability to tell cars apart; she is able to locate her car in a parking lot only by reading all the license plates until she finds her own (Damasio, Damasio, & Van Hoesen, 1982). Thus, prosopagnosia is not strictly a disorder of face recognition.

Likewise, in Chapter 2, we considered neuroimaging data showing that a particular brain site—the fusiform face area (FFA)—is specifically responsive to faces. It turns out, though, that tasks requiring subtle distinctions among birds, or among cars, also produce high levels of activation in this area (Gauthier, Skudlarski, Gore, & Anderson, 2000). Apparently, the neural tissue "specialized" for faces isn't used only for faces.

In the same way, other categories of stimuli, not just faces, can show the upside-down effect we have already described. For example, one study examined people who were highly experienced judges in dog shows, people who knew particular breeds extremely well. Diamond and Carey (1986) compared how well these judges recognized right-side-up and upside-down stimuli in each of two categories: faces and dogs in the familiar breed. Not surprisingly, performance was much worse with upside-down faces than with right-side-up faces, replicating the pattern of Figure 3.15. The critical result, though, is that performance suffered just as much with upside-down pictures of dogs. (For more on perceptual expertise, see Bukach, Gauthier & Tarr, 2006.)

It seems, therefore, that we do have a specialized recognition system, using its own brain tissue and especially sensitive to orientation. The key, though, is that this system doesn't operate only on faces. Instead, the system seems crucial whenever a task has two characteristics: The task has to involve recognizing specific individuals within a category, and the category has to be an extremely familiar one (Diamond & Carey, 1986; Gauthier, 2000; although, for an argument that this system *does* operate only on faces, see McKone, Kanwisher, & Duchaine, 2007). The recognition of faces certainly meets these requirements, but other tasks do as well. Thus, this special system is used when expert bird-watchers are recognizing individual birds, when expert dog-judges are recognizing individual dogs, and so on.

How does this second system work? Several authors have suggested that humans have one object-recognition system specialized for the recognition of a pattern's *parts* (features, geons) and the assembly of those parts into larger wholes. That's the system we've been discussing for most of this chapter. In addition, a second system is specialized for the recognition of *configurations*. This system is less able to analyze patterns into their parts and less able to recognize these parts, but it is more sensitive to larger-scale patterns. Presumably, it is this system that is crucial for the recognition of faces and the other cases discussed in this section (for a broad review, see Farah, Wilson, Drain, & Tanaka, 1998).

Damage to either of these systems would cause difficulties—but difficulties of different sorts. Damage to the second (configuration) system is presumably what underlies prosopagnosia. Damage to the first (part) system disrupts the ability to recognize words, objects, or any other target that is identified by its inventory of parts. Consistent with this proposal, prosopagnosia and object agnosia do appear to be separate disorders, with patients typically showing one of these but not the other, just as we would expect if the patient has suffered brain damage in only one of these systems (Farah et al., 1998).

Further work is needed to specify how the configurational system functions. In the meantime, it appears that the feature-net approach we have discussed in this chapter is powerful and applicable to a wide variety of patterns, but it simply is not the whole story. Some patterns, including faces, seem to involve a different sort of pattern recognition. (For examples of other research on memory for faces, see Hancock, Bruce, & Burton, 2000; Jones & Bartlett, 2009; Kanwisher, 2006; Michel, Rossion, Han, Chung, & Caldara, 2006; Rhodes, Hayward, & Winkler, 2006.)

Top-Down Influences on Object Recognition

The previous section had a two-part message. First, it seems likely that the feature-net idea is applicable to a great many domains, including the recognition of print and the recognition of three-dimensional objects. Second, there are other domains for which the feature net is not well suited. The suggestion, then, is that we need at least two recognition systems: the part-based system we've been focusing on, designed specifically to recognize objects by identifying their elements; and then a configurational system, crucial for faces and some other patterns.

In this last section, we explore a different limit on the feature net. Our concern here is with targets for which the feature net *is* useful—print, common objects, and so on. Even in this domain, it turns out that the feature net must be supplemented with additional mechanisms. This requirement doesn't undermine the importance of the feature-net idea; the net is plainly needed as part of our theoretical account. The key word, however, is "part," because we need to place the feature net within a larger theoretical frame.

The Benefits of Larger Contexts

We have already seen that letter recognition is improved by context, so that the letter *V*, for example, is easier to recognize in the context "VASE," or even the nonsense context "VIMP," than it is if presented alone. It turns out, though, that the same is true for words: These, too, are better recognized in context—in particular, in the context of a sentence.

There are many formal demonstrations of this effect (e.g., Rueckl & Oden, 1986; Spellman, Holyoak, & Morrison, 2001; Tulving & Gold, 1963; Tulving, Mandler, & Baumal, 1964), but for our purposes, an informal example will be sufficient. Imagine that we tell research participants, "I am about to show you a word very briefly on a computer screen; the word is the name of something that you can eat." If we forced the participants to guess the word at this point, they would be unlikely to name the target word. (There are, after all, many things you can eat, and so the chances are slim of guessing just the right one.) But if we now tachistoscopically show the word "CELERY," we are likely to observe a large priming effect; that is, participants are more likely to recognize "CELERY" with this cue than they would have been without the cue.

Consider what this priming involves. First, the person needs to understand each of the words in the instruction. If she did not understand the word "eat" (if, for example, she mistakenly thought we had said, "something that you can beat"), we would not get the priming. Second, the person must understand the syntax of the instruction and, specifically, the relations among the words in the instruction. Again, if she mistakenly thought we said "something that can eat you," we would expect a very different sort of priming. Third, the person has to know some facts about the world—namely, the kinds of things that can be eaten; without this knowledge, we would expect no priming.

Obviously, then, this instance of priming relies on a broad range of knowledge, and there is nothing special about this example. We could, after all, observe similar priming effects if we tell someone that the word about to be shown is the name of a historical figure, or that the word is related to the *Harry Potter* books. In each case, this instruction would facilitate perception, with the implication that in explaining these various priming effects we'll need to hook up our pattern-recognition system to a much broader library of information.

Interactive Models

In thinking about these priming effects, it is useful to distinguish two broad types of priming and, with that, two types of processing. Our focus so far has largely been on **data-driven**, or **bottom-up, processing**. That is, we have discussed how the incoming information (the "data") triggers a response by feature detectors, which in turn triggers a response by letter detectors (or geon detectors), and so on. The data take the initiative; the data get things going. Moreover, most of the priming we have considered has also been data driven: If the *TH*-detector (for example) is well primed, it is simply because of the data this detector has received in the past—that is, the inputs it has encountered recently or frequently.

But object recognition also involves **concept-driven**, or **top-down, processing**—processing that is driven by a broad pattern of knowledge and expectations, including knowledge that cannot easily be understood as an echo of frequent or recent experiences. The examples of priming given in the previous section are illustrations of top-down priming.

Most contemporary models of object recognition involve both top-down and bottom-up components and so are said to be **interactive models**. In fact, we have already mentioned one interactive model: the McClelland and Rumelhart word-recognition model. (Recall that this model has activation flowing upward from lower-level units, like letter detectors, and downward from higher-level units, like word detectors.) But this model needs to be expanded to incorporate the sort of broad knowledge effects we've now considered—priming effects that cannot be explained simply in terms of someone's stimulus history (i.e., what stimuli the person has seen recently).

To put this more broadly, concept-driven priming relies on knowledge that is separate from one's knowledge about letters, words, and letter combinations. This is why, for example, the McClelland and Rumelhart model, while interactive, is not interactive enough; that is, it does not draw on a wide enough knowledge base to handle the effects we are now considering.

Notice, though, where this brings us: The evidence is telling us that we cannot view object recognition as a self-contained process. Instead, knowledge that is external to object recognition (e.g., knowledge about what is edible) is imported into and clearly influences the process. Put differently, the "CELERY" example (and many others as well) does not depend on stimulus history, at least not in any straightforward way. Instead, what is crucial for priming is what a person knows coming into the experiment, and also how this knowledge is used.

We have, therefore, reached an important juncture. We have tried in this chapter to examine object recognition in isolation from other cognitive processes, considering how a separate object-recognition module might function, with the module then handing its product (the object it had recognized) on to subsequent processes. We have made good progress in this attempt and have described how a significant piece of object recognition might proceed. But in the end we have also run up against a problem—namely, concept-driven priming. This sort of priming depends on what is in memory and on how that knowledge is accessed and used, and so we really cannot tackle concept-driven priming until we have said a great deal more about memory, knowledge, and thought. We therefore must leave object recognition for now in order to fill in some other pieces of the puzzle. We will have more to say about object recognition in later chapters, once we have some more theoretical machinery in place.

Chapter Summary

- Visual perception is a highly active process in which the perceiver goes beyond the information given in organizing and interpreting the visual input. The process includes specifying a figure/ground organization for the input and specifying how the figure is organized in depth. To describe these processes, some investigators speak of the "logic of perception," referring to the fact that perception, like a good scientist, arrives at an interpretation that fits with all the evidence, and without appeals to coincidence.

- We easily recognize a wide range of objects in a wide range of circumstances. Our recognition is heavily influenced by context, which can determine how or whether we recognize an object. To study these achievements, investigators have often focused on the recognition of printed language, using this case as a microcosm within which to study how object recognition in general might proceed.

■ Many investigators have proposed that recognition begins with the identification of features in the (organized) input pattern. Crucial evidence for this claim comes from neuroscience studies showing that the detection of features is separate from the processes needed to assemble these features into more complex wholes.

■ To study word recognition, investigators often use tachistoscopic presentations. In these studies, words that appear frequently in the language are easier to identify, and so are words that have been recently viewed—an effect known as repetition priming. The data also show a pattern known as the word-superiority effect; this refers to the fact that words are more readily perceived than isolated letters. In addition, well-formed nonwords are more readily perceived than letter strings that do not conform to the rules of normal spelling. Another reliable pattern is that recognition errors, when they occur, are quite systematic, with the input typically perceived as being more regular than it actually is. These findings together indicate that recognition is shaped by learning, often relying on inference, and certainly influenced by the regularities that exist in our environment (e.g., the regularities of spelling patterns).

■ These results can be understood in terms of a network of detectors. Each detector collects input and fires when the input reaches a threshold level. A network of these detectors can accomplish a great deal; for example, it can interpret ambiguous inputs, recover from its own errors, and make inferences about barely viewed stimuli.

■ The feature net seems to "know" the rules of spelling and "expects" the input to conform to these rules. However, this knowledge is distributed across the entire network and emerges only through the network's parallel processing. This setup leads to enormous efficiency in our commerce with the world because it allows us to recognize patterns and objects with relatively little input and under highly diverse circumstances. But these gains come at the cost of occasional error. This trade-off may be necessary, though, if we are to cope with the informational complexity of our world.

■ A feature net can be implemented in different ways—with or without inhibitory connections, for example. With some adjustments (e.g., the addition of geon detectors), the net can also recognize three-dimensional objects. However, some stimuli—for example, faces—probably are not recognized through a feature net, but instead require a different sort of recognition system.

■ The feature net also needs to be supplemented to accommodate top-down influences on object recognition. These influences can be detected in the benefits of larger contexts in facilitating recognition, and also in forms of priming that are plainly concept-driven rather than data-driven. These other forms of priming demand an interactive model, which merges bottom-up and top-down processes.

The Workbook Connection

See the *Cognition Workbook* for further exploration in recognizing objects:

- Demonstration 3.1: Adelson's Brightness Illusion
- Demonstration 3.2: Features and Feature Combinations
- Demonstration 3.3: Inferences in Reading
- Research Methods: Dealing With Confounds
- Cognitive Psychology and Education: Speed-Reading
- Cognitive Psychology and the Law: Cross-Race Identification

Paying Attention

Consider your circumstances right now. You are paying attention to this page, reading these words. However, there are thousands of other inputs available to you, things you could pay attention to if you chose. For example, you're paying attention to the meanings of these words, but you could choose instead to look at the shapes of the letters, rather than the words themselves. You could, if you chose, contemplate the color of the paper, or its texture. If you wanted to, you could look up from the page and look at any of the people or objects in the room with you. And these are just the *visual* inputs. There are also many sounds in the room. Perhaps the radio is on, or perhaps you can hear someone at the next desk turning pages. Perhaps the room is silent, but even so, you could focus on the silence, much as a sentry listens carefully to detect intruders.

This list could easily be extended, but by now the point should be clear: The stimulus you're attending to is only one of many that are available to you, and this fact invites two crucial observations. First, it seems clear that you could choose to pay attention to any of the things just mentioned, and if you did, you would be virtually oblivious to the other things on the list. Indeed, until you read the previous paragraph, you probably were oblivious to the other stimuli we mentioned! How do you do this? How do you manage to avoid the distractors and focus your attention in just the manner you wish, selecting only one input of many? Second, there seems to be one thing you cannot do: you cannot pay attention to all of these things at once. If you start musing about your weekend, you are likely to lose track of what's on the page; if you start planning your term paper, you won't finish the reading assignment. Of course, it is possible in some circumstances to divide your attention, to deal with two different inputs at once. You can, if you choose, hum a melody while reading these words; most people can walk and chew gum at the same time; and so on. But where are the limits? When can you do two (or more) things at the same time, and when can't you?

- In this chapter, we argue that multiple mechanisms are involved in the seemingly simple act of paying attention. In particular, people must take many different steps to facilitate the processing of desired inputs; in the absence of these steps, our ability to pick up information from the world is dramatically reduced.

- Many of the steps we take in order to perceive have a "cost" attached to them: They require the commitment of mental resources. These resources are limited in availability, and this is part of the reason why we cannot pay attention to two inputs at once: This would require more resources than we have.

- Divided attention (the attempt to do two things at once) can also be understood in terms of resources: We can perform two activities at the same time, provided that the activities do not require more resources than we have available.

- Some of the mental resources we use are specialized, and so they are required only for tasks of a certain sort. Other resources are more general, needed for a wide range of tasks. The resource demand of a task can, however, be diminished through practice.

- We emphasize that attention is best understood not as a process or mechanism, but as an *achievement*. Like most achievements, paying attention involves many different elements, all of which help us to be aware of the stimuli we're interested in, and not pulled off track by irrelevant distractors.

Selective Listening

Many early studies of attention employed a task called **shadowing**. In this task, participants hear a tape recording of someone speaking and must echo this speech back, word for word, while they are listening to it. Shadowing is initially challenging, but it becomes relatively easy after a minute of practice. (You might try it, shadowing a voice on the radio or TV.)

In most experiments, the message to be shadowed, the **attended channel**, is presented through stereo headphones, so that participants hear the attended channel through, say, the right earphone. A different message—the **unattended channel**—is presented in the left earphone, and participants are instructed simply to ignore this message. This overall setup is referred to as **dichotic listening**.

Under these circumstances, participants easily follow one message, and their shadowing performance is generally near perfect. At the same time, however, they hear remarkably little from the unattended channel. If we ask them, after a minute or so of shadowing, to report what the unattended message was about, they cannot (Cherry, 1953). They cannot even tell if the unattended channel contained a coherent message or just random words. In fact, in one study, participants shadowed coherent prose in the attended channel, while in the unattended channel they heard a text in Czech, read with English pronunciation. Thus, the individual sounds (the vowels, the consonants) resembled English, but the message itself was (for an English speaker) gibberish. After a minute of shadowing, only 4 of 30 participants detected the peculiar character of the unattended message (Treisman, 1964).

More recent studies have documented a similar pattern with *visual* inputs. Participants in one study watched a TV screen that showed a team of players in white

FIGURE 4.1 Visual Attention

In this experiment, participants were instructed to keep track of the ballplayers in the white shirts. Intent on their task, they were oblivious to what the black-shirted players were doing. They also failed to see the person in the (black) gorilla suit strolling through the scene. (Figure provided by Daniel J. Simons)

shirts passing a ball back and forth; the participants had to signal each time the ball changed hands. Interwoven with these players (and visible on the same TV screen) was another team, wearing black shirts, also passing a ball back and forth; participants were instructed to ignore these. Participants easily did this selective task, and they were so intent on the white team that they didn't see other, rather salient, events that appeared on the screen, right in front of their eyes. For example, they entirely failed to notice when another player wearing a gorilla costume walked through the middle of the game, pausing briefly to thump his chest before exiting! (See Figure 4.1; Neisser & Becklen, 1975; Simons & Chabris, 1999; for a similar result in which participants fail to perceive unattended faces, see Jenkins, Lavie, & Driver, 2005).

However, people are not altogether oblivious to the unattended channel: In selective listening experiments, they easily and accurately report whether the unattended channel contained human speech, musical instruments, or silence. If the unattended channel contains human speech, they can report whether the speaker was male or female, had a high or low voice, was speaking loudly or softly. (For reviews of this early work, see Broadbent, 1958; Kahneman, 1973.) It seems, then, that physical attributes of the unattended channel are heard, even though participants seem oblivious to the unattended channel's semantic content.

Some Unattended Inputs Are Detected

However, some results do not fit this pattern. Some bits of the unattended input seem to "leak" through and get noticed. In one study, people were asked to shadow one passage while ignoring a second passage. Embedded within the unattended channel, though, was a series of names, including the participant's own name. Overall, participants heard very little of the unattended message, in keeping with the other studies mentioned. Nonetheless, about a third of them did hear their own name (Moray, 1959). As we commonly say, the name seemed to "catch" their attention. Other contents will also catch your attention, if you are suitably primed for them: Mention of a movie you just saw, or mention of your favorite restaurant, will often be noticed in the unattended channel. More generally, words with some personal importance will also be noticed (A. R. A. Conway, Cowan, & Bunting, 2001; Wood & Cowan, 1995).

These results are often referred to under the banner of the **cocktail party effect**. There you are at a party, engaged in conversation. Many other conversations are taking place in the room, but somehow you're able to "tune them out." You are aware that other people in the room are talking, but you don't have a clue what they're saying. All you hear is the single conversation you're attending, plus a buzz of background noise. But now imagine that someone a few steps away from you mentions the name of a close friend of yours. Your attention is immediately caught by this, and you find yourself listening to that other conversation and (momentarily) oblivious to the conversation you had been engaged in. This experience, easily observed outside the laboratory, is precisely parallel to the pattern of experimental data.

How can we put all of these results together? How can we explain both our general insensitivity to the unattended channel and also the cases in which the unattended channel "leaks through"?

Perceiving and the Limits on Cognitive Capacity

At the very start, we have two broad options for how we might think about attention. One option focuses on what we do with the *unattended* input. Specifically, the proposal is that we somehow block processing of the inputs we're not interested in, much as a sentry blocks the path of unwanted guests but simply stands back and allows legitimate guests to pass. This sort of proposal was central for early theories of attention, which suggested that we erect a **filter** that shields us from potential distractors. Desired information (the attended channel) is not filtered out and so goes on to receive further processing (Broadbent, 1958).

Evidence suggests we can shut out distractors in this way, but this "shutting out" seems to work on a distractor-by-distractor basis. In other words, we can inhibit our response to *this* distractor and do the same for *that* distractor, and these efforts can be quite successful. However, the same efforts are of little value if some new distractor comes along; in that case, we need to develop a new skill aimed specifically at blocking the new intruder (Fenske, Raymond, Kessler, Westoby, & Tipper, 2005; Jacoby, Lindsay, & Hessels, 2003; Milliken, Joordens, Merikle, & Seiffert, 1998; Milliken & Tipper, 1998; Reisberg, Baron, & Kemler, 1980; Tsushima, Sasaki, & Watanabe, 2006).

In addition, further evidence indicates that this is only a small part of the story. That's because not only do we block the processing of distractors, but we are also able to *promote* the processing of *desired* stimuli.

As we saw in Chapter 3, perception involves a considerable amount of activity—as you organize and interpret the incoming stimulus information. One might think that this activity would require some initiative and some resources from you, and the evidence suggests that it does.

In one experiment, participants were told that they would see large "+" shapes on a computer screen, presented for 200 milliseconds, followed by a pattern mask. If the horizontal bar of the "+" was longer than the vertical, the participants were supposed to press one button; if the vertical was longer, they had to press a different button. As a complication, participants weren't allowed to look directly at the "+." Instead, they fixated (pointed their eyes at) a mark in the center of the computer screen—a **fixation target**—and the "+" shapes were shown just off to one side.

For the first three trials of the procedure, events proceeded just as the participants expected, and the task was relatively easy. On Trial 3, for example, participants made the correct response 78% of the time. On Trial 4, though, things were slightly different: While the target "+" was on the screen, the fixation target disappeared and was replaced by one of three shapes—a triangle, a rectangle, or a cross. Then the entire configuration (the "+" target and this new shape) was replaced by a pattern mask.

Immediately after the trial, participants were asked: Was there anything different on this trial? Was anything present, or anything changed, that wasn't there on previous trials? Remarkably, 89% of the participants reported that there was no change; they had apparently failed to see anything other than the (attended) "+." To probe the participants further, the researchers then told them (correctly) that during the previous trial the fixation target had momentarily disappeared and had been replaced by a shape. The participants were then asked what that shape had been and were explicitly given the choices of a triangle, a rectangle, or a cross. The responses to this question were essentially random. Even when probed in this fashion, participants seemed not to have seen the shape that had been directly in front of their eyes (Mack & Rock, 1998; also see Mack, 2003).

What's going on in this study? Some researchers have proposed that the participants in this experiment did see the target shapes but, a moment later, couldn't *remember* what they had just seen (Wolfe, 1999). Mack and Rock, however, offer a stronger claim: They note that the participants were not expecting any shapes to appear and were not in any way prepared for these shapes. As a consequence, Mack and Rock claim, the participants literally failed to see the shapes, even though they were staring straight at them. This failure to see, caused by inattention, has been dubbed **inattentional blindness** (Mack & Rock, 1998; also see Mack, 2003).

Which of these accounts is correct? Did participants fail to see the input? Or did they see it but, just a few milliseconds later, forget what they'd seen? For purposes of theory, this distinction is crucial, but for the moment let's emphasize what the

Inattentional Blindness

Inattentional blindness is usually demonstrated in the laboratory, but has a number of real-world counterparts. Most people, for example, have experienced the peculiar situation in which they are unable to find the mayonnaise in the refrigerator (or the ketchup, or the salad dressing) even though they are staring right at the bottle! This is a situation in which the person is sufficiently absorbed in thoughts about other matters so that they make themselves blind to an otherwise salient stimulus.

two proposals have in common: By either account, our normal ability to see what's around us, and to make use of what we see, is dramatically diminished in the absence of attention.

Conscious Perception, Unconscious Perception

Mack and Rock, the investigators who documented the inattentional blindness phenomenon, draw a strong claim from these data: There is no perception, they claim, without attention. However, this claim needs an important refinement, and so, more precisely, Mack and Rock argue there is no *conscious* perception without attention (Mack & Rock, 1998, p. 14).

To see why this refinement is needed, consider the following experiment (Moore & Egeth, 1997; for other data pertinent to this claim, see Mack, 2003; Mack & Rock, 1998). Participants were shown a series of images on a computer screen; each image contained two horizontal lines surrounded by a pattern of black and white dots (see Figure 4.2A), and the participants' task was to decide which of the two lines was longer, the top one or the bottom. For the first three trials of this procedure, the background dots on the computer screen were arranged randomly. On Trial 4, however, and with no warning to participants, the pattern of dots shown was like the one in Figure 4.2B, creating a stimulus configuration that reproduces a standard geometric illusion, the Müller-Lyer illusion. Focusing their attention on the two horizontal lines, however, the participants didn't perceive this pattern. When they were asked immediately after the trial whether they had noticed any pattern in the dots, none reported seeing the pattern. They were then told directly that there had been a pattern and were asked to choose it (out of four choices available); 90% selected one of the incorrect patterns. Plainly, then, this experiment reproduces the finding of inattentional blindness.

Nonetheless, the participants were influenced by the dot pattern. In the standard Müller-Lyer display, the "fins" make the top horizontal line in Figure 4.2c appear longer than the bottom horizontal line, even though both lines are exactly the same length. The dot pattern in the Moore and Egeth displays did the same, and 95% of the participants reported that the top line in Figure 4.2B was longer than the bottom one, even though, in the display, both were the same length.

Notice, then, that the participants were completely unaware of the fins, but were still influenced by them. No participant reported seeing the fins, but virtually all responded in the length judgment in a fashion consistent with the fins. (For related data, see Russell & Driver, 2005.) The obvious conclusion, then, is that participants did perceive the fins in some way, but did not consciously perceive them. We will return to issues of conscious and unconscious perception in Chapter 15; for now, it seems attention may be needed for *conscious* perception, but perhaps you can unconsciously detect (and be influenced by) patterns in the world even in the absence of attention.

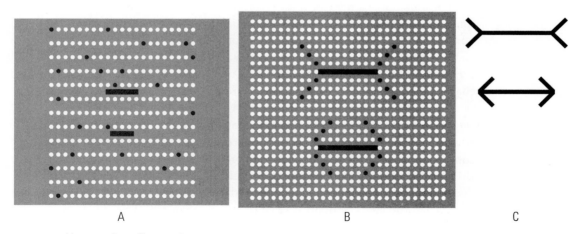

A   B   C

FIGURE 4.2 Unconscious Perception
Participants were shown a series of images, each containing a pair of horizontal lines; their task was to decide which of the two lines was longer. For the first three trials, the background dots were arranged randomly (Panel A). For the fourth trial, the dots were arranged as shown in Panel B, roughly reproducing the configuration of the Müller-Lyer illusion; Panel C shows the standard form of this illusion. The participants in this study did not perceive the "fins" consciously, but they were nonetheless influenced by the fins—judging the top horizontal line in Panel B to be longer, fully in accord with the usual misperception of this illusion.

Change Blindness

Similar conclusions emerge from studies of **change blindness**—observers' inability to detect changes in scenes they are looking directly at. In some experiments, participants are shown pairs of pictures separated by a brief blank interval (e.g., Rensink, O'Regan, & Clark, 1997). The pictures in the pair are identical except for some single aspect: an "extra" engine shown on the airplane in one picture and not in the other; a man not wearing a hat in one picture but wearing one in the other; and so on. Participants know from the start that their task is to detect these changes, but even with this clear understanding of the task, the task is quite difficult. If the change involves something central to the scene, observers may need as many as a dozen alternations between the pictures before they detect the change. If the change involves some peripheral aspect of the scene, then as many as 25 alternations may be required. (For some examples, see color insert, Figure 10.)

A related pattern emerges when participants watch movies. In one study, observers watched a movie of two women having a conversation. During the film, the camera first focused on one woman, then on the other, just as it would in an ordinary TV show or movie. The crucial element of this experiment, though, was that aspects of the scene changed every time the camera angle changed. For example, when the camera was pointing at Woman A, you could plainly see the red plates on the table between the women. When the camera was shifted to point at Woman B, just a fraction of a second later, the plates had miraculously turned white. Most observers, however, noticed none of these changes. In one experiment, a film containing a total of nine changes was shown to ten participants. Only one participant claimed to notice the changes, and when pressed, this participant merely said there was a difference in "the way people were sitting." When allowed to watch the film again and told explicitly to look out for changes, observers noticed (on average) only two of the nine changes (D. T. Levin & Simons, 1997; Shore & Klein, 2000; Simons, 2000).

Incredibly, the same result pattern can be documented with live (not filmed) events. In a remarkable study, an investigator (let's call him "Bo") approached pedestrians on a college campus and asked for directions to a certain building. During the conversation, two men carrying a door approached and deliberately walked *between* Bo and the research participant. As a result, Bo was momentarily hidden (by the door) from the participant's view, and in that moment Bo traded places with one of the men carrying the door. A second later, therefore, Bo was able to walk away, unseen, while the new fellow (who had been carrying the door) stayed behind and continued the conversation with the participant.

Roughly half of the participants failed to notice this switch. They continued the conversation as though nothing had happened—despite the fact that Bo and his replacement were wearing different clothes, had easily distinguishable voices, and so on. When asked directly whether anything odd had happened in this event, many participants commented only that it was rude that the guys carrying the door had walked right through their conversation (Simons & Ambinder, 2005; for other studies of change blindness, see Most et al., 2001, and Rensink, 2002; for similar effects with auditory stimuli, see Gregg & Samuel, 2008; Vitevitch, 2003; for studies of why some unattended stimuli nonetheless "catch" our attention, see Most, Scholl, Clifford, & Simons, 2005; for more on what we *miss* in a visual display, see color insert, Figure 11).

Early Versus Late Selection

In several paradigms, then, people seem oblivious to stimuli that are directly in front of their eyes—whether the stimuli are simple displays on a computer screen, or photographs, or movies, or real-life events. As we noted earlier, though, there are two ways we might think about these results: These studies may reveal genuine limits on *perception*, so that participants literally don't see these stimuli; or these studies may reveal limits on *memory*, so that people do see the stimuli but immediately forget what they have just seen.

Which proposal is correct? One approach to this question hinges on *when* the perceiver selects the desired input, and (correspondingly) when the perceiver ceases the processing of the unattended input. According to the **early selection** hypothesis, the attended input is identified and privileged from the start, so that the unattended input receives little analysis (and so is never perceived). According to the **late selection** hypothesis, however, all inputs receive relatively complete analysis. But it is only the attended input that reaches consciousness, or (as a related idea) it is only the attended input that is remembered.

It turns out that each hypothesis captures part of the truth. On the one side, we have already considered a case in which people seem genuinely unaware of the distractors but are nevertheless influenced by them (pp. 102–103). This seems to be a case of *late selection*, in which the distractors were perceived, but the perception—even if influential—was not conscious. But, on the other side, we can also find evidence for *early selection*, with distractor stimuli receiving little analysis, and indeed falling out of the stream of processing at a very early stage. Relevant evidence comes, for example, from studies that record the electrical activity of the brain in the milliseconds after a stimulus has arrived. These studies confirm that the brain activity for attended inputs is distinguishable from that for unattended inputs just 60 or 70 ms after the stimulus presentation—a time interval in which the earliest sensory processing is still under way (Hillyard, Vogel, & Luck, 1998). Apparently, in these cases, the attended input is privileged from the very start.

Other data also provide evidence for early selection. For example, recording from neurons in Area V4 of the visual cortex shows that the neurons are more responsive to attended inputs than to unattended ones, almost as if attention made the light areas seem brighter and dim areas seem darker (Carrasco, Ling, & Read, 2004; Carrasco, Penpeci-Talgar, & Eckstein, 2000; Reynolds, Pasternak, & Desimone, 2000). Other studies suggest that attention may modulate neural events even earlier in the stream of visual processing—perhaps as early as the lateral geniculate nucleus (O'Connor, Fukui, Pinsk, & Kastner, 2002; also see Yantis, 2008). These results argue powerfully that attention doesn't just change what we remember or what we're aware of. Attention can also literally change what we perceive.

But what accounts for this mixed pattern? Why do the data sometimes indicate late selection, and sometimes early? The answer depends in part on the nature of the attended input. If this input is particularly complex, then the processing of this input will demand a lot of effort and a lot of cognitive resources. (We will have more to say about these "resources" later in the chapter.) In this case, little effort will be left over for other stimuli, with the consequence that the other stimuli receive less processing, leading to a data pattern consistent with early selection. In contrast, if the attended input is relatively simple, processing will demand few resources, leaving more available for the unattended inputs. Here the unattended inputs will probably receive more analysis, and so we'll see the pattern of late selection (after Lavie, 1997, 2001, 2005; Macdonald & Lavie, 2008; for some challenges to this claim, though, see Mack, 2003).

Selective Priming

Whether selection is early or late, however, it's clear that looking directly at an input isn't by itself enough to allow conscious perception. But, in that case, what else is needed? Likewise, we've noted that people seem to hear little from the unattended channel during dichotic listening, but are reasonably likely to detect some inputs—such as their own name. How should we think about these facts? And, with this, we've also now suggested that "resources" are needed for perceiving, but what are those resources? Let's tackle these questions.

In Chapter 3, we proposed that recognition requires a network of detectors, and we argued that these detectors fire most readily, and most quickly, if they are suitably primed. But what does that priming involve? In some cases, priming is produced by one's visual experience—specifically, whether each detector has been used recently or frequently in the past. But as we suggested at the end of Chapter 3, priming can also come from another source: your expectations about what the stimulus will be.

The proposal, then, is that people can literally prepare themselves for perceiving by priming the suitable detectors. Let's hypothesize in addition that this priming isn't free. Instead, you must spend some effort or allocate some resources in order to do the priming, and let's suppose that these resources are in limited supply.

This simple idea helps explain several findings we've already met. Why don't participants notice the shapes in the inattentional blindness studies? It may be that they don't expect any stimulus, so they have no reason to prepare for any stimulus. As a result, the stimulus, when it's presented, falls on unprepared (thus, unresponsive) detectors.

What about selective listening? In this case, one does not want to hear the distractor, so devoting resources to the distractor would be, at best, a waste of these resources. Therefore, the detectors needed for the distractor receive no resources and so are unprimed, literally making it more difficult to hear the distractor. But why, on this account, does attention sometimes "leak," so that we do hear some aspects of the unattended input? Think about what will happen if your name is uttered on the unattended channel. The detectors for this stimulus are already primed, but this is not because you are, at that moment, expecting to hear your name. Instead, the detectors are primed simply because this is a stimulus you have often encountered in the past. Thanks to this prior exposure, the activation level of these detectors is already high; you don't need to prime them further. So these detectors will fire even if your attention is elsewhere.

Two Types of Priming

The idea, in short, is that resources are needed to prime detectors, and that those resources are in limited supply. These proposals certainly seem promising, but can we find evidence to confirm these claims directly? In a classic series of studies, Posner and Snyder (1975) gave people a straightforward task: A pair of letters was shown on a computer screen, and participants had to decide, as swiftly as they could, whether the letters were the same or different. So someone might see "A A" and answer "same," or might see "A B" and answer "different."

Before each pair, participants saw a warning signal. In the neutral condition, the warning signal was a plus sign ("+"). This signal notified participants that the stimuli were about to arrive but provided no other information. In a different condition, the warning signal was itself a letter and actually matched the stimuli to come. So someone might see the warning signal "C" followed by the pair "C C." In this case, the warning signal actually served to prime the participants for the stimuli. In a third condition, though, the warning signal was misleading. The warning signal was again a letter, but it was a letter different from the stimuli to come. Participants might see "C" followed by the pair "F F." Let's call these three conditions *neutral*, *primed*, and *misled*.

In this simple task, accuracy rates are very high. But the *speed* of responding varies from condition to condition, and we can use these speeds as a way of exploring what's going on in the participants' minds. Specifically, in each condition, Posner and Snyder recorded how quickly people responded. By comparing these **response times** (or RTs) in the *primed* and *neutral* conditions, we can ask what benefit there is from the prime. Likewise, by comparing RTs in the *misled* and *neutral* conditions, we can ask what cost there is, if any, from being misled.

Before we turn to the results, though, we need one further complication: Posner and Snyder ran this procedure in two different versions (as shown in Table 4.1). In one version, the warning signal was an excellent predictor of the upcoming stim-

TABLE 4.1 Design of Posner and Snyder's Experiment

	Type of trial	Typical Sequence		Provides repetition priming?	Provides basis for expectation?
		Warning signal	Test stimuli		
Low-validity condition	Neutral	+	AA	No	No
	Primed	G	GG	Yes	No
	Misled	H	GG	No	No
High-validity condition	Neutral	+	AA	No	No
	Primed	G	GG	Yes	Prime leads to correct expectation
	Misled	H	GG	No	Prime leads to incorrect expectation

In the low-validity condition, *misled* trials occurred four times as often as *primed* trials (80% vs. 20%). Therefore, participants had reason not to trust the primes and, correspondingly, had no reason to generate an expectation based on the primes. In the high-validity condition, things were reversed: Now *primed* trials occurred four times as often as *misled* trials. Therefore, participants had good reason to trust the primes and good reason to generate an expectation based on the prime.

uli: For example, if the warning signal was an *A*, there was an 80% chance that the upcoming stimulus pair would contain *A*s. In Posner and Snyder's terms, the warning signal provided a "high validity" prime. In a different version of the procedure, the warning signal was a poor predictor of the upcoming stimuli: If the warning signal was an *A*, there was only a 20% chance that the upcoming pair would contain *A*s. This is the "low validity" condition.

Let's consider the low-validity condition first, and let's focus on those rare occasions in which the prime did match the subsequent stimuli. That is, we are focusing on 20% of the trials and ignoring the other 80%. In this condition, the participant can't use the prime as a basis for predicting the stimuli because, after all, the prime is a poor indicator of things to come. Therefore, the prime should not lead to any specific expectations. Nonetheless, we do expect faster RTs in the *primed* condition than in the *neutral* condition: Thanks to the prime, the relevant detectors have just fired, and so the detectors should still be warmed up. When the target stimuli arrive, therefore, the detectors should fire more readily, allowing a faster response. This is, in effect, a case of repetition priming, as described in Chapter 3.

The results bear this out. RTs were reliably faster (by roughly 30 ms) in the *primed* condition than in the *neutral* condition. Apparently, then, detectors can be primed by mere exposure to a stimulus. Or, to put it differently, priming is observed even in the absence of expectations. This priming seems truly stimulus-based.

What about the *misled* condition? With a low-validity prime, misleading participants had no effect: Performance in the *misled* condition was the same as performance in the *neutral* condition. Priming the "wrong" detector, it seems, takes nothing away from the other detectors—including the detectors actually needed for that trial. This fits with our discussion in Chapter 3: Each of the various detectors works independently of the others. Thus, priming one detector obviously influences the functioning of that specific detector, but neither helps nor hinders the other detectors.

Let's look next at the high-validity primes. In this condition, people might see, for example, a "J" as the warning signal, and then the stimulus pair "J J." Presentation of the prime itself will fire the *J*-detectors, and this should, once again, "warm up" these detectors, just as the low-validity primes did. Thus, we expect a stimulus-driven benefit from the prime. However, the high-validity primes may also have another influence: High-validity primes are excellent predictors of the stimulus to come. Participants are told this at the outset, and they have lots of opportunity to see that it is true. High-validity primes will therefore produce a warm-up effect *and also* an expectation effect, whereas low-validity primes produce only the warm-up. We should therefore expect the high-validity primes to help participants more than low-validity primes—and that's exactly what the data show. The combination of warm-up and expectations, in other words, leads to faster responses than warm-up alone. From the participants' point of view, it pays to know what the upcoming stimulus might be.

Just as important, though, is what happened in the *misled* condition: With high-validity primes, responses in the *misled* condition were *slower* than responses in the *neutral* condition. That is, misleading participants actually hurt performance. As a concrete example, *F*-detection was slower if G was primed, compared to *F*-detection when the prime was simply the neutral warning signal ("+").

Explaining the Costs and Benefits

The message of these data is clear: There are two types of primes. One type is stimulus-based—produced merely by presentation of the priming stimulus, with no role for expectations. The other type of priming is expectation-based, and is created only when the participant believes the prime allows a prediction of what's to come.

These types of primes can be distinguished in several ways. First, expectation-based priming is larger in magnitude than the stimulus-based priming, leading to a greater benefit in the RT data. Second, expectation-based priming takes longer to kick in: Stimulus-based priming can be observed immediately after the prime; priming based on expectations takes roughly a half second to develop (Neely, 1977).

Third, the two types of priming can also be distinguished in terms of their "cost." Stimulus-based priming appears to be "free," and so we can prime one detector without taking anything away from the other detectors. We see this in the low-validity condition, in the fact that the *misled* trials lead to responses just as fast as those in the *neutral* trials. Expectation-based priming, however, does have a cost, as we see in the high-validity condition. Here priming the "wrong" detector does take something away from the other detectors, and so participants are worse off when they're misled than when they received no prime at all.

What produces this cost? As an analogy, think about being on a limited budget. Imagine that you have just $50 to spend on groceries. You can spend more on ice cream if you wish, but if you do, you'll have that much less to spend on other foods. Any increase in the ice cream allotment must be covered by a decrease somewhere else. This trade-off arises, though, only because of the limited budget. If you had unlimited funds, you could spend more on ice cream and still have enough money for everything else.

Expectation-based priming shows the same pattern. If the Q-detector is primed, this takes something away from the other detectors. Getting prepared for one target seems to make people less prepared for other targets. But we just said that this sort of pattern implies a limited "budget." If an unlimited supply of activation were available, one could prime the Q-detector and leave the other detectors just as they were. And that is the point: Expectation-based priming, by virtue of revealing costs when misled, reveals the presence of a **limited-capacity system**.

We can now put the pieces together. Ultimately, we need to explain the facts of **selective attention**, including the fact that while listening to one message you hear little content from other messages. To explain this, we have proposed that perceiving involves some work, and this work requires some limited mental resources. That is why you can't listen to two messages at the same time; doing so would demand more resources than you have. And now, finally, we are seeing evidence for those limited resources: The Posner and Snyder research (and many other results) reveals the workings of a limited-capacity system, just as our hypothesis demands.

Chronometric Studies and Spatial Attention

The Posner and Snyder study shows us how a person's expectations about an upcoming stimulus can influence the processing of that stimulus. But what exactly is the nature of these expectations? How precise, or how vague, are they? To see the point, imagine that participants are told, "The next stimulus will be a *T*." In this case, they know exactly what to get ready for. But now imagine that participants are told, "The next stimulus will be a letter" or "The next stimulus will be on the left side of the screen." Will these cues allow people to prepare themselves?

These issues have been examined in studies of **spatial attention**—that is, our ability to focus on a particular position in space, and thus to be better prepared for any stimulus that appears in that position. In an early study, Posner, Snyder, and Davidson (1980) required their participants simply to detect letter presentations;

the task was just to press a button as soon as a letter appeared. Participants kept their eyes pointed at a central fixation mark, and letters could appear either to the left or to the right of this mark.

For some trials, a neutral warning signal was presented, so that participants knew a trial was about to start but had no information about stimulus location. For other trials, an arrow was used as the warning signal. Sometimes the arrow pointed left, sometimes right; and the arrow was generally an accurate predictor of the location of the stimulus-to-come: If the arrow pointed right, the stimulus would be on the right side of the computer screen. (In the terms we used earlier, this is a high-validity cue.) On 20% of the trials, however, the arrow misled participants about location.

The results show a familiar pattern (Posner et al., 1980, Exp. 2): With high-validity priming, the data show a benefit from cues that correctly signal where the upcoming target will appear. Concretely, with a neutral warning signal, people took 266 ms to detect the signal. With a correct prime, they were faster: 249 ms. This isn't a huge difference, but keep the task in mind: All participants had to do was detect the input. Even with the simplest of tasks, therefore, it pays to be prepared.

What about the trials in which participants were misled? RTs in this condition averaged 297 ms, 31 ms (about 12%) slower than the neutral condition. Once again, therefore, we're seeing evidence of a limited-capacity system: In order to devote more attention to (say) the left position, one has to devote *less* attention to the right. If the stimulus then shows up on the right, one is less prepared for it—hence the cost of being misled.

Attention as a Searchlight

Studies of spatial attention suggest to some psychologists that visual attention can profitably be compared to a searchlight beam that can "shine" anywhere in the visual field. The "beam" marks the region of space for which one is prepared, so inputs within the beam are processed more efficiently and more swiftly. The beam can be wide or narrowly focused (see color insert, Figure 12), and it can be moved about at will as one explores (attends to) one aspect of the visual field or another.

Let's emphasize, though, that the searchlight idea is referring to movements of *attention*, and not movements of the eyes. Of course, eye movements do play an important role in our selection of information from the world: If we want to learn more about something, we look at it. (For more on how we move our eyes to explore a scene, see Rayner, Smith, Malcolm, & Henderson, 2009.) But even so, movements of the eyes can be separated from movements of attention, and it's attention that's moving around in the Posner et al. study. We know this because of the timing of the effects: Eye movements are surprisingly slow, requiring 180 to 200 ms. But the benefits of primes can be detected within the first 150 ms after the priming stimulus is presented. Thus, the benefits of attention occur prior to any eye movement, and so they cannot be a consequence of eye movements.

But what exactly does the "searchlight" accomplish? What is different, in our processing of an input, when the light is "shining" on that input? The answer, we've said, is priming: When we say that the searchlight of attention is shining on a stimulus, this is just another way of saying that a person is priming the relevant detectors for that stimulus. This priming allows the detectors to work more swiftly and more efficiently, promoting our perception of the input. Without this priming, the detectors would be less responsive, and this helps explain why we are much less likely to perceive unattended inputs.

Attending to Objects, or Attending to Positions

There are, however, also important differences between attention and a searchlight beam. (For a broad overview of spatial attention and the searchlight notion, see Wright & Ward, 2008.) Think about how an actual searchlight works. If, for example, a searchlight shines on a donut, then part of the beam will fall on the donut's hole and so illuminate the plate underneath the donut. Similarly, if the searchlight isn't aimed quite accurately, it may also illuminate the plate just to the left of the donut. The region illuminated by the beam, in other words, is defined purely in spatial terms: a circle of light at a particular position. That position may or may not line up with the boundaries of the object you're shining the beam on.

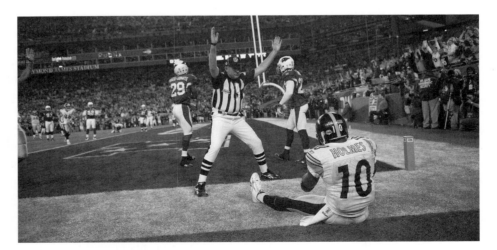

Paying Attention to (Almost) Everything
The task of a sports referee is enormously difficult: The ref must pay attention to many players, scattered across many positions, all at once, and must be alert to a wide variety of "targets" (any of the fouls the ref might need to call). In essence, he or she needs to shine an "attention spotlight" on everything! This is precisely the sort of things that most people, in the lab, cannot do—making the referees' skill quite remarkable.

Is this how attention works—so that we pay attention to whatever it is that falls in a certain region of space? In this case, we might on some occasions end up paying attention to part of this object, part of that. An alternative is that we pay attention to objects, rather than to *positions in space*. To continue the example, the target of our attention might be the donut itself, rather than the donut's location. In that case, the plate just to the left, and the bit of plate visible through the donut's hole, might be close to our focus, but they aren't part of the attended object and so aren't attended.

Which is the correct view of attention? Do we pay attention to regions in space, whatever the objects (or parts of objects) are that fall in that region? Or do we pay attention to objects? It turns out that each view captures part of the truth.

One line of evidence comes from the study of people who have suffered forms of brain damage (typically in the parietal cortex) that produce extraordinary problems in paying attention. For example, patients with **unilateral neglect syndrome** seem to ignore all inputs coming from one side of the body. A patient with neglect syndrome will eat food from only one side of the plate, will wash only half of his or her face, and will fail to locate sought-for objects if they are on the neglected side (Heilman, Watson, & Valenstein, 1985; Sieroff, Pollatsek, & Posner, 1988). This syndrome usually results from damage to the *right* parietal lobe, and so the neglect is for the *left* side of space. (Remember the brain's contralateral organization; see Chapter 2.) Thus, in the laboratory, neglect patients will read only the right half of words shown to them; that is, they will read "pigpen" as "pen," "parties" as "ties," and so on. If asked to cross out all the *E*s on a page, the patient will cross out the *E*s on only the right side of the page.

Taken at face value, these symptoms seem to support a space-based account of attention: The afflicted patient seems insensitive to all objects within a spatially defined region—namely, everything to the left of his current focus. If an object falls half within the region and half outside of it, then it's the spatially defined region that matters, not the object's boundaries. This is evident, for example, in how these patients read words—responding only to the word's right half, apparently oblivious to the word's overall boundaries.

Other evidence, however, demands further theory. In one study, patients with neglect syndrome had to respond to targets that appeared within a barbell-shaped frame. Not surprisingly, they were much more sensitive to the targets appearing within the red circle (on the right) and missed many of the targets appearing in the blue circle (on the left); this result simply confirms the patients' diagnosis. What is crucial, though, is what happened next: While the patients watched, the barbell frame was slowly spun around, so that the red circle, previously on the right, was now on the left, and the blue circle, previously on the left, was now on the right (see Figure 4.3).

What should we expect in this situation? If the patients consistently neglect a region of space, they should now be more sensitive to the right-side blue circle. A different possibility is more complicated: Perhaps these patients have a powerful bias to attend to the right side, and so initially they attend to the red circle. Once they have "locked in" to this circle, however, it is the object, and not the position in space, that

Patient initially sees:

As the patient watches:

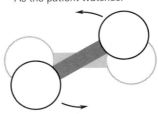

Patient now sees:

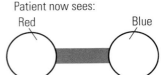

FIGURE 4.3 Space-Based or Object-Based Attention?
Patients with unilateral neglect syndrome were much more sensitive to targets appearing within the red circle (on the right) and missed many of the targets appearing within the blue circle (on the left); this observation simply confirms their clinical diagnosis. Then, as the patients watched, the "barbell" frame rotated, so that now the red circle was on the left and the blue circle was on the right. After this rotation, participants were still more sensitive to targets in the red circle (now on the left), apparently focusing on this attended object even though it had moved into their "neglected" side.

defines their focus of attention. According to this view, if the barbell form rotates, they will continue attending to the red circle (this is, after all, the focus of their attention), even though it now appears on their "neglected" side. This prediction turns out to be correct: When the barbell rotates, the patients' focus of attention seems to rotate with it (Behrmann & Tipper, 1999).

To describe these patients, therefore, we need a two-part account. First, the symptoms of neglect syndrome plainly reveal a spatially defined bias: These patients neglect half of space. But, second, once attention is directed toward a target, it is the target itself that defines the focus of attention; if the target moves, the focus moves with it. In this way, the focus of attention is object-based, not space-based. (For more on these issues, and on some of the intriguing complications in neglect syndrome, see Awh, Dhaliwal, Christensen, & Matsukura, 2001; Chen & Cave, 2006; Logie & Della Salla, 2005; Richard, Lee, & Vecera, 2008; Scholl, 2001.)

Could it be that this complex pattern appears only in neglect patients, so that the pattern is somehow a by-product of their brain damage? The answer to this is clearly no. Normal participants, too, show a mix of space-based and object-based attention. We have already seen evidence for the spatial base: The Posner et al. (1980) study and many results like it show that participants can focus on a particular region of space in preparation for a stimulus. In this situation, the stimulus has not yet appeared; there is no object to focus on. Therefore, the attention must be spatially defined.

In other cases, though, attention is heavily influenced by object boundaries. For example, in several studies participants have been shown displays with visually superimposed stimuli, as if a single television set were showing two channels at the same time (Neisser & Becklen, 1975; Simons & Chabris, 1999). Participants can easily pay attention to one of these stimuli and ignore the other. This selection cannot be space-based (because both stimuli are in the same place) and so must be object-based.

Similarly, Egly, Driver, and Rafal (1994) had their participants look at a computer screen that showed two rectangles, one on the left side of the screen and one on the right. The participants' task was to respond as soon as they saw a target at one end (top or bottom) of one of the rectangles. In the majority of trials, a cue signaled in advance where the target would appear—in which rectangle, and at which end of the rectangle. In other trials, though, the cue was misleading: It signaled a location, but the target appeared elsewhere. Sometimes the target appeared in the same rectangle as the cue, but at the rectangle's opposite end; sometimes the target appeared in the other rectangle.

Not surprisingly, participants were fastest when the cue accurately signaled where the target would be; this observation echoes other results we have already discussed. What's crucial, though, is the comparison between misleading cues that at least signaled the proper rectangle, and misleading cues that signaled the *wrong* rectangle. According to a space-based account, there should be no difference between these two cases, because the display had been arranged so that both of the targets were the same distance from the misleading cue. According to an object-based account, though, these two cases will be different. Let's say that the cue draws attention to the top of the left-hand rectangle, and the target then appears in the bottom of that rectangle. In that case, the cue at least led participants to focus on the proper rectangle, and so attention will (on an object-based account) include that rectangle. As a result, responses will be quicker in this condition than they would be if the cue signaled the wrong rectangle altogether.

The latter prediction turns out to be correct. The cues in this study didn't just draw attention to a *location*. They also drew attention to the *object* that was in that location. Hence, in this way, our description of attention needs to be object-based as well as space-based.

Perceiving and the Limits on Cognitive Capacity: An Interim Summary

Our account is growing complex, so let's pause to take stock of where we are. At the broadest level, we have suggested that two different mechanisms are involved in selective attention. One mechanism serves to *inhibit*, or block out, the processing of *unwanted* inputs; this is, in effect, a mechanism for "ignoring" inputs in which we have no interest. A second mechanism *facilitates* the processing of *desired* inputs. This is a mechanism for "paying attention."

We've also seen, though, that the mechanism for paying attention has several parts. In other words, we take many different steps to promote the processing of inputs we're interested in. If we know the target's identity in advance, we can prime the relevant detectors. If we know only *where* the target will appear, we can prime detectors for the appropriate region of space; then, once we locate the object in that region, we prime detectors for that object.

Moreover, we have suggested that there is some flexibility in *when* the selection takes place. In some circumstances, the perceiver makes an early selection of the desired input, so that the unattended input receives relatively little processing. In other circumstances, the unattended input receives a fuller analysis—even if that input never penetrates into the perceiver's conscious awareness.

In light of all these points, the term "attention" seems not to label a particular process or a particular mechanism. Instead, we probably need to think of paying attention as an *achievement*, something that you are able to do. Like many other achievements (e.g., doing well in school, staying healthy, earning a good salary), paying attention involves many elements. The exact set of elements varies from occasion to occasion. Sometimes a strong distractor is on the scene, making it essential that you inhibit your response to that distractor. Sometimes no distractors are in view, so inhibition plays a smaller role. Sometimes you know in advance what the stimulus will be, so you can prime just the right detectors. Sometimes stimuli are less predictable, so your priming must be more diffuse. In all cases, though, multiple steps are needed to ensure that you end up aware of (and able to remember) the stimuli you're interested in, and not pulled off track by irrelevant inputs.

Divided Attention

So far in this chapter, we have been emphasizing situations in which you want to focus on a single input. If other tasks and other stimuli are on the scene, they are mere distractors. Our concern, therefore, has been on how you manage to select just the desired information, while avoiding irrelevant distraction.

There are circumstances, however, in which you want to do multiple things at once, in which you want to divide your attention among various tasks or various inputs. In some cases you can do this, but your ability to perform concurrent tasks is clearly limited. Almost anyone can walk and talk simultaneously, but it is far harder to solve calculus problems while reading a history text. Why are some task combinations difficult, while others are easy?

Our first step toward answering this question is, however, already in view. We have proposed that perceiving requires resources that are in short supply; the same is presumably true for other mental tasks—remembering, reasoning, problem-solving. They, too, require resources, and without these resources, these processes cannot go forward. All of this provides a straightforward account of **divided attention**: One can

The Long History of Multitasking

Some writers lament the hectic pace at which we live our lives, and view this as a sad fact about the pressured reality of the modern world. But were things that different in earlier times? More than 2,000 years ago, Julius Caesar was praised for his ability to multitask. (That term is new, but the capacity is not.) According to the Roman historian Suetonius, Caesar could write, dictate letters, and read at the same time. Even on the most important subjects, he could dictate four letters as once, and, if he had nothing else to do, as many as seven letters at once.

perform concurrent tasks only if the sum of the tasks' demands is within the "cognitive budget." Thus, for example, solving calculus problems requires some mental resources, and so does reading a text. You have enough resources to do either one of these tasks by itself, but not enough for both; if you try to do both at the same time, you will fail.

But what are these hypothesized mental resources? Do all tasks, no matter what they involve, draw on the same mental resources? Or are mental resources somehow specialized, so that the resources required by a task depend on the exact nature of the task?

The Specificity of Resources

Some mental resources do seem relatively specialized and so are drawn on only by certain sorts of tasks. This is why it is more difficult to combine two verbal tasks than it is to combine a verbal task with a spatial task. To make this idea concrete, imagine that you are trying to read a list of words while simultaneously listening to someone give a speech. Both of these tasks draw on resources specialized for verbal tasks, and it's likely that listening to the speech will exhaust these resources. As a result, reading while listening will be impossible: The reading requires resources that aren't available. But now imagine that you are trying to look at pictures while listening to the speech. This will be much easier because picture-viewing doesn't require verbal resources, and so it won't matter if those resources have been exhausted by some other task.

This pattern—greater interference among more similar tasks—is easily demonstrated. In an early study by Allport, Antonis, and Reynolds (1972), participants heard a list of words presented through headphones into one ear, and their task was to shadow these words. At the same time, they were also presented with a second list. No immediate response was required to this second list, but later on, memory was tested for these items. In one condition, these memory items consisted of words presented into the other ear, so the participants were hearing (and shadowing) a list of words in one ear while simultaneously hearing the memory list in the other. In a second condition, the memory items were presented visually. That is, while the participants were shadowing one list of words, they were also seeing, on a screen before them, a different list of words. Finally, in a third condition, the memory items consisted of pictures, also presented on a screen.

These three conditions have similar requirements—namely, shadowing one list while memorizing another. But the first condition (hear words + hear words) involves very similar tasks; the second condition (hear words + see words) involves less similar tasks; the third condition (hear words + see pictures), even less similar tasks. If performance is limited by task-specific resources, then it seems most likely that the first pair of tasks will compete with each other for resources, and least likely that the last pair will. Thus, in terms of task-specific resources, we would expect the most interference in the first condition, the least in the third. And that is what the data show. (For further evidence, see Brooks, 1968; Hirst, 1986; Hirst & Kalmar, 1987.)

Plainly, therefore, the likelihood of interference increases when tasks are similar. Even so, we can still demonstrate interference between tasks that are completely different from each other. Evidence comes from many sources, including one often-discussed case: talking on a cell phone while driving. The conversation requires an auditory input and speech as output; the material being attended to is verbal. Driving, on the other hand, involves a visual input and hand and foot motion as output; the material being attended to is spatial. One might therefore think that there is little or no overlap in the resources required for these two tasks, and so little chance that the tasks will compete for resources.

It turns out, however, that driving and cell-phone use do interfere with each other; this is reflected, for example, in the fact that phone use has been implicated in many automobile accidents (Lamble, Kauranen, Laakso, & Summala, 1999). The interference can be observed even if the phones are of the hands-free type so that the driver's hands can remain on the steering wheel. Even with a hands-free phone, drivers engaged in cell-phone conversations are more likely to be involved in accidents, more likely to overlook traffic signals, and slower to hit the brakes when they need to (Kunar, Carter, Cohen, & Horowitz, 2008; Levy & Pashler, 2008; Strayer, Drews, & Johnston, 2003; Strayer & Drews, 2007; also see Spence & Read, 2003).

Identifying General Resources

Apparently, tasks as different as driving and talking compete with each other for some mental resource; otherwise, we have no explanation of the interference. This resource, therefore, must be fairly general in its application—so that it applies to verbal tasks and spatial ones, tasks with visual inputs and tasks with auditory inputs. But what is this general resource?

Researchers have offered various answers to this question, and it is likely that all the answers are correct. In other words, there are likely to be *several* task-general resources, with each contributing to the limits on how (or whether) we can divide attention between tasks. Some authors, for example, liken mental resources to an energy supply or a bank account, drawn on by all tasks, and we have used this analogy in much of our discussion. For example, Kahneman (1973) hypothesized that mental tasks require the expenditure of mental effort (also see Eysenck, 1982). The term "effort" was meant rather literally here, so that mental tasks require effort in about the same fashion that physical tasks do.

Other authors have offered different views, conceiving of these resources more as "mental tools" rather than as some sort of mental "energy supply" (A. Allport, 1989; Baddeley, 1986; Bourke & Duncan, 2005; Dehaene, Sergent & Changeux,

Cell Phones and Driving

The evidence is clear that cell phone use while driving increases accident risk. Some people propose that this is because one of the driver's hands is holding the phone (and therefore absent from the steering wheel). However, the risk is similar with any of the hands-free phones; apparently, then, the conversation itself creates the risk. How is this different from holding a conversation with a passenger in the car? Evidence suggests that passengers helpfully slow the pace of the conversation whenever they see that the traffic has grown more challenging; someone at the other end of a cell phone conversation is unable to make this crucial adjustment.

2003; Johnson-Laird, 1988; Just, Carpenter, & Hemphill, 1996; Norman & Shallice, 1986). For example, Pashler and Johnston have proposed a mental mechanism that is required for *selecting* and *initiating* responses, including both physical responses and mental ones (such as the beginning of a memory search or the making of a decision; McCann & Johnston, 1992; Pashler, 1991, 1992, 1996; Pashler & Johnston, 1989; but also see Tombu & Jolicoeur, 2003). This **response selector** presumably plays a key role in coordinating the timing of our various activities, and so it serves as a mental traffic cop, controlling which processes go forward at any moment in time.

The response selector can initiate only one response at a time, and so, on this proposal, divided attention often involves a system of "turn-taking." Thus, if you are trying to divide your attention between Task A and Task B, you might first select and launch some action that is part of Task A; while that is happening, Task B must be put on hold for a moment. Then, while that first step of Task A is being carried out, you can use the response selector to launch the first step for Task B. Then, while that step is being executed, you can use the selector to launch the next step of A, and so on. This back-and-forth sequence allows both tasks to go forward—but often in a slower, less efficient manner than if either was being performed on its own.

Executive Control as a Limited Resource

The response selector is concerned with the moment-by-moment timing of our various responses. A different type of general resource, required for many tasks, involves more global processes—including the processes needed for *planning* our various activities. In particular, many theorists have highlighted the role of the mind's "central executive" —a mechanism that sets goals and priorities, chooses strategies, and, in general, directs the function of many cognitive processes (Baddeley, 1986, 1996; A. R. A. Conway, Kane, & Engle, 2003; for some possible complications, see Logan, 2003).

Several proposals about the "executive" have been proposed; let's look at one in particular (Engle & Kane, 2004; Unsworth & Engle, 2007): Engle and his associates have suggested that much of our day-to-day functioning is guided by habit and prior associations. After all, most of the situations we find ourselves in resemble those we've encountered in the past, and so we don't need to start from scratch in figuring out how to behave. Instead, we can rely on the responses or strategies we've used previously.

In some cases, though, we want to behave in a fashion that's different from how we've behaved in the past—perhaps because our goals have changed, or perhaps because the situation has changed in some way that makes prior habits no longer useful. In such cases, we need to overrule the action or strategy supplied by memory. To do this, Engle proposes, we need to take steps to keep our current goal in mind, so that this goal, and not habit, will guide our actions. As a related problem, some settings contain triggers that powerfully evoke certain responses. If we wish to make some *other* response, we need to take steps to avoid the obvious trap.

Within this context, Engle's proposal is that **executive control** is a task-general mental resource needed whenever someone wants to avoid interference from previous habit. This control provides two essential functions: It works to *maintain* the desired goal in mind; simultaneously, it serves to *inhibit* automatic or habitual responses.

Engle has proposed that people differ in how effective their executive control is—with some people literally having more control over their own thought processes. We can measure someone's degree of executive control with measures of their *working-memory capacity* (WMC), and it turns out that people with a larger WMC have an advantage in many tasks, including those that involve resisting distraction and those that involve resisting habit or reflex. (We'll describe in Chapter 5 how this capacity is measured.)

In one study, participants were initially required to fix their eyes on a target (Kane, Bleckley, Conway, & Engle, 2001). When a cue arrived, participants in one condition were asked to move their eyes *toward* the cue. This was easy, because this requirement is in line with ordinary habit: Whenever a stimulus appears suddenly in our view, we tend to move our eyes toward the stimulus to inspect it, just as this condition requires. In another condition, however, participants were asked to do something more difficult: They were asked to override habit and, as soon as the cue arrived, make an eye movement in the opposite direction, *away from* the cue.

The first condition in this experiment should not require executive control; there is no need to override the habitual response. Consistent with this prediction, individuals with smaller WMC were just as fast and just as accurate in making the desired response as individuals with a larger WMC. The second condition, though, is different and should require executive control, overriding habit. And, consistent with the theory, individuals with larger WMC were uniformly more successful in the task—faster and less likely to fall into the trap of moving their eyes (contrary to instructions) toward the cue.

This eye-movement task fits well with the hypotheses we are discussing, but the task is not deeply interesting for its own sake. It is important, therefore, that measures of WMC are also correlated with a range of other tasks. Thus, individuals with a greater working-memory capacity are better at resisting distraction, and staying "on task," whenever they are working on something that is at all challenging (Kane et al., 2007). People with a larger WMC are also likely to score higher on the verbal SAT, to be better in reading comprehension and the following of directions, better at reasoning tasks and computer-language learning, and so on (Engle & Kane, 2004; Salthouse & Pink, 2008). All of this makes sense if we assume that each of these various tasks requires, as one component, an ability to maintain goals in mind and to resist various forms of interference.

Researchers have also made headway in identifying the neural underpinnings of WMC, and at least two areas of the brain appear to be involved. First, the prefrontal cortex (roughly, the brain area right behind the eyes) seems to play a crucial role in "goal maintenance"—the process of keeping one's current goal in mind. This is reflected, for example, in the finding that people who have suffered damage to the prefrontal cortex often show a pattern of "goal neglect"—falling into habit and failing to work toward their assigned goals in a particular task, even though they understand the current goals perfectly well (Duncan, Burgess, & Emslie, 1995; Duncan et al., 1996). Other evidence comes from a study in which participants had to perform a Stroop task (described later in this chapter), which requires a response *different from* the one provided by habit. Data from fMRI scans showed that activation in the prefrontal cortex increased in the seconds leading up to each trial, and the greater the activation, the lower the chance of error—that is, the *greater* the chance that participants would be able to resist the force of habit (Braver & Cohen, 2001; MacDonald, Cohen, Stenger, & Carter, 2000; for more on the prefrontal cortex, and its role as an "executive," see Aron, 2008; Stuss & Knight, 2002).

Second, different evidence suggests that other brain structures—including the anterior cingulate—may play a role in detecting situations that call for two conflicting responses. In such situations, this structure seems to trigger increased activation in other areas, including the prefrontal cortex, which then work to overcome the conflict (Botvinick, Cohen, & Carter, 2004; also see Egner, 2008).

These two brain functions—goal maintenance (supported by the prefrontal cortex) and conflict detection (supported by the anterior cingulate)—fit well with the claims that Engle and others have made about executive control. More generally, these neuroscience findings add support to the claim that there are certain processes, certain mechanisms, that will be needed for a wide range of tasks and, therefore, are the task-general mental resources described by our theories.

Divided Attention: An Interim Summary

Again, let's pause to take stock of where we are. Our consideration of *selective* attention drove us toward a several-part account, with one mechanism apparently serving to block out unwanted distractors, and then a number of other mechanisms all serving to promote the processing of interesting stimuli. Now, in our discussion of *divided* attention, we again seem to require several elements in our theory. Interference between tasks is plainly increased if the tasks are similar to each other, presumably because similar tasks overlap in their processing requirements and so make competing demands on mental resources that are specialized for that sort of task. It is on this basis, then, that our overall account of divided attention needs to take task-specific resources into account.

At the same time, interference can also be demonstrated with tasks that are entirely different from each other—driving and talking on a cell phone, for example. Thus, our account also needs to include resources general enough in their use that they're drawn on by almost any task. We've argued that there are likely to be several of these general resources: an energy supply needed for mental tasks; a response selector needed whenever a task involves the launching of successive steps; executive control, needed whenever a task requires "rising above" prior habits and tendencies; and probably others as well. No matter what the resource, though, the key principle will be the same: Tasks will interfere with each other if their combined demand for a resource is greater than the amount available—that is, if the demand exceeds the supply.

Practice

We still need to add a complication to our account—namely, the effect of *practice*. To introduce the issue, let's return to the example of talking on a cell phone while driving. For a skilled driver, this task combination is easy *if* the driving is straightforward and the conversation is relatively simple. Indeed, many drivers manage this pair of simultaneous tasks every day, without causing traffic accident after traffic accident. Things fall apart, though, the moment the conversation becomes complex or the driving becomes challenging (e.g., because the driver has to merge into traffic or negotiate a complex turn). That's when the two tasks visibly interfere with each other: Engaged in deep conversation, the driver misses a turn; while maneuvering through the intersection, the driver suddenly stops talking.

These facts can easily be fit into our framework: It seems likely that there's a close relationship between how complicated a task is and how resource-demanding it is.

The (Many) Benefits of Practice
Practice allows a person to rely on a well-polished set of routines—so that the tennis player does not need to think about how to hold her elbow, or where to plant her feet. This frees the player to pay attention to other things instead— where to aim, or which way the opponent is leaning, or even an overall strategy for the game.

Concretely, driving in ordinary circumstances makes only a light demand on executive control and only occasional demands on the response selector. Driving in a challenging situation makes a much heavier demand on these resources. The same is true for conversation: A casual chat with a friend requires few resources; a profound interview requires more. It's no wonder, then, that you can combine these tasks (driving and talking) when they're easy, but not when they're hard: Difficult driving requires a lot of resources, and so does difficult conversation. Together, they'll demand more resources than you have available.[1]

The Effects of Practice

What we've just said is true only for a skilled driver. For a *novice* driver, the task of driving is difficult all by itself, even on a straight road with no traffic. If, therefore, we ask the novice to do anything else at the same time—whether it's talking on a cell phone or even listening to the radio—we put the driver (and other cars) at substantial risk.

Why are things so different after practice than before? The main proposal should be obvious: We have already said, first of all, that mental tasks require resources, with the particular resources required, and the *amount* of those resources required, dependent on the nature of the task. Let's now add the claim that as a task becomes more practiced it requires *fewer* resources. Why should this be? Why does practice diminish a task's resource demand? Actually, the answer to these questions flows naturally from the way we've defined some of the resources. For example, the executive control that's measured by working-memory capacity (WMC) is needed whenever one has to rise above habit and do things in a new way. Early in practice, though, there are no habits to fall back on, because the task is brand-new. As a result, executive control is needed all the time. With practice, the person acquires a repertoire of habits, associations, and procedures, and so can rely more and more on these routine thoughts and actions. Thus, the demand for executive control decreases.

The same is true for the response selector. Early in practice, you have to decide what the first step of your performance should be, and then launch that step. Then you have to choose the second step and launch it. And so on. Thus, the response selector is needed a lot—for the selection and launching of each individual step. After practice, though, you can handle things differently. Because you know in advance

---

[1]As a practical note, let's emphasize that challenges like a sudden increase in the demands of driving, or a sudden shift in the conversation's complexity, can arise without warning. As a result, you never know when the conversation and driving will demand more resources than you've got (and so cause interference), and this is why most psychologists would recommend that you never talk on the cell phone while driving. If you follow that advice, then there's no risk that interference might unexpectedly arise. Whether drivers (including the psychologists themselves) heed this advice, however, is a separate matter.

what the steps of the task will be, you can approach the task with the entire sequence in mind and so use the response selector just once: to launch the whole sequence. Thus, there's no need for a series of choices ("What do I do next?") and, with that, no need for a series of launches, one for each of the task's steps. Instead, you simply do a single memory lookup ("What was the sequence of steps I used last time?"), and the response selector is needed to launch this overall routine. Once that's done, you can just run off the routine with no further need for the selector.

It is not surprising, therefore, that with practice, tasks make smaller demands on mental resources. These resources, it seems, are intimately tied up with the *control* of our mental performance—making plans for what to do, launching each step, and so on. Once a routine is established, there is less need for this control and, with that, less need for the resources.

Why Does Practice Improve Performance?

We have so far discussed why practice makes a task less resource-demanding. But what about the other obvious effect of practice—namely, the fact that it makes performance *better*? After all, there is no question that a pianist plays more beautifully after rehearsing a piece for a while, or that athletes play more skillfully after practice. Similar observations can be made for mental skills, such as solving problems, reading, or doing calculations. These, too, are more successful after practice than before. What produces this improvement?

The answer to this question has several parts, but one part hinges on the points we have already discussed, as well as the broad idea of resource availability. To understand this point, let's start with the fact that most tasks that you do have multiple components, and you will succeed in the tasks only if you can handle all the components. To continue our example of driving, a skilled driver needs to keep track of her steering *and* how fast she is going *and* how far she is from the car in front of her, and so on. If the driver neglects any of these elements, the result could be disastrous.

Cast in these terms, it appears that complex tasks, all by themselves, can create problems in divided attention: To do the task, you need to be able to divide your attention among the task's parts, and that's where practice comes in. Early in practice, the various parts of a task will each require resources, and that makes it impossible to think about all the tasks' parts at once. Thus, the novice tennis player getting ready to serve the ball will focus all his resources on how he tosses the ball upward. As a result, the player won't have any resources left over for other aspects of the serve—like choosing where to aim.

With practice, however, the elements of a task each become easier, thereby freeing up resources for dealing with other elements of the same task. This is what allows the driver (or the tennis player) to deal with multiple elements simultaneously, which is precisely what skilled performance requires.

In addition, this shift in resource demand also makes it possible to think about *new* elements of a task—elements that are beyond the reach of any novice. As an example, a skilled chess player is, of course, sensitive to the locations of the various pieces on the board and is alert to how these pieces might move in the next few steps of the game. But for the expert, these elements are so obvious, and thinking about them is so automatic, that resources are left over for other, more abstract aspects of the game: What long-term strategy does the player want to develop? Are there hints in the opponent's moves so far that might signal her long-term strategy? The novice has no resources for these "higher-order" elements, and this lack of resources places powerful limits on the quality of the novice's play.

Automaticity

In all these ways, then, practice can make tasks *easier* and also *better*. Both of these improvements are made possible by the fact that practice decreases resource demands; this decrease, in turn, comes from the fact that practice diminishes the need for moment-by-moment *control* of a task.

All of this has an important implication: If, after practice, a task is no longer drawing on mechanisms that provide control, then the task is, in a sense, *uncontrolled*. Consistent with this suggestion, many psychologists distinguish **controlled tasks** and **automatic tasks**. Controlled tasks are typically novel tasks or tasks that require considerable flexibility in one's approach. Automatic tasks, in contrast, are typically highly familiar and do not require great flexibility. The person approaches these tasks with a well-learned routine—a sequence of responses (often triggered by specific stimuli) that have gotten the job done in the past. Usually this routine has been learned through practice, but it can also be learned from some good advice or a skilled teacher. In any case, once the routine is acquired, the automatic task doesn't need to be supervised or controlled, and so it requires few resources.

We have been discussing the advantages of this **automaticity**: An automatic task is usually easy and can be readily combined with other tasks. But automaticity also has a downside: Since automatic tasks are *not* controlled, in some circumstances they can act as if they were "mental reflexes."

A striking example of this lack of control involves an effect known as **Stroop interference**. In the classic demonstration of this effect, study participants were shown a series of words and asked to name aloud the color of the ink used for each word. The trick, though, was that the words themselves were color names. So people might see the word "BLUE" printed in green ink and would have to say "green" out loud, and so on (Stroop, 1935).

This task turns out to be enormously difficult. There is a strong tendency to read the printed words themselves rather than naming the ink color, and people make many mistakes in this task. Presumably, this reflects the fact that word recognition, especially for college-age adults, is enormously well practiced and, as a consequence, can proceed automatically. This is a condition, therefore, in which mental control should be minimal, and that is certainly consistent with the errors that we observe. (For a demonstration of Stroop interference, see color insert, Figure 13; for a variant on Stroop interference, see Figure 4.4. There is, however, debate over the exact mechanisms that produce this interference; for some of that debate, see Besner & Stolz, 1999a, 1999b; Durgin, 2000; Engle & Kane, 2004; Jacoby et al., 2003; Kane & Engle, 2003. For some discussion of how automatic actions may be shaped by circumstances, see Bargh, 1989; Bargh & Chartrand, 1999.)

Where Are the Limits?

We are nearing the end of our discussion of attention, and so it again may be useful to summarize where we are. Two simple ideas lie at the heart of our account: First, tasks require resources, and second, you cannot "spend" more resources than you have. These claims are central for almost everything we have said about selective and divided attention.

How many items are in each row?	How about these rows?
# #	4 4
? ? ? ?	2 2 2 2
&	3
& &	3 3
/ / / /	1 1 1 1
#	4
? ?	2 2
/ / /	1 1 1
# # #	4 4 4
& & & &	3 3 3 3
?	2
/ /	1 1

FIGURE 4.4 **Variant on Stroop Interference**
The classic version of Stroop interferences is shown in the color insert. However, there are many variations on this effect. For example, as rapidly as you can, say out loud how many symbols there are in each row in the left column. (And so you'd say "two, four" and so on.) Now do the same for the right column. You probably find the latter task more difficult—because you have an automatic habit of *reading* the numerals rather than *counting* them.

We need to complicate this account, however, in two regards: First, there seem to be different types of resources, and second, the exact resource demand of a task depends on several different factors. What are those factors? The nature of the task matters, of course, so that the resources required by a verbal task (e.g., reading) are different from those required by a spatial task (e.g., remembering a shape). The novelty of the task and how much flexibility the task requires also matter. Connected to this, *practice* matters, with well-practiced tasks requiring fewer resources.

What, then, sets the limits on divided attention? When can you do two tasks at the same time, and when not? The answer varies, case by case. If two tasks make competing demands on task-specific resources, the result will be interference. If two tasks make competing demands on task-general resources (such as the response selector, or executive control), again the result will be interference. In addition, it will be especially difficult to combine tasks that involve similar stimuli—combining two tasks that both involve printed text, for example, or that both involve speech. This is because similar stimuli can sometimes "blur together," with a danger that you'll lose track of which elements belong in which input ("Was it the man who said 'yes,' or the woman?"; "Was the red dog in the top picture or the bottom?"). This sort of "crosstalk" (leakage of bits of one input into the other input) can itself compromise performance.

In short, it looks like we need a multipart theory of attention, with performance limited by different factors on different occasions. This draws us once more to a claim we made earlier in the chapter: Attention cannot be thought of as a skill, or a mechanism, or a capacity. Instead, attention is an *achievement*—an achievement of performing multiple activities simultaneously, or an achievement of successfully avoiding distraction when you wish to focus on a single task. And, as we have seen, this achievement rests on an intricate base, so that many skills, mechanisms, and capacities contribute to our ability to attend.

Finally, one last point. We have discussed various limits on human performance—that is, limits on how much you can do at any one time. How rigid are these limits? We have discussed the improvements in divided attention that are made possible by practice, but are there boundaries on what practice can accomplish? Can one perhaps gain new mental resources or, more plausibly, find new ways to accomplish a task in order to avoid the bottleneck created by some limited resource? At least some evidence indicates that the answer to these questions may be yes; if so, many of the claims made in this chapter must be understood as being claims about what is *usual*, and not claims about what is *possible* (Hirst, Spelke, Reaves, Caharack, & Neisser, 1980; Spelke, Hirst, & Neisser, 1976). With this, many traditions in the world—Buddhist meditation traditions, for example—claim it is possible to *train* attention so that one has better control over one's mental life; how do these claims fit into the framework we have developed in this chapter? These are issues in need of further exploration, and in truth, what is at stake here is a question about the boundaries on human potential, making these issues of deep interest for future researchers to pursue.

Chapter Summary

- People are often quite oblivious to unattended inputs; they are unable to tell if an unattended auditory input is coherent prose or random words, and they often fail altogether to detect unattended visual inputs, even though such inputs are right in front of the viewer's eyes. However, some aspects of the unattended inputs are detected. For example, people can report on the pitch of the unattended sound and whether it contained human speech or some other sort of noise. Sometimes they can also detect stimuli that are especially meaningful; some people, for example, hear their own name if it is spoken on the unattended channel.

- These results suggest that perception may require the commitment of mental resources, with some of these resources helping to prime the detectors needed for perception. This proposal is supported by studies of inattentional blindness, studies showing that perception is markedly impaired if the perceiver commits no resources to the incoming stimulus information. The proposal is also supported by results showing that we perceive more efficiently when we can anticipate the upcoming stimulus (and so can prime the relevant detectors). In many cases, this anticipation is spatial—if, for example, we know that a stimulus is about to arrive at a particular location. This priming, however, seems to draw on a limited-capacity system, and so priming one stimulus or one position takes away resources that might be spent on priming some other stimulus.

- Our ability to pay attention to certain regions of space has encouraged many researchers to compare attention to a searchlight beam, with the idea that stimuli falling "within the beam" are processed more efficiently. However, this searchlight analogy is potentially misleading. In many circumstances, we do seem to devote attention to identifiable regions of space, no matter what falls within those regions. In other circumstances, though, attention seems to be object-based, not space-based, and so we pay attention to specific objects, not specific positions.

- Perceiving, it seems, requires the commitment of resources, and so do most other mental activities. This provides a ready account of divided attention: It is possible to perform two tasks simultaneously only if the two tasks do not in combination demand more resources than are available. Some of the relevant mental resources are task-general, and so are called on by a wide variety of mental activities. These include the response selector, mental effort, and working-memory capacity. Other mental resources are task-specific, required only for tasks of a certain type.

- Divided attention is clearly influenced by practice, and so it is often easier to divide attention between familiar tasks than between unfamiliar tasks. In the extreme, practice may produce automaticity, in which a task seems to require virtually no mental resources but is also difficult to control. One proposal is that automaticity results from the fact that decisions are no longer needed for a well-practiced routine; instead, one can simply run off the entire routine, doing on this occasion just what one did on prior occasions.

The Workbook Connection

See the *Cognition Workbook* for further exploration on paying attention:

- Demonstration 4.1: Shadowing
- Demonstration 4.2: Automaticity and the Stroop Effect
- Demonstration 4.3: Color-Changing Card Trick
- Research Methods: The Power of Random Assignment
- Cognitive Psychology and Education: ADHD
- Cognitive Psychology and the Law: What Do Eyewitnesses Pay Attention to?

PART 3

Memory

In this section, we'll discuss how people learn new things and how they remember this information later. We'll also consider some of the apparent failures of memory, including cases in which people "draw a blank" and can't remember anything at all, and also cases in which people seem to remember but are actually recalling things that never happened! Throughout the section, we'll be concerned with both theoretical and practical questions—for example, questions about how students should study their class materials, and also questions about how much trust a jury can place in an eyewitness's recollection of a crime.

One theme in this section concerns the active nature of memory, and we'll discuss the crucial importance of how the learner approaches, and thinks about, material in determining whether that material will be remembered later on. As we'll see, passive exposure to information, with no intellectual engagement, leads to poor memory. We'll also consider why some forms of engagement with to-be-learned material lead to good memory and other forms do not.

The active nature of memory will also be key in our discussion of what it means to "remember." Here we'll see that in many cases what seems to be remembering is really after-the-fact reconstruction, and we'll need to consider how this reconstruction proceeds and what it implies for memory accuracy.

A second theme will be equally prominent: the role of memory connections. In Chapter 5, we'll see that at its essence learning involves the creation of connections, and the more connections formed, the better the learning. In Chapter 6, we'll explore the idea that these connections are helpful because they serve as retrieval paths later on—paths, one hopes, that will lead you from your memory search's starting point to the information you're trying to recall. As we will see, this notion has clear implications for when you will remember a previous event and when you won't.

Chapter 7 then explores a different ramification of the connections idea: Memory connections can actually be a source of memory errors. In learning, you create connections that knit together the new material with things you already know. These connections are helpful (because they serve as retrieval paths), but the more connections you create, the harder it will be to keep track of which remembered elements were contained within the episode itself and which are connected to that episode only because you connected them during the learning process. We'll ask what this means for memory accuracy overall, and we'll also discuss what one can do to minimize error and to improve the completeness and accuracy of human memory.

CHAPTER 5

The Acquisition of Memories and the Working-Memory System

How does new information—whether it's a friend's phone number or a fact you hope to memorize for the Bio exam—become established in memory? Are there ways to learn that are particularly effective? Why do we sometimes forget? And, finally, how much trust should we place in our memories? How accurate and how complete is our recollection of previous events? These questions will be our focus for the next three chapters.

In tackling these questions, there is an obvious way to organize our inquiry: Before there can be a memory, some learning must occur; that is, new information must be acquired. Therefore, **acquisition** should be our first topic for discussion. Then, once information has been acquired, it must be held in memory until it is needed. We refer to this as the **storage** phase. Finally, we *use* the information that is in memory; we *remember*. Information is somehow found in the vast warehouse that is memory and brought into active use; this is called **retrieval**.

This organization seems intuitively sensible; it fits, for example, with the way most "electronic memories" (e.g., computers) work. Information ("input") is provided to a computer (the acquisition phase). The information then resides in some dormant form, generally on the hard drive (the storage phase). Finally, the information can be brought back from this dormant form, often via a search process that hunts through the disk (the retrieval phase). And, of course, there's nothing special about a computer here; "low-tech" information storage works the same way. Think about a file drawer: Information is acquired (i.e., filed), then rests in this or that folder, and then is retrieved.

- We begin the chapter with a discussion of the broad architecture of memory. We then turn to a closer examination of one component of the model—namely, working memory.

- We emphasize the active nature of working memory— activity that is especially evident when we discuss working memory's "central executive," a mental resource that serves to order, organize, and control our mental lives.

- The active nature of memory is also evident in the process of *rehearsal*: Rehearsal is effective only if the person engages the materials in some way; this is

reflected, for example, in the contrast between deep processing (which leads to excellent memory) and mere maintenance rehearsal (which produces virtually no memory benefit).

- The activity during learning appears to establish *memory connections*, which can serve as retrieval routes when it comes time to remember the target material. For complex material, the best way to establish these connections is to seek to understand the material; the better the understanding, the better the memory will be.

Guided by this framework, we'll begin our inquiry by focusing on the acquisition of new memories, leaving discussion of storage and retrieval for later. As it turns out, though, we will soon find reasons for challenging this overall approach to memory. In discussing acquisition, for example, we might wish to ask: What is good learning? What guarantees that material is firmly recorded in memory? As we will see, evidence indicates that what is good learning depends on how the memory is to be used later on, so that good preparation for one kind of use may be poor preparation for a different kind of use. Claims about acquisition, therefore, must be interwoven with claims about retrieval. These interconnections between acquisition and retrieval will be the central theme of Chapter 6.

In the same way, we cannot separate claims about memory acquisition from claims about memory storage. This is because how you learn (acquisition) depends heavily on what you already know (information in storage). This relationship needs to be explored and explained, and it will provide a recurrent theme for both this chapter and Chapter 7.

With these caveats in view, we will nonetheless begin by describing the acquisition process. Our approach will be roughly historical. We will start with a simple model, emphasizing data collected largely in the 1970s. We will then use this as the framework for examining more recent research, adding refinements to the model as we proceed.

The Route Into Memory

For many years, theorizing in cognitive psychology was guided by a perspective known as **information processing**. Details aside, the notion was that complex mental events such as learning, remembering, or deciding actually involve a large number of discrete steps. These steps occur one by one, each with its own characteristics

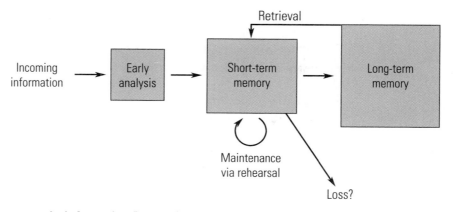

FIGURE 5.1 An Information-Processing View of Memory
In this view, the boxes represent separate events, processes, or storage spaces; arrows represent the flow of information from one process to another.

and its own job to do, and with each providing as its "output" the input to the next step in the sequence. Within this framework, theories could often be illustrated with charts such as the one in Figure 5.1. In this diagram, each enclosed shape represents a separate event or process, and the arrows represent the flow of information from one event to the next. The research goal was to make the charts more and more complete by analyzing each box into still smaller boxes, continuing until the entire process could be described in terms of its elementary components.

A great deal of information-processing theory focused on the processes through which information was detected, recognized, and entered into memory storage—that is, on the process of information acquisition. Although there was disagreement about the details, there was reasonable consensus on the bold outline of events. An early version of this model was described by Waugh and Norman (1965); later refinements were added by R. C. Atkinson and Shiffrin (1968). The consensus model came to be known as the **modal model**, and it is on this model that we will focus.

The Modal Model

According to the modal model, our information processing involves different kinds of memory, two of which are short-term memory and long-term memory. **Short-term memory** holds on to information currently in use, much as your desk contains the papers or books with which you are currently working. Just like your desk, short-term memory is limited in how much it can hold, but most important, information in short-term memory is instantly and easily available to you.

We first mentioned short-term memory in Chapter 1, although there we used the more modern term, **working memory**—a term that emphasizes the function of this memory. We noted in Chapter 1 that virtually all mental tasks rely on working memory, because virtually all mental tasks involve inputs or sequences of steps that are stretched out in time. That creates a short-lived memory demand: You need to hang on to the early parts of the input, or the early steps, while you're working on what comes next. Only then, with the later steps finished, can you put all of the pieces together.

To make this point concrete, let's return to an example we described in Chapter 1: As you read this sentence, your interpretation of the early words will depend on what comes later; therefore, you will need to store the early words for a few moments, until you have read the entire sentence. Those early words, presumably, would be stored in working memory. That way, the words (or, at least, the *meanings* of the words) are available to you when you need them at the sentence's end, when you're ready to think about what the entire sentence means.

It is in this fashion, then, that working memory provides a mental "desk space"—a resource that lets you hang on to ideas, images, and memories while you're working on them. But you also need another type of memory—one that's much larger and that includes all the information that you're not thinking about right now, but that is nonetheless part of your knowledge base. This is **long-term memory** (LTM), and it contains all of the information you remember: your memories of what you did yesterday, how you spent your childhood, a vast number of facts about various topics, the names and faces of a hundred acquaintances, and so on.

Although there is a close association between working memory and the contents of your current thinking, there is no such association for long-term memory. At any point in time, much of the material in LTM lies dormant, and so the process of retrieving information from LTM, making the information available for use, often requires some hunting and can sometimes be effortful and slow.

Working Memory and Long-Term Memory: One Memory or Two?

Many pieces of evidence demand this distinction between working memory and LTM, but much of the evidence comes from a single task. Study participants are read a series of words, like "bicycle, artichoke, radio, chair, palace." In a typical experiment, the list might contain 30 words and be presented at a rate of about one word per second. Immediately after the last word is read, participants are asked to repeat back as many words as they can. They are free to report the words in any order they choose, which is why this is referred to as a **free recall** procedure.

People usually remember 12 to 15 words in such a test, in a consistent pattern: They are extremely likely to remember the first few words on the list, something known as the **primacy effect**; and they are also likely to remember the last few words on the list, a **recency effect**. This pattern is illustrated in Figure 5.2, with a *U*-shaped curve describing the relation between position within the series (or **serial position**) and likelihood of recall (Baddeley & Hitch, 1977; Deese & Kaufman, 1957; Glanzer & Cunitz, 1966; Murdock, 1962; Postman & Phillips, 1965).

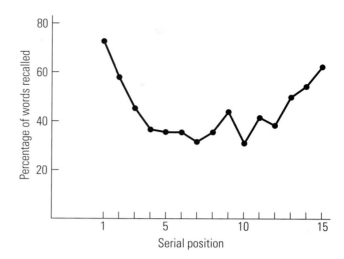

FIGURE 5.2 The U-Shaped Serial-Position Curve
Participants are read a list of words and then must recall as many of the words as they can. They are most likely to remember the first few words presented to them and the last few words. (After Glanzer & Cunitz, 1966)

This serial-position curve is easily explained by the modal model. At any point in time, according to the model, working memory contains the material someone is working on at just that moment, and during the list presentation, the participants are of course thinking about the words they are hearing. Therefore, it is these words that are in working memory. This memory, though, is limited in its size, capable of holding only five or six words. Consequently, as participants try to keep up with the list presentation, they will be placing the words *just heard* into working memory, and this will bump the previous words out of this memory. Thus, as participants proceed through the list, their working memories will, at each moment, contain only the half dozen words that arrived most recently. Any words earlier than these will have been pushed out by later arrivals.

Of course, the last few words on the list don't get bumped out of working memory, because no further input arrives to displace these words. Therefore, when the list presentation ends, those last few words stay in place. Moreover, our hypothesis is that materials in working memory are readily available—easily and quickly retrieved. When the time comes for recall, then, working memory's contents (the list's last few words) are accurately and completely recalled.

Thus, in brief, the proposal is that the list's ending is still in working memory when the list ends, and working memory's contents are easy to retrieve. This is the source of the recency effect. The primacy effect, on the other hand, comes from a different source. According to the modal model, the transfer of material from working memory to LTM depends on processes that require time and attention, so let's examine how participants allocate their attention to the list items. As participants hear the list, they do their best to be good memorizers, and so, when they hear the first word, they repeat it over and over to themselves ("bicycle, bicycle, bicycle")—a process referred to as **memory rehearsal**. When the second word arrives, they rehearse it, too ("bicycle, artichoke, bicycle, artichoke"). Likewise for the third ("bicycle, artichoke, radio, bicycle, artichoke, radio"), and so on through the list. Note, though, that the first few items on the list are privileged: For a brief moment, "bicycle" was the only word participants had to worry about, and so it had 100% of their attention lavished on it; no other word received this privilege. For a brief moment, "artichoke" had 50% of the participants' attention, more attention than any word except the first. When "radio" arrived, it had to compete with "bicycle" and "artichoke" for the participants' time, and so it received only 33% of their attention.

Words later in the list receive even less attention. Once six or seven words have been presented, the participants need to divide their attention among all of these, which means that each word receives only a small fraction of the participants' efforts. As a result, words later in the list literally are rehearsed fewer times than words early in the list—a fact we can confirm simply by asking participants to rehearse out loud (Rundus, 1971).

This easily provides an explanation of the primacy effect—that is, the observed memory advantage for the early list items. These early words didn't have to share attention with other words, and so more time and more rehearsal were devoted to these early words than to any others. This means that the early words have a greater chance of being transferred into LTM, and so a greater chance of being recalled after a delay. That's what shows up in our data as the primacy effect.

This account of the serial-position curve leads to many further predictions. First, note that the model claims that the recency portion of the curve is coming from working memory, while the other items on the list are being recalled from LTM. Therefore, any manipulation of working memory should affect recall of the recency items, but not recall of the other items on the list. To see how this works, consider a modification of our procedure. In the standard procedure, we allow participants to recite what they remember immediately after the list's end. In place of this, we can delay recall by asking participants to perform some other task prior to their report of the list items. For example, we can ask them, immediately after hearing the list, to count backward by threes, starting from 201. They do this for just 30 seconds, and then they try to recall the list.

We have hypothesized that at the end of the list working memory still contains the last few items heard from the list. But the chore of counting backward will itself require working memory (e.g., to keep track of where one is in the counting sequence). Therefore, this chore will *displace* working memory's current contents; that is, it will bump the last few list items out of working memory. As a result, these items won't benefit from the swift and easy retrieval that working memory allows, and, of course, that retrieval was the presumed source of the recency effect. On this basis, the simple chore of counting backward, even if only for a few seconds, will eliminate the recency effect. In contrast, the counting backward should have no impact on recall of the items earlier in the list: These items are (by hypothesis) being recalled from long-term memory, not working memory; and there's no reason to think the counting task will interfere with LTM. (That's because LTM, unlike working memory, is not dependent on current activity.)

Figure 5.3 shows that these predictions are correct: An activity interpolated between the list and recall essentially eliminates the recency effect, but it has no influence elsewhere in the list (Baddeley & Hitch, 1977; Glanzer & Cunitz, 1966; Postman & Phillips, 1965). In contrast, merely delaying the recall for a few seconds after the list's end, with no interpolated activity, has no impact. In this case, participants can continue rehearsing the last few items during the delay and so can maintain them in working memory. With no new materials coming in, nothing pushes the recency items out of working memory, and so, even with a delay, a normal recency effect is observed.

The model makes a different set of predictions for experiments that manipulate long-term memory rather than working memory. In this case, the manipulation should affect all performance *except* for recency. For example, what happens if we slow down the presentation of the list? Now participants will have more time to spend on all of the list items, increasing the likelihood of transfer into more permanent storage. This should improve recall for all items coming from LTM. Working memory,

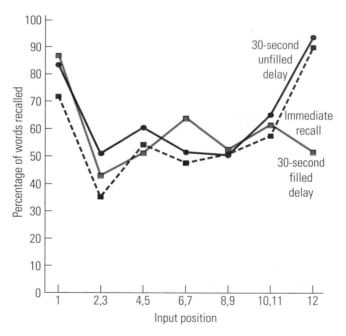

FIGURE 5.3 The Impact of Interpolated Activity on the Recency Effect
With immediate recall, or if recall is delayed by 30 seconds with no activity during this delay, a strong recency effect is detected. In contrast, if participants spend 30 seconds on some other activity between hearing the list and the subsequent memory test, the recency effect is eliminated. This interpolated activity has no impact on the pre-recency portion of the curve.

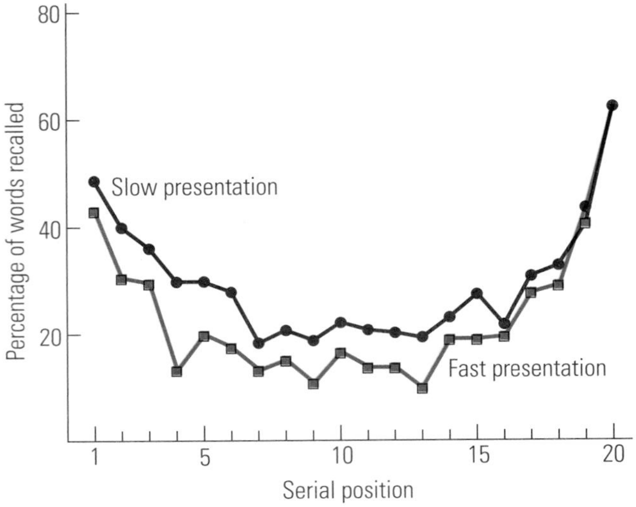

FIGURE 5.4 Rate of List Presentation and the Serial-Position Effect

Presenting the to-be-remembered materials at a slower rate improves pre-recency performance but has no effect on recency. The slow rate in this case was 9 seconds per item; the fast rate was 3 seconds per item.

in contrast, is limited by its size, not by ease of entry or ease of access. Therefore, the slower list presentation should have no influence on working-memory performance. As predicted, Figure 5.4 shows that slowing the list presentation improves retention of all the pre-recency items but does not improve the recency effect. Other variables that influence entry into long-term memory have comparable effects. Using more familiar or more common words, for example, would be expected to ease entry into long-term memory and does improve pre-recency retention, but it has no effect on recency (Sumby, 1963).

Over and over, therefore, the recency and pre-recency portions of the curve are open to separate sets of influences and obey different principles. This strongly indicates that these portions of the curve are the products of different mechanisms, just as the modal model proposes. In addition, fMRI scans suggest that memory for early items on a list depends on brain areas (in and around the hippocampus) that are associated with long-term memory; memory for later items on the list do not show this pattern (Talmi, Grady, Goshen-Gottstein, & Moscovitch, 2005). This provides further (and powerful) confirmation for our memory model.

A Closer Look at Working Memory

There is much more to be said about memory acquisition and, in particular, how materials are entered into long-term memory. Before turning to these matters, though, we should pause to consider working memory more fully. This will allow us to fill in some details about this store and to say more about this memory's function.

The Function of Working Memory

As we have discussed, virtually all mental activities require the coordination of several pieces of information. We generally start by working on these bits one at a time, and only afterward do we integrate them into a full package. For example, we earlier mentioned the reading of a sentence in which you have to decipher the sentence's early words and then place them on "hold" while working on the sentence's later words. Then, once these have been identified, you can integrate all the words to understand the full phrase. Likewise, consider a simple plan: You must first choose your goal, but then you put this choice on hold in order to concentrate on the early steps needed to reach this goal. Then, once these steps are taken, you have to think about the goal again, in order to select your next steps.

Of course, the memory making this possible is working memory. When information is currently in use or likely to be needed soon, it is held in working memory. This plainly implies that working memory will be involved in a wide range of tasks, and this suggestion has been confirmed in many studies. As we mentioned in Chapter 4 when we discussed the "general resources" needed for paying attention, some of these studies exploit the fact that working memory's capacity varies somewhat from one individual to the next. One can therefore ask about this memory's function by asking what tasks are facilitated by a slightly larger working memory, and what tasks are compromised by a smaller memory.

This research tells us, as one example, that someone with a larger-capacity working memory is likely also to be a more efficient reader, confirming the role for working memory in reading (Baddeley, Logie, Nimmo-Smith, & Brereton, 1985; Daneman & Carpenter, 1980; Just & Carpenter, 1992). Likewise, people with a larger capacity are better off in many types of reasoning skills, making it clear that working memory matters here, too. Other studies show similar positive correlations between working-memory capacity and performance on the SATs, computer-language learning, the following of directions, and more (e.g., Carpenter, Just, & Shell, 1990; Engle & Kane, 2004; Kyllonen & Cristal, 1990).

The Holding Capacity of Working Memory

The claims in the previous section rest on the fact that some people have slightly larger working memories and some have smaller. But how do we measure the capacity of someone's working memory? For many years, this capacity was measured with a **digit-span task**. In this task, people are read a series of digits (e.g., "8, 3, 4") and must immediately repeat them back. If they do this successfully, they are given a slightly longer list (e.g., "9, 2, 4, 0"). If they can repeat this one without error, they're given a still longer list, and so on. This continues until the person starts to make errors—something that usually happens when the list contains more than seven or eight items.

Procedures such as this imply that working memory's capacity is around seven items or, more cautiously, at least five items and probably not more than nine items. These estimates are often summarized by the statement that this memory holds **"7 plus-or-minus 2"** items (Chi, 1976; Dempster, 1981; G. A. Miller, 1956; Watkins, 1977).

However, these "measurements" of working memory may be misleading. If working memory can hold 7 plus-or-minus 2 items, what exactly is an "item"? Can we remember seven sentences as easily as seven words? Seven letters as easily as seven equations? In a classic paper, George Miller proposed that working memory holds 7 plus-or-minus 2 **chunks** (G. A. Miller, 1956). The term "chunk" is a deliberately unscientific-sounding term in order to remind us that a chunk does not hold a fixed quantity of information. Instead, Miller proposed, working memory holds 7 plus-or-minus 2 packages, and what those packages contain is largely up to the individual person.

The flexibility in how people "chunk" the input can easily be seen in the span test. For example, imagine that someone hears a list like "H, O, P, T, R, A, S, L, U," and so on. If the person thinks of these as individual letters, then she will remember seven of them, more or less. But if the same person reorganizes the list and, in particular, thinks of the letters as forming syllables ("HOP, TRA, SLU, . . ."), she'll remember five or six of these syllables—and therefore 15 to 18 letters.

The chunking process does have a cost attached, because some effort is required to "repackage" the materials (i.e., assemble the letters into syllables or the syllables into words), and with some amount of attention spent in this way, less attention is available for rehearsing these items (Daneman & Carpenter, 1980; Hitch, Towse, & Hutton, 2001). Even so, chunking can have enormous effects, creating considerable flexibility in what working memory can hold. This is evident, for example, in a remarkable individual studied by Chase and Ericsson (Chase & Ericsson, 1982; Ericsson, 2003). This fellow happens to be a fan of track events, and when he hears numbers, he thinks of them as finishing times for races. The sequence "3, 4, 9, 2," for example, becomes "3 minutes and 49 point 2 seconds, near world-record mile time." In this fashion, four digits become one chunk of information. This person can then retain seven finishing times (seven chunks) in memory, and this can involve 20 or 30 digits! Better still, these chunks can be grouped into larger chunks, and these into even larger chunks. For example, finishing times for individual racers can be chunked together into heats within a track meet, so that, now, four or five finishing times (more than a dozen digits) become one chunk. With strategies like this and with a considerable amount of practice, this person has increased his apparent memory span from the "normal" 7 digits to 79 digits!

However, let's be clear that what has changed through practice is merely this person's chunking strategy, not the size of working memory itself. This is evident in the fact that when tested with sequences of letters, rather than numbers, so that he can't use his chunking strategy, this individual's memory span is a (perfectly normal) six consonants. Thus, the seven-chunk limit is still in place for this man, even though (with numbers) he is able to make extraordinary use of these seven slots.

The Active Nature of Working Memory

Chunking, therefore, provides one complication in our measurement of working memory's capacity. Another complication grows out of the very nature of working memory. Specifically, the language of the modal model seems to imply that working memory is something like a box in which information is stored or, continuing our earlier desk analogy, something like a location in which information can be displayed. In this view, learning would be a matter of transferring information from one position (working memory) to another (long-term memory), as though working memory were the loading dock just outside the large memory warehouse.

In truth, though, this conception of working memory is far too static. We've already seen that some amount of repackaging takes place in working memory. And later in the chapter, we'll see that the "work" in working memory often involves sophisticated analysis of the materials to be remembered, as well as the finding of connections between these materials and other information already in storage. Given these points, the notion of a loading platform may be misleading, as is the notion of mechanical transfer between one position and another. If working memory is a place at all, it's not a mere box. It is instead more like the office of a busy librarian who is energetically categorizing, cataloguing, and cross-referencing new material.

Perhaps, therefore, we need to rethink how we *measure* this memory's capacity. The traditional span test is, in essence, designed to count the number of "slots" in working memory, with each item on the test being placed in its own slot. This method does little to measure working memory's capacity *to do things* with these slots, and this concern has led researchers to develop more dynamic measures of working memory—measures of reading span or **operation span**, designed specifically to measure the efficiency of working memory when it is "working."

For example, to measure reading span, research participants might be asked to read aloud a series of sentences, like these:

Due to his gross inadequacies, his position as director was terminated abruptly.

It is possible, of course, that life did not arise on the Earth at all.

Immediately after reading the sentences, each participant is asked to recall the final words in the sentences—in this case, "abruptly" and "all." If the participant can do this successfully with these two sentences, she is asked to do the same task with a group of three sentences, and then with four, and so on, until the limit on her performance is located.

Think about what this task involves: storing some materials (the ending words) for later use in the recall test, while simultaneously working with other materials (the full sentences). This juggling of processes, as you move from one part of the task to

$(7 \times 7) + 1 = 50$; dog
$(10 / 2) + 6 = 10$; gas
$(4 \times 2) + 1 = 9$; nose
$(3 / 1) + 1 = 5$; beat
$(5 / 5) + 1 = 2$; tree

FIGURE 5.5 Dynamic Measures of Working Memory
Operation span can be measured in several different ways. In one procedure, participants must announce whether each of these "equations" is true or false, and then recall the words that were appended to each equation. If participants can do this with two equations, we ask them to do three; if they can do that, we try four. By finding out how far they can go, we measure their working-memory capacity.

the next, is exactly what working memory must do in its functioning in day-to-day life. Therefore, performance in this test is likely to reflect the efficiency with which working memory will operate in more natural settings. (For a different way to measure working memory, see Figure 5.5.)

The data confirm this prediction. We have mentioned that people with a larger working-memory capacity (WMC) have an advantage on many other measures: the verbal SAT, tests of reasoning, reading comprehension, and so on (Ackerman, Beier, & Boyle, 2002; Cantor & Engle, 1993; Daneman & Hannon, 2001; Engle & Kane, 2004; Gathercole & Pickering, 2000; Gray, Chabris, & Braver, 2003; Howe, Rabinowitz, & Powell, 1998; Just & Carpenter, 1992). In other words, there are strong *positive correlations* between WMC and these other measures. For that matter, people with a larger WMC seem less likely to have their minds wander, and so are more likely to keep their thoughts "on task," in comparison to people with a smaller WMC (Kane et al., 2007). Related results have been found with children, and so the size of working-memory capacity is, for example, positively correlated with problem-solving performance in schoolchildren (Passolunghi, Cornoldi, & De Liberto, 1999). These correlations are obtained when the more active measure of working memory— reading span or operation span—is used. These correlations are not observed with the more traditional (and more static) span measure, confirming the advantage of the more dynamic measures. These findings, in turn, strengthen the overall claim that working memory is not a passive storage box but is instead a highly active information processor.

The Working-Memory System

Working memory's active nature is also evident in another way: in the actual structure of this memory. In Chapter 1, we introduced the idea that working memory is not a single entity, but is instead a *system* built out of several components (Baddeley, 1986, 1992; Baddeley & Hitch, 1974; Salame & Baddeley, 1982). At the center of the system is the **central executive**, a multipurpose processor capable of running many different operations on many different types of material. It is the executive that does the real "work" in working memory, and so if one has to plan a response or make a decision, these steps require the executive. But, in addition, many tasks place a different, less complicated demand on working memory—namely, that it serve as a mere "information holder," a temporary resting spot for information that isn't needed yet but soon will be. This holding-of-information is crucial for many purposes, but all it requires is mere maintenance, and there's no reason to burden the executive with this simple task. Instead, the maintenance can be provided by one of working memory's less sophisticated "helpers," leaving the executive free to work on more difficult matters.

Working memory's helpers thus serve as internal scratch pads, storing information you will need soon but don't need right now. One of these helpers is the **visuospatial buffer**, used for storing visual materials (such as mental images; see Chapter 11); another is the **articulatory rehearsal loop**, used for storing verbal material.

The Central Executive

We described the functioning of working memory's rehearsal loop in Chapter 1, but what can we say about the main player within working memory—the central executive? Here we can build on ideas introduced in Chapter 4, where we discussed the idea of *executive control*. The notion there was that certain processes are needed to control the sequence of our thoughts and actions; these processes serve to select and launch specific responses; they are needed for planning and the setting of goals, and also for the steps needed to resist falling into habit or routine. In Chapter 4, our focus was on the fact that these processes can only work on one task at a time; this

The Inner Hand, Rather than the Inner Voice
People who can speak and hear rely on the articulatory rehearsal loop as part of the working-memory system; as a result, errors in working memory are often "sound-alike errors." Members of the deaf community, in contrast, rely on a "signing rehearsal loop," using an "inner hand" rather than an "inner voice." Their errors often involve confusions between different words that happen to have similar hand-shapes when expressed in sign language.

is one of the limits on people's ability to divide their attention and do two things at once. In the current context, though, let's emphasize that these same processes serve to control our moment-by-moment awareness as we work on a task. This is precisely the function of working memory, and that leads to a simple proposal: These mental resources, needed for control of the mind's processes, *are* the central executive; put differently, the central executive is just the name we give for the use of these cognitive resources.

This proposal is supported by several lines of evidence. We know, for example, that many sites in the prefrontal cortex (PFC) are particularly active when people are engaged in tasks that make heavy use of working memory (Courtney, Petit, Maisog, Ungerleider, & Haxby, 1998; Goldman-Rakic, 1995; Huey, Krueger, & Grafman, 2006; Stuss & Knight, 2002). But exactly what function is supported by this brain tissue? We can find out by asking what symptoms result if someone has suffered brain damage in these areas, and the answer is intriguing. Often people who have suffered frontal lobe damage can still lead relatively normal lives. In much of their day-to-day behavior, they show no obvious symptoms; they perform normally on conventional tests of intelligence.

Nonetheless, with appropriate tests we can reveal the disruption that results from frontal lobe damage, and it turns out that the disruption takes several different forms. As one problem, patients with frontal lesions show a pattern of **goal neglect**—relying on habitual responses even if those responses won't move them toward their assigned goal in a particular task. Closely related is a problem known as **perseveration**. This pattern emerges in many aspects of the patients' behavior and involves a strong tendency to produce the same response over and over, even when it's plain that the task requires a change in the response. For example, in one commonly used task the patients are asked to sort a deck of cards into two piles. At the start of the task, the patients have to sort the cards according to color; later they need to switch strategies and sort according to the shapes shown on the cards. The patients have enormous difficulty making this shift, and they continue to sort by color (i.e., they *persevere* in their original pattern) even though the experimenter tells them again and again that they are placing the cards onto the wrong piles (Goldman-Rakic, 1998).

A somewhat different pattern is revealed when patients with frontal lobe damage are asked to make a copy of a drawing. For example, one patient was asked to copy Figure 5.6a; the patient produced the drawing shown in Figure 5.6b. The copy preserves many features of the original, but closer inspection reveals that the patient drew the copy with no particular plan in mind. The large rectangle that defines much of the shape was never drawn; the diagonal lines that organize the figure were drawn in a piecemeal fashion. Many details are correctly reproduced but were not drawn in any sort of order; instead, these details were added whenever they happened to catch the patient's attention (Kimberg, D'Esposito, & Farah, 1998). Another patient, asked to copy the same figure, produced the drawing shown in Figure 5.6c. This

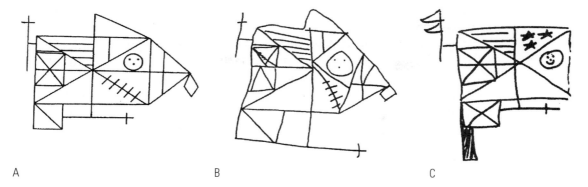

A   B   C

FIGURE 5.6 Drawings by Patients with Prefrontal Brain Damage

Two patients with damage to the prefrontal cortex were asked to copy the figure shown in Panel A. The drawing shown in Panel B, by one of the patients, is reasonably accurate, but was plainly drawn in a feature-by-feature fashion, with no overall plan in mind. The patient who drew the image in Panel C started out in a normal way but then ended up following her own artistic impulses, rather than carrying out the task as she'd first intended.

patient started to draw the figure in a normal way, but then she got swept up in her own artistic impulses, adding stars and a smiley face (Kimberg et al., 1998).

Data like these suggest that the PFC is pivotal in allowing people to plan and organize their activities (that seems to be the difficulty with the patient who drew Figure 5.6B). The PFC also seems crucial for the inhibition of impulses (lack of inhibition led to the drawing in Figure 5.6c). It also seems crucial for "turning off" responses once they have been launched (the problem in perseveration). All of these functions are likely to contribute to what we are here calling the central executive—the mental resources (or, more likely, the *set* of resources) that order, organize, and control our mental lives. (For more on this complex topic, see Duncan, et al., 2008; S. J. Gilbert & Shallice, 2002; Kane & Engle, 2003; Kimberg et al., 1998; Stuss & Levine, 2002; for more on the neural basis of working memory, see Logie & Della Salla, 2005; Ranganath & Blumenfeld, 2005.)

The Nature of Working Memory

Let's pause to take stock and to ask, in particular, how our discussion over the last few pages fits into the larger picture with which we began this chapter. With that, where are we with regard to the modal model, introduced several sections ago?

Our understanding of working memory has certainly evolved in recent years, and as we've seen, the evidence now makes it clear that working memory is not a mere box or storage container. Instead, working memory is more dynamic than that; indeed, "working memory" may actually be just the name we give to an organized set of *activities*, especially the complex activities of the central executive. (For close scrutiny of the modern view of working memory, see Jonides et al., 2008; Nee, Berman, Moore, & Jonides, 2008.)

Even so, some claims in the modal model remain unchanged. In current conceptions, working memory is still understood to be crucial for holding on to the information that you're currently thinking about, limited in its storage capacity but easily loaded and easily accessed. In addition—and still in accord with the modal model—current conceptions view working memory as being quite fragile, since each shift in attention brings new information into working memory, and newly arriving materials displace earlier items. Storage in working memory, therefore, is plainly temporary. All of this is in clear contrast to long-term memory, which is far larger in capacity, less easily loaded or accessed, and far more enduring.

With all of this said, we're ready to move on. We've discussed the broad "architecture" of memory—with a working-memory system and a long-term store, connected more or less as shown in Figure 5.1. We've also said a great deal about working memory—its structure and its function. But if we are to understand memory acquisition, we still need to tackle the most important part of the puzzle: how information becomes established in long-term memory, so that it can be remembered an hour, or a day, or even a decade after the original event of learning.

Entering Long-Term Storage: The Role of the Intent to Learn

We've already seen one important clue about how information becomes established in long-term storage: In discussing the primacy effect, we suggested that the more an item is rehearsed, the more likely it is that you will remember that item later on. In order to pursue this clue, however, we need to ask what exactly rehearsal is, and how it might work to promote memory.

Two Types of Rehearsal

The term "rehearsal" really means little beyond "thinking about." When a research participant rehearses an item on a memory list, she's simply thinking about that item—perhaps once, perhaps over and over; perhaps mechanically, or perhaps with close attention to what the item means. Clearly, therefore, there is considerable variety in the sorts of activity that count as rehearsal, and, in fact, psychologists find it useful to sort this variety into two broad types.

As one option, people can engage in **maintenance rehearsal**, in which they simply focus on the to-be-remembered items themselves, with little thought about what the items mean or how they are related to each other. This is a rote, mechanical process, recycling items in working memory simply by repeating them over and over. In contrast, **relational**, or **elaborative**, **rehearsal** involves thinking about what the to-be-remembered items mean, and how they are related to each other and to other things you already know.

In general, relational rehearsal is vastly superior to maintenance rehearsal for establishing information in memory. Indeed, in many settings maintenance rehearsal provides no long-term benefits whatsoever. As an informal demonstration of this point, consider the following common experience. You want to telephone a friend, and so you call directory assistance to get his number, or perhaps you look up the number in the telephone book. Once you've learned the number in this way, you recite it over and over to yourself while pressing the appropriate sequence of buttons on your phone. But it turns out that the line is busy, so you wait a minute or two and then try again. The moment you start to dial, though, you realize that you don't have a clue what the number is, even though you knew it perfectly well just a few seconds earlier. What went wrong? While dialing the number the first time, you held on to it via maintenance rehearsal. This kept the number in your thoughts while you were dialing, but it did nothing to establish the number in long-term storage. And when you try to dial the number the second time, it's long-term storage that you need. (For a more formal demonstration of this point, see Craik & Watkins, 1973.)

The suggestion, therefore, is that rehearsal promotes memory only if it's rehearsal of the right sort. We know from the primacy effect that in some settings more rehearsal leads to more memory. We can now qualify this assertion, though, by noting that if you spend many seconds thinking about something, but think about it only in a mindless mechanical fashion (i.e., through maintenance rehearsal), the item will not be established in your memory.

In exactly the same way, long-lasting memories are not created simply by repeated exposures to the items to be remembered. If you encounter an item over and over but, on each encounter, barely think about it (or think about it in a mechanical fashion), then this, too, will not produce a long-term memory. As a demonstration, consider the ordinary penny. Adults in the United States have probably seen pennies tens of thousands of times. Adults in other countries have seen their own coins just as often. If sheer exposure is what counts for memory, then people should remember perfectly what these coins look like.

But, of course, most people have little reason to pay attention to the penny. Pennies are a different color from the other coins, so they can be identified at a glance with no need for further scrutiny. If it's scrutiny that matters for memory, or, more broadly, *if we remember what we pay attention to and think about*, then memory for the coin should be quite poor.

The evidence on this point is clear: People's memory for the penny is remarkably bad. For example, most people know that Lincoln's head is on the "heads" side, but which way is he facing? Is it his right cheek that's visible, or his left? What other words or markings are shown on the coin? Most people do very badly with these questions; their answers to the "which way is he facing?" question are close to random (Nickerson & Adams, 1979); performance is similar for people in other countries remembering their own coins. (Also see Bekerian & Baddeley, 1980; and Rinck, 1999.)

The Need for Active Encoding

It seems, then, that it takes some work to get information into long-term memory. Merely having an item in front of your eyes is not enough—even if the item is in front of your eyes over and over and over. Likewise, having an item in your thoughts doesn't, by itself, establish a memory. That's shown by the fact that maintenance rehearsal seems entirely ineffective at promoting memory.[1]

These claims are supported by many lines of evidence, including studies of brain activity during learning. In several studies, researchers have used fMRI recording to keep track of the moment-by-moment brain activity in people who were studying a list of words (Brewer, Zhao, Desmond, Glover, & Gabrieli, 1998; Wagner, Koutstaal, & Schacter, 1999; Wagner et al., 1998). Later, the participants were able to remember some of the words they had learned, but not others, and this allowed the investigators to return to their initial recordings and compare brain activity during the learning process for words that were later remembered and words that were later forgotten. Figure 5.7 shows the results, with a clear difference during the initial encoding between these two types of words. Specifically, greater levels of brain activity (especially in the hippocampus and regions of the prefrontal cortex) were reliably associated with greater probabilities of retention later on.

These fMRI results are telling us, once again, that learning is not a passive process. Instead, activity is needed to lodge information into long-term memory, and, apparently, higher levels of this activity lead to better memory. But this demands some new questions: What is this activity? What does it accomplish? If—as it seems—*maintenance* rehearsal is a poor way to memorize, what type of rehearsal is more effective?

Incidental Learning, Intentional Learning, and Depth of Processing

Consider a student taking a course in college. The student knows that her memory for the course materials will be tested later (e.g., in the course's exams). And presumably the student will take various steps to help herself remember: She may read through her notes again and again, she may discuss the material with friends, she may try outlining the material. Will these various techniques work—so that the student will

---

[1]We should acknowledge that maintenance rehearsal does have a lasting impact if memory is tested in just the right way, and we will return to this point in Chapter 6. (See, for example, Kelly, Burton, Kato, & Akamatsu, 2001; Wixted, 1991; for accurate *penny* memory, given just the right test, see Martin & Jones, 2006.) However, this does not change the fact that maintenance rehearsal is worthless for establishing the sorts of memories one needs when simply trying to remember "Is this what I saw yesterday?" or "Is this what I heard ten minutes ago?"

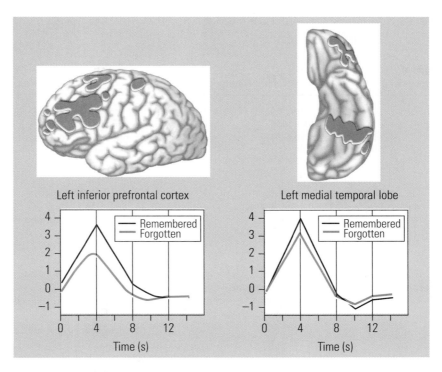

FIGURE 5.7 Brain Activity

Participants in this study were given a succession of words to memorize, and their brain activity was recorded during this initial presentation. These brain scans were then divided into two types—those showing brain activity during the encoding of words that were *remembered* later on in a subsequent test, and those showing activity during encoding of words that were *forgotten* in the test. As the figure shows, activity levels were higher, during encoding, for the later-remembered words than they were for the later-forgotten words. This confirms that whether a word is forgotten or not depends on participants' mental activity when they encountered the word in the first place.

have a complete and accurate memory when the exam takes place? And notice that the student is taking these steps in the context of wanting to memorize, hoping to memorize. How do these elements influence performance? Or, put another way, how does the *intention to memorize* influence how or how well we learn?

These questions have been addressed in many experiments, and in order to summarize the broad pattern of data, it will be helpful to present a composite experiment summarizing the results of many different studies. This composite is a bit complicated, so we have illustrated its design in Table 5.1. (An early procedure by Hyde & Jenkins, 1969, is quite close to the composite we're about to describe, but related data have been reported by Bobrow & Bower, 1969; Craik & Lockhart, 1972; Hyde & Jenkins, 1973; Jacoby, 1978; Lockhart, Craik, & Jacoby, 1976; Parkin, 1984; Slamecka & Graf, 1978; and many others.)

TABLE 5.1 Studying the Effects of Intention and the Effects of Levels of Processing on Memory

Type of processing	Incidental learning	Intentional learning
Shallow	Are these words in the same typeface? "HOUSE—trick" (*Produces poor retention*)	Are these words in the same typeface? "HOUSE—trick" *and*, in addition, you'll have to remember these words later on! (*Produces poor retention*)
Medium	Do these words rhyme? "BALL—TALL" (*Produces moderate level of retention*)	Do these words rhyme? "BALL—TALL" *and*, in addition, you'll have to remember these words later on! (*Produces moderate level of retention*)
Deep	Are these words synonyms? "CAR—AUTOMOBILE" (*Produces excellent retention*)	Are these words synonyms? "CAR—AUTOMOBILE" *and*, in addition, you'll have to remember these words later on! (*Produces excellent retention*)

Illustrated here is a composite of many procedures examining how memory performance is shaped by the intention to memorize and also by how, at the time of learning, one approaches the material to be remembered.

Some of the participants in this experiment are told that we are studying how quickly they can make judgments about letters. No indication is given that we are actually interested in memory. The participants are then shown a series of word pairs on a computer screen. For each pair, they decide as quickly as possible whether the two words are typed in the same case (both capitalized or both not) or typed in different cases. Let's refer to this as **shallow processing**, since participants are engaging the information in a relatively superficial fashion. (Other examples of shallow processing would be decisions about whether the words are printed in red or in green, high or low on the screen, and so on.) At the end of this sequence, the participants are surprised to learn that their memories are being tested, and they are asked to write down as many of the words as they can remember. This is the top left cell shown in Table 5.1. This sort of procedure assesses **incidental learning**—that is, learning in the absence of any intention to learn.

A second group of participants is given the same instructions, but with one change. Like the first group, these participants are told that we want them to make judgments about whether the words in each pair are in the same case or in different cases. This group, therefore, is also doing shallow processing. However, this group is also told that their memories will be tested, so that when the memory test arrives, it comes as no surprise. These participants, therefore, are doing shallow processing in the context of the intention to learn. This is the top right cell in Table 5.1, and it examines **intentional learning**.

A third group of participants is brought into the lab and told that we are studying how quickly people can make judgments about rhyme. If the two words shown on the computer screen rhyme, they press one button; if not, they press a different button. Again, a surprise memory test follows this presentation. These participants are doing what we might call "medium processing," and because the memory test was unexpected, this is another instance of incidental learning.

A fourth group is given the same rhyme task but is told in advance about the upcoming memory test. Members of this group are doing medium processing with the intention to memorize the words they are viewing.

The fifth and sixth groups (the bottom cells in Table 5.1) are led to do **deep processing**—that is, to think about the meaning of the items. Participants in the fifth group are shown pairs of words on a computer screen, with the instruction that they should press one button if the words on the screen are synonyms, another button if they are not. No warning is given about a memory test, and therefore these participants presumably have no intention to memorize the words. Participants in the sixth group are given the same task but are warned about the memory test, so this group is doing deep processing with the intention to learn.

What are the results of all this? Let's frame the answer in terms of Table 5.1. When the time comes for recall, participants from the bottom left cell (deep processing with no intention to learn) perform quite well, whereas participants from the top left cell (shallow processing with no intention to learn) do rather poorly. In other words, attention to meaning really pays off for recall, while attention to surface characteristics produces little memory benefit. Moderate levels of processing (attention to rhyme) produce a moderate level of recall performance.

What about the right column of the table? Here the result is quite straightforward: There is no difference between the left and right columns of the table. That is, the intention to learn seems to add nothing. For purposes of memorizing, there is no difference between shallow processing with the intention to learn and shallow processing without this intention. Likewise, there is no difference between deep processing with the intention to learn and deep processing without this intention.

The Intention to Learn

In the experiment just sketched, depth of processing had a powerful effect, such that the deeper the processing, the better the memory. However, incidental learning and intentional learning yielded identical patterns, indicating little role for the intention to learn. But let's take a closer look at the importance of intentions by considering one last group of participants. This group is told that they are about to be shown words on a computer screen, and they are asked to memorize these words. No further instructions are given, so they are free to approach this memorization in any way they choose. These participants are then shown a sequence just like the ones described in the previous section.

When people are instructed to memorize, each uses the strategy that he or she thinks best. And, in fact, different people have different beliefs about the best way to memorize. Some of us, for example, have discovered that thinking about meaning is an effective strategy and so, if asked to memorize, spontaneously draw on deep processing. Others seem to believe that the best way to memorize is by listening to the sound of the word over and over. People in this second group will end up indistinguishable from the participants in the middle right cell of Table 5.1, while people who spontaneously employ deep processing will end up equivalent to participants in the lower right cell. Of course, the participants we were discussing before had been instructed to use a particular form of processing, and the people we are now considering have "self-instructed." But as it turns out, this difference between instruction and self-instruction is irrelevant to performance.

All of this leads to the expectation that results from this "just memorize" condition will be variable, depending on how participants self-instruct—that is, depending on what strategy they choose. This prediction is correct. If participants have figured out, on their own, that attention to meaning aids memory, then they perform quite well. More precisely, they perform as well as—but no better than—participants specifically told to do deep processing. If they select a less-than-optimal strategy, then they perform at a lower level. And, in fact, many people do have peculiar beliefs about what works in placing material into memory. These people then choose their memorizing strategy on the basis of these (faulty) beliefs, and their performance on memory tests is correspondingly poor. (For studies of people's spontaneous strategies, see J. R. Anderson & Bower, 1972; A. L. Brown, 1979; Hyde & Jenkins, 1969; T. O. Nelson, 1976; Postman, 1964.)

What, therefore, should we conclude about the role of intention in guiding the learning process? Clearly, intention does matter. Someone who has no intention to learn may end up doing maintenance processing rather than elaborative processing, and this obviously will affect what is remembered. Likewise, someone who intends to learn will select the strategy she thinks best, and as we have seen, this choice of strategy will also affect the quality of memory. As a result of all this, intentional encoding usually does yield better memory than incidental encoding (e.g., Pansky, Koriat, & Goldsmith, 2005). But these effects of intention are *indirect*. The intention to learn leads people to approach the materials in a certain fashion, and it is the approach, not the intention, that matters for memory. If we can lead people to approach the materials in the same way without the intention, we get the same memory results.

The Role of Meaning and Memory Connections

Clearly, then, a great deal depends on how we engage the materials we encounter at the time of learning—whether we do deep processing, shallow processing, or mere maintenance. Indeed, the differences at stake here are quite large, so that in many experiments people are three, or four, or five times more likely to remember items that were processed deeply than they are to remember items processed in a shallow manner. But what exactly does this "engagement" with the materials accomplish? Why is it, for example, that attention to meaning leads to such good recall? Let's start with a broad proposal; we'll then need to circle back and fill in the evidence for this proposal.

Perhaps surprisingly, the benefits of deep processing may not lie in the learning process itself. Instead, deep processing may influence *subsequent* events. More precisely, attention to meaning may promote recall by virtue of facilitating *retrieval* of the memory later on. To understand this point, consider what happens whenever a library acquires a new book. On its way into the collection, the new book must be catalogued and shelved appropriately. These steps happen when the book arrives, but the cataloguing doesn't literally influence the arrival of the book into the building. The moment the book is delivered, it's physically in the library, catalogued or not, and the book doesn't become "more firmly" or "more strongly" in the library because of the cataloguing.

But the cataloguing is crucial. If the book were merely tossed on a random shelf somewhere, with no entry in the catalogue, users might never be able to find it. Indeed, without a catalogue entry, users of the library might not even realize that the book was in the building. Notice, then, that cataloguing happens at the time of arrival, but the benefit of cataloguing isn't for the arrival itself. (If the librarians all went on strike, so that no books were being catalogued, books would continue to arrive, magazines would still be delivered, and so on. Again: The *arrival* doesn't depend on cataloguing.) Instead, the benefit of cataloguing is for events subsequent to the book's arrival: Cataloguing makes it possible (and maybe makes it *easy*) to find the book later on.

The same is true for the vast library that is our memory. The task of learning is not merely a matter of placing information into long-term memory. Learning also needs to establish some appropriate indexing; it must, in effect, pave a path to the newly acquired information, so that this information can be retrieved at some future point. In essence, then, one of the main chores of memory acquisition is to lay the groundwork for memory retrieval.

But what is it that facilitates memory retrieval? There are, in fact, several ways to search through memory, but a great deal depends on memory *connections*. Connections allow one memory to trigger another, and then that memory to trigger another, so that like a series of dominoes falling, one is "led" to the sought-after information. If remembering the experimenter's shirt reminds you of materials you learned during the experiment, this will help you to locate these materials in memory. In this case, there must have been some connection in your thoughts between the shirt and the target materials, and this connection is what triggered the reminding. Likewise, if remembering the third word on a list reminds you of the fourth and fifth, these connections among the items will improve your memory performance.

This line of reasoning easily accounts for why attention to meaning promotes memory. Attention to meaning involves thinking about relationships: "What words are related in meaning to the word I'm now considering?"; "What is the relationship between the start of this story and the way the story turned out?" Thinking about points like these will help you to find (or, in some cases, to *create*) connections among your various ideas, and it's these connections, we're proposing, that really matter for memory.

Elaborate Encoding

It will take us several chapters to work through all the evidence for the claims just offered. One bit of evidence, though, is immediately accessible: On the hypotheses just sketched, attention to meaning should not be the only way to improve memory. Other strategies should have similar effects, provided that these strategies help the memorizer to establish memory connections.

As an example, consider a study by Craik and Tulving (1975). Participants were shown a word and then shown a sentence with one word left out. Their task was to decide whether the word fit into the sentence. For example, they might see the word "chicken," then the sentence "She cooked the _____." The appropriate response would be yes, since the word does fit in this sentence. After a series of these trials, there was a surprise memory test, with participants asked to remember all the words they had seen.

In this experiment, some of the sentences shown to participants were simple, while others were more elaborate. For example, a more complex sentence might be, "The great bird swooped down and carried off the struggling _____." The data showed that words were more likely to be remembered if they appeared with these rich, elaborate sentences.

To make their initial yes-or-no response to any of these sentences, the research participants obviously have to think about the meanings of the words in the sentences. This is deep processing, and if this were all that mattered for memory, then all of the words should be remembered equally. But that's not what the data show. Instead, deep and *elaborate* processing led to much better recall than deep processing alone.

Why does elaborate processing help memory? The answer hinges on memory connections. Perhaps the "great bird swooped" sentence calls to mind a barnyard scene, with the hawk carrying a chicken away. Or perhaps it calls to mind thoughts about predator–prey relationships. One way or another, the richness of this sentence offers the potential for many connections as it calls other thoughts to mind, each of which can be connected, in your thinking, to the target sentence. These connec-

Why Do Memory Connections Help?

When books arrive in a library, the librarians must *catalog* them. This doesn't facilitate the "entry" of books into the library—the books are in the building whether they are catalogued or not. But cataloguing makes the books vastly easier to find later on. Memory connections may serve the same function: The connections don't "bring" material into memory, but they do make the material findable in long-term storage later.

tions, in turn, provide potential **retrieval paths**—paths that can, in effect, guide your thoughts toward the content to be remembered. All of this seems less likely for the impoverished sentences. These will evoke fewer connections and will establish a narrower set of retrieval paths. Consequently, these sentences will be less likely to be recalled later on.

Organizing and Memorizing

Sometimes memory connections link the to-be-remembered material to other information already in memory. In other cases, the connections link one aspect of the to-be-remembered material to another aspect of the same material. Such a connection ensures that if any part of the material is recalled, then all will be recalled.

In all cases, though, the connections are important, and that leads us to ask how one goes about discovering (or creating) these connections. More than 60 years ago, a German psychologist, George Katona, argued that the key lies in *organization* (Katona, 1940). Katona's argument, in fact, was that the processes of organization and memorization are inseparable: We memorize well when we discover the order within the material. Conversely, if we find (or impose) an organization on the material, we will easily remember it. These suggestions are fully compatible with the conception we are developing, since what organization provides is, once again, memory connections.

Mnemonics

For thousands of years, people have wished for "better" memories; they have wished to learn more quickly and to remember more accurately. Motivated by these wishes, a number of techniques have been designed to "improve" memory—techniques known as **mnemonic strategies**. Some of these mnemonics are modern inventions, but most are very old, dating back to ancient Greece.

Most mnemonics involve a straightforward and familiar principle—namely, that organization helps. If an organization can be found within the materials, then this will lead to good memory. If an organization cannot be found, then often an "external" organization can be imposed on the material, with the same memory benefit.

Let us take a concrete case. You want to remember a list of largely unrelated items, perhaps the entries on your shopping list or a list of questions you want to ask when you next see your adviser. You might try to remember this list using one of the so-called **peg-word systems**. These systems begin with a well-organized structure, such as this one:

> One is a bun.
>
> Two is a shoe.
>
> Three is a tree.
>
> Four is a door.
>
> Five is a hive.
>
> Six are sticks.
>
> Seven is heaven.
>
> Eight is a gate.
>
> Nine is a line.
>
> Ten is a hen.

This rhyme provides ten "peg words" ("bun," "shoe," "tree," and so on), and in memorizing something you can "hang" the materials to be remembered on these "pegs." Let's imagine, therefore, that you are trying to memorize the list of topics you want to discuss with your adviser. If you want to discuss your unhappiness with your chemistry class, you might form an association between chemistry and the first peg, "bun." You might, for example, form a mental image of a hamburger bun floating in an Erlenmeyer flask. If you also want to discuss your after-graduation plans, you might form an association between some aspect of those plans and the next peg, "shoe." (Perhaps you might think about how you plan to pay your way after college by selling shoes.) If you continue in this fashion, then when the time comes to meet with your adviser, all you have to do is think through that silly rhyme again. When you think of "one is a bun," it is highly likely that the image of the flask (and therefore of chemistry lab) will come to mind. When you think of "two is a shoe," you'll be reminded of your job plans. And so on.

Mnemonic Strategies
To be effective, a mnemonic must provide some rich linkage among the items being memorized. Merely putting the items side-by-side is not enough.

"You simply associate each number with a word, such as 'table' and 3,476,029."

Hundreds of variations on this strategy are possible, some taught in self-help courses (you've probably seen the ads—"How to Improve Your Memory!"), some presented by corporations as part of management training, and on and on. Some mnemonic strategies rely heavily on visualization (e.g., we mentioned that you might form an image of the bun floating in the flask), others do not. (For more on visualization, see Chapter 11.) All the variations, though, employ the same basic scheme. To remember a list with no apparent organization, you impose an organization on it by employing a skeleton or scaffold that is itself tightly organized. The number rhyme provides one such scaffold, but other scaffolds are easily located. And, crucially, these systems all work: They help you to remember individual items, and they also help you to remember those items in a specific sequence (G. H. Bower, 1970, 1972; G. H. Bower & Reitman, 1972; Christen & Bjork, 1976; Higbee, 1977; Roediger, 1980; J. Ross & Lawrence, 1968; Yates, 1966). All of this confirms our central claim: Organizing improves recall. Mnemonics work because they impose an organization on the materials to be remembered, thus establishing connections between the material and some other easily remembered structure.

Mnemonics contribute to our theoretical understanding of memory, but in addition, they have important practical uses. Many students, for example, use a first-letter mnemonic to remember the standard colors of the rainbow, turning the list of seven colors (red, orange, yellow, . . .) into a single integrated unit: the name "Roy G. Biv." Likewise, many students use the sentence "King Phillip crossed the ocean to find gold and silver" to remember the taxonomic categories: kingdom, phylum, class, order, family, genus, and species. These techniques serve students well, underscoring the fact that mnemonics are indeed effective. A first-letter mnemonic, just like any other mnemonic, imposes organization and unity on a list, and here, as always, organization aids memory.

But let's also note that there's a downside to using mnemonics in educational settings. In using a mnemonic, you typically focus on just one aspect of the material to be remembered—just the first letter of the word to be remembered, for example, or (returning to an earlier case) just some specific relationship between "bun" and chemistry. This focus guarantees that the selected link receives much attention and so is well established in memory. But focusing in this way also means that you won't pay much attention to *other* aspects of the material to be remembered. As a result, you may cut short your effort toward understanding this material, and likewise your effort toward finding multiple connections between the material and other things you know.

Notice, then, that mnemonic use involves a trade-off: More attention focused on one or two memory connections means less attention spent on thinking about other connections, including the other connections that might help you to understand the material. This trade-off will be fine if you don't care very much about the meaning of the material. (Do you care why biologists count "order" as a subset of "class," rather than the other way around?) But this trade-off is troubling if you're trying to memorize material that is meaningful. In this case, you would be better served by a memory strategy that leads you to seek out *multiple* connections between the material you're trying to learn and things you already know. Indeed, this effort toward multiple links will help you in two ways. First, it will foster your understanding of the material to be remembered, and so will lead to better, richer, deeper learning. Second, the multiple links will also help you to retrieve this information later on: We've already suggested that memory connections serve as retrieval paths; and the more paths there are, the easier it will be to find the target material later.

For these reasons, mnemonic use may be ill-advised in many situations. Nonetheless, the fact remains that mnemonics are immensely useful in some settings (what were those rainbow colors?), and this in turn confirms our initial point: Organization promotes memory.

Understanding and Memorizing

So far, we've said a lot about how people memorize rather impoverished stimulus materials—lists of randomly selected words, or colors that have to be learned in exactly the right sequence. In our day-to-day lives, however, we typically want to remember more meaningful, and more complicated, material. We wish to remember the episodes we experience, the details of rich scenes we have observed, or the many-step arguments we have read in a book. Do the same memory principles apply to these cases?

The answer to this question is clearly yes. Our memory for events, or pictures, or complex bodies of knowledge is enormously dependent on our being able to organize the material to be remembered. We remember best what we have organized best; we remember poorly when we can neither find nor create an organizing scheme.

With these more complicated materials, though, and as we've already suggested, our best bet for organization is not some arbitrary skeleton like those used in peg-word systems. Instead, the optimal organization of these complex materials is generally dependent on understanding. That is, we remember best what we understand best.

There are many ways to show that this is true. For example, one can give people a sentence or paragraph to read and test their comprehension by asking questions about the material or by asking them to paraphrase the material. Sometime later, we can test their memory for this material. The results are straightforward: The better the participants' understanding of a sentence or a paragraph, the greater the likelihood that they will remember it later. The more accurately they could answer questions immediately after reading the material, the greater the chance that they will remember the material after a delay (e.g., Bransford, 1979).

This pattern can be demonstrated in the laboratory; it can also be demonstrated in people's day-to-day lives. For example, consider the material you are learning right now in the courses you are taking. Will you remember this material 5 years from now, or 10, or 20? The answer depends on how well you understand the material. One measure of understanding is the grade you earn in a course: With full and rich understanding, you are likely to earn an A; with poor understanding, your grade is likely to be lower. One would expect, therefore, that the higher someone's grade in a course, the more likely that person is to remember the course contents, even many years later. This is exactly what the data show. Plainly, the better your understanding, the better (and longer-lasting) your memory will be (M. Conway, Cohen, & Stanhope, 1992).

The relationship between understanding and memory can also be demonstrated in another way, by *manipulating* whether people understand the material or not. For example, in an experiment by Bransford and Johnson (1972, p. 722), participants read this passage:

> The procedure is actually quite simple. First you arrange items into different groups. Of course one pile may be sufficient depending on how much there is to do. If you have to go somewhere else due to lack of facilities that is the next step; otherwise you are pretty well set. It is important not to overdo things. That is, it is better to do too few things at once than too many. In the short run, this may not seem important but complications can easily arise. A mistake can be expensive as well. At first, the whole procedure will seem complicated. Soon, however, it will become just another facet of life. It is difficult to foresee any end to the necessity for this task in the immediate future, but then, one never can tell. After the procedure is completed one arranges the materials into different groups again. Then they can be put into their appropriate places. Eventually they will be used once more and the whole cycle will then have to be repeated. However, that is part of life.

You are probably puzzled by this passage; so are most research participants. The story is easy to understand, though, if we give it a title: "Doing the Laundry." In the experiment, some participants were given the title before reading the passage; others were not. Participants in the first group easily understood the passage and were able to remember it after a delay. The second group, reading the same words, were not confronting a meaningful passage and did poorly on the memory test. (For related data, see Bransford & Franks, 1971; Sulin & Dooling, 1974; for another example, see Figure 5.8.)

Similar effects can be documented with nonverbal materials. Consider the picture shown in Figure 5.9. This picture at first looks like a bunch of meaningless blotches; with some study, though, you may discover that a familiar object is depicted. Wiseman and Neisser (1974) tested people's memory for this picture. Consistent with what we have seen so far, their memory was good if they understood the picture, and bad otherwise. (Also see G. H. Bower, Karlin, & Dueck, 1975; Mandler & Ritchey, 1977; Rubin & Kontis, 1983.)

The Study of Memory Acquisition

This chapter has largely been about memory acquisition. How do we acquire new memories? How is new information, new knowledge, established in long-term memory? Or, in more pragmatic terms, what is the best, most effective, most efficient way to learn? We now can answer these questions, but in important ways our discussion has also indicated that we need to place these questions into a broader context—looking not just at acquisition, but also at the substantial contribution from the memorizer, as well as the powerful interconnections among acquisition, retrieval, and storage.

The Contribution of the Memorizer

Over and over, we have seen that memory is facilitated by organizing and understanding the materials to be remembered. Hand in hand with this, it appears that memories are not established by sheer contact with the items you're hoping to remember. If

1 4 9 1 6 2 5 3 6 4 9 6 4 8 1

FIGURE 5.8 Memory for Digits

Examine this series of digits for a moment, and then turn away from the page and try to recall all fifteen digits in their proper sequence. The chances are good that you will fail in this task—perhaps remembering the first few and last few digits, but not the entire list. Things will go differently, though, if you discover the pattern within the list. Now you'll easily be able to remember the full sequence. What is the pattern? Try thinking of the series this way: 1, 4, 9, 16, 25, 36. . . . Here, as always, organizing and understanding aid memory.

FIGURE 5.9 Comprehension Also Aids Memory for Pictures
People who perceive this picture as a pattern of meaningless blotches are unlikely to remember the picture. People who perceive the "hidden" form do remember the picture. (After Wiseman & Neisser, 1974)

people are merely exposed to the items without giving those items any thought, then subsequent recall of those items will be poor.

These points immediately draw our attention to the role played by the memorizer. If we wish to predict whether this or that event will be recalled, it is not enough to know that someone was exposed to the event. Likewise, if we wish to predict memory performance, it is not enough to describe the memory "equipment" possessed by each of us—for example, a working memory with various components, a long-term memory with a specific structure. Instead, if we wish to predict someone's recall performance, we need to pay attention to what the person was doing at the time of learning. Did she elect to do mere maintenance rehearsal, or did she engage the material in some other way? If the latter, how did she think about the material? Did she pay attention to the appearance of the words or to their meaning? If she thought about meaning, was she able to understand the material? Did she think about the material as involving separate bits, or did she find some unifying theme? These considerations are crucial for predicting the success of memory.

The contribution of the memorizer is also evident in another way. We have argued that learning depends on the person's making connections, but connections to what? If someone wants to connect the to-be-remembered material to other knowledge, to other memories, then the person needs to have that other knowledge; she needs to have other (potentially relevant) memories. Thus, what people contribute to learning also includes their own prior knowledge. If someone happens to enter the learning situation with a great deal of relevant knowledge, then she arrives with a considerable advantage—a rich framework onto which the new materials can be "hooked." If someone enters the learning situation with little relevant background, then there is no framework, nothing to connect to, and learning will be correspondingly more difficult. Thus, if we wish to predict the success of memorizing, we also need to consider what other knowledge the individual brings into the situation.

The Links Among Acquisition, Retrieval, and Storage

These points lead us to another theme of immense importance. Our emphasis in this chapter has been on memory acquisition, but we have now seen several indications that claims about acquisition cannot be separated from claims about memory storage and memory retrieval. For example, why is recall improved by organization and understanding? We have suggested that organization provides retrieval paths, making the memories "findable" later on when the time comes to remember the target information. Therefore, our claims about acquisition rest on assumptions about memory retrieval and the usefulness of memory connections within retrieval.

Likewise, we have just noted that a person's ability to learn new material depends, in part, on having a framework of prior knowledge to which the new materials can be tied. In this way, claims about memory acquisition must be coordinated with claims about the nature of what is already in storage.

The same can be said about chunking, both in working memory and in long-term storage. In most cases, chunking depends on understanding, and understanding rests on things you already know. The number series "1 4 9 1 6 . . ." (Figure 5.8) can be chunked as the squares of the digits only if you already know what the squares of the digits are. The passage about laundry is understood only by virtue of your prior knowledge about how clothing is washed. In both of these cases, therefore, chunking at the time of memory acquisition is dependent on knowledge you already have, and so again we see the interweaving of memory acquisition and knowledge already in storage.

We close this chapter, then, with a two-sided message. We have offered many claims about memory acquisition and about how memories are established. In particular, we have offered claims about the importance of memory connections, organization, and understanding. At the same time, though, these claims cannot stand by themselves. At the level of theory, our account of acquisition has already made references to the role of prior knowledge and to the nature of memory retrieval. At the level of data, we will soon see that these interactions among acquisition, knowledge, and retrieval have important implications—for learning, for forgetting, and for memory accuracy. We turn next to some of those implications.

Chapter Summary

- It is convenient to think of memorizing as having separate stages. First, one acquires new information (acquisition). Next, the information remains in storage until it is needed. Finally, the information is retrieved. However, this separation among the stages may be misleading. For example, in order to memorize new information, one forms connections between this information and things one already knows. In this fashion, the acquisition stage is intertwined with the retrieval of information already in storage.

- Information that is currently being considered is held in working memory; information that is not currently active but is nonetheless in storage is in long-term memory. Working memory is sometimes likened to the mental "desk space," long-term memory to the mental "library." The distinction between these two forms of memory is often described in terms of the modal model and has been examined in many studies of the serial-position curve. The primacy portion of this curve reflects those items that have had extra opportunity to reach long-term memory; the recency portion of this curve reflects the accurate retrieval of items currently in working memory.

- Working memory is more than a passive storage container. Instead, this is where the mind's filing, cross-referencing, and active contemplation take place. This activity is carried out by working memory's central executive. For mere storage, the executive often relies on a small number of low-level assistants, including the articulatory rehearsal loop and the visuospatial buffer, which work as mental scratch pads. The activity inherent in this overall system is reflected in the flexible way material can be chunked in working memory; the activity is also reflected in current measures of the active memory span.

- Working memory's "central executive" may simply be the name we give to a small number of mental resources that serve to order, organize, and control our mental lives. These resources rely heavily on brain tissue in the prefrontal cortex; this is reflected in the fact that damage to the prefrontal cortex causes difficulties in tasks that require someone to plan and organize their activities.

- Maintenance rehearsal serves to keep information in working memory and requires little effort, but it has little impact on subsequent recall. To maximize one's chances of recall, elaborative rehearsal is needed, in which one seeks connections within the material to be remembered, or connections between the material to be remembered and things one already knows.

- In many cases, elaborative processing takes the form of attention to meaning. This attention to meaning is called deep processing, in contrast to attention to sounds or visual form, which is considered shallow processing. Many studies have shown that deep processing leads to good memory performance later on, even if the deep processing was done with no intention of memorizing the target material. In fact, the intention to learn has no direct effect on performance; what matters instead is how someone engages or thinks about the material to be remembered.

■ Deep processing has beneficial effects by creating effective retrieval paths that can be used later on. Retrieval paths depend on connections linking one memory to another; each connection provides a path potentially leading to a target memory. Mnemonic strategies build on this idea and focus on the creation of specific memory connections, often tying the to-be-remembered material to a frame (e.g., a strongly structured poem).

■ Perhaps the best way to form memory connections is to understand the material to be remembered. In understanding, one forms many connections within the material to be remembered, and also between this material and other knowledge. With all of these retrieval paths, it becomes easy to locate this material in memory. Consistent with these suggestions, studies have shown a close correspondence between the ability to understand some material and the ability to recall that material later on; this pattern has been demonstrated with stories, visual patterns, number series, and many other sorts of stimuli.

The Workbook Connection

See the *Cognition Workbook* for further exploration of the acquisition of memories and the working-memory system:

■ Demonstration 5.1: Primary and Recency Effects
■ Demonstration 5.2: The Effects of Unattended Exposure
■ Demonstration 5.3: Depth of Processing
■ Research Methods: Replication
■ Cognitive Psychology and Education: "How Should I Study?"
■ Cognitive Psychology and the Law: The Videorecorder View

CHAPTER 6

Interconnections Between Acquisition and Retrieval

Putting information into long-term memory helps us only if we can retrieve that information later on. Otherwise, it would be like putting money into a savings account without the option of ever making withdrawals, or like writing books that could never be read. And it is equally clear that there are different ways to retrieve information from memory. We can try to recall the information ("What was the name of your tenth-grade homeroom teacher?") or to recognize it ("Was the name perhaps Miller?"). If we try to recall the information, a variety of cues may or may not be available (we might be told, as a hint, that the name began with an *M* or rhymed with "tiller").

In Chapter 5, we largely ignored these variations in retrieval. We talked as if material was well established in memory or was not, with no regard for how the material would be retrieved from memory. There is every reason to believe, however, that we cannot ignore these variations in retrieval, and in this chapter we will examine the interactions between how exactly a bit of information was learned and how it is retrieved later on.

As we will see, this examination will lead us into several crucial issues. One will involve the conscious experience of *familiarity*, and we will need to ask what causes this experience. This will in turn lead us into an intriguing set of cases in which people are influenced by memories that they aren't at all aware of—memories that are, in effect, unconscious. We will also need to consider what "optimal" learning might be: If you want to maximize your chances of recalling what you learned in a college course, or if you want to remember as much as possible about some event in your life, how should you proceed? Our discussion will guide us toward some surprising answers to this question.

- Learning does not simply place information in memory; instead, learning prepares you to retrieve the information in a particular way. As a result, learning that is good preparation for one sort of memory retrieval may be inadequate for other sorts of retrieval.

- In general, retrieval seems to be most likely if your mental perspective is the same during learning and during retrieval, just as we would expect if learning establishes retrieval paths that help you, later, only if you "travel" the same path in your effort toward locating the target material.

- Some experiences also seem to produce unconscious memories, and an examination of these "implicit memory" effects will help us understand the broad set of ways in which memory influences us and will also help us see where the feeling of familiarity comes from.

- Finally, an examination of amnesia confirms a central theme of the chapter—namely, that we cannot speak of "good" or "bad" memory in general; instead, we need to evaluate memory by considering how, and for what purposes, the memory will be used.

Learning As Preparation for Retrieval

Why should there be a relationship between the particular way you learn and the particular form of memory retrieval? The answer begins with a point that we made in Chapter 5: When you are learning, you're making connections between the newly acquired material and other representations already in your memory. These connections help you because they make the new knowledge "findable" later on. The connections, in other words, serve as *retrieval paths*: When you want to retrieve information from memory, you travel on those paths, moving from one memory to the next until you reach the target material.

These claims seem simple enough, but they have an important implication. To see this, bear in mind that retrieval paths—like any paths—have a starting point and an ending point: The path leads you from a certain Point A to a certain Point B. That's obviously useful if you want to move from A to B, but what if you're trying to reach B from somewhere else? What if you're trying to reach Point B, but at the moment you happen to be nowhere close to Point A? In that case, this path linking A and B may not help you.

As an analogy, imagine that you are trying to reach Chicago from the west. For this purpose, what you need is some highway coming in from the west. It won't be helpful that you've constructed a wonderful road coming into Chicago from the *south*. That road will be valuable in other circumstances, but it's not the path you need to get from where you are right now to where you're heading.

Do retrieval paths in memory work the same way? If so, we might find cases in which someone's learning is excellent preparation for one sort of retrieval, but useless for other types of retrieval—as if he's built a road coming in from one direction but now needs a road from another direction. Is this indeed the pattern of the data?

State-Dependent Learning

Consider a broad class of studies on **state-dependent learning** (J. E. Eich, 1980; Overton, 1985). In one such study, Godden and Baddeley (1975) asked scuba divers to learn various materials. Some of the divers learned the material while sitting on dry land; others learned the material while 20 feet underwater, hearing the material via a special communication set. Within each group, half of the divers were then tested while above water, and half were tested below (see Figure 6.1).

Underwater, the world has a different look, feel, and sound, and this could easily influence what thoughts come to mind for the divers in this situation. Imagine, for example, that a diver is feeling a bit cold while underwater. This context will lead the diver to certain thoughts, and so those thoughts will be in the diver's mind during the learning. As a result, it's likely that the diver will form some sort of memory connections between these "cold-related thoughts" and the materials he is trying to learn.

How will this influence memory performance? If this diver is back underwater at the time of the memory test, it's likely that he'll again feel cold, and this may once more lead him to "cold-related thoughts." These thoughts, in turn, are now connected (we've proposed) to the target materials, and that gives us what we want: The cold triggers certain thoughts, the thoughts are linked to the target memories, and those links will lead the diver back to those memories.

Of course, all is not lost if the diver is tested for the same memory materials *on land*. In this case, the diver might have some other links, some other memory connections, that will lead back to the target memories. However, the diver-on-land will nonetheless be at a disadvantage—with the "cold-related" thoughts not triggered, and so with no benefit from the earlier-established connections linking those thoughts to the sought-after memories.

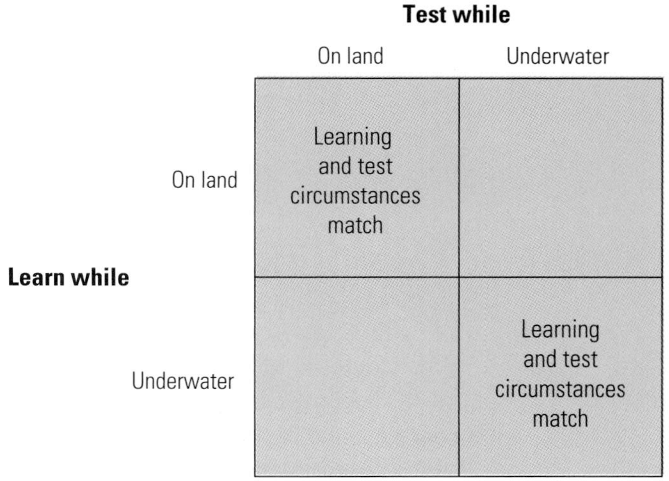

FIGURE 6.1 The Design of a State-Dependent Learning Experiment
Half of the participants (deep-sea divers) learned the test material while underwater; half learned while sitting on land. Likewise, half were tested while underwater; half were tested on land. We expect a retrieval advantage if the learning and test circumstances match. Hence, we expect better performance in the top left and bottom right cells.

	Test while	
	On land	Underwater
On land	Learning and test circumstances match	
Underwater		Learning and test circumstances match

Learn while

On this basis, we should expect that the divers who learn material while underwater should remember the material best if tested underwater; this will increase the chance that they'll be able to use the memory connections they established earlier. Likewise, the divers who learn on land should do best if tested on land. This is exactly what the data show (see Figure 6.2).

Related results have been obtained with odors present or absent during learning (Cann & Ross, 1989; Schab, 1990): Memory is best if the olfactory environment is the same during memory retrieval as it was during the initial learning. Similar data have been obtained in studies designed to mimic the real-life situation of a college student: The research participants read a two-page article on psychoimmunology, similar to the sorts of readings they might encounter in their college courses. Half the participants read the article in a quiet setting; half read it in noisy circumstances. When given a short-answer test later on, those who read the article in quiet did best if tested in quiet—67% correct answers, compared to 54% correct if tested in a noisy environment. Those who read the article in a noisy environment did better if tested in a noisy environment—62% correct, compared to 46% (Grant et al., 1998; also see Balch, Bowman, & Mohler, 1992; S. Smith, 1985; S. M. Smith & Vela, 2001).

S. M. Smith, Glenberg, and Bjork (1978) report the same pattern if learning and testing simply take place in different rooms—with the rooms differing in their visual

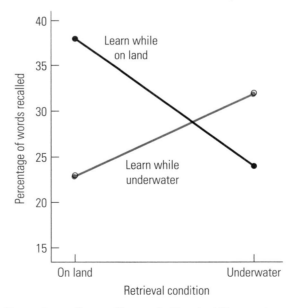

FIGURE 6.2 State Dependency From a Change in Physical Circumstances
Materials learned while on land are best recalled while on land. Materials learned while underwater are best recalled while underwater.

appearance, their sounds, and even their *scent*: The data showed that recall was best if done in the room in which the initial learning took place. Here, though, there is an interesting twist: In one procedure, the participants learned materials in one room and were tested in a different room. Just before testing, however, the participants were urged to think about the room in which they had learned—what it looked like and how it made them feel. When tested, these participants performed as well as those participants for whom there was no room change (S. Smith, 1979). What seems to matter, therefore, is not the physical context but the psychological context—a result that's entirely consistent with our account of this effect.

Changes in One's Approach to the Memory Materials

In a number of settings, then, recall performance is best if someone's state (internal or external) at the time of testing matches his state at the time of learning. As a result, we can easily demonstrate a benefit of **context reinstatement**—that is, improved memory performance if we re-create the context that was in place during learning. Let's emphasize, though, that the context has its effect only because it influences how the person thinks about the materials to be remembered; it's these thoughts, and the perspective the person has during learning, that really matter for memory, and not the physical environment. On this basis, we should be able to get a similar result with no change in physical context, but instead by manipulating someone's perspective directly.

Fisher and Craik (1977) presented their research participants with a series of word pairs. The participants were instructed to learn the second word in each pair and to use the first word in each pair only "as an aid to remembering the target words." For half of the pairs, the "context word" was semantically associated with the target word; for example, if participants were shown "cat," they were also shown the context word "dog." This association should have encouraged them to think about the words' meanings. For the other pairs, the context word was one that rhymed with the target (e.g., if shown "cat," they were also shown the context word "hat"). This association should have encouraged participants to think about the target word's sound.

When the time came for a test, participants were given either a hint concerning meaning ("Was there a word on the list associated with 'dog'?") or a hint concerning sound ("Was there a word on the list associated with 'hat'?"). Table 6.1 shows the results. Note, first, the column all the way to the right (averaging together trials with meaning hints and trials with sound hints). Consistent with the data in Chapter 5, thinking about meaning led to better memory, in this case with an impressive advantage of 30.5% to 21.5%. That is, people who thought about meaning at the time of learning remembered about 50% more than people who thought about sound. These are the data in the rightmost column in Table 6.1. But now look at the table's other two columns. If participants thought about meaning at the time of learning, they did

TABLE 6.1 Percentage of Words Recalled on Testing After Prior Association With Either Meaning or Sound

| | Type of Hint | | |
Type of processing at time of learning	Meaning	Sound	Both combined
Meaning	44%	17%	30.5%
Sound	17%	26%	21.5%

(After Fisher & Craik, 1977)

considerably better in the test if the cues provided by the experimenter concerned meaning. The same was true for sound: If they thought about sound at the time of learning, then they did better with a cue concerning the word's sound.

In fact, the table shows two separate influences on memory working at the same time: an advantage for thinking about meaning (overall, performance is better in the top row) and an advantage for matched learning and test conditions (overall, performance is best in the main diagonal of the table). In the table's top left cell, these effects combine, and here performance is better (44%) than in any other condition. These effects clash in the column showing the results of the sound hint. The advantage from thinking about meaning favors the top cell in this column; the advantage from matched learning and test conditions favors the bottom cell. As it turns out, the match effect wins over the levels-of-processing effect: "Deep but unmatched" (17%) is inferior to "not so deep, but matched" (26%). Thus, the advantage for deep processing is simply overturned in this situation.

Encoding Specificity

It is possible to view the data presented so far in a slightly different way: When you learn a list of words underwater, what goes into your memory is not just a record of those words; what's in your memory is the words *plus* some record of what you were thinking about in response to the words. In the terms we've been using, what is preserved in your memory is some record of the list of words plus the set of connections you established in thinking about the list.

This extra material in your memory can influence your search for the target information. That's what we have been emphasizing so far, in showcasing the role of the connections as retrieval paths. But this extra material can, in a sense, also change the *meaning* of what is remembered: In some situations, "memory plus *this* set of connections" has a different meaning from "memory plus *that* set of connections." That change in meaning, in turn, can have profound consequences for how you remember the past. To see this, let's consider experiments on **encoding specificity**.

In one experiment, participants read target words (e.g., "piano") in either of two contexts: "The man lifted the piano" or "The man tuned the piano." These sentences led the participants to think about the target word in a specific way, and it was this thought that was encoded into memory. In other words, what was placed in memory was not just the word "piano." Instead, what was recorded in memory was the idea of "piano as something heavy" or "piano as musical instrument."

This difference in memory content became clear when participants were later asked to recall the target words. If they had earlier seen the "lifted" sentence, they were quite likely to recall the target word if given the hint "something heavy." The hint "something with a nice sound" was much less effective. But if participants had seen the "tuned" sentence, the result reversed: Now the "nice sound" hint was effective, but the "heavy" hint was not (Barclay, Bransford, Franks, McCarrell, & Nitsch, 1974). In both cases, the memory hint was effective only if it was congruent with what was stored in memory.

This kind of demonstration has been reported in numerous forms by Endel Tulving (Tulving, 1983; also see Hunt & Ellis, 1974; Light & Carter-Sobell, 1970). Why is this called "encoding specificity"? This label reminds us that what one encodes (i.e., places into memory) is indeed specific—not just the physical stimulus as it was encountered, but the stimulus together with its context. In the experiment just described, the context would include what one thinks and understands about the word. As a result, if participants are later presented with the word in *some other context*, they ask themselves, "Does this match anything I learned previously?" and they *correctly* answer no. And we emphasize that this "no" response is indeed correct. It is as if the participants learned the word "other" and were later asked whether they had been shown the word "the." In fact, "the" does appear as part of "other"; more precisely, the letters $T\,H\,E$ do appear within the word "other." But it is the whole that people learn, not the parts. Therefore, if you've seen "other," it's entirely sensible to deny that you have seen "the" or, for that matter, "he" or "her," even though all these letter combinations are contained within "other."

Learning a list of words works in the same way. The word "piano" was contained in what the research participants learned, just as $T\,H\,E$ is contained in "other." What was learned, however, was not just this word; instead, what was learned was the broader, integrated experience: the word as the perceiver understood it. Therefore "piano-as-a-musical-instrument" *isn't* what participants learned if they saw the "lifted" sentence, and so they're correct in asserting that this item wasn't on the earlier list.

Other results show a similar pattern—including studies with nonverbal stimuli. For example, we can show people a pattern and arrange things (through instructions) so that they perceive it as a vase on a black background (Figure 6.3). A few minutes later, we show this exact picture once again, but this time we lead people to organize it differently—as two profiles against a white background. We now ask the participants whether they have ever seen this figure before.

FIGURE 6.3 The Ambiguous Vase/Profiles Figure
This figure, which we first met in Chapter 3, can be perceived either as a white vase against a black background or as two black profiles against a white background.

According to the idea of encoding specificity, what's in participants' memory is the stimulus-as-understood, the stimulus with its appropriate mental context. In this case, what's in memory will be the stimulus with a particular figure/ground organization, and that memory does not match the test stimulus (which, because of our instructions, has a *different* figure/ground organization). Therefore, participants will not recognize the stimulus as familiar—even though the same picture was in front of their eyes just moments earlier. And that is the result—with participants regularly saying they've never seen this picture before, even though they have (Kanizsa, 1979; Rock, 1983; for a number of related results, see Chapter 3).

All of this leads us back to some familiar themes. In learning new material, you establish a memory that can be retrieved in a certain way, from a certain perspective. If the perspective changes—if, in particular, your understanding of the target information changes—then the original memory may not be retrieved. In light of this, perhaps we cannot speak of "good learning" (or "less good learning") in general. Instead, what counts as good learning may depend on later events: Whether it is better to learn underwater or on land depends on where one will be tested. Whether it is better to learn while listening to jazz or while sitting in a quiet room depends on the music background of the memory test environment. Even whether it is best to attend to meaning depends to some extent on whether meaning will be prominent when the time comes for memory retrieval.

Different Forms of Memory Testing

Our discussion so far has focused on the learner's circumstances and perspective, and whether these are the same during memory retrieval as they were during the original learning. Similar conclusions emerge when we consider another way memory retrieval can vary: in the nature of the memory test itself.

Both in the laboratory and in day-to-day life, we often want to **recall** information we encountered earlier. This means that we're presented with some cue that broadly identifies the information that we seek, but then we need to come up with the information on our own: "What was the name of that great restaurant that your parents took us to?"; "Can you remember the words to that song?"; "Where were you last Saturday?"

This stands in contrast to memory tests that hinge on **recognition**. In this case, information is presented to us, and we must decide whether it's the sought-after information or not: "Is this the man who robbed you?"; "I'm sure I'll recognize the street when we get there"; "If you let me taste that wine, I'll tell you if it's the same one we had last time."

These two modes of retrieval—recall and recognition—turn out to be fundamentally different from each other. Recall, by its very nature, requires memory *search*, because you have to come up with the sought-after item on your own; you need to locate that item within memory. As a result, recall depends heavily on memory connections—because it is the connections (serving as retrieval paths) that support the search. It's no surprise, then, that forms of learning that promote connections are particularly useful for recall testing. Specifically, recall is much more likely if during the original learning you thought about relationships between the materials to be remembered and other things you already know, or between the materials to be remembered and other aspects of the learning environment. Thinking about these relationships established (or strengthened) memory connections, allowing you to find the target material later on.

Recognition, in contrast, turns out to be something of a "hybrid." To put this in concrete terms, imagine that you are taking a recognition test, and the fourth word on the test is "loon." You might say to yourself, "Yes, I remember seeing this word on the previous list, because I remember the image that came to mind when I saw this word." In this situation, you'll make a *recognition* response ("Yes, I saw this word before") because you can *recall* the earlier episode. It's no surprise, then, that this sort of recognition follows the same rules as recall, and so is more likely if you formed the relevant connections during learning.

Sometimes, though, recognition works differently. Let's say that you're taking a recognition test, and the fifth word on the test is "butler." In response to this word, you might find yourself thinking this way, "I don't recall seeing this word on the list, but this word feels extraordinarily familiar, so I guess I must have seen it recently. Therefore, it must have been on the list." In this case you do not have what's called **source memory**; that is, you do not have any recollection of the *source* of your current knowledge. But you do have a strong sense of **familiarity**, and you're willing to make an inference about where that familiarity came from. In other words, you attribute the familiarity to the earlier encounter, and thanks to this **attribution**, you will probably respond yes on the recognition test.

Familiarity and Source Memory

It seems, therefore, that we need a two-part theory of recognition, with recognition sometimes depending on *familiarity* and sometimes on *source memory* (e.g., Aggleton & Brown, 2006; Diana, Reder, Arndt, & Park, 2006; Mandler, 2008; Rugg & Yonelinas, 2003). These two types of memory can be distinguished in many ways, including the simple fact that it is possible to have either one of these without the other. For example, the "butler" case just described is one in which you have familiarity but no source memory. The same pattern can easily be observed outside of the lab. Consider the common experience in which you are walking down the street, or perhaps turn on the television, and see a familiar face. Immediately, you know the face is familiar, but you are unable to say just why the face is familiar. Is it someone you saw in a movie last month? Is it the driver of the bus you often take? You are at a loss to answer these questions; all you know is that the face is familiar.

"Familiar . . . But *Where Do I Know Him From?!?*"
The photos here all show successful film actors. The odds are good that, for some of them, you will immediately know that their faces are familiar—but be uncertain *why* the faces are familiar. You know you have seen these actors in some movie, but which one? (We'll identify these six faces at the chapter's end.)

In (maddening!) cases like these, you cannot "place" the memory, you cannot identify the episode in which the face was last encountered. But you are certain the face is familiar, even though you don't know why—a clear example of familiarity without source memory.

The inverse case (source memory without familiarity) is less common but can also be demonstrated. For example, we considered an illustration of this pattern in Chapter 2 when we discussed Capgras syndrome: In this syndrome, the patient has detailed, complete, accurate memories of the past but no sense at all of familiarity, and faces (of family members, of friends) seem hauntingly unfamiliar.

Source memory and familiarity are also distinguishable biologically. In a number of studies, participants have been asked, during a recognition test, to make a **"remember/know"** distinction—pressing one button (to indicate "remember") if they actually recall the episode of encountering a particular item, and pressing a different button ("know") if they don't recall the encounter but just have the broad feeling that the item must have been on the earlier list. In this latter case, participants are essentially saying, "This item seems very familiar, and so I *know* it was on the earlier list, even though I *don't remember* the experience of seeing it" (Gardiner, 1988; Hicks & Marsh, 1999; Jacoby, Jones, & Dolan, 1998).

We can use fMRI scans to monitor participants' brain activity while they are taking recognition tests, and these scans make it clear that "remember" and "know" judgments depend on different brain areas. The scans show heightened activity in the hippocampus when people indicate that they "remember" a particular test item, suggesting that this brain structure is crucial for source memory. In contrast, "know" responses are associated with activity in a different area—the anterior parahippocampus, with the implication that this brain site is crucial for familiarity (Aggleton & Brown, 2006; Diana, Yonelinas, & Ranganath, 2007; Dobbins, Foley, Wagner, & Schacter, 2002; Wagner, Shannon, Kahn, & Buckner, 2005; also see Rugg & Curran, 2007; Rugg & Yonelinas, 2003).

Familiarity and source memory can also be distinguished during *learning*. Specifically, if certain brain areas (e.g., the rhinal cortex) are especially active during learning, then the stimulus is likely to seem familiar later on (and so that stimulus is likely, later, to trigger a "know" response). The obvious suggestion is that this brain site plays a key role in establishing the familiarity (see color insert, Figure 14). In contrast, if other brain areas (e.g., the hippocampal region) are particularly active during learning, then there's a high probability that the person will offer a "remember" response to that stimulus when tested later on (e.g., Davachi & Dobbins, 2008; Davachi, Mitchell, & Wagner, 2003; Ranganath et al., 2003), implying that these brain sites are crucial for establishing source memory.

We still need to ask, though, what's going on in these various brain areas to create the relevant memories. Activity in the hippocampus is presumably helping to create the memory connections we have been discussing all along, and it is these connections, we've argued, that promote source memory: The connections link a memory item to other thoughts that help identify the episode (the source) in which that item was encountered, and this allows you to recall when and where you saw (or heard) that item. What about familiarity? In this case, effortful encoding, with attention paid to relationships, is not crucial. Instead, sheer exposure to a stimulus, or rote rehearsal, seems to be enough (e.g., Dobbins, Kroll, & Yonelinas, 2004). But what does this exposure accomplish? What "record" does it leave in memory? The answers to these questions turn out to be complicated, and they require some discussion of a very different sort of "memory."

Implicit Memory

It's clear that some stimuli—a face that you see, a song that you hear, a scent that reaches your nose—instantly seem familiar to you. You're sure you've encountered the stimulus before; you know that it is somehow connected to your past. But what leads to this subjective sense of familiarity? As we'll see, our best path toward this issue begins with cases in which stimuli *are* familiar (i.e., they are part of your past) but don't *feel* familiar.

Memory Without Awareness

How can we find out if someone remembers a previous event? The obvious path is to ask her: "How did the job interview go?"; "Have you ever seen *Casablanca*?"; "Is this the man who robbed you?" But as an alternative, we can expose someone to an event, then later reexpose her to the same event, and assess whether her response on the second encounter is different from the first. Specifically, we can ask whether the first encounter somehow primed the person—got her ready—for the second exposure. If so, it would seem that the person must retain some record of the first encounter— she must have some sort of memory.

In a number of studies, participants have been asked to read through a list of words, with no indication that their memories would be tested later on. (They might be told, for example, that they're merely checking the list for spelling errors.) Then, sometime later, the participants are given a **lexical-decision task**: They are shown a series of letter strings ("star," "lamb," "nire") and, for each, must indicate (by pressing one button or another) whether the string is a word in English or not. And, of course, some of the letter strings in the lexical decision task are duplicates of the words seen in the first part of the experiment (i.e., the words were on the list they checked for spelling), allowing us to ask whether this first exposure somehow primed the participants for the second encounter.

The result of such experiments is clear (e.g., Oliphant, 1983): Lexical decisions are appreciably quicker if the person has recently seen the test word; that is, lexical decision shows a pattern of **repetition priming**. Remarkably, this priming is observed even when participants have no recollection for having encountered the stimulus words before. To demonstrate this, we can show participants a list of words and then test them in two different ways. One test assesses memory directly and uses a standard recognition procedure: "Which of these words were on the list I showed you earlier?" The other test is indirect and relies on lexical decision: "Which of these letter strings form real words?" In this setup, the two tests will often yield different results. At a sufficient delay, the direct memory test is likely to show that the participants have completely forgotten the words presented earlier; their recognition performance is essentially random. According to the lexical-decision results, however, they still remember the words perfectly well—and so they show a robust priming effect. In this situation, then, participants seem to have no conscious memory of having seen the stimulus words, but they are nonetheless influenced by the earlier experience.

Other procedures show similar effects: In some studies, participants have been asked to read a list of words aloud and then later have been given a test of tachistoscopic recognition; their task here is simply to identify each word—to say what the word is (Jacoby, 1983; also Jacoby & Dallas, 1981; Winnick & Daniel, 1970). Unbeknownst to the participants, some of the words shown tachistoscopically had also been presented during the procedure's initial phase; other words were novel (i.e., had not been recently viewed). Our question is whether this earlier exposure will influence performance.

Again, the result is clear. With tachistoscopic testing, performance is considerably improved if participants have recently viewed the test word, and again, this benefit does not depend on conscious recollection: Participants show the repetition priming effect even for words that (when we ask them directly) they cannot recall seeing on the earlier list. So here, too, participants are being influenced by a specific past experience that they seem (consciously) not to remember at all—a pattern that some researchers refer to as "memory without awareness."

One last example draws on a task called **word-stem completion**. In this task, people are given three or four letters and must produce a word with this beginning. If, for example, they are given "CLA-", then "clam," "class," or "clatter" would all be acceptable responses, and the question of interest for us is which of these the person produces. It turns out (in line with the other results in this section) that people are more likely to offer a specific word if they've encountered it recently, and once again, this priming effect is observed even if participants, when tested directly, show no conscious memory of their recent encounter with that word (Graf, Mandler, & Haden, 1982).

Results like these lead psychologists to distinguish two types of memory (for reviews, see Richardson-Klavehn & Bjork, 1988; Schacter, 1987). **Explicit memories** are those usually revealed by **direct memory testing**—testing that specifically urges you to remember the past. Recall is a direct memory test; so is the standard recognition test. **Implicit memories**, however, are those typically revealed by **indirect memory testing** and are often manifested as priming effects. In this form of testing, your current behavior is demonstrably influenced by a prior event, but you

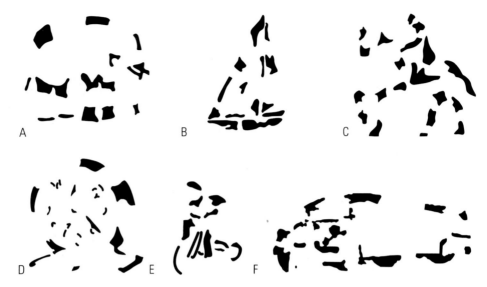

More Memory Without Awareness
Memory without awareness can be detected in many settings. These six figures show familiar objects, but they are difficult to identify. If you have seen (and identified) the figures at some point in the past, however, you are likely to have an easy time identifying them now. This will be true even if you have no conscious recollection of having seen the figures before—one more illustration of implicit memory in the absence of explicit memory. (We'll identify the figures at the chapter's end.)

may be quite unaware of this. Tachistoscopic recognition, lexical decision, word-stem completion, and many other tasks provide indirect means of assessing memory.

What exactly is implicit memory? How is implicit memory different from explicit memory? We will have more to say about these questions before we are done; first, though, we need to say more about how implicit memory *feels* from the rememberer's point of view. This will then lead us back into our discussion of familiarity and source memory.

False Fame

Jacoby, Kelley, Brown, and Jasechko (1989) presented participants with a list of names to read out loud. The participants were told nothing about a memory test; they thought the experiment was concerned with how they pronounced the names. Some time later, the participants were given the second step of the procedure. They were shown a new list of names and asked to rate each person on this list according to how famous each was. The list included some real, very famous people; some real but not-so-famous people; and also some fictional names. Crucially, the fictional names were of two types: Some were names that had occurred on the prior ("pronunciation") list, and some were simply new names. A comparison between those two types will tell us how the prior familiarization (during the pronunciation task) influenced the judgments of fame.

For some participants, the "famous" list was presented right after the "pronunciation" list; for other participants, there was a 24-hour delay between these two steps. To see how this delay matters, imagine yourself in the place of a participant in the immediate-testing condition: When you see one of the fictional-but-familiar names, you might decide, "This name sounds familiar, but that's because I just saw it on the previous list." In this case, you have a feeling that the (familiar) name is distinctive, but you also realize why it is distinctive, because you remember your earlier encounter with the name. Therefore, there's nothing here to persuade you that the name belongs to someone famous, and you respond accordingly. But now imagine that you're a participant in the other condition, with the 24-hour delay. Thanks to this time span, you may not recall the earlier episode of seeing the name in the pronunciation task. Nonetheless, the broad sense of familiarity remains, and so in this setting you might say, "This name rings a bell, and I have no idea why. I guess this must be a famous person." And this is indeed the pattern of the data: When the two lists are presented one day apart, the participants are likely to rate the made-up names as being famous.

Apparently, the participants in this study noted (correctly) that some of the names did "ring a bell" and so did have a certain feeling of familiarity. The false judgments of fame, however, come from the way the participants *interpreted* this feeling and what conclusions they drew from it. To put it simply, participants in the 24-hour-delay condition forgot the real source of the familiarity (appearance on a recently viewed list) and instead filled in a bogus source ("Maybe I saw this person in a movie?"). And it's not hard to see why they made this particular misattribution. After all, the experiment was described to them as being about fame, and other names on the list were indeed those of famous people. From the participants' point of view, therefore, it is a reasonable inference under these circumstances that any name that "rings a bell" belongs to a famous person.

This misattribution is possible, however, only because the feeling of familiarity produced by these names was relatively vague, and so open to interpretation. The suggestion, then, is that implicit memories may leave people only with a broad sense that a stimulus is somehow distinctive—that it "rings a bell" or "strikes a chord." What happens after this depends on how they interpret that feeling.

Implicit Memory and the "Illusion of Truth"

How broad is this potential for *mis*interpreting an implicit memory? Participants in one study heard a series of statements and had to judge how interesting each statement was (Begg, Anas, & Farinacci, 1992). As an example, one sentence was, "The average person in Switzerland eats about 25 pounds of cheese each year." (This is false; the average is closer to 18 pounds.) Another was, "Henry Ford forgot to put a reverse gear in his first automobile." (This is true.) After hearing these sentences, the participants were presented with some more sentences, but now they had to judge the credibility of these sentences, rating them on a scale from *certainly true* to *certainly false*. Needless to say, some of the sentences in this "truth test" were repeats from the earlier presentation; the question of interest is how sentence credibility is influenced by sentence familiarity.

The result was a propagandist's dream: Sentences heard before were more likely to be accepted as true; that is, familiarity increased credibility (Begg, Armour, & Kerr, 1985; A. S. Brown & Halliday, 1990; Fiedler, Walther, Armbruster, Fay, & Naumann, 1996; Hasher, Goldstein, & Toppino, 1977; Moons, Mackie, & Garcia-Marques, 2009; Unkelbach, 2007). To make things worse, this effect emerged even when the participants were explicitly warned in advance not to believe the sentences in the first list. In one procedure, participants were told that half of the statements had been made by men and half by women. The women's statements, they were told, were always true; the men's, always false. (Half the participants were told the reverse.) Then participants rated how interesting the sentences were, with each sentence attributed either to a man or to a woman: "Frank Foster says that house mice can run an average of 4 miles per hour" or "Gail Logan says that crocodiles sleep with their eyes open." Later, participants were presented with more sentences and had to judge their truth, with these new sentences including the earlier assertions about mice, crocodiles, and so forth.

Let's focus on the sentences initially identified as being false—in our example, Frank's claim about mice. If someone explicitly remembers this sentence ("Oh yes— Frank said such and such"), then he should judge the assertion to be false ("After all, the experimenter said that the men's statements were all lies"). But what about someone without this explicit memory? Since the person doesn't remember whether the assertion came from a man or a woman, he can't use the source as a basis for judging the sentence's veracity. Nonetheless, the person might still have an implicit memory for the sentence left over from the earlier exposure ("Gee, that statement rings a bell"), and this might increase the credibility of the statement ("I'm sure I've heard that somewhere before; I guess it must be true"). This is exactly the pattern of the data: Statements plainly identified as false when they were first heard still created the so-called **illusion of truth**; that is, these statements were subsequently judged to be more credible than sentences never heard before.

The relevance of this result to the political arena, or to advertising, should be clear. A newspaper headline inquires, "Is Mayor Wilson a crook?" Or perhaps the headline declares, "Known criminal claims Wilson is a crook!" In either case, the assertion that Wilson is a crook has now become familiar. The Begg et al. data indicate that this familiarity will, by itself, increase the likelihood that you'll later believe in Wilson's dishonesty. This will be true even if the paper merely raised the question; it will be true even if the allegation came from a disreputable source. Malicious innuendo does in fact work nasty effects (Wegner, Wenzlaff, Kerker, & Beattie, 1981).

innoculate	vs.	inoculate?
embarrass	vs.	embarass?
argument	vs.	arguement?
harass	vs.	harrass?
cemetery	vs.	cemetary?
mispell	vs.	misspell?

Familiarity and Spelling

In deciding how to spell a word, people often write out the word, then ask, "Does this look right?" This is a good strategy, but if you have regularly encountered the misspelled version of the word, these encounters will make that spelling "look right." As a result, regular encounters with the *wrong* spelling can make that spelling look right to you. This will be true even if you have no recollection of those encounters—another example of implicit memory's influence.

Attributing Implicit Memory to the Wrong Stimulus

In both the illusion-of-truth and the false-fame experiments, participants are misinterpreting a sense of familiarity: They know that a name or a sentence is familiar, but they don't realize that this is because it was on the previous list. Instead, they falsely conclude that the name is familiar because it belongs to someone famous or that the sentence is familiar because they read it in some authoritative source.

In other cases, the misinterpretation can go even further. In one experiment, participants were presented with bursts of noise and asked to judge how loud each noise was (Jacoby, Allan, Collins, & Larwill, 1988). Embedded within each burst of noise, though, was a sentence. Some of the sentences were new to participants, but—crucially—some of the sentences had been presented earlier.

In this study, memory appeared in an odd way. If a sentence was one of the previously presented ones, participants had an easier time hearing it against the backdrop of noise. This is just another case of repetition priming and so is consistent with results already described. But then the participants seemed to reason in this fashion: "Well, that sentence was easy to hear. I guess, therefore, the noise couldn't have been so loud." Likewise, for the unfamiliar sentences, they seemed to reason like this: "Gee, that noise must have been loud, since it really drowned out the sentence." As a result of these (completely unconscious) inferences, a noise that contained familiar sentences was (mis)perceived as being softer than it actually was. Noise containing novel sentences was (mis)perceived as being loud.

In this experiment, therefore, the participants seemed not to realize at all that the previously presented sentences were, in fact, familiar. All they realized is that it was easier to perceive the sentences in one condition than it was in the other, and they mistakenly attributed this difference to differing noise levels. In other words, it was the sentences that were (objectively) familiar, but there was no subjective sense of familiarity. Indeed, the implicit memory didn't at all change how participants felt about the sentences. Instead, the memory showed its influence by changing how the participants felt about an entirely different stimulus—namely, the noise in which the sentences were embedded.

Attributing Implicit Memory to the Wrong Source

One last example will illustrate the range of cases in which we are influenced by misplaced familiarity, and it is an example of some consequence. In a study by E. Brown, Deffenbacher, and Sturgill (1977), research participants witnessed a staged crime. Two or 3 days later, they were shown "mug shots" of individuals who supposedly had participated in the crime; but as it turns out, the people in these photos were different from the actual "criminals"—no mug shots were shown for the truly "guilty" individuals. Finally, after 4 or 5 more days, the participants were shown a lineup of 4 persons and asked to select from this lineup the individuals seen in Step 1—namely, the original crime. (See color insert, Figure 15.)

The data in this study show a pattern known as **source confusion**. The participants correctly realized that one of the people in the lineup looked familiar, but they were confused about the source of the familiarity. They falsely believed they had seen the person's face in the original "crime," when, in truth, they'd seen that face only in a subsequent photograph. In fact, the likelihood of this error was quite high, with 29% of the participants (falsely) selecting from the lineup an individual they had seen only in the mug shots.

Does this sort of confusion happen outside of the laboratory? It certainly does. One example comes from a court case in England in which a crime victim confidently identified a sailor as the person who had robbed him. The sailor, however, was able to prove that at the time of the crime he was many miles away. How did this mistaken identification arise? It turns out that the crime victim was a ticket agent in a train station, and the sailor had on several prior occasions purchased tickets at this station. It seems, therefore, that the ticket-seller correctly realized that the sailor's face was familiar but (unwittingly) drew the wrong conclusion about why the face was familiar (D. F. Ross, Ceci, Dunning, & Toglia, 1994). Similar examples are easy to find—both in the laboratory and in real-world examples.

Theoretical Treatments of Implicit Memory

One message coming from all of these studies is that we are often better at remembering *that* something is familiar than we are at remembering *why* it is familiar. This is why it's possible to have a sense of familiarity with no source memory ("I've seen her somewhere before, but I can't figure out where!"), and also why it's possible to be correct in judging familiarity but mistaken in judging source. The latter pattern was evident in many of the examples we have just considered, and in other cases as well (e.g., Anand & Sternthal, 1991; Peretz, Gaudreau, & Bonnel, 1998; Seamon et al., 1995; Zajonc, 1980).

In addition, it is important that in many of these studies the participants are being influenced by memories they are not aware of. In some cases, participants realize that a stimulus is somehow familiar, but they have no memory of the encounter that produced the familiarity. In other cases, people don't even have a sense of familiarity for the target stimulus; nonetheless, they're influenced by their previous encounter with the stimulus. We saw this pattern in the experiment involving noise judgments; other experiments show that participants often *prefer* a previously presented stimulus over a novel stimulus, even though they have no sense of familiarity with either stimulus. In such cases, people don't realize at all that their preference is being guided by memory (S. T. Murphy, 2001).

It does seem, then, that the phrase "memory without awareness" really is appropriate, and it does seem sensible to describe these memories as *implicit* memories. But what exactly are implicit memories? What is the content of these memories? It is to these questions that we now turn.

Implicit Memory: A Hypothesis

We argued in Chapter 4 that perceiving a stimulus causes changes in your visual system, and these changes actually make it easier to perceive the same stimulus the next time you meet it. The initial exposure raises the activation level of the relevant detectors, and this makes it easier to fire these detectors in the future. The exposure also strengthens the connections linking one detector to the next, so that communication between detectors is improved. In both of these ways, each opportunity to perceive a stimulus increases the *fluency* with which you'll recognize that stimulus on the next encounter.

Presumably, though, the same can be said for other bits of intellectual performance: Just as *perceiving* a word leads to fluency in perceiving, perhaps *thinking about the word's meaning* leads to fluency of a parallel sort. The next time you contemplate the same word's meaning, you might be a little quicker or more efficient.

The suggestion for us to consider, therefore, is that implicit memory may be a direct consequence of these practice effects and, more specifically, may be a direct reflection of the increase in **processing fluency** that results from this practice. Consider, for example, implicit memory's effect on tachistoscopic identification or on lexical decisions. These tasks require little more than the identification of the presented stimuli, and so these tasks would benefit directly from anything that speeds up processing. Thus, when we say these tasks are influenced by implicit memory, we're simply acknowledging the fact that once a stimulus has been perceived it will be easier to perceive the next time around.

To explain other implicit-memory effects, though, we need a further assumption—namely, that people are sensitive to the *degree* of processing fluency. That is, people know when they have perceived easily and when they have perceived only by expending more effort. They likewise know when a sequence of thoughts was particularly fluent and when the sequence was labored. This fluency, however, is perceived in an odd way. When a stimulus is easy to perceive (for example), people do not experience something like, "That stimulus sure was easy to recognize!" Instead, they merely register a vague sense of specialness. They feel that the stimulus "rings a bell." No matter how it is described, though, our hypothesis is that this sense of specialness has a simple cause—namely, ease in processing, brought on by fluency, which in turn was created by practice.[1]

We still need one more step in our hypothesis, but it is a step we have already introduced: When a stimulus feels special, people typically want to know why. Thus, the vague, hard-to-pinpoint feeling of specialness (again, produced by fluency) triggers an attribution process, as people seek to ask, "Why did that stimulus stand out?" In many circumstances, that question will be answered correctly, and so the specialness will be (correctly) interpreted as *familiarity* and attributed to the correct source. ("That picture seems distinctive, and I know why—it's the same picture I saw yesterday in the dentist's office.") In other situations, though, things may not go so smoothly, and so—as we have seen—people sometimes misinterpret their own processing fluency, falling prey to the errors and illusions we have been discussing.

In addition, people can detect *decreases* in their own processing fluency, as well as increases. Imagine that someone you know well changes her hairstyle or gets new eyeglasses. In such cases, you often have the uncomfortable feeling that something in your friend's appearance has changed, but you can't figure out what it is. In our terms, your friend's face was a stimulus that you had seen often, and therefore a stimulus you were fluent in perceiving. Once the stimulus is changed, however, your well-practiced steps of perceiving don't run as smoothly as they have in the past, and so the perception is less fluent than it had been. This lack of fluency is detected and gives you the "something is new" feeling. But then the attribution step fails: You cannot identify what produced this feeling (and so you end up offering various lame hypotheses: "Did you lose weight?" when, in fact, it's the eyeglasses that are new). This case therefore provides the mirror image of the cases we have been considering, in which familiarity leads to an *increase* in fluency, so that something "rings a bell" but you cannot say why.

---

[1]Actually, what people detect, and what makes a stimulus feel "special," may not be fluency per se. Instead, what they detect may be a *discrepancy* between how easy (or hard) it was to carry out some mental step and how easy (or hard) they expected it to be, in light of the context and their experience. (See, for example, Whittlesea, 2002.) A stimulus is registered as distinctive, or "rings a bell," when this discrepancy reaches too high a level. Having acknowledged this, however, we will, for simplicity's sake, ignore this complication in our discussion.

The Nature of Familiarity

All of these points provide us—at last—with a proposal for what "familiarity" is, and the proposal is surprisingly complex. One might think that familiarity is a feeling produced more or less directly when you encounter a stimulus you have met before. The findings of the last few sections, though, point toward a different proposal—namely, that "familiarity" is more like a *conclusion that you draw* rather than a *feeling* triggered by a stimulus. Specifically, the evidence suggests that a stimulus will seem familiar whenever the following list of requirements is met: First, you have encountered the stimulus before. Second, because of that prior encounter (and the "practice" it afforded), you are now faster and more efficient in your processing of that stimulus; that's what we're calling "processing fluency." Third, you detect that fluency, and this leads you to register the stimulus as somehow distinctive or special. Fourth, you reach a particular decision about that specialness—namely, that the stimulus has this distinctive quality *because* it is a stimulus you have met before in some prior episode. And then, finally, you draw a conclusion about when and where you encountered the stimulus—in the experimenter's list of words, or yesterday in the newspaper, and so on.

Let's be clear, though, that none of these steps happens consciously; you're not aware of seeking an interpretation or trying to explain why a stimulus feels distinctive. All you experience consciously is the end product of all these steps: the sense that a stimulus feels familiar. Moreover, this conclusion about a stimulus isn't one you draw capriciously; instead, you draw this conclusion, and decide a stimulus is familiar, only when you have supporting information. Thus, imagine that you encounter a stimulus that "rings a bell." You're certainly more likely to decide the stimulus is familiar if you also have an (explicit) source memory, so that you can recollect where and when you last encountered that stimulus ("I know this stimulus is familiar *because I can remembering seeing it yesterday*"). You're also more likely to decide a stimulus is familiar if the surrounding circumstances support it: If you are asked, for example, "Which of these words were on the list you saw earlier?" then the question itself gives you a cue that some of the words were recently encountered, and so you're more likely to attribute fluency to that encounter.

The fact remains, though, that judgments of familiarity can go astray, which is why we need this complicated theory. We have considered several cases in which a stimulus is objectively familiar (you've seen it recently) but does not *feel* familiar—just as our theory predicts. In these cases, you detect the fluency but attribute it to some other source ("The noise is soft" rather than "The sentence is familiar," or "That melody is lovely" rather than "The melody is familiar"). In other words, you go through all of the steps shown in the top of Figure 6.4 except for the last two: You do not attribute the fluency to a specific prior event, and so you do not experience a sense of familiarity.

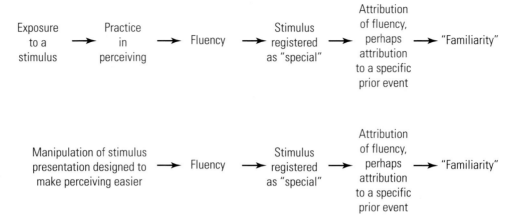

FIGURE 6.4 The Chain of Events Leading to the Sense of "Familiarity"
In the top line, practice in perceiving leads to fluency, and if the person attributes the fluency to some specific prior encounter, the stimulus will "feel familiar." The *bottom* line, however, indicates that fluency can be created in other ways: by presenting the stimulus more clearly or for a longer exposure. Once this fluency is detected, though, it can lead to steps identical to those in the top row. Hence, an "illusion of familiarity" can be created.

We can also find the opposite sort of case—in which a stimulus is not familiar (i.e., you've not seen it recently) but feels familiar anyhow—and this, too, fits with the theory. This sort of *illusion of familiarity* can be produced, for example, if the processing of a completely novel stimulus is more fluent than you expected—perhaps because the stimulus follows a pattern you've seen before, or because you've been (unconsciously) primed for the stimulus (Jacoby & Whitehouse, 1989; Whittlesea, 2002; Whittlesea, Jacoby, & Girard, 1990). In cases like these, we have the situation shown in the bottom half of Figure 6.4, and as our theory predicts, these situations do produce an illusion: Your processing of the stimulus is unexpectedly fluent; you seek an attribution for this fluency, and you are fooled into thinking the stimulus is familiar—and so you say you've seen the stimulus before, when in fact you haven't. This illusion is surely a powerful confirmation that the sense of familiarity does rest on processes like the ones we've described. (For more on fluency, see Hertwig, Herzog, Schooler, & Reimer, 2008; Oppenheimer, 2008. For a glimpse of what fluency amounts to in the nervous system, see Knowlton & Foerde, 2008.)

Memory and Familiarity: An Interim Summary

Before moving on, let's pause to put the last few sections into proper context. There can be no question that we are often influenced by the past without being aware of that influence. We often respond differently to familiar stimuli than we do to novel stimuli, even if we have no subjective feeling of familiarity. Thus, our conscious recollection seriously underestimates what is in our memories, and it seems certain that we have only begun to document the ways in which unconscious memories influence what we do, think, and feel. (For example, see Coates, Butler, & Berry, 2006, for an exploration of implicit memory's role in guiding consumer choice; for an exploration of priming effects that result from seeing items on a multiple-choice test, see Roediger & Marsh, 2005; for a discussion of memory's influence on spelling errors, see Jacoby & Hollingshead, 1990. And so on!)

In addition, the evidence is clearly telling us that there are at least two different kinds of memory: one typically conscious and deliberate, one typically unconscious and automatic. It turns out that there has been disagreement about how we should define these two types of memory, but there is no disagreement about the need for some distinction, some categorization scheme.

In fact, two further lines of evidence also speak to the need to distinguish these categories of memory. One, which we'll simply mention, involves the attempt to chart memory performance across the life span. Many studies are pertinent to this point, but in general the pattern is that implicit memory can be documented at all ages, from very early childhood to very old age. Indeed, what is remarkable is the similarity in implicit-memory performance by people at very different ages. Performance on explicit-memory tasks, in contrast, is strongly age-dependent, with children and the elderly both outperformed by those in their middle years (Graf & Masson, 1993; N. S. Newcombe, Drummey, Fox, Lie, & Ottinger-Alberts, 2000). These observations add to the evidence that a distinction is needed here, with the memory systems distinguishable developmentally as well as functionally.

The distinction is also demanded by clinical evidence—in particular, evidence from cases of brain damage. Let's take a look at that evidence.

Amnesia

A variety of injuries or illnesses can lead to a loss of memory, or **amnesia**. Some forms of amnesia are *retrograde*, meaning that they disrupt memory for things learned prior to the event that initiated the amnesia. **Retrograde amnesia** is often caused, for example, by blows to the head; often one is unable to recall events occurring just prior to the blow. Other forms of amnesia have the reverse effect, causing disruption of memory for experiences *after* the onset of amnesia; these are cases of **anterograde amnesia**. (We should note that many cases of amnesia have both retrograde and anterograde memory loss.) Here we will focus on anterograde amnesia; as we will see, this form of memory loss can tell us a great deal about the issues we have been discussing. (For more on retrograde amnesia, see A. S. Brown, 2002; M. Conway & Fthenaki, 1999; Kapur, 1999; Kopelman & Kapur, 2001; Nadel & Moscovitch, 2001; Riccio, Millin, & Gisquet-Verrier, 2003.)

We discussed a famous case of anterograde amnesia in Chapter 1: the patient H.M. (For a review of H.M.'s case, see Milner, 1966, 1970; for more recent studies, see O'Kane, Kensinger, & Corkin, 2004; Skotko et al., 2004.) H.M. suffered from profound epilepsy, and a variety of attempts at curing him had all failed. As a last resort, doctors sought to contain H.M.'s disorder by brain surgery, specifically by removing portions of the brain that seemed to be the source of the seizures. The surgery was, in a very narrow sense, a success, because it did improve the epilepsy. But more broadly the surgery was a disaster, because the cure for epilepsy came at an incredible cost: H.M. was now unable to learn anything new.

H.M. could function normally in some regards and could, for example, hold a coherent, meaningful conversation. Within the conversation, he would even talk about prior events in his life, since he was fully able to recall events that took place *prior to* the surgery. However, he could not recall anything that had taken place since the surgery. Episodes he had experienced, people he had met, books he had read—all seemed to leave no enduring record, as though nothing new could get into his long-term storage.

The severity of H.M.'s amnesia was evident in many ways, but the problem became instantly clear if a conversation with him was interrupted for some reason: If you spoke with him for a while, then (for example) left the room and came back 3 or 4 minutes later, H.M. seemed to have totally forgotten that the earlier conversation ever took place; if the earlier conversation was your first meeting with H.M., he would, after the interruption, be quite certain he was now meeting you for the very first time.

H.M.'s case was unique, but a similar amnesia can be found in patients who have been longtime alcoholics. The problem is not the alcohol itself; the problem instead is that alcoholics tend to have inadequate diets, getting most of their nutrition from whatever they are drinking. It turns out, though, that most alcoholic beverages are missing several key nutrients, including vitamin B_1 (thiamine). As a result, longtime alcoholics are vulnerable to a number of problems caused by thiamine deficiency, including a disorder known as **Korsakoff's syndrome** (Rao, Larkin, & Derr, 1986; Ritchie, 1985).

A patient suffering from Korsakoff's syndrome seems in many ways similar to H.M. There is typically little problem in remembering events that took place before the onset of alcoholism. Current topics can also be maintained in the mind as long as there is no interruption. New information, though, if displaced from the mind, is seemingly lost forever. Korsakoff's patients who have been in the hospital for decades will casually mention that they arrived only a week ago; if asked the name of the current president or events in the news, they unhesitatingly give answers appropriate for two or three decades back, whenever the disorder began (Marslen-Wilson & Teuber, 1975; Seltzer & Benson, 1974).

Learning From Amnesia

These cases of amnesia can teach us a great deal about memory. For example, what is the biological basis for memory? A partial answer comes from the fact that amnesia is typically associated with damage that involves the hippocampus and neighboring brain areas; this implies that these brain sites play a crucial role in memory. Let us be clear, though, that the evidence does not imply that the hippocampus is the "seat" of memory in the brain. We know this because damage to the hippocampus does not disrupt already-established memories. (Hippocampus damage is associated with *anterograde* amnesia, not retrograde.) Instead, the hippocampus plays its main role in memory acquisition, such that with hippocampal damage H.M. and the Korsakoff's patients seem unable to create *new* memories.

The study of amnesia can also provide important lessons about the function of memory in our daily lives. As one illustration, consider again the patient H.M. We mentioned that he can function normally in some arenas: He can, for example, hold a reasonable conversation. But he is also limited in profound ways. If, for example, in the midst of a conversation H.M. notices that the other person is smiling, he often does not know why. Was there a funny joke in the conversation a moment ago? Or did someone say something embarrassing? Or is it a smile of sympathy because someone said something sad? Because of this sort of ambiguity, H.M. lives with a constant sense of awkwardness: "Right now, I'm wondering, have I done or said anything amiss? You see, at this moment everything looks clear to me, but what happened just before? That's what worries me" (a quote from H.M. in Hilts, 1995, p. 138). Examples like this make it clear what a crucial role memory plays in many settings—including our everyday social interactions. (For further discussion of memory's role in our lives, see Chapters 1 and 7.)

The study of amnesia can also help us with a number of theoretical questions—including questions that were before us a few pages back, such as the nature of familiarity and the contrast between implicit and explicit memory.

Another Look at Amnesia: What Kind of Memory Is Disrupted?

Patients suffering from anterograde amnesia can remember events from before the amnesia's start, suggesting that there is nothing wrong with their long-term memories. The patients also seem to have intact working memories; that is how they remember events as they think about them. In H.M.'s case, for example, these intact parts of his memory are what allowed him to participate in a normal conversation: As long as the conversation was coherent and uninterrupted, he could maintain the stream of ideas in his intact working memory. It's only when there was an abrupt shift in topic or an interruption, pushing the earlier conversation out of working memory, that he needed to draw on long-term storage, and then his amnesia became fully evident.

What, then, is the problem with amnesic patients? For many years, their amnesia was described as a "disconnection syndrome." The idea was that their problem was lodged in the *connection* between working memory and long-term memory, so that they were unable to move information from working memory into long-term storage. That is why no new memories could be established.

Other evidence, though, demands significant revision in this account of amnesia, and some of the evidence has been available for a long time. In 1911, Édouard Claparède (1911/1951) reported the following incident. He was introduced to a young woman suffering from Korsakoff's amnesia, and he reached out to shake the patient's hand. However, Claparède had secretly positioned a pin in his own hand so that when they clasped hands the patient received a painful pinprick. (Respect for patient's rights would prevent any modern physician from conducting this cruel experiment, but ethical standards for physicians were apparently different in 1911.) The next day, Claparède returned and reached out to shake hands with the patient. Not surprisingly for someone with Korsakoff's amnesia, the patient initially gave no indication that she recognized Claparède or remembered anything about the prior encounter. Nevertheless, when the time came to clasp hands, the patient at the last moment abruptly withdrew her hand and would not shake hands with Claparède. Claparède asked her why, and after some confusion the patient simply said vaguely that "sometimes pins are hidden in people's hands."

This patient seemed to have no explicit memory of the prior encounter with Claparède. She did not mention the encounter in explaining her refusal to shake hands; if questioned closely about the prior encounter, she indicated no knowledge of it. Nonetheless, some sort of memory was retained. The patient knew something about the previous day's mishap but could not report on the knowledge.

This peculiar kind of remembering can be demonstrated with Korsakoff's patients in many other ways. In one experiment, Korsakoff's patients were asked a series of trivia questions (Schacter, Tulving, & Wang, 1981). For each question, possible answers were offered in a multiple-choice format, and the patient had to choose which was the right answer. If the patient did not know the answer, he was told it, and then (unbeknownst to the patient) the question was replaced in the stack. Sometime later, therefore, as the game continued, the question came up again, and this time the patient was quite likely to get it right. Apparently, the patient had "learned" the answer in the previous encounter and "remembered" the relevant information. Consistent with their diagnosis, though, the patients had no recollection of the learning: They were consistently unable to explain why their answers were correct. They did not say, "I know this bit of trivia because the same question came up just five minutes ago." Instead, they were likely to say things like, "I read about it somewhere" or "My sister once told me about it."

A different experiment makes a similar point. In a procedure by Johnson, Kim, and Risse (1985), patients with Korsakoff's amnesia heard a series of brief melodies. A short time later, they were presented with a new series and told that some of the

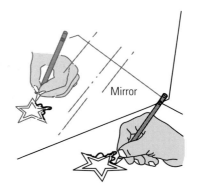

Preserved Learning in Patients with Amnesia

Anterograde amnesics (by definition) suffer from profound disruption in their explicit memories. Nonetheless, they do show many effects—and, in some cases, *benefits*—from their past experiences, indicating that they do have some form of memory. For example, patients can be trained to trace a figure that they can only see via its mirror reflection. This task is quite difficult, but the patients soon learn to do it—while all the while insisting that they have never seen this apparatus, or tried this task, before.

Mirror

tunes in the second batch were repeats from the earlier presentation. The amnesic patients' assignment was to tell which tunes were the repeats and which tunes they were hearing for the first time. As expected, these patients did poorly on this task; indeed, their memory responses were close to random. This result is, of course, consistent with their clinical diagnosis. Remarkably, though, when asked which melodies they *preferred*, the amnesic patients uniformly preferred the familiar ones. The patients had no (explicit) memory for these tunes, but a memory did emerge with indirect testing—it emerged, in this case, as a preference.

A great many studies show similar results, with amnesic patients showing profound memory loss on some measures but looking perfectly normal on other measures (N. J. Cohen & Squire, 1980; Graf & Schacter, 1985; Moscovitch, 1982; Schacter, 1996; Schacter & Tulving, 1982; Squire & McKee, 1993). Thus, on the one hand, these patients seem completely incapable of recalling episodes or events. In the terms we have been using, these patients seem to have no "explicit memory." On the other hand, these patients do learn and do remember; they seem to have intact "implicit memories." Indeed, in many tests of implicit memory, amnesic patients seem indistinguishable from ordinary individuals.

Explicit Memory Without Implicit?

The results with amnesic patients, therefore, add to the package of evidence we have been considering in this chapter. In particular, these patients provide powerful evidence that explicit memory is truly independent of implicit memory, with these patients plainly influenced (implicitly) by specific episodes in the past even though they have no conscious (explicit) recollection of the episodes.

Further data, also arguing for a separation between implicit and explicit memory, come from patients who have the reverse pattern of symptoms: implicit memory disrupted but explicit memory intact. This provides us with a so-called **double dissociation**—telling us that it's possible to interfere with explicit memory while sparing implicit, and that it's also possible to disrupt implicit memory while sparing explicit. This pattern of evidence tells us that these memory systems are indeed separate from each other. (For some reservations about this dissociation in the clinical data, though, see Aggleton & Brown, 2006.)

One study involved a patient who had suffered brain damage to the hippocampus but not the amygdala; another patient in the study had the reverse problem—damage to the amygdala but not the hippocampus (Bechara et al., 1995). These patients were exposed to a series of trials in which a particular stimulus (a blue light) was reliably followed by a loud boat horn, while other stimuli (green, yellow, or red) were not followed by the horn. Later on, the patients were exposed to the blue light on its own and their bodily arousal was measured; would they show a fright reaction in response to this stimulus? In addition, the patients were asked directly, "Which color was followed by the horn?"

The patient with damage to the hippocampus did show a fear reaction to the blue light, but when asked directly, he could not explicitly recall which of the lights had been associated with the boat horn. In contrast, the patient with damage to the amygdala showed exactly the opposite pattern. He was able to report calmly that just one of the lights had been associated with the horn, and that the light's color had been blue—demonstrating fully intact explicit memory. When presented with the blue light, however, he showed no fear response.

Related evidence comes from a patient who had damage to his occipital lobe in areas crucial for vision (Gabrieli, Fleischman, Keane, Reminger, & Morell, 1995). The patient was first shown a list of words and then tested in two different ways. In one test, the words were mixed together with new words, and the patient had to judge which words were old and which were new. In the other test, the words were presented tachistoscopically, and the question was whether the words shown earlier would be more easily identified. The results were clear-cut: In the test of explicit recognition memory, the patient performed normally; in the tachistoscopic task, however, the patient showed no evidence of repetition priming.

In both of these studies, therefore, we find evidence of diminished implicit memory (no fear response in the first study, no priming in the second), even though the patients have normal explicit memories. This is the mirror image of the pattern shown by H.M. and Korsakoff's patients, and it makes it clear that explicit and implicit memory are indeed independent from each other.

Optimal Learning

Let's put these brain-damage findings into the broader context provided by the main themes of this chapter. Throughout the chapter, we've argued that we cannot make claims about learning or memory acquisition without some reference to how the learning is going to be used later on or how the memories are going to be retrieved.

This is because we've seen, over and over, that learning that prepares you well for one sort of memory retrieval may be worthless as preparation for a different sort of retrieval. Learning that will allow you, later on, to remember well in one situation may not allow you to remember at all in a different setting. Learning that prepares you for an explicit memory test may not prepare you for an implicit test, and vice versa.

This theme is echoed in the neuropsychology data. More specifically, it would be too coarse to say that amnesia (or brain damage more generally) entirely disrupts the capacity to acquire new memories. Instead, some forms of brain damage make it difficult to acquire explicit memories; and some, implicit memories. Therefore, the nature of the disruption again depends on how the memories will be used later on, how they will be retrieved.

These points are enormously important for our theorizing about memory, but the same points also have a powerful practical implication. Right now, you are reading this material and presumably want to remember the material later on. For that matter, you are also encountering new material in other settings (perhaps in other classes you are taking), and surely you want to remember this as well. How should you study all of this information if you want to maximize your chances of retaining it for later use?

At one level, the lesson of this chapter might be that the ideal form of learning is one that is "aligned with" the approach to the material that you'll need later. If later on you'll be tested explicitly, you want to learn the material in a fashion that prepares you for that form of retrieval. If later on you'll be tested underwater or while listening to music, then, again, you want to learn the material in a way that prepares you for that context and the mental perspective it produces. If later on you'll need source memory, then you want one type of preparation; if later on you'll instead need familiarity, you might want a different type of preparation.

The problem, though, is that during learning you often don't know how you'll be approaching the material later—whether your focus during retrieval will be on meaning or on sound, whether you'll need the information implicitly or explicitly, and so on. As a result, maybe the best strategy in learning would be to employ *multiple perspectives*. To pick up an earlier analogy, imagine that you know that at some point in the future you'll want to reach Chicago, but you don't know yet whether you'll be approaching the city from the north, the south, or the west. In that case, your best bet might be to build multiple highways, so that you can reach your goal from any direction. Memory works the same way. If you initially think about a topic in different ways and in conjunction with many other ideas, then you will establish many paths leading to the target material, and so you'll be able to access that material from many different perspectives. The real pragmatic message from this chapter, then, is that this multiperspective approach may, in fact, provide the optimal learning strategy.

Chapter Summary

■ In general, the chances that someone will remember an earlier event are greatest if the physical and mental circumstances in place during memory retrieval match those in place during learning. This is reflected in the phenomenon of state-dependent learning, in which one is most likely to remember material learned while underwater if tested underwater, most likely to remember material learned while listening to music if again listening to music during the test, and so on.

■ In the same vein, if one focused on the meaning of some material while learning it, then hints concerned with meaning will be especially helpful when the time comes to recall the material. If one focused on the sound of the material during learning, then hints concerned with sound will be most helpful at the time of recall.

■ A similar pattern is reflected in the phenomenon of "encoding specificity." This term refers to the idea that one usually learns more than the specific material to be remembered itself; one also learns that material within its associated context.

■ All these results arise from the fact that learning establishes connections among memories, and these connections serve as retrieval paths. Like any path, these lead from some starting point to some target. To use the path, therefore, one must return to the appropriate starting point. In the same way, if there is a connection between two memories, then activating the first memory is likely to call the second to mind. If the first memory is not activated, however, this connection, no matter how well established, will not help in locating the second memory, just as a large highway approaching Chicago from the south will not be helpful if you are trying to reach Chicago from the north.

■ Likewise, some learning strategies are effective as preparation for some sorts of memory tests but ineffective for other sorts of tests. Some strategies, for example, are effective at establishing source memory rather than familiarity; other strategies do the reverse. Source memory is essential for recall; recognition can often be achieved either through source memory or through familiarity.

■ Different forms of learning also play a role in producing implicit and explicit memories. Implicit memories are those that influence us even when we have no awareness that we are being influenced by a specific previous event. In many cases, implicit-memory effects take the form of priming—for example, in tachistoscopic recognition or word-stem completion. But implicit memories can also influence us in other ways, producing a number of memory-based illusions.

■ Implicit memory may be the consequence of processing fluency, produced by experience in a particular task with a particular stimulus. The fluency is sometimes detected and registered as a sense of "specialness" attached to a stimulus. Often this specialness is then attributed to some cause, but this attribution can be inaccurate.

- Implicit memory is also important in understanding the pattern of symptoms in anterograde amnesia. Amnesic patients perform badly on tests requiring explicit memory and may not even recall events that happened just minutes earlier. However, they often perform at near-normal levels on tests involving implicit memory. This disparity underscores the fact that we cannot speak in general about good and bad memories, good and poor learning. Instead, learning and memory must be matched to a particular task and a particular form of test; learning and memory that are excellent for some tasks may be poor for others.

The Workbook Connection

See the *Cognition Workbook* for further exploration of interconnections between acquisition and retrieval:

- Demonstration 6.1: Retrieval Paths and Connections
- Demonstration 6.2: Encoding Specificity
- Demonstration 6.3: Priming Effects
- Research Methods: Double Dissociations
- Cognitive Psychology and Education: Familiarity Is Potentially Treacherous
- Cognitive Psychology and the Law: Unconscious Transference

The actors who appear on p. 176 are (top, from left) Jennifer Morrison, John Leguizamo, Dane Cook; (bottom, from left) Padma Lakshmi, Jeffrey Dean Morgan, and Regina Hall.

The six familiar figures on p. 180 are (A) an elephant, (B) a sailboat, (C) a horse and rider, (D) a clock, (E) a child riding a tricycle, and (F) a school bus.

Remembering Complex Events

In the last two chapters, we have said a great deal about how memory functions—how information enters storage in the first place, and then how the information is retrieved later. Almost all of the findings we have considered, though, come from studies that have used relatively simple materials: Research participants have been asked to memorize word lists or short sentences. We've probed memory for single pictures or brief bits of melody.

In our daily lives, however, we encounter much more complex materials. We encounter (and then try to remember) complicated episodes involving many actions and, often, many players. And, crucially, these episodes are integrated into the fabric of our lives: We come into these episodes already knowing things about the situation, then, afterward, we're likely to encounter other episodes and other information pertinent to the event we experienced initially.

How do these factors influence memory? What new principles do we need to include in our theories to deal with this added complexity? In this chapter, we will tackle this issue in two separate ways. First, we'll consider some of the *errors* that can arise when people try to remember episodes that are related to other things they know and have experienced. Second, we'll consider some of the factors that are directly pertinent to memory as it functions in day-to-day life. For example, we'll consider the impact of the *emotion* that is often part of an event, asking how it influences memory. We'll also consider the effect of *time*, asking how people remember events that happened years, or even decades, earlier.

- Outside the lab, we often try to remember materials that are related in some fashion to other things we know or have experienced. Over and over, we will see that this other knowledge, the knowledge we bring to a situation, helps us to remember by promoting retrieval, but it also hurts memory by promoting error.

- The memory errors produced by our prior knowledge tend to be quite systematic, and so we often end up recalling the past as more "normal," more in line with our expectations, than it actually was.

- Even if we acknowledge the memory errors, our overall assessment of memory can be quite positive. This is because our memories are accurate most of the time, and the errors that do occur can be understood as the by-products of mechanisms that generally serve us well.

- Finally, we will consider three factors that play an important role in shaping memory outside of the laboratory: our *involvement* with an event, *emotion*, and the *passage of time*. These factors require some additional principles as part of our overall theory, but they also confirm the power of more general principles—principles hinging (for example) on the role of memory connections.

Memory Errors, Memory Gaps

Where did you spend last summer? What country did you grow up in? Where were you 5 minutes ago? These are, of course, extremely easy questions. The sought-after information is in your memory, and you effortlessly retrieve the information the moment you need it. And the same is true for countless other bits of information; these, too, are at your fingertips, swiftly and easily recalled whenever you wish.

Simple observations like these testify to the breadth and efficiency of human memory, and if we want to understand memory, we need to understand how you locate these bits of information (and thousands of others just like them) so quickly and easily. But if we want to understand memory, we also need to account for some other observations. Sometimes, when you try to remember an episode, you simply draw a blank. And sometimes you recall something, but with no conviction that you're correct: "I think her nickname was Dink, but I'm not sure."

Sometimes, when you try to remember, things can go wrong in another way: You recall a past episode, but then it turns out that your memory is mistaken. Perhaps details of the event were different from the way you recall them. Or perhaps your memory is altogether wrong, misrepresenting large elements of the original episode. In some cases, you even remember entire events that never happened at all!

In this chapter, we'll consider all of these cases, including how, and how often, these errors arise. In tackling these themes, though, it will be helpful to start with some examples.

Memory Errors: Some Initial Examples

In 1992, an El Al cargo plane lost power in two of its engines just after taking off from Amsterdam's Schiphol Airport. The pilot attempted to return the plane to the airport but could not make it; a few minutes later, the plane crashed into an 11-story apartment building in the Bijlmermeer neighborhood of Amsterdam. The building collapsed and burst into flames; 43 people were killed, including the plane's entire crew.

Ten months later, researchers questioned 193 Dutch people about the crash, asking them in particular, "Did you see the television film of the moment the plane hit the apartment building?" More than half of the participants (107 of them) reported seeing the film, even though there was no such film. No camera had recorded the crash; no film (or any reenactment) was shown on television. The participants were remembering something that never took place (Crombag, Wagenaar, & van Koppen, 1996; for similar data, with people remembering a nonexistent film of the car crash that killed Princess Diana and Dodi Fayed, see Ost, Vrij, Costall, & Bull, 2002; also Jelicic et al., 2006; but for a complication, see Smeets et al., 2006).

In a follow-up study, the investigators surveyed another 93 people about the crash. These people were also asked whether they had seen the (nonexistent) TV film, and then they were asked more detailed questions about exactly what they had seen in the film: Was the plane burning when it crashed, or did it catch fire a moment later? In the film, did you see the plane come down vertically with no forward speed, or did it hit the building while still moving horizontally at a considerable speed?

Two thirds of these participants remembered seeing the film, and most of them confidently provided details about what they had seen. When asked about the plane's speed of movement, for example, only 23% prudently said that they couldn't remember. The others gave various responses, presumably based on their "memory" of the film; as it turns out, only 11% gave the correct answer.

This is not a case of one or two people making a mistake; instead, a large majority of the people questioned seemed to have a detailed recollection of the nonexistent film. In addition, let's emphasize that this plane crash was an emotional, important, and much-discussed event for these participants; the researchers were not asking them to recall a minor occurrence.

Perhaps these errors emerged simply because the research participants were trying to remember something that had taken place almost a year earlier. Is memory more accurate when the questions come after a shorter delay? In a study by Brewer and Treyens (1981), participants were asked to wait briefly in the experimenter's office prior to the procedure's start. After 35 seconds, participants were taken out of this office and told that there actually was no experimental procedure. Instead, the study was concerned with their memory for the room in which they had just been sitting.

FIGURE 7.1 The Office Used in the Brewer and Treyens Study
No books were in view in this office, but participants, biased by their expectations for what should be in a scholar's office, often remembered seeing books! (After Brewer & Treyens, 1981)

The participants' recollections of the office were plainly influenced by their prior knowledge—in this case, their knowledge about what an academic office typically contains. For example, participants surely knew in advance of the study that academic offices usually contain a desk and a chair; as it turns out, these pieces of furniture were present in this particular office. This agreement between prior knowledge and the specific experience led to accurate memory, and 29 of 30 participants correctly remembered that the office contained a desk and a chair. In other regards, however, this office was different from what the participants might have expected. Specifically, participants would expect an academic office to contain shelves filled with books, yet in this particular office no books were in view (see Figure 7.1). As it turns out, though, the participants' recall was often in line with their expectations and not with reality: Almost one third of them (9 of 30) remembered seeing books in the office when, in fact, there were none.

How could this be? How could so many Dutch participants be wrong in their recall of a significant emotional episode? How could intelligent, alert college students fail to remember what they had seen in an office just moments earlier?

Memory Errors: A Hypothesis

Memory errors can happen in many different ways, starting with errors that arise during your initial exposure to the episode to be remembered, and continuing through the moment of recall. In all cases, though, the errors involve the same simple mechanism: In Chapters 5 and 6, we emphasized the importance of memory connections, linking each bit of knowledge in your memory to other bits. Sometimes these connections tie together similar episodes, so that a given trip to the beach ends up connected in memory to your recollections of other trips. Sometimes the connections tie an episode to certain ideas—ideas, perhaps, that were part of your understanding of the episode, or ideas that were triggered by some element within the episode.

With all of these connections in place, information ends up being stored in memory in a system that looks like a vast spider web, with each bit of information connected by many threads to other bits of information elsewhere in the web. And within this spider web, there are no clear boundaries keeping the contents of one memory separate from the contents of other memories. The memories, in other words, are not stored in separate "files," each distinct from the others. What is it, therefore, that holds together the various elements within a remembered episode? It is simply the density of connections: There are many connections linking the various aspects of your "trip to the beach" to each other; there are fewer connections linking this event to other events.

As we have discussed, these connections play a crucial role in memory retrieval: Whenever you are looking for some bit of information, you follow the connections from one remembered element to the next until you find the information you want. For this reason, the connections are a good thing, and the more connections there are, the easier it will be for you to find the information you seek.

However, the same connections can also create problems for you. As you add links between the bits of this episode and the bits of that episode, you are gradually knitting these two episodes together. As a result, it becomes very easy to lose track of which bits of information were contained within which episode, and thus you become vulnerable to what we might think of as "transplant" errors in which a bit of information encountered in one context is transplanted into another context. In the same fashion, as your memory for an episode becomes more and more interwoven with other thoughts you had about the episode, it becomes difficult to keep track of which elements are linked to the episode because they were, in truth, part of the episode, and which are linked because they were merely *associated with* the episode in your thoughts. This, too, can produce transplant errors—as elements that were part of your thinking get misremembered as if they were actually part of the original experience.

Understanding Both Helps and Hurts Memory

How can we test this broad proposal? For a start, notice that this hypothesis suggests that memory connections both help and hurt recollection. They help because the connections, in their role as retrieval paths, make it easier to locate information in memory. But the same connections *hurt* because they can make it difficult to see where the remembered episode stops and other, related knowledge begins. As a result, the connections encourage **intrusion errors**—errors in which other knowledge intrudes into the remembered event.

Consistent with this view, many experiments show that factors that encourage the creation of connections do both help and hurt memory. As one example, consider the role of *understanding* itself. In one study, half of the participants in the experiment read the following passage (Owens, Bower, & Black, 1979):

> Nancy arrived at the cocktail party. She looked around the room to see who was there. She went to talk with her professor. She felt she had to talk to him but was a little nervous about just what to say. A group of people started to play charades. Nancy went over and had some refreshments. The hors d'oeuvres were good but she wasn't interested in talking to the rest of the people at the party. After a while she decided she'd had enough and left the party.

Other participants read the same passage, but with a prologue that set the stage:

> Nancy woke up feeling sick again and she wondered if she really were pregnant. How would she tell the professor she had been seeing? And the money was another problem.

All participants were then given a recall test in which they were asked to remember the sentences as exactly as they could. Table 7.1 shows the results; as can be seen, the participants who had read the prologue (the "theme condition") recalled much more of the original story. This is consistent with claims made in Chapter 5: The prologue provided a meaningful context for the remainder of the story, and this helped understanding. Understanding, in turn, promoted recall.

At the same time, the story's prologue also led participants to include many things in their recall that were not mentioned in the original episode. In fact, participants who had seen the prologue made *four times* as many intrusion errors as did participants who had not seen the prologue. For example, they might recall, "The professor had gotten Nancy pregnant." This is not part of the story but is certainly implied, and so it will probably be part of the participants' understanding of the story. It is this understanding (including the imported element) that is remembered.

TABLE 7.1 Number of Propositions Remembered by Participants

	Theme condition	Neutral condition
Studied propositions (those in story)	29.2	20.2
Inferred propositions (those not in story)	15.2	3.7

In the *theme* condition, a brief prologue set the theme for the passage that was to be remembered. (After Owens et al., 1979.)

The DRM Procedure

Similar effects, with memory connections both *helping* memory and *hurting*, can even be demonstrated with word lists, provided that the lists are arranged so that they make appropriate contact with prior knowledge. For example, in many experiments, participants have been presented with lists like this one: "bed, rest, awake, tired, dream, wake, snooze, blanket, doze, slumber, snore, nap, peace, yawn, drowsy." Then, immediately after hearing this list, participants are asked to recall as many of the words as they can.

As you may have noticed, all of the words in this list are associated with the word "sleep," and the presence of this theme helps memory: The words that are on the list are relatively easy to remember. It turns out, though, that "sleep," the root of the list, is not itself included in the list. Nonetheless, the participants spontaneously make the connection between the list words and this associated word, and this almost invariably leads to a memory error: When the time comes for recall, participants are extremely likely to recall that they heard "sleep." In fact, they are just as likely to recall "sleep" as they are to recall the actual words on the list!

The same pattern emerges in recognition testing: If participants are shown test words and asked which of these appeared in the original list, they are just as likely to recognize "sleep" as being one of the list words as they are to recognize the actually presented list words. When asked how confident they are in their memories, participants are just as confident in their (false) recognition of "sleep" as they are in their (correct) recognition of genuine list words (Roediger & McDermott, 1995, 2000; also see Brainerd & Reyna, 1998; Bruce & Winograd, 1998; Deese, 1957; McEvoy, Nelson, & Komatsu, 1999; Stadler, Roediger, & McDermott, 1999).

This paradigm is referred to as the **Deese–Roediger–McDermott** (or DRM) **procedure**, in honor of the investigators who developed it. The procedure yields striking results—with a very simple task leading to large numbers of memory errors. The errors are observed even if participants are put on their guard before the procedure begins and are told explicitly about the nature of the lists and the frequency with which these lists produce memory errors. Even with these warnings, participants still make the DRM errors (Gallo, Roberts, & Seamon, 1997; McDermott & Roediger, 1998). Apparently, the mechanisms leading to these memory errors are quite automatic, and not mechanisms that people can somehow inhibit.

Schematic Knowledge

In the DRM procedure, intrusion errors come from words (or ideas) merely associated with the materials being learned. In other settings, intrusion errors come from the background knowledge that we bring to most situations. And again, this knowledge is usually helpful: It guides us as we explore, think about, and interpret the

Schematic Knowledge

Schematic knowledge guides our attention by making sure we focus on elements that are interesting or informative within a scene. This is why you are likely to focus on the palm tree in this picture—because it is unexpected and therefore interesting. And if you focus on the palm tree, you are likely to remember it later. In this way, schematic knowledge can lead us to especially good memories for items or objects that are particularly unusual, and that therefore seize our attention.

situations we find ourselves in. But this knowledge can also be a source of memory error.

To make this concrete, imagine that you go to a restaurant with a friend. This is a familiar experience for you, and you have knowledge about what normally happens in each visit: You'll be seated; someone will bring menus; you'll order, then eat; eventually, you'll pay the check and leave. Knowledge like this is called **generic knowledge**; it's knowledge about how things unfold in general, and knowledge about what's typical in a particular sort of setting. This knowledge is often referred to by the Greek word **schema** (plural: schemata). Schemata summarize the broad pattern of what's normal in a situation: Your kitchen schema tells you that a kitchen is likely to have a stove in it, but no piano; your dentist's office schema tells you that there are likely to be magazines in the waiting room; and so on.

Schemata help us in a variety of ways. In a restaurant, for example, you're not puzzled by the fact that someone keeps filling your water glass or that someone drops by the table to ask, "How is everything?" Your schema tells you that these are normal occurrences in a restaurant, and you instantly understand how they fit into the broader script.

Schemata also help when the time comes to recall an event. Often there are gaps in your recollection—either because there were things you didn't notice in the first place, or because you have gradually forgotten some aspects of an experience. (We will say more about forgetting in a moment.) In either case, you can rely on your schemata to fill these gaps. Thus, in thinking back to your dinner at Chez Pierre, you might not remember anything about the menus. Nonetheless, you can be reasonably sure that there were menus, and that they were given to you early on and taken away after you placed your order. On this basis, you're likely to include menus within your "recall" of the dinner, even if you have no memory for seeing the menus for this particular meal. In other words, you'll (unwittingly) supplement what you actually remember with a plausible reconstruction based on your schematic knowledge. And in most cases this after-the-fact reconstruction will be correct, since schemata do, after all, describe what happens most of the time.

Evidence for Schematic Knowledge

Clearly, then, schematic knowledge helps us—guiding our understanding and allowing us to reconstruct things we cannot remember. But schematic knowledge can also hurt us, promoting errors in both our perception and our memory. Moreover, the *types* of errors produced by schemata will be quite predictable: Bear in mind here that schemata summarize the broad pattern of our experience, and so schemata tell us, in essence, what's "typical" or "ordinary" in a given situation. Any reliance on schematic knowledge, therefore, will be shaped by this information about what's "normal." Thus, if there are things you don't notice while viewing a situation or event, your schemata will allow you to fill these "gaps" with knowledge about what's normally in place in that setting. Likewise, if there are things you can't recall, your schemata will fill the gaps with knowledge about what's typical in that situation. As a result, a reliance on schemata will inevitably make the world seem more "normal" than it really is and will make the past seem more "regular" than it actually was.

Imagine, for example, that you visit a dentist's office, and this one happens not to have any magazines in the waiting room. It's possible that you won't notice this detail or that you'll forget about it after a while. What will happen, therefore, if you later try to recall this trip to the dentist? Odds are good that you'll rely on your schematic knowledge and "remember" that there were magazines (since, after all, there usually are some scattered around the waiting room). In this way, your recollection will make this dentist's office seem more typical, more ordinary, than it actually was.

This tendency toward "regularizing" the past is easily demonstrated in the laboratory. The classic demonstration, however, comes from research published many years ago by Frederick Bartlett. Bartlett presented his study participants with stories taken from the folklore of Native Americans (Bartlett, 1932). When tested later, the participants did reasonably well in recalling the gist of the stories, but they made many errors in recalling the particulars. Often the details of the original story were omitted from their recall; other details were either added to the original or changed. The pattern of errors, though, was quite systematic: The details omitted tended to be ones that made little sense to Bartlett's British participants. Likewise, aspects of the story that were unfamiliar were changed into aspects that were more familiar; steps of the story that seemed inexplicable were supplemented to make the story seem more logical.

Overall, in this study, participants' memories seem to have "cleaned up" the story they had read—making it more coherent (from their perspective), more sensible, than it first seemed. This is exactly what we would expect if the memory errors derived from the participants' attempts to understand the story and, with that, their efforts toward fitting the story into a familiar schematic frame. Elements that fit within the frame remained in their memories or could perhaps be reconstructed later. Elements that did not fit dropped out of memory or were changed.

In the same spirit, consider the Brewer and Treyens study we mentioned at the start of this chapter—the study in which participants remembered seeing bookshelves full of books, even though there were none. This error was produced by schematic knowledge: During the event itself (i.e., while the participants were sitting in the office), schematic knowledge told the participants that academic offices usually contain many books, and this biased what the participants paid attention to. (If you're already certain that the shelves contain books, why should you spend time looking at the shelves? This would only confirm something you already know.) Then, when the time came to recall the office, participants used their schema to reconstruct what the office *must* contain—a desk, a chair, and of course lots of books. In this fashion, the memory for the actual office was eclipsed by generic knowledge about what a "normal" office contains.

Likewise, think back to our other early example—the misremembered plane crash. Here, too, the memory error distorts reality by making the past seem more regular, more typical, than it really was. After all, the Dutch survey respondents probably hear about most major news events via a television broadcast, and this broadcast typically includes vivid video footage. So here, too, the past as remembered seems to have been assimilated into the pattern of the ordinary. The event as it unfolded was unusual, but the event *as remembered* is quite typical of its kind—just as we would expect if understanding and remembering were guided by our knowledge of the way things generally unfold.

Planting False Memories

The results we've been describing form a simple pattern. On the positive side, memory connections help us in multiple ways. The connections obviously serve as retrieval paths, allowing us to locate information in storage. The connections also link related ideas in our memory, and this enriches our understanding of these ideas. The connections also tie our memories to schematic knowledge, allowing us to supplement our recollection with well-informed inference.

On the negative side, though, the same memory connections can undermine memory accuracy. As we've seen, the connections can lead us to remember things as more regular than they were, in some cases "adding" elements to a memory and in other cases "subtracting" elements, so that (in either case) the memory ends up making more sense (i.e., fitting better with our schemata). The connections can, in some circumstances, even lead us to recall whole episodes (e.g., seeing a plane crash on TV) that never happened.

These errors are worrisome. As we have discussed in other contexts, we rely on memory in many aspects of our lives, and it is therefore unsettling that the memories we're relying on may be *wrong*—misrepresenting how the past unfolded. To make matters worse, the mistakes seem surprisingly frequent—with two thirds of the participants in one study remembering a nonexistent film; with one third of the participants in another study remembering books that were not there at all, and so on. Perhaps worst of all, we can easily find circumstances in which these memory errors are deeply consequential. For example, memory errors in eyewitness testimony (e.g., in identifying the wrong person as the culprit or in misreporting how an event unfolded) can potentially send an innocent person to jail and allow a guilty person to go free.

In fact, one line of research has specifically explored a sequence of events that can arise in a criminal investigation when witnesses are questioned about what they have seen. In an early study, Loftus and Palmer (1974) showed participants a series of projected slides depicting an automobile collision. Sometime later, half the participants were asked, "How fast were the cars going when they hit each other?" Others were asked, "How fast were the cars going when they smashed into each other?" The difference between these questions ("hit" vs. "smashed") is slight, but it was enough to bias the participants' estimates of speed. Participants in the first group ("hit") estimated the speed to have been 34 miles per hour; participants in the second group ("smashed") estimated 41 miles per hour. But what is critical comes next: One week later, the participants were asked in a perfectly neutral way whether they had seen any broken glass in the slides. Participants who had initially been asked the "hit" question tended to remember (correctly) that no glass was visible; only 14% said they had seen glass. Participants who had been asked the "smashed" question, though, were reasonably likely to remember glass; 32% asserted that glass was visible. It seems, therefore, that the change of just one word within the initial question can have a large effect—in this case, more than doubling the likelihood of memory error.

Across the last 30 years, researchers have tried many variations on this procedure, and broadly, all have the same effect. In some studies, participants are asked questions that merely imply how they "ought to" remember an event; the "hit" versus "smashed" experiment is one example. In other studies, participants are asked questions that contain actual misinformation about an event. For example, they might be asked, "How fast was the car going when it raced by the barn?" when, in truth, no barn was in view. In still other studies, participants have been exposed to descriptions of the target event that allegedly were written by "other witnesses," and again, these descriptions contain some misinformation (e.g., Paterson & Kemp, 2006). Finally, in other cases, participants have been asked questions about an event that required the participants themselves to *make up* the misinformation. For example, participants can be asked, "In the video, was the man bleeding from his knee or from his elbow after the fall?" Even though it was clear in the video that the man was not bleeding at all, participants are still forced to choose one of these options (e.g., Chrobak & Zaragoza, 2008; Zaragoza, Payment, Ackil, Drivadahl, & Beck, 2001).

These procedures are all variations on the same theme. In each case, the participant experiences an event and then is exposed to a misleading suggestion about how the event unfolded. Then some time is allowed to pass. At the end of this interval, the participant's memory is tested. And in each of these variations, the outcome is the same: A substantial number of participants—as many as one third of the participants in the study—end up incorporating the false suggestion into their memory for the original event. (For more on this research, see Ayers & Reder, 1998; Chan, Thomas, & Bulevich, 2009; Loftus, 2003.)

Using these procedures, researchers have led participants to remember broken glass when really there was none; to remember barns when there were no buildings at all in view; to remember blue sedans when they actually saw brown pickup trucks; and on and on. Similar procedures have altered how *people* are remembered—so that with just a few "suggestions" from the experimenter, people remember clean-shaven men as bearded, young people as old, fat people as thin, and so on (e.g., Christiaansen, Sweeney, & Ochalek, 1983; Loftus & Greene, 1980).

False Memories

False memories can be quite consequential. In one study, participants were led to believe that, as children, they had gotten ill after eating egg salad. This "memory" then changed the participants' eating habits—over the next four months, the participants ended up eating less egg salad (Geraerts et al., 2008). Obviously, false memories can persist and have lasting behavioral effects.

Are There Limits on the Misinformation Effect?

The pattern of results just described is referred to as the **misinformation effect**—because the participants' memory is being influenced by misinformation they received after an episode was over. As we have seen, misinformation can change many details of how an event is remembered, and it can even add whole objects (e.g., barns) to a memory. It turns out, though, that misinformation can do much more than this; it can create memories for entire episodes that never happened at all.

In one study, college students were told that the investigators were trying to learn how different people remember the same experience. The students were then given a list of events that they were told had been reported by their parents; the students were asked to recall these events as well as they could, so that the investigators could compare their recall with their parents' (Hyman, Husband, & Billings, 1995).

Some of the events on the list had, in fact, been reported by the participants' parents. Other events were bogus—made up by the experimenters. One of the bogus events was an overnight hospitalization for a high fever; in a different experiment, the bogus event was attending a wedding reception and accidentally spilling a bowlful of punch onto the bride's parents.

The college students were easily able to remember the genuine events (i.e., the events actually reported by their parents). In an initial interview, more than 80% of these events were recalled; by a second interview, this number had climbed to almost 90%. In the first interview, none of the students recalled the bogus events, but repeated attempts at recall changed this pattern: By the third interview, 25% of the participants were able to remember the embarrassment of spilling the punch, and many were able to supply the details of this (fictitious) episode. Other studies have yielded similar results, with participants led to recall details of particular birthday parties that, in truth, they never had (Hyman et al., 1995) or an incident of being lost in a shopping mall even though this event never took place (Loftus, 1997; Loftus & Pickrell, 1995; also see Porter, Yuille, & Lehman, 1999). In other studies, participants have been led to recall a hot-air balloon ride that, in reality, never happened, and also to recall a (fictitious) event in which they were the victim of a vicious animal attack (Loftus, 2003).

The same sort of result has been documented with children, and, in fact, evidence suggests that children are more vulnerable than adults to this sort of memory "planting." In one study, children participated in an event with "Mr. Science," a man who showed them a number of fun demonstrations. Afterward, the parents (who were not at the event) were asked to discuss the event with their children—and were, in particular, urged to discuss several elements that (unbeknownst to the parents) actually had never occurred. Later on, the children were interviewed about their visit with Mr. Science, and many of them confidently remembered the (fictitious) elements they had discussed with their parents—including a time (that never happened) in which Mr. Science put something "yucky" in their mouths, or a time in which Mr.

Science hurt the child's tummy (by pressing too hard when applying a sticker; Poole & Lindsay, 2001). Such results echo the misinformation results with adults, but they are also extremely important for their own sake, because (among other concerns) these results are relevant to children's testimony in the courtroom (Bruck & Ceci, 1999; Ceci & Bruck, 1995).

Clearly, then, entire events can be planted in someone's memory, so that the person ends up recalling—confidently and in detail—an episode that never took place. Moreover, it seems relatively easy to plant these memories: Two or three brief interviews, with no particular pressure, no effort toward coercion, are all that is needed. Indeed, in some cases merely asking a question ("Did you see the film of the plane crash?"; "How fast was the car going when it passed the barn?") is enough to cause a memory error.

Of course, it is easier to plant *plausible* memories than implausible ones (although memories for implausible events can also be planted; Hyman, 2000; Mazzoni, Loftus, & Kirsch, 2001; Pezdek, Blandon-Gitlin, & Gabbay, 2006; Scoboria, Mazzoni, Kirsch, & Jiminez, 2006; A. K. Thomas & Loftus, 2002). It is easier to plant a memory if the false suggestion is repeated, rather than delivered just once (Bruck & Ceci, 1999; Zaragoza & Mitchell, 1996). False memories are also more easily planted if the research participants don't just *hear* about the false event but, instead, are urged to *imagine* how the suggested event unfolded—an effect referred to as "imagination inflation" (Garry & Polaschek, 2000; Mazzoni & Memon, 2003; Seamon, Philbin, & Harrison, 2006; Thomas, Bulevich, & Loftus, 2003). Finally, it appears that some individuals are more susceptible than others to false memories (Bremner, Shobe, & Kihlstrom, 2000; Cann & Katz, 2005; Clancy, Schacter, McNally, & Pitmann, 2000; Heaps & Nash, 1999; Scullin, Kanaya, & Ceci, 2002).

Across all of these variations, though, the basic points remain: False memories can easily be planted through a variety of procedures, and the memory errors thus created can be large (e.g., entire events). Once the false memories are planted, the target "events" seem to be "remembered" fully and in detail. All of this raises many troubling questions—including questions about how much each of us can trust our own recollection, and also questions, as we've noted, about the degree to which the *courts* can trust the memory of eyewitnesses to crimes.

Avoiding Memory Errors

Unmistakably, then, the accuracy of our memories is far from guaranteed, and the past as we remember it may in some cases be markedly different from the past as it really was. Some of the memory errors arise because our memory for an event is connected to a schema, and this creates the risk that elements from this generic knowledge will intrude into our recollection of the target episode. Other errors arise because an episode triggers certain thoughts (e.g., a list of words triggers the idea of "sleep"), and these thoughts, now connected to the target memory, can also intrude into the recall. Still other errors arise because different episodes get linked together in memory, allowing elements of one episode to intrude into the other. (This last mechanism is crucial for the misinformation effect, so that—for example—the episode of *hearing about* an event becomes well connected with, and ends up blurring into, the episode of actually *witnessing* the event.)

Overall, though, how worried should we be about these errors? Should we, in general, be skeptical about our own recollections of the past? We will tackle these broad questions in three steps. First, while memory errors are common in the lab, how often do they occur in day-to-day life? Second, can we say more about *when* the errors will occur? Third, is there any way to *detect the errors* when they do occur? In the upcoming pages, we'll pursue each of these issues.

Accurate Memories

It would probably be a mistake to give a single broad assessment of human memory. This is because in some settings memory errors are quite likely, while in other settings they are unlikely. Nonetheless, the overall pattern of evidence suggests that in our daily lives we usually *can* trust our memories. More often than not, our recollection is complete, detailed, long-lasting, and *correct*.

Several lines of evidence are pertinent to this claim. For example, Yuille and Cutshall (1986) interviewed witnesses to an actual crime 4 to 5 months after the event. The witnesses' memory for the crime was impressively accurate despite this delay and despite the fact that the investigators used stringent criteria in evaluating the witnesses' recall: Reported ages of the perpetrators, for example, had to be within 2 years to be counted as correct; reported weights, within 5 pounds. No leeway was given for the estimation of the number of shots fired in the incident. Even with these strict rules, the witnesses were correct in 83% of the details reported about the action itself within the episode, 90% correct in their descriptions of objects on the scene. (Also see Fisher, Geiselman, & Amador, 1989; Yuille & Kim, 1987.)

Similar levels of accuracy have been observed in other studies. For example, M. Howes, Siegel, and Brown (1993) asked their adult study participants to recall events from very early in childhood. When checked, most of these memories turned out to be reasonably accurate. Likewise, Brewin, Andrews, and Gotlib (1993) summarize a number of studies showing that our autobiographical recollection is correct most of the time.

The Importance of the Retention Interval

Clearly, then, we can document cases of wonderfully accurate memory, and also examples of huge memory errors. What shapes this pattern? When is memory accurate, and when not? We have already mentioned one of the key factors—the presence of some source of intrusions into the memory; this source can be generic knowledge, or misinformation encountered after the event, or some related episode that can be confused with the event being remembered. But another—and crucial—factor is (not surprisingly) the passage of time. As the **retention interval** (the amount of time that elapses between the initial learning and the subsequent retrieval) grows, you will gradually forget more and more of the earlier event, and so you're forced to rely more and more on after-the-fact reconstruction to "plug" these gaps in the memory record, filling in with inference the bits that you cannot recall. In addition, as you forget the details of an episode, it will become more difficult to distinguish which elements were actually part of the event and which elements were merely associated with the event in your thoughts. In other words, as time goes by you will have more difficulty in **source monitoring**—that is, remembering the source of the various ideas that are associated with an event in your thoughts (e.g., M. K. Johnson, Hashtroudi, & Lindsay, 1993); this, in turn, will inevitably increase the risk of intrusion errors.

But why does the passage of time matter? Why, in brief, does forgetting happen? One possibility is **decay**. With the passage of time, memories may fade or erode. Perhaps this is because the relevant brain cells die off. Or perhaps the connections among memories need to be constantly refreshed; if not, the connections may gradually weaken. In any event, it is largely the passage of time that triggers these events.

A different possibility is that new learning somehow interferes with older learning. According to this **interference** account, less is remembered about older events because the passage of time allows new learning, and it is the new learning that disrupts the older memories.

A third hypothesis blames **retrieval failure**. After all, the retrieval of information from memory is far from guaranteed, and we argued in Chapter 6 that retrieval is most likely if your mental and physical perspective at the time of retrieval matches that in place at the time of learning. If we now assume that your perspective is likely to change more and more as time goes by, we can make a prediction about forgetting: The greater the retention interval, the greater the likelihood that your perspective has changed, and therefore the greater the likelihood of retrieval failure.

Each of these hypotheses, therefore, is compatible with the fact that longer retention intervals lead to more forgetting. But which hypothesis is correct? It turns out that they all are. There is, first of all, no doubt that retrieval failure does occur. In many circumstances, we are unable to remember some bit of information, but then, a while later, we do recall that information. Because the information eventually was retrieved, we know that it was not "erased" from memory through either decay or interference. Our initial failure to recall the information, therefore, must be counted as an example of retrieval failure.

What about decay and interference? Do they contribute to forgetting? Memories do, in fact, decay with the passage of time (e.g., Altmann & Gray, 2002; Wixted, 2004), and so decay, too, must be part of our theorizing. But at the same time, we will later look at evidence showing that some memories last an extremely long time; this tells us that decay is far from inevitable. In addition, a number of studies have directly compared the effects of decay and interference, and they show that interference, not decay, is the more prominent source of ordinary forgetting.

For example, Baddeley and Hitch (1977) asked rugby players to recall the names of the other teams they had played against over the course of a season. Not all players made it to all games because of illness, injuries, or schedule conflicts. These differences allow us to compare players for whom "two games back" means 2 weeks ago, to players for whom "two games back" means 4 weeks ago. Thus, we can look at the effects of retention interval (2 weeks vs. 4) with the number of intervening games held constant. Likewise, we can compare players for whom the game a month ago was "three games back" to players for whom a month means "one game back." Now we have the retention interval held constant, and we can look at the effects of intervening events. In this setting, Baddeley and Hitch report that the mere passage of time accounts for very little; what really matters is the number of intervening events (see Figure 7.2). This is just what we would expect if interference, and not decay, is the major contributor to forgetting.

We still need to ask, though, *why* memory interference occurs. Why can't the newly acquired information coexist with older memories? Again, the answer has several parts. As we will see in Chapter 8, new information can cause difficulties in retrieving old memories—so that *interference* can, in effect, produce its own version of *retrieval failure*. In addition, newly arriving information often gets interwoven with older information, producing the sorts of errors we have been discussing throughout this chapter. Finally, new information seems in some cases literally to

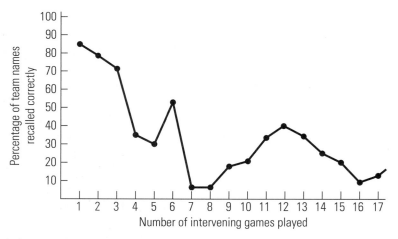

FIGURE 7.2 Forgetting From Interfering Events
Members of a rugby team were asked to recall the names of teams they had played against. Their performance was influenced by the number of games that intervened between the game to be recalled and the attempt to remember. This pattern fits with an interference view of forgetting. (After Baddeley & Hitch, 1977)

replace old information—much as you no longer save the rough draft of one of your papers once the final draft is done. In this process of **destructive updating**, the new information does not merely blur the older memory or make it difficult to locate; instead, it erases it.

Undoing Forgetting

Before we move on, we need to consider one last perspective on forgetting—namely, the proposal that certain techniques can be used to *undo* forgetting. If these techniques work, this would obviously be useful and would also be a powerful indication that old memories are not truly erased but are, instead, still in storage somewhere. This would, in turn, have profound implications for our theorizing about forgetting.

One proposal for undoing forgetting focuses on *hypnosis*, on the idea that under hypnosis witnesses to an earlier event can remember virtually everything about the event, including aspects they did not even notice (much less think about) at the time. Similar claims have been made about certain drugs—sodium amytal, for example—with the idea that these, too, help people to remember things they never could other-

Hypnosis
Hypnosis does not help people remember the past. However, hypnosis does make people more open to suggestion (and so more vulnerable to the misinformation effect) and more confident in their recall (whether the recall is accurate or not!). As a result, most courtrooms will not allow "hypnotically refreshed testimony" from eyewitnesses.

wise. Many studies have examined these claims, and the evidence is clear: Neither of these techniques improves memory. Hypnotized participants often do give detailed reports of the target event, but this isn't because they remember more; instead, they are just willing to *say* more in order to comply with the hypnotist's instructions. As a result, their "memories" are a mix of recollection, guesses, and inferences—and, of course, the hypnotized individual cannot tell you which of these are which (Dinges et al., 1992; Hilgard, 1968; Mazzoni & Lynn, 2007; M. Smith, 1982; Spiegel, 1995). Likewise, the drugs sometimes given to improve memory work largely as sedatives, and this puts an individual in a less guarded, less cautious state of mind. This state of mind allows people to report more about the past—not because they remember more, but simply because in this relaxed state they are willing to say more.

Plainly, then, neither of these techniques is an effective way to improve recollection. A more exotic proposal is suggested by reports of people whose brains have been directly stimulated, usually as part of brain surgery. Patients are typically awake during this surgery, and the surgeon uses their responses to stimulation as a way of locating certain structures and regions within the brain. Sometimes, though, when the brain is prodded or poked, the patient suddenly remembers scenes from long ago, often in clear and remarkable detail (e.g., Penfield & Roberts, 1959). Could this be the way to defeat forgetting and to recover one's "lost past"?

In fact, only a small number of patients report recollections in response to this stimulation of the brain. But the memories evoked in this fashion are extraordinary—clear and detailed, as though the patients were reliving the earlier experience. Unfortunately, though, we have no way of knowing whether these are really memories. These experiences might, for example, be hallucinations of some sort. Or these experiences might be very vivid reconstructions. Because this evidence comes from an extreme circumstance, it has been difficult to track down the historical facts to confirm (or disconfirm) these patients' recollections. Until this is done, we have no evidence that they are remembering, much less remembering accurately. Hence, we have no basis for claiming that this technique promotes memory retrieval.

On the positive side, though, there are procedures that do improve memory and that seem, therefore, to diminish forgetting. However, there is nothing exotic about these procedures. As we saw in Chapter 6, retrieval of memories from long-term storage is far from guaranteed, but in general, the retrieval is more likely if a suitable cue is provided. On this basis, researchers have explored various means of cueing memory; more specifically, they have developed a number of interview techniques intended for use in police work—to maximize the quantity and accuracy of information obtained from eyewitnesses to crimes (Fisher & Schreiber, 2007). These techniques simply provide a diverse set of retrieval cues, on the broad idea that the more cues provided, the greater the chance of finding a successful cue. The well-documented success of these techniques reminds us, once again, that some forgetting is due to retrieval failure, and so can be undone.

However, let's not overstate what these interview techniques can achieve. The techniques cannot help someone to recall details that she did not notice in the first place, nor can they undo the effects of interference (e.g., from misinformation). Likewise, these techniques still leave large gaps in what an individual can recall. It really does seem, then, that some gaps in memory are inevitable and permanent.

Memory Confidence

Can we perhaps improve memory in a different way? As we have seen, errors creep into our recall from certain sources: intrusions from schematic knowledge, for example, or a blurring-together in memory of related episodes. Can we warn people about these mechanisms, so that the errors never occur in the first place?

In some studies, researchers have tried the simple step of urging participants (either at the start of the experiment or when the time comes to recall) to be as careful as possible. Other studies have explicitly described to participants what sorts of errors are common, and urged them to avoid these errors. All of these instructions, however, have little effect (e.g., K. L. Chambers & Zaragoza, 2001; Greene, Flynn, & Loftus, 1982; Tousignant, Hall, & Loftus, 1986). The processes we have described in this chapter, the processes that lead to memory error, seem largely automatic and unavoidable.

If we cannot *prevent* the errors, can we at least *detect* the errors when they occur? Can we somehow scrutinize our own recall (or, just as important, scrutinize the memory reports we hear from others) and separate the memories that can be trusted from those that are potentially false? The evidence on this point is disappointing.

It's certainly true that we put more trust in some memories than others. Thus, we sometimes announce that we're confident in our recall ("I distinctly remember her yellow jacket; I'm sure of it"), and sometimes we say the opposite ("Gee, I think she was wearing yellow, but I'm not certain"). And the evidence suggests that we take these assessments quite seriously. In our own recall, we're more willing to take action based on confident memories than hesitant ones. The same is true when we're listening to others: In the courtroom, for example, juries place much more weight on a witness's evidence if the witness expresses confidence during the testimony; conversely, juries are usually skeptical about testimony that is hesitant or hedged. Apparently, then, juries believe that *confident* recall is likely to be *accurate* recall (Brigham & Wolfskiel, 1983; Cutler, Penrod, & Dexter, 1990; Loftus, 1979; Wells, Lindsay, & Ferguson, 1979). And it is not just juries who hold this view: Judges believe the same, and they typically instruct juries to put more faith in confident witnesses, less faith in hesitant ones (in the Unites Stated, *Neil v. Biggers*, 1972, is a key ruling on this point in federal court; many states have similar rulings in their own courts).

This is a point, however, on which common sense, juries, and the courts are all mistaken. Many studies have systematically compared people's confidence when they are reporting a correct memory with their confidence when they are reporting a false memory. This research has employed many of the procedures we have discussed in this chapter—memory for sentences, the DRM procedure, the misinformation paradigm—and also a number of studies designed to mimic the situation of an actual eyewitness to a crime. Across all of these procedures, the pattern is clear: There is little relationship between memory confidence and memory accuracy. Any attempt to categorize memories as correct or incorrect, therefore, based on the rememberer's confidence, will be riddled with errors. (For some of the evidence, see Busey, Tunnicliff, Loftus, & Loftus, 2000; Chandler, 1994; Roediger & McDermott, 1995; Sporer, Penrod, Read, & Cutler, 1995; W. B. Thompson & Mason, 1996; Wells, Luus, & Windschitl, 1994.)

How could this be? How could we be so poor in evaluating our own memories? One reason is that our confidence in a memory is influenced by variables that have no influence on accuracy. When these variables are on the scene, confidence will change (sometimes upward, sometimes downward) with no change in the accuracy level, and this will undermine any correspondence between confidence and accuracy.

For example, participants in one study witnessed a (simulated) crime and then, later, were asked if they could identify the "culprit" from a group of pictures. Some of the participants were then given feedback ("Good, you identified the suspect"); others were not. This feedback could not possibly influence the *accuracy* of the identification, because the feedback arrived only after the identification was done. But the feedback did influence *confidence*, and witnesses who had received the feedback expressed a much higher level of confidence in their choice than did witnesses who received no feedback (Douglass & Steblay, 2006; Semmler & Brewer, 2006; Wells & Bradfield, 1999; Wells, Olson, & Charman, 2002, 2003; Wright & Skzgerberg, 2007; for similar data with *children* as eyewitnesses, see Hafstad, Memon, & Logie, 2004). Thus, with confidence inflated but accuracy unchanged, the linkage between confidence and accuracy was diminished. (For other factors contributing to the disconnection between memory accuracy and memory confidence, see Lampinen, Meier, Arnal, & Leding, 2005; Sampaio & Brower, 2009; Sharman, Manning, & Garry, 2005.)

Other Efforts Toward Detecting False Memories

Perhaps we can distinguish correct memories from false memories in some other way. Investigators have, for example, considered the emotion attached to a memory. We know that people often become quite emotional when recalling the events of their lives—and so they feel proud when thinking about some past triumph, distressed when thinking about some past tragedy, and so on. Are they perhaps less emotional when remembering some memory fiction—an event that never occurred? If so, then we could use the degree of emotion as a way of distinguishing accurate memories from false ones. This, too, turns out to be a dead end. False memories, memories of events that never actually happened, can be just as upsetting, just as emotional, as memories for real events (McNally et al., 2004).

Other investigators have examined the way a memory *feels*, relying on the "remember/know" distinction that we met in Chapter 6. (This is, in essence, the difference between the two experiences: "I remember that there were books, because I recall thinking about how dusty they looked" and "I'm sure I saw books, although, to tell you the truth, I don't remember anything about what they looked like.") It turns out that a feeling of "remembering" is, in fact, more likely with correct memories than with false memories (e.g., M. Conway, Collins, Gathercole, & Anderson, 1996; Lane & Zaragoza, 1995). Put differently, false memories often arrive with only a general sense of familiarity and no recollection of a particular episode. But there are numerous exceptions to this pattern—cases in which fully correct memories arrive in your thoughts with only a feeling of knowing, and false memories arrive with a detailed sense of remembering. As a result, the subjective distinction between knowing and remembering, like the other efforts we have described, cannot serve as a reliable means of distinguishing correct memories from false ones (Frost, 2000; Holmes, Waters, & Rajaram, 1998; Roediger & McDermott, 1995).

Researchers continue to seek other means of distinguishing memory errors from accurate memory responses, but overall, the status of this research is easy to describe: A number of attributes are, in fact, associated with accurate remembering, including greater speed in responding (Dunning & Perretta, 2002, but also see Weber, Brewer, Wells, Semmler, & Keast, 2004), and, in some paradigms, somewhat greater confi-

Memory *Can* Be Accurate
This chapter has emphasized cases in which memory is inaccurate, but we can also celebrate cases in which memory is much *more* accurate, complete, and long-lasting than we ordinarily expect. In many traditional societies, for example, lore, family histories, and other cultural knowledge are transmitted orally from generation to generation, and all of this knowledge seems to be well-remembered, in enormous detail, over many years. In short, memory can sometimes be truly remarkable for its accuracy and longevity.

dence (Brewer & Wells, 2006). In each case, though, the linkage is weak enough so that in the end we have uncovered no indicator that can reliably guide us in deciding which memories to trust, and which not. For now, it seems that memory errors, when they occur, are essentially undetectable.

Memory: An Overall Assessment

Over and over in this chapter, we have seen that memory errors do occur. People sometimes confidently, sincerely, and vividly recall events that never took place. In other settings, they recall actual events, but in a fashion that is systematically different from the way the events really unfolded.

Most of these errors have been documented in the laboratory, but it is easy to identify the same sorts of errors in various real-world settings—including settings in which the stakes are extremely high. Errors by eyewitnesses to crimes, for example, have been well documented by investigators (e.g., Ceci & Bruck, 1995; Loftus & Ketcham, 1991; Schacter, 1999; Wright & Davies, 1999) and acknowledged as a problem by the U.S. Department of Justice (Connors, Lundregan, Miller, & McEwan, 1996).

One might argue, though, that these errors are simply the price we pay in order to gain other advantages. Bear in mind that the errors arise (in part) because our memories are densely interconnected with each other. This is what allows elements to be transplanted from one remembered episode to another. But the connections are there for a purpose: They are the retrieval paths that make memory search possible. Thus, to avoid the errors, we would need to restrict the connections; but if we did that, we would lose the ability to locate our own memories within long-term storage!

In addition, the memory connections that lead to error often help us in other ways. Our environment, after all, is in many ways predictable, and it is enormously useful for us to exploit that predictability. There's little point in scrutinizing a kitchen to make sure there is a stove in the room, because in the vast majority of cases there is. Why take the time, therefore, to confirm the obvious? Likewise, there's little point in taking special note that, yes, this restaurant does have menus and that, yes, people in the restaurant are eating and not having their cars repaired. These, too, are obvious points, and it would be a waste of effort to give them special notice.

On these grounds, reliance on schematic knowledge is a good thing: Schemata guide our attention to what's informative in a situation, rather than what's self-evident (e.g., Gordon, 2006), and they also guide our inferences at the time of recall. If this use of schemata sometimes leads us astray, it may be a small price to pay for the gain in efficiency that schemata allow. (For similar points, see Chapter 3.)

Finally, what about forgetting? Remarkably, this, too, may be a blessing in disguise, for sometimes it is to our advantage to remember less and to forget more. For example, think about all the times in your life when you've been with a particular friend. These episodes are related to each other in an obvious way, and so they are likely to become interconnected in your memory. This will cause difficulties if you want to remember which episode is which, and whether you had a particular conversation in this episode or in that one. However, rather than lamenting this as an example of forgetting, perhaps we should *celebrate* what's going on here: Because of the "interference," all of the episodes will merge together in your memory, so that what resides in memory is one integrated package, containing in united form all of your knowledge about your friend. This is, in fact, the way that much of your *general knowledge* is created! In other words, the same blurring together that makes it difficult to remember episodes also makes it possible to think in a general way, to think about what's in common among diverse experiences rather than what makes each experience unique. Without this blurring together, our capacity for thinking in general terms might be dramatically impaired.

It seems, then, that our overall assessment of memory can be rather upbeat. We have, to be sure, discussed a wide range of memory errors, but we have also noted that errors are the exception rather than the rule. In addition, we have now pointed out that the errors are in most cases a side product of mechanisms that otherwise help us—to locate our memories within storage, to be efficient in our contact with the world, and to form general knowledge. Thus, even with the errors, even with forgetting, it seems that human memory functions in a fashion that serves us well.

Autobiographical Memory

We began this chapter by acknowledging that much of the evidence in Chapters 5 and 6 was concerned with memory for very simple stimuli—word lists, for example, or short sentences. In this chapter, we've considered memories for more complex materials, and this has drawn our attention to the way in which someone's knowledge (whether knowledge of a general sort or knowledge about related episodes) can both improve memory and also interfere with it.

In making these points, we've considered memories in which the person was actually involved in the remembered episode, and not just an external witness (e.g., the false memory that you spilled that bowl of punch). We've also looked at studies that involved memories for emotional events (e.g., the plane crash we discussed at the chapter's start) and memory over the very long term (e.g., memories for childhood events "planted" in adult participants).

Do these three factors—involvement in the remembered event, emotion, and long delay—matter in any way, changing how or how well someone remembers? These factors are surely relevant to the sorts of remembering people do outside of the laboratory, and indeed, all three seem central for **autobiographical memory**. This is the memory that each of us has containing the full recollection of our lives, and we have argued (e.g., in Chapters 1 and 6) that this sort of memory plays a central role in shaping how each of us thinks about ourselves and, thus, how we behave. (For more on the importance of autobiographical memory, see Baddeley, Aggleton, & Conway, 2002.

For more on the distinction between these types of memory, including *biological* differences between autobiographical memory and "lab memory," see Cabeza & St. Jacques, 2007; Hodges & Graham, 2001; Kopelman & Kapur, 2001; Tulving, 1993, 2002.)

All of this leads us to ask: How do the three factors we've mentioned, each seemingly central for autobiographical memory, influence what we remember?

Memory and the Self

Having some involvement in an event, rather than passively witnessing the event, turns out to have a large effect on memory. In part, this is because involvement in the event leads to the idea that the event is relevant to you and who you are, and, in general, information relevant to the self is better remembered than information that's not self-relevant (e.g., Symons & Johnson, 1997). This **self-reference effect** emerges in many forms, including an advantage in remembering things you have said as opposed to things others have said, better memory for adjectives that apply to you relative to adjectives that do not, better memory for names of places you have visited relative to names of places you have never been, and so on.

But here, too, we can find memory errors—and the pattern of the errors is similar to what we've seen in other domains. For example, your "memory" for your own life is likely to be a mix of genuine recall and some amount of schema-based reconstruction—and so you can "remember" how you spent last Tuesday by relying on your generic knowledge about how your Tuesdays usually unfold; you can "remember" that you were excited on New Year's Eve because you believe this is your usual pattern. These reconstructions are likely to be accurate in most cases, because your **self-schema**—just like any other schema—does reflect your usual or normal behavior. Even so, this schema-based construction is (as in all other cases) open to error.

Consider the fact that most adults believe they have been reasonably consistent, reasonably stable, over their lifetimes. They believe, in other words, that they've always been pretty much the same as they are now. When the time comes to remember the past, therefore, people will rely to some extent on this belief, and so reconstruct their own history in a biased fashion—one that maximizes the (apparent) stability of their lives. Thus, people recall their past attitudes, and the past status of their romantic relationships, and their health, in a fashion that emphasizes consistency and thereby makes the past look more like the present than it really was (M. Conway & Ross, 1984; Holmberg & Homes, 1994; for related results, also showing how current views of self change memory, see L. J. Levine, 1997; G. B. Marcus, 1986; Ochsner & Schacter, 2000; M. Ross & Wilson, 2003).

It's also true that most of us would prefer to have a positive view of ourselves, including a positive view of how we have acted in the past. This, too, can shape memory. As one illustration, Bahrick, Hall, and Berger (1996) asked college students to recall their high school grades as accurately as they could, and the data showed a clear pattern of self-service: When students forgot a good grade, their (self-serving) reconstruction led them to the (correct) belief that the grade must have been a good one; consistent with this, 89% of the A's were correctly remembered. But when students forgot a poor grade, reconstruction led them to the (false) belief that the grade must have been okay; as a result, only 29% of the D's were correctly recalled. Overall, then, students consistently recalled their grades as being better than they actually were. (For other mechanisms through which current motivations can color autobiographical recall, see M. Conway & Holmes, 2004; M. Conway & Pleydell-Pearce, 2000; Forgas & East, 2003; Kunda, 1990; Mather, Shafir, & Johnson, 2000.)

Memory and Emotion

Another factor important for autobiographical memory is *emotion*. We don't get emotional when memorizing a researcher's list of words or a story that we read in the lab. But many of our experiences in life *do* cause emotion; how does this influence memory?

In general, emotion helps us to remember. At a biological level, emotional events trigger a response in the amygdala, and this in turn sets off a series of events in our bodies that promotes the process of memory **consolidation**—the process through which memories are biologically "cemented in place." Activation of the amygdala may also play a crucial role in promoting memory *retrieval*, so that the person can both

Emotional Memories

How memory is influenced by emotion probably depends on what the emotion is. In 1995, O.J. Simpson was found not guilty of murder at the end of a widely publicized trial. People who were *happy* about the verdict tended to recall what happened when the verdict was announced, but were also vulnerable to intrusion errors. People who felt *negatively* about the verdict remembered less overall, but also made fewer intrusion errors (Levine & Bluck, 2004).

recall the target event and (to some extent) reexperience the emotion associated with that event. (For reviews, see Buchanan, 2007; Dudai, 2004; Hamann, 2001; Kensinger, 2007; LaBar & Cabeza, 2006; LaBar, 2007; Öhman, 2002; Phelps, 2004.) In addition to these biological mechanisms, emotional events are likely to be important to us, virtually guaranteeing that we will pay close attention as the event unfolds, and this obviously helps memory. Moreover, we tend to mull over emotional events in the minutes (or hours) following the event, and this is tantamount to memory rehearsal. For all of these reasons, it is unsurprising that emotional events are well remembered (Reisberg & Heuer, 2004).

Many authors have argued in addition that emotion changes what we pay attention to within an event, and this changes the pattern of what is and is not remembered from an emotional episode. One proposal is that emotion leads to a "narrowing" of attention, so that in an emotional event all of one's attention will be focused on just a few aspects of the scene (Easterbrook, 1959). This helps to guarantee that these attended aspects are firmly placed into memory, but it also implies that the rest of the event, excluded from this narrowed focus, won't be remembered later. As a result, people will have good memory for the emotional event's "center" but poor memory for the event's "periphery." Many studies have documented this sort of memory narrowing, both in the laboratory and in the recollection of emotional events occurring in people's lives (e.g., Burke, Heuer, & Reisberg, 1992; Christianson, 1992; Gable & Harmon-Jones, 2008; Steblay, 1992).

Flashbulb Memories

One group of emotional memories, however, seems to be in a category all its own. These are the so-called **flashbulb memories**—memories of extraordinary clarity, typically for highly emotional events, retained despite the passage of many years. When Brown and Kulik (1977) introduced the term "flashbulbs," they pointed as a paradigm case to the memories people have of first hearing the news of President Kennedy's assassination. Their participants, interviewed more than a decade after that event, remembered it "as though it were yesterday," recalling details of where they were at the time, what they were doing, and whom they were with. Many participants were able to recall the clothing worn by people around them, the exact words uttered, and the like. Memories of comparable clarity have been reported for other, more recent events, including the news of Princess Diana's death in 1997 and the attack on the World Trade Center in 2001 (e.g., see Pillemer, 1984; Rubin & Kozin, 1984; also see Weaver, 1993; Winograd & Neisser, 1993; see color insert, Figure 16).

Flashbulb memories seem extraordinarily vivid and are rich in detail, but are these memories *correct*—that is, are they an accurate reflection of how the event really did unfold? Research indicates that some flashbulb memories contain large-scale errors. For example, Neisser and Harsch (1992) interviewed college students one day after the 1986 explosion of the space shuttle *Challenger*, asking the students how they first heard about the explosion, what they were doing at the time, and so on. They then reinterviewed these students 3 years later, asking the same questions about the shuttle explosion. The results show remarkably little agreement between the immediate and delayed reports, even with regard to major facts such as who delivered the news or where the person was when the news arrived. It appears, then, that the 3-year reports are mostly false, although it should be said that the students were highly confident about the accuracy of these reports. (For similar data, see Christianson, 1989; Talarico & Rubin, 2003; Wagenaar & Groeneweg, 1990.)

Other data, though, tell a different story, suggesting that some flashbulb memories are accurate. Why should this be? Why are some flashbulb events remembered well, while others are not? One key factor seems to be the **consequentiality** of the flashbulb event. If the event matters directly for the participant's life, then the event is more likely to be remembered accurately. If the event is inconsequential for that person, then memory accuracy will be poor. This point is well illustrated in a study that examined how accurately people remembered the 1989 San Francisco earthquake. For individuals who lived in Georgia, thousands of miles from the earthquake's epicenter, memory accuracy was quite low. For people who lived in Santa Clara (at the epicenter), the earthquake was remembered accurately and in detail (Neisser, Winograd, & Weldon, 1991; Palmer, Schreiber, & Fox, 1991). Similarly, another study examined people's memories for the unexpected resignation (in 1990) of British prime minister Margaret Thatcher. People differed widely in the accuracy of their recall for this event, but this accuracy was closely linked to their assessments of how important the event was for them: If it was important for them, they were much more likely to remember it, so that, again, consequentiality predicted accurate recollection (M. Conway et al., 1994; also see Luminet & Curci, 2009; Tinti, Schmidt, Sotgiu, Testa, & Curci, 2009).

In summary, some flashbulb memories do turn out to be marvelously accurate, while others are filled with error. From the point of view of the person doing the remembering, however, there is no difference between the accurate memories and the inaccurate ones: Both are recalled with great detail; both are recalled with enormous confidence. In both cases, the memory can be intensely emotional. This adds strength to our earlier claim that memory errors can occur even in the midst of our strongest, most confident recollection.

Traumatic Memories

Flashbulb memories tend to be highly emotional: Some people still cry when they think about Princess Diana's death, even though her death was many years ago; other people still grow angry (or, in some cases, relieved) when they think of O. J. Simpson's acquittal. But, sadly, we can easily find cases of much stronger emotion evoked by much more consequential events. How are these events remembered? If someone has witnessed wartime atrocities, for example, can we count on the accuracy of their testimony in a war crimes trial? If someone suffers through the horrors of a sexual assault, will the painful memory eventually fade? Or will the memory remain as a horrific remnant of the experience?

The evidence suggests that most traumatic events are well remembered for many years; indeed, victims of some atrocities seem plagued by a cruel enhancement of memory, leaving them with extra-vivid and long-lived recollections of the terrible event (Alexander et al., 2005; Golier, Yehuda, & Southwick, 1997; G. S. Goodman et al., 2003; Harber & Pennebaker, 1992; Horowitz & Reidbord, 1992; Peace & Porter, 2004; Pope, Hudson, Bodkin, & Oliva, 1998; Porter & Peace, 2007; Thompsen & Berntsen, 2009). In fact, people who have experienced trauma sometimes complain about having "too much" memory and wish they remembered *less*.

This enhanced memory is probably best understood in terms of the biological processes through which memories are established, with these processes apparently promoted by the conditions that accompany bodily arousal (Buchanan & Adolphs, 2004; Hamann, 2001). But this does not mean that traumatic events are always well remembered. There are, in fact, cases in which people who have suffered through extreme events have little or no recall of their experience (e.g., Arrigo & Pezdek, 1997). We need to ask, therefore, why some traumatic events—in contrast to the broader pattern—are completely forgotten.

In some cases, the forgetting of a traumatic event can be understood in terms of the person's *age*. In general, people have difficulty recalling events (traumatic or otherwise) from the first years of life. As a result, a failure to recall some early trauma may just be part of the broader pattern of **childhood amnesia**. In other cases, traumatic events are accompanied by sleep deprivation, head injuries, or alcohol and drug abuse, and each of these can disrupt memory, making it unsurprising that these traumas aren't recalled (McNally, 2003). In still other cases, the extreme stress associated with the event can disrupt the biological processes needed for establishing the memory in the first place; as a result, no memory is ever established (Hasselmo, 1999; McGaugh, 2000; Payne, Nadel, Britton, & Jacobs, 2004).

Finally, one last hypothesis is highly controversial: Several authors have argued that highly painful memories will be repressed—pushed out of awareness as a step toward self-protection. These memories, it is claimed, will not be consciously available but will still exist in a person's long-term storage and, in suitable circumstances, may be "recovered"—that is, made conscious once again. (See, for example, Freyd, 1996, 1998; Terr, 1991, 1994.)

It does seem that memories can, in fact, be "lost" for some time and then recovered (e.g., Geraerts et al., 2007). The mechanism behind this pattern, however, remains uncertain; specifically, many memory researchers are deeply skeptical about the repression idea (e.g., Kihlstrom, 2006). As one consideration, many painful events—presumably likely candidates for repression—are well remembered. In addition, when painful events are forgotten, the rate of forgetting seems similar to the rate at which ordinary events are forgotten—not what we'd expect if painful memories are especially likely to be banished through a mechanism like repression. Third, at least some of the "recovered memories" may, in fact, have been remembered all along, and so provide no evidence of repression. In these cases, the memories had appeared to be "lost" because the person refused to discuss the memories for many years (presumably because the remembered events were quite painful); the "recovery" of these memories simply reflects the fact that the person is at last willing to discuss these memories out loud. Such a recovery may be extremely consequential—emotionally and perhaps legally—but it does not tell us anything about how memory works.

Moreover, the pattern of memories lost and then found, when it does occur, may just reveal the effects of ordinary retrieval failure. This certainly is a mechanism that can hide memories from view for long periods of time, only to have the memories reemerge once a suitable retrieval cue is available. In this case, too, the recovery is of enormous importance for the person finally remembering the long-lost episodes; but again, this merely confirms the role of an already-documented memory mechanism; there is no need here for any theorizing about repression.

Finally, and most troubling, we need to acknowledge the possibility that at least some of these "recovered memories" are, in fact, false memories. After all, we know that false memories occur and that they are more likely when one is recovering the distant past than when one is trying to remember recent events. It is also worth mentioning that many recovered memories emerge only with the assistance of a therapist who is genuinely convinced that the client's psychological problems stem from childhood abuse. Even if the therapist scrupulously avoids leading questions, bias might still lead him to shape the client's memory in other ways—by giving signs of interest or concern if the client hits on the "right" line of exploration, by spending more time on topics related to the alleged memories, and so forth. In these ways, the climate within a therapeutic session could guide the client toward finding exactly the "memories" the therapist expects to find.

These are, of course, difficult issues, especially when we bear in mind that recovered memories often involve horrible episodes, such as episodes of sexual abuse; if these memories are true, therefore, they are evidence for repugnant crimes. But here, as in all cases, the veracity of recollection cannot be taken for granted. This caveat is important in evaluating any memory, and it is far more so for anyone wrestling with this sort of traumatic recollection. (For discussion of this difficult issue, see, among others, Geraerts et al., 2009; Ghetti et al., 2006; Giesbrecht et al., 2008; Kihlstrom & Schacter, 2000; Loftus & Guyer, 2002; Read, 1999.)

Long, Long-Term Remembering

Our discussion has several times touched on the fact that people sometimes seek to recall events that happened long, long ago—perhaps several decades earlier. Of course, distant events are often difficult to remember, and some of our memories from long ago will certainly turn out to be mistaken. But, impressively, memories from long ago can also turn out to be wonderfully accurate.

Bahrick, Bahrick, and Wittlinger (1975) tracked down the graduates of a particular high school—people who had graduated in the previous year, and the year before, and the year before that, and, ultimately, people who had graduated 50 years before. All of these alumni were shown photographs from their own year's high school yearbook. For each photo, they were given a group of names and had to choose the name of the person shown in the picture. The data for this "name matching" task show remarkably little forgetting; performance was approximately 90% correct if tested 3 months after graduation, the same after 7 years, and the same after 14 years. In some versions of the test, performance was still excellent after 34 years (see Figure 7.3).

Recall performance in this study was slightly worse than recognition but still impressive. When asked (in a "picture cueing" task) to come up with the names on their own, rather than choosing the correct name from a list, the participants were

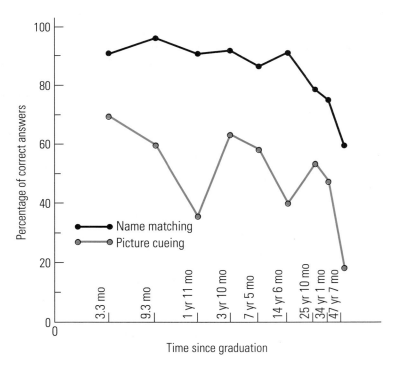

FIGURE 7.3 Memory Over the Very Long Term
People were tested for how well they remembered names and faces of their high school classmates; memory was remarkably long-lasting. (See the text for a description of the tasks.) The data do show a drop-off after 47 years, but it is unclear whether this reflects an erosion of memory or a more general drop-off in performance caused by the normal process of aging. (After Bahrick et al., 1975)

able to name 70% of the faces when tested 3 months after graduation, and 60% after 9 months. Remarkably, they were still able to name 60% of their classmates after 7 years.

As a different example, what about the material you are learning right now? You are presumably reading this textbook as part of a course on cognitive psychology. Five years from now, will you still remember things you have learned in this course? How about a decade from now? Conway, Cohen, and Stanhope (1991) explored these questions, testing students' retention of a cognitive psychology course taken years earlier. The results broadly echo the pattern we have already seen: Some forgetting of names and specific concepts was observed during the first 3 years after the course. After the third year, however, performance stabilized, so that students tested after 10 years still remembered a fair amount and, indeed, remembered just as much as did students tested after 3 years. Memory for more general facts and memory for research methods showed even less forgetting.

Some loss of memories is observed in these studies, but what is remarkable is how much people do remember, and for how long. In study after study, there is an initial period of forgetting, generally for the first 3 or 4 years. After that, performance remains impressively consistent, despite the passage of several decades. In other words, if you learn the material well enough to retain it for 3 years, odds are that you will remember it for the rest of your life. Indeed, Bahrick (1984) has claimed that memories can achieve a state of **permastore** (short for "permanent storage"), although he argues that only some memories achieve this status. Permastore is more likely, for example, if the material is extremely well learned in the first place (Bahrick, 1984; Bahrick & Hall, 1991; M. Conway, Cohen, & Stanhope, 1991, 1992). Permastore is also more likely if the person continues to learn new materials in that domain. Thus, students who take calculus courses in college are likely to remember their high school algebra even 50 years after high school (Bahrick & Hall, 1991). Some learning strategies also seem more likely to produce permastore (Bahrick, Bahrick, Bahrick, & Bahrick, 1993).

Very long-term retention is also helped by one additional factor: rehearsal. For many years, Linton (1975, 1978, 1982, 1986; also Wagenaar, 1986) has kept careful notes on the events that fill each of her days, sort of like keeping a detailed diary. After certain intervals, she selects events from the diary and tests her own memory for what transpired; this memory can then be checked against the written record. Linton reports impressive memory accuracy for these mundane events—over 65% remembered after 3 years, roughly the same after 4 years. In addition, Linton often retests her memory for a given event. This way, we can ask about the effects of rehearsing these memories, since, after all, the experience of testing memory constitutes a reencounter with the original episode. (Thus, the first test provides a rehearsal that may then benefit the second test.) This rehearsal turns out to have enormous impact. For those events previously tested (rehearsed), forgetting after 3 years was cut in half, from 32% forgotten with no rehearsals to 16% with one rehearsal.

Linton's result is important for what it tells us about forgetting, and, specifically, for what it tells us about the impact of rehearsal on forgetting. But this result also has practical implications. In Linton's study, each test served as a reminder of earlier-learned material, and so the test itself promoted long-term retention. Can tests in educational settings accomplish the same thing? That is, can tests in the classroom serve as reminders, and so help students to remember what they've learned? Several bits of evidence suggests that they can—a result that is both theoretically interesting and pragmatically useful (Carpenter, Pashler, Wixted, & Vul, 2008; Pashler, Rohrer, Cepeda, & Carpenter, 2007).

How General Are the Principles of Memory?

Where does this brief survey of autobiographical memory leave us? In some ways it seems that this form of memory is different from other sorts of remembering, but in some ways it is the same. Autobiographical memories can last for years and years, but so can memories that do not refer directly to one's own life. Autobiographical remembering is far more likely if the person occasionally revisits the target memories; these rehearsals dramatically reduce forgetting. But the same is true in nonautobiographical remembering.

Autobiographical memory is also open to error, just as other forms of remembering are. We saw this in cases of flashbulb memories that turn out to be false. We have also seen that misinformation and leading questions can plant false autobiographical memories—about birthday parties that never happened and trips to the hospital that never took place. (Also see Brown & Marsh, 2008.)

These facts strengthen a claim that has been implicit in much of our discussion over the last three chapters: Certain principles seem to apply to memory in general, quite independent of what is being remembered. All memories depend on connections. The connections promote retrieval. The connections also facilitate interference because they allow one memory to blur into another. The connections can fade with the passage of time, producing memory gaps, and the gaps are likely to be filled via reconstruction based on generic knowledge. All of these things seem to be true whether we are talking about relatively recent memories or memories from long ago, emotional memories or memories of calm events, memories for complex episodes or memories for simple word lists.

But this does not mean that all principles of memory apply to all types of remembering. As we saw in Chapter 6, for example, the rules that govern implicit memory may be different from those that govern explicit memory. And, as we have seen here, some of the factors that play a very large role in shaping autobiographical remembering (e.g., the role of emotion) may be irrelevant to other sorts of memory.

In the end, therefore, our overall theory of memory is going to need more than one level of description. We will need some principles that apply only to certain types of memory (e.g., principles specifically aimed at autobiographical remembering). But we will also need broader principles, reflecting the fact that some themes seem to apply to memory of all sorts (e.g., the importance of memory connections). As we have seen over the last three chapters, these more general principles have moved us forward considerably in our understanding of memory in many different domains and have allowed us to illuminate many aspects of learning, of memory retrieval, and of the sources of memory error.

Chapter Summary

■ Our memories are usually accurate, but errors do occur and can be quite large. In general, these errors are produced by the connections that link our memories to each other and link memories for specific episodes to other, more general knowledge. These connections help us because they serve as retrieval paths. But the connections can also "knit" separate memories together, making it difficult to keep track of which elements belong in which memory.

■ Some memory errors are produced by our understanding of an episode. The understanding promotes memory for the episode's gist but also encourages memory errors. A similar pattern emerges in the DRM procedure, in which a word related to other words on a list is (incorrectly) recalled as being part of the list. Similar effects arise from schematic knowledge. This knowledge helps us to understand an episode, but at the same time, a reliance on schematic knowledge can lead us to remember an episode as being more "regular," more "normal," than it actually was.

■ Memory errors can also arise through the misinformation effect, in which people are exposed to some (false) suggestion about a previous event. Such suggestions can easily change the details of how an event is remembered and can, in some cases, plant memories for entire episodes that never occurred at all.

■ While memory errors are easily documented, cases of accurate remembering can also be observed, and they are probably more numerous than cases involving memory error. Memory errors are more likely, though, in recalling distant events rather than recent ones. One reason for this is decay of the relevant memories; another reason is retrieval failure. Perhaps the most important source of forgetting, though, is interference.

■ People seem genuinely unable to tell apart their accurate and inaccurate memories. This is because false memories can be recalled with just as much detail, emotion, and confidence as a historically accurate memory. Memory errors also cannot be defeated with exotic techniques such as hypnosis or "memory-improving" drugs.

■ Although memory errors are troubling, they may simply be the price we pay in order to obtain other advantages. For example, many errors result from the dense network of connections that link our various memories. These connections sometimes make it difficult to recall which elements occurred in which setting, but the same connections serve as retrieval paths, and without the connections we might have great difficulty in locating our memories in long-term storage. Even forgetting may have a positive side, by virtue of trimming details from memory in a fashion that may foster abstract thinking.

■ Autobiographical memory is influenced by the same principles as any other form of memory, but it is also shaped by its own set of factors. For example, episodes connected to the self are, in general, better remembered—a pattern known as the self-reference effect.

■ Autobiographical memories are also often emotional, and this has multiple effects on memory. Emotion seems to promote memory consolidation, but it may also produce a pattern of memory narrowing. Some emotional events give rise to very clear, long-lasting memories called flashbulb memories. Despite their subjective clarity, these memories, like memories of any other sort, can contain errors and, in some cases, can be entirely inaccurate. At the extreme of emotion, trauma has mixed effects on memory. Some traumatic events are not remembered, but most traumatic events seem to be remembered for a long time and in great detail.

■ Some events can be recalled even after many years have passed. In some cases, this is because the knowledge was learned so well that it reached a state of permastore. In other cases, occasional rehearsals preserve a memory for a very long time.

The Workbook Connection

See the *Cognition Workbook* for further exploration on remembering complex events:
■ Demonstration 7.1: Associations and Memory Error
■ Demonstration 7.2: Memory Accuracy and Confidence
■ Demonstration 7.3: Childhood Amnesia
■ Research Methods: External Validity
■ Cognitive Psychology and Education: Remembering for the Long Term
■ Cognitive Psychology and the Law: Jurors' Memory

PART 4

Knowledge

In Parts 2 and 3, we saw case after case in which our interactions with the world are guided by knowledge. In perceiving, we make inferences guided by knowledge about the world's regular patterns. In attending, we anticipate inputs guided by knowledge about what's likely to occur. In learning, we connect new information to things that we already know. And so on. But what is knowledge? How is knowledge represented in the mind? How do we locate knowledge in memory when we need it?

These questions will be at the heart of this section. In Chapter 8, we'll develop a proposal for how knowledge is represented in memory and use this proposal to put some flesh on the suggestion—crucial for Chapters 5, 6, and 7—that learning consists of the creation of memory connections, and that these connections then serve as retrieval paths. In Chapter 8, we'll also return to the idea that complex processes can be built up from a network of simple elements relying on distributed representations and parallel processing. In Chapter 3, we applied this idea to the recognition of objects; here we'll apply it to the learning and use of knowledge.

In Chapter 9, we'll look at the building blocks of our knowledge—our individual concepts. We'll consider several hypotheses about what this knowledge might be, and we'll see that each hypothesis captures a part of the truth, so that we'll be driven toward a several-part theory combining the various views. In the process, we'll also be driven toward an overall framework in which our knowledge about individual concepts turns out to depend in interesting ways on our knowledge about many other concepts. As we'll see, therefore, one cannot know what a "dog" is without also understanding what an "animal" is, what a "living thing" is, and so on. As a result, connections among ideas again enter our view—this time, connections that play a central role in representing our conceptual knowledge.

Chapters 10 and 11 look at two special types of knowledge: our knowledge about language, and our knowledge about visual images. In Chapter 10, we will see that our knowledge of language is highly creative in the sense that we can produce new words and new sentences that no one has ever used before. But at the same time, the creativity is constrained, and so there are some words and sentences that are considered unacceptable by virtually any speaker. In order to understand this pattern of "constrained creativity," we'll consider the possibility that language knowledge involves abstract rules that are, in some fashion, known and honored by every user of the language.

In Chapter 11, we'll discuss the fact that mental images seem to involve representations that are qualitatively distinct from those involved in other forms of knowledge, but we will also consider some of the ways in which memory for visual appearances is governed by the same principles as other forms of knowledge.

Associative Theories of Long-Term Memory

Long-term memory is huge. It has to be, in order to contain all of the information we remember—memories for episodes and for mundane facts, phone numbers, lyrics for songs, the faces of a thousand different acquaintances, the layout of our hometown, the definitions of 50,000 to 60,000 different words, and on and on and on.

How do we ever find anything in this huge storehouse? How do we manage to locate a particular bit of information among the millions of other bits contained within this vast library? Moreover, let's bear in mind that, in most cases, the knowledge contained in your memory is instantly available to you, and so the process of searching through this vast library has to be incredibly fast. Otherwise, you wouldn't be able to use your knowledge in the ways we've described in other chapters. As just one example, imagine that, as you were reading this sentence, you needed a tenth of second to remember what the word "example" means, or the word "imagine." In that case, your reading of the sentence would be impossibly slow—and the same point applies to all the other settings in which you use your knowledge base. If this knowledge is going to be useful for you, it has to be immediately available, and this puts a strong demand on the speed-of-retrieval.

How, therefore, does memory retrieval work, and how is memory set up to support this retrieval? We have already suggested part of the answer—namely, that memory search is aided by *connections* between the materials to be learned and the things one already knows. But what are these connections? Who or what does the "traveling" on these retrieval paths? We turn now to these questions and, more broadly, to the questions of how all of our knowledge is stored in long-term memory.

■ In this chapter, we pursue the idea that connections among memories are actually the building blocks out of which memories are created.

■ This approach, with individual memories built up out of "nodes" within a "network," can explain many of the results we have discussed in the previous chapters. The approach also leads to new predictions, making it undeniable that memory does involve a system in which activation flows from one node to the next.

■ Less clear, though, is whether the spread of activation through a network is *part* of how memory search pro-

ceeds, or whether this simple mechanism might provide our *entire* account of memory search.

■ In addition to our general evaluation of network models, we'll consider two specific ways a network might represent knowledge: via a system of locally represented propositions, or via a system of distributed representations. As we'll see, there are arguments in favor of each approach, and so it is too soon to tell which is the preferred way to think about how knowledge is represented in the mind.

The Network Notion

Much of this chapter will be devoted to exploring a single idea: that memory connections provide much more than retrieval paths; instead, the connections *are* our memories. For example, you know your mother's name; this fact is recorded in your memory. The proposal to be considered is that this memory is literally represented by a memory connection, in this case a connection between some memory content representing your mother and some memory content representing the sound pattern of her name. That connection isn't some appendage to the memory. Instead, the connection *is* the memory. Likewise for all the other facts you know (e.g., the opposite of "hot," how you spent last Thanksgiving, the color of rubies), so that all of knowledge is represented via a sprawling network of these connections, a vast set of associations.

The notion that memory contains a network of associations is hardly new. The idea has been discussed, both in philosophy and in psychology, for several centuries. Modern conceptions of the network, however, differ from their predecessors in important ways; we will discuss some of these differences as we proceed. Our initial focus, though, will not be on the modern conceptions per se. Instead, we will be concerned with broader themes that motivate this approach to memory. Then, once we have discussed these issues, we will turn to some of the specific ways an associative theory might be implemented. We will first consider a form of theorizing patterned after the work of Collins and Loftus (1975) and J. R. Anderson (1976, 1980; J. R. Anderson & Bower, 1973). Later in the chapter, we will turn to a more recent version of associative theorizing, a sophisticated treatment known as "connectionism."

How Might the Network Work?

The essence of a memory network is straightforward. First, we need some means of representing individual ideas; these representations will be the **nodes** within the network, just like the knots within a fisherman's net. (In fact, the word "node" is derived from the Latin word for knot, *nodus*.) These nodes are then tied to each other via connections that we will call **associations** or **associative links**. If you like, you can think of the nodes as being akin to cities on a map, and associations as being the highways that link the cities. Learning, within this metaphor, would be similar to building a highway between two cities, or perhaps improving an existing highway so that it is more easily and quickly traveled.

In this view, what it means to search through memory is to begin at one node (one "city") and to travel via the connections until the target information is reached. Critically, not all associations are of equal strength. Some "cities" are linked by superhighways, others only by country roads. Other cities are not linked to each other at all, but you can get from one to the next by traveling via some intermediate cities. This will immediately provide part of our account for why some memories are easily called up, while others are not. For example, if asked, "When is your birthday?" you answer quickly and easily. Presumably, this is because there is a strong connection between the MY BIRTHDAY node and the node representing a specific date. This connection has been established by the fact that this date and the idea of birthdays have frequently been thought about in conjunction with each other, creating an easily traveled path from one to the other. (Throughout this chapter, we will use small capital letters when we are referring to a NODE in memory; we will use normal type when referring to the word or stimulus represented by that node.)

How do these memory connections get established? We saw in earlier chapters that ideas become linked only if during the learning episode the learner pays attention to the items to be remembered. Apparently, therefore, some active intellectual engagement is needed to create (or strengthen) the connections. And the *nature* of this engagement is crucial. For example, thinking about the material in several different ways will create multiple connections, each of which can later be used as a retrieval path. The learner will also be helped if he or she thinks about the material in distinctive ways. For example, if you establish an association between THE LIST I STUDIED EARLIER and SOME CAPITALIZED WORDS, this connection isn't very informative and probably won't help you later on to recall the words to be remembered. In contrast, an association between THE LIST I STUDIED EARLIER and, say, THE OPPOSITE OF LOVE is distinctive and will help you to remember.

Spreading Activation

Theorists speak of a node becoming activated when it has received a strong enough input signal, sort of like a lightbulb being turned on by incoming electricity. This implies that what travels through the associative links is akin to energy or fuel, and the associative links themselves can be thought of as "activation carriers"—hoses carrying the fuel or wires carrying electricity. Then, once a node has been activated, it can in turn activate other nodes: Energy will spread out from the just-activated node via its associations, and this will activate nodes connected to the just-activated node.

To put all of this more precisely, nodes receive activation from their neighbors, and as more and more activation arrives at a particular node, the **activation level** for

"Steve tried to be careful when he put the vase on the table, but it still broke."

Memory Retrieval

People have no trouble understanding this sentence because they effortlessly retrieve some helpful information from memory: They recall that vases are easy to break, but tables aren't, and this allows them to figure out what the sentence's fifteenth word is referring to. In fact, this memory retrieval is so rapid that people don't even realize that the sentence is ambiguous, and that they have chosen one interpretation over another. This is just one of the cases that reminds us that memory retrieval might be slow enough to be measured, but is still very fast—so that our knowledge is instantly available for use whenever we need it.

that node increases. Eventually, the activation level will reach the node's **response threshold**. Once this happens, we say that the node **fires**. This firing has several effects, including the fact that the node will now itself be a source of activation, sending energy to its neighbors and so activating them. In addition, firing of the node will summon attention to that node; this is what it means to "find" a node within the network.

Activation levels below the response threshold, so-called **subthreshold activation**, also have an important role to play: Activation is assumed to accumulate, so that two subthreshold inputs may add together, or **summate**, and bring the node to threshold. Likewise, if a node has been partially activated recently, it is in effect already "warmed up," so that even a weak input will be sufficient to bring the node to threshold.

These claims mesh well with points we raised in Chapter 2, when we considered how neurons communicate with each other. Neurons receive activation from other neurons; once a neuron reaches its threshold, it fires, sending activation to other neurons. All of this is precisely parallel to the suggestions we are offering here, and this invites the hope that our theorizing about the network will be easily translated into biological terms. Let's be clear that this is not a suggestion that nodes *are* neurons; instead, the biological realization of nodes is likely to be far more complicated than this. Even so, nodes (like any other construct in our theorizing!) can exist only through the functioning of neural tissue, and in this case the close parallels between the way nodes work and the way neurons work suggest that it will be a straightforward matter to translate the psychological claims into biological ones. If so, we can look forward to a point at which we will understand both how the memory network functions and how it is realized in the nervous system.

In addition, the claims we are developing here parallel those we offered in Chapter 3, when we described how a network of detectors might function in object recognition. Detectors receive their activation from other detectors; they can accumulate activation from different inputs, and once activated to threshold levels, they fire. We will return to these parallels later in this chapter, when we will argue that the network of nodes in long-term memory *includes* the network of detectors we considered in Chapter 3.

Returning to long-term storage, however, the key idea is that activation travels from node to node via the associative links. As each node becomes activated and fires, it serves as a source for further activation, spreading onward through the network. This process, known as **spreading activation**, allows us to deal with a key issue. How does one navigate through the maze of associations? If you start a search at one node, how do you decide where to go from there? Our initial proposal is that you do not "choose" at all. Instead, activation spreads out from its starting point in all directions simultaneously, flowing through whatever connections are in place. Think of fuel flowing through hoses: If two hoses radiate out from a starting point, the fuel does not "choose" the left hose or the right. If there are two hoses in place, the fuel will flow through both. This is not to say, however, that all pathways are equally effective in carrying the activation, and in fact we have already suggested that they're not. Some associative links, thanks to recent or frequent use, are particularly effective; others are less so. For that matter, perhaps some associations are "built in"—that is, are innately strong. In any event, the stronger or better-established links will carry activation more efficiently and so will be more successful at activating subsequent nodes.

Evidence Favoring the Network Approach

This sketch of the network leaves a great deal unspecified, but that is deliberate: Associative nets can be implemented in various ways, and we are not ready yet to talk about the details of any particular implementation. We first need to ask whether we are even on the right track. Is this a sensible approach at all? What can be explained in these terms?

Hints

Why do hints help us to remember? Why is it, for example, that you draw a blank if asked, "What's the capital of South Dakota?" but then remember if given the hint, "Is it perhaps a man's name?"

Here's one likely explanation. Mention of South Dakota will activate the nodes in memory that represent your knowledge about this state. Activation will then spread outward from these nodes, eventually reaching nodes that represent the capital city's name. It is possible, though, that there is only a weak connection between the SOUTH DAKOTA nodes and the nodes representing "Pierre." Perhaps you are not very familiar with South Dakota, or perhaps you haven't thought about this state or its capital for some time. In these cases, insufficient activation will flow into the PIERRE nodes, and so these nodes won't reach threshold and won't be "found."

Things will go differently if a hint is available. If you are told, "South Dakota's capital is also a man's name," this will activate the MAN'S NAME node, and so activation will spread out from this source at the same time that activation is spreading out from the SOUTH DAKOTA nodes. Therefore, the nodes for "Pierre" will now receive activation from two sources simultaneously, and this will probably be enough to lift the nodes' activation to threshold levels. In this way, question plus hint accomplishes more than the question by itself (see Figure 8.1).

Context Reinstatement

As we saw in Chapter 6, memory is best if the state you're in during memory retrieval is the same as the state you were in during learning. If you were underwater during learning, you'll have an easier time remembering what you learned if you're again underwater during the memory test. If you were thinking about sounds during learning, you'll do better if you think about sounds during the test.

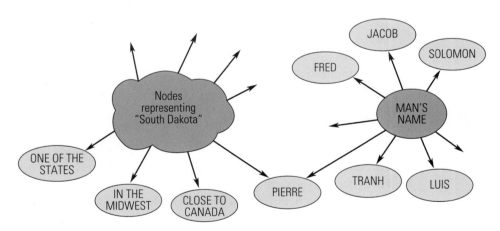

FIGURE 8.1 Activation of a Node From Two Sources
A participant is asked, "What is the capital of South Dakota?" This activates the SOUTH DAKOTA nodes, and activation spreads from there to all of the associated nodes. However, it is possible that the connection between SOUTH DAKOTA and PIERRE is weak, so PIERRE may not receive enough activation to reach threshold. Things will go differently, though, if the participant is also given the hint, "The capital is a man's name." Now the PIERRE node will receive activation from two sources: the SOUTH DAKOTA nodes and the man's name nodes. With this double input, it is more likely that the PIERRE node will reach threshold. This is why the hint ("man's name") makes the memory search easier.

Why should this be? Being underwater will bring certain thoughts to mind during the learning, and it seems likely that some of these thoughts will become associated with the materials being learned. In the terms we're using in this chapter, being underwater will activate certain thoughts, and the nodes representing these thoughts will become connected to the nodes representing the materials to be remembered.

With this base, the logic here is the same as it was in our discussion of hints. Imagine that you learn a list of words, including the word "pointer," while underwater. If asked later on, "What words were on the list?" activation will flow outward from the nodes representing your general thoughts about the list. Perhaps enough of this activation will reach the POINTER nodes to activate them, but perhaps not. If, however, you are again underwater at the time of the test, then this will trigger certain thoughts, and we just suggested that the nodes representing these thoughts may be linked to the nodes representing the learned material—including the POINTER

State-Dependent Learning

In Chaplin's classic movie *City Lights*, a drunken millionaire befriends Chaplin, but then cannot recognize him at all when sober. However, the next time the millionaire is drunk, he easily remembers his friendship with Chaplin. This pattern obviously resembles the pattern of state-dependent learning, in which memory is maximized if someone returns to the same state, during memory retrieval, that they were in during learning. However, the film, for comedic effect, glosses over the fact that drunkenness makes it hard for someone to be thoughtful or attentive—alcohol is actually a powerful impediment to learning!

nodes. As a result, the POINTER nodes will be receiving a double input: They'll receive activation from the nodes representing thoughts about the list, and also from the nodes representing the underwater thoughts. This double input makes it more likely that the POINTER nodes will be activated, leading to the memory advantage that we associate with context reinstatement.

More Direct Tests of the Network Claims

It seems, then, that the network proposal provides a natural way to bring together the evidence presented in the last few chapters. And in some ways, this should be no surprise. After all, we have been talking all along about the importance of *connections*, and the proposal now before us simply develops this idea—by being a bit more precise about what the connections are and how they work. But in addition, the network approach makes its own predictions about memory, allowing a more direct test of the claim that memory does indeed have an associative base.

Spread of Activation and Priming

A key idea of the associative network is that subthreshold activation can accumulate, so that insufficient activation received from one source can add to the insufficient activation received from another source. This is, for example, the heart of our proposal for why hints work and why context reinstatement helps memory. More direct evidence for this claim, though, comes from several paradigms, one of which is the **lexical-decision task**.

In this task (which we first met in Chapter 6), research participants are shown a series of letter sequences on a computer screen. Some of the sequences spell words; other sequences are letter strings that aren't words (e.g., "blar" or "plome" or "tuke"). The participants' task is to hit a "yes" button if the sequence spells a word and a "no" button otherwise. Presumably, they perform this task by "looking up" these letter strings in their "mental dictionary," and they base their response on whether they find the string in the dictionary or not. We can therefore use the participants' speed of response in this task as an index of how quickly they can locate the word in their memories.

Meyer and Schvaneveldt (1971; Meyer, Schvaneveldt, & Ruddy, 1974) presented their participants with *pairs* of letter strings, and participants had to respond "yes" if both strings were words and "no" otherwise. Thus, participants would say "yes" in response to "chair, bread" but "no" in response to "house, fime." In addition, if both strings were words, sometimes the words were semantically related (e.g., "nurse, doctor") and sometimes they were not ("lake, shoe"). Of central interest was how this relationship between the words would influence performance.

Consider a trial in which participants see a related pair, like "bread, butter." To choose a response, they first need to "look up" the word "bread" in memory. This means they'll search for, and presumably activate, the relevant nodes, and in this fashion they'll decide that, yes, this first string is a legitimate word. Then they're ready for the second word in the pair. But notice that in the process of looking up the first word the BREAD node in memory has now been activated. This will, we've hypothesized, trigger a spread of activation outward from this node, bringing activation to other, nearby nodes. These nearby nodes will surely include BUTTER, since the association between "bread" and "butter" is a strong one. Therefore, once BREAD is activated, some activation should also spread to the BUTTER node.

Now let's think through what happens next, when the participant turns her attention to the second word in the pair. To select a response, the participant must locate "butter" in memory. If the participant finds this word (or, more precisely, finds the relevant nodes), then she knows that this string, too, is a word, and she can hit the "yes" button. But of course the process of activating the BUTTER node has already begun, thanks to the activation this node just received from BREAD. This should accelerate the process of bringing this node to threshold (since it's already partway there!), and so it will require less time to activate. Hence, we expect quicker responses to "butter" in this context, compared to a context in which "butter" was preceded by some unrelated word—and therefore not primed.

This prediction is correct. Participants' lexical-decision responses were faster by almost 100 ms if the stimulus words were related, so that the first word could prime the second in the fashion we just described. This is exactly as we would expect on the model we are developing. (For other relevant studies, including some alternative conceptions of priming, see Hutchison, 2003; Lucas, 2000.)

Sentence Verification

When you search through the network, activation spreads from node to node to node. Search through the network, therefore, is like travel, and so the farther one must travel, the longer it should take to reach one's destination. We have already said that this search process is fast—but, even so, the process does take some time, and by measuring the time we can gain insight into the way the process unfolds.

In a classic experiment, Collins and Quillian (1969) explored this issue using a **sentence verification task**. The participants were shown sentences on a computer screen, such as "A robin is a bird" or "A robin is an animal"; or "Cats have claws" or "Cats have hearts." Mixed together with these obviously true sentences were a variety of false sentences (e.g., "A cat is a bird"). Participants had to hit a "true" or "false" button as quickly as they could.

Collins and Quillian reasoned that participants perform this task by "traveling" through the network, seeking a connection between nodes. Thus, when the participant finds the connection from the ROBIN node to the BIRD node, this confirms that there is, in fact, an associative path linking these two nodes, which tells the participant that the sentence about these two concepts is true. This travel will require little time if the two nodes are directly linked by an association, as ROBIN and BIRD probably are (see Figure 8.2). In this case, participants should answer "true" rather quickly. The travel will require more time, however, if the two nodes are connected only indirectly (e.g., ROBIN and ANIMAL), and so we should expect slower responses to sentences that require a "two-step" connection than to sentences that require a single connection.

In addition, Collins and Quillian noted that there is no point in storing in memory the fact that cats have hearts and the fact that dogs have hearts and the fact that squirrels have hearts. Instead, they proposed, it would be more efficient just to store the fact that these various creatures are animals, and then the separate fact that animals have hearts. Hence the property "has a heart" would be associated with the ANIMAL node rather than the nodes for each individual animal, and the same is true for all the other properties of animals, as shown in the figure. According to this logic, we should expect relatively slow responses to sentences like "Cats have hearts," since, to choose a response, a participant must locate the linkage from CAT to ANIMAL and then a second linkage from ANIMAL to HEART. We would expect a quicker response to "Cats have claws," because here there would be a direct connection between CAT and the node representing this property: Although all cats have claws, other animals do not, and so this information could not be entered at the higher level.

As Figure 8.3 shows, these predictions are all borne out. Responses to sentences like "A canary is a canary" take approximately 1 second (1,000 ms in Figure 8.3). This is presumably the time it takes just to read the sentence and to move one's finger on

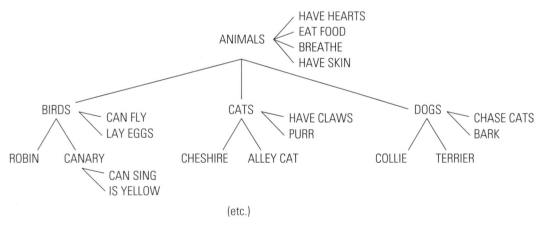

(etc.)

FIGURE 8.2 Hypothetical Memory Structure for Knowledge About Animals
Collins and Quillian proposed that the memory system avoids redundant storage of connections between CATS and HAVE HEARTS, and between DOGS and HAVE HEARTS, and so on for all the other animals. Instead, HAVE HEARTS is stored as a property of all animals. To confirm that cats have hearts, therefore, one must traverse two links: from CATS to ANIMALS, and from ANIMALS to HAVE HEARTS. (After Collins & Quillian, 1969)

the response button. Sentences like "A canary can sing" require an additional step of traversing one link in memory and yield slower responses. Sentences like "A canary can fly" require the traversing of two links, from CANARY to BIRD and then from BIRD to CAN FLY, and so they are correspondingly slower.

We should note, though, that subsequent data have clouded this picture somewhat. For example, Collins and Quillian were correct in arguing that response times depend heavily on the number of associative steps that must be traversed to support a response, but it turns out that this is not the whole story: In addition, some connections can be traversed more quickly than others. This is why participants are quicker to assent to "A robin is a bird" than to "A peacock is a bird" (Rosch, 1973, 1975; E. E. Smith, Rips, & Shoben, 1974). If we were simply to count nodes, these are both one-step connections and so should yield similar response times. In general, though, the more "typical" the exemplar (robins are typical birds, peacocks are not), the faster the response times. (We will say more about typicality in Chapter 9.)

In addition, the principle of nonredundancy envisioned by Collins and Quillian doesn't always hold. For example, the property of "having feathers" should, on their view, be associated with the BIRD node rather than (redundantly) with the ROBIN node, the PIGEON node, the EAGLE node, and so forth. This fits with the fact that responses are relatively slow to sentences like "Sparrows have feathers." Verifying this sentence requires a two-step connection—from SPARROW to BIRD and then from BIRD to HAS FEATHERS—and that's the reason for the slowness. However, it turns out that participants respond very quickly to a sentence like "Peacocks have feath-

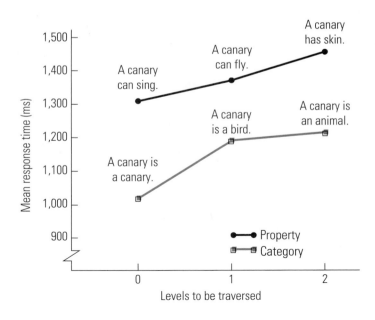

FIGURE 8.3 Time Needed to Confirm Various Semantic Facts

In a sentence verification task, participants' responses were fastest when the test required them to traverse zero links in memory ("A canary is a canary"), slower when the necessary ideas were separated by one link, and slower still if the ideas were separated by two links. (After Collins & Quillian, 1969)

ers." This is because in observing peacocks or speaking of peacocks, one often thinks about their prominent tail feathers (Conrad, 1972). Even though it is informationally redundant, a strong association between PEACOCK and FEATHERS is likely to be established.

For these (and other) reasons, psychologists have moved away from the exact model proposed by Collins and Quillian. However, this doesn't change the fact that, all other things being equal, we can predict the speed of memory access by counting the number of nodes participants must traverse in answering a question—an observation that powerfully confirms the claim that associative links play an important role in memory representation.

Degree of Fan

The speed of hunting through memory is also influenced by another factor—the nodes' *degree of fan*. To make this concrete, think about your knowledge of, say, *robins* and your knowledge of *aardvarks*. You probably know far more about robins than you do about aardvarks, and so there are more associations in your memory radiating out from the ROBIN node than there are from AARDVARK. The ROBIN node, in other words, will look like the hub of a many-spoked wheel, while the AARDVARK node will not (see Figure 8.4). In the standard terminology, ROBIN has a high **degree of fan** (many things fanning out from it), and AARDVARK has a low degree of fan.

Why should degree of fan matter? Recall that once a node is activated, the activation will spread from there, flowing through all the links radiating out from that node. In addition, it seems plausible that the quantity of activation is limited, so that each of the links only gets its "share" of the whole. (For simplicity's sake, let's assume that all of the links are equal in how effectively they carry the activation; the broad logic is the same if we don't make this assumption.) Therefore, if there are (say) just five links radiating out from AARDVARK, then each link will receive 20% of the total activation. The activation spreading outward from ROBIN, in contrast, will be much more thinly divided, and so each link will receive a smaller share of the total. And if each link receives less activation, each will carry less to the neighboring nodes. This will surely slow down the rate at which those neighbors are activated, and this will, in turn, slow down memory search.

Can we document this effect of fan? One researcher had participants memorize a set of sentences about people in locations: "The doctor is in the bank"; "The fireman is in the park"; "The lawyer is in the church"; "The lawyer is in the park"; and so on (Anderson, 1974). In the full set of sentences, some of the actors (e.g., the doctor) appeared in only one location (the bank); others (the lawyer) appeared in two locations. Likewise, some locations (the church) contained only one person; other locations (the park) contained two. In this way, the study controlled the degree of fan from the nodes representing each of these terms; there was greater fan for PARK than for CHURCH, and greater fan for LAWYER than for DOCTOR.

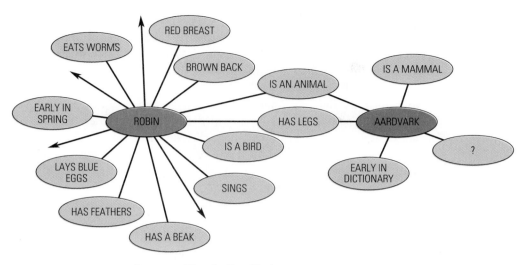

FIGURE 8.4 Degree of Fan for Two Nodes

Most people know many facts about robins, and so there are many linkages radiating out from the ROBIN node—a high degree of fan. In contrast, people typically know relatively few facts about aardvarks, and so few linkages radiate out from the AARDVARK node—a low degree of fan.

Once the participants had memorized these sentences, they were given a recognition test in which they had to decide as quickly as possible whether each of the test sentences had been presented as part of the learning set. The data showed a clear effect of fan: Response times were fastest when only one sentence mentioned a specific person or a specific place; response times were slowest when multiple sentences named a specific person or place. This is exactly what we would expect if activation were a fixed quantity; thus, the more ways divided, the less activation to each recipient. The less activation to each recipient, the longer it takes for the target node to be fully activated and so, finally, the longer for the response to be chosen. (For other research on the fan effect, and also some complications, see Anderson & Reder, 1999a, 1999b; McGuire & Maki, 2001; Radvansky, 1999; Radvansky & Zacks, 1991.)

Retrieving Information From a Network

So far, things look good for the network model. We have easily encompassed the findings described in Chapters 5, 6, and 7, and many new results confirm our claims about spreading activation and fan. In addition, the network idea offers us one further benefit: It holds the promise of explaining how we search through memory so quickly and easily.

Searching Through the Network via Associative Links

Think about how you search for information on the Internet. In most cases, you'd start with a search engine (Google, perhaps, or Yahoo), but often this does not bring you directly to the information you want. Nonetheless, you can find the desired information by using the labeled links that lead from one site to the next. Thus, imagine that your dog is ill. You might start your memory search with "dog diseases," and this might bring you to pages on veterinary medicine. However, these pages might not give you what you need, and so you might click on a link promising information on specific illnesses. That, too, might not give you what you need, but you might find a link that leads to *symptoms* of the various illnesses. This, at last, might allow you to figure out what is ailing your dog.

Of course, all this depends on having the right links and, indeed, on having a lot of links; otherwise, bridges between related topics may be omitted. But the system will collapse if there are *too many* links. Imagine that at the bottom of a Web page you find the message, "For more information, check out these sites!" and this is fol-

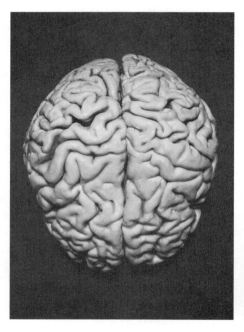

Long-Term Memory Storage
How much information is actually stored in long-term memory? No one has a good estimate, in part because we do not know what "compression algorithm" the brain uses—i.e., how the brain "packs in" the information. (To see how important this is, bear in mind that an audio CD ordinarily holds 70 minutes of music, but, if the music is "compressed" into MP3 format, the same CD can hold ten times that amount.) On anyone's account, though, long-term memory is huge, and this makes our speed of retrieving information from this storehouse truly remarkable.

lowed by a list of 343,912 links to other pages. This wouldn't be helpful, because you might need weeks to sift through the options to find the one that is useful. Presumably, though, you can find an appropriate number of links—neither too few nor too many—so that you end up with a Web page providing useful guidance to your further searching.

The network that supports your memory probably works the same way, with associative links guiding search through the network just as hyperlinks guide search through the Internet. To continue our example, let's imagine that at some prior point you have thought about the relationship between diseases and the practice of medicine, and the relationship between medicine and veterinary medicine. Therefore, the corresponding nodes will be linked, and so activating the DISEASE node will cause activation to spread to the MEDICINE node. Activation of that node will in turn activate the VETERINARY MEDICINE node, and so on, leading eventually to the material you seek.

It is also important that activation can spread from more than one source simultaneously; we relied on this claim in our discussion of hints and context reinstatement. This is actually better than what you do on the World Wide Web. It is the equivalent of looking up one Web page and finding its set of links, and then looking up a different page with its own set of links, and then, finally, asking which links appear in both sets. Obviously, this could narrow your search considerably, but with the Internet it would be a cumbersome process. In your memory, however, this process is achieved automatically: Activation will simply spread out from both of the entry points and, with no intervention and no guidance, will converge on the sought-after node.

Finding Entry Nodes

There is, however, one problem in the account just sketched. With the Internet, you launch the search process by typing some text into a search engine. How do things get launched when we're talking about searching through *memory*?

The answer to this question has several parts, but one part lies in links that tie the memory network directly to the mechanisms of perception. Specifically, some nodes within the net are **input nodes**. In their functioning, these nodes are like any others: They receive activation via associative links; once triggered, they send activation to other nodes. What is special about these input nodes, though, is that they receive most of their input activation from appropriate *detectors*, with these in turn being connected to the eyes, ears, and so on.

All of this is perfectly compatible with claims we made in Chapter 3, when we discussed how you recognize words. We suggested there that detectors for *words* might be triggered by detectors for the appropriate *letter combinations*. These in turn would be triggered by *letter detectors*, which would themselves be triggered by *feature detectors*. All we need to do now is notice that these various detectors are actually nodes within a network, functioning just like any other nodes: accumulating activation, eventually reaching threshold, and then sending activation to other nodes. And because they are nodes, there is no problem with these perceptually driven "input nodes" (the detectors) sending their activation to the long-term memory nodes we are describing in this chapter.

To put this in different words, there's really no difference between the feature net we described in Chapter 3 and the memory network we're describing here. They are seamlessly joined, with detectors (nodes that receive their input from the outside world) sending activation to memory nodes, and in that fashion allowing cues from the outside to trigger events in the memory network.

In this setting, we should acknowledge that we still need more theory to explain how inputs (especially complex, structured inputs) are recognized, and so our simple network-based proposal will be an important part of the story, but not the whole story. (For more on this point, see Chapter 3 and also Chapter 10.) Even so, we have taken a large step toward answering the question of what launches memory search in the first place. The key idea is that perceiving and identifying an input will involve, among other steps, the locating and activating of that input's node in the network. Perceiving, itself, will launch memory search.

Unpacking the Nodes

We have so far spoken of nodes as representing ideas or memories. But what does this mean? Could a node contain, for example, your full memory of last semester's courses? A node such as this would contain a lot of complex information; in that case, we would need to add to our theorizing some device capable of reading and interpreting this corpus of material. Conversely, the simpler we keep each node's informational content, the less we need to rely on some interpretive device.

Any network model needs to deal with these points, but it turns out that different models approach the issue in different ways. Therefore, to tackle these questions, we need to start distinguishing among the various *types* of associative models; in particular, we need to distinguish the most recent versions of associative theory from earlier versions. Let's start with the older perspective; we will consider the more recent innovations later.

Different Types of Associative Links

One proposal is that nodes represent single concepts—and nothing more complicated than that. This is consistent with the examples we have used so far, in which nodes have stood for concepts such as "chair" or "doctor." This still leaves many questions: How does a node represent a concept? Does the DOG node contain a brief definition of the concept "dog"? A small picture of a dog? It turns out that neither of these proposals is satisfactory, and we will need most of Chapter 9 to work through the problem of how concepts are represented in the mind.

In the meantime, though, we can use the network notion to help us with a related problem—namely, how we might represent more complex ideas, such as "George Washington was the first president" or "My favorite movie is *Casablanca.*" For that matter, how do we represent an idea as complicated as "my understanding of Darwin's theory of evolution" or a memory as complicated as "how I spent last summer"?

These complex ideas are represented, oddly enough, with more network. As a first approximation, an associative link may exist between GEORGE WASHINGTON and FIRST PRESIDENT, and a set of links may tie together MOVIE and FAVORITE and CASABLANCA. But this is too simple. How, for example, would one represent the contrast between "Sam has a dog" and "Sam is a dog"? If all we have is an association between SAM and DOG, we won't be able to tell these two ideas apart. Early theorizing sought to deal with this problem by introducing different types of associative links, with some links representing equivalence (or partial equivalence) relations and other links representing possessive relations. These links were termed *isa* links, as in "Sam isa dog," and *hasa* links, as in "A bird hasa head" or "Sam hasa dog" (Norman, Rumelhart, & Group, 1975).

Propositional Networks and ACT

There are clear limits, however, on what we can accomplish with these labeled associations. The problem is that we are able to remember, and to think about, a wide range of relationships, not just equivalence and possession. We can, for example, consider the relationship "is the opposite of" or the relationship "is analogous to," and a thousand others as well. If each type of relationship is represented by a specific type of associative link, then we'll end up with many types of links, so that we'll need a "link reader" of some sort—and that would complicate our theorizing considerably, requiring mechanisms rather different from the ones we've considered so far.

Researchers have therefore sought other mechanisms through which network models might represent complex ideas. One proposal has been developed by John Anderson (1976, 1980, 1993; Anderson & Bower, 1973), and at the center of this conception is the idea of **propositions**; these are defined as the smallest units of knowledge that can be either true or false. For example, "Children love candy" is a proposition, but "Children" is not; "Susan likes blue cars" is a proposition, but "blue cars" is not. Propositions are easily represented as sentences, but this is merely a convenience. In fact, the same proposition can be represented in a variety of different sentences: For example, "Children love candy," "Candy is loved by children," and "Kinder lieben Bonbons" all express the same proposition. For that matter, the same proposition can also be represented in various nonlinguistic forms, including a structure of nodes and linkages, and that is exactly what Anderson's model does.

Anderson's theory is embodied in a computer program known as ACT (and in later versions as ACT-R; see Anderson, 1993, 1996). Within ACT, propositions are represented as shown in Figure 8.5. The ellipses identify the propositions themselves;

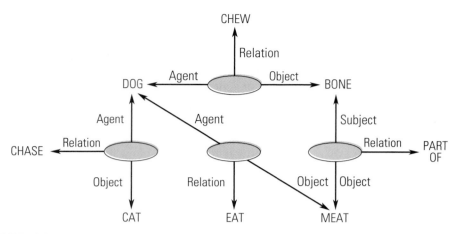

FIGURE 8.5 Network Representation of Some of the Concepts Associated With "Dog"
Your understanding of dogs—what dogs are, what they are likely to do—is represented by an interconnected network of propositions, with each proposition indicated by an ellipse. Labels on the arrows indicate each node's role within the proposition. (After J. R. Anderson, 1980)

associations connect each ellipse to the ideas that are the proposition's constituents. The associations are labeled, but only in general terms. That is, the associations are identified in terms of their syntactic role within the proposition. This allows us to distinguish the proposition "Dogs chase cats" (shown in the figure) from the proposition "Cats chase dogs" (not shown).

Figure 8.5 actually shows four propositions that, together, constitute part of the network that represents your knowledge about dogs. A complete depiction of your knowledge would include many other propositions as well, each representing some other aspect of your knowledge about what dogs are and how they behave.

To represent specific episodes or a specific object (rather than a category), ACT makes a distinction between **type nodes** and **token nodes**. "Type" refers to a general category, and type nodes are embedded in propositions true for the entire category. A "token" is a specific instance of a category, and token nodes are therefore found in propositions concerned with specific events and individuals. Note that type and token nodes are typically connected to each other as shown in Figure 8.6.

In addition, the ACT model distinguishes between timeless truths like "Jacob feeds the pigeons" and more specific statements like "Last spring, Jacob fed the pigeons in Trafalgar Square." ACT does this by incorporating time and location nodes as part of propositions, and in this fashion it can mark when and where the proposition was true. This additional information allows ACT to represent facts about specific episodes (see Figure 8.7).

The ACT model shares many claims with other network models: Nodes are connected by associative links. Some of these links are stronger than others, with the strength of the link depending on how frequently and recently it has been used.

Once a node is activated, the process of spreading activation causes the nearby nodes to become activated as well. ACT is distinctive, however, in its attempt to represent knowledge in terms of propositions, and the promise of this approach has attracted the support of many researchers in this area.

Refining Network Models

Associative theories of memory strike many investigators as being our best hypothesis about how knowledge is represented in the mind. At the same time, these models have been controversial. Let's look at some of this debate.

How Can We Test Network Models?

The evidence is clear that mechanisms such as spreading activation and subthreshold priming do play a role in memory search. However, the data presented so far do not speak to a larger and more interesting issue: Are these mechanisms merely *involved* in memory search? Or could it be that these mechanisms, by themselves, *provide our*

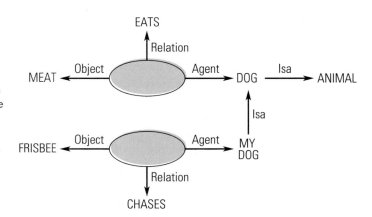

FIGURE 8.6 Networks Contain Information About Categories and About Individuals

This fragment of a network contains a type node representing dogs in general, and a token node representing a specific dog (MY DOG). The type node is linked to propositions true for all dogs; the token node is linked to propositions true only for MY DOG. That is, all dogs eat meat. Not all dogs chase Frisbees, although MY DOG does. The type node and token node are linked to each other (via an *isa* line), indicating that "my dog" is a member of the category "dogs."

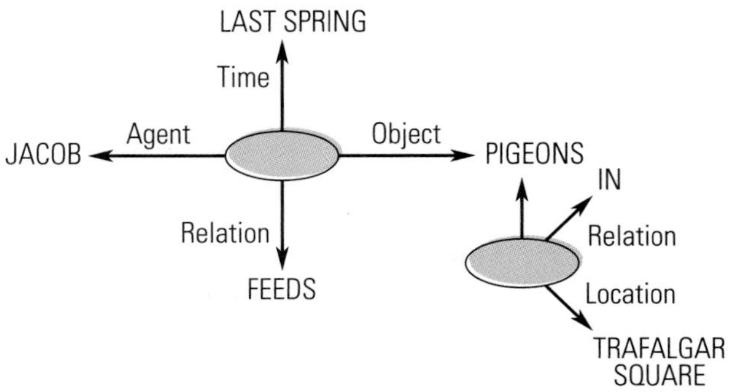

FIGURE 8.7 Representing Episodes Within a Propositional Network

In order to represent episodes, the propositional network includes time and location nodes. This fragment of a network represents two propositions— the proposition that Jacob fed pigeons last spring, and the proposition that the pigeons are in Trafalgar Square. Note that no time node is associated with the proposition about pigeons being in Trafalgar Square. Therefore, what is represented is that the feeding of the pigeons took place last spring, but that the pigeons are always in the square.

entire account of memory retrieval, so that we need no further theory? Up until now in this chapter, we've considered no mechanisms other than associations, spreading activation, and the like. Therefore, we've been on a path toward suggesting that these are the only mechanisms we'll need to explain memory retrieval. Is this suggestion right?

Perhaps the best way to address these questions might be simply to give networks a serious try. Specifically, if one has a theory of how memory operates, one powerful test of the theory would be to build a working model based on the theoretical claims and to examine how well the model performed as an information storage and retrieval device. On this basis, many psychologists are seeking to construct such models of memory, usually implemented as a computer program that functions according to the rules and procedures specified by the theory. (We mentioned earlier, for example, that Anderson's ACT model is embodied in such a system.) This allows us to see how well the computer does in "learning"—that is, in storing new information—and then in retrieving facts, based on some cue or hint. If the computer fails in these tasks or doesn't do as well as humans do, we know that something is missing (or wrong) in the theory. What if the computer succeeds? Success would indicate that the processes and strategies programmed into the computer are sufficient to accomplish the tasks of learning and remembering. This would not, by itself, show that humans use the same processes and strategies. It would, however, be a strong argument that the theory must be taken seriously as an account of human performance.

It would take us rather far afield to evaluate these modeling efforts in any detail. To make a long story short, though, it is not possible to point to an associative network that successfully simulates all of human memory. The available models work reasonably well, but all are limited in their scope, representing just a narrow slice of knowledge—knowledge about a particular topic or a particular domain. How should we think about this limitation? It could be understood as reflecting some inadequacy in the network approach. Alternatively, it could just reflect the early state of the models' evolution. With further work and refinements, perhaps these limits will be overcome.

It's too soon to know which of these interpretations is correct. What we can do in the meantime, though, is to look at some of the specific reasons why the models have (so far) been limited; this will help us understand some of the potential problems for the network approach. We'll then consider ways that a network might handle these challenges.

Retrieval Blocks and Partial Retrievals

One attractive feature of the associative net is that activation spreads out indiscriminately through all of the available connections. We need no means of directing the activation or supervising the search. Instead, we simply allow the activation to travel wherever the connections lead.

This approach keeps our theorizing simple, but do things always work in a fashion consistent with this "automatic" view? Try to think of the word that means a type of carving done on whalebone, often depicting whaling ships or whales. Try to think of the name of the navigational device used by sailors to determine the positions of stars. Try to think of the name of the Russian sled drawn by three horses. Chances are that in at least one of these cases you found yourself in a frustrated state—certain you knew the word but unable to come up with it. The word was, as they say, right on the "tip of your tongue"; following this lead, psychologists refer to this as the **TOT phenomenon**. People in the TOT state often know correctly that the word is somewhere in their vocabulary; they often correctly remember what letter the word begins with, how many syllables it has, and approximately what it sounds like. Thus, a person might remember "It's something like Sanskrit" in trying to remember "scrimshaw," or "something like secant" in trying to remember "sextant" (A. Brown, 1991; R. Brown & McNeill, 1966; Harley & Brown, 1998; W. James, 1890; Read & Bruce, 1982; Reason & Lucas, 1984; B. L. Schwartz, 1999). Similar results have been obtained when people try to recall specific names: Who played the nervous man with the knife in the shower scene in Hitchcock's *Psycho*? What was the name of the Greek orator who taught himself to speak clearly by practicing speeches with pebbles in his mouth? With clues like these, research participants are often able to recall the number of syllables in the name and the name's initial letter, but not the name itself (Brennen, Baguley, Bright, & Bruce, 1990; Hanley & Chapman, 2008; Yarmey, 1973). (Anthony Perkins was the nervous man with the knife, and the Greek orator was Demosthenes. The Russian sled is a troika.)

On first inspection, these findings seem not to fit with the network view. It seems clear that a person in the TOT state has reached the memory vicinity of the sought-after word. After all, the person is able to come up with the correct starting letter and the correct number of syllables. In addition, the nodes in this area of memory are presumably receiving a great deal of activation, given the time and effort one spends in trying to find the word. But this activation seems not to spread to the sought-after node; if it does, the activation of this node is not being recognized or acknowledged. In short, the person is in the right neighborhood; there is lots of activation on the scene, but the activation does not reach the target. All of this is peculiar if we conceive of spreading activation as a purely mechanical process whose success is guaranteed once one is in the correct memory vicinity.

Finding More Distant Connections

In the TOT state, you fail to locate a target memory despite being in the right memory vicinity with plenty of activation. Related concerns emerge in a different case—a case in which you *succeed* in locating the memory you seek.

We have already said that only some of the links radiating out from a node will be efficient carriers of activation—namely, those links that are used frequently or recently.

But realistically, what is the number of these likely to be? How many strong associations does one have, for example, to "water"? Is 100 a halfway plausible number? This is probably a gross underestimate, but it will serve for the moment. Using this estimate, think about what happens when activation spreads outward from the WATER node. One hundred new nodes each receive some activation (see Figure 8.8). If the sought-for information is directly associated with the WATER node, things will now go well: One only has to choose which among these hundred is the node one seeks.

But what if the sought-for node is not directly tied to WATER? What if it is tied by means of one intermediate step? We have already said that 100 nodes receive activation directly from WATER; now activation spreads out from these. If each of these 100 is connected to 100 more nodes, we end up with activation reaching 10,000 nodes. And, of course, if the sought-for node is still one more step removed, we need to let activation spread once again, so that now activation reaches a million nodes ($100 \times 100 \times 100$).

It seems, then, that we create problems if we let the spreading activation spread too far. Even if the spread is only three or four steps, we will end up with too many nodes

FIGURE 8.8 How Many Associations Are There to "Water"?
There is probably a huge number of linkages radiating out from each node; we have shown here only some of the ideas associated with the node for water. Each of these associations leads to some other node(s), and there are likely to be many linkages radiating out from those other nodes. If activation spreads out just one step, a large number of nodes will be activated. If activation spreads out two steps, how many nodes receive activation?

activated, and so we will lose the selective guidance we hoped for in the first place. You were hunting for one memory, but you've activated a million memories instead!

Of course, we can avoid this danger if we place limits on how far the activation can spread. In this case, we avoid the risk of activating too many nodes, but we also risk not finding the node we seek: If the activation peters out, for example, after a single link, then your memory search will never find information that is two links away from your starting point.

Winner Takes All

How should we address these challenges? Let's start with the fact that whenever you hunt through memory, activation spreads outward from the nodes representing your search's starting point. In many cases, this will activate the nodes representing the information you seek, but it will also activate many nodes irrelevant to your current concerns. What you need, therefore, is some means of narrowing things down, of picking out just a subset of the now-activated nodes. In this way, you could focus on the nodes representing the desired information and ignore the nodes representing irrelevancies.

One way to achieve this is by launching a process of *competition* among the nodes. Specifically, let's imagine a process in which each node can sometimes send out inhibition, rather than activation, to the nodes associated with it, thereby *deactivating* its neighbors rather than activating them. Let's also imagine that the more active a node is, the more strongly it will inhibit its neighbors. As a result, we might start with, say, 100 nodes activated, some more strongly than others. The most strongly activated node, however, will "shut down" the other (more weakly activated) nodes, so that many are activated initially, but only one—the strongest—survives the competition. This is called a **winner-takes-all system.**[1]

A winner-takes-all system could help us with both of the network problems we just described. Concretely, let's say that you're in a chemistry exam and trying to remember some facts about water. Your thinking about water will activate the node for this concept, and this will send activation to many nodes that are entirely irrelevant for your current purposes—the nodes representing your memory of a vacation at the lake or the nodes representing your annoyance at the rainy weather. These nodes will be shut down, however, thanks to the competition we have described: In this setting, it's likely that the node H_2O will receive activation both from the WATER node and from the CHEMISTRY node; this will make the H_2O node strong enough to win the winner-takes-all contest, shutting down the other distracting thoughts. If activation

---

[1]The terminology here is borrowed from politics. In most parliamentary systems—the United Kingdom's, for example, or Germany's—each party gets a share of power corresponding to its share of votes. If the X Party, therefore, gets 28% of the votes, then it gets 28% of the seats in Parliament. In contrast, the United States has a winner-takes-all system: If a presidential candidate gets 58% of the vote, she doesn't get just 58% of the presidency; she gets 100%.

now spreads outward from the H$_2$O node, you are likely to find the information you seek. And, crucially, with the RAINY WEATHER nodes now shut down, as well as the VACATION AT THE LAKE nodes, you won't activate *their* associated nodes, and so the distracting thoughts won't trigger other distracting thoughts. In this way, the winner-takes-all system provides a mechanism that helps keep your thoughts on track at the same time that it helps you swiftly cull through the nodes activated in your search.

Sometimes, though, this mechanism will work against you. Imagine that you are trying to remember the name of the main character in the movie *The Matrix*. You'll start by activating nodes representing your recall of the movie, and activation will then spread from there to the associated nodes. One of those nodes might be MORPHEUS, and this is close (Morpheus was in the movie) but not quite right (Morpheus wasn't the main character). But perhaps the MORPHEUS node becomes strongly activated. This launches the winner-takes-all process, which weakens the other associated nodes—which include the node you want! At this point, your early activation of MORPHEUS will actually work against your finding the information you seek. (Who was the main character, by the way?) In this fashion, the winner-takes-all system can produce a **retrieval block** and can, in particular, produce the pattern we have labeled the TOT state.

Your best bet in this situation, therefore, may be simply to give up on your search for now. This will allow the MORPHEUS activation to decay, which will weaken the inhibition now attached to this node's neighbors, which will then make it easier to activate these neighbors. (For more on competition among nodes and how, in particular, this might apply to the TOT phenomenon, see Anderson & Bell, 2001; M. C. Anderson & Spellman, 1995; L. E. James & Burke, 2000; S. K. Johnson & Anderson, 2004; Macleod & Macrae, 2001. The main character in *The Matrix* was Neo.)

The Newest Chapter: Connectionism

We've now considered one way a network model might be expanded—by adding some sort of inhibitory process. This process will occasionally interfere with memory search (as in the TOT example), but more often it will *help* memory search by avoiding the problem of having too many memories activated.

Investigators have also explored other ways to improve the network's functioning. One option is to incorporate some sort of "executive processes" similar to those introduced in Chapters 4 and 5. These processes, we've suggested, allow us to form plans and set goals, and so, plausibly, these processes might allow us to make strategic decisions about memory search—decisions about where to begin a search, for example, or decisions that might guide the flow of activation through the network. Of course, any appeal to these processes would entail a different style of theorizing than we have considered in this chapter, but we may eventually need this extra complexity if we hope to explain the full range of memory's functioning.

A different option is also being developed, and it has generated considerable excitement not just in psychology but also in computer science and philosophy. Rather than adding an "executive" to the network, this approach moves in the opposite direction and tries, in effect, to improve the network's functioning by making the network's components *simpler* rather than more complex.

Distributed Processing, Distributed Representations

In the networks we have considered so far, individual ideas are represented with **local representations**: Each node represents one idea, so that when that node is activated, you're thinking that idea, and when you're thinking about that idea, that node is activated. In contrast, **connectionist networks** rely on **distributed representations**, so that any particular idea is represented only by a pattern of activation across the network. To take a simple case, the concept "birthday" might be represented by a pattern in which nodes B, F, H, and R are firing, whereas the concept "computer" might be represented by a pattern in which nodes C, G, H, and S are firing. Note that node H is part of both of these patterns and probably part of the pattern for many other concepts as well. Therefore, we can't attach any meaning or interpretation to this node by itself; we can only learn what is being represented by looking at many other nodes simultaneously to find out what pattern of activation exists across the entire network. (For more on local and distributed representations, see Chapter 3.)

This reliance on distributed representation has important consequences for how a connectionist network functions. Imagine being asked what sort of computer you use. In order for you to respond, the idea "computer" needs to trigger the idea "MacBook" (or "Dell" or whatever it is you have). In a distributed network, this means that the many nodes representing "computer" have to manage collectively to activate the many nodes representing "MacBook." To continue our simple illustration, node C has to trigger node L at the same time that node G triggers node A, and so on, leading ultimately to the activation of the L-A-J-T combination that, let's say, represents "MacBook." In short, a network using distributed representations must employ processes that are similarly distributed, so that one widespread activation pattern can have broad enough effects to evoke a different (but equally widespread) pattern. In addition, the steps bringing this about must all occur simultaneously—in parallel—with each other, so that one entire representation can smoothly trigger the next. This is why connectionist models are said to involve **parallel distributed processing** (PDP).

This type of processing has both advantages and disadvantages. One crucial advantage comes from the fact that distributed processing, by its very nature, allows something called **simultaneous multiple constraint satisfaction**. To understand this point, let's start with the fact that mental processes in general, and memory searches in particular, often have to satisfy many demands, as illustrated in Figure 8.9. You could deal with this in any given case by trying to think through the demands one by one—seeking an idea that satisfies the first requirement, then narrowing things to just those options that also satisfy the second requirement, then narrowing things still further in light of the third requirement, and so on, continuing in this way until you'd located a solution that satisfies *all* the constraints. In many circumstances, though, this might be slow and laborious. Worse, this procedure could easily fail: Many circumstances demand some sort of compromise among the various demands, and the one-requirement-at-a-time procedure provides no way to locate that compromise.

As an alternative, it might be more efficient to tackle all of the demands at once—by letting one part of the network deal with one demand; another part, another demand; and so forth. Each part of the network would therefore "tug" you toward a particular outcome—one that would satisfy just one of the constraints. With all of these tugs working simultaneously, though, they would pull you toward a specific target that represents, in essence, the "balance point" among all of these tugs (in our example in Figure 8.9: the frying pan)—an idea, or memory, that provides the best possible compromise among the various demands.

We still might ask, however, how this balancing of the various "tugs" plays out. In fact, we've already covered this point: In the feature net described in Chapter 3, there's no mechanism in place to coordinate the various detectors. Instead, each detector does its own thing—guided by the input that it received and by its level of activation prior to receiving any input. The *CH*-detector therefore tugs the network in one direction, the *CO*-detector tugs in a different direction, and the final outcome simply reflects the sum of all these tugs. As we saw earlier, the resulting network, simple as it is, can accomplish a great deal: It acts as if it knows the rules of English spelling, it seems to have "expectations," and it acts as if it were making "inferences"

FIGURE 8.9 Satisfying Multiple Constraints
Imagine that you live in an apartment on the 10th floor of a building, and you want to hang a picture on the wall. All you need to do is bang a nail into the wall, but you have no hammer. What should you use? You need to search memory for something that is hard enough to bang a nail, lightweight enough so that you can swing it, strong enough so that it can take the impact, likely to be within your apartment, preferably belonging to you and not your roommate, and so on. If the cast-iron frying pan comes to mind, it's because the pan satisfies all these requirements. How do you manage to search through memory in order to honor all of these constraints?

to fill in missing information. But this is not because the network includes some centralized authority or some sophisticated decision-maker. Instead, the network is a fully distributed system, and what it accomplishes is simply the result of the different elements within the system each doing their individual jobs.

Learning as the Setting of Connection Weights

How do we construct models that gain the advantage from simultaneous multiple constraint satisfaction? To answer this, we first need to address a separate question. If distributed processing is going to succeed, we need to have the appropriate connections in place, so that activation will spread to the desired target rather than in some other direction. This demands that we ask: How are the connections set up in the first place? In other words, how, in a connectionist account, does learning take place?

In any associative network, knowledge is literally contained within the associations themselves. To return to an earlier example, the knowledge that "George Washington was a president" can be represented via a link between the nodes representing GEORGE WASHINGTON and those representing PRESIDENT. When we first introduced this example, we phrased it in terms of local representations, with individual nodes having specific assigned referents. The basic idea, however, is the same in a distributed system. What it means to know this fact about Washington is to have a pattern of connections among the many nodes that together represent "Washington" and the many nodes that together represent "president." Once these connections are in place, activation of either of these patterns will lead to the activation of the other.

Notice, then, that knowledge refers to a *potential* rather than to a *state*. If you know that Washington was a president, then the connections are in place so that if the "Washington" pattern of activations occurs, this will lead to the "president" pattern of activations. And, of course, this state of readiness will remain even if you happen not to be thinking about Washington right now. In this way, "knowing" something, in network terms, corresponds to how the activation will flow—if there is activation on the scene. This is different from "thinking about" something, which corresponds to which nodes are active at a particular moment, with no comment about where that activation will spread next.

On this view, "learning" must involve some sort of adjustments of the connections among nodes, so that after learning, activation will flow in a fashion that can represent the newly gained knowledge or the newly acquired skill. But in a connectionist network, these adjustments cannot be done via some central authority's intervention—because in a connectionist network there is no central authority. Instead, the adjustment must be governed entirely at the local level. In other words, the adjustment of **connection weights**—the strength of the individual connections—must be controlled entirely by mechanisms in the immediate neighborhood of each connection and influenced only by information about what's happening in that neighborhood.

Moreover, let's be clear that any bit of learning requires the adjustment of a great many connection weights: We need to adjust the connections, for example, so that the thousands of nodes representing "Washington" manage, together, to activate the thousands of nodes representing "president." Thus, learning, just like everything else in the connectionist scheme, must be a distributed process involving thousands of microscopic changes taking place all over the network, with no attempt at (and, indeed, no mechanism for) any coordination of these adjustments.

This is, to be sure, an amazing proposal. In order to achieve learning in the network, the various adjustments in connection weights must in some way end up coordinated with each other. Otherwise, adjustments at one connection might cancel out adjustments made at another! Thus, if learning is to happen at all, we need to ensure that there is some coherence in the changes made across the network. And yet, as we have said, there is no explicit mechanism in place to achieve this coordination. How, therefore, is learning possible? Here we arrive at one of the most important intellectual innovations driving connectionism forward. Connectionists have offered a number of powerful computing schemes, called "learning algorithms," that seek to accomplish learning within this setup. These schemes accomplish learning on the local level, without an executive and seem to make the entire system grow gradually and impressively smarter.

One type of learning algorithm, for example, is governed by whether neighboring nodes are activated at the same time or not. If the nodes are activated at the same time, the connection between them is strengthened; if they are activated at different times, the connection is weakened. This gives the network a means of learning what-goes-with-what in experience—learning, for example, that "Q" is usually followed by "U," that the taste of apples is usually accompanied by the sight of an apple, and so on. Another type of learning relies on feedback: In this algorithm, nodes that led to an inappropriate response receive an **error signal** from some external source, and this causes a *decrease* in the node's connections to the other nodes that led it to the error. (It as if the node were saying to its inputs, "You misled me, and so I will listen to you less carefully in the future.") In addition, the node also transmits the error signal to those same inputs, so that they can make their own adjustments. (Again, it is as if the initial node is saying, "You misled me, so you had it wrong; therefore, you should put less faith in the nodes that misled *you*.") In this fashion, the error signal is transmitted backwards through the network—starting with the nodes that immediately triggered the incorrect response, but with each node then passing the error signal back to the nodes that had caused it to fire. This process is called **back propagation**, and it allows the entire network to make use of the feedback even though each node is only being influenced by the nodes in its immediate vicinity.

Strengths and Limits for Connectionist Networks

Many psychologists and computer scientists regard connectionist models as an enormously powerful form of theorizing and a great step forward; others argue that the models are inadequate and that we should be pursuing other approaches. (For advocates of the connectionist approach, see Christiansen, Chater, & Seidenberg, 1999; Churchland & Sejnowski, 1992; McClelland & Rogers, 2003; Plaut, 2000; Rogers & McClelland, 2004; Rumelhart, 1997; Seidenberg & Zevin, 2006; for more critical views, see Fodor, 1997; Fodor & Pylyshyn, 1988; Holyoak, 1987; Lachter & Bever, 1988; Pinker, 1999.)

What arguments might sway us for or against the connectionist approach? First, many argue that connectionist models make biological sense; these models fit well, they claim, with what we know about the nervous system. In part, this is because the functioning of individual nodes resembles the functioning of individual neurons—accumulating activation, adjusting the strength of their connections to other neurons, and so on. In addition, we know that the brain relies on parallel processing, with many different processes going on simultaneously; we also know that the brain uses a "divide and conquer" strategy, with complex tasks being broken down into small components and with separate brain areas working on each component. These are exactly the operating features of a connectionist net.

Moreover, we need to take connectionist models seriously simply because of what they can accomplish. Connectionist models have so far learned to recognize patterns and—crucially—can **generalize** what they have learned in appropriate ways. Connectionist models can, it is claimed, learn the rules of English grammar, learn how to read, and even learn how to play strategic games such as backgammon. All of this has led to considerable enthusiasm for connectionist approaches.

Other investigators, however, have expressed skepticism about these claims. There is, first of all, room for debate about the biological realism of connectionist models (e.g., Bowers, 2009). Some aspects of these models surely do make biological sense, but other aspects may not. (For example, it is not clear how some of the learning algorithms are to be translated into neural terms.) Second, learning by connectionist models tends to be slow and gradual, requiring hundreds or even thousands of learning trials. Human learning, in contrast, is often much faster—including cases of nearly instantaneous insights or immediate responses to some new clue or instruction. Perhaps, therefore, we will need a model that relies on connectionism to explain gradual learning but that appeals to other mechanisms to explain rapid or insightful learning (cf. McClelland, McNaughton & O'Reilly, 1995).

Third, some critics have argued that connectionist models can learn only when the programmers stack the deck in the right way. Because the models often learn by inspecting examples, it is possible to "help" the models enormously by providing just the right examples in just the right sequence. Perhaps, then, connectionist models can't learn as we learn; more precisely, perhaps they can learn what we learn only if

Applying Connectionist Models

One of the powerful reasons for taking connectionist models seriously is what these models can accomplish. For example, a number of computer programs, set up as connectionist models, have been trained to play backgammon at world-class levels. Apparently, therefore, these models can master sophisticated, strategic, rule-governed activities.

we give them a great deal of help. (For concerns about the "psychological realism" of connectionist learning, see French, 1999; Lavric, Pizzagalli, Forstmeier, & Rippon, 2001; McCloskey & Cohen, 1989; Pinker & Prince, 1988.)

The state of the art, therefore, resembles what we saw with networks in general. There have been, to be sure, some remarkable successes for connectionist theory, with seemingly complex mental activities being successfully modeled. However, the range of these successes is still limited, and questions have been raised about whether this learning matches the learning that humans do. As a result of all this, many in the field have adopted a wait-and-see attitude about what connectionist modeling will eventually accomplish.

We leave this chapter, therefore, with some very obvious loose ends. There is no doubt that network theorizing can encompass an enormous range of memory data. Hand in hand with this, it is virtually certain that the "warehouse" of our long-term storage does rely on some sort of network representation, with activation spreading from node to node just as we have described in this chapter. What remains unsettled, though, is whether we will need other mechanisms, and more theory, beyond that provided by the network. Does the associative network serve merely as the "library" of long-term storage—with, perhaps, some other set of processes governing the use of this library? Or does the network essentially run itself? With some mix of activation and inhibition, as well as some reliance on simultaneous multiple constraint satisfaction, is it possible that the network needs no help with the processes of loading information into storage and then locating that information later on? In other words, is it possible that the operation of the network serves not just as the "library" but also as the librarian, the indexer, the assistant who retrieves books from the stacks, and the patron using the library?

We don't yet have answers to these questions, either for propositional networks (like Anderson's ACT model) or for connectionist nets. Perhaps this is not surprising, given the scale of the questions that are at stake here. In the meantime, though, we should surely take comfort from the fact that we have at least part of the puzzle under control. Our theorizing is allowing us to handle a lot of data and is leading us to new discoveries. This is, on anybody's account, a positive and promising sign.

Chapter Summary

- Many theorists have proposed that memory consists of a huge network of nodes, with each joined to others via connections or associations. An individual node becomes activated when it receives enough of an input signal to raise its activation level to its response threshold. Once activated, the node sends activation out through its connections to all the nodes connected to it.

- The network approach easily accommodates many results. For example, hints are effective because the target node can receive activation from two sources simultaneously—from nodes representing the main cue or question, and also from nodes representing the hint. The benefits of context reinstatement are explained in roughly the same fashion.

- Many specific predictions of network theorizing have been directly confirmed. For example, activating one node does seem to prime nearby nodes through the process of spreading activation. Similarly, search through the network does seem to resemble travel in the sense that greater travel distances (more connections to be traversed) require more time.

- If a node has a high degree of fan, it will be less effective in activating neighboring nodes, because each neighbor will receive only a small fraction of the activation energy radiating out from the initial node. This can, in some circumstances, impede memory search.

- The quantity of knowledge in long-term storage can make it difficult to locate any particular bit of information when needed. However, search through memory can be guided by the structure of the network itself. Once in the vicinity of the target information, connections will guide activation toward the target. To launch the search in the first place, some nodes must be tied to the mechanisms of perception, and presentation of the appropriate stimulus will trigger these nodes.

■ To store all of knowledge, the network may need more than simple associations among ideas. One proposal is that the network stores propositions, with different nodes each playing the appropriate role within the proposition.

■ To test network theories, investigators have often translated their theories into computer models. It is too soon to tell how successful these models will be, but the development of computer models has already spurred theoretical development. For example, any model based on a relatively mechanical process of spreading activation has difficulty explaining retrieval blocks or the tip-of-the-tongue phenomenon. However, an additional winner-takes-all mechanism may solve this problem.

■ Much recent effort has gone into the development of connectionist nets. These are distinctive in relying entirely on distributed processes and representations. In these models, all learning consists of the setting (and adjusting) of connection weights. One attraction of this mode of theorizing is biological realism; another is the fact that processing by a connectionist net is sensitive to many constraints simultaneously, just as the mind seems to be.

■ There continues to be debate over what network models can accomplish. There is no doubt that associations and spreading activation do play a crucial role in long-term memory, but questions remain about whether these mechanisms are sufficient to explain memory storage and memory search, or whether, alternatively, some sort of guide or executive is needed to direct the operations of the network.

The Workbook Connection

See the *Cognition Workbook* for further exploration of associative theories of long-term memory:

■ Demonstration 8.1: Activation in Memory Search
■ Demonstration 8.2: The Tip-of-the-Tongue Effect
■ Demonstration 8.3: Semantic Priming
■ Research Methods: Chronometric Studies
■ Cognitive Psychology and Education: Maximizing Interconnectedness
■ Cognitive Psychology and the Law: The Cognitive Interview

CHAPTER 9

Concepts and Generic Knowledge

No adult takes any pride in knowing what a dog is, or a house, or a tree. These concepts are so ordinary, so common, that there seems to be nothing special about knowing—and being able to think about—these simple ideas. However, ordinary concepts like these are, in an important way, the building blocks out of which all our knowledge is created, and as we've seen in previous chapters, we depend on our knowledge in many aspects of our day-to-day functioning. Thus, we know what to pay attention to in a restaurant because we understand the basic concept of "restaurant." We're able to understand a simple story about a child checking her piggy bank because we understand the concepts of "money," "shopping," and so on.

The idea, then, is that we need concepts in order to have knowledge, and we need knowledge in order to function. In this fashion, our understanding of ideas like "dog" and "house" might seem commonplace, but it is an ingredient without which cognition cannot proceed.

But what exactly does it mean to understand simple concepts like these? How is this knowledge represented in the mind? In this chapter, we'll tackle these questions, and as we will see, describing these concepts is appreciably more difficult than one might guess.

We will begin with the obvious hypothesis—that our understanding of a concept is analogous to a dictionary definition, and so, if someone knows what a triangle is, they can offer us something like a definition for triangle, and likewise for all the other concepts in each person's knowledge base. As we will see, though, we'll soon need to abandon this hypothesis, and turn to a richer—and more complicated—proposal.

- Basic concepts—like "chair" and "dog"—are the building blocks of all our knowledge. However, attempts at *defining* these concepts usually fail because we easily find exceptions to virtually any definition that might be proposed.

- This leads to the suggestion that knowledge of these concepts is cast in terms of *probabilities*, so that a creature that has wings and feathers, and that flies and lays eggs, is *probably* a bird.

- Many results are consistent with this probabilistic idea and show that the more a test case resembles the "prototype" for a category, the more likely people are to judge the case as being in that category.

- Other results, however, indicate that our conceptual knowledge includes other beliefs—beliefs that link a concept to other concepts and also specify why the concept is as it is.

- We are driven, therefore, to a multipart theory of concepts. Our conceptual knowledge must include a prototype for each category and also a set of remembered exemplars. But we also seem to have a broad set of beliefs about each concept—beliefs that provide a "theory" for why the concept takes the form it does, and we use this theory in a wide range of judgments about the concept.

Definitions: What Do We Know When We Know What a Dog Is?

We all know what a dog is. If someone sends us to the pet shop to buy a dog, we are sure to succeed. If someone tells us that a particular disease is common among dogs, we know that our pet terrier is at risk and so are the wolves in the zoo. Clearly, our store of knowledge about dogs will support these not-very-exciting achievements. But what is that knowledge?

One possibility is that we know something akin to a dictionary definition. That is, what we know is of this form: "A dog is a creature that (a) is mammalian, (b) has four legs, (c) barks, (d) wags its tail." This definition would presumably serve us well. When asked whether a candidate creature is a dog, we could use our definition as a checklist, scrutinizing the candidate for the various defining features. When told that "a dog is an animal," we would know that we had not learned anything new, because this information is already contained, presumably, within our mental definition. If we were asked what dogs, cats, and horses have in common, we could scan our definition of each one looking for common elements.

The difficulty with this proposal, however, was made clear by the 20th-century philosopher Ludwig Wittgenstein. Wittgenstein (1953) noted that philosophers had been trying for thousands of years to define terms like "virtue" and "knowledge." There had been some success, with various features identified as important aspects of these terms. However, even after thousands of years of careful thought, these terms were still without accepted, full definitions.

Perhaps this is not surprising, since these are subtle, philosophically rich terms and so are resistant to definition. Wittgenstein wondered, though, whether this really was the problem. He wondered whether we could find definitions even for simple, ordinary terms—for example, the word "game."

What is a game? Consider, for example, the game of hide-and-seek. What makes hide-and-seek a "game"? Hide-and-seek (a) is an activity most often practiced by children, (b) is engaged in for fun, (c) has certain rules, (d) involves multiple people, (e) is in some ways competitive, and (f) is played during periods of leisure. All these are plausible attributes of games, and so we seem well on our way to defining "game." But are these attributes really part of the definition of "game"? Consider (a) and (b): What about the Olympic Games? The competitors in these games are not children, and runners in marathon races do not look like they are having a great deal of fun. Consider (d) and (e): What about card games played by one person? These are played alone, without competition. Consider (f): What about professional golfers?

It seems, then, that for each clause of the definition, we can find an exception: an activity that we call a game but that does not have the relevant characteristic. And the same is true for most any concept. We might define "shoe" as an item of apparel made out of leather, designed to be worn on the foot. But what about wooden shoes? What about a shoe, designed by a master shoemaker, that is intended only for display and never for use? What about a shoe filled with cement, which therefore cannot be worn? Similarly, we might define "dog" in a way that includes four-leggedness, but what about a dog that has lost a limb in some accident? We might specify "communicates by barking" as part of the definition of dog, but what about the Egyptian basenji, which has no bark? Examples like these make it clear that even simple terms, terms denoting concepts that we use easily and often, resist being defined. In each case, we can come up with what seems to be a plausible definition, but then it is absurdly easy to find exceptions to it.

Family Resemblance

What we need, therefore, is a way of identifying concepts that highlights what the various members of a category have in common (e.g., what all dogs have in common) while simultaneously allowing exceptions to whatever rule we propose. One way to achieve this is by keeping the *content* of our definitions but being much more flexible in our *use* of the definitions. Thus, we would not say, "A dog is a creature that has fur and four legs and barks." That's because, as we've seen, there are exceptions to each of these requirements (a hairless Chihuahua? a three-legged dog? the barkless basenji?). But surely we *can* say, "A dog is a creature that *probably* has fur, four legs, and barks, and a creature without these features is *unlikely to be* a dog." This probabilistic phrasing preserves what is good about definitions—the fact that they do name sensible, relevant features. But this phrasing also allows some degree of uncertainty, some number of exceptions to the rule.

Wittgenstein's proposal was roughly along these lines. His notion was that members of a category have a **family resemblance** to each other. To understand this term,

Typicality in Families

In the Smith family, many (but not all) of the brothers have dark hair, and so dark hair is typical for the family but does not define the family. Likewise, wearing glasses is typical for the family but not a defining feature, and so is having a mustache and a big nose. Many concepts have the same profile—and so it is easy to say what is typical for the concept, but difficult (and perhaps impossible) to offer a definition for the concept.

think about the resemblance pattern in an actual family—your own, perhaps. There are probably no "defining features" for your family—features that every family member has. Nonetheless, there are features that are *common* in the family, and so, if we consider family members two or even three at a time, we can always find some shared attributes. Thus, you, your brother, and your mother might all have the family's beautiful blonde hair, the same square shoulders, and the same wide lips; as a result, you three look alike to some extent. Your sister, on the other hand, doesn't have these features; she's a narrow-lipped brunette. Nonetheless, she's still recognizable as a member of the family, because she (like you and your father) has the family's typical eye shape and the family's distinctive chin.

One way to think about this resemblance pattern is by imagining the "ideal" for each family—someone who has *all* of the family's features. (In our example, this would be someone who is blonde, has square shoulders and wide lips, and also has just the right eye and chin shapes.) In many families, this person may not exist; there may be no one who has all of the family's features, and so no one who looks like the "perfect Jones" (or the "perfect Martinez" or the "perfect Goldstein"). Nonetheless, each member of the family has at least some features in common with this ideal, and therefore some features in common with other family members. This is why the family members resemble each other, and it's also how we manage to recognize these individuals as being within the family.

"Attention, everyone! I'd like to introduce the newest member of our family."

Wittgenstein proposed that the thousands of categories we can think about—categories like "dog" or "game" or "furniture"—work in the same fashion. There may be no features that are shared by all dogs or all games, just as there are no features shared by everyone in your family. That's why a rigid definition isn't possible. Even so, we can identify "characteristic features" for each category—features that most category members have. And the more of these features an object has, the more likely we are to believe it is in the category. Family resemblance is a matter of degree, not all-or-none.

There are several ways we might translate all of this into a psychological theory, but the most influential translation was proposed by Eleanor Rosch in the mid-1970s (Rosch, 1973, 1978; Rosch & Mervis, 1975; Rosch, Mervis, Gray, Johnson, & Boyes-Braem, 1976), and it's to her model that we now turn.

Prototypes and Typicality Effects

One way to think about definitions is that they set the "boundaries" for a category. If a test case has certain attributes, then it is inside the category. If the test case does not have the defining attributes, then it is outside the category. (For discussion of this "classical" view, see G. L. Murphy, 2003; E. E. Smith, 1988.)

Prototype theory begins with a different tactic: Perhaps the best way to identify a category, to characterize a concept, is to specify the "center" of the category rather than the boundaries. Just as we spoke earlier about the "ideal" family member, perhaps the concept of "dog" (for example) is represented in the mind by some representation of the "ideal" dog, the prototype dog. In this view, all judgments about dogs are made with reference to this ideal. (See color insert, Figure 17.) For example, categorization (i.e., deciding whether something is a dog or not) would involve a comparison between a test case (the furry creature currently before your eyes) and the prototype represented in your memory. If there is no similarity between these, then the creature before you is probably not in the category; if there is considerable similarity, then you draw the opposite conclusion.

What is a prototype? In some cases, a prototype may literally represent the ideal for the category (and so, for example, the prototype diet soft drink might have zero calories but still taste great). More commonly, though, a prototype will be an average of the various category members you have encountered. Thus, the prototype dog will be the average color of the dogs you have seen, the average size of the dogs you've seen, and so forth.

Notice, then, that different people may have different prototypes. If a prototype reflects the ideal for a category, then people may disagree about what that ideal would involve. If a prototype reflects the average of the cases you have encountered, then an American's prototype for "house" might have one form, while for someone living in Japan the prototype "house" might be rather different. We will therefore need some flexibility in how we characterize prototypes. Nonetheless, in all cases the prototype will serve as the anchor, the benchmark, for our conceptual knowledge. When we reason about a concept or use our conceptual knowledge, our reasoning is done with reference to the prototype.

Fuzzy Boundaries and Graded Membership

Our hypothesis, then, is that what it means to "know" a concept is simply to have some mental representation of the concept's prototype. How does this work? We've already described how prototypes would help us in the simple task of categorization: You categorize objects by comparing them to prototypes stored in memory. If, for example, the creature now before your eyes has many attributes in common with the dog prototype, it will easily be recognized as a dog. Dogs that have fewer attributes in common with the prototype will probably cause you uncertainty about their identity. Similarly, in deciding that a particular ceramic vessel is a cup and not a bowl, you might compare the vessel to both your cup prototype and your bowl prototype. By discovering that the vessel is more similar to one than to the other, you reach a decision.

This sounds plausible enough, but there is an odd implication here: Since the category is characterized by its *center* (the prototype) and not by its *boundaries*, there's no way we can say whether something is, strictly speaking, inside of the category or outside. (To be inside or outside, you need a boundary to be inside or outside *of*!) At best, therefore, each category will have what's called a **fuzzy boundary**, with no clear specification of category membership and nonmembership.

Hand in hand with this, on this view, not all category members are equal. In the classical view, an object was either in the category or not, with no issue of being "more" in the category or "less." But on the prototype view, with its fuzzy boundaries, categorization is a matter of more or less. Objects closer to the prototype are, in effect, "better" members of the category than objects farther from the prototype. Thus, categories that depend on a prototype have **graded membership**, with some dogs being "doggier" than others, some books "bookier" than others, and so on for all the other categories you can think of.

Testing the Prototype Notion

In the **sentence verification task**, research participants are presented with a succession of sentences; their job is to indicate (by pressing the appropriate button) whether each sentence is true or false. In most experiments, what we are interested in is *how quickly* participants can do this task, and in fact their speed depends on several factors. As we saw in Chapter 8, response speed depends on the number of "steps" the participants must traverse to confirm the sentence. Participants also respond more quickly for true sentences than for false, and also more quickly for familiar categories. Most important for our purposes, though, the speed of response varies from item to item within a category. For example, response times are longer for sentences like "A penguin is a bird" than for "A robin is a bird"; longer for "An Afghan hound is a dog" than for "A German shepherd is a dog" (E. E. Smith, Rips, & Shoben, 1974).

Why should this be? According to a prototype perspective, participants make these judgments by comparing the thing mentioned (e.g., penguin) to their prototype for that category (i.e., their bird prototype). When there is much similarity between the test case and the prototype, participants can make their decisions quickly; judgments about items more distant from the prototype take more time. Given the results, it seems that penguins and Afghans are more distant from their respective prototypes than are robins and German shepherds.

Other results can also be understood in these terms. For example, in a **production task** we ask people to name as many birds or dogs as they can (Mervis, Catlin, & Rosch, 1976). According to a prototype view, they will do this production task by first locating their bird or dog prototype in memory and then asking themselves what resembles this prototype. In essence, they will start with the center of the category (the prototype) and work their way outward from there. Thus, birds close to the prototype should be mentioned first; birds farther from the prototype, later on.

Notice, then, that the first birds to be mentioned in the production task should be the birds that yielded fast response times in the verification task; that's because what matters in both tasks is proximity to the prototype. Likewise, the birds mentioned later in production should have yielded slower response times in verification. This is exactly what happens.

In fact, this sets the pattern of evidence for prototype theory: Over and over, in category after category, members of a category that are "privileged" on one task (e.g., yield the fastest response times) turn out also to be privileged on other tasks (e.g., are most likely to be mentioned). That is, various tasks *converge* in the sense that each task yields the same answer—that is, indicates the same category members as special. (For some examples of these privileged category members, see Table 9.1.)

Thus, category members mentioned early in a production task (*robin*, if someone is asked to name birds, or *apple*, if someone is asked to name fruits) are also "privileged" in a **picture-identification task**, yielding faster responses if someone is asked, "Does the next picture show you a *bird*?" or "Does the next picture show you a *fruit*?" (Rosch, Mervis, et al., 1976; E. E. Smith, Balzano, & Walker, 1978). The same category members are privileged in a **rating task**. For example, Rosch (1975; also Malt & Smith, 1984) explicitly asked participants to judge how typical various category members were for the category. In these **typicality** studies, the participants are given instructions like these: "We all know that some birds are 'birdier' than others, some

TABLE 9.1 Participants' Typicality Ratings for the Category "Fruit" and the Category "Bird"

Fruit	Rating	Bird	Rating
Apple	6.25	Robin	6.89
Peach	5.81	Bluebird	6.42
Pear	5.25	Seagull	6.26
Grape	5.13	Swallow	6.16
Strawberry	5.00	Falcon	5.74
Lemon	4.86	Mockingbird	5.47
Blueberry	4.56	Starling	5.16
Watermelon	4.06	Owl	5.00
Raisin	3.75	Vulture	4.84
Fig	3.38	Sandpiper	4.47
Coconut	3.06	Chicken	3.95
Pomegranate	2.50	Flamingo	3.37
Avocado	2.38	Albatross	3.32
Pumpkin	2.31	Penguin	2.63
Olive	2.25	Bat	1.53

Ratings were made on a 7-point scale, with 7 corresponding to the highest typicality. Note also that the least "birdy" of the birds isn't (technically speaking) a bird at all! (After Malt & Smith, 1984)

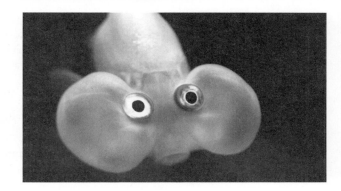

Typicality and Attractiveness

Typicality influences many judgments about category members, including *attractiveness*. Which of these pictures shows the most attractive-looking fish? Which shows the least attractive-looking? In several studies, participants' ratings of attractiveness have been correlated with (other participants') ratings of typicality—so that people prefer to look, it seems, at more-typical category members (e.g., Halberstadt & Rhodes, 2003). Plainly, the influence of typicality is rather broad.

dogs are 'doggier' than others, and so on. I'm going to present you with a list of birds or of dogs, and I want you to rate each one on the basis of how 'birdy' or 'doggy' it is." People are easily able to render these judgments, and quite consistently they rate items as being very "birdy" or "doggy" when these instances are close to the prototype (as determined in the other tasks). They rate items as being less "birdy" or "doggy" when these are farther from the prototype. This suggests that people perform this task by comparing the test item to the prototype.

A related pattern emerges if we simply ask people to *think* about categories (e.g., Rosch, 1977a). In one study, participants were asked to generate simple sentences about a category. If the category were "birds," for example, a participant might say, "I saw two birds in a tree" or "I like to feed birds in the park." Next, the experimenters rewrote these sentences, substituting for the category name either the name of a prototypical member of the category (e.g., robin) or a not-so-prototypical member (e.g., penguin). In our example, we would get "I like to feed robins in the park" and "I like to feed penguins in the park." Finally, these new, edited sentences were shown to a different group of participants; they were asked to rate how silly or implausible the sentences seemed.

A   B

Typicality and Assumptions

If people are told to think about "two birds perched in a tree," they automatically assume *typical* birds, like robins or sparrows, and so envision something like the drawing on the left. They are extremely unlikely to assume we are talking about emus or ostriches or penguins, and so will surely not envision something like the drawing on the right.

The hypothesis here is that when people think about a category they are in fact thinking about the prototype for that category. Therefore, in making up their sentences, participants will come up with statements appropriate for the prototype. It follows from this that the meaning of the sentence will be pretty much unchanged if we substitute a prototypical category member for the category name, since that will be close to what the participant had in mind in the first place. Substituting a nonprototypical member, in contrast, may yield a peculiar, even ridiculous proposition. This is fully in line with the data. When the new group of participants rated these sentences, they rated as quite ordinary the sentences into which we placed a prototypical case ("I saw two robins in a tree") and rejected as silly the sentences into which we placed a nonprototypical case ("I saw two penguins in a tree").

Basic-Level Categories

It seems, then, that certain category members are indeed "privileged," and they show this distinction in a variety of tasks—just as the prototype theory proposes. It turns out, though, that certain *types of category* are also privileged—in their structure and how they are used. To make this point concrete, imagine that we show you a picture of a chair and simply ask, "What is this?" You are likely to say that the picture shows a chair. You are less likely to offer a more specific response ("It's a Windsor chair") or a more general response ("It's an item of furniture"), although these responses would also be correct. Likewise, we might ask, "How do people get to work?" In responding, you are unlikely to say, "Some people drive Fords; some drive Toyotas." Instead, your answer is likely to use more general terms, such as "cars" and "trains" and "buses."

In keeping with these observations, Rosch and others have argued that there is a "natural" level of categorization, neither too specific nor too general, that we tend to use in our conversations and our reasoning. The special status of this **basic-level categorization** can be demonstrated in many ways. Basic-level categories are usually represented in our language via a single word, while more specific categories are identified only via a phrase. Thus, "chair" is a basic-level category, and so is "apple." The subcategories of "lawn chair" or "kitchen chair" are not basic level; neither is "Granny Smith apple" or "Golden Delicious apple." In addition, if asked to describe an object, we are likely spontaneously to use the basic-level term. If asked to explain what members of a category have in common with one another, we have an easy time with basic-level categories ("What do all chairs have in common?") but some difficulty with more-encompassing categories ("What does all furniture have in common?"). And so on.

The importance of basic-level categories also shows up in our *memory errors*. In one study, participants read a story, and then after a delay their memory for the story was tested. If the story contained specific terms, participants often (falsely) recalled that they had heard something more general. For example, the sentence "She noticed that her jeans were stained" was often misremembered as ". . . her pants were stained." Conversely, if the story contained *general* terms, these were misremembered as being more specific than they actually were (and so participants remembered hearing about "dogs" when they had actually heard about "animals"). In all cases, though, the errors

Basic versus Superordinate Labeling
What is this? The odds are good that you would answer by saying this is a "chair," using the basic-level description, rather than using the superordinate label ("It's a piece of furniture") or a more specific description ("It's a wooden desk chair"), even though these latter descriptions would certainly be correct.

tended to "revise" the story in the direction of basic-level categorization (Pansky & Koriat, 2004).

It seems, then, that basic-level categorization is important for a variety of purposes. Indeed, in studies of children who are learning how to talk, there are some indications that basic-level terms are acquired earlier than either the more specific subcategories or the more general, more encompassing categories. Thus, basic-level categories do seem to reflect a natural way to categorize the objects in our world (Rosch, Mervis, et al., 1976; for discussion and some complications, see Corter & Gluck, 1992; M. Morris & Murphy, 1990; Rogers & Patterson, 2007; Tanaka & Taylor, 1991; B. Tversky & Hemenway, 1991).

Exemplars

Let's return, though, to our main agenda. As we have seen, a broad spectrum of tasks reflects the "graded membership" of mental categories. Some members of the categories are "better" than others, and the better members are recognized more readily, mentioned more often, judged more typical, and so on. Likewise, it seems plain that typicality does guide many of our category judgments: In diagnosing diseases, for example, physicians often seem to function as if asking themselves, "How much does this case resemble a typical case of disease X? How closely does it resemble a typical case of disease Y?" The greater the resemblance to this or that diagnostic prototype,

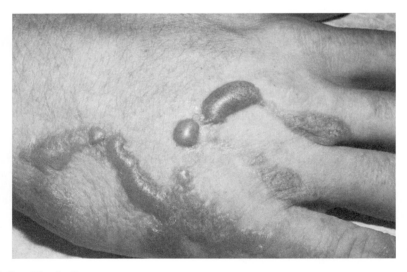

Specialized Typicality

The concepts we use everyday seem influenced by typicality, but the same is true for concepts used in more specialized setting. For example, dermatologists seem to have a good idea about what a "typical" poison ivy rash looks like, and they make their diagnosis by comparing a patient's rash to the "typical" appearance.

the more likely the diagnosis will be of that disease. (See, for example, Klayman & Brown, 1993.)

All of this is in accord with the notion that our conceptual knowledge is represented via a prototype and that we categorize by making comparisons to that prototype. It turns out, though, that prototype theory isn't the only way one can think about these data. A different perspective provides an alternative way to explain typicality effects and the graded membership of categories. In this section, we examine this alternate view.

Analogies From Remembered Exemplars

Imagine that we place a wooden object in front of you and ask, "Is this a chair?" According to the prototype view, you will answer this question by calling up your chair prototype from memory and then comparing the candidate to that prototype. If the resemblance is great, you will announce, "Yes, this is a chair." But you might make this decision in a different way. You might notice that this object is very similar to an object in your Uncle Jerry's living room, and you know that the object in Uncle Jerry's living room is a chair. After all, you've seen Uncle Jerry sitting in the thing, reading his newspaper. If Jerry's possession is a chair, and if the new object resembles Jerry's, then it is a safe bet that the new object is a chair too.

The idea here is that in some cases categorization can draw on knowledge about specific category members rather than on more general information about the overall category. In our example, the categorization is supported by memories of a specific chair, rather than remembered knowledge about chairs in general. This is referred to as **exemplar-based reasoning**, with an exemplar being defined as a specific remembered instance—in essence, an example.

The exemplar-based approach is in many ways similar to the prototype view. According to each of these proposals, you categorize objects by comparing them to a mentally represented "standard." The difference between the views lies in what that standard is: For prototype theory, the standard is the prototype—an average representing the entire category; for exemplar theory, the standard is provided by whatever example of the category comes to mind (and, of course, different examples may come to mind on different occasions). In either case, though, the process is then the same. You assess the similarity between a candidate object and this standard. If the resemblance is great, you judge the candidate as being within the relevant category; if the resemblance is minimal, you seek some alternative categorization.

Explaining Typicality Data With an Exemplar Model

We have discussed how the graded-membership pattern, so often seen in concept tasks, is consistent with the idea that concepts are represented in the mind via prototypes. It turns out, though, that an exemplar-based approach can also explain the graded-membership pattern. For illustration, consider a task in which we show people a series of pictures and ask them to decide whether each picture shows a fruit or not. We already know that they will respond more quickly for typical fruits than for less typical fruits, and we have seen how this result is handled by a prototype account. How could an exemplar model explain this finding?

According to exemplar theory, people make their judgments in this task by comparing the pictures to specific memories of fruits—that is, to specific, mentally represented examples. But how exactly will this work? Let's imagine that you're looking at a picture of some object and trying to decide whether it's a fruit or not. To make your decision, you'll try to think of a fruit exemplar that resembles the one in the picture; if you find a good match, then you know the object in the picture is a fruit. No match? Then it's not a fruit.

If the picture shows, say, an apple, then your memory search will be extremely fast: Apples are common in your experience (often seen, often eaten, often mentioned), and so you've had many opportunities to establish apple memories. Moreover, these memories will be well primed, thanks to your frequent encounters with apples. As a result, you'll easily find a memory that matches the picture, and so you will swiftly respond that, yes, the picture does show a fruit. But if the picture shows, say, a fig or a carob, then your memory search will be more difficult: You probably don't have as many memories that will match these pictures, and these memories aren't well primed. Hence your response will be appreciably slower.

A similar argument will handle the other tasks showing the graded-membership pattern—for example, the production task. Let's say that you are asked to name as many fruits as you can. You'll quickly name apples and oranges because these fruits are represented many times in your memory, thanks to the many encounters you've had with them. These memories are also well primed, making them easy to retrieve. Therefore, apple memories and orange memories will readily come to mind. Fig and carob memories, however, will have none of these advantages, and so they will come to mind less easily. In this way, your production will favor the typical fruits—not because of prototyping, but because of the pattern of what's available in memory.

Exemplars Preserve Information About Variability

It seems, therefore, that exemplar-based views can easily explain typicality effects, and so the data we have reviewed so far favor neither the prototype nor the exemplar theory; both are compatible with the evidence. Other results, however, seem to favor the exemplar view. For example, we have noted that a prototype can be thought of as the average for a category, and as such it provides a summary of what is typical or frequent for that category. But much information is lost in an average. For example, an average, by itself, doesn't tell you how variable a set is, and plainly people are sensitive to category variability (Rips, 1989; Rips & Collins, 1993). For example, imagine that you see, perhaps in a store window, a pizza that's 15 inches in diameter. Two days later, let's say, you see a pizza that's twice that size—30 inches. You are likely to take no special notice of this variation, for the simple reason that you already know that pizzas vary in size. Now imagine that you see, in a store window, a dinner plate that's 15 inches in diameter, and then, a few days later, you see another plate that's 30 inches across. Now you are likely to be surprised, and you may suspect that the larger plate isn't a plate at all. (Perhaps it's a serving platter.)

These observations remind us that you do have some knowledge about the variability within a category—and you sometimes use this variability as an aid to categorization. These points are puzzling if your categorization relies only on prototypes, but the points can easily be handled via exemplars: If you can remember both a 15-inch pizza and one that was 30 inches across, this tells you in an instant that pizzas can vary in size. For that matter, if you reflect on the full set of pizzas you have seen, you can make a reasonable assessment of how variable the set has been.

In short, a set of exemplars preserves information about variability; a prototype does not. Since people do seem sensitive to variability information, this is a strike against prototype theory and in favor of exemplars. (For further discussion of people's sensitivity to variability, see Fried & Holyoak, 1984; Nisbett, Krantz, Jepson, & Kunda, 1983.)

A Combination of Exemplars and Prototypes

Other results also suggest a reliance on exemplars. For example, people routinely "tune" their concepts to match the circumstances, and so they think about birds differently when thinking about Chinese birds than when thinking about American birds; they think about gifts differently when thinking about gifts for a student rather than gifts for a faculty member; and so on (Barsalou, 1988; Barsalou & Sewell, 1985). In fact, people can adjust their categories in fairly precise ways: not just "gift," but "gift for a 4-year-old" or "gift for a 4-year-old who recently broke her wrist" or "gift for a 4-year-old who likes sports but recently broke her wrist."

This pliability in our concepts is easy to understand if people are relying on exemplars; after all, different settings, or different perspectives, would trigger different memories and so bring different exemplars to mind. If someone is then relying on these exemplars in his reasoning, it makes sense that his reasoning will vary somewhat as he moves from one circumstance to the next, or as he shifts his perspective.

Plainly, then, some evidence favors the idea that part of our conceptual knowledge involves exemplars. But at the same time, we must not lose sight of the fact that prototypes also have their advantages. Prototypes do, after all, represent in an efficient and economical manner what's typical for a category, and there may well be circumstances in which this quick summary is quite useful. How, therefore, should we put all these pieces together? The answer is easy. We have presented the prototype and exemplar proposals as though they were mutually exclusive, so that our conceptual knowledge would consist of one form of representation or the other. But, in

Distinctions Within Categories

The chapter suggests that we have knowledge of both exemplars *and* prototypes. As a further complication, though, we also have special knowledge about distinctive individuals within a category. Thus, we know that Kermit has many frogly properties (he's green, he eats flies, he hops), but also has unusual properties that make him a rather unusual frog (since, after all, he can talk, he can sing, he's in love with a pig, and so on).

truth, it is entirely plausible that our conceptual knowledge includes *both* prototypes *and* exemplars, and so it gains the advantages of each.

In fact, the mix of exemplar and prototype knowledge may vary from person to person and from concept to concept. One person, for example, might have extensive knowledge about individual horses, and so she has many exemplars in memory; the same person might have only general information (a prototype, perhaps) about snowmobiles. Some other person might show the reverse pattern. And for all people, the pattern of knowledge might depend on the size of the category (for small categories, it is easier to think about specific exemplars), how confusable the category memories are with each other (with exemplars used when the individuals are more distinct), and also the familiarity of the category. Initially, we might know a couple of individuals within the category, and so rely on this exemplar knowledge for all our thinking about the category. With a bit more experience, though, we might start to lose track of which individual is which, so we rely more and more on prototype knowledge. Then, with even more experience, we might again become aware of individuals within the category—and so, at that point, we have an even mix of prototype and exemplar knowledge. (For discussion of these points, including how the mix of exemplars and prototypes will be shaped by various factors, see Brooks, 1990; Brooks, Norman, & Allen, 1991; Homa, Dunbar, & Nohre, 1991; Homa, Sterling, & Trepel, 1981; Minda & Smith, 2001; Rouder & Ratcliff, 2006; J. D. Smith, 2002; Vanpaemel & Storms, 2008; Whittlesea, Brooks, & Westcott, 1994.)

Indeed, it cannot be surprising that we have the option of *combining* prototype and exemplar models, because, as we've said, the two types of model are similar in crucial ways. In either case, an object before your eyes triggers some information in memory (either a specific instance, according to exemplar theory, or the prototype, according to prototype theory). In either case, you assess the resemblance between this conceptual knowledge, supplied by memory, and the novel object now before you: "Does this object resemble my sister's couch?" If so, then the object is a couch. "Does the object resemble my prototype for an ashtray?" If so, it's probably an ashtray.

In short, exemplar and prototype models rely on the exact same processes—a triggering of a memory, then a judgment of resemblance, and finally a conclusion based on this resemblance. Given these similarities, it seems sensible that we might merge the models, with each of us on any particular occasion relying on whichever sort of information (exemplar or prototype) comes to mind more readily.

The Difficulties With Categorizing via Resemblance

We are moving, it seems, toward a relatively clear-cut set of claims. For most of our concepts, definitions are not available. For many purposes, though, we would be well served by conceptual knowledge that involves prototypes and exemplars, rather than a definition. Moreover, there is no question that *typicality* plays a huge role in our thinking, with more-typical category members being "privileged" in many regards. And typicality is exactly what we would expect if category knowledge did, in fact, hinge on prototypes and exemplars.

All of this seems straightforward enough. However, there are some results that do not fit easily into this picture. The time has come to broaden our conception of concepts.

Odd Number, Even Number

In the view we have been developing, judgments of *typicality* and judgments of *category membership* both derive from the same source: resemblance to an exemplar or to a prototype. If the resemblance is great, then a test case will be judged to be typical, and it will also be judged to be a category member. If the resemblance is small, then the test case will be judged atypical and probably not a category member. Thus, typicality and category membership should go hand in hand.

As we have seen, much evidence fits with this claim. It turns out, however, that we can also find situations in which there is no relation between typicality and category membership, and this is surely inconsistent with our claims so far. As a striking example of this pattern, consider a study by Armstrong, Gleitman, and Gleitman (1983). These researchers asked their research participants to do several of the concept tasks we have been discussing—for example, sentence verification, or making explicit judgments about whether individuals were typical or not for their category. The twist, though, is that the researchers used categories for which there clearly is a definition—for example, the category "odd number." As a participant, therefore, you might be told, "We all know that some numbers are odder than others. What I want you to do is to rate each of the numbers on this list for how good an example it is for the category 'odd.'" Participants felt that this was a rather silly task, but nevertheless they were able to render these judgments and, interestingly, were just as consistent with each other using these stimuli as they were with categories like "dog" or "bird" or "fruit" (see Table 9.2).

The obvious response to this experiment is that participants knew the definition of "odd number" but were playing along in response to the experimenters' peculiar request. Even so, the fact remains that participants' judgments about typicality were in this case disconnected from their judgments about category membership: They knew that all the test numbers were in the category "odd number," but they still judged some to be more "typical" than others. Apparently, then, there is not always a link between typicality and membership. (For further data pointing to the separation between typicality judgments and judgments of category membership, see Rips & Collins, 1993.)

To put this point slightly differently, the Armstrong et al. result signals a need for caution in interpreting the other results we've considered so far in this chapter. Thus, for example, we know that people are able to judge what a typical "dog" is, or a typical "tree," or a typical "bird," and we know that they rely on these assessments of typicality in many settings. But we cannot conclude from this that knowledge about typicality is *all* people know about these categories. That's because the Armstrong et al. data remind us that it's possible to have both a basis for judging typicality *and* other knowledge about the category; the presence of one of these doesn't rule out

TABLE 9.2 Participants' Typicality Ratings for Well-Defined Categories

Even Number		Odd Number	
Stimulus	Typicality rating	Stimulus	Typicality rating
4	5.9	3	5.4
8	5.5	7	5.1
10	5.3	23	4.6
18	4.4	57	4.4
34	3.6	501	3.5
106	3.1	447	3.3

Participants rated each item on how "good an example" it was for its category. Ratings were on a 0 to 7 scale, with 7 meaning the item is a "very good example." Participants rated some even numbers as being "better examples" of even numbers than others, although mathematically this is absurd: Either a number is even (divisible by 2 without a remainder), or it is not. (After Armstrong et al., 1983) the possibility of the other. But what might this "other knowledge" be? This is clearly a point we'll need to tackle before we are through.

Lemons and Counterfeits

The example in the previous section (the category "odd number") is an unusual one—a technically defined, mathematical category. Do other categories show the same pattern? In fact, they do; and many results echo the message just described: In each case, people find it easy and "natural" to decide whether a particular object is "typical" for the category or not, but then the same people judge category membership in a fashion that's completely independent of typicality. As a result, a test case can be a category member without being typical or can be typical without being a category member. This pattern is troublesome for any theory proposing that typicality and category-membership judgments both derive from the same source.

For example, it is true that robins strike us as being closer to the typical bird than penguins do. Nonetheless, most of us are quite certain that both robins and penguins are birds. Likewise, Moby-Dick was definitely not a typical whale, but he certainly was a whale; Abraham Lincoln was not a typical American, but he was an American. These informal observations are easily confirmed in the laboratory. For example, research participants judge whales to be more typical of the concept "fish" than sea lampreys are, but the same participants respond (correctly) that sea lampreys are fish and whales are not (McCloskey & Glucksberg, 1978).

It seems, therefore, that category judgments are often not based on typicality. What are they based on? As a way of approaching the problem, let's think through some examples. Consider a lemon. Paint the lemon with red and white stripes. Is it still a lemon? Most people believe that it is. Now inject the lemon with sugar water, so that it has a sweet taste. Then run over the lemon with a truck, so that it is flat as a pancake. What have we got at this point? Do we have a striped, artificially sweet, flattened lemon? Or do we have a non-lemon? Most people still accept this poor, abused fruit as a lemon, but we should consider what this judgment entails. We have taken steps to make this object more and more distant from the prototype and also very different from any specific lemon you have ever encountered (and thus very different from any remembered exemplars). But this seems not to shake our faith that the object remains a lemon. To be sure, we have a not-easily-recognized lemon, an exceptional lemon, but it is still a lemon. Apparently, something can be a lemon with virtually no resemblance to other lemons. (For discussion of a similar case, with category members being transformed by exposure to toxic waste, see Rips, 1989.)

Here is the opposite case. Consider a perfect counterfeit $20 bill. This bill will be enormously similar to the prototype for a real $20 bill and also highly similar to any remembered exemplar of a $20 bill. Yet we still consider it to be counterfeit, not real. Apparently, resemblance to other cases is not enough to qualify this bill for mem-

Prototypes and Counterfeits
A perfect counterfeit bill might bear a strong resemblance to the prototype for a real $20 bill, but you are not confused about the concepts. After all, which would you rather receive as a gift: a stack of real bills or a stack of counterfeits? The fact that you have a preference makes it clear that you can distinguish between these two—even though, in terms of typicality, there is no difference at all.

bership in the category "real money." In fact, think about the broad category "perfect counterfeit." One can certainly imagine a prototype for this category, and of course the prototype would have to be very similar to the prototype for the category "real money." But despite this resemblance, you have no trouble keeping the categories distinct from each other: You know many things that are true for one category but not for the other, and you clearly understand, despite the near-identical prototypes, that counterfeit money is not the same thing as real money. You might be perceptually confused between a real bill and a counterfeit (because they do look alike), but you are not confused about the concepts, and you certainly know when you are thinking about one and when you are thinking about the other.

These examples underscore the distinction between typicality and category membership. In the case of the lemon, we see category membership even though the test case bears no resemblance to the prototype and, indeed, no resemblance to any of the other members of the lemon category. Conversely, one can have close resemblance to category members and high typicality without category membership (the counterfeit bill). If we take these cases at face value, then category membership cannot rest on typicality.

But can we take these cases at face value? Perhaps these cases are too playful. Perhaps people think about mutilated lemons in some artificial way, differently from how they think about more conventional concepts. Similarly, perhaps the Armstrong et al. study participants realized they were doing something bizarre in judging the odd numbers and treated the task as a game, somehow different from their customary way of thinking about concepts. So again one might ask whether the data pattern would be different with more-typical concepts in more-typical settings.

Relevant evidence for this point comes from work by Keil (1986). Keil was particularly interested in how children come to have concepts and what children's concepts do or do not include. For our purposes, this approach is ideal because it allows us to ask about concept holders who are relatively untutored and relatively naive. These preschool children have not yet learned technical definitions for their concepts, nor have they been trained to reflect on, or manipulate, their mental categories. Thus, we can use the data from children as a way of asking about concepts "uncontaminated" by education or training.

In one of Keil's studies, preschool children were asked what makes something a "coffeepot," a "raccoon," and so on. As a way of probing their beliefs, the children were asked whether it would be possible to turn a toaster into a coffeepot. Children often acknowledged that this would be possible. One would have to widen the holes in the top of the toaster and fix things so that the water would not leak out of the bottom. One would need to design a place to put the coffee grounds. But the children saw no obstacles to these various manipulations, and they were quite certain that with these adjustments in place one would have created a bona fide coffeepot.

Things were different, though, when the children were asked a parallel question—namely, whether one could, with suitable adjustments, turn a skunk into a raccoon. The children understood that we could dye the skunk's fur, teach it to climb trees, and, in general, teach it to behave in a raccoon-like fashion. Even with these provisions, the children steadfastly denied that we would have created a raccoon. A skunk that looks, sounds, and acts just like a raccoon might be a very peculiar skunk, but it is a skunk nonetheless. (For related data, see Gelman & Wellman, 1991; Keil, Smith, Simons, & Levin, 1998; Walker, 1993. For other evidence suggesting that we reason differently about naturally occurring items like raccoons and manufactured items like coffeepots, see Caramazza & Shelton, 1998; Estes, 2003; German & Barrett, 2005; Levin, Takarae, Miner, & Keil, 2001.)

What lies behind these judgments? If people are asked why the abused lemon still counts as a lemon, they are likely to mention the fact that it grew on a lemon tree, is genetically a lemon, and so on. It is these "deep" features that matter, and not the lemon's current properties. Likewise, counterfeit money is defined as such not because of its current attributes but because of its history: Real money was printed by the government in special circumstances; counterfeit money was not. And so, too, for raccoons: In the child's view, being a raccoon is not merely a function of having the relevant features; there is something deeper to raccoon-hood than that. What is this "something deeper"? In the eyes of the child, the key to being a raccoon involves (among other things) having a raccoon mommy and a raccoon daddy. Thus, a raccoon, just like lemons and counterfeit money, is defined in ways that refer to deep properties and not to mere appearances.

It appears, then, that some properties are essential for being a lemon or a raccoon, and if an object has these essential properties, it doesn't matter what the object looks like. Likewise, without these essential properties, an item is not in the category no matter what its appearance. (This is the case of the counterfeit bill.) In addition, notice that these claims about an object's "essential properties" depend on a web of other beliefs—beliefs about cause and effect and about how things come to be as they are. For example, concern about a raccoon's parentage comes into play in your thinking about raccoons only because you have certain beliefs about how biological species are created and about the role of inheritance in biological species. You do not worry about parentage when you are contemplating other categories, because you do not have the belief that inheritance matters for those categories. (In thinking through whether someone is really a doctor, you are unlikely to worry about whether she has a doctor mommy and a doctor daddy. Perhaps she does and perhaps she doesn't, but this is irrelevant to whether she is or is not a doctor.)

Likewise, in judging the category of counterfeit bills, you consider "circumstances of printing" only because of your other beliefs—beliefs, in this case, about ownership, authenticity, and monetary systems. You wouldn't consider circumstances of printing if asked whether a copy of the Lord's Prayer is "counterfeit" or not (or authentic or legitimate). Your beliefs tell you that the Lord's Prayer is the Lord's Prayer no matter where (or by whom) it's printed. What's crucial for the prayer is whether the words are the correct words, and so again, what's essential for the category depends on the category and on other beliefs you have about that category.

All of this invites several questions: How should we think about a category's "essential properties"? What are these "other beliefs" that seem to guide your thinking about what's essential for a particular category and what's superfluous? And how does typicality (which, without question, does have a powerful influence in many settings) fit into this enlarged picture? We'll turn to these issues in a moment; first, though, we need to consider a slightly different perspective on the issues that are in play here.

The Complexity of Similarity

Both the prototype and the exemplar views depend, at their base, on judgments of *resemblance*—resemblance to the prototype or to some remembered instance. Cases like the mutilated lemon and the counterfeit bill, however, suggest that resemblance may not be the key here. The mutilated lemon does not resemble the lemon prototype, but it is still a lemon. The counterfeit bill *does* resemble the prototype for real money, but it still isn't legal. These simple observations suggest that we cannot base category membership on resemblance alone.

Perhaps, though, we can preserve the resemblance notion: An abused lemon doesn't resemble the lemon prototype perceptually, but it does resemble the lemon prototype in the ways that matter. For example, the abused lemon has a DNA pattern that resembles the DNA pattern of the prototype. Likewise, the abused lemon has seeds inside it that, if planted, would grow into lemon trees; this, too, is a property of the prototype, and so it is a basis for claiming resemblance. If only we could focus on these essential properties, therefore, and ignore the superficial attributes, we could maintain the claim that category membership depends on properties shared with the prototype or shared with exemplars. In this way, we could preserve the claim that category membership depends on resemblance.

The problem, though, lies in explaining what we mean by "resembling the prototype *in the ways that matter.*" How do we decide which properties of the prototype are really important, and so should be given a lot of weight when judging resemblance, and which properties we can ignore as irrelevant? This seems once again to demand that our judgments be guided by some further knowledge—including beliefs about what it is that really matters for that category. And this brings us right back to where we were: In order to use our category knowledge, we've got to have other beliefs about what is essential for the category and what's not.

It may help to make this point more broadly, by considering what judgments of "resemblance" actually involve. One might think that two objects will be seen to resemble each other if the two objects share properties; both objects are big, for example, or both are green, or slow-moving, or whatever. And presumably, the more properties shared, the greater the resemblance. But it turns out that resemblance is far more complicated than this. To see the point, consider plums and lawn mowers; how much do these two things resemble each other? Actually, these two have many properties in common (Murphy & Medin, 1985): Both weigh less than a ton, both are found on Earth, both have an odor, both are used by people, both can be dropped, both cost less than a thousand dollars, both are bigger than a grain of sand, and so on. (For discussion, see Goldstone, 1996; N. Goodman, 1972; Markman & Gentner, 2001; Medin, Goldstone, & Gentner, 1993.) Of course, we ignore most of these shared features in judging these two entities, and so, as a result, we regard plums and lawn mowers as rather different from each other. But that brings us back to a familiar question: How do we decide which features to ignore when assessing similarity and which features to consider? How do we decide, in comparing a plum and a lawn mower, which of their features are essential and which can be ignored?

We have already suggested an answer to these questions: A decision about which features are trivial and which are crucial depends largely on one's beliefs about the concept in question. We know, for example, that what matters for being a lawn mower is suitability for getting a particular job done. Costing less than a thousand dollars is irrelevant to this function. (Imagine a lawn mower covered with diamonds; it would still be a lawn mower, wouldn't it?) Therefore, cost is an unimportant feature for lawn mowers. Cost is a critical attribute, however, for other categories (consider the category "luxury item"). Similarly, we were unimpressed by the fact that plums and lawn mowers both weigh less than a ton: Weight is not critical for either of these categories. But weight is crucial in other settings (imagine a paperweight made out of gaseous helium). Apparently, then, the importance of an attribute—cost, or weight, or whatever—varies from category to category, and it varies, in particular, according to your beliefs about what matters for that category.

But now let's tie all of this back to issues of categorization. Imagine that a furry creature stands before you, and you reason, "This creature reminds me of the animal I saw in the zoo yesterday. The sign at the zoo indicated that the animal was a gnu, so this must be one, too." This sounds like a simple case of categorization via exemplars. But the creature before your eyes is not a perfect match for the gnu in the zoo, and so you might reason this way, "The gnu in the zoo was a different color and slightly smaller. But I bet that doesn't matter. Despite the new hue, this is a gnu, too."

In this case, you have decided that color isn't a critical feature, and you categorize despite the contrast on this dimension. Things will go differently, though, in this case: "This stone in my hand reminds me of the ruby I saw yesterday. Therefore, I bet this is a ruby too. Of course, the ruby I saw yesterday was red, and this stone is green, but. . . ." You surely would not draw this conclusion, because in this case you know that it is wrong to ignore hue. Rubies are red. If a stone isn't red, it isn't a ruby. Color might not matter for gnus, but it does matter here, and our category judgments respect this fact.

Concepts as Theories

Let's pause to take stock. Early in the chapter, we saw many results indicating that our use of concepts is heavily influenced by typicality. Typicality plays a role when we are categorizing objects we have just met; it also guides us when we are reasoning about our concepts. Our theory, therefore, needs to explain how these typicality effects emerge, and the best way to do this, we suggested, is by including prototypes and exemplars in our theorizing.

At the same time, our theory of concepts also needs more than prototypes and exemplars. This is evident, for example, in the fact that some category judgments (e.g., counterfeit money, the mutilated lemon) are entirely independent of typicality, and so, quite obviously, our theory needs some other element to guide these judgments. Even when typicality is crucial, its role depends on *resemblance*. That is, typicality plays its role thanks to a judgment of resemblance between the object being assessed and some standard in memory (i.e., an exemplar or the prototype). But judgments of resemblance, in turn, depend on other knowledge—for example, knowledge about which attributes to pay attention to in judging resemblance, and which to regard as trivial. So here, too, we need some other element in the theory, guiding the assessment of resemblance.

It seems plain, then, that we're moving toward a multipart theory of concepts. On the one side, there are prototypes and exemplars, often shaping how we reason in tasks requiring conceptual knowledge. On the other side, there are other beliefs and

Categorization Outside of Typicality

Moby-Dick was not a typical whale, but he unmistakably was a whale, even so. Clearly, then, typicality can, in some settings, be separated from category membership. We are able to categorize these unusual cases, though, because—independent of typicality—we have a "theory" about what membership in the category involves.

other knowledge, guiding and supplementing our use of prototypes. But how should we characterize these other beliefs? And within this broader context, exactly what role is played by prototypes and exemplars?

Categorization Heuristics

In your day-to-day thinking about the world, it seems plausible that you'd want to rely on strategies that are as accurate as possible, strategies that would rarely lead you astray. There is a danger, though, that such strategies might be slow and take a lot of effort. If so, you might be better off with a **heuristic** strategy, one that gives up the guarantee of accuracy in order to gain some efficiency. After all, which would you prefer: to be right *all* of the time but needing 18 hours for every judgment you make, or to be right *most* of the time but able to make your judgments in a matter of moments?

We've met this trade-off between efficiency and accuracy in other contexts (e.g., in Chapters 3 and 5), and it is in fact a widespread feature of our mental lives, one that will come up again in later chapters. But in any case, the proposal to be offered here should be obvious: Categorization via resemblance is a heuristic strategy, a relatively efficient (even if imperfect) way to think about categories. What makes this strategy efficient? In most cases, resemblance to a prototype or an exemplar can be judged on the basis of relatively superficial features rather than on the basis of more abstract knowledge about a category. This emphasis on superficial characteristics is precisely what we want for a categorization heuristic: These traits can generally be judged swiftly, allowing comparisons that are quick and easy.

Like any other heuristic, however, the use of typicality will occasionally lead to error: If you rely on the bird prototype to categorize flying creatures, you may mis-identify a bat. That is the price you pay for heuristic use. But if the heuristic is well chosen, these errors will be relatively rare, and on this point, too, a reliance on typi-cality seems sensible. Prototypes, by their very nature, represent the most common features of a category, and so prototypes will be representative of most category mem-bers. Thus, categorization via prototypes will usually be accurate: Most members of the category do resemble the prototype, even if some members do not. And the same points apply to a reliance on exemplars: As we have seen, the exemplars coming to mind will usually be examples of typical category members and so, more often than not, will resemble the new category members you encounter.

This view of things, therefore, preserves a central insight of both the prototype and the exemplar views: We cannot equate typicality with membership in a category. But even so, membership and typicality are clearly related to each other: Creatures closely resembling the prototype bird are not guaranteed to be birds, but they are highly likely to be birds. This is what allows us to use typicality as a fast and efficient basis for judging category membership.

Explanatory Theories

It's easy to see, therefore, why prototypes and exemplars are so important and what function they serve. They are, in short, the sort of category knowledge we rely on when we want a judgment that is quick and efficient. Over and over, though, we have argued that there is more to category knowledge than this. What is the "more"?

Our discussion has already provided some hints about this issue. In cases we have considered, a person's understanding of a concept seems to involve a network of interwoven beliefs linking the target concept to a number of other concepts. To understand what counterfeit is, you need to know what money is, and probably what a government is, and what crime is. To understand what a raccoon is, you need to understand what parents are, and with that, you need to know some facts about life cycles, heredity, and the like.

Perhaps, therefore, we need to broaden our overall approach. We have been trying throughout this chapter to characterize concepts one by one, as though each concept could be characterized independently of other concepts. We talked about the proto-type for bird, for example, without any thought about how this prototype is related to the animal prototype or the egg prototype. Perhaps, though, we need a more holistic approach, one in which we place more emphasis on the interrelationships among concepts. This would allow us to include in our accounts the wide network of beliefs in which concepts seem to be embedded.

To see how this might play out, consider the concept "raccoon." Your knowledge about this concept probably includes a raccoon prototype and some exemplars, but it also includes a set of beliefs about raccoons: your belief that raccoons are biological creatures (and therefore made of flesh and blood, and also the offspring of adult raccoons), and also your belief that raccoons are wild animals (and therefore usually not pets, usually living in the woods), and so on. These various beliefs may not be sophisticated, and they may sometimes be inaccurate, but nonetheless they provide you with a broad cause-and-effect understanding of why raccoons are as they are. (Various authors have suggested different proposals for how we should conceptualize this web of beliefs. See, among others, Johnson-Laird, 1987; Keil, 1989, 2003; Komatsu, 1992; Lakoff, 1987; Markman & Gentner, 2001; Medin & Ortony, 1989; G. L. Murphy, 2003; Neisser, 1987; Rips & Collins, 1993; Wisniewski & Medin, 1994.)

Guided by these considerations, many authors have suggested that each of us has something that we can think of as a "theory" about raccoons—what they are, how they act, and why they are as they are—and likewise a "theory" about most of the other concepts we hold. The theories are less precise, less elaborate, than a scientist's theory, but they serve the same function: They provide a crucial knowledge base that we rely on in most of our thinking about an object, event, or category; and they allow us to understand any new facts we might encounter about the relevant object or category.

Beliefs and Categorization

Not only do we know what's typical for a category, we also have beliefs that tell us why the category is as it is. These beliefs can be documented in many ways. For example, we can imagine an airplane made out of unusual materials such as wood or ceramic, but it's absurd to think of an airplane made out of whipped cream. Why is this? We know that a plane's function depends on its aerodynamic properties, and those, in turn, depend on the plane's shape. Whipped cream wouldn't hold its shape, and so is not an option for airplane construction—a point that is obvious to us because of our background knowledge about the concept "airplane."

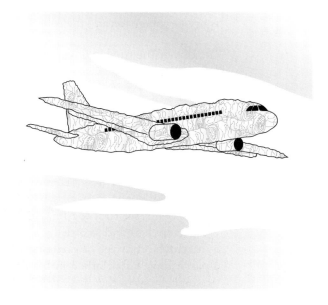

Theories and Category Coherence

A person's implicit "theories" about concepts influence him in many ways—and govern, for example, how easily or how quickly he can learn new concepts. To see how this works, imagine that you were given a group of objects and had to decide whether each belonged in Category A or Category B. Category A, you were told, included all the objects that were metal, had a regular surface, were of medium size, and were easy to grasp. Category B, on the other hand, included objects made of metal, with irregular surfaces, small, and hard to grasp. This sorting task would be difficult and cumbersome—unless we gave you another piece of information: namely, that Category A includes objects that could serve as substitutes for a hammer. With this clue, you can immediately draw on your other knowledge about hammers, and in this way you can see *why* the features are as they are. This allows much more rapid learning of the new category. Indeed, when research participants were given this "theme," they learned the category more rapidly and more accurately (Medin, 1989; Wattenmaker, Dewey, Murphy, & Medin, 1986; for related findings, see Heit & Bott, 2000; Kaplan & Murphy, 2000; Rehder & Ross, 2001).

Many other cases show the same pattern, so that in general people learn new concepts more quickly, and work more easily with those concepts, when they understand how the concepts' features hang together. Let's be clear, though, that this understanding of a concept's features rests on a broader set of cause-and-effect beliefs. You understand why "metal" and "easy to grasp" go together for the category "hammer substitutes" because you understand what a hammer is and how a hammer is used; these points, in turn, allow you to understand why the qualities of "metal" and "easy to grasp" are important for the tool's functioning. Thus, it is your beliefs and broader understanding (in essence, your "theory" about what a hammer is) that give the category its coherence, and the coherence, in turn, makes the category easier to learn.

The Use of Theories in Categorization

The influence of beliefs and background knowledge is also evident in how people *categorize* things—that is, their decisions about whether a test case is or is not in a particular category. This was crucial for our earlier examples of the abused lemon, the counterfeit bill, and the transformed raccoon. In each case, people seem to rely on their background knowledge for that category in deciding which features are crucial for the categorization and which are not; then, with the features "selected" in this fashion, a new case now before their eyes can be categorized appropriately. (For a parallel case involving the way that professional psychologists diagnose [categorize] their patients, see Kim & Ahn, 2002.)

Our background knowledge also helps us with cases that are very different from a category's prototype or exemplars. For example, imagine that you saw someone at a party jump fully clothed into a pool. Odds are good that you would decide this person belongs in the category "drunk," but why is this? Jumping into a pool in this way is surely not part of the *definition* of being drunk, nor is it part of the *prototype* (Medin & Ortony, 1989). But each of us also has certain beliefs about how drunks behave; we have, in essence, a "theory" of drunkenness. This theory allows us to think through what being drunk will cause someone to do and not to do, and on this basis we would decide that, yes, someone who jumped into the pool fully clothed probably was inebriated.

Inferences Based on Theories

Here is one more way in which theories guide our everyday concept use. If you meet my pet, Boaz, and decide that he's a dog, then you instantly know a great deal about Boaz—the sorts of things he's likely to do (bark, beg for treats, chase cats) and the sorts of things he's unlikely to do (climb trees, play chess, hibernate all winter). Likewise, if you have decided (correctly) that Boaz is a dog, and if you now learn something new about Boaz, you may be able to make broad use of that knowledge. If, for example, you learn that Boaz has sesamoid bones, you may draw the conclusion that all dogs have sesamoid bones—and that perhaps other animals do too.

These examples remind us of one of the reasons why categorization is so important: Categorization allows you to make broad use of your knowledge by applying that knowledge (e.g., knowledge about dogs in general) to the new cases you encounter (e.g., Boaz). Conversely, categorization allows you to draw broad conclusions from your experience (so that things you learn about Boaz can be applied to other dogs you meet). All of this, we emphasize, is possible only because you realize that Boaz *is a dog*; without this simple realization, you wouldn't be able to use your knowledge in this way. But how exactly does this use of knowledge proceed?

Early research indicated that inferences about categories were guided by typicality. In one study, participants who were told a new fact about robins were willing to infer that the new fact would also be true for ducks. If they were told a new fact about ducks, however, they would not extrapolate to robins (Rips, 1975). Apparently, people were willing to make inferences from the typical case to the whole category, but not from an atypical case to the category. This provides one more argument that typicality does play a crucial role in our thinking about concepts. (For discussion of *why* people are more willing to draw conclusions from typical cases, see Murphy & Ross, 2005.)

However, factors beyond typicality also influence these inferences. People are, for example, also influenced by *similarity*: If told that my dog, Boaz, has sesamoid bones, people are more comfortable concluding that wolves also have sesamoid bones than they are in concluding that cows do. The *diversity* of cases being considered also matters. If people are told that crows and ducks are vulnerable to a particular disease, they are quite willing to believe that all birds are vulnerable to the disease. If, however, people are told that crows and blackbirds are vulnerable to a disease, then they're less willing to draw the general conclusion that all birds are vulnerable (Osherson, Smith,

Wilkie, Lopez, & Shafir, 1990). Presumably, this is because crows and ducks are quite different from each other, while crows and blackbirds are less so; and the more diverse the cases being considered, the stronger the conclusion.

It turns out, though, that people's beliefs about cause and effect also play a role here, and so, once again, we meet a case of concept use being guided by the background knowledge and beliefs that accompany each concept. For example, if told that gazelle's blood contains a certain enzyme, people are willing to conclude that lion's blood contains the same enzyme. However, if told that lion's blood contains the enzyme, people are less willing to conclude that gazelle's blood does too. Why is this? In the first case but not in the second, people find it easy to imagine the property being transmitted from gazelles to lions via the food chain. Likewise, if told that grass contains a certain chemical, people are willing to believe that cows have the same chemical inside them. This makes no sense in terms of similarity or typicality, but it makes perfect sense if people are thinking of the inference in terms of cause and effect, relying on their beliefs about how these various concepts ("gazelles," "lions," "grass," etc.) are related to each other (Medin, Coley, Storms, & Hayes, 2003; also see Heit, 2000; Heit & Feeney, 2005; Rehder & Hastie, 2004).

Expertise Effects

Let's once again pause to take stock. There is no question that typicality plays a huge role in shaping how we use our conceptual knowledge. That fact led us to a proposal in which typicality was at the heart of conceptual knowledge; that was the proposal cast in terms of prototypes and exemplars. However, we quickly found limitations on this proposal, and that led us to the view that conceptual knowledge must also include other information: knowledge about how each concept is linked to other concepts, and knowledge about how the features associated with a concept are linked to each other. And we now see that this "other knowledge" influences our concept use in a variety of ways—in how people learn new concepts, how they categorize new cases they encounter, and how they reason about their categories.

This proposal about theories and background knowledge also has another important implication: People may think about different concepts in different ways. For example, most people believe that *natural kinds* (groups of objects that exist naturally in the world, like bushes or alligators or stones or mountains) are as they are because of forces of nature, forces that are relatively consistent across the years. As a result, the properties of these objects are relatively predictable: There are, in effect, certain properties that a bush must have in order to survive as a bush; certain properties that a stone must have because of its chemical composition. Things are different, though, for *artifacts*, objects made by human beings. If we wished to make a table with 15 legs rather than 4, or one made out of gold rather than wood, or even a table with a top that wasn't flat, we could do this. The design of tables, after all, is up to us; and the same is true for most artifacts.

This leads to the proposal that people will reason differently about natural kinds and artifacts—because they have different beliefs about why categories of either sort are as they are. We have already seen one result consistent with this idea: the finding that children would agree that toasters could be turned into coffeepots, but not that skunks could be turned into raccoons. Plainly, the children had different ideas about artifacts like toasters than they had about animate objects (like skunks). Other results confirm this pattern: In general, people tend to assume more homogeneity when reasoning about biological kinds (like raccoons or skunks) than when reasoning about artifacts (Atran, 1990; Coley, Medin, & Atran, 1997; Rehder & Hastie, 2001).

Related evidence comes from neuroscience: People who have suffered brain damage sometimes lose the ability to name certain objects, or to answer simple questions about these objects ("Does a whale have legs?"). Often the problem is specific to certain categories, and so some patients lose the ability to name living things but not nonliving things; other patients show the reverse pattern (Mahon & Caramazza, 2009). Indeed, sometimes the symptoms caused by brain damage are even more specific, with some patients losing the ability to answer questions about fruits and vegetables, but still able to answer questions about other objects (living or not living). These data certainly suggest that separate brain systems are responsible for different types of conceptual knowledge—and so damage to a particular brain area disrupts one type of knowledge but not others. (As one author put it, the data seem to suggest that the brain has a "produce section," and damage here disrupts knowledge just about produce [Pinker, 1994].) These points add to the argument that we may need somewhat different types of theorizing for different types of concepts.

In addition, researchers have used fMRI scans to examine what parts of the brain are activated when people are drawing on one aspect or another of their conceptual knowledge. These neuroimagery data confirm the differences among types of concepts, with different brain areas activated when people are thinking about living things and when they are thinking about nonliving things (e.g., Chao et al., 2002). Moreover, these brain scans also reveal activation in sensory and motor areas when thinking about various concepts (Mahon & Caramazza, 2009)—with a strong suggestion that our abstract conceptual knowledge is intertwined with knowledge about what particular objects look like (or sound like or feel like) and also with knowledge about how one might interact with the object. These findings fit well with another theme we have been developing—namely, that our conceptual knowledge has many elements (and so cannot be reduced, say, to just a representation of a prototype, or a definition).

Our background knowledge also influences how we think about individual concepts. For example, consider these two concepts: "woman" and "stamp collector." People reason about these concepts rather differently. They tend to assume that the category "woman" has relatively sharp boundaries (you either are a woman or you're not), that membership in the category is involuntary and immutable, and that many of the category's observable features reflect deep, unchanging attributes (such as a genetic pattern or hormone levels) that make women what they are. People make the opposite assumptions for "stamp collector"—the category has fuzzy boundaries, membership can be temporary, and so on (Prentice & Miller, 2007). In both cases, though, the rationale is straightforward: People draw on their cause-and-effect beliefs (which may or may not be accurate!) about how someone gets to be a woman or how someone gets to be a stamp collector, and then they reason about each of these categories in a fashion guided by those beliefs.

As a closely related point, this emphasis on beliefs and background knowledge suggests that people will change how they use their concepts if their background knowledge changes—and this, too, turns out to be correct. For example, a number of studies have compared "ordinary" concept users with "experts"—commercial fishermen in making judgments about fish or expert botanists in making judgments about trees. The experts are clearly influenced by their (extensive) knowledge. In one procedure, the tree experts were asked to imagine that gingko trees get disease X, and they were asked how likely it would be, on this basis, that all trees could get disease X. The response was clearly guided by the experts' knowledge: "Gingkos are so resistant to disease that if they get it, it must be a very powerful disease" (Medin et al., 2003, p. 519). The results are similar with commercial fishermen: They are much less influenced by a fish's appearance than a novice is. Instead, they pay attention to multiple relations—including the fish's habitat, its preferred food, and so on (Shafto & Coley, 2003).

Concepts: Putting the Pieces Together

Where does all of this leave us? One might think that there's nothing glorious or complicated about knowing what a dog is, or a lemon, or a fish. Our use of these concepts is effortless and ubiquitous, and so is our use of the thousands of other concepts in our repertoire. No one over the age of 4 takes special pride in knowing what an odd number is, nor do people find it challenging to make the elementary sorts of judgments we've considered throughout this chapter.

As we have seen, though, human conceptual knowledge is impressively complex. At the very least, this knowledge contains several parts. We suggested that there is likely to be a prototype for each concept, as well as a set of remembered exemplars, and that people use these for a range of fast and easy judgments about the relevant category. In addition, people seem to have a set of beliefs about each concept they hold and also, as we have now discussed, an understanding of how these beliefs fit together. Much of this knowledge reflects a person's understanding of cause-and-effect relationships in the world—and so why it is that drunks act as they do, or how it could be that enzymes found in gazelles might be transmitted to lions. These cause-and-effect beliefs influence how people categorize items and also how they reason about the objects in their world.

Apparently, then, even our simplest concepts require a multifaceted representation in our minds, and at least part of this representation (the "theory") seems reasonably sophisticated. It is all this richness, presumably, that makes human conceptual knowledge extremely powerful and flexible—and so easy to use in a remarkable range of circumstances.

Chapter Summary

- People cannot provide definitions for most of the concepts they use; this suggests that knowing a concept and being able to use it competently do not require knowing a definition. However, when trying to define a term, people mention properties that are indeed closely associated with the concept. One proposal, therefore, is that our knowledge specifies what is typical for each concept, rather than naming properties that are truly definitive for the concept. Concepts based on typicality will have a family resemblance structure, with different category members sharing features but with no features being shared by the entire group.

- Concepts may be represented in the mind via prototypes, with each prototype representing what is most typical for that category. This implies that categories will have fuzzy boundaries and graded membership, and many results are consistent with this prediction. The results converge in identifying some category members as "better" members of the category. This is reflected in sentence verification tasks, production tasks, explicit judgments of typicality, and so on.

- In addition, basic-level categories seem to be the categories we learn earliest and use most often. Basic-level categories (like "chair") are more homogeneous than their superordinate categories ("furniture") and much broader than their subordinate categories ("armchair"), and they are also usually represented by a single word.

- Typicality results can be also be explained with a model that relies on specific category exemplars, and with category judgments made by the drawing of analogies to these remembered exemplars. The exemplar model also has other advantages. It can explain our sensitivity to category variability, and it can also explain the pliability of categories, including our ability to view categories from a new perspective.

- Sometimes categorization does not depend at all on whether the test case resembles a prototype or a category exemplar. This is evident with some abstract categories ("odd number") and some weird cases (a mutilated lemon), but it is also evident with more mundane categories ("raccoon"). In these examples, categorization seems to depend on knowledge about a category's essential properties.

- Knowledge about essential properties is not just a supplement to categorization via resemblance. Instead, knowledge about essential properties may be a prerequisite for judgments of resemblance. With this knowledge, we are able to assess resemblance with regard to just those properties that truly matter for the category, and not be misled by irrelevant or accidental properties.

■ The properties that are essential for a category vary from one category to the next. The identification of these properties seems to depend on beliefs we have about the category, including causal beliefs that specify why the category features are as they are. These beliefs are implicit theories, and they describe the category not in isolation but in relation to various other concepts.

■ Prototypes and exemplars may serve as categorization heuristics, allowing efficient and usually accurate judgments about category membership. These heuristics may not be adequate, though, for some of the ways we use our category knowledge; for these, our implicit theories about the concept play a pivotal role.

The Workbook Connection

See the *Cognition Workbook* for further exploration of concepts and generic knowledge:
■ Demonstration 9.1: Defining Concepts
■ Demonstration 9.2: Assessing Typicality
■ Demonstration 9.3: Basic-Level Categories
■ Research Methods: Limits on Generalization
■ Cognitive Psychology and Education: Learning New Concepts
■ Cognitive Psychology and the Law: Defining Legal Concepts

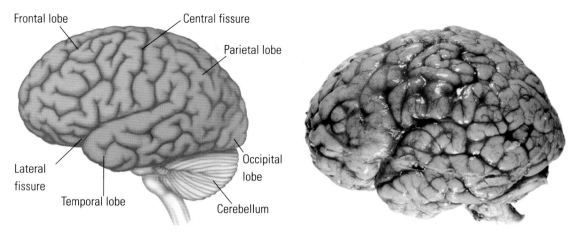

FIGURE 1 The Lobes of the Human Brain

The left panel identifies the various lobes and some of the brain's prominent features. Actual brains, however, are uniformly colored, as shown in the photograph in the right panel. The four lobes of the forebrain surround (and hide from view) the midbrain and most of the hindbrain. (The cerebellum is the only part of the hindbrain that is visible, and, in fact, the temporal lobe has been pushed upward a bit in the left panel to make the cerebellum more visible.) The side view shows the left cerebral hemisphere (the front of the head is on the left-hand side of the illustrations); the structures on the right side of the brain are similar. However, the two halves of the brain have somewhat different functions, and so the results of brain injury depend on which half is damaged. The symptoms of Capgras syndrome, for example, result from damage to specific sites on the right side of the frontal and temporal lobes.

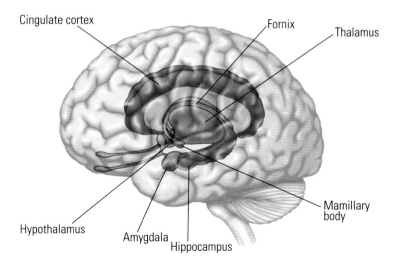

FIGURE 2 The Limbic System and the Hippocampus

Color is used in this drawing to help you visualize the arrangement of these brain structures. Imagine that the cortex is semi-transparent, allowing you to look into the brain, to see the (subcortical) structures highlighted here. The limbic system includes a number of subcortical structures that play a crucial role in learning and memory and in emotional processing.

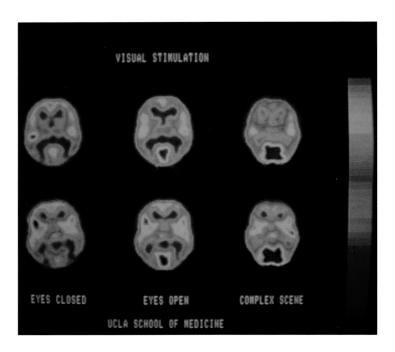

VISUAL STIMULATION

EYES CLOSED   EYES OPEN   COMPLEX SCENE

UCLA SCHOOL OF MEDICINE

FIGURE 3 PET Scan and Visual Stimulation

PET scans measure how much glucose (the brain's fuel) is being used at specific locations within the brain; this provides a measurement of each location's activity level at a certain moment in time. In the figure, the brain is viewed from above, with the front of the head at the top and the back at the bottom. As the figure shows, visual processing involves increased activity in the occipital cortex.

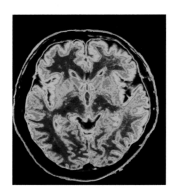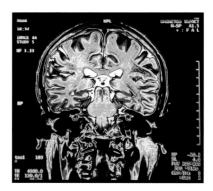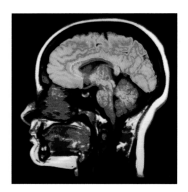

FIGURE 4 Magnetic Resonance Imaging

Magnetic resonance imaging produces magnificently detailed pictures of the brain. The left panel shows a "slice" of the brain viewed from the top of the head (the front of the head is at the top of the image); clearly visible is the longitudinal fissure, which divides the left cerebral hemisphere from the right. The middle panel shows a slice of the brain viewed from the front; again, the separation of the two hemispheres is clearly visible, and so are some of the commissures linking the two brain halves. The right panel shows a slice of the brain viewed from the side; many of the structures in the limbic system (see Figure 2) are easily seen.

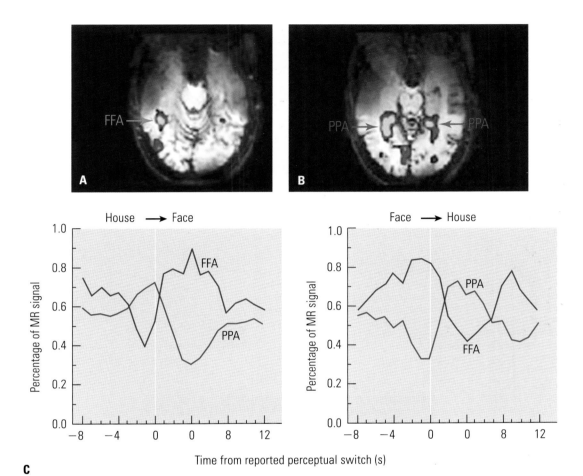

FIGURE 5 Brain Activity and Awareness

Panel A shows an fMRI scan of a person looking at *faces*. Activation levels are high in the fusiform face area (FFA), an area that is apparently more responsive to faces than to other visual stimuli. Panel B shows a scan of the same person looking at pictures of *places*; now activity levels are high in the parahippocampal place area (PPA). Panel C compares the activity in these two areas when the person has a picture of a face in front of one eye, and a picture of a house in front of the other eye. When the person becomes aware of the face, activation is higher in the FFA. When the person becomes aware of the house, activation in the PPA is higher. Thus, the activation level reflects what the person is conscious of, and not just the pattern of incoming stimulation.

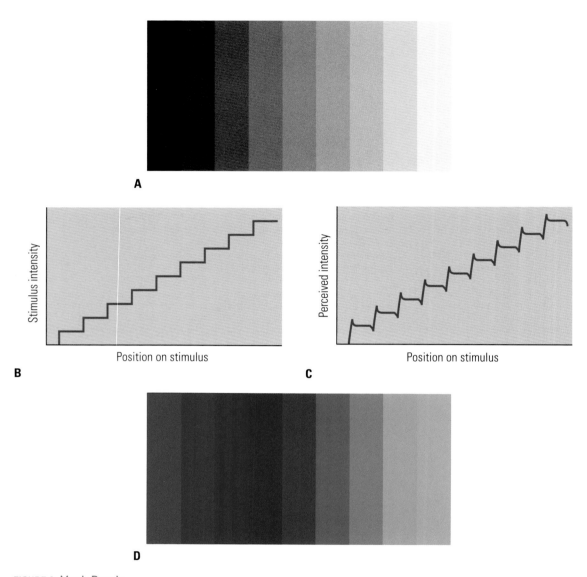

FIGURE 6 Mach Bands

In Panel A, each strip is of uniform light intensity, as shown in the graph in Panel B, which plots position against *physical light intensity*. But the strips do not appear to be uniform. For each strip, contrast makes the left edge (next to its darker neighbor) look brighter than the rest, while the right edge (next to its lighter neighbor) looks darker. As a result, the contours that separate one strip from the next are accentuated. The way the figure is perceived—its appearance—is shown graphically in Panel C. Panel D shows the same effect with hue added. Here, too, each vertical strip is uniform in brightness, but even so, the right edge of each strip (next to a bluer strip) seems redder than the rest of the strip. The left edge of each strip (next to a redder strip) seems bluer than the rest of the strip. To see that these differences are illusions, try placing some thin object (such as a toothpick or a straightened paper clip) on top of the boundary between strips. With the strips separated in this manner, the illusion disappears.

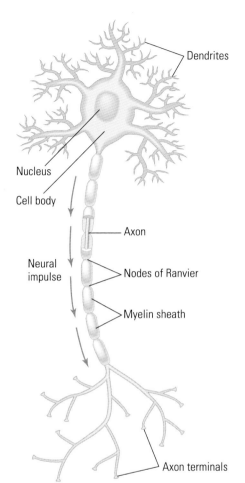

Dendrites

Nucleus

Cell body

Axon

Neural
impulse

Nodes of Ranvier

Myelin sheath

Axon terminals

A

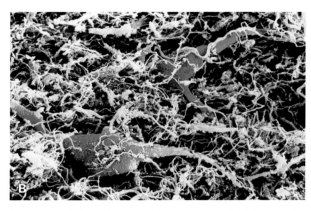

B

C

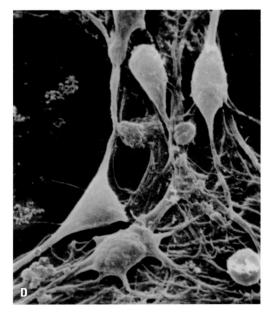

D

FIGURE 7 **Neurons**

Most neurons have three identifiable regions, as shown in Panel
A: The *dendrites* are the part of the neuron that usually detects
incoming signals. The *cell body* contains the metabolic machinery
that sustains the cell. The *axon* is the part of the neuron that
transmits a signal to another location. When the cell fires,
neurotransmitters are released from the terminal ending at the
tip of the axon (after B. Katz, 1952). We should note, though, that
neurons actually come in many different shapes and sizes. Panel
B shows neurons from the spinal cord (stained in red); Panel
C shows neurons from the cerebellum; Panel D shows neurons
from the cerebral cortex. Neurons usually have the same basic
parts (dendrites, a cell body, at least one axon), but plainly the
dimensions and configuration of these parts can vary widely!

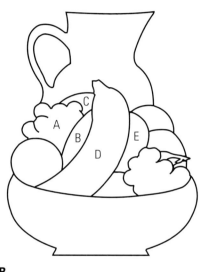

A

B

FIGURE 8 Perceptual Parsing

The text emphasizes that perception must go "beyond the information given" in important ways. Most of the examples in the text involve simple line drawings, but the same points apply to real-life scenes. For example, consider the still life (Panel A) and an overlay designating five different segments of the scene (Panel B). In order to perceive this picture correctly, the perceptual system must first decide what goes with what—for example, that Segment B and Segment E are different bits of the same object (even though they are separated by Segment D), and that Segment B and Segment A are different objects (even though they are adjacent and the same color). The perceptual system also needs to separate the figures from the ground, and so the horizontal stripes are perceived to be part of the background, continuing behind the blue vase.

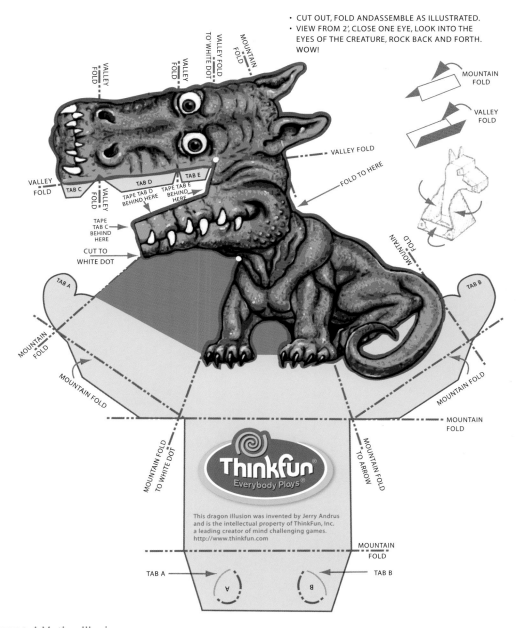

FIGURE 9 A Motion Illusion

Follow the directions at top right to assemble, then view, this 3-dimensional dragon. Watch the dragon carefully as you slowly move left or right. Odds are good that you will get a powerful motion illusion—so that the dragon moves as you move. To get a good sense of the illusion, you can view this movie: http://www.grand-illusions.com/opticalillusions/dragon_illusion/. This is a clear case in which perception is both *interpreting* and *misinterpreting* the input. Your visual system (mistakenly) registers the dragon to be convex (bulging toward you) rather than concave, and this is an understandable error (because you've probably seen very few hollow dragons in your lifetime). But then your visual system uses this faulty information to interpret the pattern of motion. The key here lies in just how far off track the visual system can go, as it "logically" interprets the input—and, in this case, interprets the input starting with a bad assumption.

FIGURE 10 Change Blindness

In some change-blindness demonstrations, participants see one picture, then a second, then the first again, then the second, and must spot the difference between the two pictures. Here we've displayed the pictures side by side, rather than putting them in alternation. Can you find the differences? For most people, it takes a surprising amount of time and effort to locate the differences—even though some of the differences are quite large. Apparently, therefore, having a stimulus directly in front of your eyes is no guarantee that you will perceive the stimulus!

FIGURE 11 A Hidden Face
A photo of a human face is hidden among these coffee beans. Can you find it? For most people, the search for the face takes time and effort. This reminds us that our perception is often selective—so that we miss rather distinctive elements within the scene. In addition, notice that before detecting the face you feel like you can easily see the entire photograph—even though you are failing to see the face. It appears, therefore, that you are in this case perceiving less than you think you do, and your sense of seeing "the entire scene" is to some extent an illusion.

FIGURE 12 Adjusting the "Beam" of Attention
Charles Allan Gilbert's painting *All Is Vanity* can be perceived either as a woman at her dressing table or as a human skull. As you shift from one of these perceptions to the other, you need to adjust the searchlight beam of attention—to a narrow beam to see details (e.g., to see the woman) or to a wider beam to see the whole scene (e.g., to see the skull).

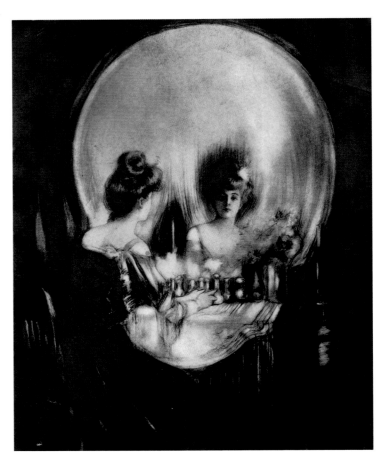

Column A	Column B
ZYP	RED
QLEKF	BLACK
SUWRG	YELLOW
XCIDB	BLUE
WOPR	RED
ZYP	GREEN
QLEKF	**YELLOW**
XCIDB	BLACK
SUWRG	BLUE
WOPR	BLACK

FIGURE 13 Stroop Interference

As rapidly as you can, name out loud the colors of the *ink* in Column A. (And so you'll say, "black, green," and so on.) Now do the same for Column B—again, naming out loud the colors of the ink. You will probably find it much easier to do this for Column A, because in Column B you experience interference from the automatic habit of reading the words.

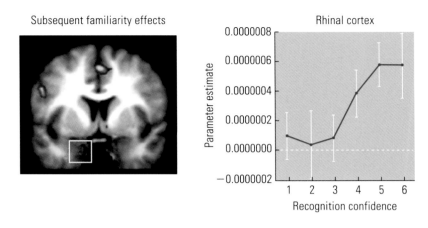

Subsequent familiarity effects

Rhinal cortex

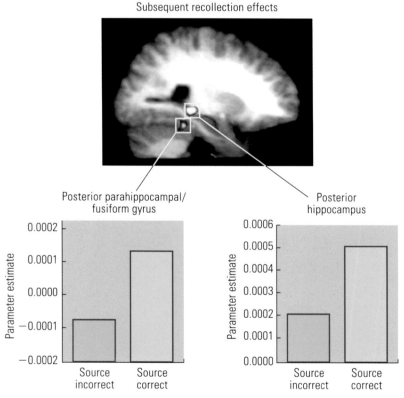

Subsequent recollection effects

Posterior parahippocampal/
fusiform gyrus

Posterior
hippocampus

FIGURE 14 Familiarity vs. Source Memory

This study involved tracking participants' brain activity during encoding and analyzing the data according to retrieval parameters. The top panel illustrates activation in the brain's rhinal cortex. If this area became highly activated during encoding, then the stimulus likely seemed familiar when participants viewed it later on. The bottom panel illustrates activation in areas in and around the hippocampus. If these areas became highly activated during encoding, then later on the participants were likely to remember having seen that stimulus.

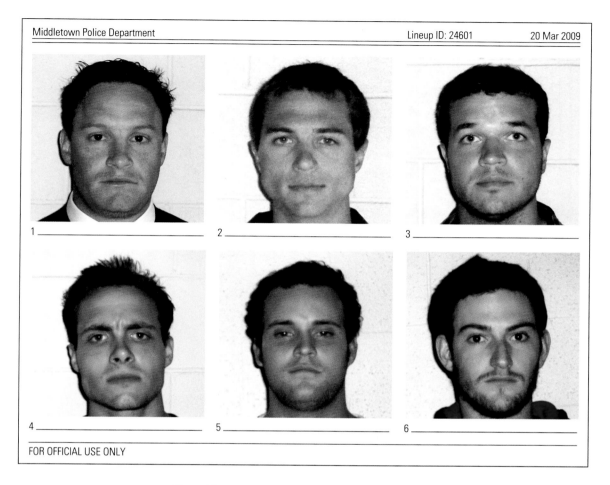

Middletown Police Department • Lineup ID: 24601 • 20 Mar 2009

1 _____ 2 _____ 3 _____

4 _____ 5 _____ 6 _____

FOR OFFICIAL USE ONLY

FIGURE 15 Photo Lineups

In criminal investigations, crucial evidence often comes from an eyewitness selecting the perpetrator from a lineup. In the United States, this is usually done with a photo lineup, like this one. The witness is told: "The perpetrator may or may not be here, and you are under no obligation to make a choice. But do you see the perpetrator here?" Eyewitnesses are usually accurate in making these judgments, but errors certainly can occur—in part because the witness might register that one of the people shown looks familiar, but then the witness makes a mistake in deciding *why* the person looks familiar.

FIGURE 16 Flashbulb Memories
People often have especially clear and long-lasting memories
for events like their first hearing about Princess Diana's death,
or the attack on the World Trade Center in September 2001.
These memories—called flashbulb memories—are vivid and
compelling, but are not always accurate.

FIGURE 17 Typicality

As the text describes, people seem to have a prototype in their minds for a category like "dog." Presumably, the German Shepherd shown here is close to that prototype, and the other dogs shown here are more distant from the prototype. It turns out, though, that many other categories also have a prototype—including the category "red." Which of these patches do you think shows the prototype for red?

A English naming

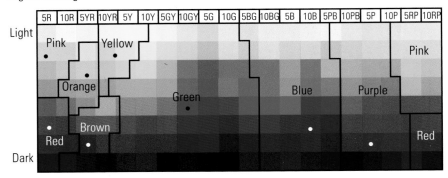

B Berinmo naming

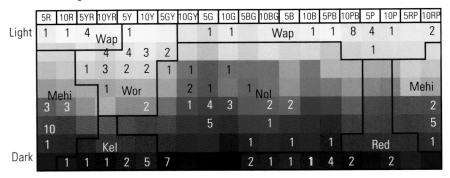

FIGURE 18 **Colors in Different Languages**

Languages differ widely in how they name the various colors. Some languages have many color terms; other languages have few. The patterns shown here summarize the results of a color-naming experiment done with English speakers (Panel A) and Berinmo speakers (Panel B). The Berinmo people, who live in Papua New Guinea, only have five different words for describing colors. Notice, then, that English distinguishes between green and blue; Berinmo does not (i.e., colors of both shades are called Nol). Likewise, English distinguishes between red and pink, but Berinmo does not (both are called Mehi). The letters and numbers along the edges of these panels refer to specific colors within the Munsell System—a common system for identifying colors. Evidence suggests that these differences, from one language to the next, have an impact on how people remember colors—so that colors that are more easily or more precisely named are easier to remember. As a result, people with larger "color vocabularies" seem to have better memories for color. In addition, these language differences may shape how people perceive color. By using different words for *blue* and *green*, English draws our attention to—and sharpens our understanding of—the boundary between these two hues. However, there is nothing special about language effects here: Similar effects can be obtained if we pay attention to this boundary in some other (nonlinguistic) fashion. It is the attention that matters, independent of how the attention is influenced.

Language

Virtually every human knows and uses a language; some of us know and use several languages. Indeed, to find a human *without* language, we need to seek out people in extraordinary circumstances—people who have suffered serious brain damage or people who have grown up completely isolated from other humans. In sharp contrast, no other species has a language comparable to ours in complexity or communicative power. In a real sense, then, knowing a language is a key part of being a human—a near-universal achievement in our species, yet unknown in its full-blown form in any other species.

Language seems no less central if we consider how it is used and what it makes possible. We use language to convey our ideas to each other, and our wishes, and our needs. Without language, our social interactions would be grossly impoverished, and cooperative endeavors would be a thousand times more difficult. Without language, the transmission of information and the acquisition of knowledge would be enormously impaired. (How much have you learned by listening to others or by reading?) Without language, there would be no science and no culture. Language is thus at the heart of, and essential for, a huge range of human activities and achievements. What is this tool, therefore, that is universal for our species, unique to our species, and crucial for so much of what our species does?

We will start by considering the elements of language—its sounds, its words, its syntax—which will help us understand what people need to know in order to be competent users of English, or Spanish, or whatever language they speak. We will then shift our focus to some of the processes people use in order to "decode" the sentences they encounter. We will turn next to the biological roots of language, and then, finally, to the ways that our language skills might shape the way that we think.

- Language can be understood as having a hierarchical structure—with phonemes put together to form morphemes, these put together to form words, and these put together to form sentences.

- At each level, we can endlessly combine and recombine units, but the combinations seem to be governed by rules of various sorts, so that some combinations of elements are rare; others seem prohibited outright. With these principles, language is *generative*, so that any user of the language can create new forms (new sound combinations, new words, new phrases).

- A different set of principles describes how, moment by moment, people interpret the sentences they hear or read; in this interpretation, people are guided by many factors, including syntax, semantics, and contextual information.

- In interpreting sentences, people seem to use a "compile as you go" strategy, trying to figure out the role of each word the moment it arrives. This approach is often efficient, but it can lead to error.

- Our extraordinary skill in using language is made possible in part by the fact that large portions of the brain are specialized for language use, making it clear that we are, in a literal sense, a "linguistic species."

- Finally, language surely influences our thoughts, but in an indirect fashion: Language is one of many ways to draw our attention to this or that aspect of the environment. This shapes our experience, which in turn shapes our cognition.

The Organization of Language

Language, at its heart, involves a special type of translation. I might, for example, want to tell you about a funny scene I saw earlier, and so I need to convert my ideas about the scene into sounds that I can utter. You, in turn, detect those sounds and need to convert them into some sort of comprehension. How does this translation—from ideas to sounds, and then back to ideas—take place?

Part of the answer lies in the fact that language is highly organized, with clear patterns in the way that various ideas are expressed. These patterns guide me when I express my ideas, and they also guide you when you're figuring out what I just said. Thus, I reliably use the word "horse" to refer to a certain type of animal. If I say, "The horse was following the cow," it reliably means that the cow was in front and the horse was behind. If I say "will follow" rather than "was following," it means the action hasn't started yet.

As speakers and listeners, therefore, we need to grasp (and rely on) these apparently reliable patterns. Indeed, this is surely a large part of what it means to "know a language" at all (e.g., to know how to speak English): We need to know what ideas are intended by the individual words, we must be able to decode the syntax, and so on. And as psychologists trying to understand language, we need to describe these patterns. How should we begin? For an initial step, let's note that language has a structure, as depicted in Figure 10.1. At the highest level of the structure (not shown in the figure) are the ideas intended by the speaker, or the ideas that the listener derives from the input. These ideas are typically expressed in **sentences**—coherent sequences of words that express the intended meaning of a speaker. Sentences, in

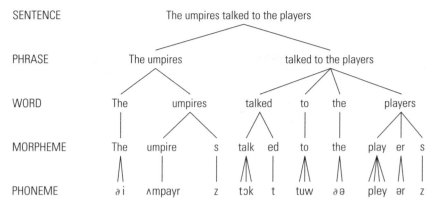

SENTENCE	The umpires talked to the players				
PHRASE	The umpires	talked to the players			
WORD	The	umpires	talked	to	the	players
MORPHEME	The	umpire	s	talk	ed	to	the	play	er	s
PHONEME	ə i	ʌmpayr	z	tɔk	t	tuw	ə ə	pley	ər	z

FIGURE 10.1 The Hierarchy of Linguistic Units

It is useful to think of language as having a hierarchical structure. At the top of the hierarchy, there are sentences. These are composed of phrases, which are themselves composed of words. The words are composed of morphemes, the smallest language units that carry meaning. When the morphemes are pronounced, the units of sound are called phonemes. In describing phonemes, the symbols correspond to the actual sounds produced, independent of how these sounds are expressed in ordinary writing.

turn, are composed of phrases, which are in turn composed of words. Words are composed of morphemes, the smallest language units that carry meaning. Some **morphemes**, like "umpire" or "talk," are units that can stand alone, and they typically refer to particular objects or ideas or actions. Other morphemes get "bound" onto these "free" morphemes, and add information crucial for interpretation. Examples of bound morphemes in Figure 10.1 are the past-tense morpheme "ed" and the plural morpheme "s."

In spoken language, morphemes, in turn, are conveyed by sounds called **phonemes**, defined as the smallest unit of sound that can serve to distinguish words in language. Some phonemes are easily represented by letters of the alphabet, but others are not, and that is why the symbols look strange in the bottom row of Figure 10.1; the symbols correspond to the actual sounds produced, independent of how those sounds are expressed in our (or any other) alphabet.

Within each of these levels, language is also organized in another way. In each level, people can combine and recombine the units to produce novel utterances—assembling the phonemes into brand-new morphemes or assembling words into brand-new phrases. Crucially, though, not all combinations are possible—so that a new breakfast cereal (for example) might be called "Klof" but would probably seem strange to English speakers if it were called "Tlof." Likewise, someone might utter the novel sentence, "I admired the lurking octopi" but almost certainly would not say, "Octupi admired the I lurking." What lies behind these points? Why are some sequences acceptable—even if strange—while others seem awkward or even unacceptable? We will need to explore these points before we are done.

Phonology

Let's begin by exploring these various forms of language organization; in the process, we will be describing what it is that someone knows when she "knows a language." We'll start at the bottom of the hierarchy depicted in Figure 10.1 and work our way up—so that we'll start, in short, with the *sounds* of speech.

The Production of Speech

In ordinary breathing, air flows quietly out of the lungs, through the larynx, and up through the nose and mouth (see Figure 10.2). However, noises are produced if this airflow is interrupted or altered, and this allows humans to produce a wide range of different sounds.

For example, within the larynx there are two flaps of muscular tissue called the "vocal folds." (These structures are also called the "vocal cords," although they are not cords at all.) The vocal folds can be rapidly opened and closed, producing a buzzing sort of vibration known as **voicing**. You can feel this vibration by putting your palm on your throat while you produce a [z] sound. You will feel no vibration, though, if you hiss like a snake, producing a sustained [s] sound. The [z] sound is voiced; the [s] is not.

You can also produce sound by narrowing the air passageway within the mouth itself. For example, hiss like a snake again and pay attention to your tongue's position.

FIGURE 10.2 The Production of Speech
In ordinary breathing, air flows out of the lungs, through the larynx, and up through the nose and mouth. To produce speech, this passageway must be constricted in a fashion that impedes or interrupts the airflow. For example, the tongue and lips control the movement of air through the oral cavity. Likewise, the uvula can be opened to allow air to move through the nose rather than the mouth.

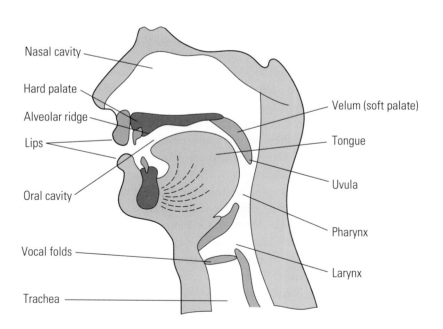

Nasal cavity

Hard palate

Alveolar ridge

Lips

Oral cavity

Vocal folds

Trachea

Velum (soft palate)

Tongue

Uvula

Pharynx

Larynx

To produce this sound, you placed your tongue's tip near the roof of your mouth, just behind your teeth; the [s] sound is the sound of the air rushing through the narrow gap you created.

If the gap is elsewhere, a different sound results. For example, to produce the [sh] sound (as in "shoot" or "shine"), the tongue is positioned so that it creates a narrow gap a bit further back in the mouth; air rushing through this gap causes the desired sound. Alternatively, the narrow gap can be more toward the front. Pronounce an [f] sound; in this case, the sound is produced by air rushing between your bottom lip and your top teeth.

These various aspects of speech production provide a basis for *categorizing* speech sounds. We can distinguish sounds, first, according to how the airflow is restricted; this is referred to as **manner of production**. Thus, as we have seen, air is allowed to move through the nose for some speech sounds but not for others. Similarly, for some speech sounds, the flow of air is fully stopped for a moment (e.g., [p], [b], and [t]). For other sounds, the air passage is restricted, but some air continues to flow (e.g., [f], [z], and [r]).

Second, we can next distinguish between sounds that are voiced—produced with the vocal folds vibrating—and those that are not. The sounds of [v], [z], and [n] (to name a few) are voiced; [f], [s], [t], and [k] are unvoiced. (You can confirm this by running the hand-on-throat test while producing each of these sounds.) Finally, sounds can be categorized according to where the airflow is restricted; this is referred to as **place of articulation**. Thus, you close your lips to produce "bilabial" sounds like [p] and [b]; you place your top teeth close to your bottom lip to produce "labiodental" sounds like [f] and [v]; and you place your tongue just behind your upper teeth to produce "alveolar" sounds like [t] and [d].

This categorization scheme allows us to describe any speech sound in terms of a few simple features. For example, the [p] sound is produced (a) with air moving through the mouth (not the nose) and with a full interruption to the flow of air, (b) without voicing, and (c) with a bilabial place of articulation. If any of these features changes—manner, voicing, or place—so does the sound's identity.

Put differently, these few features in varying combinations allow us to describe all the sounds our language needs. In English, these features are combined and recombined to produce 40 or so different phonemes. Other languages use as few as a dozen phonemes; still others, many more. (For example, there are 141 different phonemes in the language of Khoisan, spoken by the Bushmen of Africa; Halle, 1990.) In all cases, though, the phonemes are created by simple combinations of the features just described.

The Complexity of Speech Perception

These features of speech production also correspond to what listeners hear when they are listening to speech. Phonemes that differ only in one production feature sound similar to each other; phonemes that differ in multiple features sound more distinct. This is reflected in the errors people make when they try to understand speech in a noisy environment. Their misperceptions are usually off by just one feature, so that [p] is confused with [b] (a difference only in voicing), [p] with [t] (a difference only in place of articulation), and so on (G. A. Miller & Nicely, 1955; Wang & Bilger, 1973).

This makes it seem like the perception of speech may be a straightforward matter: A small number of features is sufficient to characterize any particular speech sound. All the perceiver needs to do, therefore, is detect these features; with this done, the speech sounds are identified.

As it turns out, though, speech perception is far more complicated than this. For one problem, consider Figure 10.3, which shows the moment-by-moment sound amplitudes produced by a speaker uttering a brief greeting. It is these amplitudes, in the form of air-pressure changes, that reach the ear, and so, in an important sense, the figure shows the pattern of input with which "real" speech perception begins.

Notice that within this stream of speech there are no markers to indicate where one phoneme ends and the next begins. Likewise, there are generally no gaps or signals of any sort to indicate the boundaries between successive syllables or successive

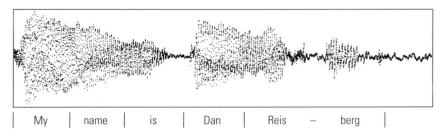

| My | name | is | Dan | Reis | — | berg |

FIGURE 10.3 The Actual Pattern of Speech

Shown here are the moment-by-moment sound amplitudes produced by the author uttering a greeting. Notice that there is no gap between the sounds carrying the word "my" and the sounds carrying "name." Nor is there a gap between the sounds carrying "name" and the sounds carrying "is." Therefore, the listener needs to figure out where one sound stops and the next begins, a process known as "segmentation."

words. Therefore, as a first step prior to phoneme identification, you need to "slice" this stream into the appropriate segments—a step known as **speech segmentation**.

For many people, this pattern comes as a surprise. As perceivers of speech, we are usually convinced that there are pauses between words, marking the word boundaries. This turns out, however, to be an illusion, and we are "hearing" pauses that, in truth, aren't there. The illusion is revealed when we physically measure the speech stream (as we did in order to create Figure 10.3) or when we listen to speech we can't understand—for example, speech in a foreign language. In the latter circumstance, we lack the skill needed to segment the stream, and so we are unable to "supply" the word boundaries. As a consequence, we hear what is really there: a continuous, uninterrupted flow of sound. That is why speech in a foreign language often sounds so fast.

Speech perception is further complicated by a phenomenon known as **coarticulation** (A. Liberman, 1970; also Daniloff & Hammarberg, 1973). This term refers to the fact that in producing speech one does not utter one phoneme at a time. Instead, the phonemes "overlap." While you are producing the [s] sound in "soup," for example, your mouth is getting ready to say the vowel. While uttering the vowel, you are already starting to move your tongue and lips and teeth into position for producing the [p].

This overlap in production allows speech to be faster and considerably more fluent. But this overlap also has important consequences for the sounds produced, and so the [s] you produce while getting ready for one upcoming vowel is actually different from the [s] you produce while getting ready for a different vowel. As a result, we can't point to a specific acoustical pattern and say, "This is the pattern of an [s] sound." Instead, the acoustical pattern is different in different contexts. Speech perception therefore has to "read past" these context differences in order to identify the phonemes produced.

These complications—the need for segmentation in a continuous speech stream, the variations caused by coarticulation, and also the variations from speaker to speaker or from occasion to occasion—make speech perception surprisingly complex. Nonetheless, we manage to perceive speech accurately and easily; how do we do it?

Part of the answer lies in the fact that the speech we encounter, day by day, is surprisingly limited in its range. Each of us knows tens of thousands of words, but most of these words are rarely used. In fact, it has been estimated that the 50 most commonly used words in English make up more than half of the words we actually hear (G. A. Miller, 1951).

In addition, the perception of speech shares a crucial attribute with all other types of perception: We don't rely only on the stimuli we receive; instead, we *supplement* this input with a wealth of other knowledge—including knowledge about what the words are in our language. Thus, on one proposal, the moment we hear the first phoneme in a word, we activate all the words in our vocabulary that have this starting sound; the moment we hear the *second* phoneme, we narrow this "cohort" of words so that we're thinking only about words that start with this pair of phonemes. Continuing in this way, speech perception ends up not just a matter of receiving and identifying sounds. Instead, it is a process in which we actively seek a match between the sounds arriving at our ears and the words actually in our vocabulary (Marslen-Wilson, 1987, 1990; Massaro, 1984; for more on how vocabulary can guide speech perception, see McClelland, Mirman & Holt, 2006).

In other cases, we are guided by knowledge of a broader sort, knowledge that relies on the broader context in which a word appears. This is evident, for example, in the **phonemic restoration effect**. To demonstrate this effect, researchers start by modifying tape-recorded sounds. For example, the [s] sound in the word "legislature" might be removed and replaced by a brief burst of noise. This now-degraded stimulus is then presented to participants, embedded in a sentence such as

> The state governors met with their respective legi*latures convening in the capital city.

When asked what they had just heard, participants reported hearing the complete word, "legislature," accompanied by a burst of noise. Apparently, they used the context to figure out what the word must have been, and then, in essence, they supplied the missing sound on their own (Repp, 1992; Samuel, 1987, 1991).

More, the participants don't just *infer* what the missing sound was; they literally seem to *"hear"* the sound. We can show this in several ways, including a procedure in which we ask participants to specify when, within the sentence, the noise burst occurred—simultaneous with the first syllable in "legislature"? the second? Remarkably, the participants cannot tell—with the clear implication that participants cannot tell which sounds within this word were truly part of the stimulus presentation and which were missing (but "supplied" by the participants themselves).

How much do context effects like these actually help us? Pollack and Pickett (1964) tape-recorded a number of naturally occurring conversations. From these recordings, they spliced out individual words and presented them, now in isolation, to their research participants. Remarkably, the participants were able to identify only half of the words. If restored to their context, though, the same stimuli were easy to identify. Apparently, the benefits of context are considerable.

Categorical Perception

The powerful effects of context remind us that speech perception (like all aspects of language use) takes place within a process in which one person is trying to convey a set of ideas to someone else, and the second person is trying to discern what those ideas are. These ideas are not just the "start point" and "end point" of the process; instead, these ideas actually shape the process, so that the listener is in effect constantly asking about the speaker, "What is she trying to say to me?"—and this question literally guides the perceptual processing.

With or without these benefits of context, though, humans are exquisitely talented in deriving information from the speech signal—and this provides yet another reminder that we are, in a deep sense, a "linguistic species." Our talent is reflected, for example, in the phenomenon of **categorical perception**, a term that refers to the fact that we are much better at hearing the differences *between* categories of sounds than we are at hearing the variations *within* a category of sounds. Said differently, we are very sensitive to the differences between, say, a [t] sound and a [d], or the differences between a [g] and a [k]. But we're surprisingly *insensitive* to differences within each of these categories, and so we have a hard time distinguishing, say, one [p] sound from another, somewhat different [p] sound. And, of course, this pattern is precisely what we want, because it allows each listener to categorize sounds with considerable accuracy, without hearing (and being distracted by) inconsequential variations within the category.

Demonstrations of categorical perception generally rely on computer-produced speech, because this allows us to ask how people perceive each stimulus in a precisely defined series. The first stimulus in the series might, for example, be a [ba] sound. Another stimulus might be a [ba] that's been distorted a tiny bit, to make it a little bit closer to a [pa] sound. A third stimulus might be a [ba] that's been distorted a bit more, so that it's a notch closer to a [pa], and so on. In this fashion we create a series of stimuli, each slightly different from the one before, ranging from a clear [ba] sound at one extreme, through a series of "compromise" sounds, until we reach at the other extreme a clear [pa] sound.

How do people perceive these various sounds? Figure 10.4A shows the pattern we might expect. After all, our stimuli are gradually shading from a clear [ba] to a clear [pa]. Therefore, as we move through the series, one might expect people to be less and less likely to identify each stimulus as a [ba], and correspondingly more and more likely to identify each as a [pa]. In the terms we used in Chapter 9, this would be a "graded-membership" pattern: Test cases close to the [ba] prototype should be reliably identified as [ba]. As we move away from this prototype, cases should be harder and harder to categorize.

The actual data, though, are shown in Figure 10.4B. Even though the stimuli are gradually changing from one extreme to another, participants "hear" an abrupt shift, so that roughly half the stimuli are reliably categorized as [ba], and half are reliably categorized as [pa]. Moreover, participants seem indifferent to the differences *within* each category. Across the first dozen stimuli, the syllables are becoming less and less [ba]-like, but this is certainly not reflected in how the listeners identify the sounds. Likewise, across the last dozen stimuli, the syllables are becoming more and more [pa]-like, but again, this is not reflected in the data. What listeners seem to hear is either a [pa], or a [ba] with no fine gradations inside of either category (Liberman, Harris, Hoffman, & Griffith, 1957; for reviews, see Handel, 1989; Yeni-Komshian, 1993).

It seems, then, that our perceptual apparatus is 'tuned' to provide us just the information we need: After all, we want to respond differently if told to "bat the ball" or "pat the ball." We'll give different answers if asked, "What's your favorite bark?" or "What's your favorite park?" And we certainly want to know whether someone said to us, "You're the best" or "You're the pest." Plainly, the difference between [b] and [p] matters to us, and this difference is clearly marked in our perception. In contrast, we usually don't care how exactly the speaker pronounced "bat" or "bark" or "best" —that's not information that matters for getting the meaning of these utterances. And, here too, our perception serves us well by largely ignoring these "subphonemic" variations.

Combining Phonemes

So far, our emphasis has been on the perception of individual phonemes, but of course language relies on *combinations* of phonemes. In English, we combine and recombine our 40 phonemes to produce thousands of different morphemes, which can themselves be combined to create word after word after word. Therefore, any speaker or listener using English needs to know both how to identify the phonemes and how to put them together into larger packages.

The step of combining phonemes would be trivial if any phoneme could be put side by side with any other. It turns out, though, that there are rules governing these combinations, and any user of the language needs to respect these rules. Thus, in English, certain sounds (such as the final sound in "going" or "flying") can occur at the end of a word but not at the beginning. Other combinations seem prohibited outright. We mentioned earlier, for example, that the sequence "tlof" seems anomalous to English-speakers; indeed, few words beginning "tl-" appear in English dictionaries. This limit, however, is simply a fact about English; it is not at all a limit on what human ears can hear or human tongues can produce. (Let's note, in fact, that there is a Northwest Indian language, *Tlingit*.)

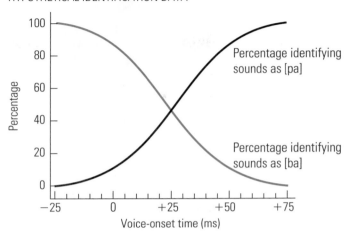

A

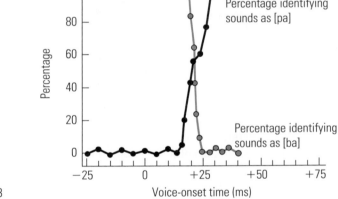

B

FIGURE 10.4 Categorical Perception

With computer speech, we can produce a variety of compromises between a [pa] and a [ba] sound, differing only in when the voicing begins (i.e., the *voice-onset time*, or *VOT*). Panel A shows a plausible prediction about how these sounds will be perceived: As the sound becomes less and less like an ordinary [ba], people should be less and less likely to perceive it as a [ba]. The bottom panel, however, shows the actual data: Research participants seem indifferent to small variations in the [ba] sound, and they categorize a sound with a 10- or 15-ms VOT in exactly the same way that they categorize a sound with a 0 VOT. The categorizations also show an abrupt categorical boundary between [pa] and [ba], although there is no corresponding abrupt change in the stimuli themselves. (After Lisker & Abramson, 1970)

Pre-Voicing

To make a [b] sound, your vocal folds start to vibrate at the same time that you start pushing air out of your lungs; for [p], you start the air moving but only begin the vibration about 60 msec later. In English, these two options (immediate voicing vs. 60-msec-delayed voicing) are the only ones we use. Some Asian languages, in contrast, rely on "pre-voicing": the vocal cords vibrate *before* the air movement begins. This is the pattern, for example, in the common Vietnamese family name *Nguyen*, and the "ng" start is the conventional way, in English spelling, to indicate this pre-voicing.

There are also rules that seem to govern the adjustments that must occur when certain phonemes are uttered one after another. For example, consider the "s" ending that marks the English plural—as in "books," "cats," "tapes," and so on. In the cases just listed, the plural is pronounced as an [s]. In other contexts, though, the plural ending is pronounced differently. Say these words out loud: "bags," "duds," "pills." If you listen carefully, you will realize that these words actually end with a [z] sound, not an [s]. The choice between these—a [z] pronunciation or an [s]—depends on how the base noun ends. If it ends with a voiced sound, then the [z] ending is used to make the plural. If the base noun ends with an unvoiced sound, then the plural is created with an [s]. (For more on phonological rules, see Chomsky & Halle, 1968; Halle, 1990.)

A speaker's obedience to these principles can be demonstrated even with novel, made-up cases. For example, I have one wug, and now I acquire another. Now, I have two . . . what? Without hesitation, people pronounce "wugs" using the [z] ending—in accord with the standard pattern. Indeed, even young children pronounce "wugs" with a [z], and so, it seems, they too have internalized—and obey—the relevant principles (Berko, 1958).

Words

The average American high school graduate knows about 45,000 different words (G. A. Miller, 1991). For college graduates, the estimate is higher: 75,000–100,000 words (Oldfield, 1963). For each of these words, the speaker must have several bits of information. The speaker needs to know the word's *sound*—that is, the sequence of phonemes that make up the word. In a literate culture, the speaker also knows the word's *orthography*—that is, the sequence of letters that make up the printed version of the word. The speaker must also know how to use the word within various phrases governed by the rules of syntax (see Figure 10.5). In addition—and quite obviously—the speaker needs to know the *meaning* of a word; he must have a *semantic representation* for the word to go with the *phonological* representation, essentially connecting the meaning to the sound. But what is this "meaning"?

Word Meaning

Most words are used to name objects or events in the world around us. The word "page," for example, refers to the sort of thing you are looking at right now; the word "reading" refers to the activity you are now engaged in; and so on. What a word refers to is called the word's **referent**. With this context, one might propose that the meaning of a word or phrase is linked to the word's (or phrase's) referent: If you know the referent of "bird," you know what the word "bird" means; if you know the referent of "football player," you know what the phrase means; and so on.

There is certainly an element of truth here, and so, if someone was clueless about what the word "page" referred to, we would suspect she did not know what the word meant. Even so, there are key differences between a word's reference and its meaning. Note, for example, that some phrases have no referent, because they refer to things that don't exist ("unicorn"? "X-ray vision"? "perfect world"?), but even so the phrases seem meaningful. In addition, sometimes a word's reference is temporary or a matter of coincidence. Thus, the referent of "president of the United States" changes at regu-

(1)	She can place the books on the table.
(2)	* She can place on the table.
(3)	* She can sleep the books on the table.
(4)	She can sleep on the table.

FIGURE 10.5 Knowing a Word
Part of what it means to "know a word" is knowing how to use a word. For example, a word like "put" demands an object, so that Sentence 1 (with an object) sounds fine, but Sentence 2 is anomalous. Other words have other demands. "Sleep," for example, does not take an object, and so Sentence 3 is anomalous, but Sentence 4 is fine.

lar intervals, but the meaning of the phrase seems more stable than that. For these (and other) reasons, word meanings must involve more than reference.

What is the "more"? Theorizing about this issue runs parallel to the points we encountered when we discussed *concepts* in Chapter 9. After all, many words do express single concepts, and more generally, one can understand a word's meaning only if one understands the relevant concepts. For present purposes, therefore, let us just say that a large part of "knowing a word" is knowing the relevant concept; we can then rely on the previous chapter for a discussion of what it means to know a concept. This may seem an inelegant proposal—but it is a proposal demanded by the complexities we encountered in Chapter 9. Conceptual knowledge turns out to be complicated—even for simple concepts like "bird" and "dog" and car." The same complications apply to *semantic* knowledge.

Building New Words

We mentioned estimates of vocabulary size for typical Americans (e.g., 45,000 words for high school graduates), but these estimates are rough at best, because the size of someone's vocabulary is quite fluid. Why is this? One reason is that new words are created all the time. This happens, for instance, whenever a new style of music or clothing demands a correspondingly new vocabulary. The world of computers offers other examples: "e-mail" is a relatively recent arrival in the language, as is "geek." Someone who wants to know something will often "google" for it, and "spam" has now become a verb (and not just a type of canned meat).

These new words don't arrive in the language as isolated entries, because language users immediately know how to create variations on each word by adding the appropriate morphemes. Imagine, for example, that you have just heard the word "hack" for the first time. You know instantly that someone who does this activity is a "hacker" and the activity itself is called "hacking," and you understand someone who says, "I've been hacked." In these ways, the added morphemes allow you to use these words in new ways—indeed, the morphemes allow you to create entirely new words. For example, the word "wave" has long been in our language, but with a few added morphemes the term "unmicrowavable" is of recent vintage (Pinker, 1994).

Once again, therefore, we need to highlight the **generativity** of language—that is, the capacity to create an endless series of new combinations, all built from the same set of fundamental units. Thus, someone who "knows English" (or, for that matter, someone who knows *any* language) has not just memorized the vocabulary of the language and perhaps some set of phrases. Instead, someone who "knows English" knows how to create new forms within the language: He knows how to combine morphemes to create new words; he knows how to "adjust" phonemes when they're put together into novel combinations; and so on. This knowledge isn't conscious—and so most English speakers could not (for example) articulate the principles governing the sequence of morphemes within a word, or why they pronounce "wugs" with a [z] sound rather than an [s]. Nonetheless, the speakers honor these principles with remarkable consistency in their day-by-day use of the language and in their day-to-day *creation* of novel words.

Syntax

The generativity of language remains in our view when we consider the upper levels in the hierarchy shown in Figure 10.1—the levels of *phrases* and *sentences*. After all, a few production features are all you need to create dozens of phonemes, and these phonemes can then be combined to produce many thousands of morphemes and an even larger number of words. But now let's consider what you can do with those words: If you have 40,000 words in your vocabulary, or 60,000, or 80,000, how many sentences can you build from those words? How many sentences are you able to understand or to produce?

Sentences can range in length from the very brief ("Go!" or "I do.") to the absurdly long. Most sentences, though, contain 20 words or fewer. With this length limit, it has been estimated that there are 100,000,000,000,000,000,000 possible sentences in English (that's 10^{20}; Pinker, 1994). (If printed in microscopic font, so that 1,000 sentences could fit on a page, this set of sentences would fill up roughly 250 trillion books—creating a library 10 million times larger than the U.S. Library of Congress.)

Syntax and Morphemes in "Jabberwocky"
In the poem "Jabberwocky," Lewis Carroll relies on proper syntax and appropriate use of morphemes to create gibberish that is wonderfully English-like. "He left it dead, and with its head / He went galumphing back."

Once again, though, there are limits on which combinations (i.e., which sequences of words) are acceptable and which not. Thus, in English one could say, "The boy hit the ball" but not "The boy hit ball the." Likewise, one could say, "The bird squashed the car" but not "The bird the car," or "The bird squashed the," or just "Squashed the car." Virtually any speaker of the language would agree these sequences have something wrong in them, suggesting that each speaker manages to follow the rules of **syntax**—rules governing the sequence of words in a phrase or sentence.

The rules of syntax provide a crucial function for us because they specify the *relationships* among the words in the sentence, and this allows us to talk about how one topic (or object or event) is related to another. Thus (to take a simple case), it's syntax that tells us who's doing what when we hear, "The boy chased the girl." Without syntax (if, for example, our sentences were merely lists of words, such as "boy, girl, chased"), we'd have no way to know who was the chaser and who was chaste.

But what is syntax? One might think the answer depends somehow on *meaning*, so that meaningful sequences are accepted as "sentences" while meaning*less* sequences are rejected as nonsentences. This suggestion, though, is plainly wrong. As one concern, many nonsentences do seem meaningful ("Me Tarzan.") In addition, consider these two sentences:

'Twas brillig, and the slithy toves did gyre and gimble in the wabe.

Colorless green ideas sleep furiously.

(The first of these is from Lewis Carroll's famous poem "Jabberwocky"; the second was penned by the important linguist Noam Chomsky.) These sentences are, of course, without meaning: Colorless things aren't green; ideas don't sleep; toves aren't slithy. Nonetheless, these sequences are sentences: Speakers of English, perhaps after a moment's reflection, regard these sequences as grammatically acceptable in a way that "Furiously sleep ideas green colorless" is not. It seems, therefore, that we need principles of syntax that are separate from considerations of semantics or sensibility.

Phrase Structure

Linguists argue that syntax needs to be understood in terms of a series of relatively abstract rules governing a sentence's structure. The rules specify the elements that must be included in the sentence and (in many languages) what the sequence of these elements must be. These rules also specify the overall organization of the sentence.

As an illustration, consider the simple sentence, "The boy loves his dog." The sentence seems to break naturally into two parts: The first two words, "the boy," identify what the sentence is about; the remaining three words ("loves his dog") then supply some information about the boy. These latter words, in turn, also break easily into two parts: the verb, "loves," and then two more words ("his dog") identifying what is loved.

This organization of the sentence can be described in terms of **phrase-structure rules.** One rule stipulates that a sentence (S) always consists of a **noun phrase** (NP) plus a **verb phrase** (VP). This is often diagrammed as an (upside-down) "tree structure," as shown in Figure 10.6, and the rule itself is often written this way:

$$S \rightarrow NP \ VP$$

Other phrase-structure rules are listed in Figure 10.7.

Linguistic Rules, Linguistic Competence

We have been discussing phrase-structure *rules*, but we need to be clear about what sort of rules these are and what these rules are *not*. We were all taught, at some stage of our education, how to talk and write "properly." We were taught never to say "ain't." Many of us were scolded for writing in the passive voice; others were reprimanded for splitting infinitives. These prohibitions are the result of **prescriptive rules**—rules

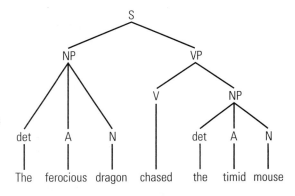

FIGURE 10.6 A Phrase-Structure Tree
The diagram shows that the overall sentence itself (S) consists of a noun phrase (NP) plus a verb phrase (VP). The noun phrase is composed of a determiner (det) followed by an adjective (A) and a noun (N). The verb phrase is composed of a verb (V) followed by a noun phrase (NP).

FIGURE 10.7 Phrase-Structure Rules
The first rule shown here indicates that a sentence (S) must consist of a noun phrase (NP) and a verb phrase (VP). A verb phrase, however, can take several forms: a verb by itself (V), or a verb followed by a noun phrase (NP), or a verb followed by a prepositional phrase (PP), and so on. Elements enclosed in parentheses are optional. An asterisk indicates that an element can be repeated, and so noun phrases can contain any number of adjectives (including none). Notice also that phrase-structure rules allow *recursion*, so that symbols can occur both on the left side of a rule (the part being defined) and the right side (the definition). Thus, a sentence must contain a verb phrase, but a verb phrase can contain a sentence, allowing complex constructions like "I believe she is the thief" or even "You heard Sam say I believe she is the thief."

describing how language is "supposed to be." Often these rules are used to mark differences between social classes—so that "upper-class" people speak "properly," but "lower-class" people don't. If one wishes to avoid being stigmatized, therefore, or wishes for membership in the elite, one tries to use these rules and to speak "proper" English.

We need to be skeptical, however, about these prescriptive rules. After all, languages change with the passage of time, and what's considered proper in one period is often different from what seems right at other times. Four hundred years ago, English speakers used the word "thou" in certain circumstances, but that construction now seems deeply old-fashioned. Prominent writers of the 18th and 19th centuries (e.g., Daniel Defoe, Ben Franklin, William Wordsworth, Henry James) commonly split their infinitives; grammarians of the early 20th century, in contrast, tried to prohibit this construction; English-speakers in the 21st century are generally indifferent to whether their infinitives are split or not. Should we therefore count split infinitives as "improper usage"? If we do, we're somehow honoring the English spoken in, say, 1926 as though it were better than the English spoken a century earlier or a century later, and it's unclear what the basis could be for such an assessment.

The rules we are concerned with in this chapter are rules of a different sort—not *prescriptive* rules but **descriptive rules**—that is, rules characterizing the language as it is ordinarily used by fluent speakers and listeners. There are strong regularities in the way English is used, and the rules we are discussing describe these patterns. No value judgment is offered (nor should one be) about whether these patterns constitute "proper" or "good" English. These patterns simply describe how English is structured—or perhaps we should say, *what English is*.

"To Boldly Go . . ."
The opening voiceover for *Star Trek* splits the infinitive "to go" with the adverb "boldly"—a point that horrified some grammarians. However, most contemporary English-speakers have no qualms about splitting infinitives.

Notice also how we go about discovering these regularities. It is, of course, important to track what is said and what is not said in ordinary language use. However, this provides evidence only of a limited sort, because the *absence* of a word or phrase in ordinary usage is difficult to interpret: If Leo never uses the word "boustrephedon," is this because he doesn't know the word or because he simply has no interest in talking about boustrephedon? If Miriam never uses the word "unmicrowavable," is this because she regards the word as illegitimate or merely because she is in the habit of using some other term to convey this idea?

In addition, spontaneous speech is filled with performance errors. Sometimes you start a sentence with one idea in mind, but then you change your idea as you are speaking. You might end up saying something like, "He went my father went yesterday," even though you realize, as you are uttering it, that the sentence contains an error. On other occasions, you slip in your production and end up saying something different from what you had intended. You might say, "They were I mean weren't fine," even though you notice (and regret) the slip the moment you produce it.

These speech errors are of considerable importance if we are studying the ways in which speech is actually produced (e.g., Dell, Burger, & Svec, 1997; Fromkin & Bernstein Ratner, 1998). However, these slips are a nuisance if we are trying to study linguistic knowledge. In most cases, you would agree that you had, in fact, made an error. In many cases, you know how to repair the error in order to produce a "correct" sentence. Clearly, therefore, your original performance, with its errors, doesn't reflect the full extent of your linguistic knowledge.

Because of considerations like these, we sometimes need to examine language **competence** rather than language **performance**, with "competence" being defined as the pattern of skills and knowledge that might be revealed under optimal circumstances (Chomsky, 1957, 1965). One way to reveal this competence is via linguistic judgments: People are asked to reflect on one structure or another and to tell us whether they find the structure acceptable or not. Note that we are not asking people whether they find the structure to be clumsy, or pleasing to the ear, or useful. Instead, we are asking them whether the structure is something that one could say, if one wished. Thus, "There's the big blue house" seems fine, but "There's house blue big the" does not. Or, to return to an earlier example, you might slip and say, "He went my father went yesterday," but you certainly know there is something wrong with this sequence. It's these "acceptability judgments" that reveal linguistic competence.

The Function of Phrase Structure

Many linguistic judgments reveal the importance of phrase-structure rules. For example, people reliably reject some sequences of words as "ungrammatical," and phrase-structure rules tell us why: The unacceptable sequences are the ones that don't follow the rules. In addition, we've noted that the words in a sentence seem to fall naturally into groups, and these groupings, too, can be explained in terms of phrase structure.

But phrase-structure rules also matter for linguistic *performance* and seem (as one crucial function) to guide our interpretations of the sentences we encounter. Specifically, the rule S → NP VP typically divides a sentence into the "doer" (the NP) and some information about that doer (the VP). If the verb phrase is rewritten VP → V NP, then the verb usually indicates the action described by the sentence, and the NP specifies the recipient of that action. In these ways, the phrase structure of a sentence provides an initial "road map" useful in understanding the sentence.

Sometimes, however, two different phrase structures can lead to the same sequence of words, and if you encounter those words you may not know which phrase structure is intended. How will this affect you? If, as we just suggested, phrase structures guide interpretation, then with multiple phrase-structures available there should be more than one way to interpret the sentence. This turns out to be correct (often with comical consequences), which confirms the role of phrase-structure rules in shaping our understanding of a sentence (see Figure 10.8).

D-structure

Phrase structure helps us untangle who-did-what-to-whom in any particular sentence. An important complication, though, arises from the sheer *variety* of sentences we encounter. We generally frame our sentences in the sequence of actor-action-recipient, but we often shift to other formats. Sometimes we shift the sequence for stylistic reasons; sometimes we rearrange the words to convey a certain emphasis or to draw attention to a particular idea ("It was the *duck* that was chased by the turkey!"). And sometimes we want to *question* a claim, rather than asserting it—and so we ask, "Did he escape the armadillo?" rather than simply commenting, "He did escape the armadillo."

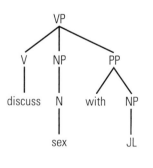
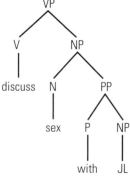

FIGURE 10.8 Phrase-Structure Ambiguity
Often the words of a sentence are compatible with more than one phrase structure; in this case, the sentence will be ambiguous. Thus, one can understand the first sentence either as describing a discussion with Jay Leno, or as describing sex with Leno; both analyses of the verb phrase are shown. Can you find both interpretations for the remaining sentences?

He wants to discuss sex with Jay Leno.
I saw the gorilla in my pajamas.
The shooting of the hunters was terrible.
They are roasting chickens.
Visiting relatives can be awful.
Two computers were reported stolen by the TV announcer.

These variations from sentence to sentence are all marked as part of a sentence's **D-structure**. (The term is derived from earlier theories that distinguished a sentence's "deep" and "surface" structures.) It is the D-structure that reflects the speaker's intentions in uttering (or writing) a sentence—including whether the sentence is a question or a comment, what the sentence's emphasis will be, and so on. The form and content of the D-structure are complex, as are the processes needed to transform the D-structure into the actual words uttered by a speaker. What is important for our purposes, though, is that there is more to a sentence than just its surface form—and so part of the task for a listener (or reader) is the "recovery" of the D-structure from the phonemes (or letters) actually encountered.

Linguistic Universals

Let's pause to take stock. We have climbed up the linguistic hierarchy—from basic features (like voicing or place of articulation) to phonemes, then to morphemes, and then to words, and finally to full sentences. At each step, we have seen how linguistic elements can be combined to create larger and more sophisticated units. In the process, we have seen how a relatively small number of elements can be used to create a vast number of combinations.

We have argued, though, that the combinations at each level seem to be rule-governed. The rules determine which units can be combined, and in what order. The rules also specify a *structure* within the larger units. And, remarkably, the rules are quite similar as we move from one language to the next.

Of course, languages differ. In English, adjectives are usually placed before the noun ("the blue house"); in Spanish, the adjective comes after the noun ("la casa azul"). Even so, there are a number of regularities across languages—even when we consider languages as diverse as, say, English, Japanese, and Turkish, or Walbiri and Kivunjo. Indeed, some have argued that these regularities constitute **linguistic universals**—that is, principles applicable to every human language (Chomsky, 1965, 1975, 1986; also see Comrie, 1981; Cook, 1988; Greenberg, Ferguson, & Moravcsik, 1978; and Hawkins, 1988).

The proposed universals are of various sorts. Some are framed in terms of probabilities. Thus, in all the world's languages, some sequences of words are quite common, while other sequences are quite rare. As an example, it is possible in English to put a sentence's object before the sentence's subject ("A bear he shot"), but this isn't the normal pattern for English—the normal pattern, instead, is subject-verb-object. And it is not only English that shows this pattern. The subject of a sentence tends to precede the object in roughly 98% of the world's languages. The sequence of subject before verb is preferred in roughly 80% of the world's languages (Crystal, 1987).

Other universals concern linguistic features that seem to come and go together. For example, if a language's preferred word order is subject-object-verb, the language is likely to form its questions by adding some words at the end of the question. If, in contrast, a language's preferred sequence is subject-verb-object (as in English), then the language will place its question words at the beginning of the question (as in, "Where did he . . . ?" or "When did they . . . ?").

The existence of these linguistic universals opens an intriguing possibility. Consider the fact that every human child learns how to speak, and, indeed, the learning process is quite rapid—with sophisticated language use in place by the time the child is 4 years old. Moreover, what is learned seems quite complex—with rules governing the combinations of phonemes and different rules governing the combinations of morphemes and the structure of phrases. How is all this complexity mastered so quickly?

We will return to the topic of language learning later in the chapter, but in the meantime, the linguistic universals offer an interesting possibility. Perhaps language learning occurs so rapidly because each child begins the process with an enormous head start: a biological heritage that somehow stipulates the broad outline of human language. In other words, the child *begins* language learning already knowing the universal rules; the task for the child, therefore, is to figure out exactly how the rules are realized within the language community in which the child is raised. The child needs to learn, for example, whether she lives in a community that prefers the subject-verb-object sequence or the subject-object-verb order. Having learned that, the child can then set the "switches" properly on the "language machinery" that she was born with and, in that way, be well on her way to speaking in the fashion that's appropriate for her language community—whether it's a community of Portuguese speakers, or Urdu, or Mandarin. Many have argued that this is the most plausible way to think about language learning, with the plausibility deriving from the fact that many of the rules we have discussed do seem, with the appropriate adjustments of parameters, universal. (For more on these points, see Bloom, 1994; Chomsky, 1957, 1965; Lidz, Waxman, & Freedman, 2003.)

Sentence Parsing

As we have discussed, a sentence's phrase structure conveys crucial information about who did what to whom; thus, once you know the phrase structure, you are well on your way to understanding the sentence. But how do you figure out the phrase structure in the first place? This would be an easy question if sentences were uniform in their structure: "The boy hit the ball. The girl chased the cat. The elephant trampled the geraniums." But, of course, sentences are more variable than this, which makes the identification of a sentence's phrase structure appreciably more difficult.

How, therefore, do you **parse** a sentence—that is, figure out each word's syntactic role? One possibility is that you wait until the sentence's end and only then go to work on figuring out the sentence's structure. With this strategy, your comprehension might be slowed a little (because of the wait for the sentence's termination), but you would avoid errors because your interpretation could be guided by full information about the sentence's content.

We've already suggested that people don't use this wait-for-all-the-information strategy in perceiving *words* (pp. 308–309). Instead, they begin the identification process as soon as they hear the word's very first phoneme. Evidence suggests the same pattern when people are interpreting *sentences*. Specifically, people seek to parse sentences as they hear them, trying to figure out the role of each word the moment they hear that word. This approach is more efficient (since there's no waiting), but it can lead to error in ways that we will describe in a moment. This turns out, therefore, to be one more case in which humans favor a strategy that is quick but occasionally misleading, in comparison to a strategy that is less efficient but more accurate. (For other illustrations of this sort of trade-off, see Chapters 3, 7, 9, and 12.)

Garden Paths

Even relatively simple sentences can be ambiguous if one is open-minded (or perverse) enough:

Mary had a little lamb. (But I was quite hungry, so I had the lamb and also a bowl of soup.)

Time flies like an arrow. (But fruit flies, in contrast, like a banana.)

Temporary ambiguity is also common inside a sentence. More precisely, the early part of a sentence is often open to multiple interpretations, but then the later part of the sentence clears things up. For instance, consider this example:

The old man the ships.

In this sentence, most people read the initial three words as a noun phrase: "the old man." However, this interpretation leaves the sentence with no verb, and so a different interpretation is needed, with the subject of the sentence being "the old" and with "man" as the verb. (Who mans the ships? It is the old, not the young. The old man the ships.) Likewise:

The secretary applauded for his efforts was soon promoted.

Here one tends to read "applauded" as the sentence's main verb, but it isn't. Instead, this sentence is just a shorthand way of answering the question, "Which secretary was soon promoted?" (Answer: "The one who was applauded for his efforts.")

These examples are referred to as **garden-path sentences**: You are initially led to one interpretation (you are, as they say, "led down the garden path"), but this interpretation then turns out to be wrong. Hence, you need to reject your first construal and seek an alternative. Here are two more examples:

Fat people eat accumulates.

Because he ran the second mile went quickly.

Garden-path sentences highlight the fact that there's some risk attached to the strategy of interpreting a sentence as it arrives. That's because the information you need in order to interpret these sentences arrives only late in the sequence, and so, to avoid an interpretive dead end, you would be well advised to remain neutral about the sentence's meaning until you've gathered enough information. That way, you'd know that "the old man" couldn't be the sentence's subject, that "applauded" couldn't be the sentence's main verb, and so on. But this is plainly not what you do. Instead, you commit yourself fairly early to one interpretation and then try to "fit" subsequent words, as they arrive, into that interpretation. This strategy is often effective, but it does lead to the "double-take" reaction when late-arriving information forces you to abandon your interpretive efforts so far. (For more on this interpret-as-you-go tendency, see Just & Carpenter, 1987, 1992; Marslen-Wilson & Tyler, 1987; Morton, 1969, 1970; Sedivy, Tanenhaus, Chambers, & Carlson, 1999.)

Syntax as a Guide to Parsing

What is it that leads us down the garden path? Why do we initially choose one interpretation, one parsing, rather than another? People actually use a bundle of different strategies. For one, they tend to assume that they will be hearing (or reading) *active* sentences rather than *passive*, and so they generally interpret a sentence's initial noun phrase as the "doer" of the action and not the recipient. As it happens, most of the sentences we encounter are active, not passive, and so this assumption is usually correct (Svartik, 1966). However, this assumption works against us whenever we do encounter a passive sentence, and that is why active sentences are usually easier to understand than passive sentences (Hornby, 1974; Slobin, 1966).

Does this mean that speakers (and writers) should always avoid passive sentences? Surely not. The assumption of active voice is only one of the factors that guide parsing, and so, in some contexts with other factors on the scene, passive sentences can be *easier* to understand, not harder (Pinker, 1994).

What are the other factors guiding parsing? It is not surprising that parsing is influenced by the function words that appear in a sentence and also by the various morphemes that signal syntactic role (Bever, 1970). For example, people easily grasp the structure of "He gliply rivitched the flidget." That's because the "-ly" morpheme indicates that "glip" is an adverb; the "-ed" identifies "rivitch" as a verb; and "the" signals that "flidget" is a noun—all excellent cues to the sentence structure.

In addition, parsing seems to be guided by a number of other strategies, including an assumption of so-called **minimal attachment**. Roughly, this means that the listener or reader proceeds through a sentence seeking the simplest phrase structure that will accommodate the words heard so far. Consider the earlier sentence, "The secretary applauded for his efforts was soon promoted." As you read "The secretary applauded," you had the option of interpreting this as a noun phrase plus the beginning of a separate clause modifying "secretary." This is, of course, the correct construal and is demanded by the way the sentence ends. However, the principle of minimal attachment led you to ignore this possibility, at least initially, and to proceed instead with a simpler interpretation—of a noun phrase + verb, with no idea of a separate embedded clause.

The tendency to misread the "secretary" sentence is also encouraged by other factors. The embedded clause is in the passive voice (the secretary was applauded by someone else); your tendency to assume active voice, therefore, worked against the correct interpretation of this sentence. Likewise, the sentence deliberately omits the helpful function words. Notice that we didn't say, "The secretary who was applauded. . . ."

With all these factors stacked against you, it's no wonder you were led to the incorrect construal. Indeed, with all these factors in place, garden-path sentences can sometimes be enormously difficult to comprehend. For example, spend a moment puzzling over this (fully grammatical) sequence:

The horse raced past the barn fell.

(If you get stuck with this sentence, try adding commas after "horse" and after "barn.")

Semantics as a Guide to Parsing

The "secretary" sentence was also complicated by one additional factor: The sentence said, "The secretary applauded for his efforts. . . ." Many people assume, in reading this sentence, that the secretary is a woman, hence "his" must refer to someone else. The suggestion, therefore, is that parsing is also guided by semantic factors, and not just syntax.

Other facts confirm this role for semantics. For example, we have already noted that it is often easier to understand an active sentence than it is to understand the corresponding passive sentence. However, this is true only if the sentence is "reversible," such as, "The dog nipped the cat." This sentence is considered reversible because the opposite sentence ("The cat nipped the dog") also makes sense. This is in contrast to sentences such as, "The elephant squashed the peanut." This sentence isn't reversible: Elephants can certainly squash peanuts, but peanuts can't squash elephants. In this case, therefore, you don't need the syntax to figure out who was the squasher and who was the squashed. Indeed, for sentences like this, there is no processing advantage for the active form relative to the passive (Slobin, 1966).

In addition, listeners and readers seem sensitive to certain statistical properties in the language. If a word has several meanings, you tend to assume its most frequent meaning whenever you encounter the word. You therefore tend to assume that "train" means the thing on tracks rather than the activity one engages in to teach tricks to a dog. Likewise, you tend to assume that "tree" refers to a type of plant rather than an activity (as in, "The hounds want to tree the raccoon"). Similarly, you tend to assume that adjectives will be followed by nouns. This isn't an obligatory pattern, but it is certainly a frequent pattern, and so the assumption seems safe.

Once again, we can see these factors in action in some of the garden-path sentences: The assumption that adjectives will be followed by nouns primes us to read the phrase "fat people" as an adjective–noun pair, and this gets us in trouble when we encounter "Fat people eat accumulates." Likewise, our reliance on frequent meanings is part of our problem in understanding sentences like "The old man ships" or "The new train quickly, but the old train more slowly."

The Extralinguistic Context

It's rare that we encounter a single, isolated sentence. Instead, sentences are uttered in some context, and the context can provide important aids for sentence understanding. Thus, the garden-path problem is much less likely to occur in the following setting:

Jack: Which horse fell?

Kate: The horse raced past the barn fell.

Factors outside of language itself—namely, the **extralinguistic context**—are also important. To see how, consider the following sentence:

Put the apple on the towel into the box.

At its start, this sentence seems to be an instruction to put an apple onto a towel; this interpretation must be abandoned, though, when the words "into the box" arrive. Now listeners realize that the box is the apple's destination; "on the towel" is simply a specification of which apple is to be moved. (Which apple should be put into the box? The one that is on the towel.) In short, this is another garden-path sentence— initially inviting one analysis, but eventually demanding another.

This confusion is avoided, however, if the sentence is uttered in the appropriate setting. Imagine that two apples are in view, as shown in Figure 10.9. In this context, a listener hearing the sentence's start ("Put the apple . . .") would immediately see the possibility for confusion (which apple is being referred to?) and so would expect the speaker to specify which apple is to be moved. When the phrase "on the towel" is uttered, then the listener immediately understands it (correctly) as the needed specification. Hence, there is no confusion and no garden path (Eberhard, Spivey-Knowlton, Sedivy, & Tanenhaus, 1995; Tanenhaus & Spivey-Knowlton, 1996).

The Use of Language: What Is Left Unsaid

What does it mean to "know a language"—to "know English," for example? As we've discussed, each language user seems somehow to know (and obey) a rich set of rules—with these rules determining which sound combinations and which sequences of words seem acceptable, and which do not. In addition, we've now seen

FIGURE 10.9 The Extralinguistic Context

"Put the apple on the towel into the box." Without the setting shown here, this sentence causes momentary confusion as the listener comes across "on the towel" before grasping the greater context of "into the box." But when the sentence is simultaneously presented with this picture, the listener finds "on the towel" useful in clearing up the ambiguity of "the apple."

that language users rely on a further set of principles whenever they perceive and understand linguistic inputs. Some of these principles are rooted in syntax (e.g., minimal attachment); others depend on semantics (e.g., knowing whether a relationship is reversible or not); others seem statistical in nature (e.g., knowing which usages are more common); and still others seem pragmatic (e.g., considerations of the extralinguistic context). These factors then seem to interact in an intricate fashion, so that our understanding of the sentences we hear (or see in print) seems guided by all of these principles at the same time.

All of this, however, still *understates* the complexity of language use and, with that, the complexity of the knowledge someone must have in order to "know a language." For illustration, note that we have said nothing about another source of information useful in parsing: the rise and fall of speech intonation and the pattern of pauses. These rhythm and pitch cues, together called **prosody**, and play an important role in speech perception. Prosody can reveal the mood of a speaker; it can also direct the listener's attention by, in effect, specifying the focus or theme of a sentence (Jackendoff, 1972). Prosody can also render unambiguous a sentence that would otherwise be entirely confusing (Beach, 1991). (Thus, garden-path sentences and ambiguous sentences are much more effective in print, where prosody provides no information.)

Likewise, we have not even touched on several other puzzles: How is language produced? How does one turn ideas, intentions, and queries into actual sentences? How does one turn the sentences into sequences of sounds? These are important issues, but we have held them to the side here. (For a review of these issues, see Dell, Burger, & Svec, 1997; Fromkin, 1993.)

Finally, what happens after one has parsed and understood an individual sentence? How is the sentence integrated with earlier sentences or subsequent sentences? Here, too, more theory is needed to explain the inferences we routinely make in ordinary conversation. If you are asked, for example, "Do you know the time?" you understand this as a request that you report the time—despite the fact that the question, understood literally, is a yes/no question about the extent of your temporal knowledge. In the same vein, consider this bit of conversation (Pinker, 1994):

Woman: I'm leaving you.
Man: Who is he?

We easily provide the soap-opera script that lies behind this exchange, but we do so by drawing on a rich fabric of additional knowledge, including knowledge of **pragmatics** (i.e., knowledge of how language is ordinarily used) and, in this case, also knowledge about the vicissitudes of romance. (For discussion, see Austin, 1962; Ervin-Tripp, 1993; Graesser, Millis, & Zwaan, 1997; Grice, 1975; Hilton, 1995; Kumon-Nakamura, Glucksberg, & Brown, 1995; Noveck & Reboul, 2008; Sperber & Wilson, 1986.)

These other topics—prosody, production, and pragmatics—are central concerns within the study of language, but for sake of brevity we need to hold them to the side here. Even so, our brief mention of these themes serves to emphasize a central

Pragmatic Assumptions

Pragmatics play an important role in our understanding of language. For example, consider this exchange: "What happened to the roast beef?" "Well, the dog sure does look happy." We understand this as a suggestion that the dog stole the meat, but what allows this interpretation? It is our assumption that conversational partners try to stay on-topic, and so we search for an interpretation about the dog comment that will link it to the question just asked.

message of this chapter: Each of us uses language all the time—to learn, to gossip, to instruct, to persuade, to express affection. We use this tool as easily as we breathe; we spend more effort in choosing our clothes in the morning than we do in choosing the words we will utter. But these observations must not hide the fact that language is a remarkably complicated tool, and we are all exquisitely skilled in its use.

The Biological Roots of Language

How is all of this possible? How is it that ordinary human beings—indeed, ordinary two-and-a-half-year-olds—manage the extraordinary task of mastering and fluently using language? We have already suggested part of the answer: Humans are equipped with extremely sophisticated neural machinery specialized for learning, and then using, language. Let's take a quick look at this machinery.

Aphasias

As we have seen in other chapters, brain damage can cause a variety of effects, depending on where and how widespread the damage is. For a number of brain sites, though, damage causes disruption of language—a disruption known as aphasia. Aphasias take many forms and are often quite specialized, with the particular symptoms being largely dependent on the locus of the brain damage. As a rough summary of the data, however, investigators find it useful to distinguish two broad classes of aphasia. Damage to the left frontal lobe of the brain, and especially a region known as Broca's area (see Figure 10.10), usually produces a pattern of symptoms known as nonfluent aphasia. In extreme cases, a patient with this disorder becomes virtually unable to utter or write a word. In less severe cases, only a part of the normal vocabulary is lost, but the patient's speech becomes labored and fragmented, and articulating each word requires special effort.

Different symptoms are associated with damage to a brain site known as **Wernicke's area** (see Figure 10.10) and usually involve a pattern known as **fluent aphasia**. In these cases patients do produce speech, but even though they talk freely and rapidly they actually say very little. The sentences they produce are reasonably grammatical but are composed largely of the little filler words that provide scant information.

Let us be clear, though, that this broad distinction—between fluent and nonfluent aphasia—captures the data only in the broadest sense. That is because, as we have seen, language use (whether for production or comprehension) involves the coordination of many different steps, many different processes. These include processes needed to "look up" word meanings in one's "mental dictionary," processes needed to figure out the structural relationships within a sentence, processes needed to integrate information gleaned about a sentence's structure with the meanings of the words within the sentence, and so on. Each of these processes relies on its own set of brain pathways, and so damage to those pathways disrupts the process. As a result,

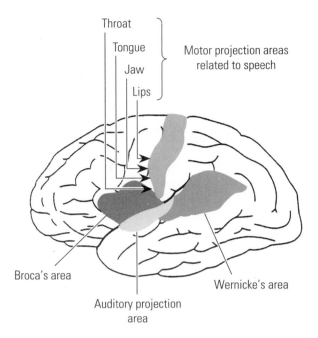

Throat
Tongue
Jaw
Lips

Motor projection areas
related to speech

FIGURE 10.10 Brain Areas Crucial for the Perception and Production of Language Many different brain regions are involved in the ordinary understanding or production of language. Many of these regions, however, are positioned close together; for most individuals, these regions are in the left cerebral hemisphere (as shown here). Broca's area is heavily involved in language production; Wernicke's area plays a crucial role in language comprehension.

Broca's area

Auditory projection area

Wernicke's area

the language loss observed in aphasia is often quite specific, with impairment just to a particular processing step (Cabeza & Nyberg, 2000; Demonet, Wise, & Frackowiak, 1993; Martin, 2003).

For example, some aphasic patients suffer from a problem known as **anomia**: They lose the ability to name various objects, as if their brain damage caused disruption to their mental dictionary. Anomias can be extraordinarily specific: Some patients can use concrete nouns but not abstract nouns; some can name animate objects but not inanimate ones; some patients lose the ability to name colors. Findings like these make it clear that certain areas of the human brain are specialized for language processing—and, more, that each of these areas is specialized for just one aspect of language processing. Apparently, then, our skill in using language rests in part on the fact that we have a considerable amount of neural apparatus devoted to precisely this task.

The Biology of Language Learning

The biological roots of language also show up in another way—the way that language is learned. As we've mentioned, this learning is remarkably fast: By the age of 3 or 4, almost every child is reasonably competent in communicating her wishes and desires and, for that matter, in communicating sophisticated beliefs. In addition, it's important to note that this learning proceeds in a normal way in an astonishingly wide range of environments. Children who talk a lot with adults learn language, and so do children who talk very little with adults. Indeed, children learn language even if their communication with adults is entirely nonlinguistic! Evidence on this last point comes from children born deaf but with no opportunity to learn sign language. (In some cases, this is because their caretakers don't know how to sign; in other cases, it is because their caretakers choose not to teach signing.) Even in these extreme cases, language emerges: Children in this situation invent their own gestural language (usually called "home sign"), and the language they invent shows many parallels to ordinary (spoken) language. For example, their invented language has many of the formal structures routinely seen in the world's existing languages, and the pattern of emergence for these invented languages follows the same sequence as that observed in ordinary language learning (Feldman, Goldin-Meadow, & Gleitman, 1978; Goldin-Meadow, 2003; Senghas, Coppola, Newport, & Supalla, 1997).

Earlier in the chapter, we suggested a way to think about these points: Perhaps children begin the language-learning process with a head start. Specifically, perhaps they are born with brain structures in place that somehow define the broad structure of human language. On this view, the learning process is one in which the child simply has to figure out how the universal structure is realized within his language community—what the parameters are for that particular language, what the vocabulary items are, and so on. This is why language learning is so fast and why the learning can proceed with truly minimal input; it is also why the various languages of the world all end up having the same basic structure.

Support for these claims comes from many sources, including the fact that certain brain structures do seem specialized for language learning, so that damage to these structures causes a disruption of language acquisition, but with few other effects. Specifically, individuals with **specific language impairment** (SLI) have normal intelligence and no problems with the muscle movements needed to produce language. Nonetheless, they are slow to learn language and, throughout their lives, have difficulty in understanding and producing many sentences. They are also impaired on tasks designed specifically to test their linguistic knowledge. They have difficulty, for example, completing passages like this one: "I like to blife. Today I blife. Tomorrow I will blife. Yesterday I did the same thing. Yesterday I _____." Most 4-year-olds know that the answer is, "Yesterday I blifed." But adults with SLI cannot do this task—apparently having failed to learn this simple rule of language (Lai, Fisher, Hurst, Vargha-Khadem, & Monaco, 2001; Pinker, 1991, 1994; van der Lely, 2005).

The Processes of Language Learning

Even with these biological contributions, though, there is no question that learning does play a crucial role in the acquisition of language. After all, children who grow up in Paris learn to speak French; children growing up in China learn Chinese. In this rather obvious way, language-learning depends on the child picking up information from her environment.

But what learning mechanisms are involved here? One might think that language learning depends heavily on imitation (so that children in Paris imitate the French-speakers around them, and so on), but, in truth, the data offer several challenges for an account hinging on imitation. For example, consider how English-speaking children learn to form the past tense. Initially, they proceed in a word-by-word fashion, and so they memorize that the past tense of "play" is "played," the past tense of "climb" is "climbed," and so on. By age 3 or so, however, children seem to realize that they don't have to memorize each word's past tense as a separate vocabulary item. Instead, they realize, they can produce the past tense by manipulating morphemes—that is, by adding the "-ed" ending onto a word. Once children make this discovery, they are able to apply this principle to many new verbs, including verbs they have never encountered before. Thus, Berko (1958) showed children a picture and told them, "Here is a man who likes to rick. Yesterday he did the same thing. Yesterday he _____" Prompted in this way, 3-year-olds unhesitatingly supply the past tense: "ricked."

However, children seem to get carried away with this pattern, and so, at this age, children's speech contains many **over-regularization errors**: They say things like, "Yesterday we goed" or "Yesterday I runned." The same thing happens with other morphemes, and so children of this age also over-generalize their use of the plural

Over-Regularization Errors
Over-regularization errors occur in many contexts. For example, children hear contractions like *aren't* for *are not*, or *isn't* for *is not*. Some children extend this pattern too far, however, and so say I *amn't* as a contraction for I *am not*. No adult would use this construction, making it clear that this form was not acquired through simple imitation.

ending: They say things like, "I have two foots" or "I lost three tooths" (Marcus et al., 1992). This pattern is interesting for many reasons, but notice that it rules out any sort of direct contribution from imitation, for the simple reason that adults almost never produce these over-regularizations. The children, therefore, are producing forms they've "invented" for themselves, and not a form they're imitating from others.

In the same way, one might think that language learning is a matter of explicit instruction, with adults somehow "teaching" their children to speak. But this too turns out to be mistaken. Studies of child–adult interaction make it plain that adults rarely correct their children's grammar, nor do they reward children in any sense when the children speak "correctly." Instead, adults usually react to the *messages* that children convey in their language—and so (for example), they respond positively to the message, "Love 'oo, Mommy," more concerned with the content than with the syntax. And in those rare occasions in which adults *do* correct children's grammar ("You shouldn't say 'holded', Susie. Say, 'held'"), children seem largely oblivious to the correction (Bellugi, 1971).

What, then, *do* the learning mechanisms involve? The answer has several parts, but a key element rests on the fact that children are exquisitely sensitive to patterns and regularities in what they hear, as though each child were an astute statistician, keeping track of the frequency-of-occurrence of this form or that. In one study, 8-month-old infants heard a 2-minute tape recording that sounded something like "bidakupadotigolabubidaku." These syllables were spoken in a monotonous tone, with no difference in stress from one syllable to the next and no pauses in between any of the syllables. But there was a pattern. The experimenters had decided in advance to designate the sequence "bidaku" as a word. Therefore, they arranged the sequences so that if the infant heard "bida," then "ku" was sure to follow. For other syllables, there was no such pattern. For instance, "daku" (the end of the nonsense word "bidaku") would sometimes be followed by "go," sometimes by "pa," and so on. Astonishingly, the babies detected these patterns and their frequencies. In a subsequent test, the babies showed no evidence of surprise if they heard the string "bidakubidakubidaku." From the babies' point of view, these were simply repetitions of a word they already knew. However, the babies did show surprise if they were presented with the string "dakupadakupadakupa." This was not a "word" they had heard before, although of course they had heard each of its syllables many times. Thus, the babies had learned the vocabulary of this made-up language. They had detected the statistical pattern of which syllables followed which, despite their rather brief, entirely passive exposure to these sounds and despite the absence of any supporting cues such as pauses or shifts in intonation (Aslin, Saffran, & Newport, 1998; Marcus, Vijayan, Rao, & Vishton, 1999; Saffran, 2003).

In addition, language-learning relies on a theme that has been in view throughout this chapter: Language has many elements (syntax, semantics, phonology, prosody, etc.), and these elements interact in ordinary language use (and so we rely on a sentence's syntactic form to figure out its meaning; we rely on semantic cues in deciphering the syntax). In the same fashion, language-learning also relies on all these elements in an interacting fashion. Thus, children rely on prosody (again: the rise and fall of pitch, the pattern of timing) as clues to syntax, and adults speaking to children helpfully exaggerate these prosodic signals, easing the children's interpretive burden. Children also rely on their vocabulary, listening for words they already know as clues helping them to process more complex strings. Likewise, children rely on their knowledge of semantic relationships as a basis for figuring out syntax—a process known as **semantic bootstrapping** (Pinker, 1987). In this way, the very complexity of language is both a burden for the child (because there's so much to learn in "learning a language"!) and an aid (because the child can use each of the elements as sources of information in trying to figure out the other elements).

Language and Thought

One last topic will bring our consideration of language to a close. There is no question that language can—and often does—shape our thoughts. To take a trivial example, if you hear someone say, "I saw a dog," this input will lead you to different ideas than if you'd heard the speaker say, "I saw a cat." In this perfectly obvious way, the language that we use (and, in this case, the language that we hear) can shape the flow of our ideas—that is, can shape what we think.

Other influences of language are, however, more interesting. For instance, verbal descriptions often provide a convenient label for a complex experience, and the labels, in turn, provide an economical way of coding, or chunking, that experience—with important consequences for memory (see Chapter 5). Thus, it is vastly easier to remember the label "tree" than it is to remember the corresponding image, easier to remember the label "trips to the zoo" than it is to remember all the details associated with those trips. In this fashion, labeling—made possible by language—has a powerful effect on memory.

Likewise, language can influence how we reason and how we make decisions. One illustration of this is in so-called "framing effects" (see Chapter 13). Thus, for just one case, a patient is more likely to choose a medical treatment if told that the treatment has a 50% chance of success than if told it has a 50% chance of failure— again, a powerful effect of language.

All of this invites a further question: If language shapes thought, then do people who speak different languages end up *thinking differently*? Some of the early evidence on this question was offered by the anthropologist Benjamin Whorf, a strong proponent of the view that the specific language we speak does force us into certain modes of thought—a claim usually known as **linguistic relativity** (Whorf, 1956). The "results" Whorf offered, however, were quite weak. He tried to show, for example, that Hopi speakers think about time differently than English speakers do, but his only evidence came from the ways that the Hopi expressed themselves when talking about different kinds of events. This evidence is without value: Perhaps the Hopi think in the same ways that English speakers do, but they express these thoughts differently because their language differs from English. In this case, the evidence indicates only that the way one expresses oneself is influenced by one's language—a conclusion that is both unsurprising and not very interesting.

More recent researchers have tried to find more rigorous tests of Whorf's proposal. One line of work has examined how we perceive the colors in our world, building on the fact that some languages have many terms for colors (red, orange, mauve, puce, salmon, fawn, ocher, etc.) and others have few (see color insert, Figure 18). Early data suggested that having a rich color vocabulary helps people to *remember* colors but does not change how the colors are *perceived* (Berlin & Key, 1969; R. Brown & Lenneberg, 1954; Heider, 1972; Rosch, 1977b). More recent findings suggest that people who speak languages with a richer color vocabulary may, in fact, perceive colors differently—making finer and more sharply defined distinctions (Özgen, 2004; Roberson, Davies, & Davidoff, 2000).

In the same fashion, languages also differ in how they describe spatial arrangement—with some languages, for example, emphasizing absolute directions (akin to north or east, which are defined in a fashion independent of which way you're currently facing), while other languages emphasize relative directions (akin to left or right, which *do* depend on which way you are facing). Several studies have suggested that these language differences lead to corresponding differences in how people remember, and perhaps how they perceive, spatial position (Majid, Bowerman, Kita, Haun, & Levinson, 2004; Pederson et al., 1998).

These data have been controversial (Gallistel, 2002; Levinson, Kita, Haun, & Rasch, 2002; Li & Gleitman, 2002; Majid, 2002). If we take the results at face value, though, what do they tell us? One possibility—in line with Whorf's original hypothesis—is that language truly "restructures" cognition, so that the language you speak determines the concepts and categories you use and, as a result, shapes what you *can* think about. On this view, there are literally some ideas that a Hopi speaker (for example) can contemplate but that a French speaker cannot, and vice versa.

A different possibility is more modest and, in truth, more plausible: The labels provided by language draw our attention to certain distinctions—so that, for example, by labeling some objects as "red," we draw attention to the distinction between red and not red. This drawing of attention makes it likely that we'll think about this distinction periodically; in essence, this provides *practice* in thinking about the distinction. The practice, in turn, will probably lead to improvement in how easily or how skillfully we think about the distinction. As a result of all this, language does end up influencing our cognition, but not because there is a direct link between the two. Instead, *language influences what we pay attention to*, and this shapes experience, which influences how and how well we think. (For more on these issues, see Hanako & Smith, 2005; Hermer-Vazquez, Spelke, & Katsnelson, 1999; Kay & Regier, 2007; Özgen & Davies, 2002; Papafragou, Li, Choi & Han, 2007; Stapel & Semin, 2007.)

If latter view is correct, then the language we speak does influence our thoughts—but not because there is something special about language. Instead, language is just one of the ways we can guide someone's attention to this or that aspect of his experience. And—consistent with this claim—we can often *undo* the effects of language by using *some other means* to redirect someone's attention. For example, English speakers and speakers of Mandarin Chinese seem initially to think about spatial relations differently—because their languages do bias them toward different interpretive habits. But the difference between English and Chinese speakers can be eradicated by a brief conversation, leading them to consider other ways one might think about space (Li & Gleitman, 2002). Likewise, some studies have observed differences in how English and Chinese speakers think about time (e.g., Boroditsky, 2001), but these differences are (at best) unreliable and have not appeared at all in several other studies (e.g., Chen, 2007; January & Kako, 2007).

Where, then, does this leave us? Having a language certainly influences cognition, and so our human language-guided thoughts are different from the thoughts of our nonlinguistic primate relatives (gorillas, chimps, etc.). In addition, speaking a *specific* language (English or Tzeltal, Mandarin or French) does influence one's thoughts—but in ways that are not at all mysterious. Of course, someone can say, "Look at the bird" and thus guide your attention to the bird. In the same fashion, your language, by virtue of having a verbal label for a category, can call your attention to this category and thus shape your experience, and thus your cognition. But this is a far cry from the claims offered by Whorf a half-century ago. Whorf's argument, as we've noted, was that language plays a unique role in shaping thought and has a lifelong impact in determining quite literally what we can or cannot think, what ideas we can or cannot entertain. There is no persuasive evidence in favor of this stronger claim.

Chapter Summary

■ All speech is built up from a few dozen phonemes; which phonemes are used varies from language to language. Phonemes in turn are built up from a small number of production features, including voicing, place of articulation, and manner of production. Phonemes can be combined to form more complex sounds, but combinations are constrained by a number of rules.

■ Speech perception is more than a matter of detecting the relevant features in the input sound stream. The perceiver needs to deal with speaker-to-speaker variation in how sounds are produced; she also needs to segment the stream of speech and cope with coarticulation. The process of speech perception is helped enormously by context, but we also have the impressive skill of categorical perception, which makes us keenly sensitive to differences between categories of speech sounds but insensitive to distinctions within each category.

- People know many thousands of words, and for each one they know the sound of the word, its syntactic role, and its semantic representation. Our understanding of words is also generative, allowing us to create limitless numbers of new words. Some new words are wholly made up (e.g., "geek"), but more often new words are created by combining familiar morphemes.

- The rules of syntax govern whether a sequence of words is grammatical. One set of rules consists of the phrase-structure rules, and the word groups identified by phrase-structure rules do correspond to natural groupings of words. Phrase-structure rules also guide interpretation. Like all the rules discussed in this chapter, though, phrase-structure rules are descriptive, not prescriptive, and are often best revealed by studies of linguistic competence rather than by studies of linguistic performance.

- To understand a sentence, a listener or reader needs to parse the sentence, determining each word's syntactic role. Evidence suggests that people parse the sentence as they see or hear each word, and this sometimes leads them into parsing errors that must be repaired later; this is revealed by garden-path sentences. Parsing is guided by syntax, semantics, and the extralinguistic context.

- The biological roots of language are revealed in many ways. The study of aphasia makes it clear that some areas of the brain are specialized for learning and using language. The rapid learning of language, in a fashion dependent on neither imitation nor explicit instruction, also speaks to the biological basis for language; this rapid learning is certainly helped by the existence of linguistic universals—structural properties shared by all languages.

- Processes of imitation and direct instruction play relatively small parts in language learning. This is evident in the fact that children produce many forms (often, over-regularization errors) that no adult produces; these forms are obviously not the result of imitation. Children also receive little direct instruction about language; adults tend to respond to the content of what children are saying, rather than its form. Language learning is, however, strongly influenced by children's remarkable sensitivity to statistical patterns in the language they hear. Children can also use their understanding of one aspect of language (e.g., phonology or vocabulary) to help them learn about other aspects (e.g., syntax).

- There has been considerable discussion about the ways in which thought might be shaped by the language one speaks. Language certainly guides and influences our thoughts, and the way a thought is formulated into words can have an effect on how we think about the thought's content. In addition, language can call our attention to a category or to a distinction, and this makes it likely that we will have experience in thinking about the category or distinction. This experience, in turn, can promote fluency in these thoughts. However, these effects are not unique to language (because other factors can also draw our attention to the category), nor are they irreversible. Hence there is no evidence that language can shape what we *can* think.

The Workbook Connection

See the *Cognition Workbook* for further exploration of language:

- Demonstration 10.1: Phonemes and Subphonemes
- Demonstration 10.2: Patterns in Language
- Demonstration 10.3: Ambiguity
- Research Methods: Methodological Opportunism
- Cognitive Psychology and Education: Writing
- Cognitive Psychology and the Law: Judicial Instructions

Visual Knowledge

People have knowledge of many different types. They know what a fish is (for example), but they also know what fish smells like when it's cooking and what a fish looks like. They know what a guitar is, but they also know what one sounds like. Likewise, people describe their *thoughts* in a variety of ways: Sometimes, they claim, their thoughts seem to be formulated in words. Sometimes, their thoughts seem more abstract—a sequence of ideas that lacks any concrete form. But sometimes, people claim, their thoughts involve a sequence of *pictures*, or *sounds*, or other sensory impressions.

What can we say about this variety? How are specific sights or sounds or smells represented in the mind? How should we think about the proposal that people sometimes "think in pictures"? In this chapter, we'll explore these questions, asking broadly about nonverbal knowledge but focusing largely on *visual* knowledge and *visual* thoughts. Our focus on visual knowledge reflects the fact that far more is known about this modality than about any other (e.g., auditory knowledge, or olfactory knowledge, or knowledge for tastes). As we proceed, though, you should keep an eye on how the questions we're asking and the data we're gathering might be applied to other forms of nonverbal knowledge.

We will begin by examining how people describe their own mental images—but we will quickly run into the limitations of this "self-report" evidence. We will turn, therefore, to more objective means of assessing imagery. Then, later in the chapter, we will consider your broader knowledge about visual appearance—how you remember the shapes, sizes, and colors of things you have seen at some distant point in the past, asking how this "sensory" information might be represented in long-term memory.

- Mental images are, in important ways, picturelike, representing in a direct fashion the spatial layout of the represented scene. It's not surprising, therefore, that there is considerable overlap between imagery and perception—in how each functions and also in their neural bases.

- However, people can also use spatial imagery, which is not visual and which may instead be represented in the mind in terms of movements, or perhaps in some more abstract format.

- Although they are picturelike, images (visual or spatial) are plainly not pictures; instead, images (like percepts) seem to be organized and already interpreted in a fashion that pictures are not.

- Even though images in working memory provide a distinctive form of representation, information about appearances in long-term memory may not be distinctive. In fact, long-term memory for sensory information seems to obey all the principles we described, in earlier chapters, for verbal or symbolic memories.

Visual Imagery

How many windows are there in your house or your apartment? Who has bushier eyebrows—Brad Pitt or Johnny Depp? For most people, questions like these seem to elicit "mental pictures." You know what Pitt and Depp look like, and you call a "picture" of each before your "mind's eye" in order to make the comparison. Likewise, you call to mind a "map" of your apartment and count the windows by inspecting this map. Many people even trace the map in the air by moving their finger around, following the imagined map's contours.

Various practical problems also seem to evoke images. There you are in the store, trying on a new sweater. Will the sweater look good with your blue pants? To decide, you will probably try to visualize the blue of the pants, using your "mind's eye" to ask how they will look with the sweater. Similarly, a friend asks you, "Was David in class yesterday?" You might try to recall by visualizing what the room looked like during the class; is David "visible" in your image?

These examples illustrate the common, everyday use of visual images—as a basis for making decisions, as an aid to remembering. But what are these images? Surely there is no tiny eye somewhere deep in your brain; thus, the phrase "mind's eye" cannot be taken literally. Likewise, mental "pictures" cannot be actual pictures; with no eye deep inside the brain, who or what would inspect such pictures?

Introspections About Images

Mental images have been described and discussed for thousands of years. However, it is only within the last century or so that psychologists have begun to gather systematic data about imagery. Among the earliest researchers was Francis Galton, who asked various people to describe their images and to rate them for vividness (Galton, 1883). In essence, Galton asked his research participants to **introspect** (or "look within") and to report on their own mental contents. The **self-report data** he obtained fit well with common sense: The participants reported that they could "inspect" their images much as they would inspect a picture. In their images, scenes were represented as if viewed from a certain position and a certain distance. They also reported that they could "read off" from the image details of color and texture. All of this implies a mode of representation that is, in many ways, picturelike, and that is of course quite consistent with our informal manner of describing mental images as "pictures in the head," to be inspected with the "mind's eye."

There was also another side of Galton's data: Galton's participants differed widely from each other. Many described images of photographic clarity, rich in detail, almost as if they were *seeing* the imaged scene rather than visualizing it. Other participants reported very sketchy images or no images at all. They were certainly able to think about the scenes or objects Galton named for them, but in no sense were they "seeing" these scenes. Their self-reports rarely included mention of color or size or viewing perspective; indeed, their reports were devoid of *any* visual qualities.

These observations are in themselves interesting: Do individuals really differ in the nature of their mental imagery? What consequences does such variety have? Are there tasks that the "visualizers" can do better than the "nonvisualizers" (or vice versa)? If so, this could provide crucial information about how visual imagery is used and what it is good for.

Before we can answer these questions, though, we must address a methodological concern raised by Galton's data—a concern that we have met before: Perhaps we shouldn't take these self-reports at face value. Perhaps all of Galton's participants had the same imagery skill, but some were cautious in how they chose to describe their imagery, while others were more extravagant. In this way, Galton's data might reveal differences in how people *talk about* their imagery rather than differences in the imagery per se.

What seems required, therefore, is a more objective means of assessing imagery—one that does not rely on the subjectivity inherent in self-reports. With this more objective approach, we could assess the differences, from one individual to the next, evident in Galton's data. Indeed, with this more objective approach, we could hope to find out exactly what images are.

Chronometric Studies of Imagery

Imagery researchers have, in the last 50 years, been keenly sensitive to these concerns about self-report, and this is why imagery experiments usually don't ask participants to *describe* their images. Instead, to gain more objective data, these experiments ask people to *do something* with their images—to read information off of them or to manipulate them in some way. We can then examine how accurate and how fast people are in their responses, and with appropriate comparisons we can use these measurements as a basis for testing hypotheses about the nature of imagery. These **chronometric** ("time-measuring") **studies** give us a much more accurate portrait of mental imagery than could ever be obtained with self-report data.

For example, chronometric studies allow us to ask what sorts of information are prominent in a mental image and what sorts are not, and we can then use these evaluations as a basis for asking how "picturelike" mental images really are. To see the logic, think about how actual, out-in-the-world pictures are different from verbal descriptions. Concretely, consider what would happen if you were asked to *write a paragraph* describing a cat. It seems likely that you would mention the distinctive features of cats—their whiskers, their claws, and so on. Your paragraph probably would not include the fact that cats have heads, since this is too obvious to be worth mentioning. But now consider, in contrast, what would happen if we asked you to *draw a sketch* of a cat. In this format, the cat's head would be prominent, for the simple reason that the head is relatively large and up front. The claws and whiskers might be less salient, because these features are small and so would not take up much space in the drawing.

The point here is that the pattern of what information is included, as well as what information is prominent, depends on the mode of presentation. For a *description* of a cat, the features that are prominent will be those that are distinctive and strongly associated with the object being described. For a *depiction*, distinctiveness and association won't matter; instead, size and position will determine what is prominent and what is not.

Against this backdrop, let's now ask what information is available in a visual image. Is it the pictorially prominent features, which would imply a depictive mode of representation, or the verbally prominent ones, implying a descriptive mode? Self-reports about imagery surely indicate a picturelike representation; is this confirmed by the data?

In a study by Kosslyn (1976), research participants were asked to form a series of mental images and to answer yes/no questions about each. For example, they were asked to form a mental image of a cat and then were asked, "Does the cat have a head? Does the cat have claws?" Participants responded to these questions quickly, but—strikingly—responses to the head question were quicker than those to the claws question. This difference suggests that information quickly available in the image follows the rules for pictures, not paragraphs. In contrast, a different group of participants was asked merely to think about cats (with no mention of imagery). These participants, when asked the same questions, gave quicker responses to claws than to head—the reverse pattern of the first group. Thus, it seems that people have the option of thinking about cats via imagery and also the option of thinking about cats without imagery; as the mode of representation changes, so does the pattern of information availability.

In a different experiment, participants were asked to memorize the fictional map shown in Figure 11.1 and, in particular, to memorize the locations of the various landmarks: the well, the straw hut, and so on (Kosslyn, Ball, & Reiser, 1978). The experimenters made sure participants had the map memorized by asking them to draw a replica of the map from memory; once they could do this, the main experi-

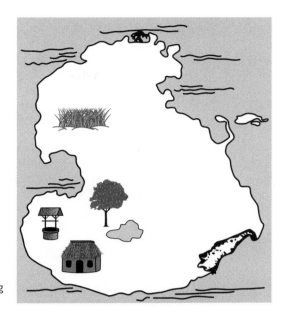

FIGURE 11.1 Map of a Fictional Island Used in Image-Scanning Experiments

Participants in the study first memorized this map, including the various landmarks (the hut, the well, the patch of grass, and so on). They then formed a mental image of this map for the scanning procedure. (After Kosslyn, 1983)

ment began. Participants were asked to form an image of the island, and to point their "mind's eye" at a specific landmark—let us say, the well. Another landmark was then mentioned, perhaps the straw hut, and participants were asked to imagine a black speck moving in a straight line from the first landmark to the second. When the speck "reached" the target, participants pressed a button, stopping a clock. This provides a measure of how long it takes to scan from the well to the hut. The same was done for the well and the tree, the hut and the patch of grass, so that we end up with "scanning times" for each of the various pairs of landmarks.

Figure 11.2 shows the results. The data from this **image-scanning procedure** clearly suggest that participants scan across their images at a constant rate, so that doubling the scanning "distance" doubles the time required for the scan, and tripling the distance triples the time required.

Similar results are obtained if participants are given a task that requires them to "zoom in" on their images (e.g., a task that requires them to inspect the image for some small detail) or a task that requires them to "zoom out" (e.g., a task that requires a more global judgment). In these studies, response times are directly proportional to the amount of zoom required, suggesting once again that travel in the imaged world resembles travel in the actual world, at least with regard to timing. As a concrete example, participants in one study were asked to imagine a mouse standing next to an elephant, and they were then asked to confirm, by inspecting their image, that the mouse had whiskers. Participants were relatively slow in responding, presumably because they first needed time to zoom in on the image in order to "see" the whiskers. Response times were faster if the participants were initially asked to imagine

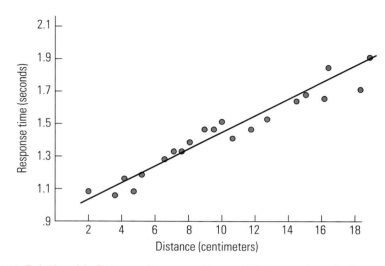

FIGURE 11.2 Relationship Between Response Time and "Distance" on the Imaged Map
Participants had to "scan" from one point on their mental image to another point; they pressed a button to indicate when their "mind's eye" had arrived at its destination. Response times were closely related to the "distance" participants had to scan across on the image, implying that mental images are similar to actual pictures in how they represent positions and distance. (After Kosslyn, 1983)

the mouse standing next to a paper clip. For this image, participants start with a "close-up" view, and so, in this setup, no zooming is needed to "see" the whiskers.

Whether you are scanning across a mental image, therefore, or zooming in on one, there is a clear relationship between "travel time" and "travel distance"—and, specifically, "traveling" a greater "distance" requires more time. This is the same relationship we would observe if we asked our participants to move their eyes across an actual map (rather than an image of one) or literally to zoom in on a real picture: In these cases, too, traveling a greater distance would require more time. All of this points toward the similarity between mental images and actual out-in-the-world pictures.

More precisely, though, these mental imagery data are telling us a great deal about the *nature* of mental images: According to these results, images represent a scene in a fashion that preserves all of the distance relationships within that scene: Points close to each other in the scene are somehow "close" to each other in the image; points that are farther apart in the scene are somehow "farther apart" in the image. Thus, in a very real sense, the image preserves the spatial layout of the represented scene. With this, the image will necessarily represent information about all the shapes and sizes within the scene, and it will also preserve a diverse set of spatial relationships (relationships such as one point being *between* two other points, or *aligned* with other points, and so on). It is in this fashion that images directly represent the *geometry* of the scene, and it is in this way that images *depict* the scene rather than describing it, and so are much more similar to *pictures* or *maps* than they are to propositional descriptions.

Mental Rotation

Other results make a similar point with regard to the *transformation* of mental images. In a series of experiments by Shepard, Cooper, and Metzler, participants were asked to decide whether displays like the one in Figure 11.3A showed two different shapes or just one shape viewed from two different perspectives. In other words, is it possible to "rotate" the form shown on the left in Figure 11.3A so that it will end up looking just like the form on the right? What about the two shapes shown in Figure 11.3B or the two in 11.3C?

To perform this **mental rotation** task, participants seem first to imagine one of the forms rotating into alignment with the other. Then, once the forms are oriented in the same way, participants can make their judgment. This step of imagined rotation takes some time; in fact, the amount of time it takes depends on how much rotation is needed. Figure 11.4 shows the data pattern, with response times clearly being influenced by how far apart the two forms were in their initial orientations. Thus, once again, imagined "movement" resembles actual movement: The farther one has to imagine a form rotating, the longer the evaluation takes (Cooper & Shepard, 1973; Shepard & Metzler, 1971).

The mental rotation task can be used to answer a number of additional questions about imagery. For example, notice that if you were to cut out the left-hand drawing in Figure 11.3A and spin it around while leaving it flat on the table, you could

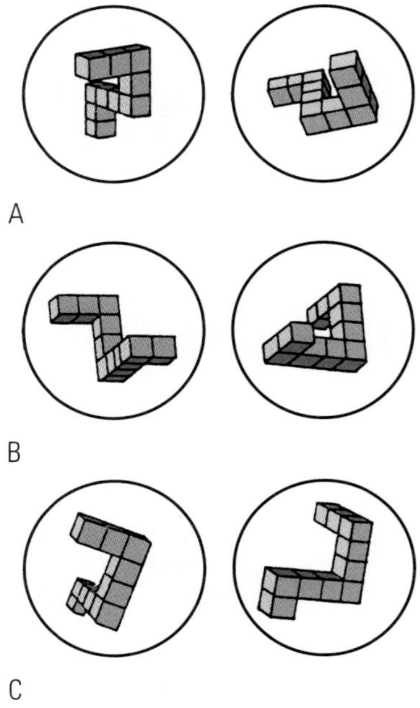

A

B

C

FIGURE 11.3 Stimuli for a Mental Rotation Experiment
Participants had to judge whether the two stimuli shown in Panel A are the same as each other but viewed from different perspectives, and likewise for the pairs shown in B and C. Participants seem to make these judgments by imagining one of the forms rotating until its position matches that of the other form. [After Shepard & Metzler, 1971]

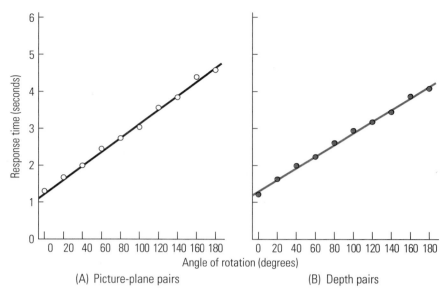

(A) Picture-plane pairs (B) Depth pairs

FIGURE 11.4 Data From a Mental Rotation Experiment

Panel A shows data from stimulus pairs requiring mental rotation in two dimensions, so that the imaged forms stay within the imagined picture plane. Panel B shows data from pairs requiring an imagined rotation in depth. The data are similar, indicating that participants can imagine three-dimensional rotations as easily, and as swiftly, as they can imagine two-dimensional rotations. In both cases, the greater the degree of rotation required, the longer the response times. (After Shepard & Metzler, 1971)

align it with the drawing on the right. The relevant rotation, therefore, is a rotation that leaves the pictures within the two-dimensional plane in which they are drawn. In contrast, the two forms shown in Figure 11.3B are identical except for a rotation in depth. No matter how you spin the *picture* on the left, it will not line up with the picture on the right. You can align these forms, but to do so you need to spin them around a vertical axis, in essence lifting them off the page.

People have no trouble with mental rotation in depth. They make very few errors (with accuracy levels around 95%), and the data resemble those obtained with picture-plane rotation. Figure 11.4A shows data from picture-plane rotation; Figure 11.4B shows data from pairs requiring depth rotation. In both cases, there is a clear relation between angle of rotation and response times, and the speed of rotation seems similar for both. Apparently, then, participants can represent three-dimensional forms in their images, and they can imagine these forms moving in depth. In some circumstances, therefore, visual images are not mental pictures; they are more like mental sculptures. (For a review, see Shepard & Cooper, 1982. For data on image scanning in three dimensions, see Pinker, 1980; Pinker & Finke, 1980.)

Avoiding Concerns About Demand Character

In mental rotation, just as in mental scanning, distance relations seem to be preserved, and so the farther the imagined "travel," the longer it takes. We have interpreted these results as revealing the way in which images represent spatial layout—with points that are more distant in the represented scene somehow being farther apart in the image. But there is another way one might try to interpret the data. Participants in these studies obviously know that movement through the world takes time and that moving a longer distance takes more time. Perhaps, therefore, the participants simply control the timing of their responses in order to re-create this "normal" pattern.

This proposal can be fleshed out in a variety of ways, but, to phrase things strongly, perhaps participants in these studies are not imagining rotations or scanning across an image at all. Instead, they might be thinking, "The experimenter just asked me to scan a long way, and I'd like to make it look like I'm obeying. I know that a long scan takes a long time, and so let me wait a moment before hitting the response button."

Why should participants act in this way? One reason is that participants in experiments usually want to be helpful, and so they do all they can to give the experimenter "good" data. As a result, they are very sensitive to the **demand character** of the experiment—that is, cues that might signal how they are "supposed to" behave in that situation (Intons-Peterson, 1983, 1999; Intons-Peterson & White, 1981). A different possibility is that this sort of "simulation" is, in fact, what imagery is really all about. Perhaps whenever someone tries to "imagine" something, he draws on his knowledge about how events in the world actually unfold, and then he does his best to simulate the event. In this case, a longer scan or a greater rotation requires more time, not because there really is some "travel" involved, but because people know that these manipulations should take more time and do their best to simulate the process (Pylyshyn, 1981).

As it turns out, though, we can set aside these concerns, allowing us to maintain the claims that we've already sketched—namely, that the scanning and rotation data are as they are *because of how images represent spatial layout*. Several lines of evidence support this claim, including (crucially) data we will turn to, later in the chapter, examining the neural bases for imagery. But, in addition, we can tackle the concern about demand character directly. In several studies, the experimenters have asked participants to make judgments about spatial layout but have taken care never to mention to participants that imagery was relevant to the task (e.g., Finke & Pinker, 1982). This should diminish the demand character of the procedure and so avoid any suggestion to participants that they should simulate some sort of "mental travel." Even without imagery instructions, though, the participants in these procedures spontaneously form images and scan across them, and their responses show the standard pattern: longer response times observed with longer scans. Apparently, this result really does emerge whenever participants are using visual imagery—whether the result is encouraged by the experimenters' instructions or not.

Interactions Between Imagery and Perception

It seems, therefore, that there really are important parallels between visual images and actual visual stimuli, and this leads to a question: If images are so much like pictures, then are the processes used to inspect images similar to those used to inspect stimuli? To put it more broadly, what is the relation between imaging and perceiving?

In a study by Segal and Fusella (1970, 1971), participants were asked to detect very faint signals—either dim visual stimuli or soft tones. On each trial, the participants' task was merely to indicate whether a signal had been presented or not. Participants did this in either of two conditions: either while forming a visual image before their "mind's eye," or while forming an auditory image before their "mind's ear." Thus, we have a 2 × 2 design: two types of signals to be detected, and two types of imagery.

Let's hypothesize that there is some overlap between imaging and perceiving—that is, there are some mental structures or mental processes used by both activities. Therefore, if these processes or structures are occupied with imaging, they are not available for perceiving, and vice versa; and so we should expect competition if participants try to do both activities at once. That is exactly what Segal and Fusella observed: Their results, shown in Figure 11.5, indicate that forming a visual image interferes with seeing, and that forming an auditory image interferes with hearing (also see Farah & Smith, 1983).

Notice, though, that the Segal and Fusella participants were trying to visualize one thing while perceiving something altogether different. What happens if participants are trying to image a stimulus related to the one they are trying to perceive?

Percentage of Detections	Visual signal	Auditory signal
While visualizing	61%	67%
While maintaining an auditory image	63%	61%

Percentage of False Alarms	Visual signal	Auditory signal
While visualizing	7.8%	3.7%
While maintaining an auditory image	3.6%	6.7%

FIGURE 11.5 Can You Visualize and See at the Same Time?
Participants were less successful in detecting a weak visual signal if they were simultaneously maintaining a visual image than if they were maintaining an auditory image. (The effect is small but highly reliable.) The reverse is true with weak auditory signals: Participants were less successful in this detection if maintaining an auditory image than if visualizing. In addition, visual images often led to "false alarms" for participants trying to detect visual signals; auditory images led to false alarms for auditory signals. (After Segal & Fusella, 1970)

Can visualizing a stimulus "pave the way" for perception? Farah (1985) had participants visualize a form (either an *H* or a *T*). A moment later, either an *H* or a *T* was actually presented, although at a very low contrast, making the letter difficult to perceive. Perception was facilitated if participants had just been visualizing the target form, and again, the effect was quite specific: Visualizing an *H* made it easier to perceive an *H*; visualizing a *T* made it easier to perceive a *T*. This result provides further confirmation of the claim that visualizing and perceiving draw on similar mechanisms, so that one of these activities can serve to prime the other. (For further discussions, see Farah, 1989; Heil, Rösler, & Hennighausen, 1993; also see McDermott & Roediger, 1994.)

Similar conclusions can be drawn from biological evidence. As we discussed in Chapter 2, we know a great deal about the specific brain structures required for vision; it turns out that many of the same structures are crucial for imagery. This can be documented in several ways, including the neuroimaging techniques that map the moment-by-moment pattern of activity in the brain. These techniques reveal that visual perception relies heavily on tissue located in the occipital cortex (and so these brain areas are highly activated whenever someone is examining a visual stimulus). It turns out that activity levels are also high in these areas when participants are visualizing a stimulus before their "mind's eye" (Behrmann, 2000; Farah, 1988; Isha & Sagi, 1995; Kosslyn, 1994; Miyashita, 1995; W. L. Thompson & Kosslyn, 2000).

More specifically, we know that different areas of the occipital cortex are involved in different aspects of visual perception, and here, too, there are important parallels between the brain activity during perception and the activity during imagery. For example, Areas V1 and V2 in the visual cortex are involved in the earliest stages of visual perception, responding to the specific low-level features of the input. It is striking, therefore, that the same areas are particularly active whenever participants are maintaining highly detailed images, and that the amount of brain tissue showing activation increases as participants imagine larger and larger objects (Behrmann, 2000; Kosslyn & Thompson, 2003). In a similar fashion, Area MT/MST in the brain is highly sensitive to motion in ordinary visual perception, and it turns out that the same brain area is particularly activated when participants are asked to *imagine* movement patterns (Goebel, Khorram-Sefat, Muckli, Hacker, & Singer, 1998). Likewise, brain areas that are especially active during the perception of faces are also highly activated when people are imagining faces (O'Craven & Kanwisher, 2000).

Further evidence comes from studies of brain damage, and here, too, we find parallels between visual perception and visual imagery. For example, in some patients brain damage has disrupted the ability to perceive color; in most cases these patients also lose the ability to imagine scenes in color. Likewise, patients who, because of brain damage, have lost the ability to perceive fine detail seem also to lose the ability to visualize fine detail; and so on (Farah, 1988; Farah, Soso, & Dasheiff, 1992; Kosslyn, 1994; we'll need to add some complications to this point later in the chapter, but in the meantime, for some contrasting data, see Behrmann, 2000; Behrmann, Moscovitch, & Winocur, 1994; G. Goldenberg, Müllbacher, & Nowak, 1995; Jankowiak, Kinsbourne, Shalev, & Bachman, 1992).

In one remarkable case, a patient had suffered a stroke and, as a result, had developed the "neglect syndrome" we described in Chapter 4: If this patient was shown a picture, he seemed to see only the right side of it; if asked to read a word, he read only the right half. The same pattern of neglect was evident in the patient's imagery: In one test, the patient was urged to visualize a familiar plaza in his city and to list the buildings "in view" in the image. If the patient imagined himself standing at the northern edge of the plaza, he listed all the buildings on the plaza's western side (i.e., on his right), but none on the eastern. If the patient imagined himself standing on the southern edge of the plaza, he listed all the sights on the plaza's eastern side, but none on the western. In both cases, therefore, he neglected the left half of the imaged scene, just as he did with perceived scenes (Bisiach & Luzzatti, 1978; Bisiach, Luzzatti, & Perani, 1979).

Still more evidence comes from a technique called **transcranial magnetic stimulation** (TMS), which we encountered in Chapter 2. The technique creates a series of strong magnetic pulses at a specific location on the scalp; this causes a (temporary!) disruption in the brain region directly underneath this scalp area (Helmuth, 2001). In this fashion, it is possible to disrupt Area V1 temporarily in an otherwise normal brain; Area V1, you may recall, is the brain area where axons from the visual system first reach the cortex (see Chapter 2). Not surprisingly, using TMS in this way causes problems in vision, but it also causes parallel problems in visual imagery, providing a powerful argument that Area V1 is crucial both for the processing of visual information and for the creation and maintenance of visual images (Kosslyn et al., 1999).

Sensory Effects in Imagery

Clearly, the neural "machinery" needed for imagery overlaps with that needed for perception. If the machinery is occupied with one of these functions, it is not available for the other. If the machinery is disrupted (permanently, by a stroke; or temporarily, by TMS), then both activities are compromised. If we scrutinize activation patterns, we find that to a large extent the same brain structures are involved in visualizing and in vision. All of this indicates an intimate relationship between imagery and perception.

This sharing of neural mechanisms between imagery and perception implies that imagery and perception should *function* in similar ways, and research indicates that this is the case. The research, in other words, seems to indicate a **functional equivalence** between many aspects of visual imagery and aspects of visual perception—that is, a series of close parallels between how these two systems function.

For example, consider **visual acuity**—that is, the ability to see fine detail. In vision, acuity is much greater at the center of the visual field than it is in the visual periphery. Can we find a comparable pattern in imagery? Is it easier to discern detail at the image's center than at its periphery?

In measurements of "two-point acuity," observers are shown two dots. If the dots are far enough apart, the observer can easily see that they are separate. When the dots are very close together, though, the observer has trouble seeing the gap between them, and so the dots seem to fuse together. We can assess acuity, therefore, by measuring how far apart the dots have to be before the observer can see that they are separate; this tells us how well the observer can perceive fine detail.

In vision, two-point acuity is greatest when people are looking directly at the dots; under these circumstances, even minuscule gaps can be detected. However, if we position the dots 10° away from someone's line of vision, acuity is far worse. What about imagery? In one study, participants were first shown two dots of the appropriate size. The dots were then removed, but participants were asked to imagine that the dots were still present. The participants then moved their eyes away from the (imagined) dots' position, and as they looked farther and farther away, they had to judge whether they could still "see" that the dots were separate. In this way, "two-point acuity" was measured with imaginary stimuli (Finke & Kosslyn, 1980).

The data show a remarkable correspondence between participants' performance with actually perceived dots and their performance with imagined dots. In both cases, acuity fell off abruptly if the dots were not in the center of vision; indeed, the pattern of falloff was virtually the same in perception and in imagery. Moreover, in vision, acuity falls off more rapidly if participants look above or below the two dots, rather than to the left or right. This pattern was also observed in the imagery condition. Thus, qualitatively and quantitatively, the imagery data match the perceptual data.

Spatial Images and Visual Images

We are building an impressive case, therefore, for a close relationship between imagery and perception. Indeed, the evidence implies that we can truly speak of imagery as being *visual* imagery, drawing on the same mechanisms and having the same traits as actual vision. Other results, however, add some complications.

A number of studies have examined imagery in people blind since birth (Carpenter & Eisenberg, 1978; Kerr, 1983; Marmor & Zabeck, 1976; also see Jonides, Kahn, & Rozin, 1975; Paivio & Okovita, 1971; Zimler & Keenan, 1983). Obviously, the procedures need to be adapted in important ways—so that (for example) the stimuli to be imaged are presented initially as sculptures to be explored with the hands, rather than as pictures to be examined visually. Once this is done, however, experimental procedures parallel to those we have described can be carried out with the blind—procedures examining how the blind scan across an image, for example, or how they imagine a form in rotation. And the data show what is by now a familiar pattern: In tests involving mental rotation or image scanning, blind individuals yield data quite similar to those obtained with sighted research participants—with response times being proportionate to the "distance" traveled, and so on.

It seems unlikely that people blind since birth are using a sense of what things "look like" to perform these tasks. Presumably, therefore, they have some other means of thinking about spatial layout and spatial relations. This "spatial imagery" might be represented in the mind in terms of a series of imagined movements, so that it is body imagery or motion imagery rather than visual imagery. (Reisberg & Logie, 1993, provide a discussion of motion-based imagery; also see Engelkamp, 1986, 1991; Logie, Engelkamp, Dehn, & Rudkin, 1999; Stevens, 2005.) Alternatively, perhaps spatial imagery is not tied to any sensory modality but is part of our broader cognition about spatial arrangements and layout.

One way or another, though, it looks like we need to distinguish between *visual* and *spatial* imagery. Visual imagery represents spatial layout in terms of how things *look*. Spatial imagery, we have just suggested, can represent spatial layout in terms of *movements*, or *body feelings*, or perhaps in some more abstract format. Blind individuals presumably use spatial imagery to carry out the tasks we have been discussing in this chapter; it seems plausible that sighted people can use either visual or spatial imagery to carry out these tasks. (For a related distinction among several types of imagery, see Kosslyn & Thompson, 1999, 2003; for other data emphasizing the importance of the visual/spatial distinction, see Hegarty, 2004; Klauer & Zhao, 2004.)

This distinction between visual and spatial imagery is also suggested by other evidence. For example, we have already noted the cases in which brain damage seems to produce similar patterns of disruption in seeing and imaging. Thus, patients who (because of brain damage) have lost their color vision also seem to lose the ability to imagine scenes in color; patients who have lost their ability to perceive motion also lose the ability to imagine movement. Results like these provide a powerful argument that the neural basis for vision overlaps heavily with that needed for imagining, and so damage to the relevant brain areas disrupts both activities. This adds to the argument that the imagery is, in important ways, *visual*.

However, there are exceptions to this pattern—cases in which brain damage causes problems in imagery but not perception, or vice versa. For example, Goldenberg et al. (1995) describe a patient whose bilateral occipital lobe lesions have produced blindness, but despite this profound deficit, the patient does well on many (but not all) imagery tasks. Similarly, investigators have documented a number of patients who do well on imagery tasks despite visual agnosia. Other patients show the pattern of "neglect syndrome" in their vision but not in their imagery (and other patients show the reverse—neglect in imagery but not in vision). And so on. (For discussion of these patients, see, for example, Bartolomeo et al., 1998; Behrmann, Moscovitch, & Winocur, 1994; Logie & Della Sala, 2005; Servos & Goodale, 1995.)

This might seem like a contradictory data pattern—with brain damage sometimes causing similar problems in imagery and in perception, and sometimes not (so that imagery is massively disrupted by the brain damage while perception is spared, or vice versa). However, there is no contradiction here. *Visual* imagery relies on brain areas that are also needed for vision, and so damage to these areas disrupts both imagery and vision. *Spatial* imagery, in contrast, relies on different brain areas, and so damage to visual areas won't interfere with this form of imagery, and damage to brain sites needed for this imagery won't interfere with vision.

Similar claims emerge if we zoom in for a closer look at the imagery tasks that brain-damaged individuals can or cannot do. L.H., for example, suffered brain damage in an automobile accident and, as a result, now has enormous difficulty in tasks requiring judgments about visual appearance—for example, judgments about *color* (Farah, Hammond, Levine, & Calvanio, 1988). In contrast, L.H. performs well on tasks like image scanning or mental rotation. More generally, he shows little disruption on tasks requiring spatial manipulations or memory for spatial positions. To make sense of L.H.'s profile, therefore, it seems once again crucial to distinguish between visual tasks and spatial ones and, correspondingly, between visual imagery and spatial imagery.

Individual Differences

Multiple lines of evidence, therefore, suggest that there are at least two types of imagery—one visual and one spatial—and, presumably, most people have the capacity for both types: They can "visualize" and they can "spatialize." But this invites a new question: When do people use one type of imagery, and when do they use the other?

Some tasks surely require one form of imagery or the other. For example, to think about *colors*, you need to imagine exactly what something *looks like*; it won't be enough just to think about shapes or spatial positions. For this case, therefore, you'll need visual, not spatial, imagery. In many other cases (including tasks like mental rotation

Eidetic Imagery

Eidetic imagery is vastly more detailed than ordinary imagery. In one study (Haber, 1969), a 10-year-old was shown a picture like this one for 30 seconds. After the picture was taken away, the boy was unexpectedly asked detail questions: How many stripes were there on the cat's tail? How many leaves on the tall flower? The child was able to give completely accurate answers, as though his memory had perfectly preserved the picture's content. Researchers estimate that 5 percent of all children are capable of this sort of imagery; the proportion is smaller in adults. We have little information, though, about how this sort of ultra-detailed imagery functions.

or scanning), either form of imagery will get the job done. (You can, for example, think about what a speck would *look like* as it zoomed across an imagined scene, or you can think about what it would *feel like* to move your finger across the scene.) In the latter situation, the choice between visual and spatial imagery will depend on many factors, including your preferences and the exact instructions you receive.

The choice between these forms of imagery will also be influenced by each individual's ability levels: Some people may be poor visualizers but good "spatializers," and they would surely rely on spatial imagery, not visual, in most tasks. And, of course, for other people, this pattern would be reversed.

How should we think about these differences from one person to the next? Recall Galton's data, mentioned early on in this chapter. If we take those data at face value, they imply that people differ markedly in their conscious experience of imaging. People with vivid imagery report that their images are truly picturelike—usually in color, quite detailed, and with all of the depicted objects viewed from a particular distance and a particular viewing angle. People without vivid imagery, in contrast, will say none of these things. Their images, they report, are not at all picturelike, and it's meaningless to ask them whether an image is in color or in black and white; their image simply isn't the sort of thing that could be in color or in black and white. Likewise, it's meaningless to ask whether their image is viewed from a particular perspective; their image is abstract in a way that makes this question inapplicable. In no sense, then, do these "non-imagers" feel like they are "seeing" with the "mind's eye." From their perspective, these figures of speech are (at best) loosely metaphorical. This stands in clear contrast to the reports offered by vivid imagers; for them, mental seeing really does seem like actual seeing.

Roughly 10% of the population will, in this fashion, "declare themselves entirely deficient in the power of seeing mental pictures" (Galton, 1883, p. 110). As William James (1890) put it, they "have no visual images at all worthy of the name" (p. 57). But what should we make of this? Is it truly the case that the various members of our species differ in whether or not they are capable of experiencing visual images?

To explore this issue, a number of studies have compared "vivid imagers" and "non-imagers" on tasks that depend on mental imagery, with the obvious prediction that people with vivid imagery will do better in these tasks and those with sparse imagery will do worse. The results, however, have often been otherwise, with many studies finding no difference between vivid imagers and sparse imagers in how they do mental rotation, how quickly or accurately they scan across their images, and so on (e.g., Ernest, 1977; A. Katz, 1983; Marks, 1983; Richardson, 1980).

Notice, though, that these tasks require *spatial* judgments or *spatial* manipulations. These are, in other words, tasks that can be performed with spatial imagery. In contrast, when people describe their images as "vivid," they are, in essence, reporting how much their image experience is like seeing. The self-report, in other words, provides an assessment of *visual* imagery. It is unsurprising, therefore, that there's no relationship between this self-report and the performance of these (spatial) tasks: There's no reason to think that how vivid someone's visual imagery is will be related to how good she is at spatial performance.

On this basis, though, there should be a relationship between image vividness and how well people perform on *visual tasks*, tasks that hinge on close judgments about what something *looks like*. And, in fact, there is. Consider, for example, the two-point acuity experiment already described. This experiment, at its heart, requires someone to imagine exactly *what something would look like*. Therefore, this task should be one performed more accurately by people with vivid mental imagery—and it is. People who describe their imagery as "vivid" yield data in this experiment in close correspondence to the perceptual data; people with less-vivid imagery do not show this correspondence (Finke & Kosslyn, 1980). Many other findings can be understood in similar terms (Cui, Jeter, Yang, Montague, & Eagleman, 2006; Kozhevnikov, Kosslyn, & Shephard, 2005; McKelvie, 1995).

All of this suggests that imagery self-reports are meaningful and do reveal genuine differences from one person to the next in the quality of their imagery experience. This in turn invites many questions: How do these differences in experience influence us? What can people "with imagery" do that people "without imagery" cannot? There is, as just one illustration, some suggestion that these differences among people may determine their career choices: Visual imagers are likely to succeed in the arts; people with spatial imagery may be better suited to careers in science or engineering (Kozhevnikov et al., 2005). These are tantalizing suggestions, and they are obviously a target for further research.

Images Are Not Pictures

At many points in this chapter, we have referred to mental images (especially *visual* images) as "mental pictures." That comparison is hardly new; the phrase was coined by Shakespeare four centuries ago and is embedded in the way most of us talk about our imagery. And, as we have seen, the comparison is in several ways appropriate: Visual images do depict a scene in a fashion that seems quite pictorial. In other ways, though, this comparison may be misleading.

To introduce this issue, let's review some points we first raised in Chapter 3, and with that, an example we first met in that chapter. Figure 11.6 shows a figure known

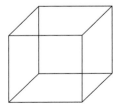

FIGURE 11.6 The Necker Cube

The cube can be perceived as if viewed from above or as if viewed from below. A version showing the two cubes broken out appears in Chapter 3 as Figure 3.1.

as the "Necker cube." The drawing of this cube—the stimulus itself—is ambiguous: It can be understood as a depiction of the (solid) cube shown as Cube A in the drawing, or it can be understood as a depiction of the cube shown as Cube B. The picture itself, in other words, doesn't specify in any way whether it shows Cube A or Cube B, and so, in this sense, the picture is neutral with regard to interpretation—and fully compatible with either interpretation.

Unlike the picture, though, our *perception* of the cube is not neutral, is not indeterminate with regard to depth. Instead, at any moment in time we perceive the cube either as similar to Cube A or as similar to Cube B. Our perception, in other words, "goes beyond the information given" by specifying a configuration in depth, a specification that in this case supplements an ambiguous drawing in order to create an unambiguous perception.

As we discussed in Chapter 3, the configuration in depth is just one of the ways that perception goes beyond the information given in a stimulus. Our perception of a stimulus also specifies a figure/ground organization, the form's orientation (e.g., identifying the form's "top"), and so on. These specifications serve to organize the form and have an enormous impact on the subjective appearance of the form, and with that, what the form is seen to resemble and what the form will evoke in memory.

We need to be clear, then, that our **percepts** (i.e., our mental representations of the stimuli we are perceiving) are in some ways similar to pictures, but in other ways different. Like pictures, percepts are *depictions*, representing key aspects of the three-dimensional layout of the world. Percepts, in other words, are not descriptions of a stimulus; instead, percepts, just like pictures, show directly what a stimulus looks like. At the same time, though, percepts are different from pictures: They are organized and unambiguous in a fashion that pictures are not.

What about visual images? Are they just like pictures—thus, neutral with regard to organization, and so open to different interpretations? Or are they organized in the way percepts seem to be, and so, in a sense, already interpreted? One line of evidence comes from studies of ambiguous figures. In one experiment, participants were first shown a series of practice stimuli to make sure that they understood what it meant to reinterpret an ambiguous figure (Chambers & Reisberg, 1985). They were then shown a drawing of one more ambiguous figure (such as the Necker cube in Figure 11.6 or the duck/rabbit in Figure 11.7); then, after this figure had been removed from view, they were asked to form a mental image of it. Once the image was formed, they were asked if they could reinterpret this image, just as they had reinterpreted the practice figures.

The results are easily summarized. Across several experiments, not one of the participants succeeded in reinterpreting his or her images: They reliably failed to find the duck in a "rabbit image" or the rabbit in a "duck image." Is it possible that they did not understand their task, or perhaps they did not remember the figure? To rule out these possibilities, participants were given a blank piece of paper immediately after their failure at reinterpreting their images and were asked to draw the figure based

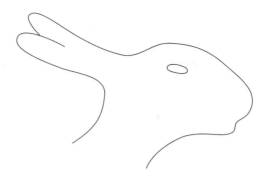

FIGURE 11.7 The Duck/Rabbit

This figure can be perceived either as a duck or as a rabbit. With the picture in view, people readily find both interpretations of the figure. If people are imaging the figure, however, they have great difficulty finding a different interpretation. That is, people imaging the "duck" have great difficulty in discovering the "rabbit"; people imaging the "rabbit" have great difficulty in discovering the "duck." Of course, once someone knows that both interpretations are possible, he can hop from one to the other. What seems enormously difficult, though, is *discovering* the alternative interpretation of the imaged figure in the first place.

on their image. Now, looking at their own drawings, all of the participants were able to reinterpret the configuration in the appropriate way. Thus, we have 100% failure in reinterpreting these forms with images, and 100% success a moment later with drawings.

Apparently, therefore, what participants "see" in their image is not a "picture"— neutral with regard to interpretation, and so open to new interpretations. Instead, images are inherently organized, just as percepts are. As such, images are entirely unambiguous and strongly resistant to reinterpretation.

Learning From Images

In some ways, the results just cited are puzzling. The Chambers and Reisberg (1985) participants universally failed to make a simple discovery from an image, but we know from other evidence that discoveries from imagery are possible. After all, common experience tells us that mental images often surprise us or remind us of something. We routinely consult our images in solving problems or in making decisions. Indeed, the history of science is filled with examples of discoveries apparently inspired by an image (see, for example, A. Miller, 1986). Many laboratory studies have also shown that people can invent new forms or new devices by inspecting and manipulating their images (R. Anderson & Helstrup, 1993; Finke, 1990; Finke & Slayton, 1988; Pinker & Finke, 1980; Thompson, Kosslyn, Hoffman, & Kooij, 2008; also see Chapter 14). What should we make of all this? Why are discoveries from imagery sometimes possible and sometimes not?

We have suggested that images (like percepts) are *organized* depictions, and so they are understood by the imager in a certain way—as having a certain top, a certain figure/ground organization, and so on. Perhaps we need to think of the mental image, therefore, as a *package* that includes both the depiction itself *and* this "perceptual reference frame" (after Peterson, Kihlstrom, Rose, & Glisky, 1992). Thus, when someone is inspecting an image, seeking a discovery, it's this package that she is inspecting, and so the discoveries must be discoveries about the package. On this basis, therefore, discoveries about the imaged form will be guided by both the depiction *and* the reference frame.

To see how this plays out, let's say that someone is visualizing the form in Figure 11.7 and thinking about it as a duck. Why doesn't this person discover that the form can also be seen as a rabbit? The image obviously contains a depiction that could allow this discovery—but that's not good enough. The image, understood as a duck, has a particular reference frame—one that identifies the form as facing-to-the-left—and this reference frame is incompatible with the sought-after rabbit. The discovery, in other words, fits with the depiction but not with the reference frame—and so it is compatible with only part of the "package." As a result, the discovery is quite unlikely.

We should be able to help participants, though, with a simple hint, one that leads them to change the image's reference frame. A hint like "try thinking about the form as facing-to-the-right" should do the trick. And, in fact, such hints—altering the image's reference frame—do have large effects, often eliciting new and dramatic discoveries (Peterson et al., 1992; Reisberg & Chambers, 1991; also see Verstijnen, Hennessey, van Leeuwen, Hamel, & Goldschmidt, 1998; Verstijnen, van Leeuwen, Goldschmidt, Hamel, & Hennessey, 1998).

Further support for this view comes from a study in which participants were asked to memorize a series of "nonsense shapes" (Reisberg & Chambers, 1991). The tenth shape in the series, presented with no special notice, was the one depicted in Figure 11.8. Participants had 5 seconds in which to memorize this shape, and then the picture was removed. Participants were next asked to form an image of the shape

FIGURE 11.8 Limitations on Learning From Imagery
Participants imaged this form, thinking of it merely as an abstract shape. When asked to imagine the form rotated by 90°, they failed to discover the familiar shape of Texas. Their understanding of the imaged form (and, in particular, their understanding of the form's "top") prevented them from recognizing the Lone Star State.

and then to imagine the shape rotated 90° clockwise. At this point, the participants were told that the shape "resembles a familiar geographic form" and were asked to identify that form.

It seems likely that participants in this procedure understood the side topmost in the original drawing as being the shape's top, and this understanding did not change when the participants imagined the rotation. As a consequence, the participants were, in this experiment, imaging the correct geometry for Texas (in other words, they had the right depiction) but with the wrong understanding, specifying the wrong top. It's not surprising, therefore, that exactly zero participants were able to discover Texas in their image.

In a subsequent experiment, participants were led through the same procedure, but this time they were explicitly instructed in how to change their understanding of the imaged form. That is, they were told directly to think of the form's left edge as being the top. With this instruction, many participants were able to discover Texas in the image. Apparently, then, the obstacle to discovery is indeed how participants understand the image. When this understanding changes, there is a corresponding change in performance.

All of these results fit with the claim that images are inherently understood in a certain way—a way that specifies, for example, which side of the form is the top,

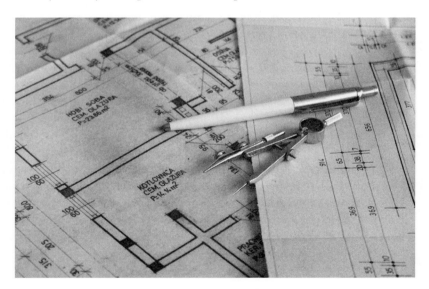

Imposing a Frame of Reference

In many professions—architecture, for example—designers *visualize* the early stages of their ideas without needing to sketch the designs on paper. Research suggests, though, that there may be limits on this image-based process, and that some discoveries (those that require a change in the reference frame) will be vastly more likely if the designers put their ideas down on paper and then inspect the drawings. This is because the drawing, on its own, has no reference frame, making it much easier for the designer to impose a new reference frame.

which side is the front, and so forth. This understanding sets boundaries on what can be discovered about the image, so that discoveries compatible with the imager's understanding of the form flow easily from the image, while discoveries incompatible with the understanding are rare.

Of course, imagers do have the option of changing how they understand the form, and when these changes occur, they have powerful effects—a range of new discoveries, compatible with the new understanding, now becomes available. Evidence suggests, however, that these changes in reference frame are surprisingly difficult and often dependent on specific instructions or specific training examples. Therefore, one's initial understanding of the form has an enormous impact on what can and cannot be discovered from an image.

Images and Pictures: An Interim Summary

Images, both visual and spatial, provide a distinctive means of representing the world, so that imagining a robot (for example) is quite different from thinking about the word "robot," or describing a robot to yourself, or merely contemplating the idea "robot." As one crucial difference, images are, as we've said, truly picturelike in the sense that they show exactly what a form looks like. This will lead you to highlight the appearance in your thoughts, and this makes it more likely that you'll be reminded of other forms having a similar appearance. Creating an image will also make some attributes of a form more prominent and others less so (the cat's head, for example, rather than its whiskers—see p. 342), and this, too, can influence what further ideas the image calls to mind. In these ways, then, putting your thoughts into imagery can literally shape the flow and sequence of your ideas.

At the same time, we have also highlighted ways in which images are *not* picturelike: Images, it seems, are inherently organized in a fashion that pictures are not, and this, too, can influence the sequence of your thoughts—with an image's reference frame guiding which discoveries do, and which do not, easily flow from an image.

Where does all this leave us? Images are different from pictures in important ways—and, in a sense, they contain more information than a picture does—but this must not distract us from how much images have in common with pictures and, likewise, the enormous overlap between imagery and perception. In short, images share crucial properties with pictures, and so they are, in many ways, certainly picturelike. Nonetheless, images are not pictures.

Long-Term Visual Memory

So far, our discussion has focused on "active" images—images currently being contemplated, images presumably held in working memory. What about visual information in long-term memory? For example, if you wish to form an image of an elephant, you need to draw on your knowledge of what an elephant looks like. What is this knowledge, and how is it represented in long-term storage? Likewise, if you recognize a picture as familiar, this is probably because you've detected a "match" between it and some memory of an earlier-viewed picture. What is the nature of this memory?

Image Information in Long-Term Memory

In Chapter 8, we suggested that your concept of "birthday" (for example) is represented by some number of nodes in long-term memory. When you think about birthdays, those nodes are activated; conversely, when those nodes are activated, you are thinking about birthdays. Perhaps we can adapt this proposal to account for long-term storage of visual information (and likewise information for the other sensory modalities).

One possibility is that nodes in long-term memory can represent entire, relatively complete pictures. Thus, to think about a mental image of an elephant, you would activate the ELEPHANT PICTURE nodes; to scrutinize an image of your father's face, you would activate the FATHER'S FACE nodes; and so on.

However, evidence speaks against this idea (e.g., Kosslyn, 1980, 1983). Instead, images seem to be stored in memory in a piecemeal fashion. To form an image, therefore, you first have to activate the nodes specifying the "image frame," which depicts the form's global shape. Then elaborations can be added to this frame, if you wish, to create a full and detailed image.

Many research results support this claim. First, images containing more parts take longer to create, just as we would expect if images are formed on a piece-by-piece basis (see Figure 11.9). Second, images containing more detail also take longer to create, in accord with our hypothesis. Third, we know that imagers have some degree of control over how complete and detailed their images will be, so that (depending on the task, the imagers' preferences, etc.) images can be quite sketchy or quite elaborate (Reisberg, 1996). This variation is easily explained if imagers first create an image frame and only then add as much detail as they want.

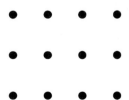

FIGURE 11.9 Columns or Rows?
This picture shows "three rows of dots." The same picture also shows "four columns of dots." There is, in short, no difference between a picture of rows and a picture of columns. There is a difference, however, between a mental image of "three rows of dots" and a mental image of "four columns." The latter image, for example, takes longer to generate and is more difficult to maintain, presumably because it contains a larger number of units—four columns, rather than three rows.

But how does the imager know *how to* construct the image—what its form should be and what it should include? The relevant information is drawn from **image files** in long-term memory. Each file contains the information needed in order to create a mental image—information about how to create the image frame, and then information about how to elaborate the frame in this way or that, if desired. How is this information represented within the image file? One proposal is that the image files contain something like a set of instructions, or even a "recipe," for creating an image. By analogy, someone could instruct you in how to create a picture by uttering the appropriate sentences: "In the top left, place a circle. Underneath it, draw a line, angling down. . . ." Such instructions would allow you to create a picture, but notice that there is nothing pictorial about the instructions themselves; the instructions are sentences, not pictures. In the same way, the instructions within an image file allow you to create a representation that, as we have already seen, is picturelike in important ways. In long-term memory, however, this information may not be at all picturelike.

Verbal Coding of Visual Materials

The proposal before us, therefore, is that visual information is represented in long-term memory in a fashion that isn't itself "visual." Instead, visual information can be represented via propositions, with these providing a "recipe" to be used, when needed, for creating an image.

In some cases, though, visual information can be represented in long-term storage in an even simpler format—namely, a verbal label. For example, consider memory for color. It is appreciably easier to remember a color if one has a label for it, so that individuals with large color vocabularies have better color memories. This leads to striking contrasts if we gather data in different cultures, capitalizing on the fact that some languages have many words for describing and categorizing colors, while other languages have only a few. It turns out that color memory is superior in those cultures with a greater number of color terms (R. Brown & Lenneberg, 1954; Rosch, 1977b), because in many cases people are remembering a verbal description for the stimuli rather than the colors themselves. (For more on the influence of color labels on color memory and color perception, see Chapter 10; also see color insert, Figure 18).

A related point was made by Carmichael, Hogan, and Walters (1932). Their research participants were shown pictures like those in the center column of Figure 11.10. Half of the participants were shown the top form and told, "This is a picture of eyeglasses." The other half were told, "This is a picture of a barbell." The participants were later required to reproduce, as carefully as they could, the pictures they had seen. Those who had understood the picture as eyeglasses produced drawings that resembled eyeglasses; those who understood the picture as weights distorted their drawings appropriately. This is again what one would expect if the participants had memorized the description, rather than the picture itself, and were re-creating the picture on the basis of this description.

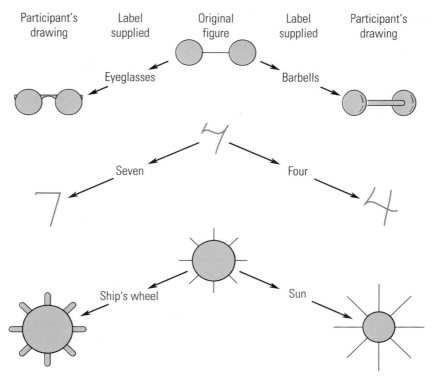

FIGURE 11.10 The Influence of Verbal Labels on Visual Memory
Participants were shown the figures in the middle column. If the top figure was presented with the label "eyeglasses," participants were later likely to reproduce the figure as shown on the left. If the figure was presented with the label "barbell," they were likely to reproduce it as shown on the right. (And so on for the other figures.) One interpretation of these data is that participants were remembering the verbal label and not the drawing itself and then, at the time of the test, reconstructed what the drawing must have been based on the remembered label.

It seems, then, that in some cases visual information may be stored in memory not via imagery but as a description of the previously viewed object. Moreover, this is a helpful strategy: Memory is improved when an appropriate label or appropriate description is available. (This is certainly true in the color-memory studies.) However, this strategy can backfire: People may end up recalling a picture in a fashion that is distorted by their understanding of it or that is perhaps selective in ways that their description was selective. In either case, though, the point is the same: Knowledge that *seems* visual may be stored in memory in some nonvisual representation.

A similar message emerges from tasks that require participants to reason about spatial position. In one study, participants were asked, "Which is farther north: Seattle or Montreal? Which is farther west: Reno, Nevada; or San Diego, California?" Many participants responded that Montreal is farther north and that San Diego is farther

Non-Spatial Reasoning

Sometimes "spatial" information is stored in a non-spatial fashion. For example, many people believe that Montreal is further north than Seattle, although the opposite is the case. Presumably, people are using this reasoning: "Montreal is in Canada; Seattle is in the United States. Canada is north of the United States. Therefore, Montreal must be north of Seattle."

west, but both of these responses are wrong. Montreal, for example, is at roughly the same latitude as Portland, Oregon, a city almost 200 miles south of Seattle (Stevens & Coupe, 1978).

These errors arise because participants seem to be reasoning this way: "Montreal is in Canada; Seattle is in the United States. Canada is north of the United States. Therefore, Montreal must be farther north than Seattle." This kind of reasoning is sensible, since it will often bring you to the correct answer. (That's because most parts of Canada are, in fact, farther north than most parts of the United States.) Even so, this reasoning will sometimes lead to error, and it does so in this case. (The logic is obviously the same for the Reno/San Diego question.)

Of course, what is of interest here is not the participants' knowledge about the longitude and latitude of these particular cities. What is important is that the sort of reasoning revealed in these studies hinges on propositional knowledge, and not on any sort of mental images or maps. Apparently, then, at least some of our spatial knowledge relies on a symbolic/propositional code. (For more on reasoning about geography, see Friedman & Brown, 2000a, 2000b.)

Imagery Helps Memory

No matter how images are stored in long-term memory, however, it is clear that images influence memory in important ways and, in general, imagery improves memory. For example, materials that evoke imagery are considerably easier to remember than materials that do not evoke imagery. This can be demonstrated in many ways, including the following two-step procedure. First, participants are presented with a list of nouns and asked to rate each noun, on a scale from 1 to 7, for how readily it evokes an image (Paivio, 1969; Paivio, Yuille, & Madigan, 1968). Examples of words receiving high ratings are "church," with an average rating of 6.63; and "elephant," rated at 6.83. Words receiving lower ratings include "context" (2.13) and "virtue" (3.33).

As a second step, we ask whether these imagery ratings, generated by one group of participants, can be used to predict memory performance with a new group of participants. The new participants are asked to memorize lists of words, using the words for which we have imagery ratings. The data reliably indicate that participants learn high-imagery words more readily than low-imagery words (Paivio, 1969; Paivio, Smythe, & Yuille, 1968).

In the same fashion, memory can be enormously aided by the use of imagery mnemonics. In one study, some participants were asked to learn pairs of words by rehearsing each pair silently. Other participants were instructed to make up a sentence for each pair of words, linking the words in some sensible way. Finally, other participants were told to form a mental image for each pair of words, with the image combining the words in some interaction. The results showed poorest recall performance by the rehearsal group, and intermediate performance by the group that generated the sentences. Both of these groups, though, did appreciably worse than the imagery group (G. H. Bower & Winzenz, 1970; for discussion of other mnemonic techniques, see Chapter 5).

If forming images helps memory, does it matter *what sort of image* one creates? Quite reliably, memory is best if the images one forms show the objects to be remembered interacting in some way, and not just side by side (Wollen, Weber, & Lowry, 1972). This is not surprising: As we saw in Chapter 5, memory is improved in general if one can find ways to organize the material; interacting images provide one means of achieving this organization.

In addition, it's sometimes suggested that imagery mnemonics are most effective if the mental "picture" is in some fashion *bizarre*, rather than just showing some ordinary interaction. Evidence for this point, however, is mixed, with some studies showing an effect of bizarreness and some studies showing the opposite. The explanation for this mixed pattern probably lies in the *sequence* of stimuli employed in these studies. If participants see only a succession of bizarre images, one after another, they cease thinking of the images as bizarre, and so bizarreness has no impact on the data. If, instead, the bizarre images are mixed together with more-common images, the bizarreness is noticed and contemplated, leading to a memory improvement. (For reviews, see Einstein, McDaniel, & Lackey, 1989; McDaniel & Einstein, 1986, 1990.)

Dual Coding

There's no question, then, that imagery improves memory. But why is this? What memory aid does imagery provide?

One proposal is that imageable materials, such as high-imagery words, will be doubly represented in memory: The word itself will be remembered, and so will the

A

B

Imagery and Relationships

Imagery is a powerful force in promoting memory. However, this benefit depends on the *relationships* shown in the image. The left picture merely shows a dog and monkey together, and would probably not help you to remember this pair. The right picture shows a specific interaction between the dog and monkey, and would likely be a great spur to memory.

corresponding picture. This pattern is referred to as **dual coding**, and the advantage of this should be obvious: When the time comes to retrieve these memories, either record—the verbal or the image—will provide the information you seek. This gives you a double chance of locating the information you need, thereby easing the process of memory search. Imagery mnemonics work in the same way by encouraging people to lay down two different memory records—a propositional record of the material, plus an image—rather than one.

Of course, framing things in this way implies that we have two different types of information in long-term storage: memories that represent the content of symbolic (and perhaps verbal) materials, and memories that represent imagery-based materials. Paivio (1971), the source of the dual-coding proposal, argues that these two types of memory differ from each other in important ways—including the information that they contain, as well as the ways they are accessed. Access to symbolic memories, he suggests, is easiest if the cue provided is a word, as in, "Do you know the word 'squirrel'?" Access to an image-based memory, in contrast, is easiest if one begins with a picture: "Do you recognize this pictured creature?" Moreover, Paivio argues, some types of information—for example, semantic associations—are more easily stored via symbolic memories. Other types of information, such as information about size or shape, are more readily accessed from the remembered images. (Also see Paivio & Csapo, 1969; Yuille, 1983.)

Memory for Pictures

Paivio (1971) also proposed that there are two separate memory systems: one containing the symbolic memories, the other containing images. However, many psychologists would reject this claim, arguing instead that there is just a single, vast, long-term memory, capable of holding diverse contents. Within this single memory, each type of content has its own traits, its own pattern of functioning. Nonetheless, there is still one unified memory system, with images and verbal memories fully and intimately interwoven—much as a single library building, with one indexing system and one set of rules, can hold both books and photographs, sound recordings as well as videos. (For discussion of this point, see Heil, Rösler, & Hennighausen, 1994.)

Thus, images in long-term storage may well be distinct from verbal memories in many ways, but even so, these two types of memory have a great deal in common, reflecting the fact that both reside within a single memory system. As a result, many of the claims we made in Chapters 5, 6, and 7 apply with equal force to visual memories and verbal memories: Recall of both memory types, for example, is dependent on memory connections; priming effects can be observed with both types of memory; encoding specificity is observed in both domains; and so on.

As an illustration of this broad point, consider memory for pictures. In many ways, the principles governing picture memory are the same as the principles governing memory for other materials. For example, we argued in Chapter 7 that participants' memories are clearly influenced by generic knowledge—knowledge about how events unfold in general. In support of this claim, Chapter 7 relied largely on evidence for verbal memories, such as memory for sentences and stories. Similar effects, though, can easily be demonstrated with pictures.

In one study, Friedman (1979) showed participants pictures of scenes such as a typical kitchen or a typical barnyard. In addition, the pictures also contained some unexpected objects. The kitchen picture, for example, included a stove and a toaster, but it also included items less often found in a kitchen, such as a fireplace. Participants were later given a recognition test in which they had to discriminate between pictures they had actually seen and altered versions of these pictures in which something had been changed.

In some of the test pictures, one of the familiar objects in the scene had been changed. For example, participants might be shown a test picture in which a different kind of stove appeared in place of the original stove, or one in which the toaster on the counter was replaced by a radio. Participants rarely noticed these changes, and so they tended (incorrectly) to respond "old" in these cases. This is sensible on schema grounds: Both the original and altered pictures were fully consistent with the kitchen schema, and so both would be compatible with a schema-based memory.

However, participants almost always noticed changes to the unexpected objects in the scene. If the originally viewed kitchen had a fireplace and the test picture did not, participants consistently detected this alteration. Again, this is predictable on schema grounds: The fireplace did not fit with the kitchen schema and so was likely to be specifically noted in memory. In fact, Friedman recorded participants' eye movements during the original presentations of the pictures. Her data showed that participants tended to look twice as long at the unexpected objects as they did at the expected ones; clearly, these objects did catch the participants' attention. (For more on schema guidance of eye movements, see Henderson & Hollingworth, 2003; Henderson, Weeks, & Hollingworth, 1999.)

In essence, then, what Friedman's participants seemed to remember was that they had seen something we might label "kitchen plus a fireplace"—a description that both identifies the relevant schema and also notes what was special about this particular instance of the schema. If recognition memory is tested with a kitchen without a fireplace, participants spot this discrepancy easily, because this picture does not fit with the remembered description. If tested with a kitchen plus or minus a toaster, this picture still fits with the "kitchen plus a fireplace" description, and so the alteration is likely not to be noticed. (Also see Pezdek, Whetstone, Reynolds, Askari, & Dougherty, 1989.)

A different line of evidence also shows schema effects in picture memory. Recall our claim that in understanding a story people place the story within a schematic frame. As we have seen, this can often lead to intrusion errors, as people import their own expectations and understanding into the story, and so they end up remembering the story as including more than it actually did.

A similar phenomenon can be demonstrated with picture memory. Intraub and her collaborators have documented a consistent pattern of **boundary extension** in picture memory (Intraub & Bodamer, 1993; Intraub & Dickinson, 2008; Intraub, Gottesman, & Bills, 1998; Intraub, Hoffman, Wetherhold, & Stoehs, 2006). That is, people remember a picture as including more than it actually did, in effect extending the boundaries of the remembered depiction. For example, participants shown the top panel in Figure 11.11 were later asked to sketch what they had seen. Two of the participants' drawings are shown at the bottom of Figure 11.11, and the boundary extension is clear: Participants remember the scene as less of a close-up view than it actually was, and correspondingly, they remember the scene as containing more of the backdrop than it actually did. This effect is observed whether participants initially see a few pictures or many, whether they are tested immediately or after a delay, and even when participants are explicitly warned about boundary extension and urged to avoid this effect.

Intraub has argued that this boundary extension arises from the way in which people perceive these pictures in the first place. In essence, people understand a picture by means of a perceptual schema (Hochberg, 1978, 1986). This schema places the picture in a larger context, informing the perceiver about the real-world scene only partially revealed by the picture. This leads to a series of expectations about

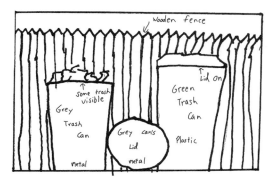

FIGURE 11.11 Boundary Extension in Picture Memory

Participants were initially shown the photograph at the top of this figure. The two panels below show the scene as drawn from memory by two different participants. The participants clearly recalled the scene as a wide-angle shot, revealing more of the background than it actually did. (After Intraub & Richardson, 1989)

what people would see if they could somehow look beyond the photograph's edges. All of this influences memory, as the memory interweaves what people saw with what they expected, or what they knew they might see if they explored further. In important ways, this effect resembles the intrusion errors, produced by knowledge schemata, observed with verbal memory.

Overall, then, it does look like picture memory follows the same rules and is influenced by the same factors as memory for verbal materials. Schema effects, for example, can be found in both domains, with people showing better memory for the schema itself than for details of the particular stimulus. Intrusion errors can be documented in both domains. Similarly, participants show primacy and recency effects when they learn a series of pictures (Tabachnick & Brotsky, 1976), just as they do when they learn a series of words (Chapter 5). Phenomena such as spread of activation and priming can be demonstrated with nonverbal materials (Kroll & Potter, 1984), just as they can be demonstrated with verbal materials (Chapter 8). In short, picture memory is distinct from other sorts of memory, but there is also enough commonality to sustain our suggestion of a single memory system, with diverse contents but with a uniform set of operating principles.

The Diversity of Knowledge

Notice, then, where the data are leading us: There can be no question that *active images*, held in working memory, are different from other mental contents. Active images contain different information than other representations do; they make different information prominent; they require a set of operations (like scanning, or rotation, or zooming) that are irrelevant to other sorts of memory contents. For materials in working memory, therefore, we really do need different types of theory to describe images and other forms of mental representation.

The situation is completely different, however, when we turn to long-term memory and consider our long-term retention for what an elephant looks like or our recollection of what an earlier-viewed picture contained. The *content* of these memories is different from, say, our memory for stories. But even so, the image-based memories seem to be stored in the same memory system as every other memory—and so are influenced by exactly the same principles. In support of this claim, we can find many commonalities in the ways people remember diverse types of knowledge. Thus, memory for faces benefits from rehearsal (Sporer, 1988), just as memory for stories does. Similarly, a separation between *familiarity* and *source memory* (see Chapter 6) can be demonstrated for remembered music or remembered faces (Brigham & Cairns, 1988; Brown, Deffenbacher, & Sturgill, 1977), just as it can be for remembered words. And across all of these domains, schema effects are observed in which memories for specific cases become entangled with more-generic knowledge. Across domains, priming effects are observed. And so on.

It would appear, therefore, that there really is just one long-term memory, with a set of rules consistently applicable to all its diverse contents. However, we must attach some reservations to this claim. In this chapter, we have focused entirely on visual memories, and one might well ask whether similar conclusions would emerge with other categories of knowledge. For example, do memories for tastes or smells benefit from rehearsal, show schema effects, and the like? Do memories for emotions or for pain benefit from deep processing? Do they show the effects we called (in Chapter 6) "implicit memory" effects? Relatively little research speaks to these issues.

It is on this basis, then, that the claims about the singularity of long-term memory must remain tentative, and that is one of the reasons why, throughout this chapter, our agenda has been both methodological and substantive. We have tried to show by example what it means to explore the idea that a certain content is distinctive in working memory, and also what it would mean to propose a separate system within long-term memory. We have also seen how things stand on these issues with regard to visual materials. However, the field awaits additional data before these issues can be resolved for other modalities.

Chapter Summary

- People differ enormously in how they describe their imagery experience, particularly the vividness of that experience. However, these self-reports are difficult to interpret, and this ambiguity has led investigators to seek more objective means of studying mental imagery.

- Chronometric studies indicate that the pattern of what information is more available and what is less available in an image closely matches the pattern of what is available in an actual picture. Likewise, the times needed to scan across an image, or to zoom in on an image to examine detail, or to imagine the form rotating, all correspond closely to the times needed for these operations with actual pictures. These results emerge even when the experimenter makes no mention of imagery, ruling out an account of these data in terms of the demand character of the experiments.

- In many settings, visual imagery seems to involve mechanisms that overlap with those used for visual perception. This is reflected in the fact that imaging one thing can make it difficult to perceive something else, or that imaging the appropriate target can prime a subsequent perception. Visual images also show sensory effects similar to those observed in vision. Further evidence comes from neuroimaging and studies of brain damage; this evidence confirms the considerable overlap between the biological basis for imagery and that for perception.

- Not all imagery, however, is visual, so that we may need to distinguish between *visual* and *spatial* imagery. This proposal is confirmed by studies of individuals with brain damage, some of whom seem to lose the capacity for visual imagery but retain their capacity for spatial imagery. This proposal may also help us understand the pattern of individual differences in imagery ability, with some individuals being particularly skilled in visual imagery, and some in spatial.

- Even when imagery is visual, mental images are picture*like*, and not actually pictures. Unlike pictures, mental images seem to be accompanied by a perceptual reference frame that guides the interpretation of the image and also influences what can be discovered about the image. Discoveries flow easily from an image if the discoveries are compatible with the imaged geometry and its reference frame; discoveries are much more difficult if the sought-after form is compatible with the imaged geometry but not the reference frame.

- To create a mental image, one draws on information stored in an image file in long-term memory. These image files can be thought of as "recipes" for the construction of a mental image, usually by first constructing a frame and then by elaborating the frame as needed. In addition, at least some information about visual appearance or spatial arrangement is stored in long-term memory in terms of verbal labels or conceptual frameworks. For example, information about the locations of cities may be stored in terms of propositions ("Montreal is in Canada; Canada is north of the United States") rather than being stored in some sort of mental map.

- Imagery helps people to remember, and so word lists are more readily recalled if the words are easily imaged; similarly, instructions to form images help people to memorize. These benefits may be the result of dual coding: storing information in both a verbal format and a format that encodes appearances; this approach doubles the chances of recalling the material later on. When you're trying to remember combinations of ideas, it is best to imagine the objects to be remembered interacting in some way. There has been some dispute over whether bizarre images are more easily remembered than ordinary images, and evidence suggests that bizarre images will have an advantage only if the other images to be remembered are not bizarre.

- Memory for pictures can be accurate, but it follows most of the same rules as any other form of memory; for example, it is influenced by schematic knowledge.

- It is unclear what other categories of memory there may be. In each case, other kinds of memory are likely to have some properties that are distinctive and also many properties that are shared with memories of other sorts.

The Workbook Connection

See the *Cognition Workbook* for further exploration of visual knowledge:

- Demonstration 11.1: Imaged Synthesis
- Demonstration 11.2: Mnemonic Strategies
- Demonstration 11.3: Auditory Imagery
- Research Methods: Expectations, Motivation, and Demand
- Cognitive Psychology and Education: Using Imagery
- Cognitive Psychology and the Law: Lineups

PART 5

Thinking

Modern humans are all members of the species *Homo sapiens*—a term that translates (from the Latin) roughly as "rational person," or perhaps "wise person" or "thinking person." Apparently, our species' capacity for thought is so central, so important, that it essentially *defines* our species. And, of course, we rely on our ability to think all the time. We draw conclusions—about whether a friend is trustworthy; whether Volvos are especially safe; whether drinking red wine leads to headaches the next morning. We make choices—to go to this college or that; to take this job or that one; to get married or not. We solve problems, whether it's figuring out a way to repair a bicycle or finding a strategy for restoring a damaged friendship.

But how do we achieve these things? How do we think? And how *well* do we think? In this section, we'll tackle these questions. We'll examine evidence showing that human judgment and reasoning are often excellent, but we'll also encounter numerous examples of bad judgment, improper reasoning, and highly inefficient problem-solving.

How should we understand this mixed pattern? One suggestion reflects a theme that has already arisen in our discussion: In a wide range of settings, humans rely on mental shortcuts—strategies that are reasonably efficient but that risk error. These shortcuts played an important part in Chapter 3, when we discussed object recognition; in Chapter 7, when we discussed memory errors; and in Chapter 9, when we discussed categorization. Similar shortcuts will emerge again in this section, and as we'll see, they play an important (and sometimes destructive) role in guiding human thought.

However, we should not overemphasize these shortcomings in human thinking, because in many circumstances people rise above the shortcuts and think carefully and well. This will, at the least, drive us toward a multilayered conception of thinking, because we'll need to describe both the shortcuts that we use and also the more careful strategies. But, in addition, we'll need to tackle the obvious question of when we rely on one type of thinking, and when the other.

Finally, one other set of issues will arise in this section: How much of our thought is conscious? Are there benefits associated with conscious thought, as opposed to unconscious thought? We will tackle these questions in Chapter 15, but we'll do this largely by pulling together points we have made in earlier chapters; in this way, Chapter 15 will provide something of a review for the text at the same time that it tackles a series of enormously important theoretical questions.

Judgment: Drawing Conclusions From Evidence

I magine that you want to cheer up your friend Allen and so you need to figure out what will do the trick, based on things you have seen Allen do or heard him say. How will you proceed? Or, as a different example, should you buy a European car or one from Japan? In this case, you have seen ads telling you something like "Buy a VW!" You'll probably try to ignore those instructions, though, in making your choice. Instead, you'll try to recall what you have heard about different car types, and draw your conclusions based on these remembered facts.

As these examples suggest, we often take actions based on knowledge that we have, in effect, created for ourselves—by drawing inferences based on things we have seen or heard. In short, we draw conclusions from our experiences, and so we need to ask: How and how well do we draw these conclusions? If we draw lessons from our experience, do we draw the *right* lessons?

In this chapter, our focus will be on **induction**, typically described as a process in which you try to go beyond the available information—drawing inferences about a pattern, based on a few examples, or making projections about novel cases, based on what you've seen so far. Inductive conclusions are never guaranteed to be true. (What if the examples you've seen so far are just atypical?) Nonetheless, if induction is done properly, the conclusions are likely to be true, and so we'll want to ask whether the ordinary use of induction is done properly or not. Thus, we'll want to compare a **descriptive account** of human induction, telling us how the process ordinarily proceeds, with a **normative account**, telling us how things *ought to go*. In this way, we'll be able to ask whether our day-to-day judgments are foolish or sensible, and whether our commonsense conclusions are justified or not.

375

- In a wide range of circumstances, people use cognitive shortcuts, or "heuristics," to make judgments. These heuristics tend to be relatively efficient, and they often lead to sensible conclusions. However, heuristic use can lead to error.

- People use these heuristics even when they are trying to be careful in their judgment, and even when they are highly motivated to be accurate. The heuristics are used both by experts and by ordinary people, and so expert judgments, too, are vulnerable to error.

- However, heuristic use is far from inevitable, and we can easily identify circumstances in which people rely on more sophisticated forms of reasoning—and so they judge covariation accurately, are sensitive to base rates, are alert to the problems of drawing a conclusion from a small sample of evidence, and so on.

- We will consider when people use their more sophisticated ("System 2") reasoning and when they rely on the heuristics ("System 1"). Evidence suggests that System 2 comes into play only if the circumstances are right and only if the case being judged contains the appropriate triggers for this form of reasoning.

Judgment Heuristics

Experience can be an extraordinary teacher; indeed, we sometimes say things like, "There's no substitute for experience." With that, we put considerable faith in the judgments that a physician makes, based on her years of experience, or the advice we hear from a car mechanic, based on the many cars he's worked on, or the suggestions of a police officer, based on what he's seen "on the streets."

But, of course, the process of education doesn't depend just on the "teacher" —it also depends on the student! If a student pays no attention in class or remembers only a few bits of what the teacher said, then it won't matter if the teacher was talented or not. Likewise for learning from daily experience: Here, too, the capacity to learn depends on the person who has that experience and (among other concerns) depends on the person's *memory*: In order to draw a conclusion based on previous observations and experiences, the person needs to recall those experiences. As a result, virtually any factor that influences memory will, sooner or later, influence the pattern of our conclusions and the quality of our judgments.

This point provides an immediate basis for caution in evaluating human judgment. Often we draw conclusions based on experiences gathered over months and even years ("I can always tell when someone is lying"; "Have you noticed that creative people are usually a little bit crazy?"; "This year's freshmen seem more mature than last year's"), and so these conclusions rest on memories stretching back across a considerable time period. If these memories are selective (how many juvenile freshmen have you overlooked?), or incomplete, or somehow distorted, then the validity of these conclusions is questionable. In fact, Chapter 7 reviewed evidence that our memories often are selective, or incomplete, or distorted, raising a question right at the start about whether we really can rely on "learning from experience."

If judgments often depend on remembered evidence, is there anything you can do to help yourself, so that memory problems are less likely to pull you off track? One option is **attribute substitution**: You use this strategy when you're trying to evaluate some point but don't have easy access to the target information. You therefore rely instead on some other aspect of experience that's more accessible and that is (you hope) a plausible substitute for the information you seek.

For example, imagine that you're trying to predict whether you'll do well in Organic Chemistry next semester. To figure this out, you might ask yourself, "How well have my friends done in this course? How many have gotten good grades, and how many have done poorly?" In this case, you're seeking information about *frequencies*—assessments of how often various events have happened in the past. However, these frequency counts may not be easily accessible for you: Surely, you've not kept a tally, in the past, of friends' Chemistry grades. Likewise, you may not be able, right now, to recall a dozen friends who've taken this course and the grade for each friend. Therefore, you may have trouble estimating the relevant frequencies.

What can you do instead? One option is that you might do a quick scan through memory, seeking relevant cases. If you easily can think of four friends who got good grades in Organic Chemistry, you'll probably conclude that this is a relatively frequent occurrence. If you can think of few friends with good grades, or if the relevant memories come to mind only slowly, you'll probably draw the opposite conclusion: This must be a rare occurrence. In this fashion, you are relying on *availability*—the ease with which things come to mind—as an index for *frequency*. Tversky and Kahneman (1973) referred to this substitution—the reliance on availability as a substitute for frequency—as the **availability heuristic**.

As a different example, imagine that you're trying to judge whether David is lying to you or not. You could, as one option, try to remember everything you know about David and everything you know about liars, asking whether David truly fits into the category "liar." However, this makes considerable demands on memory. It may be easier, therefore, to rely on attribute substitution: Rather than trying to judge David's *category membership*, you could instead think about whether David *resembles* your notion of a typical liar. If he does, you could judge him to be a liar; if not, then you count him as honest. This substitution—using resemblance in place of information about category membership—is called the **representativeness heuristic**.

The Availability Heuristic

We introduced the idea of *heuristics* in Chapter 9. Heuristics are defined as reasonably efficient strategies that usually lead us to the right answers. The key word, however, is "usually." Heuristics do allow errors, but that is simply the price one pays in order to gain efficiency. To avoid the errors, you would need a strategy that would be much slower and much more effortful.

The availability and representativeness heuristics both fit this profile. In both cases, the attribute being used (availability or resemblance) is easy to assess. In both cases, the attribute being relied on is correlated with the target dimension, so that it can serve as a proxy for the target. Events or objects that are frequent are, in fact, likely to be easily available in memory, and so usually we can rely on availability as an index for frequency. And many categories are homogeneous enough so that members of the category do resemble each other; that's why we can often rely on resemblance as a way of judging category membership. (Indeed, this was crucial for us in Chapter 9.)

Nonetheless, it is easy to find cases in which these strategies lead to error. To take a simple case, ask yourself, "Are there more words in the dictionary beginning with the letter R ('rose,' 'rock,' 'rabbit') or more words with an R in the third position ('tarp,' 'bare,' 'throw')?" Most people assert that there are more words beginning with R (Tversky & Kahneman, 1973, 1974), but the reverse is true—by a margin of at least two to one.

Why do people get this wrong—and by so much? The answer lies in availability. If you search your memory for words starting with R, many will come to mind. (Try it: How many R-words can you name in 10 seconds?) But if you search your memory for words with an R in the third position, fewer will emerge. (Again, try this for 10 seconds.) This difference, favoring the words beginning with R, arises simply because your memory is organized roughly like a dictionary is, with the words sharing a start-ing sound all grouped together. As a consequence, it's easy to search memory using "starting letter" as your cue; a search based on "R in third position" is much more dif-ficult. In this way, the organization of memory creates a bias in what's easily available, and this bias in availability leads to an error in frequency judgment.

The Wide Range of Availability Effects

Use of the availability heuristic seems sensible in the question about "R-words." After all, the question isn't very interesting, and so you probably don't want to spend much effort or time in choosing a response. But evidence suggests that people use strategies like availability in a wide range of other cases, including cases in which they're mak-ing judgments of some importance.

For example, consider the fact that people regularly overestimate the frequency of events that are, in actuality, quite rare (Attneave, 1953; Lichtenstein, Slovic, Fischhoff, Layman, & Combs, 1978). This probably plays a part in people's willing-ness to buy lottery tickets; they overestimate the likelihood of winning! Sadly, it also can play a role in more important domains. For example, there is evidence that physi-cians may, in many circumstances, overestimate the likelihood of a rare disease and, in the process, fail to pursue other, perhaps more appropriate, diagnoses. (For an example, see Elstein et al., 1986.)

What causes this pattern? Events that are unusual or peculiar are, by their nature, likely to catch your attention. You will therefore notice these events and think about them, ensuring that these events are well recorded in memory. This will, in turn, make these events easily available to you. As a consequence, if you rely on the availability heuristic, you will overestimate the frequency of these unusual events and, correspondingly, will overestimate the likelihood of similar events happening in the future.

As a different example, participants in one study were asked to recall a number of examples in their lives in which they had acted in an assertive fashion (N. Schwarz et al., 1991; also see Raghubir & Menon, 2005). Half of the participants were asked to recall 6 examples; half were asked to recall 12 examples. Then all the participants were asked some more general questions, including how assertive, overall, they thought they were.

What should we expect here? Participants will probably have an easy time coming up with 6 examples, and so, using the availability heuristic, they are likely to conclude, "Those examples came easily to mind; therefore, there must be a large number of these examples; therefore, I must be an assertive person." In contrast, participants asked for 12 examples are likely to have more difficulty generating this longer list, and so they will conclude, "If these examples are so difficult to recall, I guess the examples can't be typical for how I act."

Availability Bias

Who washes the dishes more often, you or your housemates? Most people end up overestimating the amount of housework they do—and the reason is availability. You may not be around when your housemates do their chores, but you're inevitably aware of your own vacuuming, dishwashing, and so on. As a result, there's an obvious availability bias here—with your own housekeeping more available in your memory, and so more frequent in your estimation.

Consistent with these suggestions, participants who recalled fewer examples judged themselves to be more assertive. Notice, ironically, that the participants who recalled *more* examples actually had more evidence in their view for their own assertiveness. But it's not the quantity of evidence that matters. Instead, what matters is the ease of coming up with the examples. Participants who were asked for a dozen examples had a hard time with the task *because they had been asked to do something difficult*. But participants seemed not to realize this. They reacted only to the fact that the examples were difficult to generate and, using the availability heuristic, concluded that being assertive was relatively infrequent in their past.

In this example, availability is being influenced by the experimenter's request (for 6 examples or 12). But availability can also be influenced by many other factors. Imagine that you have been asked to vote on how much money the government should spend on various research projects, all aimed at saving lives. It seems sensible that you would choose to spend your resources on the more frequent causes of death, rather than investigating rare problems, and that leads to our questions: Should we spend more on preventing death from motor vehicle accidents or death from stomach cancer? Which is more common? Should we spend more on preventing homicides or diabetes? People reliably assert that motor vehicle accidents and homicide are the

Media Bias and Frequency
People routinely overestimate the frequency of homicide and underestimate the frequency of death by diabetes. This is because diabetes rarely makes the front page (unless the deceased is someone famous). This bias in media reporting creates an imbalance in the information that's available to you, which shapes your estimate of frequency of occurrence.

Attribute Substitution

Other cases of "attribute substitution" are easy to find. For example, readers often equate ease of reading with author intelligence, figuring that smarter authors express concepts more clearly. Ironically, this means that a common strategy among students—using an impressive vocabulary—is counterproductive: the long words make the paper a bit harder to read, which may diminish the readers' estimation of the students who wrote the papers! (After Oppenheimer, 2006.)

more frequent in each pair, although the opposite is true in both cases—by a substantial margin (Combs & Slovic, 1979; Slovic, Fischhoff, & Lichtenstein, 1982).

What produces this error? In estimating the likelihood of these events, people are heavily influenced by the pattern of media coverage. Homicide makes the front page, while diabetes does not; and this is reflected in participants' estimates of frequency. Indeed, their estimates for each of the causes of death correspond rather closely to frequency of report in the media, rather than to actual frequency of occurrence. Thus, once again, we find an influence of availability. Just as some information is less available to us via the selectivity of memory, some information is less available via the selectivity of the media. And it is the available data that people use, making the media bias as important as the memory bias.

The Representativeness Heuristic

Similar points can be made about a different form of attribute substitution—namely, the representativeness heuristic, the strategy of relying on resemblance when what you're really after is a judgment of category membership. At its essence, this heuristic amounts to an assumption that the categories we encounter are relatively homogeneous. It's this assumption that leads us to act as if each member of a category is "representative" of the category—that is, each member has all of the traits that we associate with the category overall. Thus, if someone is a lawyer, we give in to the stereotype and expect her to have the traits we associate with lawyers. Conversely, if someone looks like (our idea of) a typical lawyer—that is, has "lawyer traits"—we conclude she is a lawyer.

This assumption of homogeneity leaves us quite willing to draw conclusions from a relatively small sample: If each member of a group is representative of the group, then it's fair to draw conclusions about the whole after one or two observations, and thus we agree to statements such as, "If you've seen one lawyer, you've seen 'em all."

Of course, these reasoning patterns often lead us to the correct conclusions, because many categories we encounter are homogeneous. If after one or two nights at a Marriott you conclude that most hotel rooms have Bibles in them, your conclusion is warranted. If you conclude that Sue probably is comfortable with math because she is, after all, an engineer, this conclusion, too, is probably correct; engineers are likely to be reasonably homogeneous in this particular dimension. But as with all heuristics, it is easy to find cases in which this sort of reasoning can lead to error.

Reasoning From the Population to an Instance

Imagine tossing a coin over and over, and let's say that the coin has landed heads up six times in a row. Many people (and many gamblers) believe that in this situation the coin is more likely to come up tails than heads on the next toss. But this conclusion is wrong, and this belief is commonly referred to as the "gambler's fallacy." The "logic" leading to this fallacy seems to be that if the coin is fair, then a series of tosses should contain equal numbers of heads and tails. If no tails have appeared for a while, then some are "overdue" to bring about this balance.

But how could this be? The coin has no "memory," so it has no way of knowing how long it has been since the last tails. More generally, there simply is no mechanism through which the history of the previous tosses could influence the current one. Therefore, the likelihood of a tail on toss number 7 is 50-50 (i.e., .50), just as it was on the first toss, and just as it is on every toss.

Where, then, does our (mistaken) belief come from? The explanation lies in our assumption of category homogeneity. We know that over the long haul a fair coin will produce equal numbers of heads and tails. Thus, the category of "all tosses" has this property. Our assumption of homogeneity, though, leads us to expect that any "representative" of the category will also have this property—that is, any sequence of tosses will also show the 50-50 split. But this isn't true: Some sequences of tosses are 75% heads, some are 5% heads, some are 100% heads. It is only when we combine all these sequences that the 50-50 split emerges.

A different way to say this appeals to the notion of sample size. If we examine a large number of cases (i.e., a large sample), we will find patterns close to those in the overall population. This is what statisticians refer to as the "law of large numbers," a law that states (roughly) that the larger the sample you consider is, the greater the resemblance will be between the properties of the sample and the properties of the population at large. There is, however, no "law of small numbers": There is no tendency for small samples to approximate the pattern of the population. Indeed, small samples can often stray rather far from the population values. But people seem not to appreciate this, and they act as though they expect small samples to show the pattern of the whole. (For a different perspective on the gambler's fallacy, though, see Ayton & Fischer, 2004.)

Reasoning From a Single Case to the Entire Population

If people believe categories are homogeneous, then they will expect each subset of the category, and each individual within the category, to have the properties of the category overall; this is the error we were just discussing. But if people believe categories to be homogeneous, they'll also make the opposite error: They will expect the overall category to have the properties of the individuals, and so they will be quite willing to extrapolate from a few instances to the entire set. And this error, too, is easy to document, even when people are explicitly told that the instance they are considering is not representative of the larger group.

Hamill, Wilson, and Nisbett (1980) showed their participants a videotaped interview in which a person identified as a prison guard discussed his job. In one condition, the guard was compassionate and kind, and he expressed great concern for rehabilitation. In the other condition, the guard expressed contempt for the prison inmates, and he scoffed at the idea of rehabilitation. Before seeing either of these videotapes, some participants were told that this guard was quite typical of those at the prison; other participants were told that he was quite *atypical*, chosen for the interview precisely because of his extreme views. Still other participants were given no information about whether the interviewed guard was typical or not.

Participants were later questioned about their views of the criminal justice system, and the data show that they were clearly influenced by the interview they had seen: Those who had seen the humane guard indicated that they were now more likely to believe that prison guards in general are decent people; those who had seen the inhumane guard reported more negative views of guards. What is remarkable, though, is that participants seemed largely to ignore the information about whether the interviewed guard was typical or not. Those who were explicitly told the guard was atypical were influenced by the interview just as much, and in the same way, as those who were told that the guard was typical.

Similar data are easily observed outside of the laboratory. Consider what Nisbett and Ross (1980) have referred to as "man who" arguments. Imagine that you are shopping for a new car. You have read various consumer magazines and decided, on the basis of their reports of test data and repair records, that you will buy a Smacko-brand car. You report this to your father, who is aghast. "Smacko?! You must be crazy. Why, I know a man who bought a Smacko, and the transmission fell out 2 weeks after he got it. Then the alternator went. Then the brakes. How could you possibly buy a Smacko?"

What should you make of this argument? The consumer magazines tested many cars and reported that 2% of all Smackos break down. In your father's "data," 100% of the Smackos (one out of one) break down. Should this "sample of one" outweigh the much larger sample tested by the magazine? Your father presumably believes he is offering a persuasive argument, but what is the basis for this? The only basis we can see is the presumption that the category will resemble the instance; only if that were true would reasoning from a single instance be appropriate.

If you listen to conversations around you, you will regularly hear "man who" (or "woman who") arguments. "What do you mean cigarette smoking causes cancer?! I have an aunt who smoked for 50 years, and she runs in marathons!" Often these arguments seem persuasive. But these arguments have force only by virtue of the representativeness heuristic—our assumption that categories are homogeneous, and therefore our peculiar willingness to take a small sample of data as seriously as a larger sample.

Anchoring

In sum, we often rely on shortcuts that involve one form or another of attribute substitution. Thus, we rely on availability to judge frequency; we rely on resemblance as an indicator of category membership (and also rely on category membership as a basis for expecting resemblance!). We also use other substitutes—for example, using our emotional responses to a stimulus as a basis for judging danger (Slovic & Peters, 2006), and in other cases, using the *length* of an essay as a basis for judging *how persuasive it is* (Josephs, Giesler, & Silvera, 1994).

In all cases, it's reasonable to employ these shortcuts: Yes, the shortcuts can lead to error, but they lead to the right answer more often than not, and using the shortcuts surely is easy. What's troubling, though, is that we use the shortcuts in such a wide range of settings—including cases (like medical diagnosis or making important consumer choices) in which important issues are at stake.

Perhaps, though, these shortcuts provide only a person's initial view of an issue, something like a "rough draft" of his or her ultimate conclusion. Perhaps people then revise and refine their beliefs, based on other considerations. In this case, they could enjoy the benefits of the shortcuts, but without the cost. Unfortunately, though, this optimistic view is *wrong*, thanks in part to a tendency known as **anchoring** (Tversky & Kahneman, 1974; for more recent work, see Epley & Gilovich, 2001, 2006; Janiszewski & Uy, 2008; Krosnick, Miller, & Tichy, 2004).

In many situations, we don't know the answer to a particular question, but we do have an idea about what "ballpark" the answer is in. What we can therefore do is use that initial idea as an "anchor" and then reach our answer by making some suitable

adjustment to that anchor. The problem, though, is that we usually adjust too little, and so we are more influenced by the initial anchor than we should be.

In one study, participants had to estimate how old Mahatma Gandhi was when he died. Some participants were first asked the absurdly easy question of whether Gandhi lived to the age of 140; after they'd responded, they were asked how long he actually did live. Their estimate, on average, was that he lived to be 67 years old. Other participants were first asked whether Gandhi lived past the age of 9; then they, too, had to estimate how long he lived. Given this much lower anchor, they gave appreciably lower estimates, judging on average that he lived to age 50 (Strack & Mussweiler, 1997; it turns out, by the way, that all of these estimates were off target: Gandhi was 78 when he died).

A reliance on anchors is widespread, and so this becomes an important part of our theorizing about how people make judgments. But, in addition, anchoring has another consequence: When judgment errors arise for *other* reasons, anchoring serves to cement them in place. Imagine, for example, that you're trying to judge which is more frequent in the United States—death by homicide or death by diabetes (see p. 380). You know perfectly well that homicides tend to be front-page news; diabetes, on the other hand, is rarely reported unless the victim happens to be someone famous. Because you are aware of this bias and aware of how it might have shaped your initial estimate, you might seek to adjust that estimate, and it is here that anchoring plays its role. The initial response, even though misguided, will influence subsequent judgments, making it difficult to undo the error. (For related claims, see Wilson & Brekke, 1994.)

Detecting Covariation

It cannot be surprising that we often rely on shortcuts in our thinking. After all, many judgments we need to make in life are relatively trivial, and we are often pressed for time by some aspect of the circumstances. And, as we have noted, the shortcuts usually serve us well—providing the correct answer with very little effort.

It is unsettling, though, that people use these shortcuts even when making consequential judgments and even when making judgments about familiar domains. It is also worrisome that (thanks to anchoring) the errors produced by the shortcuts can be long-lasting. As a consequence of these points, people are sometimes influenced by availability even when there's an obvious bias in what's available. Likewise, they take small samples of evidence too seriously and treat evidence as though it were representative even if told explicitly that it is not.

The impact of these shortcuts can also be seen when people are trying to make judgments about **covariation**. This term has a technical meaning, but for our purposes we can define it this way: X and Y "covary" if X tends to be on the scene whenever Y is, and if X tends to be absent whenever Y is absent. For example, exercise and stamina covary: People who do the first tend to have a lot of the second. Owning audio CDs and going to concerts also covary, although less strongly than exercise and stamina. (Some people own many CDs but rarely go to concerts.) Note, then, that covariation is a matter of degree: Covariation can be strong or weak. Covariation can also be either negative or positive. Exercise and stamina, for example, covary positively (as exercise increases, so does stamina). Exercise and body fat, in contrast, covary negatively (as exercise increases, body fat decreases).

Covariation is important for many reasons—including the fact that it's what we need to consider whenever we are checking on a belief about cause and effect. For example, does education lead to a higher-paying job? If so, then degree of education and salary should covary. Likewise, do you feel better on days in which you eat a good breakfast? If so, then the presence or absence of breakfast in a day should covary with how you feel as the day wears on. Similarly for many other cause–effect questions: Are you more likely to fall in love with someone tall? Do vertical stripes make you look thinner? Does your car start more easily if you pump the gas? These are all questions that can be addressed by asking how things covary, and they are the sorts of questions people frequently ask. So how well do we do when we think about covariation?

Illusions of Covariation

Psychologists have developed a wide variety of tests to measure personality characteristics or behavioral inclinations. One well-known example is the Rorschach test, in which participants are shown inkblots and asked to describe them. Psychologists then examine the descriptions, looking for certain patterns. A mention of humans in

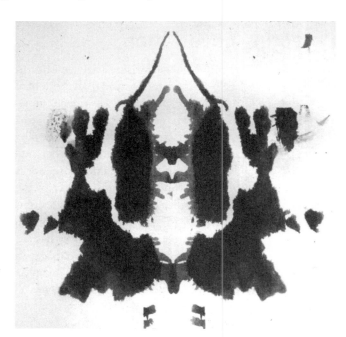

Rorschach Inkblot
Seeing "humans in motion" in an inkblot is said to indicate imagination and a rich inner life. Focusing on the white spaces around the inkblot is often seen as an indication of rebelliousness.

motion is said to indicate imagination and a rich inner life; responses that describe the white spaces around the inkblot are taken as indications of rebelliousness.

Is this valid? Do specific responses really covary with certain personality traits? And how astutely do people detect this covariation? To attack these questions, Chapman and Chapman (1971) created a number of Rorschach protocols—that is, written transcripts of a person's responses. The protocols were actually fictional, made up for this study, but they were designed to resemble real Rorschach responses. The Chapmans also made up fictional descriptions of the people who had supposedly offered these responses: One protocol was attributed to someone who "believes other people are plotting against him"; another protocol was attributed to someone who "has sexual feelings toward other men."

The Chapmans randomly paired the protocols and the personality descriptions—one protocol and one description, the next protocol and a different description. These randomly assembled protocol–profile pairs were then shown to a group of undergraduates, students who had no prior experience with the Rorschach test and who did not know the theory behind the test. These students were asked to examine the pairs and to determine what responses covaried with what traits. In particular, the students were asked which responses covaried with homosexuality.

Before pressing on, we should emphasize that the Chapmans' research was done more than three decades ago, at a time when many psychiatrists viewed homosexuality as a "disorder" to be diagnosed. Psychiatry has long since abandoned this utterly indefensible view, and so we discuss the Chapmans' research because it is a classic study of covariation, and not because it tells us anything about homosexuality.

Returning to the study itself, we know that thanks to the random pairing, there was no covariation in this set of "data" between protocols and descriptions. Nonetheless, the students reported seeing a pattern of covariation. Certain responses, they reported, seemed consistently good indicators that the respondent was a homosexual. For example, they reported that homosexual respondents were particularly likely to perceive buttocks in the inkblots. Therefore, mention of buttocks was a reasonable indicator, they claimed, of homosexuality.

Of course, there was no pattern in these (randomly assembled) data, and therefore the covariation the students were perceiving was illusory—"observed" in the data even though it was plainly not there. And oddly enough, the covariation "perceived" by these students was identical to that alleged at the time by professional clinicians. On the basis of their extensive experience with patients, clinicians were convinced that certain Rorschach responses were valid indicators of homosexuality, and the responses they mentioned were exactly the ones nominated by the participants in the laboratory study. The clinicians, like the Chapmans' participants, reported that use of the "buttocks" response did covary with sexual orientation, with homosexuals being much more likely to use this response.

Is it just a coincidence that the **illusory covariation** "detected" by the laboratory participants matches the pattern observed by the clinicians? It turns out to be no coincidence at all, because the pattern observed by the clinicians *is also illusory*. We know this because researchers have examined the Rorschach responses from homosexuals and heterosexuals and asked statistically whether the "buttocks" responses are more likely from one group than the other. It turns out that the two groups do not differ at all in the likelihood of this response, and so there is no covariation between sexual orientation and the use of the response. Thus, the clinicians are seeing a "pattern" that really isn't there. With all of their training, with their years of experience, and when they are making consequential professional judgments, the clinicians are caught by the same illusion that the lab participants are. (For related evidence, see Arkes & Harkness, 1983; Schustack & Sternberg, 1981; Shaklee & Mims, 1982; Smedslund, 1963.)

Theory-Driven and Data-Driven Detection of Covariation

In day-to-day work, a professional can accumulate great quantities of experience. A physician sees many cases of the flu; a salesperson sees many customers; a teacher sees many students. Each of these individuals, therefore, has a great opportunity to accumulate "professional wisdom" within his or her area of special expertise. The clear message of the Chapmans' data, though, is that we might be wary of this "professional wisdom." Their data remind us that professional training does not make someone immune to illusions. Professionals, just like everyone else, are capable of projecting their beliefs onto the evidence and perceiving patterns that aren't there. (For more on how expertise influences judgment, see Phillips, Klein & Sieck, 2004.)

What about nonexperts? Do we generally fall into the pattern indicated by the Chapmans' data—projecting our own biases onto the evidence we observe, and seeing only the patterns of covariation we expect to see? It's surely true that people have many false beliefs about covariation. For example, many people are convinced that there is a relationship between a person's handwriting and personality, yet no serious study has documented this covariation. Apparently, therefore, this is another example of illusory covariation (King & Koehler, 2000). Likewise, many people believe they can predict the weather by paying attention to their arthritis pain ("My knee always acts up when a storm is coming"). This, too, turns out to be groundless, and so it is another example that people are prone to perceive covariation when in truth there is none (Redelmeier & Tversky, 1996).

But what exactly causes these illusions? In a study by Jennings, Amabile, and Ross (1982), college students were asked to make covariation judgments in two types of situations: situations in which they had no prior expectations or biases, and situations in which they did. For example, in the "prior belief" (or "theory-based") case, the participants were asked to estimate how strong the covariation is between (a) children's dishonesty as measured by false report of athletic performance, and (b) children's dishonesty as measured by the amount of cheating in solving a puzzle. If a child is dishonest according to one of these indices, is she also dishonest according to the other? Or, as a different example, participants estimated the covariation between (a) how highly a student rated U.S. presidents' performance in the last decade, and (b) how highly the student rated business leaders' performance in the last decade. If you think highly of our presidents, do you also think highly of leaders in the business community?

The participants presumably made these judgments by reflecting on their prior experience and their intuitions; no new data were presented in the experimental procedure. Participants expressed these judgments by selecting a number between 0 and 100, where 0 indicated that the two traits were unrelated (i.e., did not covary) and 100 indicated that the traits covaried perfectly. Participants could also use negative values (to −100) to indicate the belief that the two traits covary, but with the presence of one indicating the absence of the other.

The participants were also asked to make a comparable judgment in a "no prior belief" (or "data-based") case—that is, with variables they had never met or considered before. For example, they were presented with ten pictures, each showing a man holding a walking stick. The heights of the men varied in the pictures, as did the length of the walking stick, and participants had to judge whether the two variables covaried, again choosing a value between −100 and +100.

Figure 12.1 shows the results from the data-based cases—that is, the cases in which participants had no prior beliefs. Here the estimates of covariation were rea-

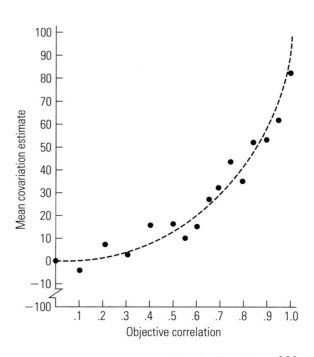

FIGURE 12.1 Assessments of Covariation in the Absence of Expectations
When research participants enter a situation with no expectations about the data, their estimates of covariation are quite orderly: The estimates grow stronger and stronger as the actual (objective) correlation grows stronger and stronger. In addition, participants give low estimates unless the actual correlation is very strong. (After Jennings, Amabile, & Ross, 1982)

sonably regular: The stronger the covariation, the stronger the estimate. The judgments also tended to be rather conservative: Estimates exceeded +30 only when the objective correlation was very strong.

Figure 12.2 shows a very different picture for the theory-based cases. The participants tended to be far more extravagant in these estimates, with estimates as high as +60 and +80. They were also far less regular in the theory-based cases, with only a weak relation between the magnitude of the estimated covariation and the magnitude of the actual covariation. For example, the "children's dishonesty" pair, mentioned earlier, is shown as the green square in the figure. In this case, the objective correlation, statistically measured, is fairly small; that is, children who are dishonest in one context are, in truth, often honest in other contexts. Participants estimated this covariation to be quite large, though, with an average estimate of almost +60. For the "presidents and business leaders" case (the green star in the figure), the objective correlation is much stronger than in the "dishonesty" pair, but participants estimated it to be much weaker.

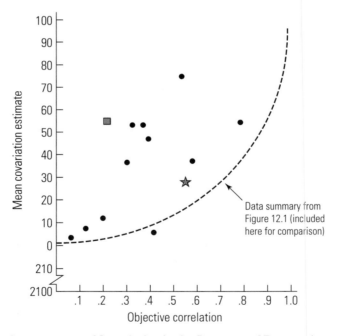

FIGURE 12.2 Assessments of Covariation in the Presence of Expectations
When participants enter a situation with expectations about the data, their estimates of covariation are often inaccurate. In this instance, participants were asked to assess the covariation in 16 cases. The square and the star indicate the two cases discussed in the text. Participants often estimated the covariation as strong even when it was quite weak, or as weak even when it was strong. The systematic pattern observed in Figure 12.1 is clearly absent here. (For purposes of comparison, this figure includes the curve describing the data from Figure 12.1.) (After Jennings, Amabile, & Ross, 1982)

At the very least, then, participants are performing differently in the theory-based and data-based judgments. The former judgments are often extravagant; the latter tend to be conservative. The data-based judgments track the objective facts fairly well; the theory-based judgments do not. Given these results, it is difficult to avoid the conclusion that theory biased what the participants "saw" in the data and that it led them to see much stronger (or weaker) covariation than was there. (Other relevant data are reviewed by Allan, 1993; Alloy & Tabachnik, 1984; Baron, 1988.)

What Causes Illusory Covariation?

Plainly, people *can* judge covariation in the absence of prior beliefs; we see that in Figure 12.1. Why, therefore, do they perform so poorly when judging covariation about familiar cases—cases for which they do have beliefs or expectations? One proposal focuses on the *evidence* people consider, rather than the process itself (Baron, 1988; Evans, 1989; Gilovich, 1991; Jennings, Amabile, & Ross, 1982). Specifically, the claim is that in making these judgments people consider only a subset of the evidence, and it's a subset that's shaped by their prior expectations. This virtually guarantees mistaken judgments, since even if the judgment process were 100% fair, a biased input would lead to a biased output.

This proposal rests on a tendency known as **confirmation bias**, a tendency to be more alert and more responsive to evidence that *confirms* one's beliefs, rather than to evidence that might *challenge* one's beliefs (Nisbett & Ross, 1980; Tweney, Doherty, & Mynatt, 1981). We will have more to say about confirmation bias in Chapter 13, and there we will consider some of the data documenting the breadth and power of this bias. For now, though, let's think through how confirmation bias applies to the assessment of covariation. Let us say, for the sake of discussion, that you have the belief that big dogs tend to be vicious. As a result of this belief, whenever you are thinking about dogs or looking at dogs, confirmation bias will lead you to notice the big dogs that are, in fact, vicious and the little dogs that are friendly. Your memory schemata will also help you to remember episodes that fit with this belief and will work against your remembering counterexamples. (Recall that one effect of memory schemata is to "regularize" our past experiences, bringing our recollections into line with our schema-based expectations; see Chapter 7.)

Thanks to these mechanisms, a biased sample of dogs is available to you—both in the dogs you perceive (because of a bias in attention) and in the dogs you remember (because of the bias in attention plus the effects of memory schemata). Therefore, if you are asked to estimate covariation between dog size and temperament, you will probably overestimate the covariation. This isn't because you are ignoring the facts, nor is it because you're incompetent in thinking about covariation. The problem instead lies in your "data"; and if the data are biased, so will be your judgment.

How alarmed should we be by these observations? It's worth bearing in mind that many social stereotypes are based on illusory covariation (e.g., the anti-Semitic

Illusory Covariations

Illusory covariations can produce, and then sustain, a wide range of beliefs—including some horrible ones that lead to racism, sexism, xenophobia, homophobia, and many other forms of narrow-minded prejudice and intolerance.

illusion that being overly concerned with money "covaries" with being Jewish, or the racist illusion that being lazy "covaries" with being black). In cases like these, the perception of illusory covariation obviously has ugly consequences. Likewise, if you're convinced that money makes people happy, and so you design your life in hopes of maximizing your wealth, then here, too, an illusion of covariation is having powerful effects. (For a glimpse of the data on the actual relationship between having money and being happy, see Myers, 2000.) Thus, the stakes are often high in judgments involving covariation, making our errors in this domain rather troubling.

Base Rates

Our assessment of covariation can also be pulled off track by another problem: our neglect of *base-rate* information. As a way of entering this issue, consider the following problem (Kahneman & Tversky, 1973; Nisbett & Ross, 1980):

> I have a friend who is a professor. He likes to write poetry, is rather shy, and is small in stature. Which of the following is his field: (a) Chinese studies or (b) psychology?

In response to this question, most people conclude that the friend is in Chinese studies, and presumably this judgment is based on something like the representativeness heuristic: The example describes someone close to many people's stereotype of a Chinese scholar, and so they draw the appropriate conclusion.

However, this judgment overlooks an important bit of information. As you can probably guess, the number of psychologists in the world is much greater than the number of scholars in Chinese studies. To see how this matters, let us assume, just for the sake of argument, that virtually all Chinese scholars—say, 90%—fit the stereotype. Let us assume further that only 5% of the psychologists fit the stereotype. In this case, "fitting the stereotype" would be high-quality **diagnostic information**—information that does indeed indicate that a person is in one category rather than another.

But now let's factor in how many psychologists there are in total, and how many Chinese scholars. We've already suggested that there are relatively few Chinese scholars in the world; even if 90% of these fit the description, this is still 90% of a small number. In contrast, merely 5% of the psychologists fit the description, but this will be 5% of a much larger number. To make this concrete, let's say there are 10,000 Chinese scholars in the United States, and 200,000 psychologists. In this case, 9,000 Chinese scholars fit the description (90% of 10,000), but 10,000 psychologists do as well (5% of 200,000). Therefore, even though the *proportion* of Chinese scholars fitting the description is larger than the proportion of psychologists (90% vs. 5%), the *number* of psychologists who fit the description is greater than the number of Chinese scholars fitting the description (10,000 vs. 9,000). As a result, chances are that the friend is a psychologist, because the description is compatible with more psychologists than Chinese scholars.

To put this point more generally, you need two types of information in order to make judgments like this one: both the diagnostic information and also the **base rate**—the overall likelihood that a particular case will be in this category or that one, independent of the diagnostic information. Often the base rate is expressed as a probability or as a percentage, and so, in our example, the base rate for "being a Chinese scholar," from the total group being considered, is 4.8%.[1]

Base rates are always important to consider, and in some cases they can overturn a conclusion suggested by the diagnostic information. This is evident in our "Chinese studies" example and is true in many other cases as well. Imagine that we are testing a new drug and discover that 70% of the patients who take this drug recover from the malady being treated. Does that mean the drug is effective? The answer depends on the base rate. In general, how many patients recover? If the answer is 70%, then the drug is having no effect whatsoever. Likewise, do good-luck charms help? Let's say that you wear your lucky socks whenever your favorite team plays, and the team has won 85% of its games. We again need to ask about base rates: How many games has your team won over the last few years? Perhaps the team has won 90% overall but only 85% when you are wearing your lucky socks; in that case, your socks are actually a jinx.

---

[1] In our example, we said that there were 10,000 Chinese scholars in the country, and 200,000 psychologists. That means the *proportion* of Chinese scholars, out of all the people we're considering, is 10,000 out of 210,000. Expressed as a decimal, that fraction equals 0.0476, or roughly 4.8%.

Base-Rate Neglect

In a classic study, Kahneman and Tversky (1973) asked participants this question: If someone is chosen at random from a group of 70 lawyers and 30 engineers, what is his profession likely to be? Participants understood perfectly well that the person is likely to be a lawyer. When asked to estimate the probability of this outcome, they sensibly responded .70. Thus, in this setting, participants made full and accurate use of the base-rate information.

Other participants were given a similar task, but with no base-rate information. They were instead given diagnostic information—brief descriptions of certain individuals—and asked, based on these descriptions, whether each individual was more likely to be a lawyer or an engineer. Some of the descriptions had, in fact, been crafted to suggest that the person was a lawyer; some suggested engineer; some were relatively neutral. For example, a description favoring the engineer stereotype described a man whose hobbies include home carpentry, sailing, and mathematical puzzles and who has no interest in political or social issues.

Not surprisingly, participants were easily able to use these descriptions, and their judgments sensibly reflected the content of the thumbnail sketches. Thus, it appears that participants are responsive to base rates if this is the only information they have, indicating that they know the base rates are relevant to this judgment. Likewise, they make appropriate use of diagnostic information if this is all they have. But now let's ask: What happens if we provide participants with both sorts of information—the base rates and the diagnostic information?

Participants in a third group were again provided with the thumbnail descriptions, but they were told, in addition, that the individuals being described had been selected at random from a group of 30 engineers and 70 lawyers. We have just seen evidence that participants understand the value of both pieces of information: the thumbnail sketch and the overall composition of the group. Therefore, we should expect the participants, when given both, to consider both and to combine these two sources of information as well as they can. If the base rate and the diagnostic information both favor the lawyer response, participants should offer this response with some confidence. If the base rate indicates one response and the diagnostic information the other response, then participants should temper their estimates accordingly.

However, this is not what the participants do. When they are provided with both types of information, participants ignore the base rate and rely only on the diagnostic information. Thus, in the lawyer/engineer problem, participants' responses were completely determined by the degree of resemblance between the individual described and their stereotype of a lawyer or an engineer. Indeed, they responded the same way if the base rates were as already described (70 lawyers, 30 engineers) or if the base rates were reversed (30 lawyers, 70 engineers). This reversal had no impact whatsoever on participants' judgments, confirming that they were indeed ignoring the base rates.

What produces this neglect of base rate? The answer, in part, is attribute substitution: When asked whether a particular person—Tom, let's say—is a lawyer or an engineer, people seem to turn this question about category membership into a question about resemblance. (In other words, they rely on the representativeness heuristic.) Thus, to ask whether Tom *is* a lawyer, they ask themselves how much Tom *resembles* (their idea of) a lawyer. This substitution is in many circumstances sensible. (Again, attribute substitution is efficient and often provides us with the right answer.) But the substitution can also cause problems: We earlier saw that the representativeness heuristic leads us to ignore sample size (pp. 383–384); we now add that the heuristic also leads us to ignore base rates.

The neglect of base rates, in turn, causes other problems. For example, someone who is insensitive to base rates will be inept in judging covariation, which means that he will be inaccurate whenever he tries to figure out cause-and-effect relationships. Likewise, base rates are crucial for questions of categorization (lawyer or engineer; Chinese scholar or psychologist), and some types of categorization are deeply consequential. For example, is a particular tumor malignant or benign? Is a patient truly suicidal or not? It turns out that experts making these decisions (physicians, psychotherapists) also show the pattern of base rate neglect (Dawes, 1988; Eddy, 1982; Klayman & Brown, 1993), highlighting just how important (and just how worrisome) this pattern can be.

Assessing the Damage

We seem to be painting a grim portrait of human judgment. We have discussed several sources of error, and we have suggested that these errors are rather widespread. Most of the studies we have cited have been run at prestigious universities, and so the participants (students at those universities) are, presumably, intelligent and motivated. The errors occur nonetheless. (For reviews, see Arkes, 1991; Einhorn & Hogarth, 1981; Gilovich, 1991.)

Even experts make these errors. We have mentioned poor diagnostic reasoning in physicians and illusory correlations in experienced therapists. Likewise, if we add just a little subtlety to our problems, analogous errors can be observed even among people with considerable training in statistics and methodology (Kahneman & Tversky, 1982a; Tversky & Kahneman, 1971, 1983; also see Mahoney & DeMonbreun, 1978; Shanteau, 1992). And as we've seen, people make these errors even when the stakes are high. In a number of studies, participants have been offered cash bonuses if they perform accurately. These incentives do have an impact on performance (Arkes, 1991; Gilovich, 1991; Hertwig & Ortmann, 2003), but even so, many errors remain. In addition, we have discussed errors in the context of medical diagnosis; other studies have documented similar errors in the professional work of highly motivated financial managers (e.g., Hilton, 2003). In these cases, the stakes are high indeed, yet the errors can still be documented.

More-Sophisticated Judgment Strategies

Could it be that human judgment is so fundamentally flawed? If so, this might help explain why warfare, racism, neglect of poverty, and environmental destruction are widespread; perhaps these consequences are the inevitable outcome of our inability to understand the facts and to draw decent conclusions. Likewise, it's no wonder that people are so ready to believe in telepathy, astrology, and a variety of bogus cures (Gilovich, 1991; King & Koehler, 2000).

Before we make these claims, however, we need to acknowledge that there is another side to our story and, with that, evidence showing that people can rise above the simple strategies we have described and avoid the errors we have catalogued. This will in turn demand a new line of questioning—asking why people sometimes rely on judgment short-cuts (with the attendant risk of error), and why people sometimes use more-sophisticated strategies.

Let's start, though, by documenting the simple but crucial fact that sometimes human judgment does rise above the heuristics we have described so far. For example, we argued earlier that people often rely on availability when they are trying to judge frequency, asking themselves, "How easily can I think of cases of type X?" in order to decide, "How common is type X?" But people don't always do this. Sometimes people are alert to the fact that they don't know much about a category, and this dissuades

Hope for the Future?
Our overall evaluation of human judgment cannot be too dismal; otherwise, how could we explain the extraordinary progress humans have made in the sciences, or the fabulous inventions humans have produced? Plainly, we are capable both of top-quality judgment at the same time that we are all-too-vulnerable to judgment errors.

them from relying on the availability heuristic. For example, how many sumo wrestlers are there in your state? If you relied on availability in answering this question, you might answer "zero" (assuming that none of your friends or relatives are sumo wrestlers). But in this situation you are probably alert to your own lack of expertise, and so you will seek some other basis for making this judgment. (For experimental demonstrations of this, see Oppenheimer, 2004; N. Schwarz, 1998; Winkielman & Schwarz, 2001.)

Similarly, consider the common reliance on the representativeness heuristic. This reliance is evident in many ways, including the fact that people are far too willing to draw conclusions from a small sample of evidence (we saw this in the power of "man who" arguments). This (and other findings) seems to suggest that people do not understand the importance of *sample size* when evaluating a pattern of evidence. Other evidence, however, makes it clear that people *do* understand sample size. As an illustration, imagine the following dialogue:

> Bart: I've got a great system for choosing lottery numbers! I chose a number yesterday, and I won!
>
> Lisa: Come on—that doesn't mean your system's great; maybe you just got lucky.

In this setting, Lisa's response sounds perfectly fine; we all know that lucky accidents do happen, and so Bart's boast does sound unjustified. But now consider this bit of dialogue:

> Marge: I've got a great system for choosing lottery numbers! I've tried it 11 times, and I won every time!
>
> Homer: Come on—that doesn't mean your system's great; maybe you just got lucky each time.

This time, Homer's response sounds odd, and Marge's boast does seem sensible. Yes, lucky accidents do happen, but they don't keep happening over and over. If something does happen over and over, therefore, it's probably not an accident.

These are easy points to grasp, and it's precisely this ease of understanding that's important here, because it reveals a comprehension of some crucial facts about sample size. Specifically, you understand these bits of dialogue only because you already know that it's dangerous to draw conclusions from a small sample of evidence. This is why you side with Lisa, not Bart. Likewise, you side with Marge because you understand that it's legitimate to draw conclusions from a larger sample; you know that a pattern in a larger set is less likely to be the result of accident.

Experimental data also make it clear that in some circumstances people are alert to the size of the data set they are considering. For example, Nisbett, Krantz, Jepson, and Kunda (1983) asked participants in one study to imagine that they had encountered a new bird, the "shreeble." The one shreeble observed so far was blue, and on this basis participants were asked how likely they thought it was that all shreebles were blue. These participants were also asked to imagine that they had encountered a new element, "floridium." Only one sample of floridium had been examined, and when heated, it burned with a blue flame. Given this evidence, the participants were asked how likely they thought it was that all floridium, when heated, burns with a blue flame. Finally, in still other trials, the same participants were told about a previously unknown tribe living on a Pacific island. One member of the tribe had been observed and was obese. With this information, the participants were asked how likely they thought it was that all members of this tribe were obese.

In each of these judgments, the research participants seemed to draw on their prior knowledge about how homogeneous these categories (heated elements, bird colors, and body sizes) are likely to be. As a result, for floridium, participants were quite willing to believe that a single instance allows generalization to the whole set, and so they asserted that all floridium would burn blue when heated. Participants were less willing to extrapolate from a single case when thinking about shreebles, and even less willing when thinking about obese islanders. For these categories, the participants were willing to draw conclusions only after they were told about several observations (several shreebles or several tribespeople) in addition to the initial case.

Clearly, therefore, people sometimes *are* sensitive to sample size, and so, apparently, they do not always use the representativeness heuristic. People could, in principle, have made their judgment about shreebles by relying on a "man who" argument (or, more precisely, "bird who"): "I know a shreeble that is blue; therefore all shreebles. . . ." But instead, people sensibly realize that shreebles may vary, and so they draw no conclusion until they have more evidence. Obviously, then, use of the heuristic is not inevitable.

Dual-Process Models

How should we think about all of this? It's certain that people do often rely on heuristics and, as a result, fall into errors—ignoring base rates, misjudging covariation, being overly influenced by what's easily available, or drawing conclusions from a tiny sample of evidence. Therefore, our theories about thinking must include a discussion of the heuristics. But, in contrast, people in many circumstances do not make the errors associated with the heuristics. Plainly, therefore, people have some means of going beyond the heuristics, and this, too, must be represented in our theories.

These considerations have led many theorists to propose **dual-process models** of thinking—models that assert people have two distinct ways of thinking about the evidence they encounter (e.g., Evans, 2003, 2006; Ferreira, Garcia-Marques, Sherman & Sherman, 2006; Kahneman, 2003; Pretz, 2008; Shafir & LeBoeuf, 2002; for thoughtful reviews, though, including some concerns about dual-process models, see De Neys, Vartanian, & Goel, 2008; Evans, 2008; Keysers et al., 2008; Kruglanski &

Orehek, 2007; Osman, 2004; for a discussion of dual-process models in *children*, see Osman & Stavy, 2006).

The various models differ in many specifics, but all propose that people have one way of thinking that is fast, effortless, and automatic; the heuristics we have described all fall into this category. The models then propose that people have another way of thinking that is slower, effortful, and applied only with deliberate intention. This is the sort of thinking that allows people to rise above the heuristics and to reach decisions that are more laborious, but also more likely to be correct.

Different names have been proposed for the two systems. In their early writings, Kahneman and Tversky distinguished between *intuition* and *reasoning* (Kahneman, 2003); others have distinguished *association-driven thought* from *rule-driven thought* (e.g., Sloman, 1996). We will rely, though, on the more neutral terms suggested by Stanovich and West (2000), and therefore we will use **System 1** as the label for the fast and automatic sort of thinking, and **System 2** as the label for the slower, more effortful thinking.

In these terms, then, the proposal is that in a wide range of situations people rely on System 1 thinking. This is a good thing, because System 1 is fast, easy, and often leads to the correct answer. However, System 1's strategies are not perfect and will in many settings lead to mistakes; this is, in essence, the price one pays for being quick and efficient. Fortunately, though, System 2 thinking, although more cumbersome, can often catch (and overrule) System 1's errors.

The Importance of Circumstances

In any specific judgment, what determines whether we use System 1 or System 2? Why is it that we sometimes rely on the shortcuts and sometimes shift into more-cautious strategies? One proposal is that people can *choose* when to rely on System 1 and when to rely on System 2. Presumably, people would elect to use the more efficient System 1 when making judgments that weren't particularly important but would shift to the less efficient, more accurate System 2 whenever a judgment really mattered.

However, we have already seen indications that this proposal is incorrect. As we have discussed, people rely on the fast-and-loose heuristics even when incentives are offered for accuracy, even when making important professional judgments, even when making medical diagnoses that may, in some cases, literally be matters of life and death. Surely people would choose to use System 2 in all these cases if they could, and yet they still rely on the heuristics and still fall into error. On these grounds, it is difficult to argue that using System 2 is a matter of deliberate choice.

Instead, the evidence suggests that System 2 comes into play only if appropriately triggered by certain cues in the problem and only if the circumstances are right. In addition, evidence suggests that System 2 can become more responsive as a result of training. After the training, System 2 appears to be "primed," so that it is more easily triggered by situational cues.

What are the circumstances that matter for System 2's operation? We've already suggested that System 2 judgments are slower than System 1's, and on this basis, it's not surprising that heuristic-based judgments (and so heuristic-based *errors*) are more likely when judgments are made under time pressure (Finucane, Alhakami, Slovic, & Johnson, 2000). We've also said that System 2 judgments require *effort*, and so this form of thinking is more likely if the person can focus attention on the judgment being made. Conversely, a reliance on heuristics and automatic interpretive habits is more likely if people are distracted or not fully alert (De Neys, 2006; Ferreira et al., 2006; D. T. Gilbert, 1989; for some complexity, though, in the role of distraction in governing heuristic use, see Chun & Kruglanski, 2006).

In addition, System 1 runs more or less "on autopilot," proceeding without much supervision or reflection. System 2, on the other hand, is more deliberate and serves often to override or inhibit these automatic tendencies. It's important, therefore, that some people are better than others at inhibiting their own mental habits when they want to. Specifically, we argued in Chapter 4 that someone's ability to control her own mental habits is linked to working-memory capacity (WMC), which in turn is linked to many standardized tests of mental ability—including the IQ test and SAT scores.

Putting these pieces together, we might expect that people with high IQs or high SATs would be more successful in using System 2 to overrule the automatic (habit-based) conclusions of System 1. Many studies confirm this prediction. For example, people with higher SATs are more likely to consider base rates, less likely to be influenced by "man who" stories, and better able to judge covariation (Stanovich & West, 1998; also De Neys, 2006; Feldman Barrett, Tugade, & Engle, 2004). We emphasize that high-SAT individuals still commit these judgment errors, but even so, they are less likely to commit the errors than those with low SATs.

The Importance of Data Format

There are few surprises in the factors just mentioned. It is not astonishing, for example, that people make more errors when they are pressed for time or distracted, nor is it amazing that smart people make fewer errors than less-smart people. But these factors are far from the whole story. We know this because even smart, undistracted, unpressured people make the errors we've described, and, often, people who are distracted, pressured, or less smart still get things right! We therefore need to ask: What *else* is needed to elicit System 2 reasoning, allowing someone to avoid judgment errors?

The answer lies in the characteristics of the specific judgment that is being made. In effect, certain characteristics in a judgment seem to trigger System 2's operation. If these triggers are present, System 2 reasoning will be observed even with time pressure and distraction, and even with people who are not especially brilliant. But if the triggers are not present, then System 1 is likely to prevail.

For example, we earlier discussed the widespread neglect of base-rate information. Presumably, this is a result of System 1 thinking, with people relying on various heuristics in judging covariation and, in the process, not taking base rates into account. However, the error is avoided, and sensitivity to base rates is markedly increased, if the base rates are presented in the right way.

In many experiments, people have been presented with base rates cast in terms of probabilities or proportions: "There is a .01 chance that people like Mary will have this disease"; "Only 5% of the people in this group are Chinese scholars." But the same information can be conveyed in terms of counts, or *frequencies*, and it turns out that people are more likely to use the base rates if they are conveyed in this "frequency format." Thus, people are more alert to a base rate phrased as "10 out of every 1,000

Problem A

Suppose that you are at a concert in a nearby town. When the concert ends, you discover that there is snow and ice on the ground. Nonetheless, you decide to drive home.

On average, 50% of college students who drive home during such weather will be in a car accident.

What is your chance of being in a car accident that day? _____%

Problem B

Suppose that you are at a concert in a nearby town. When the concert ends, you discover that there is snow and ice on the ground. Nonetheless, you decide to drive home.

The chance of a college student being in a car accident during such weather is 55% for bad drivers and 45% for good drivers.

What is your chance of being in a car accident that day? _____%

Does the Base Rate Apply to Me?

In Problem A, most people choose to ignore the 50% base rate, but this is not because they believe base rates are irrelevant to the question. Instead, they seem to reason this way: "I'm a better-than-average driver, so the 50% estimate doesn't apply to me!" This sort of reasoning is less likely, though, in Problem B, and here people are often influenced by the base rates (Chandler, Greening, Robinson, & Stoppelbein, 1999). Apparently, even if people understand the importance of base rates, they still need to be convinced the base rates actually apply to them!

cases" than they are to the same information cast as a percentage ("1%"); they're likewise more accurate in using *diagnostic* information if it is cast as a frequency ("8 correct out of 10") than they are in using the same information cast as a probability or percentage ("80%" or ".8"; Gigerenzer & Hoffrage, 1995; also Brase, 2008; Brase, Cosmides, & Tooby, 1998; Cosmides & Tooby, 1996).

There is debate about *why* frequency information is advantageous. Some scholars have explained this in terms of the biology of the brain: Our ancient ancestors, they claim, often had occasion to think in terms of frequencies, and so natural selection favored those ancestors who were more skilled in thinking in these terms (e.g., Gigerenzer & Hoffrage, 1995). We are, of course, the descendants of these individuals, and so, as a result, we are now well adapted to thinking about frequencies, but not to thinking about proportions or probabilities.

Other researchers have offered different perspectives. As one alternative, a phrasing in terms of frequencies (X number *out of a larger group of* Y number) calls attention to the fact that we need to think about *groups* of observations and subsets within those groups; it may be this cue that improves judgment, rather than the actual frequencies themselves (Evans, Handley, Perham, Over, & Thompson, 2000; Fiedler, Brinkmann, Betsch, & Wild, 2000; Girotto & Gonzalez, 2001; Lewis & Keren, 1999; Mellers, Hertwig, & Kahneman, 2001; Mellers & McGraw, 1999).

Even with this controversy, there is no question that participants' performance in dealing with judgment problems is influenced by the data format and, in particular, is improved if the data are cast in terms of frequencies (although, we note, errors still occur, even with frequencies), and this helps us to understand why human judgment about evidence is sometimes so poor and sometimes accurate. It depends on how the problem is presented, with some presentations being more "user-friendly" than others.

Codable Data

As we have seen, people have a reasonable understanding of some fundamental statistical concepts. That was the point of our fictional dialogues earlier, between Bart and Lisa, and between Marge and Homer. The dialogues captured the fact that people readily understand that accidents do happen (and hence one must be wary of a single observation, which could, after all, be the result of a fluke). They also understand that accidents don't keep happening over and over (and so one should take seriously a larger sample of evidence in which an observation has been repeated many times).

If people understand these broad points, why don't they use this understanding more often? Why do they routinely fall prey to conclusions based only on a tiny set of observations (e.g., one prison guard, or a man-who story)? One reason is that people often just don't realize that their statistical concepts are *applicable* to a judgment they're trying to make. Often they don't realize that the evidence they're contemplating can be understood as a *sample of data* drawn from a larger set of potential observations. Likewise, they often don't see that *chance* played a role in shaping the evidence they're considering. As a result, they do not bring their (System 2) understanding to bear on the evidence, and instead they rely on (System 1) heuristics.

On this basis, we would expect people to rise above their simple heuristics if the role of chance is conspicuous in the evidence they're considering and if it's obvious how to interpret, or "code," the evidence in terms of a set of independent observations (Nisbett et al., 1983). The data confirm these claims. For example, manipulations that highlight the role of chance do increase the likelihood of someone reasoning in a statistically appropriate manner. In one study, participants were asked about someone who assessed a restaurant based on just one meal; the participants were more alert to considerations of sample size if the diner chose his entrée by blindly dropping a pencil onto the menu (presumably because they realized that a different sample, and perhaps different views of the restaurant, might have emerged if the pencil had fallen on a different selection). In another study, participants were asked about a high-school student who chose what college to go to based on her campus visit; they, too, were more alert to issues of sampling if told that the student chose which classes to sit in on entirely at random (e.g., Baratgin & Noveck, 2000; Gigerenzer, 1991; Gigerenzer, Hell, and Blank, 1988; Nisbett et al., 1983; A. Tversky & Kahneman, 1982).

Likewise, people are more accurate in their judgments, less prone to heuristic use, and less prone to errors when confronting evidence that is easily understood in statistical terms. Specifically, when judging events that are readily interpreted in terms of single, repeatable observations, people are better at judging covariation, more likely to be sensitive to the size of the sample of evidence, and so on (Holland, Holyoak, Nisbett, & Thagard, 1986; Kunda & Nisbett, 1986).

For example, consider the broad domain of *sports*. Here it's usually obvious that the information we receive can be understood in statistical terms. It's clear that a team's performance in the game's first quarter is just a sample of evidence and may or may not reflect its performance in other samples (other quarters or other games). It's also clear how to measure performance (points or other sports statistics). For these reasons, the evidence is already "packaged" in a way that leads us to think in statistically sophisticated terms, and so it's no surprise that sports evidence, as well as other easily coded evidence, usually evokes System 2 thinking (Jepson, Krantz, & Nisbett, 1983).

In contrast, other evidence is less easily coded in these terms. If an employer interviews a job candidate, the employer may or may not realize that the 10 minutes of interview can be thought of as just a "sample" of evidence, and that other impressions might come from other samples (e.g., re-interviewing the person on a different day or seeing the person in another setting). It's also not clear how to quantify the employer's impressions during the interview—how to measure how responsible the candidate seemed, or how motivated, or how clever. In the eyes of most people, evidence like this doesn't lend itself to statistical treatment, and, in fact, this sort of evidence tends not to evoke System 2 thinking. Instead, the employer is likely to rely on simple heuristics in thinking about the job candidate—and to make less justifiable decisions in the process.

Background Knowledge

Sometimes a problem will evoke better reasoning, not because of cues explicit in the problem but because of knowledge that the person brings to the problem and, with that, beliefs that the person has about how the parts of the problem are related. We have already seen an example of this—in the study involving floridium, shreebles, and obese islanders (Nisbett et al., 1983). Participants came into this study with the knowledge that one sample of a chemical element is likely to resemble all other samples of that element, and so they were willing to extrapolate from just a single observation about the (fictional) element floridium. But the participants also knew that birds of a single species can vary in color (think of how the pattern of coloration varies from one parrot to the next) and that humans within a group can surely vary in height and weight. It was because of this background knowledge that participants hesitated to draw conclusions based on a single bird or a single tribesperson.

A different example involves base rates. Imagine that research participants are asked to predict whether a particular student will pass an exam or not, and they are given some diagnostic information plus the base-rate information that in the past only 30% of the students who have taken this exam passed (Ajzen, 1977; also A. Tversky & Kahneman, 1982). In this case, the participants will draw on their broad understanding of exams and passing rates, and probably they will conclude that the exam must be relatively difficult. In other words, they are likely to perceive a cause-and-effect relationship between the base rate and the case they're trying to judge ("30% pass rate" implies "hard exam," which will cause difficulties for anyone taking the exam). As a result, they're likely to use the base rate in making their judgment.

However, base rates are usually ignored when participants don't see any cause-and-effect relationship between the base rate and the case they are interested in. As an illustration, imagine, once again, that participants are asked to predict whether a particular student will pass an exam, and, as before, they are given a base rate to use. This time, though, the base rate is presented differently: Participants are told that the student they are judging was drawn from a sample of students selected by a researcher, and in this sample, it turns out, only 30% of the students are likely to pass. In this set-up, the base rate is the same as it was before (a 30% pass rate), but the rate seems arbitrary; it might have been different if the researcher had chosen a different group of students. Statistically this makes no difference, and the base rate is as useful in this situation as it was in the first setting we considered. But with no causal link perceived, the base rate is neglected. (Also see Krynski & Tenenbaum, 2007; Oppenheimer, 2004; Winkielman & Schwarz, 2001.)

In this and other experiments, then, people are likely to consider factors (like base rates, or sample size, or sample bias) that they think played a cause-and-effect role in shaping the particular case they are considering. In this way, System 2's influence depends on what people happen to believe about the "causal history" of the evidence being considered—that is, how that evidence came to be as it is. This, in turn, depends on the background knowledge people bring into the situation, background knowledge about what causes what in the world.

Training Participants to Use Statistics

Let's pause to take stock. It is remarkably easy to find evidence for heuristic use, even when people are making highly consequential judgments. But people are also capable of more-sophisticated judgment strategies, strategies that in many cases can correct the errors sometimes produced by heuristic use. This demands that we ask *when* people use these System 2 strategies to correct the heuristics, and so far our answer to this question has two parts. One group of factors depends on the broad context (the presence or absence of time pressure or distraction, how capable the person is of inhibiting her own mental habits). A second group of factors depends on the particular attributes of a particular judgment (the format of the data, whether the evidence is easily coded, whether the person has beliefs that would call up statistical concepts in interpreting the evidence, etc.).

But there are still other factors that also influence System 2's use. For example, there are some indications that people will shift into System 2 thinking if they notice that their System 1 thinking was especially slow, or clumsy, on that occasion (Alter, Oppenheimer, Epley, & Eyre, 2007). In addition—and quite optimistically—the use of System 2 can also be influenced by *training*. That is, with appropriate education it becomes easier to trigger the use of System 2 and thus to diminish the problems associated with System 1.

Fong, Krantz, and Nisbett (1986) provided research participants with just a half-hour of training, focusing on the importance of sample size. The participants were reminded that accidents do happen, but that accidents don't keep happening over and over. Therefore, a small sample of data might be the result of some accident, but a large sample probably isn't. Consequently, large samples are more reliable, more trustworthy, than small samples.

This brief bit of training was remarkably effective: Once they were trained, the participants were appreciably more likely to apply considerations of sample size to novel cases. Moreover, their application of this knowledge tended to be reasonable and appropriate. (Also see Fong & Nisbett, 1991.)

Similarly, Fong et al. conducted a telephone survey of "opinions about sports," calling students who were taking an undergraduate course in statistics. Half of the students were contacted during the first week of the semester; half were contacted during the last week. Note, though, that there was no indication to the students that the telephone interview was connected to their course; as far as the students knew, they had been selected entirely at random.

In the phone interview, one of the questions involved a comparison between how well a baseball player did in his first year and how well he did in the remainder of his career. This is, in effect, a question about sample size (with the first-year being just a sample of the player's overall performance). Did the students realize that sample size was relevant here? For those contacted early in the term, only 16% gave answers that showed any consideration of sample size. For those contacted later, the number of answers influenced by sample size more than doubled (to 37%). The quality of the answers also increased, with students being more likely to articulate the relevant principles correctly at the end of the semester than at the beginning.

It seems, then, that students' reasoning about evidence can be improved, and the improvement applies to problems in new domains and in new contexts. Training in statistics, it appears, can have widespread benefits. (For more on education effects, see Ferreira et al., 2006; Gigerenzer, Gaissmaier, Kurz-Milcke, Schwartz, & Woloshin, 2008; Lehman & Nisbett, 1990; Schunn & Anderson, 1999.)

Thinking About Evidence: Some Conclusions

How, then, should we think about the results described throughout this chapter? As we have seen, it is easy to document judgment errors in bright, motivated undergraduates or in highly trained professionals. But we have also seen evidence of more-sophisticated judgment—and so cases in which people are sensitive to sample size and sample bias, cases in which people judge covariation accurately and do consider base rates.

It's this pattern that demands a dual-process model, distinguishing between System 1 thinking and System 2 thinking. People surely don't want to use System 2 all the time; that would be too slow, too effortful, too inefficient. But they probably do want to use System 2 when the stakes are high and a judgment really matters. It's therefore troubling that System 2's use is not a matter of choice, and so, even when we're motivated to use System 2 (e.g., because the judgment is an important one), we often use System 1 nonetheless. System 2 seems to enter the scene only when circumstances allow it and only when this system is appropriately triggered.

It's therefore encouraging that we can identify various steps that *promote* System 2's use. We can, for example, change features of the environment (e.g., recasting numbers as frequencies rather than proportions), so that we seek what one paper calls "environments that make us smart" (Todd & Gigerenzer, 2007). It's also important that *training* seems to improve judgment and seems to make judgment errors less likely. The training presumably helps by making our understanding of statistical principles more prominent in memory and, therefore, easier to trigger. The training also helps us to see how our statistical intuitions apply to a range of new cases. Thus, with training, one realizes that an interview can be thought of as a small sample of data and perhaps should be trusted less than some other source of information based on a larger sample of evidence. Likewise, one can think of an athlete's rookie year in these terms, or a dancer's audition. Once the situation is coded in this fashion, the application of statistical rules is more straightforward and more likely.

We close this chapter, then, on an optimistic note. Errors in judgment are ubiquitous and often consequential. But these errors are not the result of some deep flaw in our capacity for making judgments. Instead, the errors arise largely because the situation does not trigger our (System 2) abilities for making sensible, defensible judgments. And, crucially, education can improve this state of affairs, allowing us to use better judgment in a wide range of settings. Indeed, with suitable training, it may be possible to use judgment strategies that are both accurate and efficient.

Put differently, it seems that judgment—as one might have expected—is a *skill*, a skill that we all have to some extent, and a skill that can be improved by the appropriate type of education. Errors in drawing conclusions and in making inferences are remarkably widespread, but the path is open to reducing these errors and to improving the quality of human judgment.

Chapter Summary

- Induction often relies on attribute substitution, so that (for example) people estimate frequency by relying on availability, and so they judge an observation to be frequent if they can easily think of many examples of that observation. The more available an observation is, the greater the frequency is judged to be.

- Judgments based on the availability heueristic are often accurate, but they do risk error. This is because many factors influence availability, including the pattern of what is easily retrievable from memory, bias in what we notice in our experiences, and also bias in what the media report. Even if people detect these biases, they often fail to adjust for them, because of anchoring.

- People also rely on the representativeness heuristic when they extrapolate from observations they have made. This heuristic rests on the assumption that categories are relatively homogeneous, so that any case drawn from the category will be representative of the entire group. Because of this assumption, people expect a relatively small sample of evidence to have all the properties that are associated with the entire category; one example of this is the gambler's fallacy. Similarly, people seem insensitive to the importance of sample size, and so they believe that a small sample of observations is just as informative as a large sample. In the extreme, people are willing to draw conclusions from just a single observation, as in "man who" arguments.

- People are also likely to make errors in judging covariation. In particular, their beliefs and expectations sometimes lead them to perceive illusory covariations. These errors have been demonstrated not just in novices working with unfamiliar materials but also in experts dealing with the sorts of highly familiar materials they encounter in their professional work.

- People are accurate in assessing covariation if they have no prior beliefs or expectations about the data. This suggests that people do understand the concept of covariation and understand (roughly) how to assess covariation. When people have prior beliefs, though, their judgments of covariation are sometimes extreme and often erratic. This may be attributable to the fact that confirmation bias causes people to notice and remember a biased sample of the evidence, which leads to bad covariation judgments.

- People also seem insensitive to base rates, and again, this can be demonstrated both in novices evaluating unfamiliar materials and in experts making judgments in their professional domains.

- Use of heuristics is widespread, and so are the corresponding errors. However, we can also find cases in which people rely on more-sophisticated judgment strategies, and so are alert to sample size and sample bias, and do consider base rates. This has led many theorists to propose dual-process models of thinking. One process (often called System 1) relies on fast, effortless short-cuts; another process (System 2) is slower and more effortful, but less likely to lead to error.

- System 1 thinking is more likely when people are pressed for time or distracted. System 1 thinking also seems more likely in people with lower working-memory capacity. However, System 1 thinking can be observed even in high-intelligence individuals and even in the absence of time pressure or distraction. System 1 thinking can be observed even when the matter being judged is both familiar and highly consequential.

- System 2 thinking seems more likely when the data are described in terms of frequencies rather than probabilities and also when the data are easily coded in statistical terms (as a *sample* of data, with *chance* playing a role in shaping the sample). System 2 thinking is also more likely if people bring to a situation background knowledge that helps them to code the data and to understand the cause-and-effect role of sample bias or base rates. Training in statistics also makes System 2 thinking more likely, leading us to the optimistic view that judging is a *skill* that can be improved through suitable education.

The Workbook Connection

See the *Cognition Workbook* for further exploration of judgment:
- Demonstration 12.1: Sample Size
- Demonstration 12.2: Relying on the Representative Heuristic
- Demonstration 12.3: Applying Base Rates
- Research Methods: Systematic Data Collection
- Cognitive Psychology and Education: Making People Smarter
- Cognitive Psychology and the Law: Juries' Judgment

CHAPTER 13

Reasoning: Thinking Through the Implications of What You Know

In Chapter 12, we discussed how people make judgments about evidence, and in most cases the judgments involved some element of uncertainty. Often, though, we try to draw conclusions from claims that seem solidly established. Perhaps you're already convinced, for example, that red wine gives you headaches, or that relationships based only on physical attraction rarely last. You might then want to ask: What follows from this? What implications do these claims have for your other beliefs or actions? These questions rely on **deduction**—a process through which we start with claims or assertions that we count as "given" and ask what follows from these premises.

Among its other roles, deduction allows us to make predictions about upcoming events, and this is obviously useful as we move through our daily lives. In addition, the same predictions can help keep our beliefs in touch with reality. After all, if deduction leads us to a prediction based on our beliefs, and the prediction turns out to be *wrong*, this tells us that something is off track in our beliefs—and that things we thought to be solidly established aren't so solid after all.

Does our reasoning respect this principle? If we encounter evidence confirming our beliefs, does this strengthen our convictions? If evidence challenging our beliefs should come our way, do we adjust? And what if we realize, from the start, that we are uncertain about a belief? What evidence do we seek to verify or disprove our view? Our discussion of reasoning will begin with these crucial questions.

- People often show a pattern of "confirmation bias," so that (for example) they take confirming evidence at face value but scrutinize disconfirming evidence with care, seeking flaws or ambiguity.

- Errors in logical reasoning are easy to document, and they follow patterns suggesting that people are guided by principles other than those of logic.

- People's reasoning is also heavily influenced by the *content* of what they're reasoning about, although the exact reasons for this remain uncertain.

- Overall, it appears that our theory of reasoning (like our theory of judgment) must contain multiple elements: People sometimes use logic; they sometimes rely on content-specific reasoning strategies and sometimes

on shortcuts. They sometimes also rely on mental models.

- People seem not to base most decisions on utility calculations. Instead, they try to make decisions that they feel they can explain and justify. This is why people are so sensitive to the framing of a decision, and also why decision-making is influenced by the same factors that, as we have seen, influence judgment and reasoning in general.

- We can easily document patterns in decision-making that seem to be errors—including self-contradictions and cases in which people fail to predict their own values. The chapter closes, therefore, with a consideration of whether or not people make decisions in the "right way."

Confirmation and Disconfirmation

Each of us regards many of our beliefs as solidly established, and not subject to question or refutation. We are certain that water is wet, that winters can be cold, and that chocolate is delicious. But we're far less certain about some of our other beliefs: We think that Sam would be a good secretary, but we're not sure. We believe that Sue and Harry would get along well at a dinner party, but we might be mistaken.

How should we proceed in these cases in which we're uncertain? How should we go about testing one of our beliefs? What evidence might strengthen the belief? What would undermine it? These *normative* questions—about how one ought to reason—have been discussed at length by philosophers, and one point emerging from their discussion concerns the ambiguity of *confirming* evidence and, with that, the great value of *disconfirming* evidence. To see this, imagine a rooster who believes that his crowing each morning brings the sun into the sky. The rooster might, in fact, be quite confident in this belief, because there is a large amount of confirming evidence: Day after day he has crowed, and each time the sun has risen just as expected. But, of course, we know that the rooster is wrong—his vocalizations are irrelevant for the sun's rising. Apparently, then, a belief can be many-times-confirmed and still be false, and this tells us immediately that confirmation is of uncertain value.

*Dis*confirmations, however, can be enormously informative. Imagine, for example, that the rooster decided to do the obvious experiment, and so he let one morning pass without crowing. His belief would lead him to expect that the sun would not come up that day, and so, when it did rise, this would disconfirm the rooster's expectations—and would provide information of considerable value for the rooster.

Confirmation Bias

It seems, then, that in order to evaluate a belief, it's often useful to seek out both evidence that *supports* the belief and also evidence that might *challenge* the belief. Likewise, consideration of alternative hypotheses is often helpful: In asking, "Is there another way to explain the facts?" you will sometimes discover that the evidence is open to multiple interpretations—and so provides weaker support for your belief than you initially thought.

However, despite the usefulness of disconfirmation and the utility of considering alternatives, people generally do neither. Instead, people display a pattern known as **confirmation bias**—a strong tendency to seek out confirming evidence and to rely on that evidence in drawing their conclusions. This bias emerges in numerous forms. First, when people are assessing a belief or a hypothesis, they are far more likely to seek evidence that confirms the belief than evidence that might disconfirm it. Second, when disconfirming evidence is made available to them, people often fail to use it in adjusting their beliefs. Third, when people encounter confirming evidence, they take it at face value; when they encounter disconfirming evidence, in contrast, they reinterpret the evidence to diminish its impact. Finally, people regularly fail to consider alternative hypotheses that might explain the available data just as well as their current hypothesis does. (For reviews, see Evans, 1982; Gilovich, 1991; Higgins & Bargh, 1987; Rothbart, Evans, & Fulero, 1979; Schulz-Hardt, Frey, Lüthgens, & Moscovici, 2000; Stangor & McMillan, 1992; Tweney, Doherty, & Mynatt, 1981.)

In a classic demonstration of confirmation bias, Wason (1966, 1968) presented research participants with a series of numbers, such as "2, 4, 6." The participants were told that this trio of numbers conformed to a specific rule, and their task was to figure out what the rule was. Participants were allowed to propose their own trios of numbers ("Does '8, 10, 12' follow the rule?"), and in each case the experimenter responded appropriately ("Yes, it does follow the rule" or "No, it doesn't"). Then, once participants were satisfied they had discovered the rule, they announced their "discovery."

Equal Rights are NOT SPECIAL RIGHTS

Confirmation Bias

Confirmation bias shows up in many settings. For example, bumper stickers on "our side" of an issue often seem witty, pithy, and compelling. Bumper stickers on "their side" of the same issue often seem childish, misleading, and even offensive.

The rule was, in fact, quite simple: The three numbers had to be in ascending order. Thus, "1, 3, 5" follows the rule; so does "18, 19, 236." The trio "6, 4, 2" does not follow the rule, nor does "10, 10, 10." Despite this simplicity, participants had considerable difficulty in discovering the rule, often requiring many minutes. This was in part due to the kinds of information they requested as they sought to evaluate candidate rules: To an overwhelming extent, they sought to confirm the rules they had proposed; requests for disconfirmation were relatively rare. And, it's important to note, those few participants who *did* seek out disconfirmation for their hypotheses were more likely to discover the rule! It seems, then, that confirmation bias was strongly on the scene in this experiment, and it interfered with performance. (For related data, see Mahoney & DeMonbreun, 1978; Mitroff, 1981; Mynatt, Doherty, & Tweney, 1977, 1978.)

Memory for Disconfirming Evidence

When people encounter evidence that fits with their views, they tend to accept it at face value. When people encounter disconfirming evidence, in contrast, they are often quite skeptical about it—and so they scrutinize these new observations with special care, seeking flaws or ambiguities. If possible, they find ways to reinterpret the evidence so that it doesn't challenge their beliefs. Ironically, this mental activity sometimes makes people more likely to remember disconfirming evidence than they are to remember confirming evidence (which received much less scrutiny). However, the disconfirming evidence is remembered in a fashion that robs this evidence of its force, and so it leaves the person's beliefs intact.

As an illustration, one study examined people who had placed bets on professional football games (Gilovich, 1983; also Gilovich & Douglas, 1986). The gamblers all believed that they had good strategies for picking winning teams, and their faith in these strategies was undiminished by a series of losses. Why is this? It is because the gamblers didn't remember their losses as "losses." Instead, they remembered them as mere flukes or oddball coincidences: "I was right. New York was going to win, if it hadn't been for that crazy injury to their running back"; "I was correct in picking St. Louis. They would have won except for that goofy bounce the ball took after the kickoff." In this way, winning bets were remembered as wins, but losing bets were remembered as "near wins" (Gilovich, 1991). No wonder, then, that the gamblers maintained their views despite the (seemingly) contrary evidence provided by their own empty wallets.

Belief Perseverance

Even when disconfirming evidence is undeniable and out in plain view, people sometimes do not use it, illustrating a phenomenon called **belief perseverance**. For example, participants in one study were asked to read a series of suicide notes; their task was to figure out which notes were authentic, collected by the police, and which were fake, written by other students as an exercise. As participants offered their judgments, they were provided with feedback about how well they were doing—that is, how accurate they were in detecting the authentic notes. The trick, though, was that the feedback was predetermined and had nothing to do with the participants' actual judgments. Some participants were told that they were well above average in this task (again, independent of their judgments); other participants were told the opposite—that they were much below average (L. Ross, Lepper, & Hubbard, 1975; also L. Ross & Anderson, 1982).

Later on, participants were debriefed. They were told that the feedback they had received was utterly bogus and had nothing to do with their performance. Indeed, they were shown the experimenter's instruction sheet, which had assigned them in advance to the *success* or *failure* group. They were then asked a variety of additional questions, including questions for which they had to assess their own "social sensitivity." Specifically, they were asked to rate their actual ability, as they perceived it, in tasks like the suicide-note task.

Let's emphasize that participants were making these judgments about themselves after they had been told the truth about the feedback. That is, they had been told clearly and explicitly that the feedback was randomly determined and had no credibility whatsoever. Nonetheless, participants were plainly influenced by the feedback: Those who had received the "above average" feedback continued to think of their social sensitivity as being above average, and likewise their ability to judge suicide notes. Those who had received the "below average" feedback showed the opposite pattern. The participants, in other words, persevered in their beliefs even when the basis for the belief had been completely discredited.

How does all of this connect to confirmation bias? Imagine yourself in the place of one of the participants, and let's say that we have told you that you are particularly bad at the suicide-note task. As you digest this new "information" about yourself, you'll probably ask yourself, "Could this be true? Am I perhaps less sensitive than I think I am?" To check on this possibility, you might search through your memory, looking for evidence that will help you evaluate this suggestion.

What sort of evidence will you seek? This is where confirmation bias comes into play. Because of this bias, chances are good that you will check on the researcher's information by seeking other facts or other prior episodes in your memory that might confirm your lack of social perception. As a result, you will soon have two sources of evidence for your social insensitivity: the (bogus) feedback provided by the researcher, and the supporting information you came up with yourself, thanks to your (selective) memory search. Thus, even if the researcher discredits the information he provided, you will still have the information you provided, and on this basis you might maintain your belief. (For discussion, see Nisbett & Ross, 1980; also H. Johnson & Seifert, 1994.)

Of course, in this experiment, participants could be led either to an enhanced estimate of their own social sensitivity or to a diminished estimate, depending on which false information they were given in the first place. Presumably, this is because the range of episodes in participants' memories is rather wide: In some previous episodes they have been sensitive, and in some they haven't been. Therefore, if they search through their memories seeking to confirm the hypothesis that they have been sensitive in the past, they will find confirming evidence. If they search through memory seeking to confirm the opposite hypothesis, this too will be possible. In short, they can confirm either hypothesis via a suitably selective memory search. This obviously highlights the dangers built into a selective search of the evidence and, more broadly, the danger associated with confirmation bias.

Let's also note another important implication of these results. In many studies, an investigator needs to mislead the participants in one way or another—usually to hide the experimental hypothesis or to minimize any effects of experimental demand. Then, at the end of the procedure, the investigator debriefs the participants, telling them the whole truth about the study and, in this fashion, trying to "un-do" any effects of the deception. As we've just seen, though, this debriefing may not always be effective—and so any investigator relying on deception needs to think through ways to make sure the debriefing does what it's supposed to do!

Logic

Why are people so vulnerable to confirmation bias? Is it possible that people just aren't logical in their thinking? We can find out by directly examining how well people do if we explicitly invite them to think things through in a logical manner. That will allow us to ask, in a straightforward way, whether thought tends to be logical or not.

Reasoning About Syllogisms

A number of theorists have proposed that thought does follow the rules of logic (Boole, 1854; Henle, 1962, 1978; Mill, 1874; Piaget, 1952). If we make reasoning errors, therefore, it is not because of some flaw in our thinking. Instead, the errors must come from other sources—carelessness, perhaps, or a misreading of the problem.

It turns out, however, that errors in logical reasoning are ubiquitous. If we are careless or misread problems, we do so with great frequency. This is evident, for example, in studies employing **categorical syllogisms**—a type of logical argument that begins with two assertions (the problem's **premises**) each containing a statement about a category, as shown in Figure 13.1. The syllogism can then be completed with the conclusion that follows from these premises. The cases shown in the figure are all valid syllogisms (i.e., **valid arguments**); that is, the conclusion does follow from the premises stated. In contrast, here is an example of an **invalid** syllogism:

All P are M.
All S are M.
Therefore, all S are P.

```
All M are B.
All D are M.
    Therefore, all D are B.

All X are Y.
Some A are X.
    Therefore, some A are Y.

Some A are not B.
All A are G.
    Therefore, some G are not B.
```

FIGURE 13.1 Examples of Categorical Syllogisms
All of the syllogisms shown here are valid; that is, if the two premises are true, then the conclusion must be true.

To see that this is invalid, try translating it into concrete terms, such as "All plumbers are mortal" and "All sadists are mortal." Both of these are surely true, but it doesn't follow from this that "All sadists are plumbers."

Research participants who are asked to reason about syllogisms do remarkably poorly. Chapman and Chapman (1959) gave their participants a number of syllogisms, including the one just discussed, with premises of "All P are M," and "All S are M." The vast majority of participants, 81%, endorsed the invalid conclusion "All S are P." Another 10% endorsed other invalid conclusions; only 9% got this problem right. Other studies, with other problems, yield similar data—with error rates regularly as high as 70% to 90%. (Gilhooly, 1988, provides a review.) Participants' performance is somewhat better when the syllogisms are spelled out in concrete terms, but here, too, performance remains relatively low (for the classic data, see Wilkins, 1928).

Sources of Logical Errors

Overall, then, errors in logical reasoning are extremely common. Moreover, the errors don't look at all like the product of carelessness. Instead, the errors tend to fall into a few simple categories. For example, people often show a pattern dubbed **belief bias**: If a syllogism's conclusion happens to be something people believe to be true anyhow, they are more likely to judge the conclusion as following logically from the premises. Conversely, if the conclusion happens to be something they believe to be false, they are likely to reject the conclusion as invalid (Evans, Over, & Manktelow, 1993; Klauer, Musch, & Naumer, 2000; Newstead, Pollard, Evans, & Allen, 1992; Oakhill & Garnham, 1993).

On first inspection, the pattern of belief bias seems entirely sensible: In displaying this

bias, participants are endorsing claims they believe to be true, based on the totality of their knowledge, and rejecting claims they believe to be false. This seems a reasonable thing to do (Evans & Feeney, 2004), but it is not what these logic problems require. Logic is instead concerned with more "local" issues of reasoning—specifically, whether a particular conclusion is warranted by a particular set of premises. Thus, when people show the belief-bias pattern, they are failing to distinguish between good arguments (those that are logical and persuasive) and bad ones: They are willing to endorse a bad argument if it happens to lead to conclusions they already believe to be true, and they are willing to reject a good argument if it leads to conclusions already believed to be false.

Other logical errors seem to be the result of people relying on a low-level "matching strategy" —a strategy of endorsing conclusions if the words "match" those in the premise. Thus, if a participant sees a premise such as "All A are B" and then another premise such as "All D are B," the participant is likely to accept a conclusion like "All A are D," because this conclusion "matches" the wording and structure of the premises. Likewise, a participant who sees premises like "Some A are not X" and "Some B are not X" is likely to accept a conclusion like "Some A are not B"—again, because of the "match" in wording and structure (Gilhooly, Logie, Wetherick, & Wynn, 1993; Johnson-Laird, 1983; Wetherick, 1989; an earlier version of this idea, dubbed the "atmosphere hypothesis," was proposed by Woodworth & Sells, 1935). But, of course, this "matching strategy" is illogical, and it will lead to errors like the one (already discussed) in the "plumbers and sadists" example.

It appears, then, that people's reasoning is guided by certain principles, but the principles are not the rules of logic! Put differently, it appears that scholars have simply been mistaken when they have argued that systems of formal logic describe the actual rules of thought.

Reasoning About Conditional Statements

Similar conclusions derive from research on a different aspect of logic—namely, reasoning about **conditional statements**. These are statements of the familiar "If X, then Y" format, with the first statement providing a *condition* under which the second statement is guaranteed to be true.

The rules of logic specify how one should reason about conditional statements. For example, one logical rule, called *modus ponens*, justifies conclusions in this case:

> If P is true, then Q is true.
>
> P is true.
>
> Therefore, Q must be true.

People generally reason well with problems resting on *modus ponens*, such as "If Luke waves at me, I'll be happy. Luke did wave at me. What follows from this?" People have some difficulty, though, with the logical rule called *modus tollens*, which justifies the conclusion in this case:

> If P is true, then Q is true.
>
> Q is false.
>
> Therefore, P must be false.

In very simple cases, people do understand this rule: "If Luke waves at me, I'll be happy. I'm not happy. Therefore, it must be the case that Luke didn't wave at me; if he had, I'd be happy." If we add any complexity at all, though, people are easily confused by problems resting on *modus tollens*, often rejecting conclusions if they are based on this rule (Braine & O'Brien, 1991; Rips, 1983, 1990; Taplin & Staudenmayer, 1973).

People also make other logical errors—including the error called **affirming the consequent** and the error called **denying the antecedent**. As a result of all this, performance tends to be rather poor when people are asked to reason about conditional statements. Indeed, some studies have documented error rates, when people try to draw conclusions about conditionals, as high as 80% or 90% (see Figure 13.2).

Just as with syllogisms, errors are more common if people are asked to reason about abstract problems ("If P, then Q") in comparison to performance with concrete problems ("If John plays baseball, then he is tense"). Errors are also more common if the logic problems involve negatives ("If John does not play baseball, then he won't be late"). Moreover, and again just like syllogisms, belief bias can be demonstrated: People will endorse a conclusion if they happen to believe it to be true, even if the conclusion doesn't follow from the stated premises. Conversely, people will reject a

Denying the Antecedent
The philosopher René Descartes famously argued, "I think, therefore I am." The fly's conclusion appears to follow from this—but in fact, this is the error known as "denying the antecedent."

Affirming the consequent
(1) If A is true, then B is true.
     B is true.
     Therefore, A is true.

Denying the antecedent
(2) If A is true, then B is true.
     A is not true.
     Therefore, B is not true.

Many people accept these arguments as valid, but they are not. To see this, consider some concrete cases:

(3) If the object in my hand is a frog, then the object is green.
     The object in my hand is green.
     Therefore, it is a frog.

(4) If the object in my hand is a frog, then the object is green.
     The object in my hand is not a frog.
     Therefore, it is not green.

Both of these arguments are invalid. The object could, for example, be a lime—green, but not a frog, contradicting argument 3. Likewise, a lime is not a frog, but it is nonetheless green, contradicting argument 4.

FIGURE 13.2 **Errors in Logic**
People commonly make the errors called "affirming the consequent" and "denying the antecedent." However, a moment's reflection, guided by a concrete case, makes it clear that reasoning in these patterns is, in fact, incorrect.

conclusion if they happen to believe it to be false, even if the conclusion is logically demanded by the premises. Across the board, though, reasoning about conditionals is quite poor (Evans, 1982; Evans, Newstead, & Byrne, 1993; Rips, 1990; Wason & Johnson-Laird, 1972).

The Four-Card Task

Psychologists have used many paradigms to study how people reason about "if-then" statements, but much of the research involves Wason's **four-card task** (sometimes called the **selection task**). In this task, research participants are shown four playing cards, as in Figure 13.3 (after Wason, 1966, 1968). The participants are told that each card has a number on one side and a letter on the other. Their task is to evaluate this rule: "If a card has a vowel on one side, it must have an even number on the other side." Which cards must be turned over to put this rule to the test?

Many people assert that the "A" card must be turned over to check for an even number. Others assert that the "6" card must be turned over to check for a vowel. Still

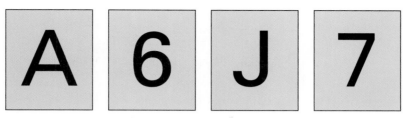

FIGURE 13.3 The Four-Card Task

Each card has a letter on one side and a number on the other side. Which cards must be turned over to check this rule: "If a card has a vowel on one side, it must have an even number on the other side"?

others assert that both of these must be turned over. In Wason's research, 46% of the participants turned over the "A" and the "6"; 33% turned over just the "A." The correct answer, however, was obtained by only 4% of the participants—turning over the "A" and the "7." In brief, then, performance is atrocious in this problem, with 96% of the participants giving wrong answers.

Why is "A and 7" the right answer? If we turn over the "A" card and find an even number, that's consistent with the rule. But if we turn it over and find an odd number, that's inconsistent. Therefore, by turning over the "A," we'll discover if this card is consistent with the rule or not. In other words, there's something to be learned by turning over this card. What about the "J"? The rule makes no claims about what is on the flip side of a consonant card, so no matter what we find on the other side, it satisfies the rule. Therefore, there's nothing to be learned by turning over this card; we already know (without flipping the card over) that it's consistent with the rule. How about the "6"? If we find a vowel on the reverse side of this card, this fits with the rule. If we find a consonant on the reverse, this also fits, since, again, the rule makes no claims about what is on the reverse of a consonant card. Therefore, we'll learn nothing by turning over the "6"; no matter what we find, it satisfies the rule. Finally, if we turn over the "7" and a consonant is on the other side, this fits with the rule. If there's a vowel on the other side, this doesn't fit. Therefore, we do want to turn over this card, because there is a chance that we might find something informative.

The Effects of Problem Content

It turns out, though, that performance is much better with some variations of the four-card task. For example, Griggs and Cox (1982) asked their participants to test this rule: "If a person is drinking beer, then the person must be over 19 years of age." As in the other studies, the participants were shown four cards and asked which cards they would need to turn over to test the rule (see Figure 13.4). In this version, participants did quite well: 73% (correctly) selected the card labeled "Drinking a beer" and also the card labeled "16 years of age." They did not select "Drinking a Coke" or "22 years of age." Griggs and Cox also tested their participants with the "standard" ver-

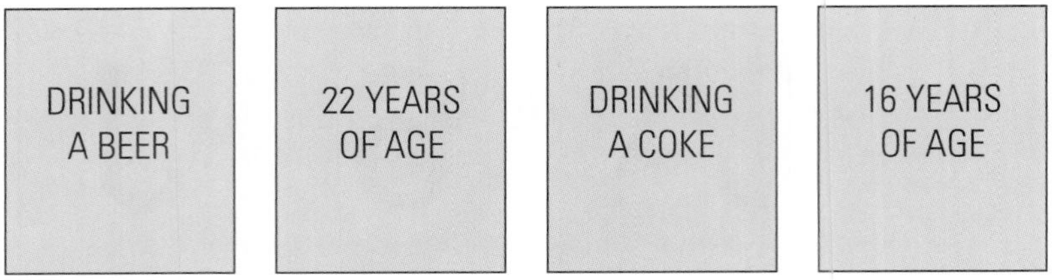

FIGURE 13.4 An Easier Version of the Four-Card Task
Participants do reasonably well with this version of the four-card task. Here each card has a person's age on one side, and what the person is drinking on the other side. The participants' task is to select the cards that one would have to turn over in order to test the following rule: "If a person is drinking beer, then the person must be over 19 years of age."

sion of the test (if vowel, then even number), and none of their participants got this problem right. (For discussion, see Cheng & Holyoak, 1985; Evans, 1982; Evans, Newstead & Byrne, 1993; Griggs, 1983; Johnson-Laird, Legrenzi, & Legrenzi, 1972; Legrenzi, Girotto & Johnson-Laird, 1993; Wason, 1983.)

These data are important for several reasons—including the fact that they provide another argument against the proposal that logic describes the rules of thought. Logic, after all, depends only on the form or syntax of the assertions being considered, and not at all on their content. (Indeed, this dependence on *form* is the basis of the term "formal logic.") Thus, in terms of logic, there's no difference between the problem shown in Figure 13.4 and the one shown in Figure 13.3—both have exactly the same form. Nonetheless, performance is markedly different with these two problems—and so, quite plainly, the content of these problems does matter. In other words, it seems that the way we think (and *how well* we think) depends on what we're thinking about—that is, it depends on the meaning and pragmatics of the material we're contemplating. But all of that simply demands the next question: *How* does the content influence us?

Detecting Cheaters

Investigators have offered a variety of proposals for why some versions of the four-card problem are difficult and others are easy, and the data do not allow a clear choice among these views. Indeed, in the end, we may need to seek some combination of these views in order to encompass the full data pattern.

One proposal comes from an evolutionary perspective on psychology, a perspective we first met in Chapter 12. According to this perspective, many questions in psychology are better understood if we think about how the relevant skills and processes have been shaped by evolutionary pressures over the last million years or so. To apply this perspective to the broad topic of reasoning, several investigators have argued this way: Our ancient ancestors didn't have to reason about whether or not all *A* are *B*, nor did they have to reason about vowels and even numbers. Instead, our ancestors had to worry about issues like social interactions, including issues of betrayal and cheating: "I asked you to do something. Have you done it, or have you betrayed me?"; "None of our clan is supposed to eat more than one share of meat; is Joe perhaps cheating and eating too much?"

If our ancestors needed to reason about these issues, then any individuals who were particularly skilled in this reasoning might have had a survival advantage, and so, little by little, those who were skillful would become more numerous, and those without the skill would die off. In the end, only those skillful at social reasoning would be left. And, of course, we are the biological heirs of these survivors, and so we inherited their skills.

According to this proposal, therefore, people in the modern world will reason well about a logical rule whenever they understand that rule as involving cheating, betrayal, or the like (Cosmides, 1989; Cummins, 2004; Cummins & Allen, 1998; Gigerenzer & Hug, 1992). In this case, the skills that people have (thanks to their biology) will be well matched to the reasoning problem, and this will lead to good performance.

This claim is certainly consistent with the data we have seen so far: The "over 19 and drinking beer" problem, for example, involves the detection of "cheaters" and yields good performance. Other results also confirm that good performance is observed with problems that can be understood as "detecting cheaters"—even if the problems involve unfamiliar situations or principles (Cosmides, 1989; Gigerenzer & Hug, 1992; but also see N. Liberman & Klar, 1996).

Pragmatic Reasoning Schemata

Other investigators offer different hypotheses about the four-card problem. Cheng and Holyoak (1985), for example, have proposed that thinking generally depends on pragmatic rules that people have learned from their day-to-day experience. Thus, for example, people learn from experience that certain rules apply to any situation that involves *permission*. These rules include "If one wishes to take a certain action, then one must have permission" and "If one has permission to take a certain action, then one may take the action." These rules are similar to the rules of logic, and so they can be used to guide reasoning. Let's emphasize, though, that these rules only support thinking about situations of the right sort—situations involving permission. In this way, these pragmatic reasoning rules are more concrete than the rules of logic.

People also have **pragmatic reasoning schemata** for other sorts of situations—situations involving *obligations* or situations involving *cause-and-effect* relationships. In these cases, too, the pragmatic reasoning rules, gained from experience, guide people in the sorts of reasoning they need to do in their everyday existence (Cheng & Holyoak, 1985; Cheng, Holyoak, Nisbett, & Oliver, 1986; Nisbett, 1993).

How does all of this apply to the four-card problem? The original version of this problem contained no practical or meaningful relations; the rule of "if a vowel, then an even number" is completely arbitrary. The problem is therefore unlikely to evoke a reasoning schema, and this leaves participants at a loss: With their primary reasoning strategy not called into play, it is no wonder that they do poorly on this task.

According to this view, we should be able to improve performance on the four-card task by altering the problem so that it will trigger a pragmatic reasoning schema. Then people will be able to employ their usual means of reasoning and should perform quite well. To this end, participants in one experiment were shown the cards illustrated in Figure 13.5. Their task was to decide which cards to turn over to test the rule, "If the form says 'ENTERING' on one side, then the other side includes cholera among the list of diseases."

For half of the participants, this problem was given with no further rationale. The prediction here is that no schema will be evoked and performance should be poor. The other participants, however, were given a rationale designed to trigger the permission schema. These participants were told that the cards listed diseases against which airline passengers had been inoculated. In addition, they were told that cholera inoculation was required of all passengers seeking to enter the country. These participants were then given the same rule as stated above, but now the rule can be understood in permission terms—something like, "If a passenger wishes to enter the country, he or she must first receive a cholera inoculation." With this rationale in view, the problem should trigger a schema, and participants should perform well.

The data were consistent with these predictions. Participants did well with the rationale versions of this problem, averaging about 90% correct. Without the rationale, they did poorly (about 60%). Thus, in this and in other experiments, people do seem to reason well if a reasoning schema is called into play, but otherwise they reason poorly.

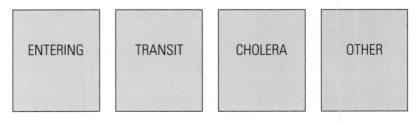

FIGURE 13.5 **The Role of a Rationale in the Four-Card Problem**
Participants were asked which cards they would need to turn over to find out if the following rule is true: "If the form says 'ENTERING' on one side, then the other side includes cholera among the list of diseases." Participants perform well on this problem if they are provided with a rationale; otherwise they perform poorly.

Yet another approach to the four-card data begins with the fact that "if-then" sentences are actually ambiguous (Ahn & Graham, 1999). For example, consider these two sentences:

> If Jacob passed his driver's test, then it's legal for him to drive.
> If Solomon is eligible for jury duty, then he is over 21.

The two sentences seem to have the same structure, but they're actually quite different. To see this, think about what you'd conclude in each case if you knew that the condition (the "if" part) was *false*. In the first sentence, the "if" part identifies a **necessary condition**—something that must be true for the rest of the sentence to be true. Therefore, "has passed" implies "is legal," and "has not passed" means "is not legal." In the second sentence, in contrast, the "if" part identifies a **sufficient condition**—something that, if true, guarantees the conclusion is true. As a result, "eligible" does imply "over 21," but "*not* eligible" does not mean "*not* over 21." After all, Solomon might not be a U.S. citizen, and so he couldn't serve on a jury—but that would tell us nothing about his age.

How does this connect to the four-card problem? Some versions of the problem (like the "drinking beer" version) invite an interpretation that involves *sufficiency*, and this triggers a pattern of reasoning that's similar to the way logicians define the "if-then" relationship. It's no wonder, then, that these problems lead to a high proportion of "correct" answers (answers in line with those endorsed by logicians). Other problems invite different interpretations, and so they trigger different patterns of reasoning. And still other problems (like the original "vowel and even number" version) are ambiguous with regard to interpretation, and so different participants interpret the problem in different ways, yielding a chaotic pattern of results. (For related proposals, see Almor & Sloman, 2000; Girotto, 2004; Oaksford & Chater, 1995; Polk & Newell, 1995; Sperber, Cara, & Girotto, 1995.)

Where, then, does all of this leave us? There is no question that some versions of the four-card problem produce miserable levels of performance, while other versions yield excellent performance. Is this because of a biologically rooted skill of thinking about "cheating," or a skill, gained from experience, of reasoning about pragmatically defined goals? Or is it a reflection of the way that the problem's content leads us to interpret the "if-then" relationship? It is difficult to say, largely because these conceptions overlap heavily in their predictions about which versions of the task will be easy and which will be hard. It is no surprise, therefore, that researchers have not been able to devise tests that favor one of these theoretical accounts over the others. In the meantime, though, one thing is clear: A purely formal account of our reasoning—one that emphasizes only the logical form of the problems we face, and not the content of those problems—does not mesh with the way humans reason.

Deductive Logic: An Interim Summary

Before pressing on, let's summarize where we are. We've been asking, in essence, how people reason: What rules do people rely on? What principles do people follow? The answer to these questions seems to have several parts. First, it's obvious that some people, in some circumstances, can use the rules of logic. Logic teachers, for example, can obviously use these rules. Even those untutored in logic can handle simple logic problems. Imagine, for example, that we tell people, "If G is true, then H is true. G happens to be true." With no difficulty, and even with this abstract, unfamiliar problem, people draw the conclusion (based on *modus ponens*) that H, too, must be true—fully in accordance with the rules laid out by logicians.

More commonly, people rely on less-formal reasoning strategies, although, as we have seen, there is debate over what the other strategies are. Perhaps these other strategies are reasoning skills specifically shaped by evolution, skills that we use whenever we are thinking about cheaters, betrayal, and so on. Perhaps, instead, the other strategies are pragmatic reasoning schemata, used whenever a problem can be understood in terms of pragmatic goals. Or perhaps the reasoning skills are more general but still dependent on the problem's content as an aid toward figuring out whether the situation involves necessary conditions, sufficient conditions, or both. In all cases, though, these other reasoning strategies are sophisticated enough so that they generally yield conclusions identical to those endorsed by logical rules.

But this isn't all. Our account of reasoning also needs a third layer, one describing the way people reason when these relatively sophisticated reasoning strategies are not triggered. For example, people seem to rely on the matching strategy if they don't know how else to proceed. Likewise, if people can't figure out a problem, they try to help themselves by "smuggling in" other knowledge external to the problem. In this case, they show the pattern that we earlier called "belief bias." This inclusion of other knowledge isn't warranted according to logic, but it may be someone's best bet if no other plan is available.

Putting all of this together, the suggestion is that the rules of logic, some sort of content-specific reasoning strategies, and various shortcuts may all coexist in our mental repertoire, and each will surface in appropriate circumstances. Some of these approaches to reasoning (like the matching strategy) are relatively primitive, but it seems that the more "sophisticated" strategies come into play only when appropriately triggered—by cues signaling that a problem involves permission, or by content specifying that the condition is a *sufficient* one, and so forth.

Note the parallels between all of this and the pattern we saw in Chapter 12: In both judgment and reasoning, it seems, our theory requires multiple parts. In both cases, sophisticated thinking is possible even for people who have not been formally trained. However, this sophisticated thinking isn't always used, and it seems to play a role only in the "right" circumstances (e.g., if the problem contains the right triggers). Likewise, in reasoning as in judgment, we find that better-quality reasoning is associated with higher levels of intellectual ability (Evans, Handley, Neilens, & Over, 2007), although even the smartest people are vulnerable to reasoning errors. We can also document—in judgment and in reasoning—that *different neural systems* are involved in different specific tasks, with some neural systems especially active when people are relying on heuristics, different systems active when people are relying on the detection and resolution of conflict, and so on (Goel, 2007). This obviously adds to our claim that people reason (or make judgments) in different ways on different occasions. And, finally, in both reasoning and judgment people often rely on relatively primitive strategies when they don't see how else to tackle the problem. These strategies may produce error, but they probably work more often than not, and at least they are efficient.

Mental Models

It seems, then, that different reasoning strategies exist side by side in the mind and are called into play in different situations. If we sometimes reason poorly, this is largely because we are using inappropriate strategies. If we can change the situation (so that different strategies are triggered), reasoning can be much improved.

It is against this backdrop that we consider one further reasoning strategy that people use—a strategy of creating and then reasoning about **mental models**. In other words, people sometimes may not rely on rules rooted in our evolutionary past, or rules induced from pragmatic experience, or rules of any sort. Instead, they may try to reason by thinking about concrete and specific cases. To see how this might work, let's return for the moment to categorical syllogisms like this one:

> All of the artists are beekeepers.
> Some of the beekeepers are chemists.

What follows from these premises? One way to think about this problem is to imagine a room full of people. Some of the people in the room are artists (perhaps you imagine them as wearing sweatshirts with a big *A* on the front). Others in the room are not artists (they have no sweatshirts). Perhaps you then imagine all of the artists as having a bee perched on their heads, and perhaps you also imagine some non-artists as having bees on their heads as well. (After all, the premise said that all artists are beekeepers, but it didn't say that all beekeepers are artists.) Continuing in this fashion, you will end up imagining a little world, or a mental model, in which all of the premises are fulfilled (see Figure 13.6). You can then inspect this model in order to ask what else is true about it: Once the premises are fulfilled, what other claims are entailed? Does it follow, for example, that some artists are chemists? (As it turns out, this conclusion doesn't follow from these premises, and so it would be invalid. You might confirm this by constructing a suitable mental model—"staffing" the imagined room as needed.) Other premises can also be represented in this fashion. For exam-

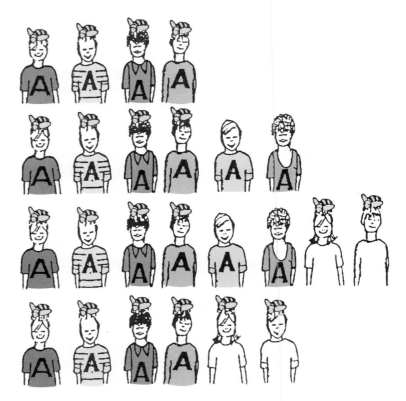

FIGURE 13.6 Mental Models of a Premise

Many premises can be modeled in more than one way. For example, shown here are several possible models for the premise "Some of the artists are beekeepers." In other words, each row within the figure depicts a situation in which this premise is true. Artists are shown with *A*s on their shirts; non-artists don't have *A*s. Beekeepers are shown with bees on their heads; non-beekeepers are bare-headed.

ple, if the premise were "No artists are beekeepers," you could imagine a room divided by a barrier, with the artists on one side and the beekeepers on the other.

Johnson-Laird and his colleagues have argued that mental models are widely used in reasoning. Broadly put, the idea is that one first constructs a mental model of a problem (or perhaps multiple models). Next one scrutinizes the model, seeking to discover what conclusions follow from the modeled premises. Finally, one can check on these conclusions by trying to construct counterexamples—models that are compatible with the premises but not with the proposed conclusion. If no counterexamples are found, then one concludes that the conclusion is valid (Johnson-Laird, 1990, 2001, 2004; Johnson-Laird & Byrne, 1989, 1991; also Klauer et al., 2000).

Participants in reasoning studies sometimes, on their own, mention the use of such models. One participant commented, "I thought of all the little artists in the room and imagined that they all had beekeeper's hats on." As more formal evidence, though, the mental-model approach leads to a number of predictions about reasoning performance, and many of these predictions have been confirmed. For example, some premises can be modeled in more than one way, and people trying to reason about these premises will have to examine multiple models, or else keep track of mental models with "optional" parts. One would expect this to make a problem more difficult, and this is indeed the case: The greater the number of models needed in reasoning through the problem, the more likely errors are to occur (Johnson-Laird, Byrne, & Tabossi, 1989; Johnson-Laird & Steedman, 1978).

Researchers have also suggested a role for mental models in other forms of reasoning, including reasoning about conditional problems (Evans, 1993; Johnson-Laird, Byrne, & Schaeken, 1992; Legrenzi et al., 1993). Hence, mental models take their place as part of the repertoire of human reasoning strategies. This obviously invites future researchers to explore more fully the pattern of triggers that lead us on one occasion to use one strategy, and on another occasion some other strategy. (For further discussion of mental models, see Evans, 1993; Ford, 1995; Goldvarg & Johnson-Laird, 2000; Johnson-Laird et al., 1992; Johnson-Laird, Legrenzi, Girotto, Legrenzi, & Caverni, 1999; Johnson-Laird & Savary, 1999; Rips, 1986, 1989.)

Decision-Making

We turn now to one last category of reasoning: reasoning about choices. How do we choose what courses to take next semester or what movie to see on Saturday? How do we choose which candidate to support in an election? How do we choose an apartment or a job? Choices like these fill our lives, leading us to ask: How do people make decisions?

Utility Theory

Each of us has his or her own values—things we like, things we prize, or conversely, things we hope to avoid. Likewise, each of us has a series of goals—things we hope to accomplish or things we hope to see. The obvious suggestion, then, is that we use these values and goals in making decisions. In choosing courses for next semester, for example, you will choose courses that are interesting (something you value) and also courses that help fill the requirements for your major (one of your goals). In choosing a medical treatment, you will hope to avoid pain, and you will also hope to retain your physical capacities as long as possible.

To put this a bit more formally, each decision will have certain costs attached to it (i.e., consequences that will carry us farther from our goals) and also certain benefits (consequences moving us toward our goals and providing us with things we value). In deciding, we weigh the costs against the benefits and seek a path that will minimize the former and maximize the latter. When we have several options open to us, we will presumably choose the one that provides the most favorable balance of benefits and costs.

This weighing of benefits against costs allows us to accommodate the fact that many decisions involve trade-offs of one sort or another. Should you go to Miami for your vacation this year, or to Tucson? The weather is better in Tucson, but the flight to Miami is less expensive. Hence, you must trade off the more desirable weather against the more attractive plane fare. Likewise, should you drive a less comfortable car if it happens to pollute less? Here the trade-off is between your comfort and protection of the environment.

Notice that these trade-offs involve factors that are, to say the least, highly disparate—comfort versus pollution, the pleasure made possible by good weather versus the $50 you might save in airfare. Can you really translate your pleasure into dollar amounts? Is your pleasure worth more than or less than $50? Likewise, how do you compare a 10% reduction in comfort with a 0.0001% reduction in pollution levels? In these examples (and, indeed, in most decisions), comparing these factors seems like the proverbial comparison of apples and oranges: The values at stake seem incommensurable.

Somehow, though, we do make these comparisons. We have to, if we are going to make these choices. Presumably, we compare them in a rather subjective way by asking how important each factor is to us. This is often expressed as the subjective **utility** of each factor, meaning, quite simply, the value of that factor for us. These utilities can then be summed (e.g., the utility of a pleasant vacation minus the "disutility" of spending more on airfare) to evaluate the overall utility for each outcome. These summed utilities for the various options can then be compared to each other, with the goal of selecting the option with the greatest overall utility.

In most decisions, though, there is also a degree of uncertainty or risk. Is Professor X an interesting instructor? Four of your friends have said she is, but two have said she is not. How should you factor these mixed reviews into your decision? Should you go to Miami for your vacation? At this time of year, you know that there's some chance of rain; do you want to take the risk?

One way to think about these risks follows a model formalized by von Neumann and Morgenstern (1947). Within their model, one calculates the **expected value** of each option using this simple equation:

$$\text{Expected value} = (\text{probability of a particular outcome}) \times (\text{utility of the outcome})$$

Thus, imagine that I offer to sell you a lottery ticket. The ticket costs $5 but gives you a one-in-a-hundred chance of winning $200. In this case, the expected value of the ticket is (.01 × $200), or $2. At a cost of $5, then, I'm selling the ticket for more than it is worth.

With more-complicated decisions, you will calculate the expected value of each factor and then add these up to compute the overall expected value associated with a particular choice. Let's say that you are choosing courses for next year. Course 1 looks interesting but also has a heavy workload. To evaluate this course, therefore, you will first need to estimate the subjective utility of taking an interesting course and also the disutility of being burdened by a heavy workload. Next, you will have to factor in the uncertainties. Perhaps there is a 70% chance that the course will be interesting but a 90% chance that it will have a heavy workload. In this case, the overall utility for this course will be (.70 × the utility of an interesting course) minus (.90 × the disutility of a heavy workload). You could then make similar calculations for the other courses available to you and choose the one with the greatest expected value.

All of this points the way toward a theory of choice, and it is a theory endorsed by most modern economists: The claim is that in making choices we seek to maximize utility—that is, to gain as much as we can of those things we value, and to avoid those things we don't like. We do this by consistently selecting the option with the greatest expected utility, calculated as described. (For discussion, see von Neumann & Morgenstern, 1947; also see Baron, 1988; Savage, 1954.)

Framing of Outcomes

Many of our choices and decisions do follow the principle of **utility maximization**. Which would you rather have—$90 or $100? Which gamble would you prefer—a 1% chance of winning a prize or a 5% chance of winning the same prize? In each case, we are appropriately sensitive to both the value of the "payoff" associated with a decision (i.e., its utility) and also the probability of a payoff.

However, an enormous number of studies show that in many circumstances we are not utility maximizers and, more broadly, that we are profoundly influenced by factors having little to do with utilities. In the process, we regularly make choices that are flatly inconsistent with other choices we have made. We will first review a number of these cases, and then we'll turn to how a theory of choice might accommodate them.

Consider the problem posed in Figure 13.7. Research participants show a clear preference in choosing between these two programs, and 72% choose Program A (Tversky & Kahneman, 1987). But now consider the problem posed in Figure 13.8. This problem is the same as the one in Figure 13.7; 200 people saved out of 600 is identical to 400 dead out of 600. Therefore, the utilities involved in this problem have not changed one bit. Nonetheless, this change in how the problem is phrased—that is, the **frame** of the decision—has a huge impact on participants' choices. In Figure 13.7, the problem is framed positively—in terms of *gains*, with each of the programs being described in terms of *lives saved*, and here participants favor Program A by almost a 3-to-1 margin. In Figure 13.8, the exact same problem is framed negatively—in terms of *losses*, with each of the programs being described in terms of *lives lost*, and now the pattern of preferences reverses—with 78% of participants opting for Program B.

It should be emphasized that there is nothing wrong with participants' individual choices. In either Figure 13.7 or Figure 13.8, there is no "right answer," and one can persuasively defend either the decision to avoid risk (by selecting Program A) or the decision to take the chance (by choosing Program B). The problem lies in the contradiction created by choosing Program A in one context and Program B in the

Imagine that the United States is preparing for the outbreak of an unusual Asian disease, which is expected to kill 600 people. Two alternative programs to combat the disease have been proposed. Assume that the exact scientific estimates of the consequences of the programs are as follows:

If Program A is adopted, 200 people will be saved.

If Program B is adopted, there is a one-third probability that 600 people will be saved, and a two-thirds probability that no people will be saved.

FIGURE 13.7 The Asian Disease Problem: Positive Frame

There is clearly no right answer to this question; one could defend selecting the "risky" choice (Program B) or the less rewarding but less risky choice (Program A). The clear majority of people, however, lean toward Program A, with 72% choosing it over Program B. Note that this problem is "positively" framed in terms of lives "saved."

other context. Indeed, if a single participant is given both frames on slightly different occasions, the participant is quite likely to contradict himself. For that matter, if we wanted to manipulate someone's evaluation of these programs (if, for example, we wanted to manipulate voters or shoppers), then framing effects provide an effective way to do this.

Framing effects of this sort are easy to demonstrate. Consider, for example, the two problems shown in Figure 13.9. When participants are given the first problem, almost three quarters of them (72%) choose the first option—the sure gain of $100. Participants contemplating the second problem generally choose the second option, with only 36% selecting the sure loss of $100 (Tversky & Kahneman, 1987). Note,

Imagine that the United States is preparing for the outbreak of an unusual Asian disease, which is expected to kill 600 people. Two alternative programs to combat the disease have been proposed. Assume that the exact scientific estimates of the consequences of the programs are as follows:

If Program A is adopted, 400 people will die.

If Program B is adopted, there is a one-third probability that nobody will die, and a two-thirds probability that 600 people will die.

FIGURE 13.8 The Asian Disease Problem: Negative Frame

This problem is identical in content to the one shown in Figure 13.7: 400 dead out of 600 people is the same as 200 saved out of 600. Nonetheless, people react to the problem shown here rather differently than they do to the one in Figure 13.7. In the "lives saved" version, 72% choose Program A. In the "will die" version, 78% choose Program B. Thus, by changing the phrasing we reverse the pattern of people's preferences.

though, that the problems are once again identical. Both pose the question of whether you would rather end up with a certain $400 or with an even chance between $300 and $500. Despite this equivalence, participants treat these problems very differently, preferring the sure thing in one case and the gamble in the other.

Across these (and many other) examples, there is a consistent pattern to framing effects. If the frame casts a choice in terms of losses (i.e., a negative frame), decision-makers tend to be **risk-seeking**; that is, they are quite willing to gamble, presumably in hopes of avoiding or reducing the loss. When the Asian disease problem (for example) is cast in terms of lives lost, people choose the gamble that's inherent in Program B, apparently attracted by the (slim) possibility that with this program they may avoid the loss. Likewise, Problem 2 in Figure 13.9 casts the options in terms of financial losses, and this, too, triggers risk-seeking: Here people reliably choose the 50-50 gamble over the sure loss.

The pattern of preferences reverses, though, with a positive frame—that is, if the frame casts the same choice in terms of gains. When contemplating gains, decision-makers tend to be **risk-averse**, not risk-seeking. In other words, they refuse to gamble, choosing instead to hold tight to what they already have. Thus, Figure 13.7 casts the Asian disease problem in terms of gains (the number of people saved), and this leads people to prefer the risk-free choice (Program A) over the gamble offered by Program B. (And likewise for Problem 1 in Figure 13.9.)

In almost every case, people tend to be risk-seeking when contemplating losses (especially *large* losses; Harinck, Van Dijk, Van Beest, & Mersmann, 2007), and risk-averse when contemplating gains. And we should emphasize that there is nothing wrong with either of these strategies by itself: If someone prefers to be risk-seeking,

---

Problem 1

Assume yourself richer by $300 than you are today. You have to choose between:
   a sure gain of $100
   50% chance to gain $200 and 50% chance to gain nothing

Problem 2

Assume yourself richer by $500 than you are today. You have to choose between:
   a sure loss of $100
   50% chance to lose nothing and 50% chance to lose $200

FIGURE 13.9 Framing Effects in Monetary Choices

These two problems are identical. In both cases, the first option leaves you with $400, while the second option leaves you with an even chance between $300 and $500. Despite this identity, people prefer the first option in Problem 1 (72% select this option) and the second option in Problem 2 (64% select this option). Once again, by changing the frames we reverse the pattern of preferences.

this is fine; if someone prefers to be risk-averse, this is okay too. The problem arises, though, when people flip-flop between these strategies, depending on how the problem is framed. The flip-flopping, as we have seen, leaves people wide open to manipulation, to inconsistency, and to self-contradiction.

Framing of Questions and Evidence

So far we have shown that people are influenced by how a problem's outcomes are framed. We can demonstrate related effects by changing how the question itself is framed. For example, imagine that you serve on a jury in a relatively messy divorce case; the parents are battling over who will get custody of their only child. The two parents have the attributes listed in Figure 13.10. To which parent will you award sole custody of the child?

Research participants asked this question tend to favor Parent B by a 64% to 36% margin. After all, this parent does have a close relationship with the child and has a good income. Note, though, that we have asked to which parent you would *award* custody. Things are different if we ask participants to which parent they would *deny* custody. This is, in obvious ways, the same question: If you are awarding custody to one parent, you are simultaneously denying it to the other parent. But in this case,

Imagine that you serve on the jury of an only-child sole-custody case following a relatively messy divorce. The facts of the case are complicated by ambiguous economic, social, and emotional considerations, and you decide to base your decision entirely on the following few observations. To which parent would you award sole custody of the child?

Parent A   average income
average health
average working hours
reasonable rapport with the child
relatively stable social life

Parent B   above-average income
very close relationship with the child
extremely active social life
lots of work-related travel
minor health problems

FIGURE 13.10 The Influence of How a Question Is Formed

When asked the question shown here, 64% of the research participants decided to award custody to Parent B. Other participants, however, were asked a different question: "To which parent would you deny sole custody?" Asked this question, 55% of the participants chose to deny custody to Parent B (and so, by default, to award custody to Parent A). Thus, with the "award" question, a majority votes for granting custody to Parent B; with the "deny" question, a majority votes for granting custody to Parent A.

55% of the participants choose to deny custody to Parent B (and so, by default, end up awarding custody to Parent A). Thus, the decision is simply reversed: With the "award" question, the majority of participants awards custody to Parent B. With the "deny" question, the majority denies custody to Parent B—and so gives custody to Parent A.

This effect has been observed in a number of contexts, including decisions involving monetary gambles, decisions about which courses a student will take, and decisions about political candidates (Shafir, 1993; also Downs & Shafir, 1999). As a related effect, people rate a basketball player more highly if the player has made 75% of his free throws, compared to their ratings of a player who has missed 25% of his free throws. They are more likely to endorse a medical treatment with a "50% success rate" than they are to endorse one with a "50% failure rate." And so on (Levin & Gaeth, 1988; Levin, Schnittjer, & Thee, 1988; also Dunning & Parpal, 1989).

None of this makes any sense from the perspective of utility theory, since these differences in framing should, on most accounts, have no impact on the expected utilities of the options. Yet these differences in framing can dramatically change people's choices and in many cases can actually reverse their pattern of preferences. (For further, related evidence, see Lichtenstein & Slovic, 2006; Mellers, Chang, Birnbaum, & Ordóñez, 1992; Schneider, 1992; Schwarz, 1999; Wedell & Bockenholt, 1990.)

Maximizing Utility Versus Seeing Reasons

How should we think about all of this? One broad possibility is that people are trying to use (something like) utility calculations when making their decisions, but they just aren't very good at it. As a result, people can be pulled off track by various distractions or complications, including how the consequences of a decision are framed or how the question they're pondering is framed.

A different possibility, though, is more radical: Perhaps, in making decisions, the maximization of utility is not our goal. Instead, our goal is simply to make decisions that we feel good about, decisions that we think are reasonable and justified. This view of decision-making is called **reason-based choice**; to see how the account plays out, consider a study by Shafir, Simonson, and Tversky (1993). Half their participants were asked to consider Scenario A in Figure 13.11. In this scenario, 66% of the participants said that they would buy the Sony; only 34% said that they would instead wait until they had learned about other models.

Other participants, though, were presented with Scenario B. In this situation, 27% choose the Aiwa, 27% choose the Sony, and a much larger number—46%—choose to wait until they'd learned about other models. How should we think about this? From a utility perspective, the results from Scenario A tell us that the perceived value of the Sony is greater than the perceived value of continued shopping; that's why (by a margin of 2-to-1) participants choose to buy. But the choices in Scenario

Scenario A

Suppose you are considering buying a compact disc player and have not yet decided which model to buy. You pass a store that is having a 1-day clearance sale. It offers a popular Sony player for just $99, well below the list price. Do you

a. buy the Sony player?
b. wait until you learn more about the various models?

Scenario B

Suppose you are considering buying a compact disc player and have not yet decided which model to buy. You pass a store that is having a 1-day clearance sale. It offers a popular Sony player for just $99 and a top-of-the-line Aiwa player for just $169, both well below the list price. Do you

a. buy the Sony player?
b. buy the Aiwa player?
c. wait until you learn more about the various models?

FIGURE 13.11 The Influence of Other Alternatives on Decision-Making
When subjects were given the choice shown in Scenario A, 66% chose to buy the Sony player, and only 34% chose to continue shopping. In Scenario B, however, 46% of the subjects chose to continue shopping, and only 27% chose to buy the Sony. Thus, in the first context subjects think that the Sony is a better choice than continued shopping, but in the second choice they think that continued shopping is a better choice than buying the Sony.

B show the reverse preference—with continued shopping preferable to either the Sony or the Aiwa (again, by almost two-to-one). It seems, then, that participants are simply flip-flopping: The purchase of the Sony is preferable to continued shopping in one case; continued shopping is preferable to purchasing the Sony in the other.

If we calculate utilities, therefore, people are being foolish. Things make much more sense, though, if we assume that people are really looking for *reasons* for their decisions. When only the Sony is available, there are compelling arguments for buying it. (It's a popular model, it's available at a good price; it's available at that price for just 1 day.) But when both the Sony and the Aiwa are available, it's harder to find persuasive arguments for buying one rather than the other. (Both, after all, are available at a good price for just 1 day. The Sony is cheaper, which is attractive, but the Aiwa is top-of-the-line.) With no good argument in view for preferring one of these models, people buy neither.

These data come from laboratory studies in which people are making hypothetical and unfamiliar decisions. Can we observe the same pattern outside of the lab? Redelmeier and Shafir (1995) gave medical doctors a problem identical in format to the Aiwa/Sony problem just discussed. Specifically, they described a patient's history and then, in one condition, offered two options for treatment—(a) a specific medication, or (b) a referral for possible surgery. In a second condition, they offered *three* options for treatment—(a) the medication, (b) an *alternative* medication, or (c), a referral for surgery.

The results in this study were virtually identical to the Aiwa/Sony results. When the medical doctors were choosing between one drug and surgery, many thought the drug was worth a try, and only 53% referred the patient for surgery. When the doctors had three choices, though, they found it difficult to justify choosing either drug over the other, and so most—72%—opted for surgery instead. This is, of course, the same pattern we have already seen: When the doctors couldn't justify one drug option over the other, they chose neither. (Also see J. Schwartz, Chapman, & Brewer, 2004; for a related demonstration with medical doctors, see Tversky & Shafir, 1992; for further discussion of the problems inherent in utility calculations, see Ariely & Norton, 2007. People also have other goals that guide their decision-making, in addition to the goal of choosing options that seem justified—see, for example, Higgins, 2005; Tyler, 2005.)

The Reasoning in Reason-Based Choice

The claim of reason-based choice suggests that we make a decision only when we see compelling reasons for that decision. On that basis, our decision-making is dependent on our capacity to find reasons and to judge those reasons persuasive. Therefore, any factor that influences our thinking in general (our ability to make judgments, our ability to reason) should have a direct impact on decision-making.

For example, we suggested earlier that confirmation bias plays a large role whenever we're evaluating an argument. We would expect, therefore, that confirmation bias will also influence decision-making, and it does. To see this in action, let's reconsider a problem already discussed: the divorce/custody problem shown in Figure 13.10. Half the research participants presented with this problem are asked to which parent they would award custody. These participants, influenced by confirmation bias, ask themselves, "What would justify giving custody to one parent or another?" This draws their attention to one subset of the parental attributes—for example, Parent B's close relationship with the child, and this in turn leads them to favor awarding custody to Parent B.

The other half of the participants are asked to which parent they would deny custody; with confirmation bias in place, this leads them to ask, "What would justify denying custody to one parent or another?" This question draws attention to a different subset of attributes—for example, Parent B's travel schedule or health problems. Thus, these participants easily find a basis for denying custody to Parent B. (For related discussion, see Legrenzi et al., 1993.)

Similarly, we know that judgment often relies on shortcut strategies such as the representativeness heuristic. If decision-making depends on judgment, then decision-making, too, should show a reliance on representativeness. This also is easy to confirm. Several studies have allowed participants to experience two different events and then asked them to decide which experience they'd like to *repeat*. In making this decision, participants seem to focus on a small number of "representative moments" within the experience, much as one might try to summarize a week's vacation in Rome with just one or two snapshots (Kahneman, 2003; Kahneman, Fredrickson, Schreiber, & Redelmeier, 1993; Schreiber & Kahneman, 2000; for a related finding, see Do, Rupert, & Wolford, 2008).

Of course, sometimes your vacation snapshots provide a distorted picture of how your vacation actually unfolded—your two glorious photos of that afternoon by the Trevi Fountain provide no indication of the three rainy days stuck in your hotel or that awful bus ride. In the same way, your "mental snapshots"—the few "representative moments" you consider when thinking back about an event—may not reflect what the event, overall, really involved. As a result, decisions based on "representative moments" can sometimes be unwise. Indeed, in some experiments, participants seem to prefer a more-obnoxious event (one involving more pain or more disgust) over a less-obnoxious one, simply because their remembered "snapshots" leave them with a distorted sense of their experiences. This finding resembles the cases we considered in Chapter 12—in which people drew erroneous conclusions because they were focusing on one or two bits of evidence ("I know a man who . . .") that actually didn't reflect the larger pattern of their experiences. Once again, therefore, we see that decision-making involves the same processes (e.g., the representativeness heuristic)—and is open to the same errors—that we have discussed in other settings. All of this is just as we'd expect if decision-making relies not on utility calculations but on the same strategies used for all sorts of reasoning and judgment.

Emotion

It seems, therefore, that the choices people make are governed by familiar principles—confirmation bias and a reliance on System 1 thinking, including the representativeness heuristic. None of this makes sense on the basis of utility calculations, but it is just what we would expect from the perspective of reason-based choice.

In addition, this emphasis on how people justify decisions calls our attention to another group of factors, factors that concern *emotion*. As one example, should someone trade in his bicycle for a newer, shinier version of the same bicycle? Most people say yes. Should someone trade in his wedding ring for a newer, shinier version of the same ring? Most people say no, because the emotional meaning associated with a wedding ring makes this decision rather different from the bicycle decision (Medin, Schwartz, Blok, & Birnbaum, 1999; also see Kahneman, Diener, & Schwarz, 1999; G. Loewenstein, Weber, Hsee, & Welch, 2001; Slovic, Finucane, Peters, & MacGregor, 2002; Weber & Johnson, 2009).

In the same vein, in judging risks people often seem to base their judgments not on some sort of calculation but instead largely on their feelings. Thus, for example, someone's assessment of how risky nuclear power really is turns out to be closely related to the amount of dread she experiences when thinking about a nuclear accident (Fischhoff, Slovic, & Lichtenstein, 1978). Indeed, some authors have suggested that many judgments and much decision-making rest on an "affect heuristic" (Finucane, Alhakami, Slovic, & Johnson, 2000; Slovic et al., 2002). The idea of this heuristic is that people often make judgments like "How risky is this?" or "How promising is this?" or "How much should I pay for this?" largely by asking themselves, much more simply, "How good (or bad) does this make me feel?"

Related to this is the fact that decision-making is also influenced by the complex emotion of *regret*. Specifically, people seem powerfully motivated to avoid regret, and so one of the strong forces guiding a decision is the effort toward choosing a course of action that minimizes the chances for regret later on. Indeed, this may be one of the reasons why people care so much about making decisions they feel they can explain and justify: It may be the best defense against subsequent regret. (For more on the avoidance of regret, see Connolly & Zeelenberg, 2002; Gilovich & Medvec, 1995; Gilovich, Medvec, & Kahneman, 1998; Kahneman & Miller, 1986; Kahneman & Tversky, 1982b; Medvec, Madey, & Gilovich, 1995; Mellers, Schwartz, & Ritov, 1999.)

But *how* do these emotions influence us? Is our decision-making guided by some calm, detached appraisal, allowing us to reflect on what emotions we will feel at some future point? Or is decision-making itself an emotional experience, so that the decisions are guided by how we feel at the time of making the decision? Several points favor the latter proposal. For example, consider the effect of framing (pp. 429–433). Framing effects are powerful, but even so, not everyone shows these effects, allowing us to ask which people do and which people do not fall prey to how a decision is framed (de Martino et al., 2006; Kahneman & Frederick, 2006).

It turns out that people are more likely to show the effects of framing if, during the decision, their amygdala (a brain area crucial for emotional evaluation) is especially activated. They're more likely to make decisions *inconsistent* with the frame if, during the decision, there is a greater degree of activation in the anterior cingulate cortex, a brain area that plays a key role in detecting conflict (including emotional conflict) within our mental processes. These points seem to suggest that different frames literally change a person's emotional response to a decision, and this in turn plays a role in whether the person will be influenced by that frame.

Likewise, Damasio (1994) has argued for an explicit and direct role of emotion in decision-making. To see his point, let's start with the undeniable fact that certain memories can cause a strong bodily reaction: In remembering a scary movie, for example, we might once again become tense and our palms might begin to sweat. In remembering a romantic encounter, we might once again become aroused. In the same fashion, *anticipated* events can also produce bodily arousal, and Damasio sug-

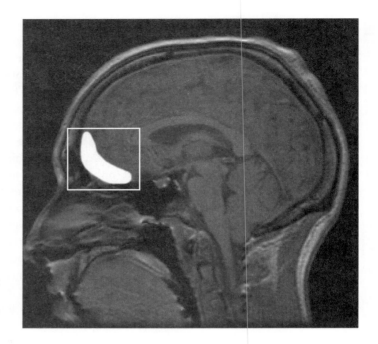

Orbitofrontal Cortex
According to Damasio, the orbitofrontal cortex plays a crucial role in allowing us to interpret the emotions associated with a stimulus or idea.

gests that we use these bodily sensations—**somatic markers**, as he calls them—as a guide to decision-making. In making a choice, he argues, we literally rely on our "gut feelings" to assess our various options, and this pulls us toward options associated with positive feelings and away from ones that trigger negative feelings.

Damasio argues, in addition, that a particular region of the brain—the orbitofrontal cortex (at the base of the frontal lobe, just above the eyes)—is crucial in our use of these somatic markers, because it is this brain region that allows us to interpret the emotions associated with various stimuli and various ideas. Evidence comes from patients who have suffered damage to the orbitofrontal cortex. In one study, participants were required to choose cards from one stack or another; each card, when turned over, showed the amount of money the participant had won or lost on that trial. The cards in one stack often showed large payoffs, but sometimes they showed huge penalties, and so, overall, it was better to choose cards from the other stack (which had smaller payoffs but much smaller penalties). Participants *without* orbitofrontal damage gradually figured this out as they worked their way through the task, and so they ended up making most of their choices from the less risky stack. Participants *with* orbitofrontal damage, in contrast, continued (unwisely) to favor the risky deck (Damasio, 1994; Naqvi, Shiv, & Bechara, 2006; also see Bechara, Damasio, Tranel, & Damasio, 2005; Coricelli, Dolan, & Sirigu, 2007; Maia & McClelland, 2005).

Apparently, then, the brain-damaged patients were less sensitive to risks and penalties, but why is this? Damasio's claim is that it is because they were not able to interpret the somatic markers associated with the risk—and so they didn't detect or use the "gut feeling" that could have warned them against a dangerous choice. This proposal gains support from another aspect of the experiment: As the gambling task progressed, the experimenters measured the participants' moment-by-moment bodily arousal. After some experience with the risky cards, participants *without* brain damage showed increased levels of arousal *before* they turned over a card in the risky stack. Apparently, they were anticipating the danger before it arrived and reacting emotionally to the perceived risk. Patients *with* brain damage, however, showed no emotional response before they turned over each card (although they did react once the card was in view). This fits with the claim that they were not anticipating the emotional response to each card, and so anticipation (via the use of somatic markers) could not influence their assessment of risk (Damasio, 1994).

Predicting Our Own Values

This emphasis on emotion raises yet another set of questions: How good are people at anticipating their own emotions? Are we accurate in these predictions—and therefore sensible in making the decisions that rest on these forecasts?

We have noted, for example, that our decision-making is often influenced by the possibility of regret. Specifically, we try to avoid making decisions that we might regret afterward. Notice, though, that this strategy rests on a prediction about the future: "If I do X and it turns out badly, how much will I regret the decision later?" It's relevant, therefore, that people are often *inaccurate* in forecasting their future regrets and tend to overestimate how much they'll later regret their errors (D. Gilbert, Morewedge, Risen, & Wilson, 2004). As a result, people probably give more weight to "regret avoidance" than they should, since they're working to avoid something that, in the end, really won't be that bad.

In the same way, imagine that you are choosing between two apartments that you might rent for next year. One is cheaper and larger but faces a noisy street. Will you just grow used to the noise, so that it ceases to bother you? If so, then you should take the apartment. Or will the noise grow more and more obnoxious to you as the weeks pass? If so, you should pay the extra money for the other apartment. Notice, then, that this decision also involves a prediction about the future—in this case, a prediction about how your likes and dislikes will change as time goes by.

Several studies suggest that people are rather inept at making this sort of prediction; in particular, people tend to underestimate the likelihood that they'll simply get used to new possessions or new features in their environment (Kahneman & Snell, 1992; Hsee & Hastie, 2005; G. Loewenstein & Schkade, 1999; Sevdalis & Harvey, 2007; Wilson, Wheatley, Meyers, Gilbert, & Axsom, 2000). Thus, to name a few examples, researchers have shown that people generally mis-predict how they will feel after "breaking up with a romantic partner, losing an election, receiving a gift, learning they have a serious illness, failure to secure a promotion, scoring well on an exam," and so on (D. Gilbert & Ebert, 2002, p. 503). Notice that this list includes

Framing Effects

As psychologists, we need to make sure that our studies reflect behavior as it occurs in the "real world" (i.e., outside of the laboratory). It's important to mention, therefore, that framing effects and mistakes about probabilities can be documented in many real-world settings—including studies done in casinos with actual gamblers (e.g., Slovic, 1995).

both negative events and positive ones. For the negative events, people are often convinced that things that bother them now will continue to bother them in the future, underestimating their ability to adapt. Similarly, for positive events, people seem to assume that things that please them now will continue to bring pleasure in the future (and so they're willing to pay for the better car or the higher-quality speakers, assuming that these will give them continued pleasure in the long term). But here, too, people underestimate their ability to adapt and, as a result, probably end up spending money for things that provide only short-term pleasure.

Normative Theories of Decision-Making

Where, then, does all of this leave us? In Chapter 12 and in the first half of this chapter, we saw that people often make errors in judgment and reasoning. It now appears that people may be just as clumsy in their decision-making, relying on strategies that leave them open to manipulation and self-contradiction. Just as bad, their decisions often rely on inaccurate forecasts, and so they take steps to avoid regrets that, in reality, they wouldn't have felt anyhow; they pay for expensive toys that will only bring short-term pleasure.

In fact, some investigators draw strong conclusions from these findings. Perhaps people really are incompetent in making decisions. Perhaps people consistently do make unwise choices, in part because they don't know what will make them happy and what won't. Perhaps people don't know what's best for them and so, in truth, might be better served by having someone else make their choices for them! (See, for example, Gilbert, 2006; Hsee, Hastie, & Chen, 2008; for an intriguingly different view, however, see Keys & Schwartz, 2007; Weber & Johnson, 2009.)

These are, of course, strong (and fascinating) claims, but we might ask: Are some of these problems avoidable? One might imagine that people could learn what does or does not make them happy and use these insights to guide their future decisions (although, for a pessimistic view of this point, see Gilbert, 2006). Likewise, one might imagine that people might learn to use better, "more rational" decision-making strategies. For example, perhaps people could be persuaded (or trained) to rely on utility calculations in their decision-making, rather than seeking reasons for their decisions. This might be an improvement, because utility calculations are (among other advantages) immune to framing effects, allowing people to avoid the self-contradictions that can occur when they shift from one decision frame to another (Baron, 1988, 1998; Larrick, Nisbett, & Morgan, 1993).

Even here, though, there are complications, because some would argue that there are decisions that must not be reduced to questions of utility. For example, consider choices involving morality—choices about theft or homicide, or choices about respecting other people's rights. Should one calculate the utility of "doing the moral thing"? If so, then perhaps there is some other utility (e.g., a large enough bribe) that would outweigh the demands of morality. For many people, this seems an inappropriate way to talk about moral values, but it is the right way to talk about moral decisions if utility theory is our guide. (For an intriguing exploration of this point, see Baron & Leshner, 2000.)

Moral values can be treated differently, however, within a theory of decision-making resting on justification. From this perspective, one shouldn't ask the "economic" question, "What gain would justify an immoral act?" Instead, one should ask the question, "What argument, or principle, would justify such an act?" And from this perspective there may be no payoff, no matter how large, to justify immorality. Instead, the only justification for an immoral action would be something like an even stronger, more compelling moral claim.

This seems to be an attractive position, and it suggests that reason-based choice can be defended as a normative theory—the way we *ought to* make decisions—even if this decision strategy has other problems associated with it (e.g., vulnerability to framing effects). Perhaps, therefore, in making decisions based on justification, we do expose ourselves to manipulation and self-contradiction, but even so, we might still be making decisions the "right way"!

Let's be clear, though, that we are not hoping to settle these issues here—including whether or not decisions should be based on utility calculations, and whether, ultimately, people will find ways to make themselves happy. Nonetheless, it's clear that the study of decision-making raises deep and complex questions. It is a straightforward matter to study *how* people make decisions, but this in turn raises fascinating questions about whether we make the decisions we should.

Chapter Summary

■ Reasoning often shows a pattern of confirmation bias: People tend to seek evidence that might confirm their beliefs rather than evidence that might challenge their beliefs. When evidence challenging a belief is in view, it tends to be underused or reinterpreted. One manifestation of confirmation bias is belief perseverance, a pattern in which people continue to believe a claim even after the basis for the claim has been discredited. This is probably because people engage in a biased memory search, seeking to confirm the claim. The evidence provided by this search then remains even when the original basis for the claim is removed.

■ People's performance with logic problems such as categorical syllogisms or problems involving conditional statements is often quite poor. The errors are not the product of carelessness; instead, many errors are due either to belief bias or to a "matching strategy."

■ Performance is also poor in the four-card task. People perform well, however, with some variations of this problem, and this makes it clear that reasoning is not guided by formal rules but is instead influenced by problem content. One proposal is that this effect should be understood in evolutionary terms, with people being skilled at reasoning about issues of cheating or betrayal; this is a type of reasoning, it is claimed, for which we are biologically well prepared. A different proposal is that our reasoning relies on pragmatic reasoning schemata; these summarize our experience in reasoning about situations involving permission, obligation, and so on. Reasoning performance will be good, therefore, if one of these schemata is triggered. Yet another proposal is that the content of a problem influences how we interpret the "if-then" relationship, with important consequences in how we reason about that relationship.

■ Apparently, theories of reasoning need multiple layers. People can be trained to reason according to the rules of formal logic. In addition, people without training do have reasonably sophisticated reasoning skills, but these skills play a role only if they are triggered by the problem's content. People also have less-sophisticated strategies that they employ when their reasoning skills are not triggered. Finally, people can also reason using mental models, in which they construct an imagined model of a situation and then inspect this model to evaluate possible conclusions.

■ According to utility theory, people make decisions by calculating the expected utility or expected value of each of their options. Evidence suggests, though, that decisions are often influenced by factors that have nothing to do with utilities—for example, how the question is framed or how the possible outcomes are described. If the outcomes are described as potential gains, decision-makers tend to be risk-averse; if they are described as potential losses, decision-makers tend to be risk-seeking.

- Some investigators have proposed that our goal in making decisions is not to max-imize utility but, instead, to make decisions that we think are reasonable or justified. Therefore, we are influenced by any factor that makes an argument in favor of an option seem more compelling. Thus, confirmation bias influences decision-making, just as it influences reasoning in general. Representativeness shapes how we evaluate our options in decision-making, and so on.

- Decisions are also clearly influenced by emotion. This influence is evident in decision-makers' efforts toward avoiding regret; it is also evident in decision-makers' reliance on their own bodily sensations as a cue for evaluating their various options.

- Decision-makers are surprisingly inept, however, at predicting their own future reactions. This is true both for predictions of regret (e.g., how much regret one will feel if a decision turns out badly) and for predictions of values (e.g., whether one will still like the new car, or still be annoyed by the street noise in an apartment after some time has passed).

- Decision-making guided by perceived justification may lead to self-contradiction and may leave us open to external manipulation (because of frame effects). But this approach to decision-making may be appropriate nonetheless, and discussion about the normative theory of decision-making (how we should make decisions) is ongoing.

The Workbook Connection

See the *Cognition Workbook* for further exploration of reasoning:
- Demonstration 13.1: Framing Questions
- Demonstration 13.2: The Effect of Content on Reasoning
- Demonstration 13.3: Mental Accounting
- Research Methods: The Community of Scientists
- Cognitive Psychology and Education: Choosing Your Courses
- Cognitive Psychology and the Law: Judgment Biases in the Courtroom

Solving Problems

In Chapter 12, we considered the processes through which people form new beliefs, based on information they have encountered. In Chapter 13, we examined how people reason about these beliefs—what inferences they draw and how they adjust their beliefs (or fail to) as new evidence comes in. We then considered how people use their beliefs as a basis for choosing among options or for selecting a course of action. In other words, we considered how people make decisions.

Once we have taken all these steps, though—that is, once we've formed a belief, drawn out its implications, and chosen a course of action—what happens next? In some cases, this is a straightforward matter. If you decide to buy one jacket rather than another, your next steps will be easy: You go to the store and get the jacket. In many other cases, though, what you select is a *goal*, and that still leaves the question of how you will reach that goal. This is the domain of **problem-solving**, the process through which you figure out how to reach your goals, starting from your current state.

We solve problems all the time. "I want to reach the store, but Tom borrowed my car. How should I get there?" "I really want Amy to notice me; how should I arrange it?" "I'm trying to prove this theorem. How can I do it, starting from these premises?" In this chapter, we will examine how people solve problems like these—including practical problems and academic ones, trivial problems and consequential ones, the well-defined and the diffuse. We will begin by considering strategies relevant to problems of all sorts. We will then discuss more-specialized strategies, applicable to only some sorts of problems, and we'll ask both how ordinary people solve problems and also how experts do. We'll next turn to the issue of how people *define* the problems they are working on. As we will see, many problems can be defined in more than one way, and the definition turns out to be crucial for how (or whether) the problem is solved. Then, at last, we'll turn to a special type of problem-solving—problem solving that is *creative*—and ask just what creativity involves.

- Often we solve problems by using general heuristics that help us to narrow our search for the problem's solution. One of these is means–end analysis, which often leads us to divide problems into a series of simpler subproblems.

- In other cases, we solve problems by drawing analogies based on problems we've solved in the past. As helpful as they are, however, analogies are often underused.

- Training can improve someone's skill in problem-solving. The training can draw someone's attention to a problem's deep structure, which promotes analogy use. Training can also help someone see how a problem can be divided into subproblems.

- Experts consistently attend to a problem's deep structure and are quite sensitive to a problem's parts. Experts also benefit from their highly cross-referenced knowledge in their domain of expertise.

- Problem-solving is often stymied by how people approach the problem in the first place, and that leads to a question of how people find new and creative approaches to problems.

- When closely examined, creative approaches seem to be the result of the same processes that are evident in "ordinary" problem-solving—processes hinging on analogies, heuristics, and the like. Hence, the creative *product* is often extraordinary, but the creative *process* may not be.

General Problem-Solving Methods

It is obvious that some problems require special expertise. If you are trying to achieve some bit of genetic engineering, you need the relevant training in biology and biochemistry. If you are trying to repair a computer, you need knowledge of electronics. Some problems, though, draw on more general skills and strategies that are available to all of us. What are these strategies?

Problem-Solving as Search

Many researchers find it useful to compare problem-solving to a process of search, as though you were navigating through a maze, seeking a path toward your goal. Some paths will (eventually) lead to the goal, but others will lead to dead ends or to the wrong goal. Some paths will be relatively direct; others will be long and circuitous. In all cases, though, your job is to select the best path, allowing you to get from your starting point to your target.

Building on this idea of "problem-solving as search," Newell and Simon (1972) described problem-solving as starting with an **initial state** (the knowledge and resources you have at the outset) and working toward a **goal state**. To move from the initial state to the goal, the problem-solver has a set of **operators**—that is, tools or actions that can change her current state. In addition, there is likely to be a set of **path constraints**, ruling out some options or some solutions. These constraints might take the form of resource limitations (e.g., limited time or money) or other limits (e.g., ethical limits on what you can do).

Given an initial state, the operators, and the path constraints, there is a limited number of intermediate states that one can reach en route to the goal. For example, consider the "Hobbits and Orcs" problem described in Figure 14.1. Figure 14.2 shows the states one can reach, early on, in solving this problem. Notice that these states can be depicted as a tree, with each step leading to more and more branches. All of these branches together form the **problem space**—that is, the set of all states that can be reached in solving this problem. In these terms, what one is seeking in solving a problem is quite literally a path through this space, leading, step-by-step, from the initial state to the goal.

One option in solving a problem would be to trace through the entire problem space, exploring each branch in turn. This approach would guarantee that you would eventually find the solution (if the problem were solvable at all). For most of the problems we face, however, this sort of "brute force" approach would be hopeless. Consider, for example, the game of chess: Your goal is to win the game, so how should you proceed? Let's say that you move first. In opening the game, you have exactly 20 moves available to you. For each of these, your opponent has 20 possible responses. Therefore, for the first cycle of play there are 400 possibilities (20 × 20) for how things might go. If you are going to choose the best move, you need to inspect all 400 of these possibilities.

Your best move, however, probably depends on what you are planning to do next—it depends on what defense you are looking to establish or what attack you are planning to launch. Therefore, in evaluating your options you will probably want to ask, "Will this lead me where I want to go?" and that requires some looking ahead. Before you select your move, then, you might want to think through three or four cycles of play, and not just one.

There are 400 possibilities for how the first cycle can unfold, but there are more options for subsequent cycles as the pieces get spread out, leaving more room to move. Let's estimate, therefore, that there are 30 different moves you might make next and, for each of these, 30 possible responses from your opponent. Thus, for two cycles of play there are 360,000 (400 × 30 × 30) possible outcomes. If, at that point, there are now 40 options open to you, and 40 possible responses for each, three cycles of play leave us with 576,000,000 different options; four cycles of play, 921,600,000,000

Five Orcs and five Hobbits are on the east bank of the Muddy River. They need to cross to the west bank and have located a boat. In each crossing, at least one creature must be in the boat, but no more than three creatures will fit in the boat.

And, of course, if the Orcs ever outnumber the Hobbits on either side of the river, they will eat the Hobbits! Therefore, in designing the crossing we must make certain that the Hobbits are never outnumbered, either on the east bank of the river or on the west.

How can the creatures get across without any Hobbits being eaten?

FIGURE 14.1 The "Hobbits and Orcs" Problem
This problem has been used in many studies of problem-solving strategies. Can you solve it?

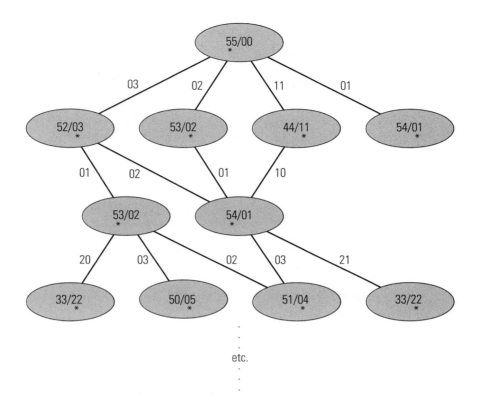

FIGURE 14.2 The Problem Space for the "Hobbits and Orcs" Problem
Each circle shows a possible problem state. The state 54/01, for example, indicates that five Hobbits and four Orcs are on the east bank; there are no Hobbits, but one Orc, on the west bank. The star shows the position of the boat. The numbers alongside of each line indicate the number of creatures in the boat during each river crossing. The move 02, for example, transports no Hobbits, but two Orcs. The problem states shown here are all the legal states. (Other states, and other moves, would result in some of the Hobbits being eaten.) Thus, there are four "legal" moves one can make, starting from the initial state. From these, there are four possible moves one can make, but these lead to just two problem states (53/02 and 54/01). From these two states, there are four new states that can be reached, and so on. We have here illustrated the first three moves that can be made in solving this problem; the shortest path to the problem's solution involves 11 moves.

options. If you are truly seeking the best possible move, maybe you should consider all 921 billion of these to find the best one. (For further discussion, see Gilhooly, 1988; Newell & Simon, 1972.)

This proliferation of moves seems to rule out the strategy of "check every option." If you needed 1 second to evaluate each sequence, you would still need 256 million hours to evaluate the full set of possibilities for four cycles of play. And, of course, there is nothing special about chess. Let's say that you are having dinner with Percy and you want him to think you are witty. Your problem is to find things to say that will achieve this goal. How many possibilities are there for sentences you might utter? How many possible rejoinders are available to Percy? How many responses could you then make? Again, the number is vast. If you consider them all, searching for the best choice, you will impress Percy with your long pauses—but not with your wit.

In light of these calculations, it would obviously be helpful if you could somehow narrow your search, so that you consider only a subset of your options rather than searching the entire problem space. Of course, this would involve an element of risk: If you consider only some options, you take the risk of overlooking the best option. However, you may have no choice about this, since the alternative—the strategy of considering every option—would be absurd for most problems.

In short, what you need is a problem-solving heuristic. Heuristics are strategies that are efficient, but at the cost of occasional errors. In the domain of problem-solving, a heuristic is a strategy that guides you through the problem space—narrowing your search, but (one hopes) in a fashion that still leads you to the problem's solution. What problem-solving heuristics do we employ?

General Problem-Solving Heuristics

Several problem-solving heuristics are revealed if we simply ask people to think out loud while working on a problem such as the "Hobbits and Orcs" problem in Figure 14.1 or the "Tower of Hanoi" problem in Figure 14.3. By inspecting the running commentaries—or **problem-solving protocols**—that people produce while they are working on these problems, we can identify some of the strategies that these problem-solvers rely on.

For example, one often-used heuristic is the so-called **hill-climbing strategy**. To understand the term, imagine that you are hiking through the woods and trying to figure out which trail leads to the mountaintop. You obviously need to climb uphill to reach the top, and so whenever you come to a fork in the trail, you select the path that is going uphill. The hill-climbing strategy works the same way: At each point, you simply choose the option that moves you in the direction of your goal.

This strategy is helpful for some problems. Imagine that there is a bad smell in your house, and you are trying to figure out where it's coming from. You might stand at the doorway between the kitchen and the dining room, and then decide in which direction the smell is stronger. If it is stronger in the kitchen, then that is the direction to explore. If the smell gets stronger as you approach the sink, then you explore that area. By always moving in the direction of the stronger smell, you will eventually discover the smell's source.

This strategy, however, is of limited use, because many problems require that you start by moving *away* from your goal; only then, from this new position, can the problem be solved. We have illustrated this in Figure 14.4, and other examples are easy to find. For instance, if you want Mingus to notice you more, it might help if you go away for a while; that way, he will be more likely to notice you when you come

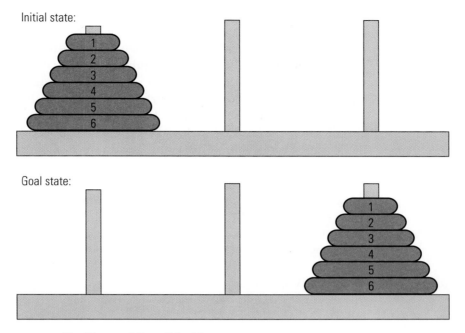

FIGURE 14.3 The "Tower of Hanoi" Problem

The rings on the left pole need to be moved so that they end up on the right pole, as shown. The rings must be moved one at a time, and with each move, a ring can be placed only on a larger ring. Thus, Ring 1 can be placed on top of Ring 2, but Ring 2 can never be placed on Ring 1. Can you solve this?

FIGURE 14.4 Limits on the Hill-Climbing Strategy

According to the hill-climbing strategy, the dog should, at each step, choose a path that moves it closer and closer to the goal. However, this strategy will fail here because the dog needs first to move away from the bone (toward the open gate) in order to reach the bone.

back. This ploy would never be discovered, though, if you relied on the hill-climbing strategy.

Despite these limitations, people often rely on a hill-climbing strategy. As a result, they have difficulties whenever a problem requires them to "move backward in order to go forward"—that is, whenever the problem requires them to move (briefly) away from their goal in order (ultimately) to reach the goal. For example, solving the "Hobbits and Orcs" problem (Figure 14.1) requires, at various points, that one carry creatures from the east bank back to the west—that is, from the goal state back to the initial state. These points of "backward movement" turn out to be very difficult for people. Often, at these points, people become convinced they are on the wrong track, and they seek some other solution to the problem: "This must be the wrong strategy; I'm going the wrong way." (See, for example, Jeffries, Polson, Razran, & Atwood, 1977; J. Thomas, 1974.)

Fortunately, though, people also have other, more sophisticated heuristics available to them. For example, people often rely on a strategy called **means–end analysis**. To use this strategy, one starts by comparing the current state and the goal state. One then asks, "What means do I have available to get from here to there?" To see how this plays out, consider this commonsense example, offered by Newell and Simon (1972):

> I want to take my son to nursery school. What's the difference between what I have and what I want? One of distance. What changes distance? My automobile. My automobile won't work. What is needed to make it work? A new battery. What has new batteries? An auto repair shop. I want the repair shop to put in a new battery; but the shop doesn't know I need one. What is the difficulty? One of communication. What allows communication? A telephone. . . . (p. 416)

As this example illustrates, a means–end analysis can actually provide two different benefits. First, the analysis obviously highlights *differences* between where you are right now and where you want to be, and in this way it helps you see exactly what you need to do to solve the problem. Second, a means–end analysis will, as in this example, often lead you to break up a problem into smaller **subproblems**, each with its own goal. By solving the subproblems one by one, you address the larger problem. In fact, some have suggested that this identification of subproblems is itself a powerful problem-solving heuristic: By breaking a problem into smaller pieces, we make the initial problem easier to solve.

A related idea is that one can often solve a problem by using the *goal* as the starting point, rather than the problem's initial state, so that, in essence, one solves the problem by **working backward** from the goal. This strategy is quite useful, for example, for the water-lilies problem described in Figure 14.5. Here, too, one is using means–end analysis, but now in reverse—asking how the goal state can be made more similar to the current state.

Water lilies are growing on Blue Lake. The water lilies grow rapidly, so that the amount of water surface covered by lilies doubles every 24 hours.

On the 1st day of summer, there was just one water lily. On the 90th day of the summer, the lake was entirely covered. On what day was the lake half covered?

FIGURE 14.5 The Water-Lilies Problem
Working backward from the goal is useful in solving this problem. Can you solve it?

A variety of evidence suggests that means—end analysis and working backward are commonly used strategies. For example, both strategies appear frequently in people's problem-solving protocols. And this turns out to be sensible, because these two strategies are often effective and are applicable to a large number of problems.

Mental Models and Mental Images

In many cases, it helps to translate a problem into concrete terms, perhaps relying on a mental image or a mental model (Cooper, 1990; Palmer, 1977; Shepard & Feng, 1972). Indeed, the histories of science, art, and engineering are all filled with instances in which great discoveries or innovations appear to have emerged from the use of imagery (A. Miller, 1986; S. Reed, 1993; Shepard, 1988; also see Finke, 1990, 1993; Finke & Slayton, 1988).

As a simple example of how models and images can help us, consider the bookworm problem described in Figure 14.6. Most people try an algebraic solution to this problem (width of each volume, multiplied by the number of volumes, divided by the worm's eating rate) and end up with the wrong answer. People generally get this problem right, though, if they start by visualizing the arrangement. With this done, they can discern the actual positions of the worm's starting point and end point, and this usually takes them to the correct answer (see Figure 14.7).

Solomon is proud of his 26-volume encyclopedia, placed neatly, with the volumes in alphabetical order, on his bookshelf. Solomon doesn't realize, though, that there's a bookworm sitting on the front cover of the A volume. The bookworm begins chewing his way through the pages on the shortest possible path toward the back cover of the Z volume.

Each volume is 3 inches thick (including pages and covers), so that the entire set of volumes requires 78 inches of bookshelf. The bookworm chews through the pages and covers at a steady rate of ¾ of an inch per month. How long will it take before the bookworm reaches the back cover of the Z volume?

FIGURE 14.6 The Bookworm Problem
People who try an algebraic solution to this problem often end up with the wrong answer.

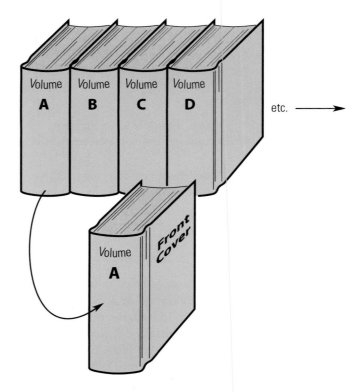

FIGURE 14.7 Diagram for the Bookworm Problem

When the bookworm problem is illustrated, as shown here, people more easily solve it. Notice that a worm, starting on the front cover of the *A* volume, would not have to chew through volume *A*'s pages in moving toward the *Z* volume. Likewise, at the end of the worm's travel, he would reach the back cover of the *Z* volume before penetrating the *Z* volume!

Pictures and Diagrams

It's likely that someone could figure out the bookworm problem either by inspecting a picture (like the one in Figure 14.7) or by inspecting a mental image of the problem's layout, and indeed, for many purposes pictures and images may be interchangeable. Consistent with this idea, several studies have found no difference between problem-solving via picture and problem-solving via imagery (J. R. Anderson, 1993; R. Anderson & Helstrup, 1993; S. Reed, 1993).

For other purposes, though, there are important differences between mental images and pictures, with some problems more readily solved via imagery, and other problems showing the reverse. For example, mental images have the advantage of being more easily modified than diagrams: If one wishes to make a form larger or a different shape, this is easy in imagination; one can, after all, imagine anything one wishes. Likewise, one can easily imagine moving patterns; it is much harder to depict motion with a diagram. Therefore, if a problem solution depends on motion, then the problem may be more easily solved with imagery than with a picture.

Sometimes, though, pictures are more helpful than images. We know, for example, that elaborate or detailed forms are difficult to image clearly. If a problem depends on such forms, problem-solving via image will be difficult. Likewise, we argued in Chapter 11 that there are certain limits on what can be discovered from a mental image, limits that are created by the image's "perceptual reference frame." One can escape these limits, though, by drawing a picture based on the image. The picture allows the perceiver to "start fresh" in interpreting the form, and this can often lead to new perspectives or new ideas. The advantage of "externalizing" the image can easily be demonstrated in the laboratory (see Chapter 11; also see Reisberg, 2000); it can also be demonstrated in real-world settings—for example, with architects who gain by sketching out their designs rather than by trying to work out the design entirely "in their heads" (Verstijnen, Hennessey, van Leeuwen, Hamel, & Goldschmidt, 1998).

Relying on Past Knowledge

Our discussion so far has focused on strategies that apply to problem-solving in general, problem-solving of all sorts. But problem-solving also draws on more specialized strategies, as well as on knowledge about particular domains.

Problem-Solving via Analogy

Often, in solving a problem, we are reminded of some other problem we have already solved, and this will tell us, by analogy, how to solve the problem now before us. In this way, we derive the unknown solution from one that is already known.

Many lines of evidence highlight just how helpful analogies can be. In the history of science, for example, analogies have often played an important role—with scientists furthering their understanding of the heart by comparing it to a pump, extending their knowledge of gases by comparing the molecules to billiard balls, and so on (Gentner & Jeziorski, 1989). Likewise, analogies are also useful as a teaching tool—with the atom being described to students as (roughly) resembling the solar system, or with memory being compared to a library, and the like—and the data suggest that analogies like these are genuinely helpful to students (Donnelly & McDaniel, 1993; although also see Donnelly & McDaniel, 2000). Indeed, one recent study examined how mathematics teachers use analogies in their classrooms. The results suggest that American teachers may, overall, be less effective in their use of analogies than teachers from, say, Hong Kong or Japan; intriguingly, this may provide part of the reason why American students seem to learn mathematics less well than their counterparts in other countries (Richland, Zur, & Holyoak, 2007).

In addition, analogies are enormously helpful in problem-solving. For example, the tumor problem (see Figure 14.8) is quite difficult, but people generally solve it if they are able to use an analogy: Gick and Holyoak (1980) first had their participants read about a related situation (see Figure 14.9) and then presented them with the tumor problem. When participants were encouraged to use this hint, 75% were able to solve the tumor problem. For participants not given the hint, only 10% solved the tumor problem.

Suppose you are a doctor faced with a patient who has a malignant tumor in his stomach. To operate on the patient is impossible, but unless the tumor is destroyed the patient will die. A kind of ray, at a sufficiently high intensity, can destroy the tumor. Unfortunately, at this intensity the healthy tissue that the rays pass through on the way to the tumor will also be destroyed. At lower intensities the rays are harmless to healthy tissue but will not affect the tumor. How can the rays be used to destroy the tumor without injuring the healthy tissue?

FIGURE 14.8 **The Tumor Problem**

The tumor problem, designed by Duncker (1945), has been studied extensively. Can you solve it? One solution is to aim multiple low-intensity rays at the tumor, each from a different angle. The rays will meet at the site of the tumor and so, at just that location, will sum to full strength.

A dictator ruled a country from a strong fortress, and a rebel general, hoping to liberate the country, vowed to capture the fortress. The general knew that an attack by his entire army would capture the fortress, but he also knew that the dictator had planted mines on each of the many roads leading to the fortress. The mines were set so that small groups of soldiers could pass over them safely, since the dictator needed to move his own troops to and from the fortress. However, any large force would detonate the mines, blowing them up and also destroying the neighboring villages.

The general knew, therefore, that he couldn't just march his army up one of the roads to the fortress. Instead, he devised a simple plan. He divided his army into small groups and dispatched each group to the head of a different road. When all were ready, he gave the signal and each group marched up a different road to the fortress, with all the groups arriving at the fortress at the same time. In this way, the general captured the fortress and overthrew the dictator.

FIGURE 14.9 **The "General and Fortress" Problem**

This problem is analogous in its structure to the tumor problem (Figure 14.8). If people read this problem and then try the tumor problem, they are far more likely to solve the latter. (After Gick & Holyoak, 1980)

Difficulties in Finding an Appropriate Analogy

Despite the clear benefit of using analogies, people routinely fail to use them. For example, Gick and Holyoak had another group of participants read the "general and fortress" story, but no further hints were given. In particular, these participants were not told that this story was relevant to the tumor problem. Only 30% solved the tumor problem—far fewer than the 75% explicitly told that the fortress story was relevant to their task.

Similarly, Reed (1977; Reed, Ernst, & Banerji, 1974) first had participants solve the "jealous husbands" problem shown in Figure 14.10; the participants were then

> Three jealous husbands and their wives have to cross a river. However, the boat they plan to use is so small that it can hold no more than two persons. Find the simplest schedule of crossing that will permit all six persons to cross the river so that no woman is left in the company of any other woman's husband unless her own husband is present. It is assumed that all passengers on the boat disembark before the next trip and that at least one person has to be in the boat for each crossing.

FIGURE 14.10 The "Jealous Husbands" Problem

If the experimenter points out the relationship between the "jealous husbands" problem and the "Hobbits and Orcs" problem (Figure 14.1), then participants benefit from first solving the "jealous husbands" problem. If this relationship is not pointed out to participants, however, they show no benefit from this "training." (After S. Reed et al., 1974)

asked to solve the "Hobbits and Orcs" problem (Figure 14.1). When the close relationship between these two problems was pointed out to the participants, they were considerably faster in solving the "Hobbits and Orcs" problem. But, remarkably, if this relationship was not explicitly pointed out, they showed no benefit at all from this "training." (See also Hayes & Simon, 1977; B. Ross, 1984, 1987, 1989; Weisberg, DiCamillo, & Phillips, 1978.)

Apparently, then, people do use analogies if suitably instructed, but spontaneous, uninstructed use of analogies seems relatively rare. Why is this? Part of the answer lies in how people search through their memories when seeking an analogy. In solving a problem about tumors, people seem to ask themselves, "What else do I know about tumors?" This will help them remember other situations in which they thought about or learned about tumors, but of course this memory search won't lead them to the "general and fortress" problem. This (potential) analogue will therefore lie dormant in memory and provide no help. Likewise, Hobbit problems remind people of other Hobbit problems, even though problems on other topics might point the way to a solution.

Consistent with this perspective, people solving Hobbit problems will spontaneously use analogies if the previously studied problems also involved Hobbits. In this case, the (rather obvious) relation between the current problem and the prior problems guarantees that the former will call the latter to mind. People are less likely to draw analogies if they have previously solved problems involving actors of a different sort. (For relevant evidence, see Bassok, 1996; Bassok, Wu, & Olseth, 1995; Cummins, 1992; Holyoak & Koh, 1987; Novick, 1988; B. Ross, 1984, 1987; Spencer & Weisberg, 1986; Wharton, Holyoak, Downing, & Lange, 1994.)

Similarities between the current problem and a previously studied case also help people in another way: In order to create, or even to understand, an analogy, people need to get beyond the superficial features of the problem and think instead about the principles governing the problem. Put differently, people can use analogies only if they figure out how to **map** the prior case onto the problem now being solved—only if they realize, for example, that converging groups of soldiers correspond to converging rays, and that a fortress-to-be-captured corresponds to a tumor-to-be-destroyed. This mapping process is sometimes difficult, and failures to figure out the mapping are common, providing another reason why people regularly fail to find, and fail to use, analogies. (For discussion of how this process of mapping unfolds, see French, 2002; Gentner, 1983, 1989; Holyoak, 1984; Holyoak & Thagard, 1989; Markman, 1997; VanLehn, 1998.)

Of course, mapping one problem onto another is easier if the two problems are similar in their particulars: If you have recently solved one "Hobbits and Orcs" problem, it is easy to apply this experience to a new "Hobbits and Orcs" problem. What you earlier learned about Hobbits can be mapped onto the new Hobbits, and what you earlier discovered about boats is immediately applicable to the boat in the current problem. If, instead, you have recently solved the "jealous husbands" problem (Figure 14.10), then the principles learned in this experience might be applicable to the new problem, but only via a step of translation (Hobbits become husbands; "cannot outnumber" is replaced with "cannot be left alone with"). This is therefore further reason why analogy use is facilitated by similarity between the target problem and the analogous case drawn from memory. (For discussion of still other factors impeding or facilitating the use of analogies, see Bassok et al., 1995; Blanchette & Dunbar, 2000; Gick & Holyoak, 1980; Needham & Begg, 1991; Novick & Holyoak, 1991.)

Strategies to Make Analogy Use More Likely

These claims point toward several suggestions for how we might promote analogy use and thus improve problem-solving. Let's start with the memory search. When considering the tumor problem presented in Figure 14.8 (for example), people seem to ask themselves, "What else do I know about tumors?" But surely there is nothing inevitable about this, and presumably people could, with suitable instruction, learn to ask themselves a different question along the lines of, "How can I bring forces to bear on a specific target without losing the forces while they're on their way to the target?" With this question, people might well be reminded of a suitable analogue, even if the analogue differs from the current problem in a dozen superficial ways.

Similarly, let's be clear that analogies usually depend on a problem's "deep structure"—the pattern of causal relationships within the problem, and how the problem's parts are interrelated. The problem's "surface structure"—how the causal relationships are manifested—is largely irrelevant. Perhaps we can promote analogy use, therefore, by urging people to pay attention to the deep structure from the very start, rather than attending to the problem's superficial content. In this way, a proper orientation, when working on a problem, might help both in the locating of analogues and also in the mapping of one problem onto another.

Several studies confirm these optimistic predictions. For example, Cummins (1992) presented participants with a series of algebra word problems. Participants in one group were asked to analyze these training problems one by one; these participants tended to categorize the problems in terms of superficial features and were unlikely, later on, to apply these analogies to new problems. Participants in a second group were explicitly asked to *compare* the training problems to each other. These participants tended to describe and categorize the problems in terms of their structures; in other words, they paid attention to each problem's underlying dynamic. These participants were much more likely to use the problems as a basis for analogies when later solving new problems.

Likewise, Needham and Begg (1991) presented their participants with a series of training problems. Some participants were told that they would need to recall these problems later on and were encouraged to work hard at remembering them. Other participants were encouraged to work at *understanding* each solution, so that they would be able to explain it later to another person. When the time came for the test problems, participants in the second group were much more likely to transfer what they had earlier learned. As a result, those who had taken the "understand" approach were able to solve 90% of the test problems; participants who had taken the "memorize" approach solved only 69%. (For related data, ways in which different forms of training can enhance analogy use, see Catrambone, Craig, & Nersessian, 2006; Kurtz & Loewenstein, 2007; Lane & Schooler, 2004; Loewenstein, Thompson, & Gentner, 1999; Pedrone, Hummel & Holyoak, 2001.)

For purposes of problem-solving, therefore, there is a preferred way to learn. In essence, you want to attend to the structure of a problem rather than to its surface; this increases the likelihood of finding analogies later on, and thus the likelihood of benefiting from analogies. One way to achieve this is by comparing problems to each other, seeking parallels and points of similarity. The same benefit is observed if you simply spend time thinking about why a problem's solution *is* a solution—that is, why the solution gets the job done. People are also helped by getting the right training problems—problems that call attention to underlying structures. Thus, there seem to be many ways to promote analogy use—ways that provide people both with the relevant analogues and with the "sagacity to apply the knowledge to a new problem" (Needham & Begg, 1991, p. 544; after W. James, 1890).

Expert Problem-Solvers

In obvious ways, then, our discussion of problem-solving has important implications for education. To make this concrete, let's say that we want students to be better problem-solvers; how should we proceed? First, we could teach our students some of the heuristics that appear useful for problem-solving in general. Second, analogies are plainly helpful in problem-solving, and so we could provide students with experience in the relevant domains so that they would have a basis from which to draw analogies. Third, we now see that this training may have little effect unless we take steps to ensure that students will *use* this knowledge when it is needed. This is why we need to encourage students to approach the training problems in an appropriate way, and also to provide a basis for seeing the mapping between the training and test problems.

Will these training steps truly improve problem-solving? One way to ask is by examining *expert* problem-solvers; if they use the techniques we have already discussed, this would support the claim that these techniques are valuable and should be the focus of training. If, however, experts use some other techniques, then perhaps these, too, could be developed with novices through the appropriate education.

In fact, expert problem-solvers do use many of the techniques we've discussed. For example, we have claimed that it is helpful to think about problems in terms of their deep structure, and this is, it turns out, the way experts think about problems. This is evident in many studies, including one in which novices and experts were asked to categorize simple physics problems (Chi, Feltovich, & Glaser, 1981). The novices tended to place together all the problems involving inclined planes, all the problems involving springs, and so on, in each case focusing on the surface form of the problem, independent of what physical principles were needed to solve the problem. In contrast, the experts (Ph.D. students in physics) ignored these details of the problems and, instead, sorted according to the physical principles relevant to the problem's solution. (Also see Cummins, 1992; Hardiman, Dufresne, & Mestre, 1989; Hinsley, Hayes, & Simon, 1977; Phillips et al., 2004; Reeves & Weisberg, 1994.)

We have also claimed that attention to a problem's structure promotes analogy use, and so, if experts are more attentive to this structure, then they should be more likely to use analogies. Several studies indicate that this is correct. For example, Novick and Holyoak (1991) examined their participants' skill in using mathematical analogies. They first provided the participants with a training problem; the participants then tried to solve several analogous problems. The data showed that participants with greater "math expertise" (measured via quantitative SAT scores) were, in fact, more likely to discover and use analogies. There was no relationship between analogy use and verbal SAT scores; what seems to matter, therefore, is not some sort of generalized skill. Instead, analogy use depends specifically on expertise within the relevant domain. (For related results, see Clement, 1982; Novick, 1988.)

Chunking and Subgoals

Experts also have another advantage, and it once again leads to a suggestion about how to *train* people so that they can become better problem-solvers. We mentioned earlier in the chapter that it is often helpful to break a problem into subproblems, so that the problem can be solved part by part rather than all at once. Related, it is often helpful to create subgoals while working on a problem, and to work on these rather than aiming only at the problem's ultimate goal. It turns out that these, too, are tech-

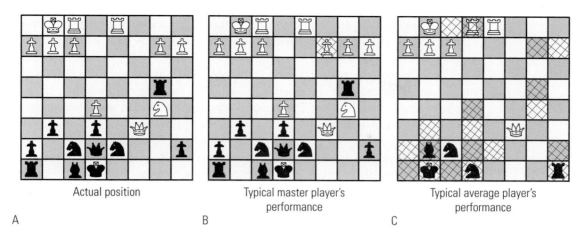

Actual position   Typical master player's performance   Typical average player's performance

A   B   C

FIGURE 14.11 Remembering Patterns

Experienced chess players who viewed the pattern in A for five seconds were easily able to memorize it; novices could not. This is because the experts were able to organize the pattern into meaningful chunks, lightening their memory load. Cross-hatched squares indicate memory errors.

niques often used by experts; crucially, these techniques are supported by the experts' understanding of the problem's deep structure.

Classic evidence on this point comes from studies of chess experts (De Groot, 1965, 1966; also see Chase & Simon, 1973), and the data show that these experts are particularly skilled in *organizing* a chess game—in seeing the structure of the game, understanding its parts, and perceiving how these parts are related to each other. This is revealed, for example, in how chess masters remember board positions. In one procedure, chess masters were able to remember the positions of 20 pieces after viewing the board for just 5 seconds; novices remembered many fewer (Figure 14.11). In addition, there was a strong pattern to the experts' recollection: In recalling the layout of the board, the experts would place four or five pieces in their proper positions, then pause, then recall another group, then pause, and so on. In each case, the group of pieces was one that made "tactical sense"—for example, the pieces involved in a "forked" attack, a chain of mutually defending pieces, and the like.

Plainly, the masters had memorized the board in terms of higher-order units, and not the individual pieces. These units, in turn, were defined according to their strategic function within the game. Consistent with this suggestion, the masters showed no memory advantage if asked to memorize random configurations of chess pieces. In this case, there were no sensible groupings, and so the masters were unable to organize (and thus memorize) the board. (Also see Gobet & Simon, 1996a, 1996b; but then see Gobet & Simon, 2000; Lassiter, 2000; Reingold, Charness, Pomplun, & Stampe, 2001.) And, of course, this pattern is not limited to chess experts: Similar results have been observed in other arenas, with masters in the game of Go showing a huge advantage for memorizing meaningful board positions (J. Reitman, 1976), and experts in electronics showing a similar advantage in memorizing circuit diagrams (Egan & Schwartz, 1979; for related data in SCRABBLE experts, see Tuffiash, Roring, & Ericsson, 2007).

Crucially, though, this perception of higher-order units doesn't just help memory; it also helps organize the expert's thinking. By focusing on the units and how they're related to each other, the expert keeps track of broad strategies without getting bogged down in the details. Likewise, these units help set subgoals for the expert: Having perceived a group of pieces as a coordinated attack, the expert sets the subgoal of preparing for the attack. Having perceived another group of pieces as "the early development of a pin," the expert creates the subgoal of avoiding the pin. In these ways, the higher-order units lend structure to the expert's thinking and guide the expert in choosing the next move.

Can nonexperts be trained to use subgoals in this way? Participants in one study were shown a new mathematical procedure, useful for calculating probabilities. For some of the participants, key steps of the procedure were labeled in a fashion that highlighted the function of those steps; for other participants, no labels were provided (Catrambone, 1998). Importantly, these labels had been chosen so that they didn't just add detail to the solution; instead, the labels were chosen so as to highlight the problem's structure, and so they potentially helped the participants to divide the procedure into meaningful parts and to see the role of each part within the larger solution. And, in fact, the labels were quite useful: Participants given the labels were better able to use this new procedure in solving novel problems, including novel problems that (superficially) differed from the training problems in a variety of ways.

The Nature of Expertise

We have now suggested that experts have several advantages in comparison to novices, including a greater use of analogies and a greater reliance on subgoals. And, as we have seen, various training programs can convey these advantages to nonexperts, making them better problem-solvers.

Let's be clear, though, that a few training sessions encouraging the use of analogies or subgoals won't turn someone into a problem-solving expert. That's because experts also have other advantages, including the simple fact that they know much more about their domains of expertise than novices do. Indeed, Hayes (1985) estimates that it takes at least 10 years to become an expert in a domain, presumably because it takes that long to accumulate the relevant experience (also see Holding, 1985). Moreover, experts don't rely on experience alone; they also gain their expertise through years of deliberate practice—paying careful attention to what they are doing, seeking feedback, and seeking explicit instruction. It seems to be these activities, and not just the experience itself, that allows experts to gain their extraordinary breadth of knowledge and their extraordinary skill (Ericsson & Ward, 2007).

There are also indications that experts *organize* their knowledge more effectively than novices. In particular, studies indicate that experts' knowledge is heavily cross-referenced, so that each bit of information has associations to many other bits (e.g., Bédard & Chi, 1992; Eylon & Reif, 1984; Heller & Reif, 1984). As a result, not only do experts know more, but they have faster, more effective access to what they know.

Experts may also differ from novices in the *strategies* they use (Lemaire & Siegler, 1995; Schunn, McGregor, & Saner, 2005). The key here is not that experts know strategies that novices don't. Instead, experts make better choices in which strategies they use, and they are also more effective in using the strategies—executing the strategies with greater skill and greater efficiency.

Finally, experts are also well practiced in working in their domain, well practiced in solving problems. This practice helps the experts to sharpen their skills (cf. Ericsson, 2005) and also helps them to establish certain routines for dealing with commonplace tasks. These routines, in turn, often allow an expert to recognize a new problem as being functionally identical to ones met earlier; with this done, the expert will give the problem no further thought, relying instead on the well-rehearsed routine. (For discussion, see J. R. Anderson, 1987; Ericsson, Krampe, & Tesch-Römer, 1993.)

Defining the Problem

It seems, then, that there are many differences between experts and novices, but one crucial difference lies in how each group's members *define* the problems they encounter. Novices usually define problems in terms of their superficial features, and this guides how they think about the problem and how they try to solve it. Experts, in contrast, define a problem in their area of expertise in terms of the problem's deep structure or underlying dynamic. As a result, the experts are more likely to break the problem into meaningful parts, more likely to realize what other problems are analogous to the current problem, so more likely to benefit from analogies.

Notice, therefore, that there are better and worse ways to define a problem—ways that will lead to a solution, and ways that will obstruct it. But what does it mean to "define" a problem? And what determines how we define the problems we encounter? We turn next to these crucial questions.

Ill-Defined and Well-Defined Problems

For many problems, the initial state, goal state, and operators are clearly defined from the start. In the "Hobbits and Orcs" problem (Figure 14.1), you know exactly where all the creatures stand at the beginning of the problem. You know exactly where you want the creatures to be at the problem's end. And you know exactly what operators you have available.

Many problems—including problems we encounter in our day-to-day lives—are rather different. We all hope for peace in the world, but what exactly will this goal look like? There will be no fighting, of course, but what other traits will the goal have? Will the nations currently on the map still be in place? How will disputes be settled? How will resources be allocated? It is also unclear what the operators should be for reaching this goal. Should we try making diplomatic adjustments? Or would economic measures be more effective—perhaps some pattern of commerce through which nations become more dependent on each other?

Problems like this one are said to be **ill-defined**, with no clear statement at the outset of how the goal should be characterized or what steps one might try in reaching that goal. Many problems are ill-defined—for example: "having a good time while on vacation," "saving money for college," or "choosing a good paper topic" (Halpern, 1984; Kahney, 1986; W. Reitman, 1964; Schraw, Dunkle, & Bendixen, 1995; Simon, 1973).

Problem-solvers have several options available when they confront ill-defined problems. One option is the creation of subgoals, because for many ill-defined problems there may be well-defined subproblems; by solving each of these, one can move toward solving the overall problem. A different strategy is to add some structure to the problem—by adding extra constraints or extra assumptions. In this way, you might gradually render the problem **well-defined** instead of ill-defined—perhaps with a narrower set of options in how you might approach the problem, but with a clearly specified goal state and, eventually, with a manageable set of operators to try.

Functional Fixedness

Even for well-defined problems, there is often more than one way to understand the problem. We have already met an example of this in the contrast between superficial and deeper-level descriptions of a problem. But other examples are easy to find.

For example, consider the candle problem presented in Figure 14.12. To solve this problem, you need to cease thinking of the box as a container. You need instead to think of it as a potential platform, and so solving the problem depends heavily on how the box is represented.

As a way of emphasizing this point, we can compare two groups of research participants. One group is given the equipment shown in Figure 14.12: some matches, a box of tacks, and a candle. This configuration (implicitly) underscores the box's conventional function—namely, as a container. As a result, this configuration increases **functional fixedness**—that is, the tendency to be rigid in how one thinks about an object's function. With this fixedness in place, the problem is rarely solved.

Other participants are given the same tools, but configured differently. They are given some matches, a pile of tacks, the box (now empty), and a candle. In this setting, the participants are less likely to think of the box as a container for the tacks, and so they are less likely to think of the box *as a container*. And in this setting, they are more likely to solve the problem (Duncker, 1945; also Adamson, 1952; Glucksberg & Danks, 1968; Weisberg & Suls, 1973; for an exploration of just how widespread

You are given the objects shown: a candle, a book of matches, and a box of tacks. Your task is to find a way to attach the candle to the wall of the room, at eye level, so that it will burn properly and illuminate the room.

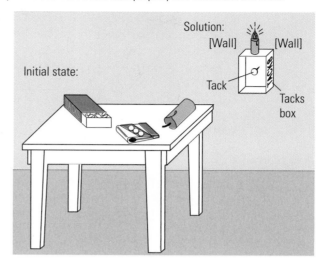

FIGURE 14.12 The Candle Problem
What makes this problem difficult is the tendency to think of the box of tacks as a box—that is, as a container. The problem is readily solved, though, once you think of the box as a potential platform.

this phenomenon is, see German & Barrett, 2005, for a demonstration of fixedness in a group of hunter-horticulturalists living in the Amazon region of Ecuador!).

Functional fixedness is also evident in studies of the two-string problem (see Figure 14.13). Few participants solve this problem, presumably because they are thinking of the pliers as a tool for grabbing and holding. To solve the problem, the pliers need to play a much simpler role, serving only as a weight, and participants will realize this only if they ignore the pliers' customary function. And, once again, we can make this problem even more difficult if we take steps to emphasize the pliers' standard function—if, for example, we use the pliers to pull a tack out of the table-top while instructing the participant in the overall task. Under these circumstances, fixedness is maximal, and virtually no participants solve the problem.

Einstellung

In the cases just described, people start out with a specific perspective on a problem and then seem unable to set that perspective aside. As a result, they're less likely to find the problem's solution. A related problem arises when people approach a problem in a sensible way but then, as they start to work on the problem, get locked into a particular line of thinking. In this case, too, people can end up being the victim of their own assumptions, rigidly following a path that no longer serves them well.

Psychologists use various terms to describe this rigidity in problem-solving. Some investigators speak of a **problem-solving set**—the collection of beliefs and assump-

You enter a room in which two strings are hanging from the ceiling and a pair of pliers is lying on a table. Your task is to tie the two strings together. Unfortunately, though, the strings are positioned far enough apart so that you can't grab one string and hold on to it while reaching for the other. How can you tie them together?

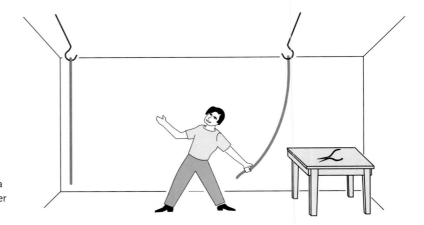

FIGURE 14.13 The Two-String Problem
To solve the problem, you should tie the pliers to one string, then push them gently away from the other string. Then grab the second string and wait until the pliers, as a pendulum, swing back to you. (After Maier, 1931)

tions a person makes about a problem—with the notion that once the person has a set, it is difficult for him to shift to a new one. Other investigators use the term **Einstellung**, the German word for "attitude," to describe the problem-solver's perspective (including his beliefs, his habits, his preferred strategies, and so on).

The effects of Einstellung are easy to demonstrate—including data drawn from the so-called water-jar problem. In this problem, you are given three jars: Jar A, which holds 18 ounces; Jar B, which holds 43 ounces; and Jar C, which holds 10 ounces. You have access to an unlimited supply of water. You also have a large, uncalibrated bucket. Your task is to pour exactly 5 ounces of water into the bucket. How would you do it?

The solution is to fill Jar B (43 ounces), then to pour water from Jar B into Jar A (which holds 18). Now Jar B contains 25 ounces of water. From this, fill Jar C (which holds 10 ounces); 15 ounces of water remains in Jar B. Dump Jar C, then fill it again from Jar B. Now 5 ounces of water remains in Jar B, so you are done (Figure 14.14).

Once participants have solved this problem, we give them a new problem. Jar A now holds 9 ounces, Jar B holds 42, and Jar C holds 6. The goal is to end up with 21 ounces. We then give participants a third problem: Jar A holds 21; B holds 127; C holds 3; the goal is 100 ounces. The series of problems is carefully designed such that all can be solved in the same way: One starts by filling the largest jar (B), pouring from it once into the middle-sized jar (A), then pouring from it twice into the smallest jar (C), leaving the desired amount.

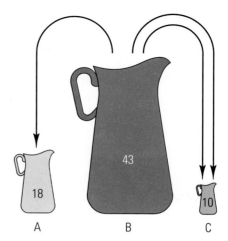

FIGURE 14.14 The Water-Jar Problem
Your task is to fill another container with exactly 5 ounces of water, with vessels A, B, and C as you only measuring tools. How would *you* solve the problem?

A   B   C

After solving four problems of this form, participants are given one more problem: Jar A holds 18 ounces; Jar B holds 48 ounces; Jar C holds 4 ounces. The goal is 22 ounces. Participants generally solve this problem the same way they have solved the previous problems. They apparently fail to see that a different, more direct route to the goal is possible—by filling A, filling C, and then combining these (18 + 4). Their prior success in using the same procedure over and over renders them blind to the more efficient alternative.

More troubling, consider what happens if participants are given the training problems just described, all solved via the same path, and then given this problem: Jar A holds 28 ounces; Jar B holds 76; Jar C holds 3. The goal is 25 ounces. The participants attack this problem by using their tried-and-true method: B, minus A, minus C twice. But this time the method fails (yielding 42 ounces, instead of the desired 25). When participants realize this, they are often stymied; their well-practiced routine won't work here, and they fail to see the much simpler path that would work (28 minus 3 equals 25). Remarkably, 64% of the participants fail to solve this problem, thanks to their history of using a now-inapplicable strategy (Luchins, 1942; Luchins & Luchins, 1950, 1959).

Notice that in a sense participants are doing something sensible here: Once you discover a strategy that "gets the job done," you might as well use that strategy. Correspondingly, once you discover a strategy that works, there is little reason to continue hunting for other, alternative strategies. It is a little unsettling, though, that this mechanization of problem-solving prevents people from discovering other, simpler strategies. Worse, this mechanization actually interferes with problem-solving: Once they have learned one strategy for solving water-jar problems, people seem less able to discover new strategies. When a new problem arrives that cannot be solved with the prior formula, performance suffers.

"Outside the Box"

Another often-discussed example of a problem-solving set involves the nine-dot problem, illustrated in Figure 14.15. People routinely fail to solve this problem, because—according to some interpretations—they (mistakenly) assume that the lines they draw need to stay inside the "square" defined by the dots. In fact, this problem is likely to be the source of the common cliché, "You need to think outside of the box."

Ironically, though, this is probably the wrong account of the nine-dot problem. In one study, participants were told explicitly that to solve this problem their lines would need to go outside the square. This hint, however, provided little benefit: 12 out of the 15 participants were still unable to find the solution (Weisberg & Alba, 1981). Apparently, then, mistaken beliefs about "the box" are not the obstacle here, because even when we eradicate these beliefs, performance remains poor.

Nonetheless, the expression "think outside the box" does get the broad idea right, because to solve this problem people do need to shift away from their initial approach and to jettison their initial assumptions. More specifically, most people assume, in tackling the nine-dot problem, that the lines they draw must begin and end on dots. People also have the idea that they'll need to maximize the number of dots "canceled" with each move; as a result, they seek solutions in which each line cancels a full row or column of dots. It turns out, though, that both of these assumptions are wrong, and so, guided by these mistaken beliefs, people find this problem quite hard (Kershaw & Ohlsson, 2004; MacGregor, Ormerod, & Chronicle, 2001).

In this problem, therefore, people seem to be victims of their own problem-solving set; to find the problem's solution, they need to change that set. This makes

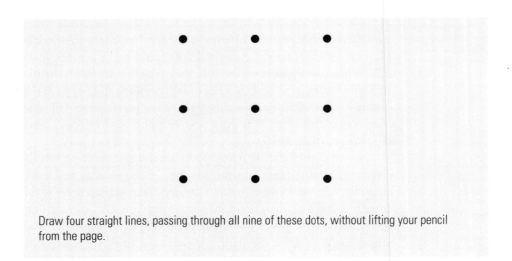

Draw four straight lines, passing through all nine of these dots, without lifting your pencil from the page.

FIGURE 14.15 The Nine-Dot Problem
Most people have difficulty with this problem, probably because of an inappropriate problem-solving set.

it sound like a set is a bad thing, blocking the discovery of a solution. We need to remind ourselves, therefore, that sets also provide enormous benefits. This is because (as we mentioned early on) most problems offer a huge number of options as you seek the solution—an enormous number of moves you might try or approaches you might consider. A problem-solving set helps you, therefore, by narrowing your options, which in turn eases the search for a solution. Thus, in solving the nine-dot problem, you didn't waste any time wondering whether you should try drawing the lines while holding the pencil between your toes, or whether the problem was hard because you were sitting down while you worked on it and should have been standing up. Likewise, you didn't consider the option of waiting for Martians to visit, so that they could whisper the solution in your ear. These are all foolish ideas, so you brushed past them. But what identifies them as foolish? It is your problem-solving set, which tells you, among other things, which options are plausible, which are physically possible, and the like.

In short, there are both benefits and costs to a problem-solving set. A set can blind you to important options, and so it can be an obstacle. But a set also blinds you to a wide range of futile strategies, and this is a good thing: It allows you to focus, much more productively, on options that are likely to work out. Indeed, without a set, you might be so distracted by silly notions that even the simplest problem would become insoluble.

Creativity

Approaching a problem with a productive set (the right assumptions, the right representation) can help us in important ways. Approaching a problem with the wrong set, in contrast, can make the problem enormously difficult. Worse, if one does start with the wrong representation, it is hard to shift gears, thanks to phenomena like Einstellung. All of this demands that we ask: How does one find an appropriate problem-solving set? How does one figure out how to approach a problem?

Case Studies of Creativity

We have already noted that a problem's solution can, in many cases, be suggested by an analogy to a previously solved problem. In the same fashion, a *set* can be suggested by analogy. If the current problem reminds you of a previously solved case, you are likely to adopt the same set that worked previously: You will make the same assumptions and try the same operations as you did on the prior occasion. What if no analogy comes to mind? In this case, you will be forced to use some less insightful, more laborious strategy—perhaps trial and error, or hill-climbing, or working backward from the problem's solution.

Surely, though, there is more to problem-solving than this. What about cases of insight or cases in which one suddenly finds a new and creative way to approach a

Creativity and Problem-Solving
Artist Henry Moore has produced many sculptures over his lifetime, and these works are considered to be enormously creative. Remarkably, though, the "ordinary" problem-solving skills we have discussed in this chapter may play a crucial role in this extraordinary creativity.

problem? These don't seem like cases of searching through memory for an analogy or cases based on heuristic use. What, then, can we say about these cases?

One way to approach these questions is by examining individuals who have undeniably been enormously creative—great artists like Picasso and Bach, or innovative scientists like Charles Darwin and Marie Curie. These are people who found innovative ways to approach their work, whether that work was in art or in science. Perhaps, therefore, by studying these people we can find out how new approaches to a problem can be found, how new sets can be established. We might then be able to draw hints from this about the nature of creativity when it arises—on a much smaller scale—in day-to-day life. With that, we'll be able to tackle the question with which we began this section—the question of how one finds a good approach to a problem, rather than a futile one; an appropriate problem-solving set rather than one that will block progress.

Many researchers have examined the creativity of individuals like Picasso and Darwin, and this inquiry reveals that highly creative people tend to have certain things in common, so that, perhaps, we can think of these shared elements as "prerequisites" for great creativity. These individuals, first of all, need to have knowledge and skills in their domain. If one doesn't know a lot of chemistry, one cannot be a creative chemist.

If one is not a skilled storyteller, one cannot be a creative novelist, and so on. Second, to be creative, one must be the "right sort of person." That is, one must have certain intellectual capacities (e.g., creative people tend to be intelligent) and also certain personality traits, including a willingness to take risks, a willingness to ignore criticism, an ability to tolerate ambiguous findings or situations, and an inclination not to "follow the crowd." Third, highly creative people tend to be motivated by the pleasure of their work rather than by the promise of external rewards. With this, highly creative people tend to work extremely hard on their endeavors and to produce a lot of their product, whether that product is poems, paintings, or scientific papers. Fourth, there is an important sense in which highly creative people have been "in the right place at the right time"—that is, in environments that allowed them freedom, that provided them with the appropriate supports, and that offered them problems that were "ripe" for solution with the resources available. (For discussion of these "prerequisites" for creativity, see Amabile, 2001; Gruber & Wallace, 2001; Nakamura & Csikszentmihalyi, 2001; Sternberg, 2001; Sternberg & Dess, 2001; Stokes, 2001; Ward, 2001.)

Notice, then, that creativity involves factors outside of the person, as well as the person's own capacities and skills. The external environment, for example, is the source of the relevant knowledge and often defines the problem itself; this is why many authors have suggested that we need a "sociocultural approach" to creativity—one that considers the social, cultural, and historical context, as well as the processes unfolding inside the creative individual's mind (e.g., Sawyer, 2006). Even so, we still need to ask: What does go on in a creative mind? If one has all the prerequisites just listed, what happens next to produce the creative step forward?

One proposal was offered many years ago by Wallas (1926), who argued that creative thought proceeds through four stages. In the first stage, **preparation**, the problem-solver gathers information about the problem. This stage is typically characterized by periods of effortful, often frustrating work on the problem, generally with little progress. In the second stage, **incubation**, the problem-solver sets the problem to the side and seems not to be working on it. Wallas argued, though, that the problem-solver was continuing to work on the problem during this stage, albeit unconsciously. Thus, the problem solution is continuing to develop, unseen, just as the baby bird develops, unseen, inside the egg. This period of incubation leads to the third stage, **illumination**, in which some key insight or new idea emerges, paving the way for the fourth stage, **verification**, in which one confirms that the new idea really does lead to a problem solution and works out the details.

The Moment of Illumination

There are certainly elements of truth in Wallas's ideas, but we should not take his "four-stage" notion too literally. As one concern, historical evidence suggests that many creative discoveries either don't include the four steps or, if they do, include them in a complex, back-and-forth sequence (Weisberg, 1986). Likewise, the moment of great illumination, celebrated in Wallas's proposal, may be more myth than reality: When we examine truly creative discoveries (Watson and Crick's discovery of the double helix; Calder's invention of the mobile as a form of sculpture; etc.), we find that these new ideas developed through a succession of "mini-insights," each moving the process forward in some way rather than springing forth, full-blown, from some remarkable "Aha!" moment (Sawyer, 2006).

For that matter, what exactly does the "Aha!" experience—a moment in which people feel they've made a great leap forward—involve? Wallas proposed that this moment indicates the arrival of the solution or, at least, the arrival of the insight that would lead to the solution. But is this right? Metcalfe (1986; Metcalfe & Weibe, 1987) gave her participants a series of "insight problems" like those shown in Figure 14.16. As participants worked on each problem, they rated their progress by using a judgment of "warmth" ("I'm getting warmer . . . , I'm getting warmer. . . ."). These ratings did capture the "moment of insight": Initially, the participants didn't have a clue how to proceed and gave warmth ratings of 1 or 2; then, rather abruptly, they saw how to solve the problem, and at that instant their warmth ratings shot up to the top of the scale.

To understand this pattern, though, we need to look separately at those participants who subsequently announced the correct solution to the problem and those who announced an *incorrect* solution. As you can see in Figure 14.17, the pattern is the same for these two groups. Thus, some participants abruptly announced that they were getting "hot" and, moments later, solved the problem. Other participants

Problem 1
A stranger approached a museum curator and offered him an ancient bronze coin. The coin had an authentic appearance and was marked with the date 544 B.C. The curator had happily made acquisitions from suspicious sources before, but this time he promptly called the police and had the stranger arrested. Why?

Problem 2
A landscape gardener is given instructions to plant four special trees so that each one is exactly the same distance from each of the others. How should the trees be arranged?

FIGURE 14.16 Insight Problems

As participants worked on these problems, they were asked to judge their progress by using an assessment of "warmth" ("I'm getting warmer . . . , I'm getting warmer . . . , I'm getting hot!"). For the first problem, you must realize that no one in the year 544 B.C. knew that it was 544 B.C.; that is, no one could have known that Christ would be born exactly 544 years later. For the second problem, the gardener needs to plant one of the trees at the top of a tall mound, and then plant the other three around the base of the mound, with the three together forming an equilateral triangle, and with the four forming a triangle-based pyramid (i.e., a tetrahedron).

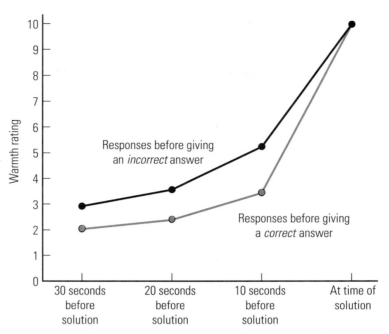

FIGURE 14.17 Self-assessments of Progress While Solving Insight Problems
Initially, participants had little idea about how to proceed with these problems and gave very low "warmth" ratings. Then, abruptly, they saw how to solve the problem, and at that moment their warmth ratings shot up to the top of the scale. An important point, though, is that the same pattern was observed for participants who then announced a correct solution to the problem and for those who then announced an *incorrect* solution. Thus, it seems that participants really can't tell when they are on the verge of correctly solving a problem. Sometimes they shout, "Aha!" only to slam into a dead end a moment later.

made the same announcement and, moments later, slammed into a dead end. Indeed, if there is any difference at all between these two groups, it appears that the participants who are on the wrong track are more confident in their progress than those who are on the right track.

In short, then, when we say, "Aha!" it means only that we've discovered a new approach, one that we've not yet considered. This is by itself important, because often a new approach is just what we need. But there is nothing magical about the "moment of illumination." This moment doesn't signal the fact that we have at last discovered the problem's solution, or even that we have discovered a path leading to the solution. Instead, it means only that we've discovered something new to try, with no guarantee whatsoever that this "something new" will be helpful. (For more on insight, illumination, and how one overcomes a problem-solving impasse, see Chronicle, MacGregor, & Ormerod, 2004; Jones, 2003; Knoblich, Ohlsson, & Raney, 2001; Sternberg & Davidson, 1995; for discussion of the neural mechanisms underlying insight, see Bowden, Jung-Beeman, Fleck & Kounios, 2005.)

Incubation

What about Wallas's second stage, the stage of incubation? In this stage, problem-solvers seem to set the problem aside, but they (allegedly) continue to work on it unconsciously and, as a result, make considerable progress.

Many people find this an appealing idea, since most of us have had an experience along these lines: You are working on a problem but getting nowhere. After a while, you give up and turn your thoughts to other matters. Sometime later, though, you try the problem again and are able to solve it. Or perhaps, later on, you are thinking about something altogether different when the solution suddenly pops into your thoughts.

Many examples of this pattern have been recorded, with a number of authors pointing out that great scientific discoveries have often been made in this manner (e.g., Kohler, 1969). As a more modest example, consider the tip-of-the-tongue (TOT) phenomenon, which we described in Chapter 8. In this phenomenon, you are struggling to think of a specific word but can't. Often your best strategy is to give up and try again later. When you do, there is a reasonable likelihood that the word will come to you.

It turns out, though, that the incubation effect is somewhat unreliable: Many studies do show that time away from a problem helps in finding the problem's solution, but other studies find no effect (Dodds, Ward, & Smith, 2007; Sio & Ormerod, 2009). More important, it's not clear *why* the interruption aids problem solving, and the answer probably involves a broad mix of factors. For one, in Chapter 8 we described the process of *spreading activation*, through which one memory can activate related memories. It is possible that when consciously working on a problem, people try to direct this flow of activation—and may end up directing it in unproductive ways. When someone is not actively thinking about a problem, in contrast, the activation can flow wherever the memory connections take it, and this may lead to new ideas being activated (cf. Ash & Wiley, 2006; Bowden et al., 2005; Schooler, Ohlsson, & Brooks, 1993). Of course, this process provides no guarantee that *helpful* or *productive* ideas will come to mind, only that *more* (and perhaps unanticipated) ideas will be activated. In this fashion, incubation is like illumination—a source of new possibilities, which may or may not pay off.

In addition, time away from a problem may be helpful for other reasons having little to do with Wallas's notion of incubation. For example, the interruption may allow problem-solvers to gather new information—perhaps because, during the time away from the problem, they stumble across some clue in the environment or in their own memories. In other cases, the interruption may simply allow problem-solvers a fresh start on a problem. Their early efforts with a problem may have been tiring or frustrating, and the interruption may provide an opportunity for this frustration or fatigue to dissipate. Likewise, their early efforts with a problem may have been dominated by a particular approach, a particular set. If they put the problem aside for a while, it is possible for them to forget these earlier tactics, and this will free them to explore other, more productive avenues.

In fact, there is direct evidence for this "forgetting" effect. Smith and Blankenship (1989, 1991; also Segal, 2004; Vul & Pashler, 2007) gave their participants playful puzzles to solve. Clues were given for each problem, but for many of the problems the clues were designed to be misleading. Control participants had a minute to work on each puzzle; other participants worked on each puzzle for 30 seconds, then were interrupted, and later returned to the puzzle for an additional 30 seconds.

This interruption did improve performance, so that problem solution was more likely for the "incubation" group. Crucially, though, Smith and Blankenship also tested participants' memory for the misleading clues, and the researchers found that the incubation participants were less likely to remember the clues. Smith and Blankenship argued that this forgetting is what created the "incubation" advantage: After the interruption, participants were no longer misled by the bad clues, and their performance improved accordingly. (For closely related evidence, see Vul & Pashler, 2007.)

The Nature of Creativity

Where does all of this leave us? We entered this section with the question of how one chooses the proper set, the proper approach, when solving a problem. We linked this to the question of creativity simply because one essential element of creativity is the ability to define problems in a new and valuable fashion—a fashion that opens up new possibilities or points the way toward solutions for problems that had previously been regarded as insoluble. Hence, if we understand creativity, we understand (among other things) how one finds new and productive ways to define and approach a problem.

It would seem, though, that the cognitive processes involved in creativity are quite similar to those involved in other, more mundane forms of problem-solving—and this is, in some ways, an amazing claim. After all, one stands in awe of creative geniuses like da Vinci, Einstein, and Beethoven. So remarkable are their accomplishments, so different from what you and I produce, that it is natural to assume their thought processes are no less distinctive. You and I, equipped with heuristics, analogies, and subgoals, have troubles enough with Hobbits and Orcs. It seems unlikely, therefore, that the same intellectual tools could have led to the creativity obvious in great works of art, great innovations of science, and great inventions. The presumption, then, is that this creativity must arise from some other source—some different form of thinking, some other approach to problem-solving.

The evidence, however, is otherwise. When we examine Darwin's notebooks or Picasso's early sketches, we discover that they relied on analogies and hints and heuristics, and a lot of hard work, just as the rest of us do (Gruber, 1981; Sawyer, 2006; Weisberg, 1986). Likewise, when we examine processes like illumination and incubation, we realize that these processes are less mysterious than they first seem. As we have seen, the "Aha!" feeling of illumination reflects only the fact that a person has discovered new things to try, new approaches to explore, in working on a problem. These new approaches may have been triggered by an analogy or by an association in memory, and crucially, these new approaches bring no guarantee of success. In many cases, people stumble onto a new approach and shout "Aha!" only to discover that the new approach leads them no closer to their goal.

Similarly, the topic of incubation has fascinated many authors, and much has been written about the role of incubation within the creative process. However, the evidence for incubation is uneven: It is unclear whether time off from a problem provides any consistent benefit, in contrast to continued effort on the same problem. Even when an "incubation" effect is observed, the process is not a magical one. Instead, incubation seems best explained in terms of the ordinary mechanism of spreading activation, as well as the dissipation of fatigue, opportunity for discovering new clues, forgetting of previous false starts, and the like.

Of course, highly creative people do have certain advantages. For example, as experts in their domains, they have memories that are highly cross-referenced (pp. 460–61), and this allows them to find and use associations that other people might miss. Similarly, highly creative people seem to have an advantage in finding novel associations for an idea; this is the base for what is commonly called "divergent thinking" (Guilford, 1967, 1979; see Figure 14.18; for a related notion, see Figure 14.19).

Tests of divergent thinking require you to think of new uses for simple objects or new ways to think about familiar ideas. How many different uses can you think of for a brick?

As a paperweight.
As the shadow-caster in a sundial (if positioned appropriately).
As a means of writing messages on a sidewalk.
As a stepladder (if you want to grab something just slightly out of reach).
As a nutcracker.
As a pendulum useful for solving the two-string problem.

Choose five names, at random, from the telephone directory. In how many different ways could these names be classified?

According to the number of syllables.
According to whether there is an even or odd number of vowels.
Accordng to whether their third letter is in the last third of the alphabet.
According to whether they rhyme with things that are edible.

FIGURE 14.18 **Creativity as Divergent Thinking**
Guilford (1967, 1979) argued that creativity lies in the ability to take an idea in a new, unprecedented direction. Among its other items, his test of creativity asks people to think of new uses for a familiar object. Some possible responses are listed here.

For each trio of words, think of a fourth word that is related to each of the first three. For example, for the trio "snow, down, out," the answer would be "fall" ("snowfall"; "downfall"; "fallout").

1. off   top   tail

2. ache   sweet   burn

3. dark   shot   sun

4. arm   coal   peach

5. tug   gravy   show

FIGURE 14.19 Creativity as the Ability to Find New Connections

Mednick (1962; Mednick & Mednick, 1967) argued that creativity lies in the ability to find new connections among ideas. This ability is measured in the Remote Associates Test, for which some sample items are shown here. The solutions are (1) "spin" ("spin-off"; "topspin"; "tailspin"); (2) "heart"; (3) "glasses"; (4) "pit"; (5) "boat."

Some early theorists, in fact, suggested that divergent thinking is the essence of creativity. This view is probably overstated, but even so, the sort of memory search involved in divergent thinking surely contributes to creativity (Baer, 1993; Barron & Huntingdon, 1981).

Even with these advantages in memory search, however, highly creative individuals do seem to be using the same search processes as everyone else: spreading activation, triggering associated ideas in memory. Yes, they are better at the process than the rest of us are, and so they're less likely to trigger the same memories again and again, and more likely to trigger new ideas. But even so, the fact remains that there's no "special" creativity mechanism here; there's just a greater level of skill in using the "standard machinery" of memory search.

In light of all of this, is it possible that there really is nothing special about the mental processes underlying creativity? To be sure, the creative *product* is extraordinary, but could it be that this product is the result of the same processes, the same forms of thinking, as more "ordinary" thought? Many authors have endorsed this idea, arguing that we need no special mental mechanisms to explain creativity. (See, for example, J. Goldenberg, Mazursky, & Solomon, 1999; Klahr & Simon, 2001; Simonton, 2003; Sternberg, 1988; Weisberg, 1986, 1988.) The "ingredients" of creativity, in other words, are available to all of us—or perhaps *would* be available if we simply acquired expertise in the relevant domain.

What, then, is so special about Newton or Michelangelo or Bach? The possibility before us is that these individuals did not rely on some special intellectual tools or some extraordinary thought processes in attaining their towering greatness. What distinguished these extraordinary individuals, therefore, was simply that they had *all* of the right tools and *all* of the right ingredients—including intellectual tools, certain personality characteristics, the right cultural setting and social supports, and so on. In other words, what makes certain scientists, and artists, and inventors great is that they have the heuristics, and the expertise, and the appropriately cross-referenced memory, and the right training and opportunities, and the appropriate personal traits, and plenty of motivation. Of course, very few people have all these ingredients, and it is the convergence of these elements that may, perhaps, be the recipe for achieving monumental creativity.

Chapter Summary

■ Problem-solving is often likened to a process of search in which one seeks a path leading from a starting point to the goal. In many problems, though, there are far too many paths to allow examination of each, and this is why problem-solving heuristics are crucial. Heuristics applicable to a wide range of problems include hill-climbing, means–end analysis, and working backward from the goal.

■ Problem-solving is also often aided by mental models, visual images, or diagrams. For some purposes, these work equally well, but each has its own advantages. Visual images are easily adjusted if one wishes to change the size or position of some element. Diagrams, in contrast, have the advantage of standing independent of our interpretation of them, and thus they can facilitate reinterpretation.

■ Analogies to earlier-solved problems are often helpful, but nonetheless, analogies seem to be underused by many problem-solvers. Analogy use is most likely if the current problem is similar in superficial ways to the (potential) analogue; these similarities help remind the problem-solver of the analogue, and they also help her map the analogue onto the current problem. Analogy use can be promoted, however, by suitable instruction. For example, people are more likely to find analogues (and so more likely to solve problems) if they focus on a problem's deep structure rather than its surface characteristics.

■ Experts in a domain generally pay more attention to a problem's underlying structure, rather than its surface form, and this helps the experts find and use analogies. Focusing on the problem's underlying structure also helps the experts to break the problem into subproblems.

■ The likelihood of solving a problem is enormously influenced by how someone perceives or defines the problem. The problem definition can include unnoticed assumptions about the form the solution must take, assumptions about the use or function of elements contained within the problem, and assumptions about what types of procedures one should try in solving the problem. These various forms of problem-solving sets are usually helpful, because they guide the problem-solver away from pointless lines of attack on the problem. But the problem-solving set can also be an obstacle to problem-solving—if, for example, the solution requires a change in the set. Thus, problem-solving sets in the form of functional fixedness or Einstellung can often be significant obstacles to problem solution.

■ Investigators interested in creativity have often relied on detailed case studies of famous creative individuals. These case studies are said to reflect four stages of problem-solving: preparation, incubation, illumination, and verification.

■ However, researchers are skeptical about these four stages, and careful studies of creativity have provided little evidence to suggest that creativity involves special or exotic processes. For example, incubation is often mentioned as a form of unconscious problem-solving, but studies indicate that the benefits of incubation, when they occur, can be understood in simpler terms: recovery from fatigue or the forgetting of unfruitful earlier approaches. In the same way, the moment of illumination seems to indicate only that the problem-solver has located a new approach to a problem; in many cases, this new approach ends up leading to a dead end.

■ In light of these data, many authors have suggested that creativity may simply be the extraordinary product that results from an assembly of ordinary elements—elements that include cognitive processes (memory search through spreading activation, heuristics, etc.), and also emotional and personality characteristics that foster the processes and circumstances needed for creativity.

The Workbook Connection

See the *Cognition Workbook* for further exploration of problem-solving:

■ Demonstration 14.1: Analogies
■ Demonstration 14.2: Incubation
■ Demonstration 14.3: Verbalization and Problem-Solving
■ Research Methods: Defining the Dependent Variable
■ Cognitive Psychology and Education: Making Better Problem Solvers
■ Cognitive Psychology and the Law: Problem-Solving in the Courts

Conscious Thought, Unconscious Thought

It was a bit more than a century ago that the field of psychology emerged as a separate discipline, distinct from philosophy or biology. And in those early years of our field, the topic of consciousness was a central concern: In Wilhelm Wundt's laboratory in Germany, researchers sought to understand the "elements" of consciousness; William James, in America, sought to understand the "stream" of consciousness.

However, the young field of psychology soon rejected this focus on consciousness, arguing that this research was subjective and unscientific. By the early 20th century, therefore, the topic of consciousness was largely gone from mainstream psychological research (although *theorizing* about consciousness, without much experimentation, continued, particularly among clinical psychologists).

Over the last few decades, though, it has become clear that a scientific investigation of consciousness is possible, and armed with new tools and new conceptualizations, researchers have made enormous advances in their understanding of what consciousness is, how it functions, and how the brain makes consciousness possible. Ironically, much of this progress has come not from examining consciousness directly, but from studying what happens in the absence of conscious awareness. This strategy has allowed us to detail the sorts of circumstances in which consciousness seems not to be needed; this, in turn, has allowed valuable insights into when consciousness *is* needed and, with that, just what it is that consciousness contributes to our mental lives. This understanding of what consciousness is *for* has illuminated questions about what consciousness *is*.

Let's acknowledge at the start, though, that there is still much about consciousness that we do not understand and, indeed, still disagreement about how consciousness should be defined and studied. With that, there is still disagree-

- Throughout this text, we have discussed processes that provide an unnoticed support structure for cognition. We begin, therefore, by reviewing themes from earlier chapters, in order to ask what sorts of things are accomplished within the "cognitive unconscious."

- Overall, it appears that we can perform a task unconsciously if we arrive at the task with an already-established routine, directly applicable to that task, and if the routine can be guided by strong habits or by powerful cues within the situation.

- This reliance on unconscious operations is fast and efficient, but these operations are also inflexible and difficult to control. They free us to pay attention to higher-order aspects of a task, but also leave us ignorant about the sources of our ideas, beliefs, and memories.

- From a biological perspective, we know that most operations of the brain are made possible by highly specialized modules. These modules can be interrelated by means of workspace neurons, literally connecting one area of the brain to another and allowing the integration of different processing streams.

- The workspace neurons create a "global workspace," and this is literally what makes consciousness possible; the operations of this workspace fit well with many things we know to be true about consciousness.

- However, profound questions remain about how (or whether) the global workspace makes possible the subjective experience that for many theorists is the defining element of consciousness.

ment about whether we should distinguish different types of consciousness or, at least, different sorts of things that might be included under the broad label of "consciousness."

We will return to these conceptual issues later in the chapter. For now, we'll proceed with this rough definition: Consciousness is a state of awareness of sensations or ideas, such that we can reflect on those sensations and ideas, know what it "feels like" to experience these sensations and ideas, and can, in many cases, report to others that we are aware of the sensations and ideas. As we'll see later, this broad definition has certain problems, but it will serve us well enough as an initial guide for our discussion.

The Cognitive Unconscious

Throughout this book, we've seen that our intellectual lives require an elaborate "support structure." Thinking, remembering, and categorizing (to name just a few of our intellectual achievements) all feel like they're quick and effortless, but, as we have discussed, these activities depend on a great deal of work taking place "behind the scenes." In a sense, describing this behind-the-scenes action has been one of the main concerns of this text.

Psychologists refer to this behind-the-scenes activity as the **cognitive unconscious**—activity of which we are completely unaware but that makes possible our ordinary interactions with the world. Let's emphasize, though, that the cognitive unconscious is rather different from the sort of thing that many people have in mind when they speak of "unconscious" thoughts or memories. Roughly 100 years ago,

Sigmund Freud proposed that people defend themselves from anxiety by pushing certain ideas out of consciousness—and so into the unconscious mind. Moreover, Freud argued that the unconscious mind has its own goals and its own logic, separate from those of the conscious mind. Most modern psychologists, however, believe that the evidence for Freud's claims is (at best) unpersuasive, and the unconscious mechanisms proposed by contemporary theorists are very different from Freud's: Processes that unfold in the cognitive unconscious are in no sense threatening, nor are they actively suppressed. These processes don't have an agenda separate from that of the conscious mind; instead, the cognitive unconscious serves and supports the conscious mind; specifically, it involves the underlying processes that make conscious experience possible. In this way, the cognitive unconscious may seem less exotic than the unconscious that Freud envisioned, but, as we'll see, the cognitive unconscious is rich, powerful, and intriguing!

Unconscious Processes, Conscious Products

It seems obvious that we're aware of the *products* created within our minds—and so we're aware of and can report on what our beliefs are, or what conclusions we've reached, or what we're perceiving at any given moment. Many investigators have proposed, though, that we are unaware of the *processes* that led to these products—and so we do not know and cannot report on the steps that led us to our beliefs or conclusions or perceptions. (For discussion of the process/product distinction, see G. A. Miller, 1962; Neisser, 1967; Nisbett & Wilson, 1977; E. Smith & Miller, 1978; White, 1988.)

For example, consider these mundane bits of memory retrieval: What is your mother's first name? What is your father's first name? Odds are that the answers just popped into your mind. You presumably had no awareness of searching through memory, of "traveling" from node to node within a network. You surely had no awareness of activation spreading out from the node for MOTHER'S NAME—activation that then facilitated the retrieval of your father's name. Yet, as we saw in Chapter 8, there is reason to believe that all of these processes were relevant to this bit of memory retrieval. The processes, however, were hidden from your view; all that you were aware of was the product—in this case, the two sought-after names.

As a different example, imagine that we briefly show the stimulus "CORN" to one group of people and the stimulus "CQRN" to a second group. As we discussed in Chapter 3, both groups are likely to perceive the stimulus as "CORN" and, in all likelihood, won't know whether they were in the first group (and so correctly perceived the stimulus) or in the second (so that, guided by an inference, they *mis*perceived the stimulus). Thus, both groups are aware of the product created by their minds (and so both groups have the experience of "seeing" the word "CORN"), but they're entirely unaware of the processes and are, in essence, clueless about whether the stimulus was actually perceived or merely inferred.

Similar themes emerged in Chapter 7, when we discussed memory errors. As we saw in that chapter, people often do make memory errors and cannot detect these errors. More specifically, people usually cannot tell when they are genuinely remembering something and when they have instead inferred (or assumed or imagined) that something happened. This is, therefore, another case in which people are aware of a product (a belief about the past) but not the process (and so they cannot tell apart events that come into their mind because of a bona fide memory, and events that come into their mind because of an inference or assumption).

The Influence of Unconscious Attributions

The role of the cognitive unconscious is also evident in studies of implicit memory (Chapter 6). In these studies, participants are plainly being influenced by events they cannot consciously recall. Moreover, this influence often seems to require several steps of reasoning: "That name rings a bell, and I'm not sure why. But the experimenter is asking me about famous names, and there are other famous names on this list in front of me. I guess, therefore, that this one must also be the name of some famous person." This inference surely sounds like something that we want to count as "thinking," but it is thinking, the evidence suggests, of which we are entirely unaware.

A similar pattern is evident in cases involving source confusion (Chapter 6). In these cases, someone seems to reason this way: "That face looks familiar to me, and the police think it's likely that this is the person who robbed me. I guess, therefore, that the face is familiar because I saw this person at the robbery." But it's not this reasoning that the person is aware of. Instead, the person simply (and sometimes falsely) "remembers" seeing the person at the robbery, and so he can end up, in some circumstances, being an unwitting victim of his own mistaken inference.

These examples suggest that our unconscious thinking can sometimes be rather sophisticated—with layers of inference and reasoning. This sophistication is particularly evident when the unconscious thinking involves a **causal attribution**—that is, reasoning about the cause to which we should attribute some fact. ("The name rings a bell because it belongs to someone famous." "The face looks familiar because I saw that person at the robbery.")

As another example of unconscious causal reasoning, consider an early experiment by Nisbett and Schachter (1966). Their participants were asked to endure a series of electric shocks, with each shock being slightly more severe than the one before. The question of interest was how far into the series the participants would go. What was the maximum shock they would voluntarily accept?

Before beginning the series of shocks, some of the participants were given a pill that, they were told, would diminish the pain but would also have several side effects: The pill would cause their hands to shake, butterflies in the stomach, irregular breathing, and the like. Of course, none of this was true. The pill was a placebo and had no analgesic properties, nor did it produce any of these side effects. Even so, this inert pill was remarkably effective: Participants given the pill and told about its side effects were willing to accept four times as much amperage as control participants.

Why was the placebo so effective? Nisbett and Schachter proposed that their control participants noticed that their hands were shaking, that their stomachs were upset, and so on. (These are standard reactions to electric shock.) The participants then used these self-observations as evidence in judging that they were quite uncomfortable in the experiment. It is as if participants said to themselves, "Oh look, I'm trembling! I guess I must be scared. Therefore, these shocks must really be bothering me." This led them to terminate the shock series relatively early. Placebo participants, in contrast, attributed the same physical symptoms to the pill. "Oh look, I'm trembling! That's just what the experimenter said the pill would do. I guess I can stop worrying, therefore, about the trembling. Let me look for some other indication of whether the shock is bothering me." As a consequence, these participants were less influenced by their own physical symptoms and less influenced by what, in Chapter 13, we called "somatic markers." They detected these markers but discounted them, attributing them to the pill and not to the shock. In essence, they overruled the evidence of their own anxiety and so misread their own internal state. (For related studies, see Nisbett & Wilson, 1977; Wilson, 2002; Wilson & Dunn, 2004.)

Of course, participants' reasoning about the pill was entirely unconscious. We know that they were thinking about the pill, because participants who received the pill (plus the instructions about the side effects) behaved in a fashion markedly different from other participants. But the participants seemed to be entirely unaware of this thinking. When they were specifically asked why they had accepted so much shock, they rarely mentioned the pill. When asked directly, "While you were taking the shock, did you think about the pill at all?" they responded with answers like, "No, I was too worried about the shock to think of anything else."

Note also the *complexity* of the unconscious thinking in this experiment. The participants are reasoning about themselves in an intellectually sophisticated manner: observing "symptoms," generating hypotheses about those symptoms, drawing conclusions, and so on. As it turns out, in this case the participants reached erroneous conclusions, because they had been misled about the pill by the experimenter. But that takes nothing away from what they are doing intellectually—and unconsciously.

Mistaken Introspections

It does seem useful, then, to distinguish between the (unconscious) processes involved in thought and the (conscious) products that result from these processes. It turns out that this distinction isn't always clear-cut, but even so, the distinction does support a useful rule of thumb about what we're aware of in our mental lives and what we're not. Thus, we arrive at a conclusion, but the steps leading to the conclusion are hidden from view. We reach a decision, but again, we are unable to introspect about the processes leading to that decision.

Sometimes, however, the processes of thought do seem to be conscious. Sometimes you reason carefully and deliberately, weighing each step and scrutinizing each bit of logic. This surely sounds like a case in which your thoughts *are* conscious. Remarkably, though, this sense of knowing one's own thoughts may, in some cases, be an illusion. You feel like the processes were conscious, so that you know why you reached a conclusion or why you made a particular decision, but you may be mistaken!

We have just discussed one example of this pattern: In the Nisbett and Schachter (1966) study, participants steadfastly denied that their willingness to undergo shock was influenced by the pill they had taken. Apparently, then, the participants had some beliefs about why they had acted as they did, and their beliefs were *wrong*—systematically ruling out a factor (the pill) that, in truth, was having an enormous impact.

Related examples are easy to find. Participants in one study read a brief excerpt from John Updike's novel *Rabbit Run*. They were then asked to describe what emotional impact the excerpt had on them, and they were also asked why the excerpt had the impact it did: Which sentences or which images, within the excerpt, led to the emotional "kick"? The participants were impressively consistent in their judgments, with 86% pointing to a particular passage (describing the messiness of a baby's crib) as playing an important role in creating the emotional tone of the passage. However, it appears that the participants' judgments were simply wrong. Another group of participants read the same excerpt, but minus the bit about the crib. These participants reacted to the overall excerpt in exactly the same way as had the earlier group. Apparently, the bit about the crib was not crucial at all (Nisbett & Wilson, 1977; for other, more recent data, see Bargh, 2005; Greenwald & Banaji, 1995).

In studies like these, participants think they know why they acted as they did, but they are mistaken. Their self-reports are offered with full confidence, and in many cases the participants report that they carefully and deliberately thought about their actions, and so the various causes and influences were, it seems, out in plain view. Nonetheless, from our perspective as researchers, we can see that these introspective reports are wrong—ignoring factors we know to be crucial, highlighting factors we know to be irrelevant.

How could these introspections get so far off track? The answer starts with the fact that we've already showcased—namely, that the processes of thought are often unconscious. People seeking to introspect, therefore, have no way to inspect these processes, and so, if they're going to explain their own behavior, they need some other source of information. That other source is likely to be an *after-the-fact reconstruction*. Roughly put, people reason in this fashion: "Why did I act that way? I have no direct information, but perhaps I can draw on my broad knowledge about why, in general, people might act in certain ways in this situation. From that base, I can make some plausible inferences about why I acted as I did." Thus, for example: "I know that, in general, passages about babies or passages about squalor can be emotionally moving; I bet that's what moved me in reading this passage."

Notice two things here. First, these after-the-fact reconstructions will sometimes be *correct*. That's because in many ways people do understand the factors that matter in a situation: "Why am I angry at Gail? She just insulted me, and I know that, in general, people tend to get angry when they've been insulted. I bet, therefore, that I'm angry because she insulted me." In cases like this one, an inference based on generic knowledge may well lead to the correct interpretation of one's own state.

However, in other cases these reconstructions will be totally wrong (as in the experiments we've mentioned). The reconstructions will go off track, for example, if someone has mistaken beliefs about why, in general, people act in certain ways in a certain setting; in that case, inferences based on these beliefs will be problematic. Likewise, the reconstructions will go off track if the person simply hasn't noticed some relevant factor in the current setting; here, too, someone's inferences (oblivious to that factor) will yield mistaken interpretations.

Second, it's striking that these after-the-fact reconstructions don't "feel like" inferences. When research participants (or people in general) explain their own behaviors,

Fallible Perceptions and Reasoning
Many people criticized the tobacco industry for using the icon of Joe Camel to attract younger smokers. The industry argued that this icon had little effect on young smokers, and sometimes pointed, as evidence, to the fact that the smokers, when asked, "Why did you start smoking?" rarely mentioned Joe Camel. As the chapter suggests, though, we need to be cautious interpreting the smokers' introspection because they might simply be *wrong* about what it was that led them to start smoking.

they're usually convinced that they are simply remembering their own mental processes based on some sort of "direct inspection" of what went on in their own minds. These reconstructions, in other words, feel like genuine "introspections." The evidence we've reviewed, however, suggests that these subjective feelings are mistaken, and so, ironically, this is one more case in which people are conscious of the product and not the process. They are aware of the conclusion ("I acted as I did because . . .") but not aware of the process that led them to the conclusion. Hence, they continue to believe (falsely) that the conclusion rests on an introspection, when, in truth, it rests on an after-the-fact reconstruction. Hand in hand with this, they continue to believe confidently that they know themselves, even though, in reality, their self-perception is (in these cases at least) focusing on entirely the wrong factors. (For more on this process of "self-interpretation," see Cooney & Gazzaniga, 2003.)

Unconscious Guides to Conscious Thinking

Sometimes, though, we surely are aware of our own thoughts. Sometimes we make decisions based on a clear, well-articulated "inner dialogue" with ourselves. Sometimes we make discoveries based on a visual image that we carefully (and consciously!) scrutinized. Even here, though, there is a role for the cognitive unconscious, because even here an elaborate unconscious support structure is needed—a support structure that exists at the "fringe" or the "horizon" of our conscious thoughts (Husserl, 1931; W. James, 1890).

Evidence for this unnoticed fringe comes from many sources, including a wide variety of cases in which our thoughts seem guided or influenced by an "unseen hand." For example, in our description of problem-solving (Chapter 14), we emphasized the role of *set*—unnoticed assumptions and definitions that guide our search for the problem's solution. Even when the problem-solving is conscious and deliberate, even when we "think out loud" about the steps of the problem solution, we are guided by a set. For the most part this is a good thing, because the set keeps us focused, protecting us from distracting and unproductive lines of thought. But as we have seen, the set can sometimes be an obstacle to problem-solving, and the fact that the set is unconscious makes it all the more difficult to overcome the obstacle: The problem-solver cannot easily pause and reflect on the set, and so she cannot alter the problematic beliefs or abandon the misleading assumptions.

Similarly, in our discussion of decision-making (Chapter 13), we emphasized the importance of the decision's *frame*. You might be completely focused on the decision and fully aware of your options and your efforts toward choosing among them. Nonetheless, the evidence suggests that you will be heavily influenced by the unnoticed framing of the decision—the way the options are described and the way the question itself is posed. You don't think about the framing itself, but the framing unmistakably colors your thoughts about the decision and plays a large role in determining the outcome of those thoughts.

Likewise, we noted in Chapter 10 that words and sentences can often be interpreted in more than one way. But when we form our thoughts into words, the thoughts are unambiguous. Thus, when you think, "I was looking for the sage," you are not puzzled about whether you are hunting for a wise fellow or some herbs to flavor the turkey. Likewise, if you were to think, "I saw the man with the binoculars," you might not even detect the ambiguity. In both cases, you are protected from confusion by a context of other ideas, beliefs, and expectations. These other ideas might not be noticed directly, and so the context they provide is an unconscious one. Even so, these other ideas set the context for the idea you are consciously focusing on, and they guide your understanding of the conscious idea.

In all of these ways, then, our deliberate, conscious thinking—about problems, decisions, images, or words—is guided by an unnoticed framework. Thus, we are aware that we are thinking about the sage, but not aware of how this thinking is shaped by assumptions or associations lying in the background. We are conscious that we are working on a problem, but not conscious of how our set guides our approach to the problem. In case after case, the unconscious mental framework protects us from uncertainty and ambiguity, and it shapes both the content and the sequence of our thoughts.

Blind Sight and Amnesia

One last line of evidence for unconscious processes comes from patients who have suffered brain damage. Consider, for example, the cases of memory pathology described in Chapter 6. Patients suffering from Korsakoff's syndrome, for example, often have no conscious awareness of events they have witnessed or things they have done. If asked directly about these events, the patients will insist that they have no recollection. If asked to perform tasks that require recollection, the patients will fail. Yet the patients do remember these events in some sense: On tests of *implicit* memory, the

Ambiguity in the World
We often fail to detect the ambiguity we encounter—such as the two ways to interpret "Out of order." This is because we (unconsciously) supply a framework that guides our interpretation.

amnesic patients seem quite normal, making it clear that they are influenced in their present beliefs and behaviors by the specific content of the prior episodes. Thus, it seems that people with amnesia can remember and can be influenced by their memories, with no conscious awareness that they are recalling the past. This is a pattern that Jacoby and Witherspoon (1982) dubbed "memory without awareness."

A similar pattern is evident in the phenomenon of **blind sight**. This is a pattern observed in patients who have experienced damage to the striate cortex. As a result of this brain damage, these patients are, for all practical purposes, blind: If asked to move around a room, they will bump into objects; they do not react to flashes of bright light; and so on. In one experiment, however, visual stimuli were presented to these patients, and they were forced to guess whether the stimuli were (for example) *X*s or *O*s, circles or squares. Quite reliably, these patients "guessed" correctly (Rees, Kreiman, & Koch, 2002; Weiskrantz, 1986, 1997). Similarly, if the patients were forced to guess where various objects were placed and to reach toward those objects, they tended to reach in the right direction with the appropriate hand position (given the shape and size of the target object). The patients did this, all the while asserting that they could not see the targets and insisting that they were reaching out at random. Thus, it seems that these patients can, in a sense, "see," but they are not aware of seeing. (For related data, also showing a sharp distinction between a patient's conscious perception of the world and her ability to gather and use visual information, see Goodale & Milner, 2004; Logie & Della Salla, 2005.)

The Disadvantages of Unconscious Processing

Where, then, does all of this leave us? Clearly, a huge range of activities, including rather complex activities, can be accomplished unconsciously. So why do we need consciousness at all? What function is served by consciousness? And related to this, what things *can't* we do unconsciously?

The Nature of Unconscious Performance

One way to tackle these questions is by scrutinizing the various activities we can perform without consciousness and asking what they have in common. In rough terms, two broad factors can be identified. First, the various cases of unconscious processing all seem to rely on well-established routines doing a well-defined job in an identifiable domain. We are, for example, unaware of the machinery needed for memory search—but notice that this is machinery needed *for memory search*; it has that specific job to do. We are likewise unaware of the processes needed to make inferences about perceptual inputs—but, again, these are inferences of a specialized sort, used for just one purpose: figuring out what the input was. Similarly, we are unaware of the processes that assign a "cause" to some detected effect (e.g., processes that attribute perceptual fluency to a particular encounter in the past), but, again, these are presumably processes that have this function and no other. In each case, the processes are impressive—but they carry out just one job, and the job is relatively specialized.

Second, and perhaps more important, in all the cases of unconscious processing that we've considered, people seem to be doing just what the situation requires—guided either by the situation itself or by prior habit. When people have (unconsciously) drawn conclusions, the conclusions tend to be the ones favored by familiarity or by the situation itself. Likewise, when people have made responses—like reaching for an object that they cannot consciously see or noting the meaning of a word that they did not consciously perceive—they are making the familiar response, the ordinary response for that situation.

The Limits of Unconscious Performance

These points lead to an obvious proposal about unconscious processing and also an obvious proposal about *conscious* processing. Specifically, perhaps we can perform tasks unconsciously—even sophisticated, complex tasks—if we arrive at the task with an already-established routine, directly applicable to that task, and if the routine can be guided entirely by strong habits or powerful cues within the situation. These routines can be highly efficient, but they are also inflexible, relying on customary, habitual, or stimulus-governed actions, and not subject to control.

These points imply that there will be clear limits on our unconscious processes. In particular, the inflexibility in our unconscious routines will make it difficult—and perhaps impossible—to tune or adjust the routine. Indeed, the inflexibility can make it difficult for us to turn off the routine even when we want to. As an illustration, consider the workings of memory: The inferences used to fill gaps in memory (both during encoding and during retrieval) are often helpful, but they can occasionally lead to memory error (Chapter 7). Knowing this, however, is no protection at all. Just as one cannot choose to avoid a perceptual illusion, one cannot choose to avoid memory error. The process of making inferences is automatic and effortless, and it is also irresistible.

Similarly, the inflexibility in routine makes it all too easy for us to become victims of habit, relying on our customary actions or customary thought patterns even when we hope to avoid them. This is one of the reasons why problem-solving sets (Chapter 14) are so powerful and so difficult to break out of. It is also the reason why **action slips**—doing something different from what you intend—take the form that they do: In most cases, these slips involve doing what's *normal* or *habitual* in a situation, rather than what you want to do on that occasion. For example, you are in the car, driving to the store. You intend to turn left at the corner, but, distracted for a moment, you turn right, taking the route that you frequently take on your way to school. Action slips like this one almost invariably involve the intrusion of a strong and familiar habit, slipping into what's "normal" even if it's not, at that moment, what you intend (Norman, 1981; Reason, 1990; also see Langer, 1989). All of this is just what we would expect if routine is forceful, automatic, and uncontrolled.

The Advantages of Unconscious Performance

At the same time, unconscious performance—inflexible as it often is—also has its advantages. For one, it allows mental tasks to run much more quickly, and we have seen many indications that speed is a desirable feature in our intellectual functioning. (This is, of course, one of the reasons we so often draw on mental shortcuts of one sort or another; see Chapters 9, 12, 13, and 14.) In addition, the routine allows a withdrawal of attention from the task, and this allows you to devote your attention instead to other, more pressing matters.

What makes this withdrawal of attention possible? We first met the answer in Chapter 4: When you're learning a new task, you need to monitor each step, so that you'll know when it's time to start the next step. Then you need to *choose* the next step and get it started. Obviously, this gives you close control over how things proceed, but this need for supervision of the task makes the performance quite demanding.

After some practice, however, things are different. The steps needed for the task are still there, but you don't think about them one by one. That's because you have stored in memory a complete routine that specifies what all the steps should be and when each step should be initiated. All you need to do, therefore, is launch the routine, and from that point forward you let the familiar sequence unfold. Thus, with no need for monitoring or decisions, you can do the task without paying close attention to it.

Autopilot
By doing things on "autopilot," we give up close control of the activity, but ensure that our thoughts are free to focus on other matters.

In short, practice allows you to perform a task while allocating your resources elsewhere, and this has important benefits. When you're in the midst of a conversation, for example, you need, again and again, to search through memory to find suitable words for expressing your intended meaning. In this setting, you'd be distracted and slowed if you had to think through the mechanics of this memory search. Better, then, to keep those mechanics hidden from view. What you want to have in your awareness are the words resulting from the search, and not the search itself.

On this basis, the invisibility of our mental processes is often a good thing: It allows us to keep our attention focused on the things that matter (like choosing what ideas to convey in the conversation) without having to worry about the details (like how to find the exact words in memory). In Chapter 14, we discussed how this focus on "higher-order" aspects of a task is useful for experts; we now see that it is just as useful for nonexperts performing ordinary tasks.

The Function of Consciousness

We still need to tackle the (hard!) question of what consciousness *is*, but our efforts toward answering that question will surely be informed by our understanding of what consciousness *is for*. In particular, we have now seen that unconscious processing carries both advantages and disadvantages: Unconscious routine is efficient and requires few mental resources, but it is also inflexible and difficult to control. Similarly, our lack of awareness for our own mental processes probably buys us speed and certainly spares us distraction, but it also leaves us ignorant about our mental processes in a fashion that can sometimes be disruptive—making it impossible for us to distinguish genuine memories from reconstructions or actual perceptions from mere inferences, even when we want to.

It is a small step from these points to a proposal for the purpose of consciousness. Before we take that step, though, we need to add one last perspective on these issues.

The Cognitive Neuroscience of Consciousness

In the last decade or so, there has been an avalanche of intriguing research on the relationship between consciousness and brain function. Some of this research has focused on cases of brain damage, including the cases of amnesia or blind sight mentioned earlier in this chapter. Other research has asked, roughly, what changes in the brain when someone becomes conscious of a stimulus; in other words, what are the **neural correlates** of consciousness (Atkinson, Thomas, & Cleeremans, 2000; Baars & Franklin, 2003; Bogen, 1995; Chalmers, 1998; Crick & Koch, 1995; Dehaene & Naccache, 2001; Kim & Blake, 2005; Rees et al., 2002)? As we'll see, consideration of these neural correlates will lead us directly back to the question of what consciousness is for.

Research on the neural correlates of consciousness typically relies on the neuroimaging techniques we described in Chapter 2, as well as on various techniques for measuring the electrical activity of the brain. This research has asked (for example) how the pattern of brain activity changes when someone shifts his attention from one idea to another or has asked what differences in brain activity we can observe if a stimulus is in front of someone's eyes but unnoticed, in contrast to a case in which the person has noticed and is thinking about that stimulus.

Data from these approaches have led many researchers to endorse one version or another of the **neuronal workspace hypothesis**. In broad outline, here is the proposal: As we first discussed in Chapter 2, different areas within the brain seem highly specialized in their function. The various aspects of visual perception, for example, depend on multiple brain areas, with one area specialized for the perception of color, another for the perception of movement, another for the perception of faces, and so on. Each of these areas does its own job, and the activity in each area is highly transient: The neurons respond to the current inputs and then move on, ready to respond to the next set of inputs.

For many purposes, though, we need to sustain the activity in these various systems (e.g., for prolonged scrutiny), and we also need to integrate the activity of the different systems into a coherent whole. What makes this possible is *attention*, probably implemented biologically through top-down activation controlled by the prefrontal cortex (Maia & Cleeremans, 2005). This activation can *amplify* the activity within specific neural systems, and it also can *sustain* that activity. In addition, attention seems to *link* the activity of different neural systems, binding these into a single representation. Thus, for example, a moving stimulus in front of our eyes will trigger a response in one brain area; a red stimulus will trigger a response in another area. In the absence of attention, these two neural responses will be independent of each other. However, if we are paying attention to a single stimulus that is red and moving, the neurons in these two systems fire in synchrony (see Chapter 2), and when neurons fire in this coordinated fashion, the brain seems to register this as a linkage among the different processing areas. As a result, these attributes are bound together, so that we end up correctly perceiving the stimulus as a unified whole.

This large-scale integration of different neural processes is supported by "workspace neurons," neurons that literally connect one area of the brain to another. The integration—and so the information carried by these neurons—is selective, so it's certainly not the case that every bit of neural activity gets linked to every other bit. Instead, various mechanisms create a competition among different brain processes, and the "winner" in this competition (typically, the most active process) is communicated to other brain areas, while other information is not. In addition, bear in mind that attention can be used to amplify activity, and so it can govern how this competition plays out. In this way, the information flow is *limited* (because of the competition) but is also to some extent *controllable*, by virtue of what the person chooses to pay attention to.

With this backdrop, we're ready for our hypothesis: The integrated activity, made possible by the workspace neurons, literally provides the biological basis for consciousness. Let's be clear, though, that the workspace neurons themselves don't carry the *content* of consciousness. The content—the sense of seeing something red, the sense of seeing something moving—is presumably represented in the same neurons, the same processing modules, that analyzed the perceptual information in the first place. But what the workspace neurons do is glue these bits together, creating a unified experience and allowing the exchange of information from one module to the next. (For a number of specific versions of this hypothesis, see Baars, 1988; Baars & Franklin, 2003; Cooney & Gazzaniga, 2003; Crick & Koch, 2003; Dehaene & Naccache, 2001; Engel & Singer, 2001; Maia & Cleeremans, 2005; Roser & Gazzaniga, 2004.)

The Function of the Neuronal Workspace

Overall, then, the proposal is that the neuronal workspace, supported by attention, provides the biological basis for conscious experience. Stimuli become conscious when they are linked to each other in the dynamic, coherent representation that the workspace provides.

What does this linkage do for us? What does it make possible? For one, it provides a basis for explaining some basic facts about conscious experience itself. For instance, it is important that our conscious experience feels unitary and coherent: We are not aware of redness and also aware of movement, and of roundness, and of closeness. Instead, we are aware of a single experience in which the red apple rolls slowly by us. Of course, this integrated coherence is just what the workspace allows: one representation, constructed from the coordinated activity of many processing components (Roser & Gazzaniga, 2004).

Likewise, we are not conscious of every aspect of our experience—so that we might focus on the rose's color but fail to notice its thorns. Moreover, we can typically *choose* what we're going to focus on (so that we might, when picking up the rose, decide to pay attention to those thorns!). These observations are easily accommodated by the workspace model: The information carried by the workspace neurons is, we've said, governed by a competition (and so is limited) and also shaped by how someone focuses her attention. In this way, the properties of the workspace readily map onto the properties of our experience.

The workspace also makes possible a range of important behaviors (Dehaene & Naccache, 2001). First, the workspace, supported by attention, allows us to maintain a mental representation in an active state for an extended period of time. In other words, the workspace makes it possible for us to continue thinking about a stimulus or an idea even after the specific trigger for that idea is removed. We can, therefore, link the workspace proposal to our claims about working memory (Chapter 5) and to the brain areas associated with working memory's function—specifically, the prefrontal cortex (or PFC; Goldman-Rakic, 1987; for other evidence linking activation in the PFC to conscious awareness, see McIntosh, Rajah, & Lobaugh, 1999; Miller & Cohen, 2001). This seems appropriate, since working memory is traditionally understood as the memory that holds materials you're currently *working on*, and this presumably means materials currently within your conscious awareness.

In addition, the workspace allows us to compare what's going on in one neural system with what's going on in others. This allows us to reflect on *relationships* and *combinations* among various inputs or ideas, and this in turn allows us to produce *new* combinations of ideas or new combinations of operations. Thus, the neural mechanisms underlying consciousness are just the right sort to allow us to produce *novel thoughts*, thoughts that allow us to rise above habit or routine. In this way, the workspace allows us to escape one of the limits that, as we've discussed, seems to characterize *un*conscious processing.

The workspace also helps us escape another limit of unconscious processing. We said earlier that unconscious processes are generally guided by prior habits or cues within the situation rather than by current goals. Indeed, if there is some conflict between prior habit and current goals, this seems to have little influence on the unconscious process. In contrast, conscious thought is guided by a sense of one's goals, and it can launch exactly the behavior that will lead to those goals.

How might the workspace support this sensitivity to current goals? By linking the various processing modules, the workspace makes it possible to compare what's going on in one module with what's going on elsewhere in the brain, and this allows us to detect conflict—if, for example, two simultaneous stimuli are triggering incompatible responses, or if a stimulus is triggering a response incompatible with our goals. This, in turn, allows us (again, by adjusting how we pay attention) to adjust processing in one system in light of what is going on in other systems. Biologically, these adjustments are probably made possible by circuits involving the **anterior cingulate cortex** (ACC), a structure that we know (from other data) plays a crucial role in detecting conflicts among different brain systems (Botvinick, Cohen, & Carter, 2004; van Veen & Carter, 2006; for more connecting the functioning of the ACC to conscious awareness, see Dehaene et al., 2003; but for some complications, see Mayr, 2004).

The neuronal workspace idea may also help with another puzzle—understanding the relationship between being *awake* and being *asleep*. When we are asleep (and not dreaming), we are not conscious of the passing of time, not conscious of any ongoing stream of thought, and not conscious of many events taking place in our vicinity. This is not, however, because the brain is less active during sleep than it is when we're awake; brain activity during sleep is, in fact, quite intense. What, then, is the difference between the "sleeping brain" and the "awake brain"? When we are in non-REM sleep (and so presumably not dreaming), evidence suggests that communication breaks down between different parts of the cortex, so that the brain's various activities are not coordinated with each other. Our suggestion is that this communication (mediated by the neuronal workspace) is crucial for consciousness, and so

Sleep and Brain Communication

The workspace idea may help us understand the difference between being *awake* and being *asleep*. When we are asleep, our brains are active but communication among brain areas breaks down—and it may be this communication that is essential for consciousness.

it makes sense that sleeping people, having temporarily lost this communication, are not conscious of their state or their circumstances (Massimini et al., 2005).

Consciousness as Justification for Action

Dehaene and Naccache (2001) argue that conscious experience also has another function, and this function, too, is made possible by the characteristics of the neuronal workspace. Specifically, they argue that conscious experience is what allows us to produce *spontaneous* and *intentional* behavior.

To understand this point, consider the blind-sight patients. We have so far emphasized the fact that these patients are sensitive to some visual information, and this tells us something important: Apparently, some aspects of vision can go forward with no conscious awareness and with no conscious supervision. But it's also striking that these patients insist that they are blind, and their behaviors are consistent with this self-assessment: They are fearful of walking across a room (lest they bump into something), they fail to react to many stimuli, and so on.

Note the puzzle here: If, as it seems, these patients can see (at least to some extent), why don't they *use* the information that they gain by vision—for example, to guide their reaching or to navigate across the room? The evidence suggests that these patients see enough so that they reach correctly, when they do reach. Why, then, don't they reach out on their own when they want to grab something? Why do they reach (in the right direction, with the right hand shape) only when the experimenter insists that they try? Or, to put this more generally, why don't they use their (unconscious) perception of the visual world to guide their actions? Is it possible that perceptual information has to be *conscious* before someone puts that information to use? (For further discussion of this puzzle, see Dennett, 1992; Goodale & Milner, 2004; Weiskrantz, 1997.)

Roughly the same questions can be asked about people who suffer from amnesia. We have emphasized how much amnesic patients do remember, when properly tested (i.e., with tests of implicit memory). But it's also important that people with amnesia do not use this (implicitly) remembered information. Thus, for example, amnesic patients will insist that they do not know the route to the hospital cafeteria, and so they won't go to the cafeteria on their own. However, if we demand that they *guess* which way one turns to get to the cafeteria, they typically guess correctly. Once again, therefore, we might ask: Why don't the amnesic patients spontaneously use their (implicit) memories? Why do they reveal their knowledge only when we insist that they guess? Is it possible that remembered information has to be conscious before it is put to use?

Closely related questions arise when we consider data from people with no brain damage—such as ordinary college students. Participants in one study were shown a list of words and then, later, were tested in either of two ways (Graf, Mandler, & Haden, 1982). Some were explicitly asked to recall the earlier list and were given word stems as cues: "What word on the prior list began 'CLE'?" Other participants were tested indirectly: "Tell me the first word that comes to mind beginning 'CLE.'"

The results show rather poor memory in the explicit test, but much better performance in the implicit test. This observation echoes many findings we have reviewed: We often have implicit memories for episodes we have explicitly forgotten. But note that there is something peculiar in this result: Participants could, in principle, proceed this way: "I don't recall any words from the list beginning 'CLE.' Perhaps I'll just guess. Let's see: What words come to mind that begin 'CLE'?" In this way, participants could use their implicit memory to supplement what they remember explicitly. If they did this, then the performance difference between the two conditions would be erased; performance on the explicit test would be just as good as performance on the implicit test. Given the results, however, participants are obviously not using this strategy. For some reason, participants in this situation seem unable or unwilling to use their implicit memories to guide explicit responding.

What is going on in all of these cases? Here is one plausible answer: In many situations, we need to take action based on remembered or perceived information. In some cases, the action is overt (walking across the room or making a verbal response); at other times, the action is mental (reaching a decision or drawing a conclusion). In either setting, though, it seems not enough merely to have access to the relevant information. In addition, we also seem to need some justification, some reason, to take the information seriously.

By analogy, imagine that you are trying to remember some prior event, and some misty thoughts about that event come to mind. You vaguely recall that friends were present on the target occasion; you have a dim idea that food was served. You might hesitate to voice these thoughts, though, because you are not convinced that these thoughts are *memories*. (Perhaps they are chance associations or dreams you once had.) Thus, you will report your memory only if you're satisfied that you are, in fact, remembering. In other words, in order to report on your recollection, you need more than the remembered information. You also need some reason to believe that the remembered information is credible.

What convinces us that the remembered information is credible? The answer, perhaps, is our conscious experience. The idea, in other words, is that we will generally take action based on some information only if we are conscious of the information, and only if the conscious experience has the right qualities. More specifically, when the experience that accompanies a memory or a perception is rich and detailed, this convinces us that the presented information is more than a passing fantasy, more than a chance association, more than a mere hunch. In that situation, we're likely to take the information seriously and take action based on the information. However, when the conscious presentation is impoverished, as it seems to be in blind sight or in amnesia, we fail to take seriously the information

"Real" Memories?

Is this a "dagger of the mind"? Macbeth's confusion over the dagger—whether it is real or imagined—hinges on the same considerations that we use in deciding whether a perception or a memory is "real" and can be taken seriously. In each case, we seek a confluence of inputs, checking one aspect of our experience against other aspects.

provided to us by our own eyes or our own memory, and so we are paralyzed into inactivity. (For related discussion, see M. K. Johnson, 1988; Johnson, Hashtroudi, & Lindsay, 1993.)

How can these points be linked to the biological claims about the neuronal workspace? One possibility is that the integration of information within the workspace provides exactly the corroboration we need in deciding to take a memory or perception seriously. The integration allows us to see that the information provided by vision is confirmed by touch, that the information gained from our senses is consistent with our other beliefs, and so on. It's this convergence of cues that persuades us that the perception or memory is real, and not just a passing thought.

In Shakespeare's play, Macbeth asks himself whether the dagger he sees is real or "a dagger of the mind, a false creation proceeding from a heat-oppressed brain" (Act 2, Scene 1). He tries to decide by checking the visual information against other cues, asking whether the dagger is "sensible to feeling as to sight." The idea we're discussing here is the same: It is the confluence of inputs, provided by the neuronal workspace, that we use to decide whether ideas and perceptions and memories are "false creations" or true to reality. And it is only after we decide that they are real that we use them as a basis for action.

Consciousness: What Is Left Unsaid

Let's put all of these pieces together. From a biological perspective, we know that the various operations in the brain are made possible by the simultaneous action of numerous, specialized brain regions, each performing its own part of the whole. We also know that attention serves to unite these various modules via the neuronal workspace. This workspace integrates the diverse elements, allowing comparisons and combinations of the processing components. The integration also allows the detection of conflict—when one module is pulling toward one response and a different module is pulling toward another. And when conflict is detected (thanks to the anterior cingulate cortex), steps can be taken to overcome the problem—by, for example, inhibiting a habitual act so that the preferred (but nonhabitual) act can dominate.

All of these points about the brain fit well with the points we would make from a psychological perspective. We have seen that an enormous amount of mental work can be done—and perhaps has to be done—by unconscious processes. These processes rely on separate, self-contained modules and are enormously efficient, but they are also inflexible. We also know that these separate processes are influenced by attention. Specifically, paying attention to an input or an idea brings the input or idea into consciousness, where we can hold it or compare it with other ideas, potentially allowing the executive control that lets us be flexible and lets us rise above habit in ways not possible in unconscious processing.

The proposal, therefore, is that consciousness is intertwined with the processes through which we pay attention; indeed, there may be little difference in many circumstances between "paying attention" to something and "becoming conscious" of it. (Although see Koch & Tsuchiya, 2007.) Then, when we do pay attention to an idea or an input or a memory, this provides an integration and organization of separate processing streams, which, as we have discussed, creates the potential for flexibility, new ideas, and sustained attention. It also creates the sort of rich representation needed to justify the launching of action.

Let's emphasize, though, that these suggestions still leave many puzzles untouched—and this may be inevitable, because (as we indicated at the chapter's start) scholars still disagree about some key conceptual issues in this domain. For example, many investigators insist that consciousness can be understood only from a first-person perspective—what it actually *feels like* to have certain experiences. In our discussion, in contrast, we have focused instead on what consciousness *allows*—that is, the behaviors (and thoughts and decisions) that are made possible by consciousness. This choice of focus was guided by the available data, and in this chapter we've been pursuing the questions that are genuinely illuminated by the results coming from recent research. But should we be content with this focus (and, therefore, with the ongoing research)? Or, perhaps, do the studies we've been describing skip by an essential element of consciousness—the subjectivity that seems to distinguish a conscious being from a "zombie" who acts just like a conscious being, but with no "inner experience"? In other words, in focusing on what consciousness makes possible and not on how consciousness feels, have we perhaps dodged what Chalmers (1996, 1998) has called the "hard problem" of consciousness? (For a glimpse of how philosophers wrestle with these issues, see, for example, Block, 2001; Chalmers, 1996, 1998; Dennett, 2001. For an example of psychologists exploring the distinction between "executive control" and "conscious experience," see Feldman Barrett, Tugade, & Engle, 2004.)

Along with these ideas, some theorists have suggested that we need to distinguish *types* of conscious experience, and it is plausible that our discussion in this chapter has addressed some types and not others. For example, Block (1997, 2005) has argued for a distinction between "phenomenal" and "access" consciousness—the first concerned with the subjective experience of being conscious, and the second concerned with the functional consequences of consciousness (i.e., what consciousness allows). Clearly, this chapter has been more concerned with the second of these than the first. Likewise, Pinker (1997; also see Jackendoff, 1987) offers a three-way distinction. First, there is "sentience" (or, on Damasio's, 1999, account, "core consciousness"); this term covers the subjective feelings of what it is like, in the here and now, to experience something—what chocolate really tastes like, how red actually looks, what it is to feel pain, and so on. Second, there is "access to information," which is the ability to use and report on one's own mental experience. Third is "self-knowledge" (or, in Damasio's terms, "extended consciousness"), which is, as the term implies, awareness of oneself as an individual, and which includes people's memories and also their sense of the future. Again, this chapter has focused on only one of these (the second) and neglected the other two.

In light of these various concerns, it seems likely that in this chapter we have discussed *part of* the problem of consciousness and left other parts untouched. Indeed, it is possible that some aspects of consciousness can be studied by means of data collection and scientific research, while other aspects require other forms of inquiry (e.g., philosophical analysis—see, for example, Dehaene & Changeux, 2004). Even so, there can be no question that the data we have reviewed in this chapter, and the conclusions that flow from these data, provide powerful insights into the nature of consciousness, and these data will certainly inform any future discussions of this profound and complex issue. This by itself—the mere fact that research can address these extraordinarily difficult issues—has to be a source of enormous satisfaction for investigators working on these intriguing problems.

Chapter Summary

■ An enormous amount of cognitive processing happens "behind the scenes," in the cognitive unconscious. In many cases, we are conscious only of the products that result from our mental processes; the processes themselves are unconscious. This is reflected in the fact that we are not conscious of searching through memory; we are aware only of the results produced by that search. Similarly, we cannot tell when we have truly perceived a word and when we have merely inferred the word's presence.

■ Unconscious processing can be rather sophisticated. For example, implicit memory influences us without our being aware that we are remembering at all, and this influence is typically mediated by a complex process through which we attribute a feeling of familiarity to a particular cause. Unconscious attributions can also shape how we interpret and react to our own bodily states.

■ Even when our thinking is conscious, we are still influenced by unconscious guides that shape and direct our thought. This is evident in the effects of framing in decision-making and the effects of perceptual reference frames in perception and imagery.

■ Still further evidence for unconscious achievements comes from the study of blind sight and amnesia; in both cases, patients seem to have knowledge (gained from perception or from memory) but no conscious awareness of that knowledge.

■ The cognitive unconscious allows enormous efficiency, but at the cost of flexibility or control. Likewise, the cognitive unconscious keeps us from being distracted by the details of our mental processes, but in some cases there is a cost to our ignorance about how our mental processes unfolded and how we arrived at a particular memory or a particular perception. These trade-offs point the way toward the function of consciousness: Conscious thinking is less efficient but more controllable, and it is also better informed by information about process.

■ The neuronal workplace hypothesis begins with the fact that most of the processing in the brain is carried out by separate, specialized modules. When we pay attention to a stimulus, however, the neurons in the various modules are linked by means of workspace neurons. This linkage amplifies and sustains the processing within individual modules, and it allows integration and comparison of the various modules. This integration, it is proposed, is what makes consciousness possible. The integration provides the basis for the unity in our experience; it also allows flexibility and the detection of conflict.

■ Consciousness may also give us a sense that we have adequate justification for taking an action. This may be why amnesic patients seem unable to take action based on what they (unconsciously) recall and why blind-sight patients seem unable to respond to what they (unconsciously) see.

■ Several theorists have argued that we must distinguish types of conscious experience. The considerations in this chapter bear more directly on "access" consciousness, which is the matter of how information is accessed and used within the mind. The chapter has had less to say about "phenomenal" consciousness, which is concerned with the subjective experience of being conscious.

The Workbook Connection

See the *Cognition Workbook* for further exploration of conscious and unconscious thought:

■ Demonstration 15.1: Practice and the Cognitive Unconscious
■ Demonstration 15.2: The Quality of Consciousness
■ Research Methods: Introspection
■ Cognitive Psychology and Education: Mindfulness
■ Cognitive Psychology and the Law: Unconscious Thinking

Glossary

ACC See *anterior cingulate cortex.*

acquisition The process of placing new information into *long-term memory.*

action potential A brief change in the electrical potential of an *axon*, which is the physical basis of the nervous impulse.

action slip An error in which someone performs some behavior, or makes some response, that is different from the behavior or response intended.

activation level A measure of the current activation state for a *node* or *detector*. Activation level is increased if the node or detector receives the appropriate input from its associated nodes or detectors; activation level will be high if input has been received frequently or recently.

acuity The ability to discern fine detail. See also *visual acuity.*

ad hoc category A mental category made up on the spot in response to a specific question.

adjustment The process through which we "tune" the first-available estimate for some fact in order to reach our final estimate. Evidence suggests that we tend to adjust too little, and so the initial estimate serves as an "anchor" that has a powerful effect on our judgment. Also see *anchoring.*

affirming the consequent An error often made in logical reasoning. The error begins with these two premises: (a) "If A then B," and (b) "B is true." The error consists of drawing the false conclusion that (c) "A must therefore be true." Compare with *denying the antecedent.*

agnosia A disturbance in a person's ability to identify familiar objects.

all-or-none law The principle stating that a *neuron* or *detector* either *fires* completely or does not fire at all; no intermediate responses are possible.

ambiguous figure A drawing that can be readily perceived in more than one way.

amnesia A broad inability to remember events within a certain category, due in many cases to brain damage.

amygdala An almond-shaped structure in the *limbic system* that plays a central role in emotion and in the evaluation of stimuli.

anarthria A disorder characterized by an inability to control the muscles needed for ordinary speech. Anarthric individuals cannot speak, although other aspects of language functioning are unimpaired.

anchoring A tendency to use the first-available estimate for some fact as a reference point for that fact, and then perhaps to make some (small) adjustment from that reference point in determining our final estimate. As a result of anchoring, the first-available estimate often has a powerful influence on us, even if that estimate comes from a source that gives it little credibility. Also see *adjustment.*

anecdotal evidence Data or results collected informally, without documentation, and without care, so as to ensure a large enough and representative sample. This evidence often takes the form of informal reports or narratives (i.e., anecdotes) relayed in conversation.

anomia A disruption of language abilities, usually resulting from specific brain damage, in which the individual loses the ability to name objects, including highly familiar objects.

anterior cingulate cortex (ACC) A brain structure known to play a crucial role in detecting and resolving conflicts among different brain systems.

anterograde amnesia An inability to remember experiences that occurred *after* the event that triggered the memory disruption. Often contrasted with *retrograde amnesia.*

aphasia A disruption to language capacities, often caused by brain damage.

apraxia A disturbance in the initiation or organization of voluntary action.

Area V1 The site on the *occipital lobe* where axons from the *lateral geniculate nucleus* first reach the cerebral cortex.

articulatory rehearsal loop One of the low-level assistants hypothesized as part of the *working-memory system*. This loop draws on *subvocalized* (covert) speech, which serves to create a record in the *phonological buffer*. Materials in this buffer then fade, but they can be refreshed by another cycle of covert speech, with this cycle being initiated by working memory's *central executive.*

association cortex The traditional name for the portion of the human *cortex* outside of the *primary motor* and *primary sensory projection areas.*

associations Functional connections that are hypothesized to link *nodes* within a mental network or *detectors* within a detector network; these associations are often hypothesized as the "carriers" of activation, from one node or detector to the next.

associative links See *associations.*

attended channel In *selective attention* experiments, research participants are exposed to simultaneous inputs and instructed to ignore all of these except one. The attended channel is the input to which participants are instructed to pay attention. Often contrasted with *unattended channel.*

attribute substitution A commonly used strategy in which someone needs one type of information but relies instead on a more-accessible form of information. This strategy works well if the more-accessible form of information is, in fact, well correlated with the desired information. An example is the case in which someone needs information about how frequent an event is in the world and relies instead on how easily he or she can think of examples of the event.

attribution The step of explaining a feeling or event, usually by identifying the factors or the earlier event that is the cause of the current feeling or event.

autobiographical memory The aspect of memory that records the episodes and events in a person's life.

automatic tasks Tasks that are well practiced and that do not require flexibility; these tasks usually require little or no attention, and they can be carried out if the person is also busy with some other task. Usually contrasted with *controlled tasks*.

automaticity A state achieved by some tasks and some forms of processing, in which the task can be performed with little or no attention. Automatized actions can, in many cases, be combined with other activities without interference. Automatized actions are also often difficult to control, leading many to refer to them as "mental reflexes."

availability heuristic A strategy used to judge the frequency of a certain type of object or the likelihood of a certain type of event. The first step is to assess the ease with which examples of the object or event come to mind; this "availability" of examples is then used as an index of frequency or likelihood.

axon The part of a *neuron* that transmits a signal to another location.

back propagation A learning procedure, common in *connectionist networks*, in which an error signal is used to adjust the inputs to a *node* within the network (so that the node will be less responsive in the future to the inputs that led it to the inappropriate response). The *error signal* is then transmitted to those same inputs, so that they can make their own similar adjustments. In this way, the error signal is transmitted backwards through the network, starting with the nodes that immediately triggered the incorrect response, but with each node then passing the error signal back to the nodes that caused it to *fire*.

base-rate information Information about the broad likelihood of a particular type of event (also referred to as "prior probability"). Often contrasted with *diagnostic information*.

baseline level A standard or basis for comparison, often assessed by some measurement before an experimental manipulation takes place, or with a group that never receives the experimental manipulation.

basic-level categorization A level of categorization hypothesized as the "natural" and most informative level, neither too specific nor too general. It is proposed that we tend to use basic-level terms (such as "chair," rather than the more general "furniture" or the more specific "armchair") in our ordinary conversation and in our reasoning.

behaviorist theory Broad principles concerned with how behavior changes in response to different configurations of stimuli (including stimuli often called "rewards" and "punishments"). In its early days, behaviorist theory sought to avoid mentalistic terms.

belief bias A tendency, within logical reasoning, to endorse a conclusion if the conclusion happens to be something one believes is true anyhow. In displaying this tendency, people seem to ignore both the premises of the logical argument and logic itself, and they rely instead on their broader pattern of beliefs about what is true and what is not.

belief perseverance A tendency to continue endorsing some assertion or claim, even when the clearly available evidence completely undermines that claim.

bigram A pair of letters. For example, the word "FLAT" contains the bigrams *FL, LA,* and *AT*.

binding problem The problem of reuniting the various elements of a scene, given the fact that these elements are initially dealt with by different systems in the brain.

binocular rivalry A pattern that arises when the input to one eye cannot be integrated with the input to the other eye. In this circumstance, the person tends to be aware of only one eye's input at a time.

bipolar cell A *neuron* in the eye. Bipolar cells receive their input from the *photoreceptors* and transmit their output to the retinal *ganglion cells*.

blind sight A pattern resulting from brain damage, in which the person seems unable to see in all or part of his or her field of vision but can correctly respond to visual inputs when required to by an experimenter.

BOLD (blood oxygenation level dependent) A measure of how much oxygen the brain's hemoglobin is carrying in specific parts of the brain; this provides a quantitative basis for comparing activity levels in different brain areas.

bottom-up processing See *data-driven processing*.

boundaries Limits on the generalizability of a particular result.

boundary extension A tendency for people to remember pictures as being less "zoomed in" (and thus having wider boundaries) than they actually are.

Broca's area An area usually in the left *frontal lobe* of the brain; damage here typically causes *nonfluent aphasia*.

Capgras syndrome A rare disorder, resulting from specific forms of brain damage, in which the afflicted person recognizes the people in his or her world but denies that they are who they appear to be. Instead, the person insists, these familiar individuals are well-disguised impostors.

catch trials A step within a research paradigm in which the target stimulus is absent (so that the correct response is "absent") or in which a stimulus requires a "no" response. Catch trials are included within a study to guarantee that the participant is taking the task seriously, and not just responding in the same fashion on every trial.

categorical perception The tendency to hear speech sounds "merely" as members of a category—the category of "z" sounds, the category of "p" sounds, and so on. As a consequence, one tends to hear sounds *within* the category as being rather similar to each other; sounds from different categories, however, are perceived as quite different.

categorical syllogism A logical argument containing two *premises* and a conclusion, and concerned with the properties of, and relations between, categories. An example is, "All trees are plants. All plants require nourishment. Therefore, all trees require nourishment." This is a valid syllogism, since the truth of the premises guarantees the truth of the conclusion.

causal attribution An interpretation of a thought or behavior in which one decides what caused the behavior.

ceiling level A level of performance in a task that is near the maximum level possible. (In many tasks, this is performance near 100%.)

cell body The area of the cell containing the nucleus and the metabolic machinery that sustains the cell.

center–surround cell A *neuron* in the visual system that has a "donut-shaped" *receptive field*; stimulation in the center of the receptive field has one effect on the cell, whereas stimulation in the surrounding ring has the opposite effect.

central executive The hypothesized director of the *working-memory system*. This is the component of the system needed for any interpretation or analysis; in contrast, mere storage of materials can be provided by *working memory's* assistants, which work under the control of the central executive.

central fissure The separation dividing the *frontal lobes* on each side of the brain from the *parietal lobes*.

cerebellum The largest area of the *hindbrain*, crucial for the coordi-nation of bodily movements and balance.

cerebral hemisphere One of the two hemispherical brain structures—one on the left side, one on the right—that constitute the major part of the *forebrain* in mammals.

change blindness A pattern in which perceivers either do not see, or take a long time to see, large-scale changes in a visual stimulus. This pattern reveals how little we perceive, even from stimuli in plain view, if we are not specifically attending to the target information.

childhood amnesia The pattern of not remembering the first 3 or 4 years of one's life. This pattern is very common; a century ago, it was explained in terms of repression of anxious events in those years; more recent accounts focus on the psychological and biological immaturity of 3- and 4-year-olds, which makes them less able to form new episodic memories.

chronometric study Literally "time measurement" study; generally, a study that measures the amount of time a task takes, often used as a means of examining the task's components or used as a means of examining which brain events are simultaneous with specific mental events.

chunk The hypothetical storage unit in *working memory*; it is estimated that working memory can hold *7 plus-or-minus 2* chunks. An unspecified quantity of information can be contained within each chunk, since the content of each chunk depends on how the memorizer has organized the materials to be remembered.

coarticulation A trait of speech pro-duction in which the way a sound is produced is altered slightly by the immediately previous and imme-diately following sounds. Because of this "overlap" in speech produc-tion, the acoustic properties of each speech sound vary according to the context in which that sound appears.

cocktail party effect A term often used to describe a pattern in which one seems to "tune out" all conversa-tions reaching his or her ear *except for* the conversation he or she wishes to pay attention to; however, if some salient stimulus (such as the person's name) appears in one of the other conversations, the person is reason-ably likely to detect this stimulus.

cognitive neuroscience The study of the biological basis for cognitive functioning.

cognitive unconscious The broad set of mental activities of which we are completely unaware that makes possible our ordinary thinking, remembering, reasoning, and so on.

commissure One of the thick bundles of fibers via which information is sent back and forth between the two *cerebral hemispheres*.

competence The pattern of skills and knowledge that might be revealed under optimal circumstances. Often contrasted with *performance*.

computerized axial tomography (CT scanning) A *neuroimaging technique* that uses X-rays to construct a precise three-dimensional image of the brain's anatomy.

concept-driven processing A type of processing in which the sequence of mental events is influenced by a broad pattern of knowledge and expectations (sometimes referred to as *top-down processing*). Often con-trasted with *data-driven processing*.

concurrent articulation task A requirement that someone speak or mime speech while doing some other task. In many cases, the person is required to say "Tah-Tah-Tah" over and over, or "one, two, three, one, two, three." These procedures occupy the muscles and control mechanisms needed for speech, and so they prevent the person from using these resources for *subvocalization*.

conditional statement A statement of the format "If X then Y," with the first statement (the "if" clause) pro-viding a condition under which the second statement (the "then" clause) is guaranteed to be true.

cone A photoreceptor that is able to discriminate hues and that has high *acuity*. Cones are concentrated in the *retina*'s *fovea* and become less frequent in the visual periphery. Often contrasted with *rod*.

confirmation bias A family of effects in which people seem more sensitive to evidence that confirms their beliefs than they are to evidence that challenges their beliefs. Thus, if people are given a choice about what sort of information they would like in order to evaluate their beliefs, they request information that is likely to confirm their beliefs. Likewise, if they are presented with both confirming and disconfirming evidence, they are more likely to pay attention to, to be influenced by, and to remember the confirming evidence, rather than the disconfirming.

confound A variable other than the independent variable that could potentially explain the pattern of observed results. For example, if participants always serve in the control *condition* first and the *experimental condition* second, then any differences between these conditions might be due to either the *independent variable* or an effect of practice (favoring the experimental condition, which came second). In this case, practice would be a confound.

conjunction error An error in perception in which someone correctly perceives what features are present but misperceives how the features are joined, so that (for example) a red circle and a green square might be misperceived as a red square and a green circle.

connection weight The strength of a connection between two *nodes* in a network. The greater the connection weight, the more efficiently activation will flow from one node to the other.

connectionism An approach to theorizing about the mind that relies on *parallel distributed processing* among

elements that provide a *distributed representation* of the information being considered.

connectionist networks See *connectionism*.

consequentiality The perceived importance of an event, or the perception of how widespread and long-lasting the event's effects will be.

consolidation The biological process through which new memories are "cemented in place," acquiring some degree of permanence through the creation of new (or altered) neural connections.

content morpheme A *morpheme* that carries meaning. Often contrasted with *function morpheme*.

context reinstatement A procedure in which someone is led to the same mental and emotional state he or she was in during some previous event; context reinstatement can often promote accurate recollection.

contralateral control A pattern in which the left half of the brain controls the right half of the body, and the right half of the brain controls the left half of the body.

control condition A condition in which research participants are not exposed to the experimental manipulation, thereby serving as a basis for comparison with participants in the *experimental condition* (who are thus exposed to the experimental manipulation).

controlled tasks Tasks that are novel or that require flexibility in one's approach; these tasks usually require attention, and so they cannot be carried out if the person is also busy with some other task. Usually contrasted with *automatic tasks*.

convergent data A pattern in which different experimental procedures all yield results pointing toward the same conclusion, so that the results "converge" on that conclusion.

conversion error An error in which people convert statements from one form into another—for example, treating "All A are B" as though it

were identical to "All B are A," or treating "If A then B" as though it were identical to "If B then A."

convolutions The wrinkles visible in the *cortex* that allow the enormous surface area of the human brain to be stuffed into the relatively small volume of the skull.

cornea The transparent tissue at the front of each eye that plays an important role in focusing the incoming light.

corpus callosum The largest of the *commissures* linking the left and right *cerebral hemispheres*.

cortex The outermost surface of the brain.

counterbalance To ensure that any potential *confound* will have an equal effect on all the experimental conditions, so that any difference between the conditions cannot possibly be due to the confound. Thus, an experimenter might have exposed half the participants to the *control condition* first and half to the *experimental condition* first. In this case, practice favors the experimental condition for the first half of the participants and favors the control condition for the second half of the participants. Therefore, practice should have an equal impact on the two conditions and so cannot be a source of difference between them, because the experimenter has counterbalanced the effect of practice.

CT scanning See *computerized axial tomography*.

covariation A relationship between two variables such that the presence (or magnitude) of one variable can be predicted from the presence (or magnitude) of the other. Covariation can be positive or negative. If positive, then increases in one variable occur when increases in the other occur. If negative, then decreases in one variable occur when decreases in the other occur.

data-driven processing A type of processing in which the sequence of mental events is determined largely by the pattern of incoming information (sometimes referred to as *bottom-up processing*). Often contrasted with *concept-driven processing*.

decay theory of forgetting The hypothesis that with the passage of time, memories may fade or erode.

deduction A process through which we start with claims, or general assertions, and ask what follows from these *premises*. Often contrasted with *induction*.

deep processing A mode of thinking about material in which one pays attention to the meaning and implications of the material; deep processing typically leads to excellent memory retention. Often contrasted with *shallow processing*.

Deese–Roediger–McDermott (DRM) procedure A commonly used experimental procedure for eliciting and studying memory errors. In this procedure, a person sees or hears a list of words that are all related to a single theme; however, the word that names the theme is not itself included. Nonetheless, people are very likely to remember later that the theme word was presented.

degree of fan The number of *associative links* radiating out from a *node*. If there are more links (high degree of fan), then each of the associated nodes will receive only a small fraction of the activation flowing outward from the node.

demand character Cues within an experiment that signal to the participant how he or she is "supposed to" respond.

dendrites The part of a *neuron* that usually detects the incoming signal.

denying the antecedent An error often made in logical reasoning. The error begins with these two premises: (a) "If A then B," and (b) "A is false." The error consists of drawing the false conclusion that (c) "B must therefore also be false." Often contrasted with *affirming the consequent*.

dependent variable The variable that the researcher observes or measures to determine if the *independent variable* has an effect or influence. The dependent variable can take many forms (e.g., speed of responding, number of errors, type of errors, a biological measure such as brain activation at a certain site).

descriptive account An account that tells us how things are, as opposed to how they should be. Often contrasted with *normative account*.

descriptive rules Rules that simply describe the regularities in a pattern of observations, with no commentary on whether the pattern is "proper," "correct," or "desirable."

destructive updating The hypothesized mechanism through which new learning or new information on a topic replaces old knowledge or information in memory, so that the old information is erased or destroyed by the newer input.

detector A *node* within a processing network that *fires* primarily in response to a specific target contained within the incoming perceptual information.

diagnostic information Information about an individual case indicating whether the case belongs in one category or another. Often contrasted with *base-rate information*.

dichotic listening A task in which research participants hear two simultaneous verbal messages—one presented via headphones to the left ear, a second presented to the right ear. In typical experiments, participants are asked to pay attention to one of these inputs (the *attended channel*) and urged to ignore the other.

digit-span task A task often used for measuring *working memory*'s storage capacity. Research participants are read a series of digits (e.g., "8 3 4") and must immediately repeat them back. If they do this successfully, they are given a slightly longer list (e.g., "9 2 4 0"), and so forth. The length of the longest list a person can remember in this fashion is that person's digit span.

direct memory testing A form of memory testing in which people are asked explicitly to remember some previous event. *Recall* and standard *recognition* testing are both forms of direct memory testing. Often contrasted with *indirect memory testing*.

distributed knowledge Information stored via a *distributed representation*.

distributed representation A mode of representing ideas or contents in which there is no one *node* representing the content, and no one place where the content is stored. Instead, the content is represented via a pattern of simultaneous activity across many nodes. Those same nodes will also participate in other patterns, and so those same nodes will also be part of other distributed representations. Often contrasted with *local representation*.

divided attention The skill of performing multiple tasks simultaneously.

doctrine of formal disciplines In educational philosophy, the notion that the best way to train the mind is to provide education in disciplines such as logic, math, and linguistics (i.e., disciplines that hinge on formal structures).

double dissociation An argument used by researchers to prove that two processes or two structures are truly distinct. To make this argument, one must show that each of the processes or structures can be disrupted without in any way interfering with the other.

double-blind procedure A procedure in which neither the research participant nor the person administering the study knows which condition of the study the participant is in (e.g., receiving medication or a placebo; being in the experimental group or the control group). In this case, there is no risk that the person administering the study can convey to the participant how the participant is "supposed to" behave in the study.

D-structure The underlying and abstract representation of a speaker's intended meaning in uttering a *sentence*.

dual-coding theory A theory that imaginable materials, such as high-imagery words, will be doubly represented in memory: The word itself will be remembered, and so will the corresponding mental image.

dual-process model Any model of thinking that claims we have two distinct means of making judgments—one of which is fast, efficient, but prone to error, and one that is slower, more effortful, but also more accurate.

early selection A proposal that *selective attention* operates at an early stage of processing, so that the unattended inputs receive little analysis.

edge enhancement A process created by *lateral inhibition* in which the *neurons* in the visual system give exaggerated responses to edges of surfaces.

Einstellung The phenomenon in *problem-solving* in which people develop a certain attitude or perspective on a problem and then approach all subsequent problems with the same rigid attitude.

elaborative rehearsal A way of engaging materials to be remembered, such that one pays attention to what the materials mean and how they are related to each other, or to other things in the surroundings, or to other things one already knows. Often contrasted with *maintenance rehearsal*.

encoding specificity The tendency, when memorizing, to place in memory both the materials to be learned and also some amount of the context of those materials. As a result, these materials will be recognized as familiar, later on, only if the materials appear again in a similar context.

error signal A form of input to a network (or some other system) in which the strength of the input is proportional to the difference between the response produced and the response demanded by the environment. If the response produced

was correct, then the error signal will be zero. The signal can then be used to adjust the network or system so that the error signal will be smaller (i.e., the error will be smaller) in the future.

excitatory connection A link from one *node*, or one *detector*, to another, such that activation of one node activates the other. Often contrasted with *inhibitory connection*.

executive control The mental resources and processes used to set goals, choose task priorities, and avoid conflict among competing habits or responses.

exemplar-based reasoning Reasoning that draws on knowledge about specific category members, rather than drawing on more-general information about the overall category.

expected value An estimate of the value of choosing a particular option, calculated as the likely value of that option, if it is obtained, multiplied by the probability of gaining that value. (Also referred to as "expected utility.")

experimental condition A condition in which research participants are exposed to an experimental manipulation, thereby serving as a basis for comparison with participants in the *control condition* so that the researcher can learn whether the experimental manipulation changes the participants' thoughts, feelings, or behavior.

explicit memory A memory revealed by *direct memory testing* and typically accompanied by the conviction that one is remembering a specific prior episode. Often contrasted with *implicit memory*.

external validity The quality of a research design that ensures that the data accurately reflect the circumstances outside of the study that the researcher hopes to understand. External validity requires that the research participants, the research task, and the research stimuli are all appropriately representative of the people, tasks, and stimuli to which

the researcher wants to *generalize* the results.

extralinguistic context The social and physical setting in which a *sentence* is encountered; usually, cues within this setting guide the interpretation of the sentence.

false alarm A detection even though the specified target is actually absent.

false memory A memory, sincerely reported, that misrepresents how an event actually unfolded. In some cases, a false memory can be wholly false and can report an event that never happened at all.

familiarity In some circumstances, the subjective feeling that one has encountered a stimulus before; in other circumstances, the objective fact that one has indeed encountered a stimulus before and is now in some way influenced by that encounter, whether or not one recalls that encounter or feels that the stimulus is familiar.

family resemblance The notion that members of a category (e.g., all dogs, all games) resemble each other. In general, family resemblance relies on some number of *features* being shared by any group of category members, even though these features may not be shared by all members of the category. Therefore, the basis for family resemblance may shift from one subset of the category to another.

feature One of the small set of elements out of which more-complicated patterns are composed.

feature net A system for recognizing patterns that involves a network of *detectors*, with detectors for features as the initial layer in the system.

figure/ground organization The processing step in which the perceiver determines which aspects of the stimulus belong to the central object (or "figure") and which aspects belong to the background (or "ground").

file-drawer problem The concern that *null findings* or disappointing findings are not published and are, so to speak, placed in a file drawer and forgotten. This problem can create a situation in which the published research is not representative of the full pattern of evidence.

filter A hypothetical mechanism that would block potential distractors from further processing.

fire To respond in a discrete and specific way—as when a *neuron*, after receiving a strong enough stimulus, sends a signal down its *axon*, which in turn causes a release of *neurotransmitter* from the membrane at the end of the axon.

fixation target A visual mark (such as a dot or a plus sign) at which one points one's eyes (or "fixates"). Fixation targets are used to help people control their eye position.

flashbulb memory A memory of extraordinary clarity, typically for some highly emotional event, retained despite the passage of many years.

fluent aphasia A disruption of language, caused by brain damage, in which afflicted individuals are able to produce speech but the speech is not meaningful, and the individuals are not able to understand what is said to them. Often contrasted with *nonfluent aphasia*.

fMRI scanning See *functional magnetic resonance imaging*.

forebrain One of the three main structures (along with the *hindbrain* and the *midbrain*) of the brain; the forebrain plays a crucial role in supporting intellectual functioning.

form perception The process through which one sees what the basic shape, size, and position of an object are.

four-card task See *selection task*.

fovea The center of the *retina*; when one looks at an object, one is lining up that object with the fovea.

frame Aspects of how a decision is phrased that are, in fact, irrelevant to the decision but that influence people's choices nonetheless.

free recall A method of assessing memory. The person being tested is asked to come up with as many items as possible from a particular source (such as "the list you heard earlier" or "things you saw yesterday"), in any sequence.

frequency estimate People's assessment of how often they have encountered examples of a particular category and how likely they are to encounter new examples of that category.

frontal lobe The lobe in each *cerebral hemisphere* that includes the *prefrontal area* and the *primary motor projection area*.

function morpheme A *morpheme* that signals a relation between words within a sentence, such as the morpheme "s" indicating a plural, or the morpheme "ed" indicating past tense. Often contrasted with *content morpheme*.

functional equivalence A series of close parallels in how two systems work—how they respond to inputs, what errors they make, and so on. An example is the functional equivalence between vision and visual imagery.

functional fixedness A tendency to be rigid in how one thinks about an object's function. This generally involves a strong tendency to think of an object only in terms of its *typical* function.

functional magnetic resonance imaging (fMRI) A neuroimaging technique that uses magnetic fields to construct a detailed three-dimensional representation of the activity levels in different areas of the brain at a particular moment in time.

fusiform face area (FFA) A brain area apparently specialized for the perception of faces.

fuzzy boundary A distinction between categories that identifies each instance only as more or less likely to be in a category, rather than specifying whether each instance is or is not included in the category.

gamma-band oscillation A particular rhythm of *firing* that seems to signal in the nervous system when different parts of the visual system are all responding to the same stimulus.

ganglion cell A *neuron* in the eye. The ganglion cells receive their input from the *bipolar cells*, and then the *axons* of the ganglion cells gather together to form the *optic nerve*, carrying information back to the *lateral geniculate nucleus*.

garden-path sentence A sentence that initially leads the reader to one understanding of how the sentence's words are related, but that then requires a change in this understanding in order to comprehend the sentence. Examples are "The old man ships" and "The horse raced past the barn fell."

generalize The step of making claims about people, tasks, and stimuli other than those scrutinized within a research study. This generalization is legitimate only if the study has *external validity*.

generativity The idea that one can combine and recombine basic units to create (or "generate") new and more-complex entities. Linguistic rules, for example, are generative, and so they govern how a limited number of words can be combined and recombined to produce a vast number of sentences.

generic knowledge Knowledge of a general sort, as opposed to knowledge about specific episodes. Often contrasted with *episodic knowledge*.

geon One of the basic shapes proposed as the building blocks of all complex three-dimensional forms. Geons take the form of cylinders, cones, blocks, and the like, and they are combined to form "geon assemblies." These are then combined to produce entire objects.

goal neglect A pattern of behavior in which one fails to keep one's goal in mind, so that (for example) one relies on habitual responses even if those responses will not move the person toward the goal.

goal state The state one is working toward in trying to solve a problem. Often contrasted with *initial state*.

graded membership The idea that some members of a category are "better" members and therefore are more firmly in the category than other members.

grammatical Conforming to the rules that govern the sequence of words acceptable within the language.

heuristic A strategy that is reasonably efficient and works most of the time. In using a heuristic, one is in effect choosing to accept some risk of error in order to gain efficiency.

hill-climbing strategy A commonly used strategy in *problem-solving*. If people use this strategy, then whenever their efforts toward solving a problem give them a choice, they will choose the option that carries them closer to the goal.

hindbrain One of the three main structures (along with the *forebrain* and the *midbrain*) of the brain; the hindbrain sits atop the spinal cord and includes several structures crucial for controlling key life functions.

hippocampus A structure in the *temporal lobe* that is involved in *long-term memory* and spatial memory.

hypothalamus A small structure at the base of the *forebrain* that plays a vital role in the control of motivated behaviors such as eating, drinking, and sexual activity.

ill-defined problem A problem for which the goal state is specified only in general terms and the operators available for reaching the goal state are not obvious at the start. Often contrasted with *well-defined problem*.

illumination The third in a series of stages often hypothesized as crucial for creativity. The first stage is *preparation*; the second, *incubation*. Illumination is the stage in which some new key insight or new idea suddenly comes to mind.

illusion of truth An effect of *implicit memory* in which claims that are familiar end up seeming more plausible.

illusory covariation A pattern that people "perceive" in data, leading them to believe that the presence of one factor allows them to predict the presence of another factor. However, this perception occurs even in the absence of any genuine relationship between these two factors. As an example, people perceive that a child's willingness to cheat in an academic setting is an indicator that the child will also be willing to cheat in athletic contests. However, this perception is incorrect, and so the covariation that people perceive is "illusory."

image file Visual information stored in *long-term memory*, specifying what a particular object or shape looks like. Information within the image file can then be used as a "recipe" or set of instructions for how to construct an active image of this object or shape.

image-scanning procedure An experimental procedure in which participants are asked to form a specific mental image and then are asked to scan, with their "mind's eye," from one point in the image to another. By timing these scans, the experimenter can determine how long "travel" takes across a mental image.

implicit memory A memory revealed by *indirect memory testing* usually manifest as *priming* effects in which current performance is guided or facilitated by previous experiences. Implicit memories are often accompanied by no conscious realization that one is, in fact, being influenced by specific past experiences. Often contrasted with *explicit memory*.

inattentional blindness A pattern in which perceivers seem literally not to see visual stimuli right in front of their eyes; this pattern is caused by the participants' attending to some other stimulus and not expecting the target to appear.

incidental learning Learning that takes place in the absence of any intention to learn and, correspondingly, in the absence of any expectation of a subsequent memory test.

incubation The second in a series of stages often hypothesized as crucial for creativity. The first stage is *preparation*; the third, *illumination*. Incubation consists of (hypothesized) events that occur when one puts a problem being worked on out of one's conscious thoughts, but continues nonetheless to work on the problem unconsciously. Many current psychologists are skeptical about this process, and they propose alternative accounts for data ostensibly documenting incubation.

independent variable In an experimental study, the variable that the researcher deliberately manipulates to ask whether it has an impact on the target variable. Outside of experimental studies, the independent variable can involve some preexisting difference (e.g., the participants' age or sex), allowing the researcher to ask if this preexisting difference influences the target variable. Sometimes called the "predictor variable."

indirect memory testing A form of memory testing in which research participants are not told that their memories are being tested. Instead, they are tested in a fashion in which previous experiences can influence current behavior. Examples of indirect tests include *word-stem completion*, the *lexical-decision task*, and *tachistoscopic* recognition. Often contrasted with *direct memory testing*.

induction A pattern of reasoning in which one seeks to draw general claims from specific bits of evidence. Often contrasted with *deduction*.

information processing A particular approach to theorizing in which complex mental events, such as learning, remembering, and deciding, are understood as being built up out of a large number of discrete steps. These steps occur one by one, with each providing as its "output" the input to the next step in the sequence.

inhibitory connection A link from one *node*, or one *detector*, to another, such that activation of one node decreases the *activation level* of the other. Often contrasted with *excitatory connection*.

initial state The state one begins in, in working toward the solution of a problem. *Problem-solving* can be understood as the attempt to move, with various operations, from the initial state to the *goal state*.

input node A *node*, within a network, that receives at least part of its activation from *detectors* sensitive to events in the external world.

insensitivity A property of an experiment that makes the experiment unable to detect differences. An experiment can be insensitive, for example, if the procedure is too easy, so that *performance* is at *ceiling levels*.

integrative agnosia A disorder caused by a specific form of damage to the *parietal lobe*; people with this disorder appear relatively normal in tasks requiring them to detect whether specific *features* are present in a display, but they are impaired in tasks that require them to judge how the features are bound together to form complex objects.

intentional learning The acquisition of memories in a setting in which people know that their memory for the information will be tested later.

interactive model A model of cognitive processing that relies on an ongoing interplay between *data-driven* and *concept-driven processing*.

interference theory of forgetting The hypothesis that materials are lost from memory because of interference from other materials also in memory. Interference that is caused by materials learned prior to the learning episode is called "proactive interference"; interference that is caused by materials learned after the learning episode is called "retroactive interference."

internal validity The quality of a research study in measuring what it intends to measure. A study is internally valid if the *dependent variables* measure what they are intended to measure, and if the pattern of results in the dependent variables can be attributed to the *independent variables* (and not to some *confound*).

interrater reliability The degree of agreement between two or more individuals who have each independently assessed some target quality. Thus, two individuals might judge how beautiful various faces are, and then the agreement between the two raters could be calculated.

introspection The process through which one "looks within," to observe and record the contents of one's own mental life.

intrusion error A memory error in which one recalls elements not part of the original episode that one is trying to remember.

invalid In the context of research design, the determination that a study does not measure what it intends to measure (in which case the study lacks internal validity) or does not reflect the circumstances outside of the lab that the researcher hoped to explore (in which case the study lacks *external validity*).

Korsakoff's syndrome A clinical syndrome characterized primarily by dense *anterograde amnesia*. Korsakoff's syndrome is caused by damage to specific brain regions, and it is often precipitated by a form of malnutrition common among long-term alcoholics.

late selection A proposal that *selective attention* operates at a late stage of processing, so that the unattended inputs receive considerable analysis.

lateral fissure The separation dividing the *frontal lobes* on each side of the brain from the *temporal lobes*.

lateral geniculate nucleus (LGN) An important way station in the thalamus that is the first destination for visual information sent from the eyeball to the brain.

lateral inhibition A pattern in which cells, when stimulated, inhibit the activity of neighboring cells. In the visual system, lateral inhibition in the *optic nerve* creates *edge enhancement*.

lens The transparent tissue located near the front of each eye that plays an important role in focusing the incoming light. Muscles control the degree of curvature of the lens, allowing the eye to form a sharp image on the *retina*.

lesion A specific area of tissue damage.

lexical-decision task A test in which participants are shown strings of letters and must indicate, as quickly as possible, whether each string of letters is a word in English or not. It is supposed that people perform this task by "looking up" these strings in their "mental dictionary."

limbic system A set of brain structures including the *amygdala*, *hippocampus*, and parts of the *thalamus*. The limbic system is believed to be involved in the control of emotional behavior and motivation, and it also plays a key role in learning and memory.

limited-capacity system A group of processes in which resources are limited so that extra resources supplied to one process must be balanced by a withdrawal of resources somewhere else, with the result that the total resources expended do not exceed some limit.

linguistic relativity The proposal that the language that we speak shapes our thought, because the structure and vocabulary of our language create certain ways of thinking about the world.

linguistic universal A rule that appears to apply to every human language.

local representation A representation of information that is encoded in some small number of identifiable *nodes*. Local representations are sometimes spoken of as "one idea per node" or "one content per location." Often contrasted with *distributed representation*.

localization of function The research endeavor of determining what specific job is performed by a particular region of the brain.

long-term memory (LTM) The storage system in which we hold all of our knowledge and all of our memories. Long-term memory contains memories that are not currently activated; those that are activated are represented in *working memory*.

longitudinal fissure The separation dividing the brain's left *cerebral hemisphere* from the right.

M cells Specialized cells within the *optic nerve* that provide the input for the *magnocellular cells* in the *lateral geniculate nucleus*. Often contrasted with *P cells*.

magnetic resonance imaging (MRI) A *neuroimaging technique* that uses magnetic fields (created by radio waves) to construct a detailed three-dimensional representation of brain tissue. Like *CT scans*, MRI scans reveal the brain's anatomy, but they are much more precise than CT scans.

magnocellular cells Cells in the *lateral geniculate nucleus* specialized for the perception of motion and depth. Often contrasted with *parvocellular cells*.

maintenance rehearsal A rote, mechanical process in which items are continually cycled through *working memory*, merely by being repeated over and over. Also called "item-specific rehearsal," and often contrasted with *elaborative rehearsal*.

manner of production The way in which a speaker momentarily obstructs the flow of air out of the lungs to produce a speech sound. This obstruction can take several forms. For example, the airflow can be fully stopped for a moment, as it is in the [t] or [b] sound; or the air can continue to flow, as it does in the pronunciation of [f] or [v].

map To figure out how aspects of one situation or argument correspond to aspects of some other situation or argument.

mask A visual presentation used to interrupt the processing of another visual stimulus.

massed learning A memorization strategy in which a research participant works on memorizing for a solid block of time. Often contrasted with *spaced learning*; akin to "cramming."

matching strategy A shortcut apparently used in reasoning tasks; to use this strategy, the person selects a conclusion that contains the same words (e.g., "not," "some," "all") as the *premises*.

means–end analysis A strategy used in *problem-solving* in which the person is guided, step-by-step, by a comparison of the difference, at that moment, between the current state and the *goal state*, and a consideration of the *operators* available.

memory rehearsal Any mental activity that has the effect of maintaining information in *working memory*. Two types of rehearsal are often distinguished: *maintenance rehearsal* and *elaborative rehearsal*.

mental accounting A process that seems to guide our decision-making, in which different choices and different resources are kept separate, so that gains in one "account" (for example) do not influence choices about a different account.

mental model An internal representation in which an abstract description is translated into a relatively concrete representation, with that representation serving to illustrate how that abstract state of affairs might be realized.

mental rotation A process that participants seem to use in comparing one imaged form to another. To make the comparison, participants seem to imagine one form rotating into alignment with the other, so that the forms can be compared.

metacognitive judgment A judgment in which one must stand back from a particular mental activity and comment on the activity, rather than participating in it.

metalinguistic judgment A particular type of *metacognitive judgment* in which one must stand back from

one's ordinary language use and comment on language or linguistic processes.

midbrain One of the three main structures (along with the *forebrain* and the *hindbrain*) of the brain; the midbrain plays an important role in coordinating movements, and it also contains structures that serve as "relay" stations for information arriving from the sensory organs.

minimal attachment A *heuristic* used in *sentence* perception. The listener or reader proceeds through the sentence seeking the simplest possible phrase structure that will accommodate the words heard so far.

misinformation effect An effect in which research participants' reports about an earlier event are influenced by misinformation they received after experiencing the event. In the extreme, misinformation can be used to create *false memories* concerning an entire event that, in truth, never occurred.

mnemonic strategy A technique designed to improve memory accuracy and to make learning easier; in general, mnemonic strategies seek in one fashion or another to help memory by imposing an organization on the materials to be learned.

modal model A nickname for a specific conception of the "architecture" of memory. In this model, *working memory* serves both as the storage site for material now being contemplated and also as the "loading platform" for *long-term memory*. Information can reach working memory through the processes of perception, or it can be drawn from long-term memory. Once in working memory, material can be further processed, or it can simply be recycled for subsequent use.

modus ponens A logical rule stipulating that from the two premises "If P then Q" and "P is true," one can draw the conclusion "Therefore, Q is true." Often contrasted with *modus tollens*.

modus tollens A logical rule stipulating that from the two premises "If

P then Q" and "Q is false," one can draw the conclusion "Therefore, P is false." Often contrasted with *modus ponens*.

morpheme The smallest language unit that carries meaning. Psycholinguists distinguish *content morphemes* (the primary carriers of meaning) from *function morphemes* (which specify the relations among words).

MRI See *magnetic resonance imaging*.

movement rule A rule that describes one aspect of our knowledge about *sentence* structure. Movement rules govern, for example, how the sentence "Can he do it?" is formed from the base of "He can do it."

necessary condition A condition that *must* be fulfilled in order for a certain consequence to occur. However, necessary conditions may not guarantee that the consequence will occur, since it may be true that other conditions must also be met. Often contrasted with *sufficient condition*.

Necker cube One of the classic *ambiguous figures*; the figure is a two-dimensional drawing that can be perceived either as a cube viewed from above or as a cube viewed from below.

neglect syndrome See *unilateral neglect syndrome*.

neural correlate An event in the nervous system that occurs at the same time as, and may be the biological basis of, a specific mental event or state.

neural net model An alternative term for connectionist models, reflecting the hypothesized parallels between this sort of computer model and the functioning of the nervous system.

neural synchrony A pattern of *firing* by *neurons* in which neurons in one brain area fire at the same time as neurons in another area; the brain seems to use this pattern as an indication that the neurons in different areas are firing in response to the same stimulus.

neuroimaging technique A method for examining either the structure or the activation pattern within a living brain.

neuron An individual cell within the nervous system.

neuronal workspace hypothesis A specific claim about how the brain makes conscious experience possible; the proposal is that "workspace neurons" link together the activity of various specialized brain areas, and this linkage makes possible integration and comparison of different types of information.

neuropsychology The branch of psychology concerned with the relation between various forms of brain dysfunction and various aspects of mental functioning. Neuropsychologists study, for example, *amnesia*, *agnosia*, and *aphasia*.

neurotransmitter One of the chemicals released by *neurons* in order to stimulate adjacent neurons. See also *synapse*.

neutral depiction A representation that directly reflects the layout and appearance of an object or scene (and so is, on this basis, a "depiction"), but without adding any specifications about how that depiction is to be understood (and so is, on this basis, "neutral"). Often contrasted with *organized depiction*.

node An individual unit within an associative network. In a scheme employing *local representations*, nodes represent single ideas or concepts. In a scheme employing *distributed representations*, ideas or contents are represented by a pattern of activation across a wide number of nodes; the same nodes may also participate in other patterns and therefore in other representations.

nonfluent aphasia A disruption of language, caused by brain damage, in which someone loses the ability to speak or write with any fluency. Often contrasted with *fluent aphasia*.

normative account An account that tells how things ought to be, as opposed to how they are. Also referred to as "prescriptive account"; often contrasted with *descriptive account*.

noun phrase One of the constituents of a phrase structure that defines a *sentence*.

null finding A result showing no difference between groups or between conditions. A null finding may indicate either (1) that there is no difference, or (2) that the study was not sensitive enough to detect a difference.

object recognition The steps or processes through which we identify the objects we encounter in the world around us.

occipital lobe The rearmost lobe in each *cerebral hemisphere*, which includes the primary visual projection area.

operation span A measure of *working memory's* capacity. This measure turns out to be predictive of performance in many other tasks, presumably because these tasks all rely on working memory.

operator A tool or action that one can use, in *problem-solving*, to move from the problem's *initial state* to the *goal state*.

optic nerve The bundle of nerve fibers, formed from the *retina's ganglion cells*, that carries information from the eyeball to the brain.

organized depiction A representation that directly reflects the layout and appearance of an object or scene (and so is, on this basis, a "depiction"), but that also adds some specifications about how the depiction is to be understood (e.g., where the form's top is, what the form's *figure/ground organization* is). Often contrasted with *neutral depiction*.

over-regularization error An error in which one perceives or remembers a word or event as being closer to the "norm" than it really is. For example, misspelled words are read as though they were spelled correctly; atypical events are misremembered in a fashion that brings them closer to more-typical events; words with an irregular past tense (such as "ran") are replaced with a regular past tense ("runned").

P cells Specialized cells within the *optic nerve* that provide the input for the *parvocellular cells* in the *lateral geniculate nucleus*. Often contrasted with *M cells*.

parahippocampal place area (PPA) A brain area apparently specialized for the perception of places.

parallel distributed processing A system of handling information in which many steps happen at once (i.e., in parallel) and in which various aspects of the problem or task are represented only in a distributed fashion.

parallel processing A system in which many steps are going on at the same time. Usually contrasted with *serial processing*.

parietal lobe The lobe in each *cerebral hemisphere* that lies between the *occipital* and *frontal* lobes and includes some of the *primary sensory projection area*, as well as circuits that are crucial for the control of attention.

parsing The process through which one divides an input into its appropriate elements—for example, divides the stream of incoming speech into its constituent words.

parvocellular cells Cells in the *lateral geniculate nucleus* specialized for the perception of patterns. Often contrasted with *magnocellular cells*.

path constraint A limit that rules out some operation in *problem-solving*. Path constraints might take the form of resource limitations (limited time to spend on the problem, or limited money) or limits of other sorts (perhaps ethical limits on what one can do).

peer-review process The process through which scientific papers are evaluated before they are judged to be of suitably high quality to be published in the field's scholarly journals. The papers are reviewed by individuals who are experts on the topic—in essence, peers of the authors of the papers being reviewed.

peg-word systems A type of *mnemonic strategy* using words or locations as "pegs" on which one "hangs" the materials to be remembered.

percept An internal representation of the world that results from perceiving; percepts are *organized depictions*.

perceptual reference frame The set of specifications about how a form is to be understood that provides the organization in an *organized depiction*.

performance The actual behavior someone produces (including the errors he or she makes) under ordinary circumstances. Often contrasted with *competence*.

permastore A hypothesized state in which individual memories are held in storage forever (hence, the state can be considered "permanent storage").

perseveration A pattern of responding in which one produces the same response over and over, even though one knows that the task requires a change in response. This pattern is often observed in patients with brain damage in the *frontal lobe*.

PET scanning See *positron emission tomography*.

phonemes The basic categories of sound used to convey language. For example, the words "peg" and "beg" differ in their initial phoneme—[p] in one case, [b] in the other.

phonemic restoration effect A pattern in which people "hear" *phonemes* that actually are not presented but that are highly likely in that context. Thus, if one is presented with the word "legislature" but with the [s] sound replaced by a cough, one is likely to hear the [s] sound anyhow.

phonological buffer A passive storage device that serves as part of the *articulatory rehearsal loop*. The phonological buffer serves as part of the mechanisms ordinarily needed for hearing. In rehearsal, however, the buffer is loaded by means of *subvocalization*. Materials within the buffer then fade, but they can

be refreshed by new covert speech under the control of the *central executive*.

phonology The study of the sounds that are used to convey language.

photoreceptor A cell on the *retina* that responds directly to the incoming light; photoreceptors are of two kinds: *rods* and *cones*.

phrase-structure ambiguity Ambiguity in how a *sentence* should be interpreted, resulting from the fact that more than one phrase structure is compatible with the sentence. An example of such ambiguity is, "I saw the bird with my binoculars."

phrase-structure rule A constraint that governs the pattern of branching in a phrase-structure tree. Equivalently, phrase-structure rules govern what the constituents must be for any syntactic element of a *sentence*.

picture-identification task A task in which a person is shown simple pictures (often line drawings) and must indicate, as rapidly as possible, what the picture shows (e.g., "a dog," "a truck"). Responses tend to be faster if the objects shown are typical of their category.

place of articulation The position at which a speaker momentarily obstructs the flow of air out of the lungs to produce a speech sound. For example, the place of articulation for the [b] sound is the lips; the place of articulation for the [d] sound is created by the tongue briefly touching the roof of the mouth.

positron emission tomography (PET scanning) A *neuroimaging technique* that determines how much glucose (the brain's fuel) is being used by specific areas of the brain at a particular moment in time.

postsynaptic membrane The cell membrane of the *neuron* "receiving" information across the *synapse*. Often contrasted with *presynaptic membrane*.

pragmatic reasoning schema A collection of rules, derived from ordinary practical experience, that defines what inferences are appropriate in a specific situation. These reasoning schemata are usually defined in terms of a goal or theme, and so one schema defines the rules appropriate for reasoning about situations involving "permission," whereas a different schema defines the rules appropriate for thinking about situations involving cause-and-effect relations.

pragmatic rule A rule that governs how language is ordinarily used, as well as how this language will be interpreted. As an example, "Do you know the time?" is literally a question about one's knowledge, but this question is interpreted as a request that one report what time it is.

pragmatics A term referring to knowledge of how language is ordinarily used, knowledge (for example) that tells most English speakers that "Can you pass me the salt?" is actually a request for the salt, not an inquiry about someone's arm strength.

prefrontal area The frontmost part of the *frontal lobe*, crucial for planning and the organization of behavior.

prefrontal cortex The outer surface (*cortex*) of the frontmost part of the brain (i.e., the frontmost part of the *frontal lobe*). This brain area has many functions but is crucial for the planning of complex or novel behaviors, and so this brain area is often mentioned as the main site underlying the brain's executive functions.

premise A *proposition* that is assumed to be true in a logic problem; the problem asks what conclusion follows from its premises.

preparation The first in a series of stages often hypothesized as crucial for creativity. The second stage is *incubation*; the third, *illumination*. Preparation is the stage in which one commences effortful work on the problem, often with little progress.

prescriptive rules Rules describing how things are supposed to be

instead of how they are. Often called *normative* rules and contrasted with *descriptive rules*.

presynaptic membrane The cell membrane of the *neuron* "sending" information across the *synapse*. Often contrasted with *postsynaptic membrane*.

primacy effect An often-observed advantage in remembering the early-presented materials within a sequence of materials. This advantage is generally attributed to the fact that one can focus attention on these items, because at the beginning of a sequence one is obviously not trying to divide attention between these items and other items in the series. Often contrasted with *recency effect*.

primary motor projection areas The strip of tissue, located at the rear of the *frontal lobe*, that is the departure point for nerve cells that send their signals to lower portions of the brain and spinal cord, which ultimately result in muscle movement.

primary projection areas Regions of the *cortex* that serve as the brain's receiving station for sensory information or as a dispatching station for motor commands.

primary sensory projection areas The main points of arrival in the *cortex* for information arriving from the eyes, ears, and other sense organs.

priming A process through which one input or cue prepares a person for an upcoming input or cue.

problem-solving A process in which one begins with a goal and seeks some steps that will lead toward that goal.

problem-solving protocol A record of how someone seeks to solve a problem; the record is created by simply asking the person to think aloud while working on the problem. The written record of this thinking-aloud is the protocol.

problem-solving set The starting assumptions that a person uses when trying to solve a new problem. These assumptions are often helpful,

because they guide the person away from pointless strategies. But these assumptions can sometimes steer the person away from worthwhile strategies, and so they can be an obstacle to problem-solving.

problem space The set of all states that can be reached in solving a problem, as one moves, by means of the problem's *operators*, from the problem's *initial state* toward the problem's *goal state*.

process-pure task A task that relies on only a single mental process. If tasks are "process-pure," then we can interpret the properties of task performance as revealing the properties of the underlying process. If tasks are not process-pure, however, we cannot interpret performance as revealing the properties of a specific process.

processing fluency An improvement in the speed or ease of processing that results from prior practice in using those same processing steps.

production task An experimental procedure used in studying concepts, in which the person is asked to name as many examples (e.g., as many fruits) as possible.

proposition The smallest unit of knowledge that can be either true or false. Propositions are often expressed via simple sentences, but this is merely a convenience.

prosody The pattern of pauses and pitch changes that characterize speech production. Prosody can be used to emphasize elements of a spoken *sentence*, to highlight the sentence's intended structure, or to signal the difference between a question and an assertion.

prosopagnosia A syndrome in which patients lose their ability to recognize faces and to make other fine-grained discriminations within a highly familiar category, even though their other visual abilities seem relatively intact.

prototype theory The claim that mental categories are represented by means of a single "best example," or prototype, identifying the "center" of the category. In this view, decisions about category membership, and inferences about the category, are made with reference to this best example, often an average of the examples of that category that one has actually encountered.

pseudoword A letter string designed to resemble an actual word, even though it is not. Examples include "blar," "plome," and "tuke."

random assignment A procedure in which participants are assigned on a random basis to one condition or another. This ensures that there will be no systematic differences, at the start of the experiment, between the participants in the various conditions. If differences are then observed at the end of the experiment, the researcher knows that the differences were caused by something inside of the experiment itself. Random assignment is required because participants inevitably differ from each other in various ways; random assignment ensures, however, that these differences are equally represented in all conditions (i.e., that all conditions have a mix of early-arrived participants and late-arrivals, a mix of motivated participants and less-motivated ones, etc.).

rating task A task in which research participants must evaluate some item or category with reference to some dimension, usually expressing their response in terms of some number. For example, participants might be asked to evaluate birds for how *typical* they are within the category of "birds," using a "1" response to indicate "very typical" and a "7" response to indicate "very atypical."

reason-based choice A proposal for how people make decisions. The central idea is that people make a choice when—and only when—they detect what they believe to be a persuasive reason for making that choice.

recall The task of memory *retrieval* in which the rememberer must

come up with the desired materials, sometimes in response to a cue that names the context in which these materials were earlier encountered ("Name the pictures you saw earlier"), sometimes in response to a question that requires the sought-after information ("Name a fruit" or "What is the state capital of California?"). Often contrasted with *recognition*.

recency effect The tendency to remember materials that occur late in a series.

receptive field The portion of the visual field to which a cell within the visual system responds. If the appropriately shaped stimulus appears in the appropriate position, the cell's *firing* rate will change. The cell's firing rate will not change if the stimulus is of the wrong form or is in the wrong position.

recognition The task of memory *retrieval* in which the items to be remembered are presented and the person must decide whether or not the item was encountered in some earlier circumstance. Thus, for example, one might be asked, "Have you ever seen this person before?" or "Is this the poster you saw in the office yesterday?" Often contrasted with *recall*.

recognition by components model A model (often referred to by its initials, RBC) of *object recognition*. In this model, a crucial role is played by *geons*, the (hypothesized) basic building blocks out of which all the objects we recognize are constructed.

recognition threshold The briefest exposure to a stimulus that still allows accurate recognition of that stimulus. For words, the recognition threshold typically lies between 10 and 40 ms. Words shown for longer durations are usually easily perceived; words shown for briefer durations are typically difficult to perceive.

reconstruction A process in which one draws on broad patterns of knowledge in order to figure out how a prior event actually unfolded.

In some circumstances, we rely on reconstruction to fill gaps in what we recall; in other circumstances, we rely on reconstruction because it requires less effort than actual *recall*.

recursion A property of rule systems that allows a symbol to appear both on the left side of a definition (the part being defined) and on the right side (the part providing the definition). Recursive rules within *syntax*, for example, allow a *sentence* to include another sentence as one of its constituents, as in the following example: "Solomon says that Jacob is talented."

referent The actual object, action, or event in the world that a word refers to.

rehearsal loop See *articulatory rehearsal loop*.

relational rehearsal A form of mental processing in which one thinks about the relations, or connections, between ideas. This rehearsal will later guide memory search.

"remember/know" A distinction between two experiences one can have in recalling a past event. If one "remembers" having encountered a stimulus before, then one usually can offer information about that encounter, including when, where, and how it occurred. If one merely "knows" that one has encountered a stimulus before, then one is likely to have a sense of familiarity with the stimulus but may have no idea when or where the stimulus was last encountered.

repetition priming A pattern of *priming* that occurs simply because a stimulus is presented a second time; processing is more efficient on the second presentation.

replication A procedure of repeating an experiment (often with small variations) to ensure that the result is reliable.

representativeness heuristic A strategy often used in making judgments about categories. This strategy is broadly equivalent to making the assumption that in general, the instances of a category will resemble the prototype for that category and, likewise, that the prototype resembles each instance.

response selector A (hypothesized) mental resource needed for the selection and initiation of a wide range of responses, including overt responses (e.g., moving in a particular way) and covert responses (e.g., initiating a memory search).

response threshold The quantity of information, or quantity of activation, needed in order to trigger a response.

response time The amount of time (usually measured in milliseconds) needed for a person to respond to a particular event (such as a question or a cue to press a specific button).

retention interval The amount of time that passes between the initial learning of some material and the subsequent memory *retrieval* of that material.

retina The light-sensitive tissue that lines the back of the eyeball.

retrieval The process of locating information in memory and activating that information for use.

retrieval block A circumstance in which a person seems unable to retrieve a bit of information that he or she knows reasonably well.

retrieval failure A mechanism that probably contributes to a great deal of forgetting. Retrieval failure occurs when a memory is, in fact, in long-term storage, but one is unable to locate that memory when trying to retrieve it.

retrieval path A connection (or series of connections) that can lead to a sought-after memory in long-term storage.

retrograde amnesia An inability to remember experiences that occurred *before* the event that triggered the memory disruption. Often contrasted with *anterograde amnesia*.

review article A scholarly report that summarizes the results of many different research papers, seeking to synthesize those results into a coherent pattern.

risk aversion A tendency toward avoiding risk. People tend to be risk-averse when contemplating gains, choosing instead to hold tight to what they already have. Often contrasted with *risk seeking*.

risk seeking A tendency toward seeking out risk. People tend to be risk-seeking when contemplating losses, because they are willing to gamble in hopes of avoiding (or diminishing) their losses. Often contrasted with *risk aversion*.

rod A *photoreceptor* that is sensitive to very low light levels but that is unable to discriminate hues and that has relatively poor *acuity*. Often contrasted with *cone*.

schema (pl. schemata) A pattern of knowledge describing what is typical or frequent in a particular situation. For example, a "kitchen schema" would stipulate that a stove and refrigerator are likely to be present, whereas a coffeemaker may be or may not be present, and a piano is likely not to be present.

selection task An experimental procedure, commonly used to study reasoning, in which a person is presented with four cards with certain information on either side of the card. The person is also given a rule that may describe the cards, and the person's task is to decide which cards must be turned over to find out if the rule describes the cards or not. Also called the "four-card task."

selective attention The skill through which one pays attention to one input or one task while ignoring other stimuli that are also on the scene.

selective deficit A limitation in someone's abilities that appears in some domains or on some tasks, but not in others; the limitations help specify the nature of the problem leading to the deficit.

self-reference effect The tendency to have better memory for information relevant to oneself than for other sorts of material.

self-report data A form of evidence in which the person is asked directly about his or her own thoughts or experiences.

self-schema The set of interwoven beliefs and memories that constitute one's beliefs about oneself and one's memories for the self-relevant events one has experienced.

self-selected group A group of participants who are in a particular condition within a study because they put themselves in that condition. In some cases, participants choose which condition to be in. In other cases, they have some trait (e.g., showing up late; arriving only in the evening) that causes them to be put into a particular condition. In all cases, there is a risk that these participants are different from other conditions at the start of the experiment—which is presumably why these participants put themselves into the condition they did. If the study then shows the participants to be different from the other conditions at the end of the experiment, this is ambiguous: It could be because of the effects of the study or because of the preexisting difference.

semantic bootstrapping An important process in language learning in which someone (usually a child) uses knowledge of semantic relationships as a basis for figuring out the *syntax* of the language.

sentence A sequence of words that conforms to the rules of syntax (and so has the right constituents in the right sequence).

sentence verification task An experimental procedure, used for studying memory, in which participants are given simple sentences (e.g., "Cats are animals") and must respond as quickly as possible whether the sentence is true or false.

sequential lineup A procedure used for eyewitness identification in which the witness sees faces one by one and cannot see the next face until he has made a yes or no decision about the face now in view.

serial position A data pattern summarizing the relationship between some performance measure (often, likelihood of *recall*) and the order in which the test materials were presented. In memory studies, the serial position curve tends to be U-shaped, with people best able to recall the first-presented items (the *primacy effect*) and also the last-presented items (the *recency effect*).

serial processing A system in which only one step happens at a time (and so the steps go on in a series). Usually contrasted with *parallel processing*.

7 plus-or-minus 2 A number often offered as an estimate of the holding capacity of *working memory*.

shadowing A task in which research participants are required to repeat back a verbal input, word for word, as they hear it.

shallow processing A mode of thinking about material in which one pays attention only to appearances and other superficial aspects of the material; shallow processing typically leads to poor memory retention. Often contrasted with *deep processing*.

short-term memory An older term for what is now called *working memory*.

simultaneous multiple constraint satisfaction An attribute of much of our thinking, in which we seem able to find solutions to problems, or answers to questions, that satisfy several requirements ("multiple constraints"), using a search process that seems to be guided by all of these requirements at the same time.

single-cell recording A technique for recording the moment-by-moment *activation level* of an individual *neuron* within a healthy, normally functioning brain.

somatic markers States of the body used in decision-making. For example, a tight stomach and an accelerated heart rate when someone is thinking about an option can signal that person that the option has risk associated with it.

source confusion A memory error in which one misremembers where a bit of information was learned or where a particular stimulus was last encountered.

source memory A form of memory that allows one to recollect the episode in which learning took place or the time and place in which a particular stimulus was encountered.

source monitoring The process of keeping track of when and where one encountered some bit of information (i.e., keeping track of the source of that information).

spaced learning A memorization strategy in which a research participant works on memorizing for a while, then does something else, then returns to memorizing, then does something else, and so on. Often contrasted with *massed learning*.

span test A procedure used for measuring *working memory*'s holding capacity. In newer studies, the *operation span* test is used.

spatial attention The mechanism through which we allocate processing resources to particular positions in space, so that we more efficiently process any inputs from that region in space.

specific language impairment A genetically rooted syndrome in which individuals seem to have normal intelligence but problems in learning the rules of language.

speech segmentation The process through which a stream of speech is "sliced" into its constituent words and, within words, into the constituent *phonemes*.

spreading activation A process through which activation travels from one *node* to another, via *associative links*. As each node becomes activated, it serves as a source for further activation, spreading onward through the network.

state-dependent learning A phenomenon in which learning seems linked to the person's mental, emotional, or biological state during the learning. As a result of this linkage, the learning is most likely to show its effects when the person is again in that mental, emotional, or biological state.

storage The state in which a memory, once acquired, remains dormant until it is retrieved.

Stroop interference A classic demonstration of *automaticity* in which people are asked to name the color of ink used to print a word, and the word itself is a different color name. For example, research participants might see the word "yellow" printed in blue ink and be required to say "blue." Considerable interference is observed in this task, with participants apparently being unable to ignore the word's content, even though it is irrelevant to their task.

subcortical Beneath the surface of the brain (i.e., underneath the *cortex*).

subliminal prime A *prime* that is presented so quickly that it is not consciously detected; such primes nonetheless can have an impact on subsequent perceptions or thoughts.

subproblem A subdivision of a problem being solved. Subproblems are produced when a person tries to solve a problem by breaking it into components or steps, each with its own goal, but so that solving all the subproblems results in solution of the overall problem.

subthreshold activation Activation levels below *response threshold*. Subthreshold activation, by definition, will not trigger a response; nonetheless, this activation is important because it can accumulate, leading eventually to an *activation level* that exceeds the response threshold.

subvocalization Covert speech, in which one goes through the motions of speaking, or perhaps forms a detailed motor plan for speech movements, but without making any sound.

sufficient condition A condition that, if satisfied, guarantees that a certain consequence will occur. However, sufficient conditions may not be necessary for that consequence (since the same consequence might occur for some other reasons). Often contrasted with *necessary condition*.

summation The addition of two or more separate inputs so that the effect of these combined inputs is greater than the effect of any one of the inputs by itself.

surface structure The representation of a *sentence* that is actually expressed in speech. In some treatments, this structure is referred to as "s-structure." Often contrasted with *underlying structure*.

synapse The area that includes the *presynaptic membrane* of one *neuron*, the *postsynaptic membrane* of another neuron, and the tiny gap between them. The presynaptic membrane releases a small amount of *neurotransmitter* that drifts across the gap and stimulates the postsynaptic membrane.

syntax Rules governing the sequences and combinations of words in the formation of phrases and *sentences*.

System 1 A commonly used name for judgment and reasoning strategies that are fast and effortless, but prone to error.

System 2 A commonly used name for judgment and reasoning strategies that are slower and require more effort than System 1 strategies do, but are less prone to error.

tachistoscope A device that allows the presentation of stimuli for precisely controlled amounts of time, including very brief presentations.

temporal lobe The lobe of the *cortex* lying inward and down from the temples. The temporal lobe in each *cerebral hemisphere* includes the primary auditory projection area, *Wernicke's area*, and, subcortically, the *amygdala* and *hippocampus*.

thalamus A part of the lower portion of the *forebrain* that serves as a major relay and integration center for sensory information.

threshold The activity level at which a cell or *detector* responds, or "fires."

TMS See *transcranial magnetic stimulation*.

token node A *node* that represents a specific example or instance of a category and therefore is used in propositions concerned with specific events and individuals. Often contrasted with *type node*.

top-down processing See *concept-driven processing*.

TOT phenomenon An often-observed effect in which people are unable to remember a particular word, even though they are certain that the word (typically identified via its definition) is in their vocabulary. People in this state often can remember the starting letter for the word and its number of syllables, and they insist that the word is on the "tip of their tongue" (hence the "TOT" label).

transcendental method A logic for theorizing first proposed by the philosopher Immanuel Kant. To use this method, one first observes the effects or consequences of a process, and then asks, What must the concept have been in order to bring about these effects?

transcranial magnetic stimulation (TMS) A technique in which a series of strong magnetic pulses at a specific location on the scalp cause temporary disruption in the brain region directly underneath this scalp area.

type node A *node* that represents a general category and therefore is embedded in propositions that are true for the entire category. Often contrasted with *token node*.

typicality The degree to which a particular case (an object, or a situation, or an event) is typical for its kind.

unattended channel A stimulus (or group of stimuli) that a person is not trying to perceive. Ordinarily, little information is understood or remembered from the unattended channel. Often contrasted with *attended channel*.

underlying structure An abstract representation of the *sentence* to be expressed; sometimes called "deep structure" (or "d-structure"). Often contrasted with *surface structure*.

unilateral neglect syndrome A pattern of symptoms in which patients ignore all inputs coming from one side of space. Patients with this syndrome put only one of their arms into their jackets, eat food from only one half of their plates, read only one half of words (e.g., they might read "output" as "put"), and so on.

utility A measure of the value that an individual puts on a particular outcome; this measure can then be used to compare various outcomes, allowing choices to be based on these comparisons.

utility maximization The proposal that people make decisions by selecting the option that has the greatest *utility*.

V1 See *Area V1*.

valid argument An argument for which the conclusion follows from the *premise*, in accord with the rules of logic or the principles of statistics and research methods.

verb phrase One of the constituents of a phrase structure that defines a *sentence*.

verification One of the four steps commonly hypothesized as part of creative *problem-solving*; in this step, one confirms that a new idea really does lead to a problem solution, and one works out the details.

viewpoint-dependent recognition A process in which the ease or success of *recognition* depends on the perceiver's particular viewing angle or distance with regard to the target object.

viewpoint-independent recognition A process in which the ease or success of *recognition* does *not* depend on the perceiver's particular viewing angle or distance with regard to the target object.

visual acuity A measure of one's ability to see fine detail.

visual search task A commonly used laboratory task in which research participants are asked to search for a specific target (e.g., a shape, or a shape of a certain color) within a field of other stimuli; usually the researcher is interested in how quickly the participants can locate the target.

visuospatial buffer One of the low-level assistants used as part of the *working-memory system*. This buffer plays an important role in storing visual or spatial representations, including visual images.

voice-onset time (VOT) The time that elapses between the start of a speech sound and the onset of *voicing*. VOT is the main feature distinguishing "voiced" consonants (such as [b], with a near-zero VOT) and "unvoiced" consonants (such as [p], with a VOT of approximately 60 ms).

voicing One of the properties that distinguishes different categories of speech sounds. A sound is considered "voiced" if the vocal folds are vibrating while the sound is produced. If the vocal folds start vibrating sometime after the sound begins (i.e., with a long *voice-onset time*), the sound is considered "unvoiced."

weapon-focus effect A pattern, often alleged for witnesses to violent crimes, in which one pays close attention to some crucial detail (such as the weapon within a crime scene) to the exclusion of much else.

well-defined problem A problem for which the *goal state* is clearly specified at the start and the operators available for reaching that goal are clearly identified. Often contrasted with *ill-defined problem*.

Wernicke's area An area usually in the left *frontal lobe* of the brain; damage here typically causes *fluent aphasia*.

what system The system of visual circuits and pathways leading from the visual *cortex* to the *temporal lobe* and especially involved in object recognition. Often contrasted with the *where system*.

where system The system of visual circuits and pathways leading from the visual *cortex* to the *parietal lobe* and especially involved in the spatial localization of objects and in the coordination of movements. Often contrasted with the *what system*.

winner-takes-all system A process in which a stronger node inhibits weaker ones, so that the stronger node comes more and more to dominate the weaker nodes.

word-stem completion A task in which people are given the beginning of a word (e.g., "TOM") and must provide a word that starts with the letters provided. In some versions of the task, only one solution is possible, and so performance is measured by counting the number of words completed. In other versions of the task, several solutions are possible for each stem, and performance is assessed by determining which of the responses fulfill some other criterion.

word-superiority effect The data pattern in which research participants are more accurate and more efficient in recognizing words (and word-like letter strings) than they are in recognizing individual letters.

working backward A commonly used *problem-solving* strategy in which the person begins with the *goal state* and tries to figure out what transformations or operations would make this state more similar to the problem's starting point (the *initial state*).

working memory The storage system in which information is held while that information is being worked on. All indications are that working memory is a system, not a single entity, and that information is held here via active processes, not via some sort of passive storage. Formerly called "short-term memory."

working-memory system A system of mental resources used for holding information in an easily accessible form. The *central executive* is at the heart of this system, and the executive then relies on a number of low-level assistants, including the *visuospatial buffer* and the *articulatory rehearsal loop*.

References

Ackerman, P. L., Beier, M. E., & Boyle, M. O. (2002). Individual differences in working memory within a nomological network of cognitive and perceptual speed abilities. *Journal of Experimental Psychology: General, 131,* 567–589.

Adamson, R. (1952). Functional fixedness as related to problem solving: A repetition of three experiments. *Journal of Experimental Psychology, 44,* 288–291.

Aggleton, J. P., & Brown, M. W. (2006). Interleaving brain systems for episodic and recognition memory. *Trends in Cognitive Sciences, 10,* 455–463.

Aggleton, J. P., & Shaw, C. (1996). Amnesia and recognition memory: A re-analysis of psychometric data. *Neuropsychologia, 34,* 51–62.

Ahn, W.-K., & Graham, L. M. (1999). The impact of necessity and sufficiency in the Wason four-card task. *Psychological Science, 10,* 237–242.

Ajzen, I. (1977). Intuitive theories of events and the effects of base-rate information on prediction. *Journal of Personality & Social Psychology, 35,* 303–314.

Alexander, K. W., Quas, J. A., Goodman, G. S., Ghetti, S., Edelstein, R. S., Redlich, A. D., et al. (2005). Traumatic impact predicts long-term memory for documented child sexual abuse. *Psychological Science, 16,* 33–40.

Allan, L. (1993). Human contingency judgments: Rule based or associative. *Psychological Bulletin, 114,* 435–448.

Alloy, L. B., & Tabachnik, N. (1984). Assessment of covariation by humans and animals: The joint influence of prior expectations and current situational information. *Psychological Review, 91,* 112–149.

Allport, A. (1989). Visual attention. In M. Posner (Ed.), *Foundations of cognitive science* (pp. 631–682). Cambridge, MA: MIT Press.

Allport, D., Antonis, B., & Reynolds, P. (1972). On the division of attention: A disproof of the single channel hypothesis. *Quarterly Journal of Experimental Psychology, 24,* 225–235.

Almor, A., & Sloman, S. A. (2000). Reasoning versus text processing in the Wason selection task: A nondeontic perspective on perspective effects. *Memory & Cognition, 28,* 1060–1070.

Alter, A. L., Oppenheimer, D. M., Epley, N., & Eyre, R. N. (2007). Overcoming intuition: Metacognitive difficulty activates analytic reasoning. *Journal of Experimental Psychology: General, 136,* 569–576.

Altmann, E. M., & Gray, W. D. (2002). Forgetting to remember: The functional relationship of decay and interference. *Psychological Science, 13,* 27–33.

Amabile, T. M. (2001). Beyond talent: John Irving and the passionate craft of creativity. *American Psychologist, 56,* 333–336.

Anand, P., & Sternthal, B. (1991). Perceptual fluency and affect without recognition. *Memory & Cognition, 19,* 293–300.

Anderson, J. R. (1974). Verbatim and propositional representation of sentences in immediate and long-term memory. *Journal of Verbal Learning and Verbal Behavior, 13,* 149–162.

Anderson, J. R. (1976). *Language, memory, and thought.* Hillsdale, NJ: Erlbaum.

Anderson, J. R. (1980). *Cognitive psychology and its implications.* San Francisco: Freeman.

Anderson, J. R. (1987). Skill acquisition: Compilation of weak-method problem solutions. *Psychological Review, 94,* 192–210.

Anderson, J. R. (1993). Problem solving and learning. *American Psychologist, 48,* 35–44.

Anderson, J. R. (1996). ACT: A simple theory of complex cognition. *American Psychologist, 51,* 355–365.

Anderson, J. R., & Bower, G. H. (1972). Recognition and retrieval processes in free recall. *Psychological Review, 79,* 97–123.

Anderson, J. R., & Bower, G. H. (1973). *Human associative memory.* Washington, DC: Winston.

Anderson, J. R., & Reder, L. M. (1999a). The fan effect: New results and new theories. *Journal of Experimental Psychology: General, 128,* 186–197.

Anderson, J. R., & Reder, L. M. (1999b). Process, not representation: Reply to Radvansky (1999). *Journal of Experimental Psychology: General, 128,* 207–210.

Anderson, M. C., & Bell, T. (2001). Forgetting our facts: The role of inhibitory processes in the loss of propositional knowledge. *Journal of Experimental Psychology: General, 130,* 544–570.

Anderson, M. C., Bjork, R., & Bjork, E. (1994). Remembering can cause forgetting: Retrieval dynamics in long-term memory. *Journal of Experimental Psychology: Learning, Memory and Cognition, 20,* 1063–1087.

Anderson, M. C., Bjork, R. A., & Bjork, E. L. (2000). Retrieval-induced forgetting. Evidence for a recall-specific mechanism. *Psychonomic Bulletin & Review, 7,* 522–530.

Anderson, M. C., & McCulloch, K. C. (1999). Integration as a general boundary condition on retrieval-induced forgetting. *Journal of Experimental Psychology: Learning, Memory and Cognition, 25,* 608–629.

Anderson, M. C., & Spellman, B. (1995). On the status of inhibitory mechanisms in cognition: Memory retrieval as a model case. *Psychological Review, 102,* 68–100.

Anderson, R., & Helstrup, T. (1993). Visual discovery in mind and on paper. *Memory & Cognition, 21,* 283–293.

Ariely, D., & Norton, M. (2007). How actions create—not just reveal—preferences. *Trends in Cognitive Sciences, 12,* 13–16.

Arkes, H. (1991). Costs and benefits of judgment errors: Implications for debiasing. *Psychological Bulletin, 110,* 486–498.

Arkes, H., & Harkness, A. (1983). Estimates of contingency between two dichotomous variables. *Journal of Experimental Psychology: General, 112,* 117–135.

Armstrong, S. L., Gleitman, L. R., & Gleitman, H. (1983). What some concepts might not be. *Cognition, 13,* 263–308.

Aron, A. (2008). Progress in executive-function research. *Current Directions in Psychological Science, 17,* 124–129.

Arrigo, J. M., & Pezdek, K. (1997). Lessons from the study of psychogenic amnesia. *Current Directions in Psychological Science, 6,* 148–152.

Ash, I. K., & Wiley, J. (2006). The nature of restructuring in insight: An individual-differences approach. *Psychonomic Bulletin & Review, 13,* 66–73.

Ashbridge, E., Walsh, V., & Cowey, A. (1997). Temporal aspects of visual search studied by transcranial magnetic stimulation. *Neuropsychologia, 35,* 1121–1131.

Aslin, R. N., Saffran, J. R., & Newport, E. L. (1998). Computation of conditional probability statistics by 8-month-old infants. *Psychological Science, 9,* 321–324.

Atkinson, A. P., Thomas, M. S. C., & Cleeremans, A. (2000). Consciousness: Mapping the theoretical landscape. *Trends in Cognitive Sciences, 4,* 372–382.

Atkinson, R. C., & Shiffrin, R. M. (1968). Human memory: A proposed system and its control processes. In K. W. S. Spence &. J. T. Spence (Eds.), *The psychology of learning and motivation* (pp. 89–105). New York: Academic Press.

Atran, S. (1990). *Cognitive foundations of natural history.* New York: Cambridge University Press.

Attneave, F. (1953). Psychological probability as a function of experienced frequency. *Journal of Experimental Psychology, 46,* 81–86.

Austin, J. (1962). *How to do things with words.* Cambridge, MA: Harvard University Press.

Awh, E., Dhaliwal, H., Christensen, S., & Matsukura, M. (2001). Evidence for two components of object-based selection. *Psychological Science, 12,* 329–334.

Ayers, M. S., & Reder, L. M. (1998). A theoretical review of the misinformation effect: Predictions from an activation-based model. *Psychonomic Bulletin & Review, 5,* 1–21.

Ayton, P., & Fischer, I. (2004). The hot hand fallacy and the gambler's fallacy: Two faces of subjective randomness. *Memory & Cognition, 32,* 1369–1378.

Baars, B. J. (1988). Momentary forgetting as a "resetting" of a conscious global workspace due to competition between incompatible contexts. In M. J. Horowitz (Ed.), *Psychodynamics and cognition* (pp. 269–293). Chicago: University of Chicago Press.

Baars, B. J., & Franklin, S. (2003). How conscious experience and working memory interact. *Trends in Cognitive Sciences, 7,* 166–172.

Baddeley, A. D. (1986). *Working memory.* Oxford, England: Clarendon.

Baddeley, A. D. (1992). Is working memory working? The fifteenth Bartlett lecture. *Quarterly Journal of Experimental Psychology, 44A,* 1–31.

Baddeley, A. (1996). Exploring the central executive. *Quarterly Journal of Experimental Psychology: Human Experimental Psychology, 49A,* 5–28.

Baddeley, A. D. (1999). *Essentials of human memory.* Hove, England: Psychology Press.

Baddeley, A. D., Aggleton, J. P., & Conway, M. A. (Eds.). (2002). *Episodic memory: New directions in research.* New York: Oxford University Press.

Baddeley, A. D., Gathercole, S., & Papagno, C. (1998). The phonological loop as a language learning device. *Psychological Review, 105,* 158–173.

Baddeley, A. D., & Hitch, G. (1974). Working memory. In G. Bower (Ed.), *Recent advances in learning and motivation* (pp. 47–90). New York: Academic Press.

Baddeley, A. D., & Hitch, G. (1977). Recency re-examined. In S. Dornic (Ed.), *Attention and performance VI* (pp. 646–667). Hillsdale, NJ: Erlbaum.

Baddeley, A. D., Logie, R. H., Nimmo-Smith, I., & Brereton, J. (1985). Components of fluent reading. *Journal of Memory and Language, 24,* 119–131.

Baer, J. (1993). *Creativity and divergent thinking: A task-specific approach.* Hillsdale, NJ: Erlbaum.

Bahrick, H. (1984). Semantic memory content in permastore: 50 years of memory for Spanish learned in school. *Journal of Experimental Psychology: General, 113,* 1–29.

Bahrick, H., Bahrick, L., Bahrick, A., & Bahrick, P. (1993). Maintenance of foreign language vocabulary and the spacing effect. *Psychological Science, 4,* 316–321.

Bahrick, H., Bahrick, P. O., & Wittlinger, R. P. (1975). Fifty years of memory for names and faces: A cross-sectional approach. *Journal of Experimental Psychology: General, 104,* 54–75.

Bahrick, H., & Hall, L. (1991). Lifetime maintenance of high school mathematics content. *Journal of Experimental Psychology: General, 120,* 20–33.

Bahrick, H., Hall, L. K., & Berger, S. A. (1996). Accuracy and distortion in memory for high school grades. *Psychological Science, 7,* 265–271.

Balch, W., Bowman, K., & Mohler, L. (1992). Music-dependent memory in immediate and delayed word recall. *Memory & Cognition, 20,* 21–28.

Baratgin, J., & Noveck, I. A. (2000). Not only base rates are neglected in the engineer-lawyer problem: An investigation of reasoners' underutilization of complementarity. *Memory & Cognition, 28,* 79–91.

Barclay, J., Bransford, J., Franks, J., McCarrell, N., & Nitsch, K. (1974). Comprehension and semantic flexibility. *Journal of Verbal Learning & Verbal Behavior, 13,* 471–481.

Baragh, J. (2005). Toward demystifying the nonconscious control of social behavior. In Hasslin, R., Uleman, J., & Bargh, J. (Eds.), *The new unconscious* (pp. 37–58). New York: Oxford University Press.

Bargh, J. A. (1989). Conditional automaticity: Varieties of automatic influence in social perception and cognition. In J. Uleman & J. Bargh (Eds.), *Unintended thought* (pp. 3–51). New York: Guilford.

Bargh, J. A., & Chartrand, T. L. (1999). The unbearable automaticity of being. *American Psychologist, 54,* 462–479.

Baron, J. (1988). *Thinking and reasoning.* Cambridge, England: Cambridge University Press.

Baron, J. (1998). *Judgment misguided: Intuition and error in public decision making.* New York: Oxford University Press.

Baron, J., & Leshner, S. (2000). How serious are expressions of protected values? *Journal of Experimental Psychology: Applied, 6,* 183–194.

Barron, F., & Huntingdon, D. M. (1981). Creativity, intelligence, and personality. *Annual Review of Psychology, 32,* 439–476.

Barsalou, L. (1988). The content and organization of autobiographical memories. In U. Neisser & E. Winograd (Eds.), *Remembering reconsidered* (pp. 193–243). Cambridge, England: Cambridge University Press.

Barsalou, L., & Sewell, D. R. (1985). Contrasting the representation of scripts and categories. *Journal of Memory and Language, 24,* 646–665.

Bartlett, F. C. (1932). *Remembering: A study in experimental and social psychology.* Cambridge, England: Cambridge University Press.

Bartolomeo, P., Bachoud-Levi, A-C., De Gelder, B., Denes, G., Barba, G. D., Brugieres, P., et al. (1998). Multiple-domain dissociation between impaired visual perception and preserved mental imagery in a patient with bilateral extrastriate lesions. *Neuropsychologia, 36*(3), 239–249.

Bassok, M. (1996). Using content to interpret structure: Effects on analogical transfer. *Current Directions in Psychological Science, 5,* 54–57.

Bassok, M., Wu, L.-L., & Olseth, K. (1995). Judging a book by its cover: Interpretive effects of content on problem-solving transfer. *Memory & Cognition, 23,* 354–367.

Beach, C. M. (1991). The interpretation of prosodic patterns at points of syntactic structural ambiguity: Evidence for cue trading relations. *Journal of Memory and Language, 30,* 644–663.

Bechara, A., Damasio, H., & Damasio, A. R. (2003). Role of the amygdala in decision-making. *Annals of the New York Academy of Sciences, 985,* 356–369.

Bechara, A., Damasio, H., Tranel, D., & Damasio, A. R. (2005). The Iowa Gambling Task and the somatic marker hypothesis: Some questions and answers. *Trends in Cognitive Sciences, 9,* 159–162.

Bechara, A., Tranel, D., Damasio, H., Adolphs, R., Rockland, C., & Damasio, A. (1995). Double dissociation of conditioning and declarative knowledge relative to the amygdala and hippocampus in humans. *Science, 269,* 1115–1118.

Bédard, J., & Chi, M. (1992). Expertise. *Current Directions in Psychological Science, 1,* 135–139.

Begg, I., Anas, A., & Farinacci, S. (1992). Dissociation of processes in belief: Source recollection, statement familiarity, and the illusion of truth. *Journal of Experimental Psychology: General, 121,* 446–458.

Begg, I., Armour, V., & Kerr, T. (1985). On believing what we remember. *Canadian Journal of Behavioral Science, 17,* 199–214.

Behrmann, M. (2000). The mind's eye mapped onto the brain's matter. *Current Directions in Psychological Science, 9,* 50–54.

Behrmann, M., & Avidan, G. (2005). Congenital prosopagnosia: Face-blind from birth. *Trends in Cognitive Sciences, 9,* 180–187.

Behrmann, M., Moscovitch, M., & Winocur, G. (1994). Intact visual imagery and impaired visual perception in a patient with visual agnosia. *Journal of Experimental Psychology: Human Perception and Performance, 20,* 1068–1087.

Behrmann, M., Peterson, M. A., Moscovitch, M., & Suzuki, S. (2006). Independent representation of parts and relations between them: Evidence from integrative agnosia. *Journal of Experimental Psychology: Human Perception and Performance, 32,* 1169–1184.

Behrmann, M., & Tipper, S. (1999). Attention accesses multiple reference frames: Evidence from visual neglect. *Journal of Experimental Psychology: Human Perception and Performance, 25,* 83–101.

Bekerian, D. A., & Baddeley, A. D. (1980). Saturation advertising and the repetition effect. *Journal of Verbal Learning & Verbal Behavior, 19,* 17–25.

Bellugi, U. (1971). Simplification in children's language. In R. Huxley & E. Ingram (Eds.), *Language acquisition: Models and methods.* New York: Academic Press.

Berko, J. (1958). The child's learning of English morphology. *Word, 14,* 150–177.

Berlin, B., & Key, P. (1969). *Basic color terms: Their universality and evolution.* Berkeley: University of California Press.

Besner, D., & Stolz, J. A. (1999a). Unconsciously controlled processing: The Stroop effect reconsidered. *Psychonomic Bulletin & Review, 6,* 449–455.

Besner, D., & Stolz, J. A. (1999b). What kind of attention modulates the Stroop effect? *Psychonomic Bulletin & Review, 6,* 99–104.

Bever, T. (1970). The cognitive basis for linguistic structures. In J. R. Hayes (Ed.), *Cognition and the devel-*

opment of language (pp. 279–362). New York: Wiley.

Biederman, I. (1985). Human vision understanding: Recent research and a theory. *Computer Vision, Graphics, and Image Processing, 32,* 29–73.

Biederman, I. (1987). Recognition by components: A theory of human image understanding. *Psychological Review, 94,* 115–147.

Biederman, I. (1990). Higher-level vision. In D. Osherson, S. Kosslyn, & J. Hollerbach (Eds.), *An invitation to cognitive science: Visual cognition and action, Vol. 2* (pp. 41–72). Cambridge, MA: MIT Press.

Bisiach, E., & Luzzatti, C. (1978). Unilateral neglect of representational space. *Cortex, 14,* 129–133.

Bisiach, E., Luzzatti, C., & Perani, D. (1979). Unilateral neglect, representational schema, and consciousness. *Brain, 102,* 609–618.

Blanchette, I., & Dunbar, K. (2000). How analogies are generated: The roles of structural and superficial similarity. *Memory & Cognition, 28,* 108–124.

Block, N. (1997). Biology vs. computation in the study of consciousness. *Behavioral and Brain Sciences, 20,* 1.

Block, N. (2001). Paradox and cross purposes in recent work on consciousness. *Cognition, 79,* 197–219.

Block, N. (2005). Two neural correlates of consciousness. *Trends in Cognitive Sciences, 9,* 46–52.

Bloom, P. (Ed.). (1994). *Language acquisition.* Cambridge, MA: MIT Press.

Blount, G. (1986). Dangerousness of patients with Capgras Syndrome. *Nebraska Medical Journal, 71,* 207.

Bobrow, S., & Bower, G. H. (1969). Comprehension and recall of sentences. *Journal of Experimental Psychology, 80,* 455–461.

Bogen, J. E. (1995). On the neurophysiology of consciousness: I. An overview. *Consciousness & Cognition: An International Journal, 4,* 52–62.

Boole, G. (1854). *An investigation of the laws of thought, on which are founded the mathematical theories of logic and probabilities.* London: Maberly.

Bornstein, B. (1963). Prosopagnosia. In L. Halpern (Ed.), *Problems of dynamic neurology* (pp. 283–318). Jerusalem: Hadassah Medical Organization.

Bornstein, B., Sroka, H., & Munitz, H. (1969). Prosopagnosia with animal face agnosia. *Cortex, 5,* 164–169.

Boroditsky, L. (2001). Does language shape thought? Mandarin and English speakers' conceptions of time. *Cognitive Psychology, 43,* 1–22.

Botvinick, M. M., Cohen, J. D., & Carter, C. S. (2004). Conflict monitoring and anterior cingulate cortex: An update. *Trends in Cognitive Sciences, 8,* 539–546.

Bourke, P. A., & Duncan, J. (2005). Effect of template complexity on visual search and dual-task performance. *Psychological Science, 16,* 208–213.

Bowden, E., Jung-Beeman, M., Fleck, J., & Kounios, J. (2005). New approaches to demystifying insight. *Trends in Cognitive Sciences, 9,* 322–328.

Bower, G. H. (1970). Analysis of a mnemonic device. *American Scientist, 58,* 496–510.

Bower, G. H. (1972). Mental imagery and associative learning. In L. W. Gregg (Ed.), *Cognition in learning and memory* (pp. 51–88). New York: Wiley.

Bower, G. H., Karlin, M. B., & Dueck, A. (1975). Comprehension and memory for pictures. *Memory & Cognition, 3,* 216–220.

Bower, G. H., & Reitman, J. S. (1972). Mnemonic elaboration in multilist learning. *Journal of Verbal Learning and Verbal Behavior, 11,* 478–485.

Bower, G. H., & Winzenz, D. (1970). Comparison of associative learning strategies. *Psychonomic Science, 20,* 119–120.

Bower, J. M., & Parsons, L. M. (2003). Rethinking the "lesser brain." *Scientific American, 289*(August), 50–57.

Bowers, J. (2009). On the biological plausibility of grandmother cells: Implications for neural network theories in psychology and neuroscience. *Psychological Review, 116,* 220–251.

Braine, M., & O'Brien, D. (1991). A theory of if: A lexical entry, reasoning program, and pragmatic principles. *Psychological Review, 98,* 182–203.

Brainerd, C. J., & Reyna, V. F. (1998). When things that were never experienced are easier to "remember" than things that were. *Psychological Science, 9,* 484–490.

Bransford, J. (1979). *Human cognition: Learning, understanding and remembering.* Belmont, CA: Wadsworth.

Bransford, J., & Franks, J. J. (1971). The abstraction of linguistic ideas. *Cognitive Psychology, 2,* 331–350.

Bransford, J., & Johnson, M. K. (1972). Contextual prerequisites for understanding: Some investigations of comprehension and recall. *Journal of Verbal Learning and Verbal Behavior, 11,* 717–726.

Brase, G. (2008). Frequency interpretation of ambiguous statistical information facilitates Bayesian reasoning. *Psychonomic Bulletin & Review, 15,* 284–289.

Brase, G. L., Cosmides, L., & Tooby, J. (1998). Individuation, counting and statistical inference: The role of frequency and whole-object representations in judgment under uncertainty. *Journal of Experimental Psychology: General, 127,* 3–21.

Braver, T. S., & Cohen, J. D. (2001). Working memory, cognitive control, and the prefrontal cortex: Computational and empirical studies. *Cognitive Processing, 2,* 25–55.

Bremner, J. D., Shobe, K., & Kihlstrom, J. F. (2000). False memories in women with self-reported childhood sexual abuse: An empirical study. *Psychological Science, 11,* 333–337.

Brennen, T., Baguley, T., Bright, J., & Bruce, V. (1990). Resolving semantically induced tip-of-the-tongue states for proper nouns. *Memory & Cognition, 18,* 339–347.

Brewer, J., Zhao, Z., Desmond, J., Glover, G., & Gabrieli, J. (1998). Making memories: Brain activity that predicts how well visual experience will be remembered. *Science, 281,* 1185–1187.

Brewer, N., & Wells, G. L. (2006). The confidence-accuracy relationship in eyewitness identification: Effects of lineup instructions, foil similarity, and target-absent base rates. *Journal of Experimental Psychology: Applied, 12,* 11–30.

Brewer, W., & Treyens, J. C. (1981). Role of schemata in memory for places. *Cognitive Psychology, 13,* 207–230.

Brewin, C. R., Andrews, B., & Gotlib, I. (1993). Psychopathology and early experience: A reappraisal of retrospective reports. *Psychological Bulletin, 113,* 82–98.

Brigham, J., & Cairns, D. L. (1988). The effect of mugshot inspections on eyewitness identification accuracy. *Journal of Applied Social Psychology, 18,* 1394–1410.

Brigham, J., & Wolfskiel, M. P. (1983). Opinions of attorneys and law enforcement personnel on the accuracy of eyewitness identification. *Law and Human Behavior, 7,* 337–349.

Broadbent, D. E. (1958). *Perception and communication.* London: Pergamon.

Brooks, L. (1968). Spatial and verbal components of the act of recall. *Canadian Journal of Psychology, 22,* 349–368.

Brooks, L. (1990). Concept formation and particularizing learning. In P. Hanson (Ed.), *Information, language and cognition* (pp. 141–167). Vancouver: University of British Columbia Press.

Brooks, L., Norman, G., & Allen, S. (1991). Role of specific similarity in a medical diagnostic task. *Journal of Experimental Psychology: General, 120,* 278–287.

Brown, A. (1991). A review of the tip-of-the-tongue experience. *Psychological Bulletin, 109,* 204–223.

Brown, A., & Marsh, E. (2008). Evoking false beliefs about autobiographical experience. *Psychonomic Bulletin & Review, 15,* 186–190.

Brown, A. L. (1979). Theories of memory and the problems of development: Activity, growth, and knowledge. In L. S. Cermak & F. I. M. Craik (Eds.), *Levels of processing in human memory* (pp. 225–258). Hillsdale, NJ: Erlbaum.

Brown, A. S. (2002). Consolidation theory and retrograde amnesia in humans. *Psychonomic Bulletin & Review, 9,* 403–425.

Brown, A. S., & Halliday, H. E. (1990, November). *Multiple-choice tests: Pondering incorrect alternatives can be hazardous to your knowledge.* Paper presented at the meeting of the Psychonomic Society, New Orleans, LA.

Brown, E., Deffenbacher, K., & Sturgill, W. (1977). Memory for faces and the circumstances of encounter. *Journal of Applied Psychology, 62,* 311–318.

Brown, R., & Kulik, J. (1977). Flashbulb memories. *Cognition, 5,* 73–99.

Brown, R., & Lenneberg, E. H. (1954). A study in language and cognition. *Journal of Abnormal and Social Psychology, 49,* 454–462.

Brown, R., & McNeill, D. (1966). The "tip of the tongue" phenomenon. *Journal of Verbal Learning and Verbal Behavior, 5,* 325–337.

Bruce, D., & Winograd, E. (1998). Remembering Deese's 1959 articles: The Zeitgeist, the sociology of sciences, and false memories. *Psychonomic Bulletin & Review, 5,* 615–624.

Bruck, M., & Ceci, S. J. (1999). The suggestibility of children's memory. *Annual Review of Psychology, 50,* 419–440.

Bruner, J. S. (1973). *Beyond the information given.* New York: Norton.

Buchanan, T. (2007). Retrieval of emotional memories. *Psychological Bulletin, 133,* 761–779.

Buchanan, T. W., & Adolphs, R. (2004). The neuroanatomy of emotional memory in humans. In D. Reisberg & P. Hertel (Eds.), *Memory and emotion* (pp. 42–75). New York: Oxford University Press.

Bukach, C., Gauthier, I., & Tarr, M. J. (2006). Beyond faces and modularity: The power of an expertise framework. *Trends in Cognitive Sciences, 10,* 159–166.

Bundesen, C., Kyllingsbaek, S., & Larsen, A. (2003). Independent encoding of colors and shapes from two stimuli. *Psychonomic Bulletin & Review, 10,* 474–479.

Burke, A., Heuer, F., & Reisberg, D. (1992). Remembering emotional events. *Memory & Cognition, 20,* 277–290.

Burton, A. M., Young, A., Bruce, V., Johnston, R., & Ellis, A. (1991). Understanding covert recognition. *Cognition, 39,* 129–166.

Buschman, T. J., & Miller, E. K. (2007). Top-down and bottom-up control of attention in the prefrontal and posterior parietal cortices. *Science, 315,* 1860.

Busey, T. A., Tunnicliff, J., Loftus, G. R., & Loftus, E. F. (2000). Accounts of the confidence-accuracy relation in recognition memory. *Memory & Cognition, 7,* 26–48.

Buzsáki, G., & Draguhn, A. (2004). Neuronal oscillations in cortical networks. *Science, 304,* 1926–1929.

Cabeza, R., & Nyberg, L. (2000). Imaging cognition II: An empirical review of 275 PET and fMRI studies. *Journal of Cognitive Neuroscience, 12,* 1–47.

Cabeza, R., & St. Jacques, P. (2007). Functional neuroimaging of autobiographical memory. *Trends in Cognitive Sciences, 11,* 219–227.

Cann, A., & Ross, D. (1989). Olfactory stimuli as context cues in human memory. *American Journal of Psychology, 2,* 91–102.

Cann, D. R., & Katz, A. N. (2005). Habitual acceptance of misinformation: Examination of individual differences and source attributions. *Memory & Cognition, 33*, 405–417.

Cantor, J., & Engle, R. (1993). Working-memory capacity as long-term memory activation: An individual-differences approach. *Journal of Experimental Psychology: Learning, Memory and Cognition, 19*, 1101–1114.

Capgras, J., & Reboul-Lachaux, J. (1923). L'illusion des "sosies" dans un delire systematise chronique. *Bulletine de Societe Clinique de Medicine Mentale, 11*, 6–16.

Caramazza, A., & Shelton, J. (1998). Domain-specific knowledge systems in the brain: The animate-inanimate distinction. *Journal of Cognitive Neuroscience, 10*, 1–34.

Carmichael, L. C., Hogan, H. P., & Walters, A. A. (1932). An experimental study of the effect of language on the reproduction of visually perceived form. *Journal of Experimental Psychology, 15*, 73–86.

Carpenter, P., & Eisenberg, P. (1978). Mental rotation and the frame of reference in blind and sighted individuals. *Perception & Psychophysics, 23*, 117–124.

Carpenter, P., Just, M., & Shell, P. (1990). What one intelligence test measures: A theoretical account of the processing in the Raven Progressive Matrices Test. *Psychological Review, 97*, 404–431.

Carpenter, S., Pashler, H., Wixted, J., & Vul, E. (2008). The effects of tests on learning and forgetting. *Memory & Cognition, 36*, 438–448.

Carrasco, M., Ling, S., & Read, S. (2004). Attention alters appearance. *Nature Neuroscience, 7*, 308–313.

Carrasco, M., Penpeci-Talgar, C., & Eckstein, M. (2000). Spatial covert attention increases contrast sensitivity across the CSF: Support for signal enhancement. *Vision Research, 40*, 1203–1215.

Catrambone, R. (1998). The subgoal learning model: Creating better examples so that students can solve novel problems. *Journal of Experimental Psychology: General, 127*, 355–376.

Catrambone, R., Craig, D., & Nersessian, N. (2006). The role of perceptually represented structure in analogical problem solving. *Memory & Cognition, 34*, 1126–1132.

Cattell, J. M. (1885). Über die Zeit der Erkennung and Benennung von Schriftzeichen, Bildern and Farben. *Philosophische Studien, 2*, 635–650.

Cave, K. R., & Bichot, N. P. (1999). Visuospatial attention: Beyond a spotlight model. *Psychonomic Bulletin and Review, 6*, 204–223.

Ceci, S., & Bruck, M. (1995). *Jeopardy in the courtroom: A scientific analysis of children's testimony.* Washington, DC: American Psychological Association.

Chalmers, D. (1996). *The conscious mind.* New York: Oxford University Press.

Chalmers, D. (1998). What is a neural correlate of consciousness? In T. Metzinger (Ed.), *Neural correlates of consciousness: Empirical and conceptual issues* (pp. 17–39). Cambridge, MA: MIT Press.

Chambers, D., & Reisberg, D. (1985). Can mental images be ambiguous? *Journal of Experimental Psychology: Human Perception and Performance, 11*, 317–328.

Chambers, K. L., & Zaragoza, M. S. (2001). Intended and unintended effects of explicit warnings on eyewitness suggestibility: Evidence from source identification tests. *Memory & Cognition, 29*, 1120–1129.

Chan, J., Thomas, A., & Bulevich, J. (2009). Recalling a witnessed event increases eyewitness suggestibility: The reversed testing effect. *Psychological Science, 20*, 66–73.

Chandler, C. (1994). Studying related pictures can reduce accuracy, but increase confidence, in a modified recognition test. *Memory & Cognition, 22*, 273–280.

Chandler, C., Greening, L., Robinson, L. J., & Stoppelbein, L. (1999). It can't happen to me . . . or can it? Conditional base rates affect subjective probability judgments. *Journal of Experimental Psychology: Applied, 5*, 361–378.

Chao, L., Weisberg, J., & Martin, A. (2002). Experience-dependent modulation of category related cortical activity. *Cerebral Cortex, 12*, 545–551.

Chapman, J., & Chapman, L. J. (1959). Atmosphere effect re-examined. *Journal of Experimental Psychology, 58*, 220–226.

Chapman, L. J., & Chapman, J. (1971). Test results are what you think they are. *Psychology Today, 5*, 106–110.

Charniak, E. (1972). *Toward a model of children's story comprehension.* Unpublished doctoral dissertation, Massachusetts Institute of Technology, Cambridge, MA.

Chase, W., & Ericsson, K. A. (1982). Skill and working memory. In G. H. Bower (Ed.), *The psychology of learning and motivation* (pp. 1–58). New York: Academic Press.

Chase, W., & Simon, H. (1973). Perception in chess. *Cognitive Psychology, 4*, 55–81.

Chen, J.-Y. (2007). Do Chinese and English speakers think about time differently? Failure of replicating Boroditsky (2001). *Cognition, 104*, 427–436.

Chen, Z., & Cave, K. R. (2006). Reinstating object-based attention under positional certainty: The importance of subjective parsing. *Perception and Psychophysics, 68*, 992–1003.

Cheng, P., & Holyoak, K. J. (1985). Pragmatic reasoning schemas. *Cognitive Psychology, 17*, 391–416.

Cheng, P., Holyoak, K. J., Nisbett, R. E., & Oliver, L. M. (1986). Pragmatic versus syntactic approaches to training deductive reasoning. *Cognitive Psychology, 18*, 293–328.

Cherry, E. C. (1953). Some experiments on the recognition of speech with one and with two ears. *Journal of the Acoustical Society of America, 25*, 975–979.

Chi, M. (1976). Short-term memory limitations in children: Capacity or processing deficits? *Memory & Cognition, 4*, 559–572.

Chi, M., Feltovich, P., & Glaser, R. (1981). Categorization and representation of physics problems by experts and novices. *Cognitive Science, 5,* 121–152.

Chomsky, N. (1957). *Syntactic structures.* The Hague, Netherlands: Mouton.

Chomsky, N. (1965). *Aspects of a theory of syntax.* Cambridge, MA: MIT Press.

Chomsky, N. (1975). *Reflections on language.* London: Temple-Smith.

Chomsky, N. (1986). *Knowledge of language: Its nature, origin and use.* New York: Praeger.

Chomsky, N., & Halle, M. (1968). *The sound pattern of English.* New York: Harper & Row.

Christen, F., & Bjork, R. A. (1976). *On updating the loci in the method of loci.* Paper presented at the meeting of the Psychonomic Society, St. Louis, MO.

Christiaansen, R., Sweeney, J., & Ochalek, K. (1983). Influencing eyewitness descriptions. *Law and Human Behavior, 7,* 59–65.

Christiansen, M. H., Chater, N., & Seidenberg, M. S. (Eds.). (1999). Connectionist models of human language processing: Progress and prospects [Special issue]. *Cognitive Science, 23*(4).

Christianson, S.-Å. (1989). Flashbulb memories: Special, but not so special. *Memory & Cognition, 17,* 435–443.

Christianson, S.-Å. (1992). Emotional stress and eyewitness memory: A critical review. *Psychological Bulletin, 112,* 284–309.

Chroback, Q. M., & Zaragoza, M. S. (2008). Inventing stories: Forcing witnesses to fabricate entire fictitious events leads to freely reported false memories. *Psychonomics Bulletin and Review, 15,* 1190–1195.

Chronicle, E. P., MacGregor, J. N., & Ormerod, T. C. (2004). What makes an insight problem? The roles of heuristics, goal conception, and solution recoding in knowledge-lean problems. *Journal of Experimental Psychology: Learning, Memory, & Cognition, 30,* 14–27.

Chun, W. Y., & Kruglanski, A. W. (2006). The role of task demands and processing resources in the use of base-rate and individuating information. *Journal of Personality and Social Psychology, 91,* 205–217.

Churchland, P., & Sejnowski, T. J. (1992). *The computational brain.* Cambridge, MA: MIT Press.

Clancy, S. A., Schacter, D. L., McNally, R. J., & Pitmann, R. K. (2000). False recognition in women reporting recovered memories of sexual abuse. *Psychological Science, 11,* 26–31.

Claparède, E. (1951). Reconnaissance et moiité. In D. Rapaport (Ed.), *Organization and pathology of thought* (pp. 58–75). New York: Columbia University Press. (Original work published in 1911.)

Clement, J. (1982, August). *Analogical reasoning patterns in expert problem solving.* Paper presented at the 4th Annual Conference of the Cognitive Science Society, Ann Arbor, MI.

Coates, S. L., Butler, L. T., & Berry, D. C. (2006). Implicit memory and consumer choice: The mediating role of brand familiarity. *Applied Cognitive Psychology 20*(8), 1101–1116.

Cohen, N. J., & Squire, L. R. (1980). Preserved learning and retention of pattern analyzing skill in amnesics: Dissociation of knowing how and knowing that. *Science, 210,* 207–210.

Coley, J. D., Medin, D. L., & Atran, S. (1997). Does rank have its privilege? Inductive inferences within folkbiological taxonomies. *Cognition, 64,* 73–112.

Collins, A. M., & Loftus, E. F. (1975). A spreading activation theory of semantic processing. *Psychological Review, 82,* 407–428.

Collins, A. M., & Quillian, M. R. (1969). Retrieval time from semantic memory. *Journal of Verbal Learning and Verbal Behavior, 8,* 240–247.

Combs, B., & Slovic, P. (1979). Causes of death: Biased newspaper coverage and biased judgments. *Journalism Quarterly, 56,* 837–843, 849.

Comrie, B. (1981). *Language universals and linguistic typology.* Chicago: University of Chicago Press.

Connolly, T., & Zeelenberg, M. (2002). Regret in decision making. *Current Directions in Psychological Science, 11,* 212–216.

Connors, E., Lundregan, T., Miller, N., & McEwan, T. (1996). *Convicted by juries, exonerated by science: Case studies in the use of DNA evidence to establish innocence after trial.* Alexandria, VA: National Institute of Justice.

Conrad, C. (1972). Cognitive economy in semantic memory. *Journal of Experimental Psychology, 92,* 149–154.

Conway, A. R. A., Cowan, N., & Bunting, M. (2001). The cocktail party phenomenon revisited: The importance of working memory capacity. *Psychonomic Bulletin & Review, 8,* 331–335.

Conway, A. R. A., Kane, M. J., & Engle, R. W. (2003). Working memory capacity and its relation to general intelligence. *Trends in Cognitive Sciences, 7,* 547–552.

Conway, M., Anderson, S., Larsen, S., Donnelly, C., McDaniel, M., McClelland, A. G. R., et al. (1994). The formation of flashbulb memories. *Memory & Cognition, 22,* 326–343.

Conway, M., Cohen, G., & Stanhope, N. (1991). On the very long-term retention of knowledge acquired through formal education: Twelve years of cognitive psychology. *Journal of Experimental Psychology: General, 120,* 395–409.

Conway, M., Cohen, G., & Stanhope, N. (1992). Why is it that university grades do not predict very long term retention? *Journal of Experimental Psychology: General, 121,* 382–384.

Conway, M., Collins, A. F., Gathercole, S., & Anderson, S. J. (1996). Recollections of true and false autobiographical memories. *Journal of Experimental Psychology: General, 125,* 69–98.

Conway, M., & Fthenaki, K. (1999). Disruption and loss of autobiographical memory. In L. S. Cermak (Ed.), *Handbook of neuropsychology: Memory*. Amsterdam: Elsevier.

Conway, M., & Holmes, A. (2004). Psychosocial stages and the accessibility of autobiographical memories across the life cycle. *Journal of Personality*, 72, 461–480.

Conway, M., & Pleydell-Pearce, C. W. (2000). The construction of autobiographical memories in the self-memory system. *Psychological Review*, 107, 261–288.

Conway, M., & Ross, M. (1984). Getting what you want by revising what you had. *Journal of Personality and Social Psychology*, 39, 406–415.

Cook, V. J. (1988). *Chomsky's universal grammar: An introduction*. Cambridge, MA: Basil Blackwell.

Cooney, J. W., & Gazzaniga, M. S. (2003). Neurological disorders and the structure of human consciousness. *Trends in Cognitive Sciences*, 7, 161–165.

Cooper, L. (1990). Mental representation of three-dimensional objects in visual problem solving and recognition. *Journal of Experimental Psychology: Learning, Memory and Cognition*, 16, 1097–1106.

Cooper, L., & Shepard, R. N. (1973). Chronometric studies of the rotation of mental images. In W. G. Chase (Ed.), *Visual information processing* (pp. 75–176). New York: Academic Press.

Coricelli, G., Dolan, R., & Sirigu, A. (2007). Brain, emotion and decision making: The paradigmatic example of regret. *Trends in Cognitive Sciences*, 11, 258–265.

Corter, J., & Gluck, M. (1992). Explaining basic categories: Feature predictability and information. *Psychological Bulletin*, 111, 291–303.

Cosmides, L. (1989). The logic of social exchange: Has natural selection shaped how humans reason? Studies with the Wason selection task. *Cognition*, 31, 187–276.

Cosmides, L., & Tooby, J. (1996). Are humans good intuitive statisticians after all? Rethinking some conclusions from the literature on judgment. *Cognition*, 58, 1–73.

Courtney, S. M., Petit, L., Maisog, J. M., Ungerleider, L. G., & Haxby, J. V. (1998). An area specialized for spatial working memory in human frontal cortex. *Science*, 279, 1347–1351.

Craik, F. I. M., & Lockhart, R. S. (1972). Levels of processing: A framework for memory research. *Journal of Verbal Learning and Verbal Behavior*, 11, 671–684.

Craik, F. I. M., & Tulving, E. (1975). Depth of processing and the retention of words in episodic memory. *Journal of Experimental Psychology: General*, 104, 269–294.

Craik, F. I. M., & Watkins, M. J. (1973). The role of rehearsal in short-term memory. *Journal of Verbal Learning and Verbal Behavior*, 12, 599–607.

Crick, F., & Koch, C. (1995). Are we aware of neural activity in primary visual cortex? *Nature*, 375, 121–123.

Crick, F., & Koch, C. (2003). A framework for consciousness. *Nature Neuroscience*, 6, 119–126.

Crombag, H. F. M., Wagenaar, W. A., & van Koppen, P. J. (1996). Crashing memories and the problem of "source monitoring." *Applied Cognitive Psychology*, 10, 95–104.

Crystal, D. (1987). *The Cambridge encyclopedia of language*. Cambridge: Cambridge University Press.

Csibra, G., Davis, G., Spratling, M. W., & Johnson, M. H. (2000). Gamma oscillations and object processing in the infant brain. *Science*, 290, 1582–1585.

Cui, X., Jeter, C., Yang, D., Montague, P. R., & Eagleman, D. M. (2006). Vividness of mental imagery: Individual variability can be measured objectively. *Vision Research*, 47, 474–478.

Cummins, D. (1992). Role of analogical reasoning in induction of problem categories. *Journal of Experimental Psychology: Learning, Memory and Cognition*, 18, 1103–1124.

Cummins, D. D. (2004). The evolution of reasoning. In J. P. Leighton & R. J. Sternberg (Eds.), *The nature of reasoning* (pp. 339–374). New York: Cambridge University Press.

Cummins, D., & Allen, C. (Eds.). (1998). *The evolution of mind*. New York: Oxford University Press.

Cutler, B. L., Penrod, S. D., & Dexter, H. R. (1990). Juror sensitivity to eyewitness identification evidence. *Law and Human Behavior*, 14, 185–191.

Dalai Lama. (2005). *The universe in a single atom: The convergence of science and spirituality*. New York: Broadway Books.

Damasio, A., Damasio, H., & Van Hoesen, G. W. (1982). Prosopagnosia: Anatomic basis and behavioral mechanisms. *Neurology*, 32, 331–341.

Damasio, A. R. (1994). *Descartes' error: Emotion, reason, and the human brain*. New York: Putnam.

Damasio, A. R. (1999). *The feeling of what happens: Body and emotion in the making of consciousness* (1st ed.). New York: Harcourt Brace.

Damasio, A. R., Tranel, D., & Damasio, H. (1989). Disorders of visual recognition. In H. Goodglass & A. R. Damasio (Eds.), *Handbook of neuropsychology*, Vol. 2 (pp. 317–332). New York: Elsevier.

Damasio, A. R., Tranel, D., & Damasio, H. (1990). Face agnosia and the neural substrates of memory. *Annual Review of Neuroscience*, 13, 89–109.

Daneman, M., & Carpenter, P. (1980). Individual differences in working memory and reading. *Journal of Verbal Learning and Verbal Behavior*, 19, 450–466.

Daneman, M., & Hannon, B. (2001). Using working memory theory to investigate the construct validity of multiple-choice reading comprehension tests such as the SAT. *Journal of Experimental Psychology: General, 130,* 208–223.

Daniloff, R., & Hammarberg, R. (1973). On defining coarticulation. *Journal of Phonetics, 1,* 185–194.

Davachi, L., & Dobbins, I. (2008). Declarative memory. *Current Directions in Psychological Science, 17,* 112–118.

Davachi, L., Mitchell, J., & Wagner, A. (2003). Multiple routes to memory: Distinct medial temporal lobe processes build item and source memories. *Proceedings of the National Academy of Science, 100,* 2157–2162.

Dawes, R. M. (1988). *Rational choice in an uncertain world.* San Diego, CA: Harcourt Brace Jovanovich.

Deese, J. (1957). Serial organization in the recall of disconnected items. *Psychological Reports, 3,* 577–582.

Deese, J., & Kaufman, R. A. (1957). Serial effects in recall of unorganized and sequentially organized verbal material. *Journal of Experimental Psychology, 54,* 180–187.

De Groot, A. (1965). *Thought and choice in chess.* The Hague, Netherlands: Mouton.

De Groot, A. (1966). Perception and memory versus thought: Some old ideas and recent findings. In B. Kleinmuntz (Ed.), *Problem solving* (pp. 19–50). New York: Wiley.

Dehaene, S., Artiges, E., Naccache, L., Martelli, C., Viard, A., Schurhoff, F., et al. (2003). Conscious and subliminal conflicts in normal subjects and patients with schizophrenia: The role of the anterior cingulate. *Proceedings of the National Academy of Sciences, USA, 100,* 13722–13727.

Dehaene, S., & Changeux, J.-P. (2004). Neural mechanisms for access consciousness. In M. Gazzaniga (Ed.), *The cognitive neurosciences III.* Cambridge, MA: MIT Press.

Dehaene, S., & Naccache, L. (2001). Toward a cognitive neuroscience of consciousness: Basic evidence and a workspace framework. *Cognition, 79,* 1–37.

Dehaene, S., Sergent, C., & Changeux, J. (2003). A neuronal network model linking subjective reports and objective physiological data during conscious perception. *Proceedings of the National Academy of Science, USA, 100,* 8520–8525.

Dell, G. S., Burger, L. K., & Svec, W. R. (1997). Language production and serial order: A function analysis and a model. *Psychological Review, 104,* 123–147.

de Martino, B., et al. (2006). Frames, biases and rational decision-making in the human brain. *Science, 313,* 684–687.

Demonet, J. F., Wise, R. A., & Frackowiak, R. S. J. (1993). Language functions explored in normal subjects by positron emission tomography: A critical review. *Human Brain Mapping, 1,* 39–47.

Dempster, F. N. (1981). Memory span: Sources of individual and developmental differences. *Psychological Bulletin, 89,* 63–100.

De Neys, W. (2006). Dual processing in reasoning: Two systems but one reasoner. *Psychological Science, 17,* 428–433.

De Neys, W., Vartanian, O., & Goel, V. (2008). Smarter than we think: When our brains detect that we are biased. *Psychological Science, 19,* 483–489.

Dennett, D. (1992). *Consciousness explained.* Boston: Little, Brown.

Dennett, D. (2001). Are we explaining consciousness yet? *Cognition, 79,* 221–237.

De Renzi, E., Faglioni, P., Grossi, D., & Nichelli, P. (1991). Apperceptive and associative forms of prosopagnosia. *Cortex, 27,* 213–221.

Diamond, R., & Carey, S. (1986). Why faces are and are not special: An effect of expertise. *Journal of Experimental Psychology: General, 115,* 107–117.

Diana, R., Yonelinas, A., & Ranganath, C. (2007). Imaging recollection and familiarity in the medial temporal lobe: A three-component model. *Trends in Cognitive Sciences, 11,* 379–386.

Diana, R. A., Reder, L. M., Arndt, J., & Park, H. (2006). Models of recognition: A review of arguments in favor of a dual-process account. *Psychonomics Bulletin & Review, 13,* 1–21.

Dinges, D., Whitehouse, W., Orne, E., Powell, J., Orne, M., & Erdelyi, M. (1992). Evaluation of hypnotic memory enhancement (hypermnesia and reminiscence) using multitrial forced recall. *Journal of Experimental Psychology: Learning, Memory and Cognition, 18,* 1139–1147.

Do, A., Rupert, A., & Wolford, G. (2008). Evaluations of pleasurable experiences: The peak-end rule. *Psychonomic Bulletin & Review, 15,* 96–98.

Dobbins, I. G., Foley, H., Wagner, A. D., & Schacter, D. L. (2002). Executive control during episodic retrieval: Multiple prefrontal processes subserve source memory. *Neuron, 35,* 989–996.

Dobbins, I. G., Kroll, N. E., & Yonelinas, A. (2004). Dissociating familiarity from recollection using rote rehearsal. *Memory & Cognition, 32,* 932–944.

Dodds, R., Ward, T., & Smith, S. (2007). A review of the experimental literature on incubation in problem solving and creativity. In M. Runco (Ed.), *Creative research handbook,* 3rd ed. Cresskill, NJ: Hampton.

Donnelly, C., & McDaniel, M. A. (1993). Use of analogy in learning scientific concepts. *Journal of Experimental Psychology: Learning, Memory and Cognition, 19,* 975–986.

Donnelly, C. M., & McDaniel, M. A. (2000). Analogy with knowledgeable learners: When analogy confers benefits and exacts costs. *Psychonomic Bulletin & Review, 7,* 537–543.

Douglass, A. B., & Steblay, N. (2006). Memory distortion in eyewitnesses: A meta-analysis of the post-identification feedback effect. *Applied Cognitive Psychology, 20,* 859–870.

Downs, J., & Shafir, E. (1999). Why some are perceived as more confident and more insecure, more reckless and more cautious, more trusting and more suspicious, than others: Enriched and impoverished options in social judgment. *Psychonomic Bulletin & Review, 6*, 598–610.

Dudai, Y. (2004). The neurobiology of consolidations, or, how stable is the engram. *Annual Review of Psychology, 55*, 51–86.

Dumit, J. (2004). *Picturing personhood: Brain scans and biomedical identity.* Princeton, NJ: Princeton University Press.

Duncan, J. (1995). Attention, intelligence, and the frontal lobes. In M. S. Gazzaniga (Ed.), *The cognitive neurosciences* (pp. 721–733). Cambridge, MA: MIT Press.

Duncan, J., Burgess, P., & Emslie, H. (1995). Fluid intelligence after frontal lobe lesions. *Neuropsychologia, 33*, 261–268.

Duncan, J., Emslie, H., Williams, P., Johnson, R., & Freer, C. (1996). Intelligence and the frontal lobe: The organization of goal-directed behavior. *Cognitive Psychology, 30*, 257–303.

Duncan, J., Parr, A., Woolgar, A., Thompson, R., Bright, P., Cox, S., Bishop, S. & Nimmo-Smith, I. (2008) Goal neglect and Spearman's g: Competing parts of a complex task. *Journal of Experimental Psychology: General, 137*, 131–148.

Duncker, K. (1945). *On problem-solving* (Psychological Monographs: General and Applied, Vol. 58, No. 5 [whole no. 270]). Washington, DC: American Psychological Association.

Dunning, D., & Parpal, M. (1989). Mental addition versus subtraction in counterfactual reasoning. *Journal of Personality and Social Psychology, 57*, 5–15.

Dunning, D., & Perretta, S. (2002). Automaticity and eyewitness accuracy: A 10- to 12-second rule for distinguishing accurate from inaccurate positive identifications.

Journal of Applied Psychology, 87, 951–962.

Durgin, F. H. (2000). The reverse Stroop effect. *Psychonomic Bulletin & Review, 7*, 121–125.

Easterbrook, J. A. (1959). The effect of emotion on cue utilization and the organization of behavior. *Psychological Review, 66*, 183–201.

Eberhard, K. M., Spivey-Knowlton, M. J., Sedivy, J. C., & Tanenhaus, M. K. (1995). Eye movements as a window into real-time spoken language comprehension in natural contexts. *Journal of Psycholinguistic Research, 24*, 409–436.

Eddy, D. M. (1982). Probabilistic reasoning in clinical medicine: Problems and opportunities. In D. Kahneman, P. Slovic, & A. Tversky (Eds.), *Judgment under uncertainty: Heuristics and biases* (pp. 249–267). Cambridge, England: Cambridge University Press.

Edelstyn, N. M. J., & Oyebode, F. (1999). A review of the phenomenology and cognitive neuropsychological origins of the Capgras Syndrome. *International Journal of Geriatric Psychiatry, 14*, 48–59.

Egan, D., & Schwartz, B. (1979). Chunking in the recall of symbolic drawings. *Memory & Cognition, 7*, 149–158.

Egly, R., Driver, J., & Rafal, R. D. (1994). Shifting visual attention between objects and locations: Evidence from normal and parietal lesion subjects. *Journal of Experimental Psychology: General, 123*, 161–177.

Egner, T. (2008). Multiple conflict-driven control mechanisms in the human brain. *Trends in Cognitive Sciences, 12*, 374–380.

Eich, J. E. (1980). The cue-dependent nature of state dependent retrieval. *Memory & Cognition, 8*, 157–173.

Einhorn, H., & Hogarth, R. (1981). Behavioral decision theory: Processes of judgment and choice. *Annual Review of Psychology, 32*, 53–88.

Einstein, G. O., McDaniel, M. A., & Lackey, S. (1989). Bizarre imagery, interference, and distinctiveness. *Journal of Experimental Psychology: Learning, Memory, and Cognition, 15*, 137–146.

Elliott, M. A., & Müller, H. J. (2000). Evidence for 40-Hz oscillatory short-term visual memory revealed by human reaction-time measurements. *Journal of Experimental Psychology: Learning, Memory and Cognition, 26*, 7093–7718.

Ellis, H. D., & De Pauw, K. W. (1994). The cognitive neuropsychiatric origins of the Capgras delusion. In A. S. David & J. C. Cutting (Eds.), *The neuropsychology of schizophrenia* (pp. 317–335). Hillsdale, NJ: Erlbaum.

Ellis, H. D., & Lewis, M. B. (2001). Capgras delusion: A window on face recognition. *Trends in Cognitive Sciences, 5*, 149–156.

Ellis, H. D., & Young, A. (1990). Accounting for delusional misidentifications. *British Journal of Psychiatry, 157*, 239–248.

Elstein, A., Holzman, G., Ravitch, M., Metheny, W., Holmes, M., Hoppe, R., et al. (1986). Comparison of physicians' decisions regarding estrogen replacement therapy for menopausal women and decisions derived from a decision analytic model. *American Journal of Medicine, 80*, 246–258.

Engel, A. K., & Singer, W. (2001). Temporal binding and the neural correlates of sensory awareness. *Trends in Cognitive Sciences, 5*, 16–25.

Engelkamp, J. (1986). Motor programs as part of the meaning of verbal items. In I. Kurcz, E. Shugar, & J. H. Danks (Eds.), *Knowledge and language* (pp. 115–137). Amsterdam: North-Holland.

Engelkamp, J. (1991). Imagery and enactment in paired-associate learning. In R. H. Logie & M. Denis (Eds.), *Mental images in human cognition* (pp. 119–128). Amsterdam: Elsevier.

Engle, R. W., & Kane, M. J. (2004). Executive attention, working memory capacity, and a two-factor theory of cognitive control. In B. Ross (Ed.), *The psychology of learning and motivation 44* (pp. 145–199). New York: Elsevier.

Epley, N., & Gilovich, T. (2001). Putting adjustment back in the anchoring and adjustment heuristic: Differential processing of self-generated and experimenter-provided anchors. *Psychological Science, 12,* 391–396.

Epley, N., & Gilovich, T. (2006). The anchoring-and-adjustment heuristic: Why the adjustments are insufficient. *Psychological Science, 17,* 311–318.

Ericsson, K., Krampe, R. T. & Tesch-Römer, C. (1993). The role of deliberate practice in the acquisition of expert performance. *Psychological Review, 10,* 363–406.

Ericsson, K. A. (2005). Recent advances in expertise research: A commentary on the contributions to the special issue. *Applied Cognitive Psychology, 19,* 233–241.

Ericsson, K. A. (2003). Exceptional memorizers: Made, not born. *Trends in Cognitive Sciences, 7,* 233–235.

Ericsson, K. A., & Ward, P. (2007). Capturing the naturally occurring superior performance of experts in the laboratory: Toward a science of expert and exceptional performance. *Current Directions in Psychological Science, 16,* 346–350.

Ernest, C. (1977). Imagery ability and cognition: A critical review. *Journal of Mental Imagery, 2,* 181–216.

Ervin-Tripp, S. (1993). Conversational discourse. In J. B. Gleason & N. B. Ratner (Eds.), *Psycholinguistics* (pp. 237–270). New York: Harcourt Brace Jovanovich.

Estes, Z. (2003). Domain differences in the structure of artifactual and natural categories. *Memory & Cognition, 31,* 199–214.

Evans, J. S. B. T. (1982). *The psychology of deductive reasoning.* London: Routledge & Kegan Paul.

Evans, J. S. B. T. (1989). *Bias in human reasoning.* Hillsdale, NJ: Erlbaum.

Evans, J. S. B. T. (1993). The mental model theory of conditional reasoning: Critical appraisal and revision. *Cognition, 48,* 1–20.

Evans, J. S. B. T. (2003). In two minds: Dual-process accounts of reasoning. *Trends in Cognitive Sciences, 7,* 454–459.

Evans, J. S. B. T., & Feeney, A. (2004). The role of prior belief in reasoning. In J. P. Leighton & R. J. Sternberg (Eds.), *The nature of reasoning* (pp. 78–102). New York: Cambridge University Press.

Evans, J. S. B. T., Handley, S. J., Perham, N., Over, D. E., & Thompson, V. A. (2000). Frequency versus probability formats in statistical word problems. *Cognition, 77,* 197–213.

Evans, J. S. B. T., Newstead, S. E., & Byrne, R. M. J. (1993). *Human reasoning: The psychology of deduction.* London: Erlbaum.

Evans, J. S. B. T., Over, D., & Manktelow, K. (1993). Reasoning, decision making and rationality. *Cognition, 49,* 165–187.

Evans, Jonathan St. B.T. (2006). The heuristic-analytic theory of reasoning: Extension and evaluation. *Psychonomics Bulletin & Review, 13,* 378–395.

Evans, J. St. B. T. (2008). Dual-processing accounts of reasoning, judgment, and social cognition. *Annual Review of Psychology, 59,* 255–278.

Evans, J. St. B. T., Handley, S., Neilens, H., & Over, D. (2007). Thinking about conditions: A study of individual differences. *Memory & Cognition, 35,* 1772–1784.

Eylon, B., & Reif, F. (1984). Effects of knowledge organization on task performance. *Cognition and Instruction, 1,* 5–44.

Eysenck, M. W. (1982). *Attention and arousal: Cognition and performance.* Berlin: Springer.

Farah, M. J. (1985). Psychophysical evidence for a shared representational medium for mental images and percepts. *Journal of Experimental Psychology: General, 114,* 91–103.

Farah, M. J. (1988). Is visual imagery really visual? Overlooked evidence from neuropsychology. *Psychological Review, 95,* 307–317.

Farah, M. J. (1989). Mechanisms of imagery-perception interaction. *Journal of Experimental Psychology: Human Perception and Performance, 15,* 203–211.

Farah, M. J. (1990). *Visual agnosia: Disorders of object recognition and what they tell us about normal vision.* Cambridge, MA: MIT Press.

Farah, M. J., Hammond, K. M., Levine, D. N., & Calvanio, R. (1988). Visual and spatial mental imagery: Dissociable systems of representation. *Cognitive Psychology, 20,* 439–462.

Farah, M. J., & Smith, A. (1983). Perceptual interference and facilitation with auditory imagery. *Perception & Psychophysics, 33,* 475–478.

Farah, M. J., Soso, M., & Dasheiff, R. (1992). Visual angle of the mind's eye before and after unilateral occipital lobectomy. *Journal of Experimental Psychology: Human Perception and Performance, 18,* 241–246.

Farah, M. J., Wilson, K. D., Drain, M., & Tanaka, J. (1998). What is "special" about face perception? *Psychological Review, 105,* 482–498.

Feldman, H., Goldin-Meadow, S., & Gleitman, L. R. (1978). Beyond Herodotus: The creation of language by linguistically deprived deaf children. In A. Lock (Ed.), *Action, gesture, and symbol: The emergence of language* (pp. 351–414). London: Academic Press.

Feldman Barrett, L., Tugade, M. M., & Engle, R. W. (2004). Individual differences in working memory capacity and dual-process theories of the mind. *Psychological Bulletin, 130,* 553–573.

Fenske, M. J., Raymond, J. E., Kessler, K., Westoby, N., & Tipper, S. P. (2005). Attentional inhibition has social-emotional consequences for unfamiliar faces. *Psychological Science, 16*, 753–758.

Ferreira, M. B., Garcia-Marques, L., Sherman, S. J., & Sherman, J. W. (2006). Automatic and controlled components of judgment and decision. *Journal of Personality & Social Psychology, 91*, 797–813.

Fiedler, K., Brinkmann, B., Betsch, T., & Wild, B. (2000). A sampling approach to biases in conditional probability judgments: Beyond base rate neglect and statistical format. *Journal of Experimental Psychology: General, 129*, 399–418.

Fiedler, K., Walther, E., Armbruster, T., Fay, D., & Naumann, U. (1996). Do you really know what you have seen? Intrusion errors and presuppositions effects on constructive memory. *Journal of Experimental Social Psychology, 2*, 484–511.

Finke, R. (1990). *Creative imagery: Discoveries and inventions in visualization.* Hillsdale, NJ: Erlbaum.

Finke, R. (1993). Mental imagery and creative discovery. In B. Roskos-Ewoldsen, M. J. Intons-Peterson, & R. Anderson (Eds.), *Imagery, creativity, and discovery* (pp. 255–285). New York: North-Holland.

Finke, R., & Kosslyn, S. M. (1980). Mental imagery acuity in the peripheral visual field. *Journal of Experimental Psychology: Human Perception and Performance, 6*, 126–139.

Finke, R. A., & Pinker, S. (1982). Spontaneous imagery scanning in mental extrapolation. *Journal of Experimental Psychology: Learning, Memory, & Cognition, 8*, 142–147.

Finke, R., & Slayton, K. (1988). Explorations of creative visual synthesis in mental imagery. *Memory & Cognition, 16*, 252–257.

Finucane, M. L., Alhakami, A., Slovic, P., & Johnson, S. M. (2000). The affect heuristic in judgments of risks and benefits. *Journal of Behavioral Decision Making, 13*, 1–17.

Fischhoff, B., Slovic, P., & Lichtenstein, S. (1978). Fault trees: Sensitivity of estimated failure probabilities to problem representation. *Journal of Experimental Psychology: Human Perception & Performance, 4*, 330–344.

Fisher, R., & Craik, F. I. M. (1977). The interaction between encoding and retrieval operations in cued recall. *Journal of Experimental Psychology: Human Learning and Memory, 3*, 701–711.

Fisher, R., Geiselman, R., & Amador, M. (1989). Field tests of the cognitive interview: Enhancing the recollection of actual victims and witnesses of crime. *Journal of Applied Psychology, 74*, 722–727.

Fisher, R., & Schreiber, N. (2007). Interview protocols to improve eyewitness memory. In M. P. Toglia et al. (Eds.), *Handbook of eyewitness psychology.* Mahwah, NJ: Erlbaum.

Fodor, J. (1997). Connectionism and the problem of systematicity (continued): Why Smolensky's solution still doesn't work. *Cognition, 62*, 109–119.

Fodor, J., & Pylyshyn, Z. W. (1988). Connectionism and cognitive architecture: A critical analysis. *Cognition, 28*, 3–71.

Fong, G., Krantz, D., & Nisbett, R. (1986). The effects of statistical training on thinking about everyday problems. *Cognitive Psychology, 18*, 253–292.

Fong, G., & Nisbett, R. (1991). Immediate and delayed transfer of training effects in statistical reasoning. *Journal of Experimental Psychology: General, 120*, 34–45.

Ford, M. (1995). Two modes of mental representation and problem solution in syllogistic reasoning. *Cognition, 54*, 1–71.

Forgas, J., & East, R. (2003). Affective influences on social judgments and decisions: Implicit and explicit processes. In J. P. Forgas and K. D. Williams (Eds.), *Social judgments: Implicit and explicit processes* (pp. 198–226). New York: Cambridge University Press.

French, R. M. (1999). Catastrophic forgetting in connectionist networks. *Trends in Cognitive Science, 3*, 128–135.

French, R. M. (2002). The computational modeling of analogy-making. *Trends in Cognitive Sciences, 6*, 200–205.

Freyd, J. J. (1996). *Betrayal trauma: The logic of forgetting childhood abuse.* Cambridge, MA: Harvard University Press.

Freyd, J. J. (1998). Science in the memory debate. *Ethics & Behavior, 8*, 101–113.

Fried, L. S., & Holyoak, K. J. (1984). Induction of category distributions: A framework for classification learning. *Journal of Experimental Psychology: Learning, Memory and Cognition, 10*, 234–257.

Friedman, A. (1979). Framing pictures: The role of knowledge in automatized encoding and memory for gist. *Journal of Experimental Psychology: General, 108*, 316–355.

Friedman, A., & Brown, N. R. (2000a). Reasoning about geography. *Journal of Experimental Psychology: General, 129*, 193–219.

Friedman, A., & Brown, N. R. (2000b). Updating geographical knowledge: Principles of coherence and inertia. *Journal of Experimental Psychology: Learning, Memory and Cognition, 26*, 900–914.

Fries, P., Reynolds, J. H., Rorie, A. E., & Desimone, R. (2001). Modulation of oscillatory neural synchronization by selective visual attention. *Science, 291*, 1560–1563.

Fromkin, V. (1993). Speech production. In J. B. Gleason & N. B. Ratner (Eds.), *Psycholinguistics* (pp. 271–300). New York: Harcourt Brace Jovanovich.

Fromkin, V., & Bernstein Ratner, N. (1998). Speech production. In J. Berko-Gleason & N. Bernstein Ratner (Eds.), *Psycholinguistics* (pp. 309–346). Orlando, FL: Harcourt Brace.

Frost, P. (2000). The quality of false memory over time: Is memory for misinformation "remembered" or "known"? *Psychonomic Bulletin & Review, 7*, 531–536.

Gable, P. A., & Harmon-Jones, E. (2008). Approach-motivated positive affect reduces breadth of attention. *Psychological Science, 19*, 476–482.

Gabrieli, J., Fleischman, D., Keane, M., Reminger, S., & Morrell, F. (1995). Double dissociation between memory systems underlying explicit and implicit memory in the human brain. *Psychological Science, 6*, 76–82.

Gallistel, C. R. (2002). Language and spatial frames of reference in mind and brain. *Trends in Cognitive Sciences, 6*, 321–322.

Gallo, D. A., Roberts, M. J., & Seamon, J. G. (1997). Remembering words not presented in lists: Can we avoid creating false memories? *Psychonomic Bulletin & Review, 4*, 271–276.

Galton, F. (1883). *Inquiries into human faculty.* London: Dent.

Gardiner, J. M. (1988). Functional aspects of recollective experience. *Memory & Cognition, 16*, 309–313.

Garry, M., & Polaschek, D. L. L. (2000). Imagination and memory. *Current Directions in Psychological Science, 9*, 6–10.

Gathercole, S. E., & Pickering, S. J. (2000). Assessment of working memory in six- and seven-year-old children. *Journal of Educational Psychology, 92*, 377–390.

Gathercole, S. E., Service, E., Hitch, G., Adams, A.-M., & Martin, A. J. (1999). Phonological short-term memory and vocabulary development: Further evidence on the nature of the relationship. *Applied Cognitive Psychology, 13*, 65–77.

Gauthier, I. L., Skudlarski, P., Gore, J. C., & Anderson, A. W. (2000). Expertise for cars and birds recruits brain areas involved in face recognition. *Nature Neuroscience, 3*, 191–197.

Gazzaniga, M. S., Ivry, R. B., & Mangun, G. R. (2002). *Cognitive neuroscience: The biology of the mind* (2nd ed.). New York: Norton.

Gelman, S., & Wellman, H. (1991). Insides and essences: Early understandings of the non-obvious. *Cognition, 38*, 213–244.

Gentner, D. (1983). Structure mapping: A theoretical framework for analogy. *Cognitive Science, 7*, 155–170.

Gentner, D. (1989). The mechanisms of analogical learning. In S. Vosniadou & A. Ortony (Eds.), *Similarity, analogy, and thought* (pp. 199–241). Cambridge, England: Cambridge University Press.

Gentner, D., & Jeziorski, M. (1989). Historical shifts in the use of analogy in science. In B. Gholson, W. Shadish, R. Neimeyer, & A. Houts (Eds.), *Psychology of science: Contributions to metascience* (pp. 296–325). Cambridge, England: Cambridge University Press.

Geraerts, E., Bernstein, D., Merckelbach, H., Linders, C., Raymaekers, L., & Loftus, E. F. (2008). Lasting false beliefs and their behavioral consequences. *Psychological Science, 19*, 749–753.

Geraerts, E., Lindsay, D. S., Merckelbach, H., Jelicic, M., Raymaekers, L., Arnold, M. M., et al. (2009). Cognitive mechanisms underlying recovered-memory experiences of childhood sexual abuse. *Psychological Science, 20*, 92–99.

Geraerts, E., Schooler, J. W., Merckelbach, H., Jelicic, M., Hauer, B., & Ambadar, Z. (2007). The reality of recovered memories: Corroborating continuous and discontinuous memories of child sexual abuse. *Psychological Science, 18*, 564–568.

German, T., & Barrett, H. C. (2005). Functional fixedness in a technologically sparse culture. *Psychological Science, 16*, 1–5.

Ghetti, S., Edelstein, R. S., Goodman, G. S., Cordon, I. M., Quas, J. A., Alexander, K. W., et al. (2006). What can subjective forgetting tell us about memory for childhood trauma? *Memory & Cognition, 34*, 1011–1025.

Gibson, E., Bishop, C., Schiff, W., & Smith, J. (1964). Comparison of meaningfulness and pronounceability as grouping principles in the perception and retention of verbal material. *Journal of Experimental Psychology, 67*, 173–182.

Gick, M., & Holyoak, K. J. (1980). Analogical problem solving. *Cognitive Psychology, 12*, 306–355.

Giesbrecht, T., Lynn, S. J., Lilienfeld, S., & Merckelbach, H. (2008). Cognitive processes in dissociation: An analysis of core theoretical assumptions. *Psychological Bulletin, 134*, 617–647.

Gigerenzer, G. (1991). From tools to theories: A heuristic of discovery in cognitive psychology. *Psychological Review, 98*, 254–267.

Gigerenzer, G., Gaissmaier, W., Kurz-Milcke, E., Schwartz, L. M., & Woloshin, S. (2008). Helping doctors and patients make sense of health statistics. *Psychological Science in the Public Interest, 8*, 53–96.

Gigerenzer, G., Hell, W., & Blank, H. (1988). Presentation and content: The use of base rates as a continuous variable. *Journal of Experimental Psychology: Human Perception and Performance, 14*, 513–525.

Gigerenzer, G., & Hoffrage, U. (1995). How to improve Bayesian reasoning without instruction: Frequency formats. *Psychological Review, 102*, 684–704.

Gigerenzer, G., & Hug, K. (1992). Domain-specific reasoning: Social contracts, cheating and perspective change. *Cognition, 43*, 127–172.

Gilbert, D. (2006). *Stumbling on happiness.* New York: Random House.

Gilbert, D., & Ebert, J. E. J. (2002). Decisions and revisions: The affective forecasting of changeable outcomes. *Journal of Personality and Social Psychology, 82*, 503–514.

Gilbert, D., Morewedge, C. K., Risen, J. L., & Wilson, T. D. (2004). Looking forward to looking backward. *Psychological Science, 15,* 346–350.

Gilbert, D. T. (1989). Thinking lightly about others: Automatic components of the social inference process. In J. S. Uleman & J. A. Bargh (Eds.), *Unintended thought* (pp. 189–211). New York: Guilford.

Gilbert, S. J., & Shallice, T. (2002). Task switching: A PDP model. *Cognitive Psychology, 44,* 297–337.

Gilhooly, K. J. (1988). *Thinking: Direct, undirected and creative* (2nd ed.). New York: Academic Press.

Gilhooly, K. J., Logie, R. H., Wetherick, N., & Wynn, V. (1993). Working memory and strategies in syllogistic-reasoning tasks. *Memory & Cognition, 21,* 115–124.

Gilovich, T. (1983). Biased evaluation and persistence in gambling. *Journal of Personality & Social Psychology, 44,* 1110–1126.

Gilovich, T. (1991). *How we know what isn't so.* New York: Free Press.

Gilovich, T., & Douglas, C. (1986). Biased evaluations of randomly determined gambling outcomes. *Journal of Experimental Social Psychology, 22,* 228–241.

Gilovich, T., & Medvec, V. H. (1995). The experience of regret: What, when and why. *Psychological Review, 102,* 379–395.

Gilovich, T., Medvec, V. H., & Kahneman, D. (1998). Varieties of regret: A debate and partial resolution. *Psychological Review, 105,* 602–605.

Girotto, V. (2004). Task understanding. In J. P. Leighton & R. J. Sternberg (Eds.), *The nature of reasoning* (pp. 103–128). New York: Cambridge University Press.

Girotto, V., & Gonzalez, M. (2001). Solving probabilistic and statistical problems: A matter of information structure and question form. *Cognition, 78,* 247–276.

Glanzer, M., & Cunitz, A. R. (1966). Two storage mechanisms in free recall. *Journal of Verbal Learning and Verbal Behavior, 5,* 351–360.

Glisky, E. L., Polster, M. R., & Routhieaux, B. C. (1995). Double dissociation between item and source memory. *Neuropsychology, 9,* 229–235.

Glucksberg, S., & Danks, J. (1968). Effects of discriminative labels and of nonsense labels upon availability of novel function. *Journal of Verbal Learning and Verbal Behavior, 7,* 72–76.

Gobet, F., & Simon, H. A. (2000). Reply to Lassiter. *Psychological Science, 11,* 174–175.

Godden, D. R., & Baddeley, A. D. (1975). Context-dependent memory in two natural environments: On land and underwater. *British Journal of Psychology, 66,* 325–332.

Goebel, R., Khorram-Sefat, D., Muckli, L., Hacker, H., & Singer, W. (1998). The constructive nature of vision: Direct evidence from functional magnetic resonance imaging studies of apparent motion and motion imagery. *European Journal of Neuroscience, 10,* 1563–1573.

Goel, V. (2007). Anatomy of deductive reasoning. *Trends in Cognitive Sciences, 11,* 435–441.

Goldenberg, G., Müllbacher, W., & Nowak, A. (1995). Imagery without perception—A case study of anosognosia for cortical blindness. *Neuropsychologia, 33,* 1373–1382.

Goldenberg, J., Mazursky, D., & Solomon, S. (1999). Creative sparks. *Science, 285,* 1495–1496.

Goldin-Meadow, S. (2003). *The resilience of language: What gesture creation in deaf children can tell us about how all children learn language.* New York: Psychology Press.

Goldman-Rakic, P. S. (1987). Development of cortical circuitry and cognitive function. *Child Development, 58,* 601–622.

Goldman-Rakic, P. S. (1995). Architecture of the prefrontal cortex and the central executive. In J. Grafman & K. J. Holyoak (Eds.), *Structure and functions of the human prefrontal cortex* (Annals of the New York Academy of Sciences, Vol. 769, pp. 71–83). New York: New York Academy of Sciences.

Goldman-Rakic, P. S. (1998). The prefrontal landscape: Implications of functional architecture for understanding human mentation and the central executive. In A. C. Roberts & T. W. Robbins (Eds.), *The prefrontal cortex: Executive and cognitive functions* (pp. 87–102). New York: Oxford University Press.

Goldstone, R. (1996). Alignment-based nonmonotonicities in similarity. *Journal of Experimental Psychology: Learning, Memory and Cognition, 22,* 988–1001.

Goldvarg, Y., & Johnson-Laird, P. N. (2000). Illusions in modal reasoning. *Memory & Cognition, 28,* 282–294.

Goodale, M. A. (1995). The cortical organization of visual perception and visuomotor control. In S. M. Kosslyn & D. Osherson (Eds.), *Visual cognition: An invitation to cognitive science* (2nd ed., pp. 167–213). Cambridge, MA: MIT Press.

Goodale, M. A., & Milner, A. D. (2004). *Sight unseen.* New York: Oxford University Press.

Goodman, G. S., Ghetti, S., Quas, J. A., Edelstein, R. S., Alexander, K. W., Redlich, A., D., et al. (2003). A prospective study of memory for child sexual abuse: New findings relevant to the repressed-memory controversy. *Psychological Science, 14,* 113–118.

Goodman, N. (1972). Seven strictures on similarity. In N. Goodman (Ed.), *Problems and projects* (pp. 437–446). New York: Bobbs-Merrill.

Gordon, R. D. (2006). Selective attention during scene perception: Evidence from negative priming. *Memory & Cognition, 34,* 1484–1494.

Graesser, A. C., Millis, K. K., & Zwaan, R. A. (1997). Discourse comprehension. *Annual Review of Psychology, 48,* 163–189.

Graf, P., Mandler, G., & Haden, P. E. (1982). Simulating amnesic symptoms in normals. *Science, 218,* 1243–1244.

Graf, P., & Masson, M. (Eds.). (1993). *Implicit memory: New directions in cognition, development and neuropsychology.* Hillsdale, NJ: Erlbaum.

Graf, P., & Schacter, D. L. (1985). Implicit and explicit memory for new associations in normal and amnesic subjects. *Journal of Experimental Psychology: Learning, Memory and Cognition, 11,* 501–518.

Grainger, J., & Whitney, C. (2004). Does the huamn mnid raed wrods as a wlohe? *Trends in Cognitive Sciences, 8,* 58–59.

Grainger, J., Rey, A., & Dufau, S. (2008). Letter perception: from pixels to pandemonium. *Trends in Cognitive Sciences, 12,* 381–387.

Grant, H. M., Bredahl, L. C., Clay, J., Ferrie, J. E., Groves, J. E., McDorman, T. A., et al. (1998). Context-dependent memory for meaningful material: Information for students. *Applied Cognitive Psychology, 12,* 617–623.

Gray, J. R., Chabris, C. F., & Braver, T. S. (2003). Neural mechanisms of general fluid intelligence. *Nature Neuroscience, 6,* 316–322.

Greenberg, J., Ferguson, C., & Moravcsik, E. (Eds.). (1978). *Universals of human language.* Stanford, CA: Stanford University Press.

Greene, E., Flynn, M., & Loftus, E. F. (1982). Inducing resistance of misleading information. *Journal of Verbal Learning and Verbal Behavior, 21,* 207–219.

Greenwald, A., & Banaji, M. (1995). Implicit social cognition: Attitudes, self-esteem and stereotypes. *Psychological Review, 102,* 4–27.

Gregg, M. K., & Samuel, A. G. (2008). Change deafness and the organizational properties of sounds. *Journal of Experimental Psychology: Human Perception & Performance, 34,* 974–991.

Grice, H. P. (1975). Logic and conversation. In P. Cole & J. L. Morgan (Eds.), *Syntax and semantics 3: Speech acts* (pp. 41–58). New York: Academic Press.

Griggs, R. (1983). The role of problem content in the selection task and in the THOG problem. In J. S. B.

Evans (Ed.), *Thinking and reasoning: Psychological approaches* (pp. 17–43). London: Routledge & Kegan Paul.

Griggs, R., & Cox, J. R. (1982). The elusive thematic-materials effect in Wason's selection task. *British Journal of Psychology, 73,* 407–420.

Grill-Spector, K., & Sayres, R. (2008). Object recognition: Insights from advances in fMRI methods. *Current Directions in Psychological Science, 17,* 73–79.

Gruber, H. E. (1981). *Darwin on man: A psychological study of scientific creativity* (2nd ed.). Chicago: University of Chicago Press.

Gruber, H. E., & Wallace, D. B. (2001). Creative work: The case of Charles Darwin. *American Psychologist, 56,* 346–349.

Guilford, J. (1967). *The nature of human intelligence.* New York: Scribner.

Guilford, J. (1979). Some incubated thoughts on incubation. *Journal of Creative Behavior, 13,* 1–8.

Haber, R. N. (1969). Eidetic images. *Scientific American, 220,* 36–44.

Hafstad, G. S., Memon, A., & Logie, R. H. (2004). Post-identification feedback, confidence, and recollections of witnessing conditions in child witnesses. *Applied Cognitive Psychology, 18,* 901–912.

Halberstadt, J. & Rhodes, G. (2003). It's not just average faces that are attractive: Computer-manipulated averageness makes birds, fish, and automobiles attractive. *Psychonomic Bulletin & Review, 10,* 149–156.

Halle, M. (1990). Phonology. In D. Osherson & H. Lasnik (Eds.), *Language: An invitation to cognitive science* (pp. 43–68). Cambridge, MA: MIT Press.

Halpern, D. (1984). *Thought and knowledge: An introduction to critical thinking.* Hillsdale, NJ: Erlbaum.

Hamann, S. (2001). Cognitive and neural mechanisms of emotional memory. *Trends in Cognitive Sciences, 5,* 394–400.

Hamill, R., Wilson, T. D., & Nisbett, R. E. (1980). Insensitivity to sample bias: Generalizing from atypical

cases. *Journal of Personality and Social Psychology, 39,* 578–589.

Hanako, Y., & Smith, L. B. (2005). Linguistic cues enhance the learning of perceptual cues. *Psychological Science, 16,* 90–95.

Hancock, P. J. B., Bruce, V., & Burton, A. M. (2000). Recognition of unfamiliar faces. *Trends in Cognitive Sciences, 4,* 330–344.

Handel, S. (1989). *Listening: An introduction to the perception of auditory events.* Cambridge, MA: MIT Press.

Hanley, J. R., & Chapman, E. (2008). Partial knowledge in a tip-of-the-tongue state about two- and three-word proper names. *Psychonomic Bulletin & Review, 15,* 156–160.

Harber, K. D., & Pennebaker, J. W. (1992). Overcoming traumatic memories. In S.-Å. Christianson (Ed.), *The handbook of emotion and memory: Research and theory* (pp. 359–387). Hillsdale, NJ: Erlbaum.

Hardiman, P., Dufresne, R., & Mestre, J. (1989). The relation between problem categorization and problem solving among experts and novices. *Memory & Cognition, 17,* 627–638.

Harinck, F., Van Dijk, E., Van Beest, I., & Mersmann, P. (2007). When gains loom larger than losses: Reversed loss aversion for small amounts of money. *Psychological Science, 18,* 1099–1105.

Harley, T. A., & Bown, H. E. (1998). What causes a tip-of-the-tongue state? Evidence for lexical neighbourhood effects in speech production. *British Journal of Psychology, 89,* 151–174.

Harwood, D. G., Barker, W. W., Ownby, R. L., & Duara, R. (1999). Prevalence and correlates of Capgras syndrome in Alzheimer's disease. *International Journal of Geriatric Psychiatry, 14,* 415–420.

Hasher, L., Goldstein, D., & Toppino, T. (1977). Frequency and the conference of referential validity. *Journal of Verbal Learning and Verbal Behavior, 16,* 107–112.

Hasselmo, M. E. (1999). Neuromodulation: Acetylcholine and memory consolidation. *Trends in Cognitive Science, 6,* 351–359.

Hawkins, J. (Ed.). (1988). *Explaining language universals.* London: Basil Blackwell.

Hayes, J. (1985). Three problems in teaching general skills. In S. Chipman, J. Segal, & R. Glaser (Eds.), *Thinking and learning skills* (pp. 391–406). Hillsdale, NJ: Erlbaum.

Hayes, J., & Simon, H. (1977). Psychological differences among problem solving isomorphs. In N. Castellan, D. Pisoni, & G. Potts (Eds.), *Cognitive theory* (pp. 21–42). Hillsdale, NJ: Erlbaum.

Hayward, W., & Williams, P. (2000). Viewpoint dependence and object discriminability. *Psychological Science, 11,* 7–12.

Heaps, C., & Nash, M. (1999). Individual differences in imagination inflation. *Psychonomic Bulletin & Review, 6,* 313–318.

Heaps, C. M., & Nash, M. (2001). Comparing recollective experience in true and false autobiographical memories. *Journal of Experimental Psychology: Learning, Memory and Cognition, 27,* 920–930.

Hegarty, M. (2004). Mechanical reasoning by mental simulation. *Trends in Cognitive Sciences, 8,* 280–285.

Heider, E. R. (1972). Universals in color naming and memory. *Journal of Experimental Psychology, 93,* 10–20.

Heil, M., Rösler, F., & Hennighausen, E. (1993). Imagery-perception interaction depends on the shape of the image: A reply to Farah. *Journal of Experimental Psychology: Human Perception and Performance, 19,* 1313–1319.

Heil, M., Rösler, F., & Hennighausen, E. (1994). Dynamics of activation in long-term memory: The retrieval of verbal, pictorial, spatial and color information. *Journal of Experimental Psychology: Learning, Memory and Cognition, 20,* 169–184.

Heilman, K., Watson, R., & Valenstein, E. (1985). Neglect and related disorders. In K. Heilman & E. Valenstein (Eds.), *Clinical neuropsychology* (pp. 243–293). New York: Oxford University Press.

Heit, E. (2000). Properties of inductive reasoning. *Psychonomic Bulletin & Review, 7,* 569–592.

Heit, E., & Bott, L. (2000). Knowledge selection in category learning. In D. L. Medin (Ed.), *The psychology of learning and motivation: Advances in research and theory,* Vol. 39 (pp. 163–199). San Diego, CA: Academic Press.

Heit, E., & Feeney, A. (2005). Relations between premise similarity and inductive strength. *Psychonomic Bulletin & Review, 12,* 340–344.

Heller, J., & Reif, F. (1984). Prescribing effective human problem-solving processes: Problem description in physics. *Cognition and Instruction, 1,* 177–216.

Helmuth, L. (2001). Boosting brain activity from the outside in. *Science, 292,* 1284–1286.

Henderson, J. M. & Hollingworth, A. (2003). Global transsaccadic change blindness during scene perception. *Psychological Science, 14,* 493–497.

Henderson, J. M., Weeks, P. A., Jr., & Hollingworth. A. (1999). The effects of semantic consistency on eye movements during complex scene viewing. *Journal of Experimental Psychology: Human Perception and Performance, 25,* 210–228.

Henle, M. (1962). On the relation between logic and thinking. *Psychological Review, 69,* 366–378.

Henle, M. (1978). Foreword. In R. Revlin & R. Mayer (Eds.), *Human reasoning* (pp. xiii–xviii). New York: Wiley.

Hermer-Vasquez, L., Spelke, E. S., & Katsnelson, A. S. (1999). Sources of flexibility in human cognition: Dual-task studies of space and language. *Cognitive Psychology, 39,* 3–36.

Hertwig, R., Herzog, S. M., Schooler, L. J., & Reimer, T. (2008). Fluency heuristic: A model of how the mind exploits a by-product of information retrieval. *Journal of Experimental Psychology: Learning, Memory & Cognition, 34,* 1191–1206.

Hertwig, R., & Ortmann, A. (2003). Economists' and psychologists' experimental practices: How they differ, why they differ, and how they could converge. In I. Brocas & J. D. Carrillo (Eds.), *The psychology of economic decisions: Rationality and well-being,* Vol. 1 (pp. 253–272). New York: Oxford University Press.

Hicks, J. L., & Marsh, R. L. (1999). Remember-Know judgments can depend on how memory is tested. *Psychonomic Bulletin & Review, 6,* 117–122.

Higbee, K. L. (1977). *Your memory: How it works and how to improve it.* Englewood Cliffs, NJ: Prentice-Hall.

Higgins, E. T., & Bargh, J. A. (1987). Social cognition and social perception. *Annual Review of Psychology, 38,* 1–95.

Higgins, T. (2005). Value from regulatory fit. *Current Directions in Psychological Science, 14,* 209–213.

Hilgard, E. R. (1968). *The experience of hypnosis.* New York: Harcourt Brace Jovanovich.

Hillyard, S. A., Vogel, E. K., & Luck, S. J. (1998). Sensory gain control (amplification) as a mechanism of selective attention: Electrophysiological and neuroimaging evidence. *Philosophical Transactions of the Royal Society: Biological Sciences, 353,* 1257–1270.

Hilton, D. (1995). The social context of reasoning: Conversational inference and rational judgment. *Psychological Bulletin, 118,* 248–271.

Hilton, D. J. (2003). Psychology and the financial markets: Applications to understanding and remedying irrational decision-making. In I. Brocas & J. D. Carrillo (Eds.), *The psychology of economic decisions: Rationality and well-being,* Vol. 1 (pp. 273–297). New York: Oxford University Press.

Hilts, P. J. (1995). *Memory's ghost: The strange tale of Mr. M and the nature of memory.* New York: Simon & Schuster.

Hinsley, D., Hayes, J., & Simon, H. (1977). From words to equations: Meaning and representation in algebra word problems. In P. Carpenter & M. Just (Eds.), *Cognitive processes in comprehension* (pp. 89–106). Hillsdale, NJ: Erlbaum.

Hirst, W. (1986). The psychology of attention. In J. E. LeDoux & W. Hirst (Eds.), *Mind and brain* (pp. 105–141). Cambridge, England: Cambridge University Press.

Hirst, W., & Kalmar, D. (1987). Characterizing attentional resources. *Journal of Experimental Psychology: General, 116*, 68–81.

Hirst, W., Spelke, E., Reaves, C., Caharack, G., & Neisser, U. (1980). Dividing attention without alternation or automaticity. *Journal of Experimental Psychology: General, 109*, 98–117.

Hitch, G. J., Towse, J. N., & Hutton, U. (2001). What limits children's working memory span? Theoretical accounts and applications for scholastic development. *Journal of Experimental Psychology: General, 130*, 184–198.

Hochberg, J. (1978). *Perception* (2nd ed.). Englewood Cliffs, NJ: Prentice-Hall.

Hochberg, J. (1986). Representation of motion and space in video and cinematic displays. In K. J. Boff, L. Kaufman, & J. P. Thomas (Eds.), *Handbook of perception and human performance*, Vol. 1 (pp. 22:1–22:64). New York: Wiley.

Hodges, J. R., & Graham, K. S. (2001). Episodic memory: Insights from semantic dementia. In A. D. Baddeley, J. P. Aggleton, & M. A. Conway (Eds.), *Episodic memory: New directions in research* (pp. 132–152). New York: Oxford University Press.

Holding, D. (1985). *The psychology of chess*. Hillsdale, NJ: Erlbaum.

Holland, J. H., Holyoak, K. F., Nisbett, R. E., & Thagard, P. R. (1986). *Induction*. Cambridge, MA: MIT Press.

Holmberg, D., & Homes, J. G. (1994). Reconstruction of relationship memories: A mental models approach. In N. Schwarz & S. Sudman (Eds.), *Autobiographical memory and the validity of retrospective reports* (pp. 267–288). New York: Springer.

Holmes, J. B., Waters, H. S., & Rajaram, S. (1998). The phenomenology of false memories: Episodic content and confidence. *Journal of Experimental Psychology: Learning, Memory and Cognition, 24*, 1026–1040.

Holyoak, K. J. (1984). Analogical thinking and human intelligence. In R. J. Sternberg (Ed.), *Advances in the psychology of human intelligence* (pp. 199–230). Hillsdale, NJ: Erlbaum.

Holyoak, K. J. (1987). Review of parallel distributed processing. *Science, 236*, 992.

Holyoak, K. J., & Koh, H. (1987). Surface and structural similarity in analogical transfer. *Memory & Cognition, 15*, 332–340.

Holyoak, K. J., & Thagard, P. (1989). Analogical mapping by constraint satisfaction. *Cognitive Science, 13*, 295–355.

Homa, D., Dunbar, S., & Nohre, L. (1991). Instance frequency, categorization, and the modulating effect of experience. *Journal of Experimental Psychology: Learning, Memory and Cognition, 17*, 444–458.

Homa, D., Sterling, S., & Trepel, L. (1981). Limitation of exemplar-based generalization and the abstraction of categorical information. *Journal of Experimental Psychology: Human Learning and Memory, 7*, 418–439.

Hornby, P. (1974). Surface structure and presupposition. *Journal of Verbal Learning and Verbal Behavior, 13*, 530–538.

Horowitz, M. J., & Reidbord, S. P. (1992). Memory, emotion, and response to trauma. In S.-Å. Christianson (Ed.), *The handbook of emotion and memory: Research and theory* (pp. 343–357). Hillsdale, NJ: Erlbaum.

Howe, M. L., Rabinowitz, F. M., & Powell, T. L. (1998). Individual differences in working memory and reasoning-remembering relationships in solving class-inclusion problems. *Memory & Cognition, 26*, 1089–1101.

Howes, M., Siegel, M., & Brown, F. (1993). Early childhood memories: Accuracy and affect. *Cognition, 47*, 95–119.

Hsee, C., & Hastie, R. (2005). Decision and experience: Why don't we choose what makes us happy? *Trends in Cognitive Sciences, 10*, 31–37.

Hsee, C. K., Hastie, R., & Chen, J. (2008). Hedonomics: Briding decision research with happiness research. *Perspectives on Psychological Science, 3*, 224–243.

Hubel, D. (1963). The visual cortex of the brain. *Scientific American, 209*(November), 54–62.

Hubel, D., & Wiesel, T. (1959). Receptive fields of single neurones in the cat's visual cortex. *Journal of Physiology, 148*, 574–591.

Hubel, D., & Wiesel, T. (1968). Receptive fields and functional architecture of monkey striate cortex. *Journal of Physiology, 195*, 215–243.

Huey, E. D., Krueger, F., & Grafman, J. (2006). Representations in the human prefrontal cortex. *Current Directions in Psychological Science, 5*, 167–171.

Hummel, J., & Biederman, I. (1992). Dynamic binding in a neural network for shape recognition. *Psychological Review, 99*, 480–517.

Hummel, J. E., & Stankiewicz, B. J. (1998). Two roles for attention in shape perception: A structural description model of visual scrutiny. *Visual Cognition, 5*, 49–79.

Hunt, R., & Ellis, H. D. (1974). Recognition memory and degree of semantic contextual change. *Journal of Experimental Psychology, 103*, 1153–1159.

Husserl, E. (1931). *Ideas*. New York: Collier.

Hutchison, K. A. (2003). Is semantic priming due to association strength or feature overlap? A *micro* analytic review. *Psychonomic Bulletin & Review, 10*, 785–813.

Hyde, T. S., & Jenkins, J. J. (1969). Differential effects of incidental tasks on the organization of recall of a list of highly associated words. *Journal of Experimental Psychology, 82*, 472–481.

Hyde, T. S., & Jenkins, J. J. (1973). Recall for words as a function of semantic, graphic, and syntactic orienting tasks. *Journal of Verbal Learning and Verbal Behavior, 12*, 471–480.

Hyman, I. E., Jr. (2000). Creating false autobiographical memories: Why people believe their memory errors. In E. Winograd, R. Fivush, & W. Hirst (Eds.), *Ecological approaches to cognition: Essays in honor of Ulric Neisser.* Hillsdale, NJ: Erlbaum.

Hyman, I. E., Jr., Husband, T., & Billings, F. (1995). False memories of childhood experiences. *Applied Cognitive Psychology, 9*, 181–198.

Intons-Peterson, M. J. (1983). Imagery paradigms: How vulnerable are they to experimenters' expectations? *Journal of Experimental Psychology: Human Perception & Performance, 9*, 394–412.

Intons-Peterson, M. J. (1999). Comments and caveats about "scanning visual mental images." *Cahiers de Psychologie Cognitive, 18*, 534–540.

Intons-Peterson, M., & White, A. (1981). Experimenter naiveté and imaginal judgments. *Journal of Experimental Psychology: Human Perception and Performance, 7*, 833–843.

Intraub, H., & Bodamer, J. (1993). Boundary extension: Fundamental aspect of pictorial representation or encoding artifact? *Journal of Experimental Psychology: Learning, Memory and Cognition, 19*, 1387–1397.

Intraub, H., & Dickinson, C. A. (2008). False memory 1/20th of a second later. *Psychological Science, 19*, 1007–1014.

Intraub, H., Gottesman, C. V., & Bills, A. J. (1998). Effects of perceiving and imagining scenes on memory for pictures. *Journal of Experimental Psychology: Learning, Memory and Cognition, 24*, 1–16.

Intraub, H., Hoffman, J. E., Wetherhold, C. J., & Stoehs, S.-A. (2006). More than meets the eye: The effect of planned fixations on scene representation. *Perception and Psychophysics, 68*, 759–769.

Intraub, H., & Richardson, M. (1989). Wide-angle memories of close-up scenes. *Journal of Experimental Psychology: Learning, Memory and Cognition, 15*, 179–187.

Isha, A., & Sagi, D. (1995). Common mechanisms of visual imagery and perception. *Science, 268*, 1772–1774.

Jackendoff, R. (1972). *Semantic interpretation in generative grammar.* Cambridge, MA: MIT Press.

Jackendoff, R. (1987). *Consciousness and the computational mind.* Cambridge, MA: MIT Press.

Jacoby, L., & Hollingshead, A. (1990). Reading student essays may be hazardous to your spelling: Effects of reading incorrectly and correctly spelled words. *Canadian Journal of Psychology, 44*, 345–358.

Jacoby, L., & Whitehouse, K. (1989). An illusion of memory: False recognition influenced by unconscious perception. *Journal of Experimental Psychology: General, 118*, 126–135.

Jacoby, L. L. (1978). On interpreting the effects of repetition: Solving a problem versus remembering a solution. *Journal of Verbal Learning and Verbal Behavior, 17*, 649–667.

Jacoby, L. L. (1983). Remembering the data: Analyzing interactive processes in reading. *Journal of Verbal Learning and Verbal Behavior, 22*, 485–508.

Jacoby, L. L., Allan, L., Collins, J., & Larwill, L. (1988). Memory influences subjective experience: Noise judgments. *Journal of Experimental Psychology: Learning, Memory and Cognition, 14*, 240–247.

Jacoby, L. L., & Dallas, M. (1981). On the relationship between autobiographical memory and perceptual learning. *Journal of Experimental Psychology: General, 3*, 306–340.

Jacoby, L. L., Jones, T. C., & Dolan, P. O. (1998). Two effects of repetition: Support for a dual process model of know judgments and exclusion errors. *Psychonomic Bulletin & Review, 5*, 705–509.

Jacoby, L. L., Kelley, C. M., Brown, J., & Jasechko, J. (1989). Becoming famous overnight: Limits on the ability to avoid unconscious influences of the past. *Journal of Personality and Social Psychology, 56*, 326–338.

Jacoby, L. L., Lindsay, D. S., & Hessels, S. (2003). Item-specific control of automatic processes: Stroop process dissociations. *Psychonomic Bulletin & Review, 10*, 638–644.

Jacoby, L. L., & Witherspoon, D. (1982). Remembering without awareness. *Canadian Journal of Psychology, 36*, 300–324.

James, L. E., & Burke, D. M. (2000). Phonological priming effects on word retrieval and Tip-of-the-Tongue experiences in young and older adults. *Journal of Experimental Psychology: Learning, Memory and Cognition, 26*, 1378–1391.

James, W. (1890). *The principles of psychology*, Vol. 2. New York: Dover.

Janiszewski, C., & Uy, D. (2008). Precision of the anchor influences the amount of adjustment. *Psychological Science, 19*, 121–127.

Jankowiak, J., Kinsbourne, M., Shalev, R. S., & Bachman, D. L. (1992). Preserved visual imagery and categorization in a case of associative visual agnosia. *Journal of Cognitive Neuroscience, 4*, 119–131.

January, D., & Kako, E. (2007). Re-evaluating evidence for linguistic relativity: Reply to Boroditsky (2001). *Cognition, 104*, 417–426.

Jeffries, R., Polson, P., Razran, L., & Atwood, M. (1977). A process model for missionaries-cannibals and other river-crossing problems. *Cognitive Psychology, 9*, 412–440.

Jelicic, M., Smeets, T., Peters, M., Candel, I., Horselenberg, R., & Merckelbach, H. (2006). Assassination of a controversial politician:

Remembering details from another non-existent film. *Applied Cognitive Psychology, 20,* 591–596.

Jenkins, R., Lavie, N., & Driver, J. (2005). Recognition memory for distractor faces depends on attentional load at exposure. *Psychological Bulletin & Review, 12,* 314–320.

Jennings, D. L., Amabile, T. M., & Ross, L. (1982). Informal covariation assessment: Data-based versus theory-based judgments. In D. Kahneman, P. Slovic, & A. Tversky (Eds.), *Judgments under uncertainty: Heuristics and biases* (pp. 211–230). Cambridge, England: Cambridge University Press.

Jepson, D., Krantz, D., & Nisbett, R. (1983). Inductive reasoning: Competence or skill? *Behavioral and Brain Sciences, 6,* 494–501.

Johnson, H., & Seifert, C. (1994). Sources of the continued influence effect: When misinformation affects later inferences. *Journal of Experimental Psychology: Learning, Memory and Cognition, 20,* 1420–1436.

Johnson, M. K. (1988). Reality monitoring: An experimental phenomenological approach. *Journal of Experimental Psychology: General, 117,* 390–394.

Johnson, M. K., Hashtroudi, S., & Lindsay, S. (1993). Source monitoring. *Psychological Bulletin, 114,* 3–28.

Johnson, M. K., Kim, J. K., & Risse, G. (1985). Do alcoholic Korsakoff's syndrome patients acquire affective reactions? *Journal of Experimental Psychology: Learning, Memory and Cognition, 11,* 27–36.

Johnson, S. K., & Anderson, M. C. (2004). The role of inhibitory control in forgetting semantic knowledge. *Psychological Science, 15,* 448–453.

Johnson-Laird, P. N. (1983). *Mental models.* Cambridge, MA: Harvard University Press.

Johnson-Laird, P. N. (1987). The mental representation of the meaning of words. *Cognition, 25,* 189–211.

Johnson-Laird, P. N. (1988). A computational analysis of consciousness.

In A. Marcel & E. Bisiach (Eds.), *Consciousness in contemporary science* (pp. 357–368). Oxford, England: Oxford University Press.

Johnson-Laird, P. N. (1990). Mental models. In M. Posner (Ed.), *Foundations of cognitive science* (pp. 469–500). Cambridge, MA: Bradford.

Johnson-Laird, P. N. (2001). Mental models and deduction. *Trends in Cognitive Sciences, 5,* 434–442.

Johnson-Laird, P. N. (2004). Mental models and reasoning. In J. P. Leighton & R. J. Sternberg (Eds.), *The nature of reasoning* (pp. 169–204). New York: Cambridge University Press.

Johnson-Laird, P. N., & Byrne, R. (1989). Only reasoning. *Journal of Memory and Language, 28,* 313–330.

Johnson-Laird, P. N., & Byrne, R. (1991). *Deduction.* Hillsdale, NJ: Erlbaum.

Johnson-Laird, P. N., Byrne, R. M. J., & Schaeken, W. (1992). Propositional reasoning by model. *Psychological Review, 99,* 418–439.

Johnson-Laird, P. N., Byrne, R., & Tabossi, P. (1989). Reasoning by model: The case of multiple quantification. *Psychological Review, 96,* 658–673.

Johnson-Laird, P. N., Legrenzi, P., Girotto, V., Legrenzi, M. S., & Caverni, J.-P. (1999). Naive probability: A mental model theory of extensional reasoning. *Psychological Review, 106,* 62–88.

Johnson-Laird, P. N., Legrenzi, P., & Legrenzi, M. S. (1972). Reasoning and a sense of reality. *British Journal of Psychology, 63,* 395–400.

Johnson-Laird, P. N., & Savary, F. (1999). Illusory inferences: A novel class of erroneous deductions. *Cognition, 71,* 191–229.

Johnson-Laird, P. N., & Steedman, M. (1978). The psychology of syllogisms. *Cognitive Psychology, 10,* 64–99.

Jones, G. (2003). Testing two cognitive theories of insight. *Journal of Experi-*

mental Psychology: Learning, Memory and Cognition, 29, 1017–1027.

Jones, T. C., & Bartlett, J. C. (2009). When false recognition is out of control: The case of facial conjunctions. *Memory & Cognition, 37,* 143–157.

Jonides, J., Kahn, R., & Rozin, P. (1975). Imagery instructions improve memory in blind subjects. *Bulletin of the Psychonomic Society, 5,* 424–426.

Jonides, J., Lacey, S. C., & Nee, D. E. (2005). Processes of working memory in mind and brain. *Current Directions in Psychological Science, 14,* 2–5.

Jonides, J., Lewis, R., Nee, D. E., Lustig, C. A., Berman, M. G., & Moore, K. S. (2008). The mind and brain of short-term memory. *Annual Review of Psychology, 59,* 193–224.

Jonides, J., Nee, D. E., & Berman, M. G. (2006). What has functional neuroimaging told us about the mind? So many examples, so little space. *Cortex, 42,* 414–427.

Josephs, R., Giesler, R. B., & Silvera, D. (1994). Judgment by quantity. *Journal of Experimental Psychology: General, 123,* 21–32.

Just, M., & Carpenter, P. (1987). *The psychology of reading and language comprehension.* Boston: Allyn & Bacon.

Just, M., & Carpenter, P. (1992). A capacity theory of comprehension: Individual differences in working memory. *Psychological Review, 99,* 122–149.

Just, M., Carpenter, P. A., & Hemphill, D. D. (1996). Constraints on processing capacity: Architectural or implementational? In D. Steier & T. Mitchell (Eds.), *Mind matters: A tribute to Allen Newell* (pp. 141–178). Mahwah, NJ: Erlbaum.

Kahneman, D. (1973). *Attention and effort.* Englewood Cliffs, NJ: Prentice-Hall.

Kahneman, D. (2003). A perspective on judgment and choice: Mapping bounded rationality. *American Psychologist, 58,* 697–720.

Kahneman, D., Diener, E., & Schwarz, N. (Eds.). (1999). *Well-being: The foundations of hedonic psychology.* New York: Russell Sage Foundation.

Kahneman, D., & Frederick, S. (2006). Frames and brains: Elicitation and the control of response tendencies. *Trends in Cognitive Sciences, 11,* 45–46.

Kahneman, D., Fredrickson, B., Schreiber, C., & Redelmeier, D. (1993). When more pain is preferred to less: Adding a better end. *Psychological Science, 4,* 401–405.

Kahneman, D., & Miller, D. (1986). Norm theory: Comparing reality to its alternatives. *Psychological Review, 93,* 136–153.

Kahneman, D., & Snell, J. (1992). Predicting a changing taste: Do people know what they will like? *Journal of Behavioral Decision Making, 5,* 187–200.

Kahneman, D., & Tversky, A. (1973). On the psychology of prediction. *Psychological Review, 80,* 237–251.

Kahneman, D., & Tversky, A. (1982a). On the study of statistical intuitions. *Cognition, 11,* 237–251.

Kahneman, D., & Tversky, A. (1982b). The simulation heuristic. In D. Kahneman, P. Slovic, & A. Tversky (Eds.), *Judgment under uncertainty: Heuristics and biases* (pp. 201–208). New York: Cambridge University Press.

Kahney, H. (1986). *Problem solving: A cognitive approach.* Milton Keynes, England: Open University Press.

Kane, M. J., Bleckley, M., Conway, A. R. A., & Engle, R. W. (2001). A controlled-attention view of working-memory capacity. *Journal of Experimental Psychology: General, 130,* 169–183.

Kane, M. J., Brown, L. H., McVay, J. C., Silvia, P. J., Myin-Germeys, I., & Kwapil, T. R. (2007). For whom the mind wanders, and when: An experience-sampling study of working memory and executive control in daily life. *Psychological Science, 18,* 614–621.

Kane, M. J., & Engle, R. W. (2003). Working-memory capacity and the control of attention: The contributions of goal neglect, response competition, and task set to Stroop interference. *Journal of Experimental Psychology: General, 132,* 47–70.

Kanizsa, G. (1979). *Organization in vision.* New York: Praeger.

Kanwisher, N. (2006). What's in a face? *Science, 311,* 617–618.

Kaplan, A. S., & Murphy, G. L. (2000). Category learning with minimal prior knowledge. *Journal of Experimental Psychology: Learning, Memory, & Cognition, 26,* 829–846.

Kapur, N. (1999). Syndromes of retrograde amnesia. *Psychological Bulletin, 125,* 800–825.

Katona, G. (1940). *Organizing and memorizing.* New York: Columbia University Press.

Katz, A. (1983). What does it mean to be a high imager? In J. Yuille (Ed.), *Imagery, memory and cognition* (pp. 39–63). Hillsdale, NJ: Erlbaum.

Katz, B. (1952). The nerve impulse. *Scientific American, 187*(November), 55–64.

Kay, P., & Regier, T. (2007). Color naming universals: The case of Berinmo. *Cognition, 102,* 289–298.

Keil, F. C. (1986). The acquisition of natural-kind and artifact terms. In W. Demopoulos & A. Marras (Eds.), *Language, learning, and concept acquisition* (pp. 133–153). Norwood, NJ: Ablex.

Keil, F. C. (1989). *Concepts, kinds, and cognitive development.* Cambridge, MA: MIT Press.

Keil, F. C. (2003). Folkscience: Coarse interpretations of a complex reality. *Trends in Cognitive Sciences, 7,* 368–373.

Keil, F. C., Smith, W. C., Simons, D. J., & Levin, D. T. (1998). Two dogmas of conceptual empiricism: Implications for hybrid models of the structure of knowledge. *Cognition, 65,* 103–135.

Kelly, S. W., Burton, A. M., Kato, T., & Akamatsu, S. (2001). Incidental learning of real-world regularities. *Psychological Science, 12,* 86–89.

Kensinger, E. (2007). Negative emotion enhances memory accuracy. *Current Directions in Psychological Science, 16,* 213–218.

Kerr, N. H. (1983). The role of vision in "visual imagery" experiments: Evidence from the congenitally blind. *Journal of Experimental Psychology: General, 112,* 265–277.

Kershaw, T. C., & Ohlsson, S. (2004). Multiple causes of difficulty in insight: The case of the nine-dot problem. *Journal of Experimental Psychology: Learning, Memory, & Cognition, 30,* 3–13.

Keys, D., & Schwartz, B. (2007). "Leaky" rationality: How research on behavioral decision making challenges normative standards of rationality. *Perspectives on Psychological Science, 2,* 162–180.

Keysers, C., Cohen, J., Donald, M., Guth, W., John, E., et al. (2008). Explicit and implicit strategies in decision making. In C. Engel & W. Singer (Eds.), *Better than conscious? Decision making, the human mind, and implications for institutions* (pp. 225–258). Cambridge, MA: MIT Press.

Kihlstrom, J. F. (2006). Trauma and memory revisited. In B. Uttl, N. Ohta, & A. Siegenthaler (Eds.), *Memory and emotion: Interdisciplinary perspectives* (pp. 259–291). Malden, MA: Blackwell.

Kihlstrom, J. F., & Schacter, D. L. (2000). Functional amnesia. In F. Boller & J. Grafman (Eds.), *Handbook of neuropsychology* (2nd ed., Vol. 2, pp. 409–427). Amsterdam: Elsevier.

Kim, C.-Y., & Blake, R. (2005). Psychophysical magic: Rendering the visible "invisible." *Trends in Cognitive Sciences, 9,* 381–388.

Kim, N. S., & Ahn, W.-K. (2002). Clinical psychologists' theory-based representations of mental disorders predict their diagnostic reasoning and memory. *Journal of Experimental Psychology: General, 131,* 451–476.

Kimberg, D. Y., D'Esposito, M., & Farah, M. J. (1998). Cognitive functions in the prefrontal cortex in working memory and executive control. *Current Directions in Psychological Science, 6,* 185–192.

King, R. N., & Koehler, D. J. (2000). Illusory correlations in graphological inference. *Journal of Experimental Psychology: Applied, 6,* 336–348.

Klahr, D., & Simon, H. A. (2001). What have psychologists (and others) discovered about the process of scientific discovery? *Current Directions in Psychological Science, 10,* 75–79.

Klauer, K. C., Musch, J., & Naumer, B. (2000). On belief bias in syllogistic reasoning. *Psychological Review, 107,* 852–884.

Klauer, K. C., & Zhao, Z. (2004). Double dissociations in visual and spatial short-term memory. *Journal of Experimental Psychology: General, 133,* 355–381.

Klayman, J., & Brown, K. (1993). Debias the environment instead of the judge: An alternative approach to reducing error in diagnostic (and other) judgment. *Cognition, 49,* 97–122.

Knoblich, G., Ohlsson, S., & Raney, G. E. (2001). An eye movement study of insight problem solving. *Memory & Cognition, 29,* 1000–1009.

Knowlton, B., & Foerde, K. (2008). Neural representations of nondeclarative memories. *Current Directions in Psychological Science, 17,* 107–111.

Koch, C., & Tsuchiya, N. (2007). Attention and consciousness: Two distinct brain processes. *Trends in Cognitive Sciences, 11,* 16–22.

Kohler, W. (1969). *The task of Gestalt psychology.* Princeton, NJ: Princeton University Press.

Komatsu, L. (1992). Recent views of conceptual structure. *Psychological Bulletin, 112,* 500–526.

Kopelman, M. D., & Kapur, N. (2001). The loss of episodic memories in retrograde amnesia: Single-case and group studies. In A. D. Baddeley, J. P. Aggleton, & M. A. Conway (Eds.), *Episodic memory: New directions in research* (pp. 110–131). New York: Oxford University Press.

Kosslyn, S. M. (1976). Can imagery be distinguished from other forms of internal representation? Evidence from studies of information retrieval times. *Memory & Cognition, 4,* 291–297.

Kosslyn, S. M. (1980). *Image and mind.* Cambridge, MA: Harvard University Press.

Kosslyn, S. M. (1983). *Ghosts in the mind's machine.* New York: Norton.

Kosslyn, S. M. (1994). *Image and brain: The resolution of the imagery debate.* Cambridge, MA: MIT Press.

Kosslyn, S. M., Ball, T. M., & Reiser, B. J. (1978). Visual images preserve metric spatial information: Evidence from studies of image scanning. *Journal of Experimental Psychology: Human Perception and Performance, 4,* 1–20.

Kosslyn, S. M., Pascual-Leone, A., Felician, O., Camposano, S., Keenan, J. P., Thompson, W. L., et al. (1999). The role of area 17 in visual imagery: Convergent evidence from PET and rTMS. *Science, 284,* 167–170.

Kosslyn, S. M., & Thompson, W. L. (1999). Shared mechanisms in visual imagery and visual perception: Insights from cognitive neuroscience. In M. S. Gazzaniga (Ed.), *The new cognitive neurosciences* (pp. 975–986). Cambridge, MA: MIT Press.

Kosslyn, S. M., & Thompson, W. L. (2003). When is early visual cortex activated during mental imagery? *Psychological Bulletin, 129,* 723–746.

Kozhevnikov, M., Kosslyn, S., & Shephard, J. (2005). Spatial versus object visualizers: A new characterization of visual cognitive style. *Memory & Cognition, 33,* 710–726.

Kroll, J. F., & Potter, M. C. (1984). Recognizing words, pictures, and concepts: A comparison of lexical, object, and reality decisions. *Journal of Verbal Learning and Verbal Behavior, 23,* 39–66.

Krosnick, J., Miller, J., & Tichy, M. (2004). A recognized need for ballot reform: Effects of candidate name order. In A. Crigler, M. Just, & E. McCaffery (Eds.), *Rethinking the vote: The politics and prospects of American election reform* (pp. 51–74). New York: Oxford University Press.

Kruglanski, A., & Orehek, E. (2007). Partitioning the domain of social inference: Dual mode and systems models and their alternatives. *Annual Review of Psychology, 58,* 291–316.

Krynski, T., & Tenenbaum, J. (2007). The role of causality in judgment under uncertainty. *Journal of Experimental Psychology: General, 136,* 430–450.

Kumon-Nakamura, S., Glucksberg, S., & Brown, M. (1995). How about another piece of pie: The allusional pretense theory of discourse irony. *Journal of Experimental Psychology: General, 124,* 3–21.

Kunar, M., Carter, R., Cohen, M., & Horowitz, T. (2008). Telephone conversation impairs sustained visual attention via a central bottleneck. *Psychonomic Bulletin & Review, 15,* 1135–1140.

Kunda, Z. (1990). The case for motivated reasoning. *Psychological Bulletin, 108,* 480–498.

Kunda, Z., & Nisbett, R. E. (1986). The psychometrics of everyday life. *Cognitive Psychology, 18,* 195–224.

Kurtz, K., & Loewenstein, J. (2007). Converging on a new role for analogy in problem solving and retrieval: When two problems are better than one. *Memory & Cognition, 35,* 334–341.

Kyllonen, P. C., & Cristal, R. E. (1990). Reasoning ability is (little more than) working-memory capacity? *Intelligence, 14,* 389–433.

LaBar, K. (2007). Beyond fear: Emotional memory mechanisms in the human brain. *Current Directions in Psychological Science, 16,* 173–177.

LaBar, K., & Cabeza, R. (2006). Cognitive neuroscience of emotional memory. *Nature Reviews Neuroscience, 7*, 54–64.

Lachter, J., & Bever, T. G. (1988). The relation between linguistic structure and associative theories of language learning—A critique of some connectionist learning models. *Cognition, 28*, 195–247.

Lai, C. S., Fisher, S. E., Hurst, J. A., Vargha-Khadem, F., & Monaco, A. P. (2001). A forkhead-domain gene is mutated in a severe speech and language disorder. *Nature, 413*, 519–522.

Lakoff, G. (1987). Cognitive models and prototype theory. In U. Neisser (Ed.), *Concepts and conceptual development* (pp. 63–100). Cambridge, England: Cambridge University Press.

Lamble, D., Kauranen, T., Laakso, M., & Summala, H. (1999). Cognitive load and detection thresholds in car following situations: Safety implications for using mobile (cellular) telephones while driving. *Accident Analysis & Prevention, 31*, 617–623.

Lampinen, J., Meier, C., Arnal, J., & Leding, J. (2005). Compelling untruths: Content borrowing and vivid false memories. *Journal of Experimental Psychology: Learning, Memory & Cognition, 31*, 954–963.

Lane, S., & Zaragoza, M. (1995). The recollective experience of cross-modality confusion errors. *Memory & Cognition, 23*, 607–610.

Lane, S. M., & Schooler, J. W. (2004). Skimming the surface: Verbal overshadowing of analogical retrieval. *Psychological Science, 15*, 715–719.

Langer, E. (1989). *Mindfulness*. Reading, MA: Addison-Wesley.

Larrick, R., Nisbett, R., & Morgan, J. (1993). Who uses the normative rules of choice? In R. Nisbet (Ed.), *Rules for reasoning* (pp. 277–294). Hillsdale, NJ: Erlbaum.

Lassiter, G. D. (2000). The relative contributions of recognition and search-evaluation processes in high-level chess performance: Comment on Gobet and Simon. *Psychological Science, 11*, 172–174.

Lavie, N. (1997). Visual feature integration and focused attention: Response competition from multiple distractor features. *Perception & Psychophysics, 59*, 543–556.

Lavie, N. (2001). Capacity limits in selective attention: Behavioral evidence and implications for neural activity. In J. Braun, C. Koch, & J. L. Davis (Eds.), *Visual attention and cortical circuits* (pp. 49–68). Cambridge, MA: MIT Press.

Lavie, N. (2005). Distracted and confused? Selective attention under load. *Trends in Cognitive Sciences, 9*, 75–82.

Lavric, A., Pizzagalli, D., Forstmeier, S., & Rippon, G. (2001). Mapping dissociations in verb morphology. *Trends in Cognitive Sciences, 5*, 301–308.

Legrenzi, P., Girotto, V., & Johnson-Laird, P. (1993). Focussing in reasoning and decision making. *Cognition, 49*, 37–66.

Lehman, D. R., & Nisbett, R. (1990). A longitudinal study of the effects of undergraduate education on reasoning. *Developmental Psychology, 26*, 952–960.

Lemaire, P., & Siegler, R. (1995). Four aspects of strategic change: Contributions to children's learning of multiplication. *Journal of Experimental Psychology: General, 124*, 83–97.

Levin, D., Takarae, Y., Miner, A., & Keil, F. (2001). Efficient visual search by category: Specifying the features that mark the difference between artifacts and animals in preattentive vision. *Perception and Psychophysics, 63*, 676–697.

Levin, D. T., & Simons, D. J. (1997). Failure to detect changes to attended objects in motion pictures. *Psychonomic Bulletin & Review, 4*, 501–506.

Levin, I., & Gaeth, G. (1988). How consumers are affected by the framing of attribute information before and after consuming the product. *Journal of Consumer Research, 15*, 374–378.

Levin, I., Schnittjer, S., & Thee, S. (1988). Information framing effects in social and personal decisions. *Journal of Experimental Social Psychology, 24*, 520–529.

Levine, L. & Bluck S. (2004). Painting with broad strokes: Happiness and the malleability of event memory. *Cognition and Emotion, 18*, 559–574.

Levine, L. J. (1997). Reconstructing memory for emotions. *Journal of Experimental Psychology: General, 126*, 165–177.

Levinson, S. C., Kita, S., Haun, D. B. M., & Rasch, B. H. (2002). Returning the tables: Language affects spatial reasoning. *Cognition, 84*, 155–188.

Levy, J., & Pashler, H. (2008). Task prioritisation in multitasking duringn driving: Opportunity to abort a concurrent task does not insulate braking responses from dual-task slowing. *Applied Cognitive Psychology, 22*, 507–525.

Lewis, C., & Keren, G. (1999). On the difficulties underlying Bayesian reasoning: A comment on Gigerenzer and Hoffrage. *Psychological Review, 106*, 411–416.

Li, P., & Gleitman, L. R. (2002). Turning the tables: Language and spatial reasoning. *Cognition, 83*, 265–294.

Liberman, A. (1970). The grammars of speech and language. *Cognitive Psychology, 1*, 301–323.

Liberman, A., Harris, K., Hoffman, H., & Griffith, B. (1957). The discrimination of speech sounds within and across phoneme boundaries. *Journal of Experimental Psychology, 54*, 358–368.

Liberman, N., & Klar, Y. (1996). Hypothesis testing in Wason's selection task: Social exchange cheating detection or task understanding. *Cognition, 58*, 127–156.

Lichtenstein, S., & Slovic, P. (2006). *The construction of preference*. New York: Cambridge University Press.

Lichtenstein, S., Slovic, P., Fischhoff, B., Layman, M., & Combs, B.

(1978). Judged frequency of lethal events. *Journal of Experimental Psychology: Human Learning and Memory, 4*, 551–578.

Lidz, J., Waxman, S., & Freedman, J. (2003). What infants know about syntax but couldn't have learned: Experimental evidence for syntactic structure at 18 months. *Cognition, 89*, B65–B73.

Light, L. L., & Carter-Sobell, L. (1970). Effects of changed semantic context on recognition memory. *Journal of Verbal Learning and Verbal Behavior, 9*, 1–11.

Linton, M. (1975). Memory for real-world events. In D. A. Norman & D. E. Rumelhart (Eds.), *Explorations in cognition* (pp. 376–404). San Francisco: Freeman.

Linton, M. (1978). Real world memory after six years: An in vivo study of very long term memory. In M. M. Gruneberg, P. E. Morris, & R. N. Sykes (Eds.), *Practical aspects of memory* (pp. 69–76). London: Academic Press.

Linton, M. (1982). Transformations of memory in everyday life. In U. Neisser (Ed.), *Memory observed: Remembering in natural contexts* (pp. 77–92). San Francisco: Freeman.

Linton, M. (1986). Ways of searching and the contents of memory. In D. C. Rubin (Ed.), *Autobiographical memory* (pp. 50–67). Cambridge, England: Cambridge University Press.

Lisker, L., & Abramson, A. (1970). *The voicing dimension: Some experiments in comparative phonetics.* Paper presented at the Proceedings of the Sixth International Congress of Phonetic Sciences, Prague.

Lockhart, R. S., Craik, F. I. M., & Jacoby, L. (1976). Depth of processing, recall, and recognition. In J. Brown (Ed.), *Recall and recognition* (pp. 75–102). New York: Wiley.

Loewenstein, G., & Schkade, D. (1999). Wouldn't it be nice? Predicting future feelings. In D. Kahneman, E. Diener, & N. Schwarz (Eds.), *Well-being: The foundations of hedonic psychology* (pp. 85–105). New York: Russell Sage Foundation.

Loewenstein, G., Weber, E. U., Hsee, C. K., & Welch, N. (2001). Risk as feelings. *Psychological Bulletin, 127*, 267–286.

Loewenstein, J., Thompson, L., & Gentner, D. (1999). Analogical encoding facilitates knowledge transfer in negotiation. *Psychonomic Bulletin & Review, 6*, 586–597.

Loftus, E., & Greene, E. (1980). Warning: Even memory for faces may be contagious. *Law and Human Behavior, 4*, 323–334.

Loftus, E. F. (1979). *Eyewitness testimony.* Cambridge, MA: Harvard University Press.

Loftus, E. F. (1997). Memory for a past that never was. *Current Directions in Psychological Science, 6*, 60–64.

Loftus, E. F. (2003). Make-believe memories. *American Psychologist, 58*, 867–873.

Loftus, E. F., & Guyer, M. J. (2002). Who abused Jane Doe? The hazards of the single case history. *Skeptical Inquirer, 26*, 24–32.

Loftus, E. F., & Ketcham, K. (1991). *Witness for the defense: The accused, the eyewitness, and the expert who puts memory on trial.* New York: St. Martin's.

Loftus, E. F., & Pickrell, J. E. (1995). The formation of false memories. *Psychiatric Annals, 25*, 720–725.

Logan, G. D. (2003). Executive control of thought and action: In search of the wild homunculus. *Current Directions in Psychological Science, 12*, 45–48.

Logie, R. H., & Della Salla, S. (2005). Disorders of visuospatial working memory. In P. Shah & A. Miyake (Eds.), *The Cambridge handbook of visuospatial thinking* (pp. 81–120). New York: Cambridge University Press.

Logie, R. H., Engelkamp, J., Dehn, D., & Rudkin, S. (1999). Actions, mental actions, and working memory. In M. Denis, C. Cornoldi, J. Engelkamp, M. De Vega, & R.

H. Logie (Eds.), *Imagery, language, and the representation of space* (pp. 161–184). Hove, England: Psychology Press.

Lucas, M. (2000). Semantic priming without association: A meta-analytic review. *Psychonomic Bulletin & Review, 7*, 618–630.

Luchins, A. (1942). *Mechanization in problem solving: The effect of Einstellung.* (Psychological Monographs, Vol. 54, No. 6 [whole no. 248]). Evanston, IL: American Psychological Association.

Luchins, A., & Luchins, E. (1950). New experimental attempts at preventing mechanization in problem solving. *Journal of General Psychology, 42*, 279–297.

Luchins, A., & Luchins, E. (1959). *Rigidity of behavior: A variational approach to the effects of Einstellung.* Eugene: University of Oregon Books.

Luminet, O., & Curci, A. (Eds.). (2009). *Flashbulb memories: New issues and new perspectives.* New York: Psychology Press.

MacDonald, A. W., Cohen, J. D., Stenger, V. A., & Carter, C. S. (2000). Dissociating the role of dorso-lateral prefrontal cortex and anterior cingulate cortex in cognitive control. *Science, 288*, 1835–1837.

MacDonald, J., & Lavie, N. (2008). Load induced blindness. *Journal of Experimental Psychology: Human Perception & Performance, 34*, 1078–1091.

MacGregor, J. N., Ormerod, T. C., & Chronicle, E. P. (2001). Information processing and insight: A process model of performance on the 9-dot and related problems. *Journal of Experimental Psychology: Learning, Memory and Cognition, 27*, 176–201.

Mack, A. (2003). Inattentional blindness: Looking without seeing. *Current Directions in Psychological Science, 12*, 180–184.

Mack, A., & Rock, I. (1998). *Inattentional blindness.* Cambridge, MA: MIT Press.

MacLeod, M. D., & Macrae, C. N. (2001). Gone but not forgotten: The transient nature of retrieval-induced forgetting. *Psychological Science, 12,* 148–152.

Mahon, B., & Caramazza, A. (2009). Concepts and categories: A cogniive neuropsychological perspective. *Annual Review of Psychology, 60,* 27–51.

Mahoney, M., & DeMonbreun, B. (1978). Problem-solving bias in scientists. *Cognitive Therapy and Research, 1,* 229–238.

Maia, T., & Cleeremans, A. (2005). Consciousness: Converging insights from connectionist modeling and neuroscience. *Trends in Cognitive Sciences, 9,* 397–404.

Maia, T. V., & McClelland, J. L. (2005). The somatic marker hypothesis: Still many questions but no answers. *Trends in Cognitive Sciences, 9,* 162–164.

Maier, N. R. F. (1931). Reasoning in humans: II. The solution of a problem and its appearance in consciousness. *Journal of Comparative Psychology, 12,* 181–194.

Majid, A. (2002). Frames of reference and language concepts. *Trends in Cognitive Sciences, 6,* 503–504.

Majid, A., Bowerman, M., Kita, S., Haun, D. B. M., & Levinson, S. (2004). Can language restructure cognition? The case for space. *Trends in Cognitive Sciences, 8,* 108–114.

Malt, B. C., & Smith, E. E. (1984). Correlated properties in natural categories. *Journal of Verbal Learning and Verbal Behavior, 23,* 250–269.

Mandler, G. (2008). Familiarity breeds attempts: A critical review of dual-process theories of recognition. *Perspectives on Psychological Science, 3,* 390–399.

Mandler, J. M., & Ritchey, G. H. (1977). Long-term memory for pictures. *Journal of Experimental Psychology: Human Learning and Memory, 3,* 386–396.

Marcus, G. B. (1986). Stability and change in political attitudes: Observe, recall, and "explain." *Political Behavior, 8,* 21–44.

Marcus, G. F., Pinker, S., Ullman, M., Hollander, M., Rosen, T., & Xu, F. (1992). *Overregularization in language acquisition* (Monographs of the Society for Research in Child Development, Vol. 57, No. 4 [serial no. 228]). Chicago: University of Chicago Press.

Marcus, G. F., Vijayan, S., Rao, S. B., & Vishton, P. M. (1999). Rule learning by seven-month-old infants. *Science, 283,* 77–80.

Markman, A. B. (1997). Constraints on analogical inference. *Cognitive Science, 21,* 373–418.

Markman, A. B., & Gentner, D. (2001). Thinking. *Annual Review of Psychology, 52,* 223–247.

Marks, D. (1983). Mental imagery and consciousness: A theoretical review. In A. Sheikh (Ed.), *Imagery: Current theory, research and application* (pp. 96–130). New York: Wiley.

Marmor, G. S., & Zabeck, L. A. (1976). Mental rotation by the blind: Does mental rotation depend on visual imagery? *Journal of Experimental Psychology: Human Perception and Performance, 2,* 515–521.

Marslen-Wilson, W. D. (1987). Functional parallelism in spoken word recognition. *Cognition, 25,* 71–102.

Marslen-Wilson, W. D. (1990). Activation, competition, and frequency in lexical access. In G. T. Altmann (Ed.), *Cognitive models of speech processing: Psycholinguistic and computational perspectives* (pp. 148–172). Cambridge, MA: MIT Press.

Marslen-Wilson, W. D., & Teuber, H. L. (1975). Memory for remote events in anterograde amnesia: Recognition of public figures from news photographs. *Neuropsychologia, 13,* 353–364.

Marslen-Wilson, W. D., & Tyler, L. (1987). Against modularity. In J. L. Garfield (Ed.), *Modularity in knowledge representation and natural-language understanding* (pp. 37–62). Cambridge, MA: MIT Press.

Martin, M., & Jones, G. V. (2006). Visual sharpness contingency in recognition memory for orientation: Mnemonic illusion suppressed by sensory signature. *Journal of Experimental Psychology: General, 135,* 542–552.

Martin, R. C. (2003). Language processing: Functional organization and neuroanatomical basis. *Annual Review of Psychology, 54,* 55–89.

Massaro, D. (1994). Psychological aspects of speech perception. In M. A. Gernsbacher (Ed.), *Handbook of psycholinguistics* (pp. 219–263). New York: Academic Press.

Massimini, M., Ferrarelli, F., Huber, R., Esser, S., Singh, H., & Tononi, G. (2005). Breakdown of cortical effective connectivity during sleep. *Science, 309,* 2228–2232.

Mather, M., Shafir, E., & Johnson, M. K. (2000). Misremembrance of options past: Source monitoring and choice. *Psychological Science, 11,* 132–138.

Mayr, U. (2004). Conflict, consciousness, and control. *Trends in Cognitive Sciences, 8,* 145–148.

Mazzoni, G., Loftus, E. F., & Kirsch, I. (2001). Changing beliefs about implausible autobiographical events. *Journal of Experimental Psychology: Applied, 7,* 51–59.

Mazzoni, G., & Lynn, S. (2007). Using hypnosis in eyewitness memory. In D. Ross, M. Toglia, R. Lindsay, & D. Read (Eds.), *Handbook of eyewitness memory: Vol. 1. Memory for events.* Mahwah, NJ: Erlbaum.

Mazzoni, G., & Memon, A. (2003). Imagination can create false autobiographical memories. *Psychological Science, 14,* 186–188.

McCann, R., & Johnston, J. (1992). Locus of the single-channel bottleneck in dual-task interference. *Journal of Experimental Psychology: Human Perception and Performance, 18,* 471–484.

McClelland, J., Mirman, D., & Holt, L. (2006). Are there interactive processes in speech perception? *Trends in Cognitive Sciences, 10*, 363–369.

McClelland, J., & Rogers, T. (2003). The parallel-distributed processing approach to semantic cognition. *Nature Reviews Neuroscience, 4*, 310–322.

McClelland, J. L., McNaughton, B. C., & O'Reilly, R. C. (1995). Why there are complementary learning systems in the hippocampus and neocortex: Insights from the successes and failures of connectionist models of learning and memory. *Psychological Review, 102*, 419–457.

McClelland, J. L., & Rumelhart, D. E. (1981). An interactive model of context effects in letter perception. Part 1. An account of basic findings. *Psychological Review, 88*, 375–407.

McCloskey, M., & Cohen, N. J. (1989). Catastrophic interference in connectionist networks: The sequential learning problem. In G. H. Bower (Ed.), *The psychology of learning and motivation*, Vol. 23 (pp. 109–165). New York: Academic Press.

McCloskey, M., & Glucksberg, S. (1978). Natural categories. Well-defined or fuzzy sets? *Memory & Cognition, 6*, 462–472.

McDaniel, M., & Einstein, G. (1986). Bizarre imagery as an effective mnemonic aid: The importance of distinctiveness. *Journal of Experimental Psychology: Learning, Memory and Cognition, 12*, 54–65.

McDaniel, M., & Einstein, G. (1990). Bizarre imagery: Mnemonic benefits and theoretical implications. In R. Logie & M. Denis (Eds.), *Mental images in human cognition* (pp. 183–192). New York: North Holland.

McDermott, K., & Roediger, H. (1994). Effects of imagery on perceptual implicit memory tests. *Journal of Experimental Psychology: Learning, Memory and Cognition, 20*, 1379–1390.

McDermott, K. B., & Roediger, H. L. (1998). False recognition of associates can be resistant to an explicit warning to subjects and an immediate recognition probe. *Journal of Memory & Language, 39*, 508–520.

McEvoy, C. L., Nelson, D., & Komatsu, T. (1999). What is the connection between true and false memories? The differential role of interitem associations in recall and recognition. *Journal of Experimental Psychology: Learning, Memory and Cognition, 25*, 1177–1194.

McGaugh, J. L. (2000). Memory—A century of consolidation. *Science, 287*, 248–251.

McGuire, M. J., & Maki, R. H. (2001). When knowing more means less: The effect of fan on metamemory judgment. *Journal of Experimental Psychology: Learning, Memory and Cognition, 27*, 1172–1179.

McIntosh, A. R., Rajah, M. N., & Lobaugh, N. J. (1999). Interactions of prefrontal cortex in relation to awareness in sensory learning. *Science, 284*, 1531–1533.

McKelvie, S. (1995). The VVIQ as a psychometric test of individual differences in visual imagery vividness: A critical quantitative review and plea for direction. *Journal of Mental Imagery, 19*(3&4), 1–106.

McKone, E., Kanwisher, N., & Duchaine, B. C. (2007). Can generic expertise explain special processing for faces? *Trends in Cognitive Sciences, 11*, 8–15.

McNally, R. J. (2003). Recovering memories of trauma: A view from the laboratory. *Current Directions in Psychological Science, 12*, 32–35.

McNally, R. J., Lasko, N., Clancy, S. A., Macklin, M. L., Pitman, R. K., & Orr, S. P. (2004). Psychophysiological responding during script-driven imagery in people reporting abduction by space aliens. *Psychological Science, 15*, 493–497.

Meadows, J. C. (1974). Disturbed perception of colours associated with localized cerebral lesions. *Brain, 97*, 615–632.

Medin, D. L. (1989). Concepts and conceptual structure. *American Psychologist, 44*, 1469–1481.

Medin, D. L., Coley, J. D., Storms, G., & Hayes, B. K. (2003). A relevance theory of induction. *Psychonomic Bulletin & Review, 10*, 517–532.

Medin, D. L., Goldstone, R., & Gentner, D. (1993). Respects for similarity. *Psychological Review, 100*, 254–278.

Medin, D. L., & Ortony, A. (1989). Psychological essentialism. In S. Vosniadou & A. Ortony (Eds.), *Similarity and analogical reasoning* (pp. 179–195). New York: Cambridge University Press.

Medin, D. L., Schwartz, H., Blok, S. V., & Birnbaum, L. A. (1999). The semantic side of decision making. *Psychonomic Bulletin & Review, 6*, 562–569.

Mednick, S. (1962). The associative basis of the creative process. *Psychological Review, 69*, 220–232.

Mednick, S., & Mednick, M. (1967). *Examiner's manual, Remote Associates Test*. Boston: Houghton Mifflin.

Medvec, V. H., Madey, S. F., & Gilovich, T. (1995). When less is more: Counterfactual thinking and satisfaction among Olympic medalists. *Journal of Personality & Social Psychology, 60*, 603–610.

Mellers, B., Chang, S.-J., Birnbaum, M., & Ordóñez, L. (1992). Preferences, prices, and ratings in risky decision making. *Journal of Experimental Psychology: Human Perception and Performance, 18*, 347–361.

Mellers, B., Hertwig, R., & Kahneman, D. (2001). Do frequency representations eliminate conjunction effects? An exercise in adversarial collaboration. *Psychological Science, 12*, 269–275.

Mellers, B., Schwartz, A., & Ritov, I. (1999). Emotion-based choice. *Journal of Experimental Psychology: General, 128*, 332–345.

Mellers, B. A., & McGraw, A. P. (1999). How to improve Bayesian reasoning: Comment on Gigerenzer and Hoffrage. *Psychological Review, 106*, 417–424.

Mervis, C. B., Catlin, J., & Rosch, E. (1976). Relationships among goodness-of-example, category norms and word frequency. *Bulletin of the Psychonomic Society, 7*, 268–284.

Metcalfe, J. (1986). Premonitions of insight predict impending error. *Journal of Experimental Psychology: Learning, Memory and Cognition, 12*, 623–634.

Metcalfe, J., & Weibe, D. (1987). Intuition in insight and noninsight problem solving. *Memory & Cognition, 15*, 238–246.

Meyer, D. E., & Schvaneveldt, R. W. (1971). Facilitation in recognizing pairs of words: Evidence of a dependence between retrieval operations. *Journal of Experimental Psychology, 90*, 227–234.

Meyer, D. E., Schvaneveldt, R. W., & Ruddy, M. G. (1974). Functions of graphemic and phonemic codes in visual word recognition. *Memory & Cognition, 2*, 309–321.

Michel, C., Rossion, B., Han, J., Chung, C.-S., & Caldara, R. (2006). Holistic processing is finely tuned for faces of one's own race. *Psychological Science, 17*, 608–615.

Mill, J. S. (1874). *A system of logic* (8th ed.). New York: Harper.

Miller, A. (1986). *Imagery in scientific thought*. Cambridge, MA: MIT Press.

Miller, E. K., & Cohen, J. D. (2001). An integrative theory of prefrontal cortex function. *Annual Review of Neuroscience, 24*, 167–202.

Miller, G. A. (1951). *Language and communication*. New York: McGraw-Hill.

Miller, G. A. (1956). The magical number seven plus or minus two: Some limits on our capacity for processing information. *Psychological Review, 63*, 81–97.

Miller, G. A. (1962). *Psychology: The science of mental life*. New York: Harper & Row.

Miller, G. A. (1991). *The science of words*. New York: Freeman.

Miller, G. A., Bruner, J. S., & Postman, L. (1954). Familiarity of letter sequences and tachistoscopic identification. *Journal of General Psychology, 50*, 129–139.

Miller, G. A., Galanter, E., & Pribram, K. (1960). *Plans and the structure of behavior*. New York: Holt, Rinehart and Winston.

Miller, G. A., & Nicely, P. (1955). An analysis of perceptual confusions among some English consonants. *Journal of the Acoustical Society of America, 27*, 338–352.

Milliken, B., Joordens, S., Merikle, P., & Seiffert, A. (1998). Selective attention: A reevaluation of the implications of negative priming. *Psychological Review, 105*, 203–229.

Milliken, B., & Tipper, S. (1998). Attention and inhibition. In H. Pashler (Ed.), *Attention* (pp. 191–221). Hove, England: Psychology Press.

Milner, B. (1966). Amnesia following operation on the temporal lobes. In C. W. M. Whitty & O. L. Zangwill (Eds.), *Amnesia* (pp. 109–133). London: Butterworths.

Milner, B. (1970). Memory and the medial temporal regions of the brain. In K. H. Pribram & D. E. Broadbent (Eds.), *Biology of memory* (pp. 29–48). New York: Academic Press.

Minda, J. P., & Smith, J. D. (2001). Prototypes in category learning: The effects of category size, category structure and stimulus complexity. *Journal of Experimental Psychology: Learning, Memory and Cognition, 27*, 775–799.

Mitroff, I. (1981). Scientists and confirmation bias. In R. Tweney, M. Doherty, & C. Mynatt (Eds.), *On scientific thinking* (pp. 170–175). New York: Columbia University Press.

Miyashita, Y. (1995). How the brain creates imagery: Projection to primary visual cortex. *Science, 268*, 1719–1720.

Moons, W. G., Mackie, D. M., & Garcia-Marques, T. (2009). The impact of repetition-induced familarity on agreement with weak and strong arguments. *Journal of Personality & Social Psychology, 96*, 32–44.

Moore, C. M., & Egeth, H. (1997). Perception without attention: Evidence of grouping under conditions of inattention. *Journal of Experimental Psychology: Human Perception and Performance, 23*, 339–352.

Moray, N. (1959). Attention in dichotic listening: Affective cues and the influence of instructions. *Quarterly Journal of Experimental Psychology, 11*, 56–60.

Morris, M., & Murphy, G. (1990). Converging operations on a basic level in event taxonomies. *Memory & Cognition, 18*, 407–418.

Morton, J. (1969). Interaction of information in word recognition. *Psychological Review, 76*, 165–178.

Morton, J. (1970). A functional model of human memory. In D. Norman (Ed.), *Models of human memory* (pp. 203–254). New York: Academic Press.

Moscovitch, M. (1982). Multiple dissociations of function in amnesia. In L. S. Cermak (Ed.), *Human memory and amnesia* (pp. 337–370). Hillsdale, NJ: Erlbaum.

Most, S. B., Scholl, B. J., Clifford, E. R., & Simons, D. J. (2005). What you see is what you set: Sustained inattentional blindness and the capture of awareness. *Psychological Review, 112*, 217–242.

Most, S. B., Simons, D. J., Scholl, B. J., Jimenez, R., Clifford, E., & Chabris, C. F. (2001). How not to be seen: The contribution of similarity and selective ignoring to sustained inattentional blindness. *Psychological Science, 12*, 9–17.

Murdock, B. B., Jr. (1962). The serial position effect of free recall. *Journal of Experimental Psychology, 64*, 482–488.

Murphy, G. L. (2003). *The big book of concepts*. Cambridge, MA: MIT Press.

Murphy, G. L., & Medin, D. L. (1985). The role of theories in conceptual coherence. *Psychological Review, 92*, 289–316.

Murphy, G. L., & Ross, B. H. (2005). The two faces of typicality in category-based induction. *Cognition, 95*, 175–200.

Murphy, S. T. (2001). Feeling without thinking: Affective primacy and the nonconscious processing of emotion. In J. A. Bargh & D. K. Apsley (Eds.), *Unraveling the complexities of social life: A festschrift in honor of Robert B. Zajonc* (pp. 39–53). Washington, DC: American Psychological Association.

Myers, D. G. (2000). *The American paradox: Spiritual hunger in an age of plenty*. New Haven, CT: Yale University Press.

Mynatt, C., Doherty, M., & Tweney, R. (1977). Confirmation bias in a simulated research environment: An experimental study of scientific inference. *Quarterly Journal of Experimental Psychology, 29*, 85–95.

Mynatt, C., Doherty, M., & Tweney, R. (1978). Consequences of confirmation and disconfirmation in a simulated research environment. *Quarterly Journal of Experimental Psychology, 30*, 395–406.

Nadel, L., & Jacobs, W. J. (1998). Traumatic memory is special. *Current Directions in Psychological Science, 7*, 154–157.

Nadel, L., & Moscovitch, M. (2001). The hippocampal complex and long-term memory revisited. *Trends in Cognitive Sciences, 5*, 228–230.

Nakamura, J., & Csikszentmihalyi, M. (2001). Catalytic creativity: The case of Linus Pauling. *American Psychologist, 56*, 337–341.

Naqvi, N., Shiv, B., & Bechara, A. (2006). The role of emotion in decision making. *Current Directions in Psychological Science, 15*, 260–264.

Nee, D., Berman, M., Moore, K., & Jonides, J. (2008). Neuroscientific evidence about the distinction between short- and long-term memory. *Current Directions in Psycholkogical Science, 17*, 102–106.

Needham, D., & Begg, I. (1991). Problem-oriented training promotes spontaneous analogical transfer:

Memory-oriented training promotes memory for training. *Memory & Cognition, 19*, 543–557.

Neely, J. H. (1977). Semantic priming and retrieval from lexical memory: Role of inhibitionless spreading activation and limited capacity attention. *Journal of Experimental Psychology: General, 106*, 226–254.

Neisser, U. (1967). *Cognitive psychology*. New York: Appleton-Century-Crofts.

Neisser, U. (1987). From direct perception to conceptual structure. In U. Neisser (Ed.), *Concepts and conceptual development* (pp. 11–24). Cambridge, England: Cambridge University Press.

Neisser, U., & Becklen, R. (1975). Selective looking: Attending to visually significant events. *Cognitive Psychology, 7*, 480–494.

Neisser, U., & Harsch, N. (1992). Phantom flashbulbs: False recollections of hearing the news about *Challenger*. In E. Winograd & U. Neisser (Eds.), *Affect and accuracy in recall: Studies of "flashbulb" memories* (pp. 9–31). Cambridge, England: Cambridge University Press.

Neisser, U., Winograd, E., & Weldon, M. S. (1991, November). *Remembering the earthquake: "What I experienced" vs. "How I heard the news."* Paper presented at the meeting of the Psychonomic Society, San Francisco, CA.

Nelson, T. O. (1976). Reinforcement and human memory. In W. K. Estes (Ed.), *Handbook of learning and cognitive processes*, Vol. 3. Hillsdale, NJ: Erlbaum.

Newcombe, F., Ratcliff, G., & Damasio, H. (1987). Dissociable visual and spatial impairments following right posterior cerebral lesions: Clinical, neuropsychological and anatomical evidence. *Neuropsychologia, 25*, 149–161.

Newcombe, N. S., Drummey, A. B., Fox, N. A., Lie, E., & Ottinger-Alberts, W. (2000). Remembering early childhood: How much, how, and why

(or why not). *Current Directions in Psychological Science, 9*, 55–58.

Newell, A., & Simon, H. (1972). *Human problem solving*. Englewood Cliffs, NJ: Prentice-Hall.

Newstead, S., Pollard, P., Evans, J., & Allen, J. (1992). The source of belief bias effects in syllogistic reasoning. *Cognition, 45*, 257–284.

Nickerson, R. S., & Adams, M. J. (1979). Long-term memory for a common object. *Cognitive Psychology, 11*, 287–307.

Nisbett, R. (Ed.). (1993). *Rules for reasoning*. Hillsdale, NJ: Erlbaum.

Nisbett, R., Krantz, D. H., Jepson, C., & Kunda, Z. (1983). The use of statistical heuristics in everyday inductive reasoning. *Psychological Review, 90*, 339–363.

Nisbett, R., & Ross, L. (1980). *Human inference: Strategies and shortcomings of social judgment*. Englewood Cliffs, NJ: Prentice-Hall.

Nisbett, R., & Schachter, S. (1966). Cognitive manipulation of pain. *Journal of Experimental Social Psychology, 2*, 277–236.

Nisbett, R., & Wilson, T. (1977). Telling more than we can know: Verbal reports on mental processes. *Psychological Review, 84*, 231–259.

Norman, D., Rumelhart, D. E., & Group, T. L. R. (1975). *Explorations in cognition*. San Francisco: Freeman.

Norman, D., & Shallice, T. (1986). Attention to action: Willed and automatic control of behavior. In R. Davidson, G. Schwartz, & D. Shapiro (Eds.), *Consciousness and self-regulation* (pp. 1–18). New York: Plenum.

Norman, D. A. (1981). Categorization of action slips. *Psychological Review, 88*, 1–15.

Norman, K., Polyn, S., Detre, G., & Haxby, J. (2006). Beyond mind-reading: Multi-voxel pattern analysis of fMRI data. *Trends in Cognitive Sciences, 10*, 424–430.

Noveck, I., & Reboul, A. (2008). Experimental pragmatics: A Gricean turn in the study of language. *Trends in Cognitive Sciences, 12*, 425–431.

Novick, L. (1988). Analogical transfer, problem similarity and expertise. *Journal of Experimental Psychology: Learning, Memory and Cognition, 14*, 510–520.

Novick, L., & Holyoak, K. (1991). Mathematical problem solving by analogy. *Journal of Experimental Psychology: Learning, Memory and Cognition, 17*, 398–415.

Oakhill, J., & Garnham, A. (1993). On theories of belief bias in syllogistic reasoning. *Cognition, 46*, 87–92.

Oaksford, M., & Chater, N. (1995). Information gain explains relevance which explains the selection task. *Cognition, 57*, 97–108.

Ochsner, K. N., & Schacter, D. L. (2000). A social cognitive neuroscience approach to emotion and memory. In J. C. Borod (Ed.), *The neuropsychology of emotion* (pp. 163–193). New York: Oxford University Press.

O'Connor, D., Fukui, M., Pinsk, M., & Kastner, S. (2002). Attention modulates responses in the human lateral geniculate nucleus. *Nature Neuroscience, 5*, 1203–1209.

O'Connor, M., Walbridge, M., Sandson, T., & Alexander, M. (1996). A neuropsychological analysis of Capgras syndrome. *Neuropsychiatry, Neuropsychology, and Behavioral Neurology, 9*, 265–271.

O'Craven, K. M., & Kanwisher, N. (2000). Mental imagery of faces and places activates corresponding stimulus-specific brain regions. *Journal of Cognitive Neuroscience, 12*, 1013–1023.

Öhman, A. (2002). Automaticity and the amygdala: Nonconscious responses to emotional faces. *Current Directions in Psychological Science, 11*, 62–66.

O'Kane, G., Kensinger, E. A., & Corkin, S. (2004). Evidence for semantic learning in profound amnesia: An investigation with patient H.M. *Hippocampus, 14*(4), 417–425.

Oldfield, R. (1963). Individual vocabulary and semantic currency: A preliminary study. *British Journal of Social and Clinical Psychology, 2*, 122–130.

Oliphant, G. W. (1983). Repetition and recency effects in word recognition. *Australian Journal of Psychology, 35*, 393–403.

Oppenheimer, D. M. (2004). Spontaneous discounting of availability in frequency judgment tasks. *Psychological Science, 15*, 100–105.

Oppenheimer, D. M. (2006). Consequences of erudite vernacular utilized irrespective of necessity: Problems with using long words needlessly. *Applied Cognitive Psychology, 20*, 139–156.

Oppenheimer, D. M. (2008). The secret life of fluency. *Trends in Cognitive Sciences, 12*, 237–241.

Osherson, D. N., Smith, E. E., Wilkie, O., Lopez, A., & Shafir, E. (1990). Category-based induction. *Psychological Review, 97*, 185–200.

Osman, M. (2004). An evaluation of dual-process theories of reasoning. *Psychonomic Bulletin & Review, 11*, 988–1010.

Osman, M., & Stavy, R. (2006). Development of intuitive rules: Evaluating the application of the dual-system framework to understanding children's intuitive reasoning. *Psychonomic Bulletin & Review, 13*, 935–953.

Ost, J., Vrij, A., Costall, A., & Bull, R. (2002). Crashing memories and reality monitoring: Distinguishing between perceptions, imaginations and "false memories." *Applied Cognitive Psychology, 16*, 125–134.

Overton, D. (1985). Contextual stimulus effects of drugs and internal states. In P. D. Balsam & A. Tomie (Eds.), *Context and learning* (pp. 357–384). Hillsdale, NJ: Erlbaum.

Owens, J., Bower, G. H., & Black, J. B. (1979). The "soap opera" effect in story recall. *Memory & Cognition, 7*, 185–191.

Özgen, E. (2004). Language, learning, and color perception. *Current Directions in Psychological Science, 13*, 95–98.

Özgen, E., & Davies, I. R. L. (2002). Acquisition of categorical color perception: A perceptual learning approach to the linguistic relativity hypothesis. *Journal of Experimental Psychology: General, 131*, 477–493.

Paivio, A. (1969). Mental imagery in associative learning and memory. *Psychological Review, 76*, 241–263.

Paivio, A. (1971). *Imagery and verbal processes.* New York: Holt, Rinehart & Winston.

Paivio, A., & Csapo, K. (1969). Concrete image and verbal memory codes. *Journal of Experimental Psychology, 80*, 279–285.

Paivio, A., & Okovita, H. W. (1971). Word imagery modalities and associative learning in blind and sighted subjects. *Journal of Verbal Learning and Verbal Behavior, 10*, 506–510.

Paivio, A., Smythe, P. C., & Yuille, J. C. (1968). Imagery versus meaningfulness of nouns in paired-associate learning. *Canadian Journal of Psychology, 22*, 427–441.

Paivio, A., Yuille, J. C., & Madigan, S. (1968). *Concreteness, imagery, and meaningfulness values for 925 nouns* (Journal of Experimental Psychology Monograph Supplement, Vol. 76, No. 1, Pt. 2). [Washington, DC]: American Psychological Association.

Palmer, S. (1977). Hierarchical structure in perceptual representation. *Cognitive Psychology, 9*, 441–474.

Palmer, S., Schreiber, C., & Fox, C. (1991, November). *Remembering the earthquake: "Flashbulb" memory for experienced vs. reported events.* Paper presented at the meeting of the Psychonomic Society, San Francisco, CA.

Pansky, A., & Koriat, A. (2004). The basic-level convergence effect in memory distortions. *Psychological Science, 15*, 52–59.

Pansky, A., Koriat, A., & Goldsmith, M. (2005). Eyewitness recall and testimony. In N. Brewer & K. Williams (Eds.), *Psychology and law: An empirical perspective* (pp. 93–150). New York: Guildford Press.

Papafragou, A., Li, P., Choi, Y., & Han, C-h. (2007). Evidentiality in language and cognition. *Cognition, 103*, 253–299.

Parkin, A. J. (1984). Levels of processing, context, and facilitation of pronunciation. *Acta Psychologia, 55*, 19–29.

Pashler, H. (1991). Dual-task interference and elementary mental mechanisms. In D. E. Meyer & S. Kornblum (Eds.), *Attention and performance XIV* (pp. 245–264). Hillsdale, NJ: Erlbaum.

Pashler, H. (1992). Attentional limitations in doing two tasks at the same time. *Current Directions in Psychological Science, 1*, 44–47.

Pashler, H. (1996). Structures, processes and the flow of information. In E. Bjork & R. Bjork (Eds.), *Handbook of perception and cognition*, 2nd ed., Vol. 10: *Memory* (pp. 3–29). San Diego, CA: Academic Press.

Pashler, H., & Johnston, J. (1989). Interference between temporally overlapping tasks: Chronometric evidence for central postponement with or without response grouping. *Quarterly Journal of Experimental Psychology, 41A*, 19–45.

Pashler, H., Rohrer, D., Cepeda, N., & Carpenter, S. (2007). Enhancing learning and retarding forgetting: Choices and consequences. *Psychonomic Bulletin & Review, 14*, 187–193.

Passolunghi, M. C., Cornoldi, C., & De Liberto, S. (1999). Working memory and intrusions of irrelevant information in a group of specific poor problem solvers. *Memory & Cognition, 27*, 779–790.

Paterson, H. M., & Kemp, R. I. (2006). Comparing methods of encountering post-event information: The power of co-witness suggestion. *Applied Cognitive Psychology, 20*, 1083–1099.

Payne, J. D., Nadel, L., Britton, W. B., & Jacobs, W. J. (2004). The bio-psychology of trauma and memory. In D. Reisberg & P. Hertel (Eds.), *Memory and emotion* (pp. 76–128). New York: Oxford University Press.

Peace, K. A., & Porter, S. (2004). A longitudinal investigation of the reliability of memories for trauma and other emotional experiences. *Applied Cognitive Psychology, 18*, 143–1159.

Pederson, E., Danziger, E., Wilkins, D., Levinson, S., Kita, S., & Senft, G. (1998). Semantic typology and spatial conceptualization. *Language, 74*, 557–589.

Pedrone, R., Hummel, J. E., & Holyoak, K. J. (2001). The use of diagrams in analogical problem solving. *Memory & Cognition, 29*, 214–221.

Peissig, J., & Tarr, M. J. (2007). Visual object recognition: Do we know more now than we did 20 years ago? *Annual Review of Psychology, 58*, 75–96.

Penfield, W., & Roberts, L. (1959). *Speech and brain mechanisms*. Princeton, NJ: Princeton University Press.

Peretz, I., Gaudreau, D., & Bonnel, A.-M. (1998). Exposure effects on music preference and recognition. *Memory & Cognition, 26*, 884–902.

Peterson, M., Kihlstrom, J. F., Rose, P., & Glisky, M. (1992). Mental images can be ambiguous: Reconstruals and reference-frame reversals. *Memory & Cognition, 20*, 107–123.

Pezdek, K., Blandon-Gitlin, I., & Gabbay, P. (2006). Imagination and memory: Does imagining implausible events lead to false autobiographical memories? *Psychonomic Bulletin & Review, 13*, 764–769.

Pezdek, K., Whetstone, T., Reynolds, K., Askari, N., & Dougherty, T. (1989). Memory for real-world scenes: The role of consistency with schema expectation. *Journal of Experimental Psychology: Learning, Memory, and Cognition, 15*, 587–595.

Phelps, E. (2004). Human emotion and memory: Interactions of the amygdala and hippocampal complex. *Current Opinion in Neurobiology, 14*, 198–202.

Phillips, J., KIein, G., & Sieck, W. (2004). Expertise in judgment and decision making: A case for training intuitive decision skills. In D. Koehler & N. Harvey (Eds.), *Blackwell handbook of judgment and decision making* (pp. 297–315). Malden, MA: Blackwell.

Piaget, J. (1952). *The origins of intelligence in children*. New York: International Universities Press.

Pickel, K. L. (1999). Distinguishing eyewitness descriptions of perceived objects from descriptions of imagined objects. *Applied Cognitive Psychology, 13*, 399–413.

Pillemer, D. B. (1984). Flashbulb memories of the assassination attempt on President Reagan. *Cognition, 16*, 63–80.

Pinker, S. (1980). Mental imagery and the third dimension. *Journal of Experimental Psychology: General, 109*, 354–371.

Pinker, S. (1987). The bootstrapping problem in language acquisition. In B. MacWhinney (Ed.), *Mechanisms of language acquisition* (pp. 339–441). Hillsdale, NJ: Erlbaum.

Pinker, S. (1991). Rules of language. *Science, 253*, 530–535.

Pinker, S. (1994). *The language instinct*. New York: Penguin.

Pinker, S. (1997). *How the mind works*. New York: Norton.

Pinker, S. (1999). *Words and rules: The ingredients of language*. New York: Basic Books.

Pinker, S., & Finke, R. (1980). Emergent two-dimensional patterns in images in depth. *Journal of Experimental Psychology: Human Perception and Performance, 6*, 244–264.

Pinker, S., & Prince, A. (1988). On language and connectionism: Analysis of a parallel distributed processing model of language acquisition. *Cognition, 28*, 73–193.

Plaut, D. C. (2000). Connectionism. In A. E. Kazdin (Ed.), *Encyclopedia of psychology* (pp. 265–268). Washington, DC: American Psychological Association.

Polk, T., & Newell, A. (1995). Deduction as verbal reasoning. *Psychological Review, 102,* 533–566.

Pollack, I., & Pickett, J. (1964). Intelligibility of excerpts from fluent speech: Auditory versus structural context. *Journal of Verbal Learning and Verbal Behavior, 3,* 79–84.

Poole, D. A., & Lindsay, D. S. (2001). Children's eyewitness reports after exposure to misinformation from parents. *Journal of Experimental Psychology: Applied, 7,* 27–50.

Pope, H. G., Hudson, J. I., Bodkin, J. A., & Oliva, P. (1998). Questionable validity of "dissociative amnesia" in trauma victims. *British Journal of Psychiatry, 172,* 210–215.

Porter, S., & Peace, K. A. (2007). The scars of memory: A prospective, longitudinal investigation of the consistency of traumatic and positive emotional memories in adulthood. *Psychological Science, 18*(5), 435–441.

Porter, S., Yuille, J. C., & Lehman, D. R. (1999). The nature of real, implanted, and fabricated memories for emotional childhood events: Implications for the false memory debate. *Law and Human Behavior, 23,* 517–538.

Posner, M., & Snyder, C. (1975). Facilitation and inhibition in the processing of signals. In P. Rabbitt & S. Dornic (Eds.), *Attention and performance V* (pp. 669–682). New York: Academic Press.

Posner, M., Snyder, C., & Davidson, B. (1980). Attention and the detection of signals. *Journal of Experimental Psychology: General, 109,* 160–174.

Postman, L. (1964). Short-term memory and incidental learning. In A. W. Melton (Ed.), *Categories of human learning* (pp. 146–201). New York: Academic Press.

Postman, L., & Phillips, L. W. (1965). Short-term temporal changes in free recall. *Quarterly Journal of Experimental Psychology, 17,* 132–138.

Prentice, D. A., & Miller, D. T. (2007). Psychological essentialism of human categories. *Current Directions in Psychological Science, 16,* 202–206.

Pretz, J. (2008). Intuition versus analysis: Strategy and experience in complex everyday problem solving. *Memory & Cognition, 36,* 554–566.

Pylyshyn, Z. (1981). The imagery debate: Analogue media versus tacit knowledge. In N. Block (Ed.), *Imagery* (pp. 151–206). Cambridge, MA: MIT Press.

Quinlan, P. T. (2003). Visual feature integration theory: Past, present and future. *Psychological Bulletin, 129,* 643–673.

Radvansky, G. A. (1999). The fan effect: A tale of two theories. *Journal of Experimental Psychology: General, 128,* 198–206.

Radvansky, G. A., & Zacks, R. T. (1991). Mental models and the fan effect. *Journal of Experimental Psychology: Learning, Memory and Cognition, 17,* 940–953.

Raghubir, P., & Menon, G. (2005). When and why is ease of retrieval informative? *Memory & Cognition, 33,* 821–832.

Ramachandran, V. S., & Blakeslee, S. (1998). *Phantoms in the brain.* New York: Morrow.

Ranganath, C., & Blumenfeld, R. S. (2005). Doubts about double dissociations between short- and long-term memory. *Trends in Cognitive Sciences, 9,* 374–380.

Ranganath, C., Yonelinas, A. P., Cohen, M. X., Dy, C. J., Tom, S., & D'Esposito, M. (2003). Dissociable correlates for familiarity and recollection within the medial temporal lobes. *Neuropsychologia, 42,* 2–13.

Rao, G. A., Larkin, E. C., & Derr, R. F. (1986). Biologic effects of chronic ethanol consumption related to a deficient intake of carbohydrates. *Alcohol and Alcoholism, 21,* 369–373.

Rayner, K., Smith, T. J., Malcolm, G. L., & Henderson, J. M. (2009). Eye movements and visual encoding during scene perception. *Psychological Science, 20,* 6–10.

Read, J. D. (1999). The recovered/false memory debate: Three steps

forward, two steps back? *Expert Evidence, 7,* 1–24.

Read, J. D., & Bruce, D. (1982). Longitudinal tracking of difficult memory retrievals. *Cognitive Psychology, 14,* 280–300.

Reason, J. T. (1990). *Human error.* Cambridge, England: Cambridge University Press.

Reason, J. T., & Lucas, D. (1984). Using cognitive diaries to investigate naturally occurring memory blocks. In J. E. Harris & P. E. Morris (Eds.), *Everyday memory actions and absent-mindedness* (pp. 53–70). London: Academic Press.

Redelmeier, D. A., & Shafir, E. (1995). Medical decision making in situations that offer multiple alternatives. *Journal of the American Medical Association, 273,* 302–305.

Redelmeier, D. A., & Tversky, A. (1996). On the belief that arthritis pain is related to the weather. *Proceedings of the National Academic of Sciences, USA, 93,* 2895–2896.

Reed, J. M., & Squire, L. R. (1997). Impaired recognition memory in patients with lesions limited to the hippocampal formation. *Behavioral Neuroscience, 111,* 667–675.

Reed, S. (1977). Facilitation of problem solving. In J. N. Castellan, D. Pisoni, & G. R. Potts (Eds.), *Cognitive theory* (pp. 3–20). Hillsdale, NJ: Erlbaum.

Reed, S. (1993). Imagery and discovery. In B. Roskos-Ewoldsen, M. J. Intons-Peterson, & R. Anderson (Eds.), *Imagery, creativity, and discovery: A cognitive perspective* (pp. 287–312). New York: North-Holland.

Reed, S., Ernst, G., & Banerji, R. (1974). The role of analogy in transfer between similar problem states. *Cognitive Psychology, 6,* 436–450.

Rees, G., Kreiman, G., & Koch, C. (2002). Neural correlates of consciousness in humans. *Nature Reviews Neuroscience, 3,* 261–270.

Reeves, L., & Weisberg, R. (1994). The role of content and abstract information in analogical transfer. *Psychological Bulletin, 115*, 381–400.

Rehder, B., & Hastie, R. (2001). Causal knowledge and categories: The effects of causal beliefs on categorization, induction, and similarity. *Journal of Experimental Psychology: General, 130*, 323–360.

Rehder, B., & Hastie, R. (2004). Category coherence and category-based property induction. *Cognition, 91*, 113–153.

Rehder, B., & Ross, B. H. (2001). Abstract coherent categories. *Journal of Experimental Psychology: Learning, Memory, & Cognition, 27*, 1261–1275.

Reicher, G. M. (1969). Perceptual recognition as a function of meaningfulness of stimulus material. *Journal of Experimental Psychology, 81*, 275–280.

Reingold, E. M., Charness, N., Pomplun, M., & Stampe, D. M. (2001). Visual span in expert chess players: Evidence from eye movements. *Psychological Science, 12*, 48–55.

Reisberg, D. (1996). The non-ambiguity of mental images. In C. Cornold, R. H. Logie, M. Brandimonte, G. Kaufmann & D. Reisberg (Eds.), *Stretching the imagination: Representation and transformation in mental imagery* (pp. 119–171). New York: Oxford University Press.

Reisberg, D. (2000). The detachment gain: The advantage of thinking out loud. In B. Landau, J. Sabini, E. Newport, & J. Jonides (Eds.), *Perception, cognition and language: Essays in honor of Henry and Lila Gleitman* (pp. 139–156). Cambridge, MA: MIT Press.

Reisberg, D., Baron, J., & Kemler, D. (1980). Overcoming Stroop interference: The effects of practice on distractor potency. *Journal of Experimental Psychology: Human Perception and Performance, 6*, 140–150.

Reisberg, D., & Chambers, D. (1991). Neither pictures nor propositions: What can we learn from a mental image? *Canadian Journal of Psychology, 45*, 288–302.

Reisberg, D., & Heuer, F. (2004). Memory for emotional events. In D. Reisberg & P. Hertel (Eds.), *Memory and emotion* (pp. 3–41). New York: Oxford University Press.

Reisberg, D., & Logie, R. H. (1993). The in's and out's of working memory: Escaping the boundaries on imagery function. In B. Roskos-Ewoldsen, M. Intons-Peterson, & R. Anderson (Eds.), *Imagery, creativity and discovery: A cognitive approach* (pp. 39–76). Amsterdam: Elsevier.

Reitman, J. (1976). Skilled perception in Go: Deducing memory structures from inter-response times. *Cognitive Psychology, 8*, 336–356.

Reitman, W. (1964). Heuristic decision procedures, open constraints, and the structure of ill-defined problems. In M. Shelley & G. Bryan (Eds.), *Human judgments and optimality* (pp. 282–315). New York: Wiley.

Rensink, R. A. (2002). Change detection. *Annual Review of Psychology, 53*, 245–277.

Rensink, R. A., O'Regan, J. K., & Clark, J. J. (1997). To see or not to see: The need for attention to perceive changes in scenes. *Psychological Science, 8*, 368–373.

Repp, B. (1992). Perceptual restoration of a "missing" speech sound: Auditory induction or illusion? *Perception & Psychophysics, 51*, 14–32.

Reynolds, J. H., Pasternak, T., & Desimone, R. (2000). Attention increases sensitivity of V4 neurons. *Neuron, 26*, 703–714.

Rhodes, G., Brake, S., & Atkinson, A. (1993). What's lost in inverted faces? *Cognition, 47*, 25–57.

Rhodes, G., Hayward, W., & Winkler, C. (2006). Expert face coding: Configural and component coding of own-race and other-race faces. *Psychonomic Bulletin & Review, 13*, 499–505.

Riccio, D. C., Millin, P. M., & Gisquet-Verrier, P. (2003). Retrograde amnesia: Forgetting back. *Current Directions in Psychological Science, 12*, 41–44.

Richard, A. M., Lee, H., & Vecera, S. P. (2008). Attentional spreading in object-based attention. *Journal of Experimental Psychology: Human Perception & Performance, 34*, 842–853.

Richardson, J. (1980). *Mental imagery and human memory*. New York: St. Martin's.

Richardson-Klavehn, A., & Bjork, R. A. (1988). Measures of memory. *Annual Review of Psychology, 39*, 475–543.

Richland, L., Zur, O., & Holyoak, K. (2007). Cognitive supports for analogies in the mathematics classroom. *Science, 316*, 1128–1129.

Riesenhuber, M., & Poggio, T. (1999). Hierarchical models of object recognition in cortex. *Nature Neuroscience, 2*, 1019–1025.

Riesenhuber, M., & Poggio, T. (2002). Neural mechanisms of object recognition. *Current Opinion in Neurobiology, 12*, 162–168.

Rinck, M. (1999). Memory for everyday objects: Where are the digits on numerical keypads? *Applied Cognitive Psychology, 13*, 329–350.

Rips, L. (1975). Inductive judgements about natural categories. *Journal of Verbal Learning and Verbal Behavior, 14*, 665–681.

Rips, L. (1983). Cognitive processes in propositional reasoning. *Psychological Review, 90*, 38–71.

Rips, L. (1986). Mental muddles. In M. Brand & R. Harnish (Eds.), *The representation of knowledge and belief* (pp. 258–286). Tucson: University of Arizona Press.

Rips, L. (1989). Similarity, typicality, and categorization. In S. Vosniadou & A. Ortony (Eds.), *Similarity and analogical reasoning* (pp. 21–59). Cambridge, England: Cambridge University Press.

Rips, L. (1990). Reasoning. *Annual Review of Psychology, 41*, 321–353.

Rips, L., & Collins, A. (1993). Categories and resemblance. *Journal of*

Experimental Psychology: General, 122, 468–489.

Ritchie, J. M. (1985). The aliphatic alcohols. In A. G. Gilman, L. S. Goodman, T. W. Rall, & F. Murad (Eds.), *The pharmacological basis of therapeutics* (pp. 372–386). New York: Macmillan.

Roberson, D., Davies, I., & Davidoff, J. (2000). Color categories are not universal: Replications and new evidence from a stone-age culture. *Journal of Experimental Psychology: General, 129*, 369–398.

Robertson, L., Treisman, A., Friedman-Hill, S., & Grabowecky, M. (1997). The interaction of spatial and object pathways: Evidence from Balint's syndrome. *Journal of Cognitive Neuroscience, 9*, 295–317.

Rock, I. (1983). *The logic of perception.* Cambridge, MA: MIT Press.

Roediger, H. L. (1980). The effectiveness of four mnemonics in ordering recall. *Journal of Experimental Psychology: Human Learning and Memory, 6*, 558–567.

Roediger, H. L., & Marsh, E. (2005). The positive and negative consequences of multiple-choice testing. *Journal of Experimental Psychology: Learning, Memory & Cognition, 31*, 1155–1159.

Roediger, H. L., & McDermott, K. (1995). Creating false memories: Remembering words not presented in lists. *Journal of Experimental Psychology: Learning, Memory and Cognition, 21*, 803–814.

Roediger, H. L., & McDermott, K. (2000). Tricks of memory. *Current Directions in Psychological Science, 9*, 123–127.

Rogers, T., & McClelland, J. (2004). *Semantic cognition: A parallel distributed processing approach.* Cambridge, MA: MIT Press.

Rogers, T., & Patterson, K. (2007). Object categorization: Reversals and explanations of the basic-level advantage. *Journal of Experimental Psychology: General, 136*, 451–469.

Rosch, E. (1973). On the internal structure of perceptual and semantic categories. In T. E. Moore (Ed.), *Cognitive development and the acquisition of language* (pp. 111–144). New York: Academic Press.

Rosch, E. (1975). Cognitive representations of semantic categories. *Journal of Experimental Psychology: General, 104*, 192–233.

Rosch, E. (1977a). Human categorization. In N. Warren (Ed.), *Advances in cross-cultural psychology* (pp. 1–49). London: Academic Press.

Rosch, E. (1977b). Linguistic relativity. In P. Johnson-Laird & P. Wason (Eds.), *Thinking: Readings in cognitive science* (pp. 501–519). New York: Cambridge University Press.

Rosch, E. (1978). Principles of categorization. In E. Rosch & B. B. Lloyd (Eds.), *Cognition and categorization* (pp. 27–48). Hillsdale, NJ: Erlbaum.

Rosch, E., & Mervis, C. B. (1975). Family resemblances. Studies in the internal structure of categories. *Cognitive Psychology, 7*, 573–605.

Rosch, E., Mervis, C. B., Gray, W., Johnson, D., & Boyes-Braem, P. (1976). Basic objects in natural categories. *Cognitive Psychology, 3*, 382–439.

Roser, M., & Gazzaniga, M. S. (2004). Automatic brains—Interpretive minds. *Current Directions in Psychological Science, 13*, 56–59.

Ross, B. (1984). Remindings and their effects in learning a cognitive skill. *Cognitive Psychology, 16*, 371–416.

Ross, B. (1987). This is like that: The use of earlier problems and the separation and similarity effects. *Journal of Experimental Psychology: Learning, Memory and Cognition, 13*, 629–639.

Ross, B. (1989). Distinguishing types of superficial similarities: Different effects on the access and use of earlier problems. *Journal of Experimental Psychology: Learning, Memory and Cognition, 15*, 456–468.

Ross, D. F., Ceci, S. J., Dunning, D., & Toglia, M. P. (1994). Unconscious transference and lineup identification: Toward a memory blending approach. In D. F. Ross & J. D. Read (Eds.), *Adult eyewitness testimony: Current trends and developments* (pp. 80–100). New York: Cambridge University Press.

Ross, J., & Lawrence, K. A. (1968). Some observations on memory artifice. *Psychonomic Science, 13*, 107–108.

Ross, L., & Anderson, C. (1982). Shortcomings in the attribution process: On the origins and maintenance of erroneous social assessments. In D. Kahneman, P. Slovic, & A. Tversky (Eds.), *Judgment under uncertainty: Heuristics and biases* (pp. 129–152). New York: Cambridge University Press.

Ross, L., Lepper, M., & Hubbard, M. (1975). Perseverance in self perception and social perception: Biased attributional processes in the debriefing paradigm. *Journal of Personality and Social Psychology, 32*, 880–892.

Ross, M., & Wilson, A. E. (2003). Autobiographical memory and conceptions of self: Getting better all the time. *Current Directions in Psychological Science, 12*, 66–69.

Rothbart, M., Evans, M., & Fulero, S. (1979). Recall for confirming events: Memory processes and the maintenance of social stereotypes. *Journal of Experimental Social Psychology, 15*, 343–355.

Rouder, J. N., & Ratcliff, R. (2006). Comparing exemplar- and rule-based theories of categorization. *Current Directions in Psychological Science, 5*, 9–13.

Rubin, D. C., & Kontis, T. S. (1983). A schema for common cents. *Memory & Cognition, 11*, 335–341.

Rubin, D. C., & Kozin, M. (1984). Vivid memories. *Cognition, 16*, 81–95.

Rueckl, J. G., & Oden, G. C. (1986). The integration of contextual and featural information during word identification. *Journal of Memory and Language, 25*, 445–460.

Rugg, M., & Curran, T. (2007). Event-related potentials and recognition memory. *Trends in Cognitive Sciences, 11,* 251–257.

Rugg, M. D., & Yonelinas, A. P. (2003). Human recognition memory: A cognitive neuroscience perspective. *Trends in Cognitive Sciences, 7,* 313–319.

Rumelhart, D. E. (1997). The architecture of mind: A connectionist approach. In J. Haugeland (Ed.), *Mind design 2: Philosophy, psychology, artificial intelligence* (2nd rev. & enlarged ed.). Cambridge, MA: MIT Press.

Rumelhart, D. E., & Siple, P. (1974). Process of recognizing tachistoscopically presented words. *Psychological Review, 81,* 99–118.

Rundus, D. (1971). Analysis of rehearsal processes in free recall. *Journal of Experimental Psychology, 89,* 63–77.

Russell, C., & Driver, J. (2005). New indirect measures of "inattentive" visual grouping in a change-detection task. *Perception & Psychophysics, 67,* 606–623.

Saalmann, Y., Pigarev, I., & Vidyasagar, T. (2007). Neural mechanisms of visual attention: How top-down feedback highlights relevant locations. *Science, 316,* 1612–1615.

Saffran, J. R. (2003). Statistical language learning: Mechanisms and constraints. *Current Directions in Psychological Science, 12,* 110–114.

Salame, P., & Baddeley, A. D. (1982). Disruption of short-term memory by unattended speech: Implications for the structure of working memory. *Journal of Verbal Learning and Verbal Behavior, 21,* 150–164.

Salthouse, T., & Pink, J. (2008). Why is working memory related to fluid intelligence? *Psychonomic Bulletin & Review, 15,* 364–371.

Sampaio, C., & Brewer, W. (2009). The role of unconscious memory errors in judgments of confidence for sentence recognition. *Memory & Cognition, 37,* 158–163.

Samuel, A. G. (1987). Lexical uniqueness effects on phonemic restoration.

Journal of Memory and Language, 26, 36–56.

Samuel, A. G. (1991). A further examination of attentional effects in the phonemic restoration illusion. *Quarterly Journal of Experimental Psychology: Human Experimental Psychology, 43,* 679–699.

Savage, J. (1954). *The foundation of statistics.* New York: Wiley.

Sawyer, R. K. (2006). *Explaining creativity: The science of human innovation.* New York: Oxford University Press.

Schab, F. (1990). Odors and the remembrance of things past. *Journal of Experimental Psychology: Learning, Memory and Cognition, 16,* 648–655.

Schacter, D. (1987). Implicit memory: History and current status. *Journal of Experimental Psychology: Learning, Memory and Cognition, 13,* 501–518.

Schacter, D. (1996). *Searching for memory: The brain, the mind and the past.* New York: Basic Books.

Schacter, D. (1999). The seven sins of memory. *American Psychologist, 54,* 182–203.

Schacter, D., & Tulving, E. (1982). Amnesia and memory research. In L. S. Cermak (Ed.), *Human memory and amnesia* (pp. 1–32). Hillsdale, NJ: Erlbaum.

Schacter, D., Tulving, E., & Wang, P. (1981). *Source amnesia: New methods and illustrative data.* Paper presented at the meeting of the International Neuropsychological Society, Atlanta, GA.

Schkade, D. A., & Kahneman, D. (1998). Does living in California make people happy? A focusing illusion in judgments of life satisfaction. *Psychological Science, 9,* 340–346.

Schneider, S. (1992). Framing and conflict: Aspiration level contingency, the status quo, and current theories of risky choice. *Journal of Experimental Psychology: Learning, Memory and Cognition, 18,* 1040–1057.

Scholl, B. J. (2001). Objects and attention: The state of the art. *Cognition, 80,* 1–46.

Schooler, J., Ohlsson, S., & Brooks, K. (1993). Thoughts beyond words: When language overshadows insight. *Journal of Experimental Psychology: General, 122,* 166–183.

Schraw, G., Dunkle, M., & Bendixen, L. (1995). Cognitive processes in well-defined and ill-defined problem solving. *Applied Cognitive Psychology, 9,* 523–538.

Schreiber, C. A., & Kahneman, D. (2000). Determinants of the remembered utility of aversive sounds. *Journal of Experimental Psychology: General, 129,* 27–42.

Schulz-Hardt, S., Frey, D., Lüthgens, C., & Moscovici, S. (2000). Biased information search in group decision making. *Journal of Personality and Social Psychology, 78,* 655–669.

Schunn, C., McGregor, M., & Saner, L. (2005). Expertise in ill-defined problem-solving domains as effective strategy use. *Memory & Cognition, 33,* 1377–1387.

Schunn, C. D., & Anderson, J. R. (1999). The generality/specificity of expertise in scientific reasoning. *Cognitive Science, 23,* 337–370.

Schustack, M., & Sternberg, R. (1981). Evaluation of evidence in causal inference. *Journal of Experimental Psychology: General, 110,* 101–120.

Schwartz, B., E. A. Wasserman, & S. J. Robbins (2002). *Psychology of learning and behavior,* 5th ed. New York: Norton.

Schwartz, B. L. (1999). Sparkling at the end of the tongue: The etiology of tip-of-the-tongue phenomenology. *Psychonomic Bulletin & Review, 5,* 379–393.

Schwartz, J., Chapman, G., & Brewer, N. (2004). The effects of accountability on bias in physician decision making: Going from bad to worse. *Psychonomic Bulletin & Review, 11,* 173–178.

Schwarz, N. (1998). Accessible content and accessibility experiences: The interplay of declarative and experiential information in judgments. *Personality and Social Psychology Review, 2,* 87–99.

Schwarz, N. (1999). Self-reports: How the questions shape the answers. *American Psychologist, 54,* 93–105.

Schwarz, N., Bless, H., Strack, F., Klumpp, G., Rittenauer-Schatka, H., & Simons, A. (1991). Ease of retrieval as information: Another look at the availability heuristic. *Journal of Personality & Social Psychology, 61,* 195–202.

Scoboria, A., Mazzoni, G., Kirsch, I., & Jimenez, S. (2006). The effects of prevalence and script information on plausibility, belief, and memory of autobiographical events. *Applied Cognitive Psychology, 20,* 1049–1064.

Scullin, M. H., Kanaya, T., & Ceci, S. J. (2002). Measurement of individual differences in children's susceptibility across situations. *Journal of Experimental Psychology: Applied, 8,* 233–246.

Seamon, J., Williams, P., Crowley, M., Kim, I., Langer, S., Orne, P., et al. (1995). The mere exposure effect is based on implicit memory: Effects of stimulus type, encoding conditions, and number of exposures on recognition and affect judgments. *Journal of Experimental Psychology: Learning, Memory and Cognition, 21,* 711–721.

Seamon, J. G., Philbin, M. M., & Harrison, L. G. (2006). Do you remember proposing marriage to the Pepsi machine? False recollections from a campus walk. *Psychonomic Bulletin & Review, 13,* 752–755.

Sedivy, J. C., Tanenhaus, M. K., Chambers, C. G., & Carlson, G. N. (1999). Achieving incremental semantic interpretation through contextual representation. *Cognition, 71,* 109–147.

Segal, E. (2004). Incubation in insight problem solving. *Creative Research Journal, 16,* 141–148.

Segal, S., & Fusella, V. (1970). Influence of imaged pictures and sounds in detection of visual and auditory signals. *Journal of Experimental Psychology, 83,* 458–474.

Segal, S., & Fusella, V. (1971). Effect of images in six sense modalities on detection of visual signal from noise. *Psychonomic Science, 24,* 55–56.

Seidenberg, M., & Zevin, J. (2006). Connectionist models in developmental cognitive neuroscience: Critical periods and the paradox of success. In Y. Munakata & M. Johnson (Eds.), *Processes of change in brain and cognitive development: Attention and performance XXI.* New York: Oxford University Press.

Selfridge, O. (1955). *Pattern recognition and modern computers.* Proceedings of the Western Joint Computer Conference, Los Angeles, CA.

Selfridge, O. (1959). Pandemonium: A paradigm for learning. In D. Blake & A. Uttley (Eds.), *The mechanisation of thought processes: Proceedings of a symposium held at the National Physics Laboratory* (pp. 511–529). London: H. M. Stationery Office.

Seltzer, B., & Benson, D. F. (1974). The temporal pattern of retrograde amnesia in Korsakoff's Disease. *Neurology, 24,* 527–530.

Semmler, C., & Brewer, N. (2006). Postidentification feedback effects on face recognition confidence: Evidence for metacognitive influences. *Applied Cognitive Psychology, 20,* 895–916.

Senghas, A., Coppola, M., Newport, E. L., & Supalla, A. (1997). *Argument structure in Nicaraguan Sign Language: The emergence of grammatical devices.* (Proceedings of the Boston University Conference on Language Development, 21.) Boston: Cascadilla.

Servos, P., & Goodale, M. A. (1995). Preserved visual imagery in visual form agnosia. *Neuropsychologia, 33,* 1383–1394.

Sevdalis, N., & Harvey, N. (2007). Biased forecasting of postdecisional affect. *Psychological Science, 18,* 678–681.

Shafir, E. (1993). Choosing versus rejecting: Why some options are both better and worse than others. *Memory & Cognition, 21,* 546–556.

Shafir, E., & LeBoeuf, R. A. (2002). Rationality. *Annual Review of Psychology, 53,* 491–517.

Shafto, P., & Coley, J. D. (2003). Development of categorization and reasoning in the natural world: Novices to experts, naive similarity to ecological knowledge. *Journal of Experimental Psychology: Learning, Memory and Cognition, 29,* 641–649.

Shaklee, H., & Mims, M. (1982). Sources of error in judging event covariations. *Journal of Experimental Psychology: Learning, Memory and Cognition, 8,* 208–224.

Shanteau, J. (1992). The psychology of experts: An alternative view. In G. Wright & F. Bolger (Eds.), *Expertise and decision support* (pp. 11–23). New York: Plenum.

Sharman, S., Manning, C., & Garry, M. (2005). Explain this: Explaining childhood events inflates confidence for those events. *Applied Cognitive Psychology, 19,* 67–74.

Shepard, R. N. (1988). The imagination of the scientist. In K. Egan & D. Nadaner (Eds.), *Imagination and education* (pp. 153–185). New York: Teachers College Press.

Shepard, R. N., & Cooper, L. A. (1982). *Mental images and their transformations.* Cambridge, MA: MIT Press.

Shepard, R. N., & Feng, C. (1972). A chronometric study of mental paper folding. *Cognitive Psychology, 3,* 228–243.

Shepard, R. N., & Metzler, J. (1971). Mental rotation of three-dimensional objects. *Science, 171,* 701–703.

Shore, D. I., & Klein, R. M. (2000). The effects of scene inversion on change blindness. *Journal of General Psychology, 127,* 27–43.

Sieroff, E., Pollatsek, A., & Posner, M. (1988). Recognition of visual letter strings following damage to the posterior visual spatial attention system. *Cognitive Neuropsychology, 5,* 427–449.

Silbersweig, D. A., Stern, E., Frith, C., Cahill, C., Holmes, A., Grootoonk, S., et al. (1995). A functional neuro-anatomy of hallucinations in schizophrenia. *Nature, 378,* 176–179.

Simon, H. (1973). The structure of ill-defined problems. *Artificial Intelligence, 4,* 181–201.

Simons, D. J. (2000). Attentional capture and inattentional blindness. *Trends in Cognitive Science, 4,* 147–155.

Simons, D. J., & Ambinder, M. S. (2005). Change blindness: Theory and consequences. *Current Directions in Psychological Science, 14,* 44–48.

Simons, D. J., & Chabris, C. F. (1999). Gorillas in our midst: Sustained inattentional blindness for dynamic events. *Perception, 28,* 1059–1074.

Simons, D. J., & Levin, D. T. (1998). Failure to detect changes to people during a real-world interaction. *Psychonomic Bulletin & Review, 5,* 644–649.

Simonton, D. K. (2003). Scientific creativity as constrained stochastic behavior: The integration of product, person, and process perspectives. *Psychological Bulletin, 129,* 475–494.

Sio, U. N., & Ormerod, T. C. (2009). Does incubation enhance problem solving? A meta-analytic review. *Psychological Bulletin, 135,* 94–120.

Skotko, B. G., Kensinger, E. A., Locascio, J. J., Einstein, G., Rubin, D. C., Tupler, L. A., et al. (2004). Puzzling thoughts for H.M.: Can new semantic information be anchored to old semantic memories? *Neuropsychology, 18*(4), 756–769.

Slamecka, N. J., & Graf, P. (1978). The generation effect: Delineation of a phenomenon. *Journal of Experimental Psychology: Human Learning and Memory, 4,* 592–604.

Slobin, D. (1966). Grammatical transformations and sentence comprehension in childhood and adulthood. *Journal of Verbal Learning and Verbal Behavior, 5,* 219–227.

Sloman, S. A. (1996). The empirical case for two systems of reasoning. *Psychological Bulletin, 119,* 3–22.

Slovic., P. (1995). The construction of preference. *American Psychologist, 50,* 364–371.

Slovic, P., Finucane, M., Peters, E., & MacGregor, D. G. (2002). The affect heuristic. In T. Gilovich, D. Griffin, & D. Kahneman (Eds.), *Heuristics and biases* (pp. 397–420). New York: Cambridge University Press.

Slovic, P., Fischhoff, B., & Lichtenstein, S. (1982). Facts versus fears: Understanding perceived risk. In D. Kahneman, P. Slovic, & A. Tversky (Eds.), *Judgment under uncertainty: Heuristics and biases* (pp. 463–489). Cambridge, England: Cambridge University Press.

Slovic, P., & Peters, E. (2006). Risk perception and affect. *Current Directions in Psychological Science, 15,* 322–325.

Smedslund, J. (1963). The concept of correlation in adults. *Scandinavian Journal of Psychology, 4,* 165–173.

Smeets, T., Jelicic, M., Peters, M. J. V., Candel, I., Horselenberg, R., & Merckelbach, H. (2006). "Of course I remember seeing that film"—How ambiguous questions generate crashing memories. *Applied Cognitive Psychology, 20,* 779–789.

Smith, E., & Miller, F. (1978). Limits on perception of cognitive processes: A reply to Nisbett & Wilson. *Psychological Review, 85,* 355–362.

Smith, E. E. (1988). Concepts and thought. In R. J. Sternberg & E. E. Smith (Eds.), *The psychology of human thought* (pp. 19–49). Cambridge, England: Cambridge University Press.

Smith, E. E., Balzano, G. J., & Walker, J. H. (1978). Nominal, perceptual, and semantic codes in picture categorization. In J. W. Cotton & R. L. Klatzky (Eds.), *Semantic factors in cognition.* Hillsdale, NJ: Erlbaum.

Smith, E. E., Rips, L. J., & Shoben, E. J. (1974). Structure and process in

semantic memory: A featural model for semantic decisions. *Psychological Review, 81,* 214–241.

Smith, J. D. (2002). Exemplar theory's predicted typicality gradient can be tested and disconfirmed. *Psychological Science, 13,* 437–442.

Smith, M. (1982). *Hypnotic memory enhancement of witnesses: Does it work?* Paper presented at the meeting of the Psychonomic Society, Minneapolis, MN.

Smith, S. (1979). Remembering in and out of context. *Journal of Experimental Psychology: Human Learning and Memory, 5,* 460–471.

Smith, S. (1985). Background music and context-dependent memory. *American Journal of Psychology, 6,* 591–603.

Smith, S. M., & Blankenship, S. E. (1989). Incubation effects. *Bulletin of the Psychonomic Society, 27,* 311–314.

Smith, S. M., & Blankenship, S. (1991). Incubation and the persistence of fixation in problem solving. *American Journal of Psychology, 104,* 61–87.

Smith, S. M., Glenberg, A., & Bjork, R. A. (1978). Environmental context and human memory. *Memory & Cognition, 6,* 342–353.

Smith, S. M., & Vela, E. (2001). Environmental context-dependent memory: A review and meta-analysis. *Psychonomic Bulletin & Review, 8,* 203–220.

Spelke, E., Hirst, W., & Neisser, U. (1976). Skills of divided attention. *Cognition, 4,* 215–230.

Spellman, B. A., Holyoak, K. J., & Morrison, R. G. (2001). Analogical priming via semantic relations. *Memory & Cognition, 29,* 383–393.

Spence, C., & Read, L. (2003). Speech shadowing while driving: On the difficulty of splitting attention between eye and ear. *Psychological Science, 14,* 251–256.

Spencer, R., & Weisberg, R. (1986). Is analogy sufficient to facilitate transfer during problem solving? *Memory & Cognition, 14,* 442–449.

Sperber, D., Cara, F., & Girotto, V. (1995). Relevance theory explains the selection task. *Cognition, 57,* 31–95.

Sperber, D., & Wilson, D. (1986). *Relevance: Communication and cognition.* Cambridge, MA: Harvard University Press.

Spiegel, D. (1995). Hypnosis and suggestion. In D. L. Schacter, J. T. Coyle, G. D. Fischbach, M.-M. Mesulam, & L. E. Sullivan (Eds.), *Memory distortion: How minds, brains and societies reconstruct the past* (pp. 129–149). Cambridge, MA: Harvard University Press.

Sporer, S. (1988). Long-term improvement of facial recognition through visual rehearsal. In M. Gruneberg, P. Morris, & R. Sykes (Eds.), *Practical aspects of memory: Current research and issues* (pp. 182–188). New York: Wiley.

Sporer, S., Penrod, S., Read, D., & Cutler, B. (1995). Choosing, confidence, and accuracy: A meta-analysis of the confidence-accuracy relation in eyewitness identification studies. *Psychological Bulletin, 118,* 315–327.

Squire, L., & McKee, R. (1993). Declarative and nondeclarative memory in opposition: When prior events influence amnesic patients more than normal subjects. *Memory & Cognition, 21,* 424–430.

Stadler, M. A., Roediger, H. L., & McDermott, K. B. (1999). Norms for word lists that create false memories. *Memory & Cognition, 27,* 494–500.

Stangor, C., & McMillan, D. (1992). Memory for expectancy-congruent and expectancy-incongruent information: A review of the social and social developmental literatures. *Psychological Bulletin, 111,* 42–61.

Stanovich, K. E., & West, R. F. (1998). Who uses base rates and P(Du,H)? An analysis of individual differences. *Memory & Cognition, 26,* 161–179.

Stanovich, K. E., & West, R. F. (2000). Individual differences in reasoning: Implications for the rationality debate. *Behavioral and Brain Sciences, 23,* 645–665.

Stapel, D., & Semin, G. (2007). The magic spell of language: Linguistic categories and their perceptual consequences. *Journal of Personality and Social Psychology, 93,* 23–33.

Steblay, N. J. (1992). A meta-analytic review of the weapon focus effect. *Law and Human Behavior, 16,* 413–424.

Sternberg, R. J. (1988). A three-facet model of creativity. In R. J. Sternberg (Ed.), *The nature of creativity* (pp. 125–147). Cambridge, England: Cambridge University Press.

Sternberg, R. J. (2001). What is the common thread of creativity? Its dialectical relation to intelligence and wisdom. *American Psychologist, 56,* 360–362.

Sternberg, R. J., & Davidson, J. E. (Eds.). (1995). *The nature of insight.* Cambridge, MA: MIT Press.

Sternberg, R. J., & Dess, N. K. (2001). Creativity for the new millennium. *American Psychologist, 56,* 332.

Stevens, A., & Coupe, P. (1978). Distortions in judged spatial relations. *Cognitive Psychology, 10,* 422–437.

Stevens, J. A. (2005). Interference effects demonstrate distinct roles for visual and motor imagery during the mental representation of human action. *Cognition, 95,* 329–350.

Stokes, P. (2001). Variability, constraints and creativity: Shedding light on Claude Monet. *American Psychologist, 56,* 355–359.

Strack, F., & Mussweiler, T. (1997). Explaining the enigmatic anchoring effect: Mechanisms of selective accessibility. *Journal of Personality & Social Psychology, 73,* 437–446.

Strayer, D. L., & Drews, F. A. (2007). Cell-phone-induced driver distraction. *Current Directions in Psychological Science, 16,* 128–131.

Strayer, D. L., Drews, F. A., & Johnston, W. A. (2003). Cell phone induced failures of visual attention during simulated driving. *Journal of Experimental Psychology: Applied, 9,* 23–32.

Stroop, J. R. (1935). Studies of interference in serial verbal reaction. *Journal of Experimental Psychology, 18,* 643–662.

Stuss, D., & Knight, R. T. (Eds.). (2002). *Principles of frontal lobe function.* New York: Oxford University Press.

Sulin, R. A., & Dooling, D. J. (1974). Intrusion of a thematic idea in retention of prose. *Journal of Experimental Psychology, 103,* 255–262.

Sumby, W. H. (1963). Word frequency and serial position effects. *Journal of Verbal Learning and Verbal Behavior, 1,* 443–450.

Stuss, D. T., & Levine, B. (2002). Adult clinical neuropsychology: Lessons from studies of the frontal lobes. *Annual Review of Psychology, 53,* 401–433.

Svartik, J. (1966). *On voice in the English verb.* The Hague, Netherlands: Mouton.

Symons, C. S., & Johnson, B. T. (1997). The self-reference effect in memory: A meta-analysis. *Psychological Bulletin, 121,* 371–394.

Tabachnick, B., & Brotsky, S. (1976). Free recall and complexity of pictorial stimuli. *Memory & Cognition, 4,* 466–470.

Talarico, J. M., & Rubin, D. C. (2003). Confidence, not consistency, characterizes flashbulb memories. *Psychological Science, 14,* 455–461.

Talmi, D., Grady, C. L., Goshen-Gottstein, Y., & Moscovitch, M. (2005). Neuroimaging the serial position curve: A test of single-store versus dual-store models. *Psychological Science, 16,* 716–723.

Tanaka, J. W., & Taylor, M. (1991). Object categories and expertise: Is the basic level in the eye of the beholder? *Cognitive Psychology, 23,* 457–482.

Tanenhaus, M. K., & Spivey-Knowlton, M. J. (1996). Eye-tracking. *Language & Cognitive Processes, 11,* 583–588.

Taplin, J., & Staudenmayer, H. (1973). Interpretation of abstract conditional sentences in deductive reasoning. *Journal of Verbal Learning and Verbal Behavior, 12*, 530–542.

Tarr, M. (1995). Rotating objects to recognize them: A case study on the role of viewpoint dependency in the recognition of three-dimensional objects. *Psychonomic Bulletin & Review, 2*, 55–82.

Tarr, M. (1999). News on views: Pandemonium revisited. *Nature Neuroscience, 2*, 932–935.

Tarr, M., & Bülthoff, H. (1998). Image-based object recognition in man, monkey and machine. *Cognition, 67*, 1–208.

Terr, L. C. (1991). Acute responses to external events and posttraumatic stress disorders. In M. Lewis (Ed.), *Child and adolescent psychiatry: A comprehensive textbook* (pp. 755–763). Baltimore: Williams & Wilkins.

Terr, L. C. (1994). *Unchained memories: The stories of traumatic memories, lost and found.* New York: Basic Books.

Thomas, A. K., Bulevich, J. B., & Loftus, E. F. (2003). Exploring the role of repetition and sensory elaboration in the imagination inflation effect. *Memory & Cognition, 31*, 630–640.

Thomas, A. K., & Loftus, E. F. (2002). Creating bizarre false memories through imagination. *Memory & Cognition, 30*, 423–431.

Thomas, J. (1974). An analysis of behavior in the Hobbits-Orcs problem. *Cognitive Psychology, 6*, 257–269.

Thompson, P. (1980). Margaret Thatcher: A new illusion. *Perception, 9*, 483–484.

Thompson, W. B., & Mason, S. E. (1996). Instability of individual differences in the association between confidence judgments and memory performance. *Memory & Cognition, 24*, 226–234.

Thompson, W. L., & Kosslyn, S. M. (2000). Neural systems activated during visual mental imagery: A review and meta-analyses. In J. Mazziotta & A. Toga (Eds.), *Brain mapping II: The applications* (pp. 535–560). New York: Academic Press.

Thompson, W. L., Kosslyn, S. M., Hoffman, M. S., & Kooij, K. v. d. (2008). Inspecting visual mental images: Can people "see" implicit properties as easily in imagery and perception? *Memory & Cognition, 36*, 1024–1032.

Thomsen, D. K., & Berntsen, D. (2009). The long-term impact of emotionally stressful events on memory characteristics and life story. *Applied Cognitive Psychology, 23*, 579–598.

Tinti, C., Schmidt, S., Sotgiu, I., Testa, S., & Curci, A. (2009). The role of importance/consequentiality appraisal in flashbulb memory formation: The case of the death of Pope John Paul II. *Applied Cognitive Psychology, 23*, 236–253.

Todd, P. M., & Gigerenzer, G. (2007). Environments that make us smart. *Current Directions in Psychological Science, 16*, 167–171.

Tombu, M., & Jolicoeur, P. (2003). A central capacity sharing model of dual-task performance. *Journal of Experimental Psychology: Human Perception & Performance, 29*, 3–18.

Tong, F., Nakayama, K., Vaughan, J. T., & Kanwisher, N. (1998). Binocular rivalry and visual awareness in human extrastriate cortex. *Neuron, 21*, 753–759.

Tousignant, J., Hall, D., & Loftus, E. (1986). Discrepancy detection and vulnerability to misleading postevent information. *Memory & Cognition, 14*, 329–338.

Treisman, A. (1964). Verbal cues, language, and meaning in selective attention. *American Journal of Psychology, 77*, 206–219.

Treisman, A., & Gelade, G. (1980). A feature-integration theory of attention. *Cognitive Psychology, 12*, 97–136.

Treisman, A., & Souther, J. (1985). Search asymmetry: A diagnostic for preattentive processing of separable features. *Journal of Experimental Psychology: General, 114*, 285–310.

Treisman, A., Sykes, M., & Gelade, G. (1977). Selective attention and stimulus integration. In S. Dornic (Ed.), *Attention and performance VI* (pp. 333–361). Hillsdale, NJ: Erlbaum.

Tsushima, Y., Sasaki, Y., & Watanabe, T. (2006). Greater disruption due to failure of inhibitory control on an ambiguous distractor. *Science, 314*, 1786–1788.

Tuffiash, M., Roring, R., & Ericsson, K. A. (2007). Expert performance in SCRABBLE: Implications for the study of the structure and acquisition of complex skills. *Journal of Experimental Psychology: Applied, 13*, 124–134.

Tulving, E. (1983). *Elements of episodic memory.* Oxford: Oxford University Press.

Tulving, E. (1993). What is episodic memory? *Current Directions in Psychological Science, 2*, 67–70.

Tulving, E. (2002). Episodic memory: From mind to brain. *Annual Review of Psychology, 53*, 1–25.

Tulving, E., & Gold, C. (1963). Stimulus information and contextual information as determinants of tachistoscopic recognition of words. *Journal of Experimental Psychology, 92*, 319–327.

Tulving, E., Mandler, G., & Baumal, R. (1964). Interaction of two sources of information in tachistoscopic word recognition. *Canadian Journal of Psychology, 18*, 62–71.

Tversky, A., & Kahneman, D. (1971). Belief in the law of small numbers. *Psychological Bulletin, 76*, 105–110.

Tversky, A., & Kahneman, D. (1973). Availability: A heuristic for judging frequency and probability. *Cognitive Psychology, 5*, 207–232.

Tversky, A., & Kahneman, D. (1974). Judgments under uncertainty: Heuristics and biases. *Science, 185*, 1124–1131.

Tversky, A., & Kahneman, D. (1982). Evidential impact of base rates. In D. Kahneman, P. Slovic, & A. Tversky (Eds.), *Judgment under uncertainty: Heuristics and biases* (pp. 153–160). New York: Cambridge University Press.

Tversky, A., & Kahneman, D. (1983). Extensional versus intuitive reasoning: The conjunction fallacy in probability judgment. *Psychological Review, 90,* 293–315.

Tversky, A., & Kahneman, D. (1987). Rational choice and the framing of decisions. In R. Hogarth & M. Reder (Eds.), *Rational choice: The contrast between economics and psychology* (pp. 67–94). Chicago: University of Chicago Press.

Tversky, A., & Shafir, E. (1992). Choice under conflict: The dynamics of deferred decision. *Psychological Science, 3,* 358–361.

Tversky, B., & Hemenway, K. (1991). Parts and the basic level in natural categories and artificial stimuli: Comments on Murphy (1991). *Memory & Cognition, 19,* 439–442.

Tweney, R. D., Doherty, M. E., & Mynatt, C. R. (1981). *On scientific thinking.* New York: Columbia University Press.

Tyler, T. (2005). *Procedural justice.* Burlington, VT: Aldershot.

Uleman, J., & Bargh, J. (Eds.). (1989). *Unintended thought.* New York: Guilford.

Ullman, S. (2007). Object recognition and segmentation by a fragment-based hierarchy. *Trends in Cognitive Science, 11,* 58–64.

Ungerleider, L. G., & Haxby, J. V. (1994). "What" and "where" in the human brain. *Current Opinions in Neurobiology, 4,* 157–165.

Ungerleider, L. G., & Mishkin, M. (1982). Two cortical visual systems. In D. J. Ingle, M. A. Goodale, & R. J. W. Mansfield (Eds.), *Analysis of visual behavior* (pp. 549–586). Cambridge, MA: MIT Press.

Unkelbach, C. (2007). Reversing the truth effect: Learning the interpretation of processing fluency in judgments of truth. *Journal of Experimental Psychology: Learning, Memory and Cognition, 33,* 219–230.

Unsworth, N., & Engle, R. (2007). The nature of individual differences in working memory capacity: Active maintenance in primary memory and controlled search in secondary memory. *Psychological Review, 114,* 104–132.

Uttal, W. (2001). *The new phrenology: The limits of localizing cognitive processes in the brain.* Cambridge, MA: MIT Press/Bradford Books.

Valentine, T. (1988). Upside-down faces: A review of the effects of inversion upon face recognition. *British Journal of Psychology, 79,* 471–491.

Van der Lely, H. (2005). Domain-specific cognitive systems: Insight from grammatical-SLI. *Trends in Cognitive Science, 9,* 53–59.

Van Essen, D. C., & DeYoe, E. A. (1995). Concurrent processing in the primate visual cortex. In M. S. Gazzaniga (Ed.), *The cognitive neurosciences* (pp. 383–400). Cambridge, MA: MIT Press.

VanLehn, K. (1998). Analogy events: How examples are used during problem solving. *Cognitive Science, 22,* 347–388.

Van Overschelde, J. P., & Healy, A. F. (2001). Learning of nondomain facts in high- and low-knowledge domains. *Journal of Experimental Psychology: Learning, Memory and Cognition, 27,* 1160–1171.

Vanpaemel, W., & Storms, G. (2008). In search of abstraction: The varying abstraction model of categorization, *Psychonomic Bulletin & Review, 15,* 732–749.

van Veen, V., & Carter, C. (2006). Conflict and cognitive control in the brain. *Current Directions in Psychological Science, 15,* 237–240.

Verstijnen, I. M., Hennessey, J. M., van Leeuwen, C., Hamel, R., & Goldschmidt, G. (1998). Sketching and creative discovery. *Design Studies, 19,* 519–546.

Verstijnen, I. M., van Leeuwen, C., Goldschmidt, G., Hamel, R., & Hennessey, J. M. (1998). Creative discovery in imagery and perception: Combining is relatively easy, restructuring takes a sketch. *Acta Psychologica, 99,* 177–200.

Vitevitch, M. S. (2003). Change deafness: The inability to detect changes between two voices. *Journal of Experimental Psychology: Human Perception and Performance, 29,* 333–342.

von Neumann, J., & Morgenstern, O. (1947). *Theory of games and economic behavior.* Princeton, NJ: Princeton University Press.

Vul, E., & Pashler, H. (2007). Incubation benefits only after people have been misdirected. *Memory & Cognition, 35,* 701–710.

Vuong, Q. C., & Tarr, M. (2004). Rotation direction affects object recognition. *Vision Research, 44,* 1717–1730.

Wade, C. (2006). Some cautions about jumping on the brain-scan bandwagon. *The APS Observer, 19,* 23–24.

Wagenaar, W. A. (1986). My memory: A study of autobiographical memory over six years. *Cognitive Psychology, 18,* 225–252.

Wagenaar, W. A., & Groeneweg, J. (1990). The memory of concentration camp survivors. *Applied Cognitive Psychology, 4,* 77–88.

Wagner, A., Shannon, B., Kahn, I., & Buckner, R. (2005). Parietal lobe contributions to episodic memory retrieval. *Trends in Cognitive Sciences, 9,* 445–453.

Wagner, A. D., Koutstaal, W., & Schacter, D. L. (1999). When encoding yields remembering: Insights from event-related neuroimaging. *Philosophical Transactions of the Royal Society of London, Biology, 354,* 1307–1324.

Wagner, A. D., Schacter, D. L., Rotte, M., Koutstaal, W., Maril, A., Dale, A., et al. (1998). Building memories: Remembering and forgetting of verbal experiences as predicted by brain activity. *Science, 281,* 1188–1191.

Walker, S. (1993). Supernatural beliefs, natural kinds, and conceptual structure. *Memory & Cognition, 20,* 655–662.

Wallas, G. (1926). *The art of thought.* New York: Harcourt, Brace.

Wallis, G., & Bülthoff, H. (1999). Learning to recognize objects. *Trends in Cognitive Sciences, 3,* 22–31.

Wang, M., & Bilger, R. (1973). Consonant confusion in noise: A study of perceptual features. *Journal of the Acoustical Society of America, 54,* 1248–1266.

Ward, T. B. (2001). Creative cognition, conceptual combination, and the creative writing of Stephen R. Donaldson. *American Psychologist, 56,* 350–354.

Wason, P. (1966). Reasoning. In B. Foss (Ed.), *New horizons in psychology* (pp. 135–151). Middlesex, England: Penguin.

Wason, P. (1968). Reasoning about a rule. *Quarterly Journal of Experimental Psychology, 20,* 273–281.

Wason, P. (1983). Realism and rationality in the selection task. In J. S. B. Evans (Ed.), *Thinking and reasoning: Psychological approaches* (pp. 44–75). London: Routledge & Kegan Paul.

Wason, P., & Johnson-Laird, P. (1972). *Psychology of reasoning: Structure and content.* Cambridge, MA: Harvard University Press.

Watkins, M. J. (1977). The intricacy of memory span. *Memory & Cognition, 5,* 529–534.

Wattenmaker, W. D., Dewey, G. I., Murphy, T. D., & Medin, D. L. (1986). Linear separability and concept learning: Context, relational properties, and concept naturalness. *Cognitive Psychology, 18,* 158–194.

Waugh, N. C., & Norman, D. A. (1965). Primary memory. *Psychological Review, 72,* 89–104.

Weaver, C. (1993). Do you need a "flash" to form a flashbulb memory? *Journal of Experimental Psychology: General, 122,* 39–46.

Weber, E., & Johnson, E. (2009). Mindful judgment and decision making. *Annual Review of Psychology, 60,* 53–85.

Weber, N., Brewer, N., Wells, G., Semmler, C., & Keast, A. (2004). Eyewitness identification accuracy and response latency: The unruly 10–12-second rule. *Journal of Experimental Psychology: Applied, 10,* 139–147.

Wedell, D., & Bockenholt, U. (1990). Moderation of preference reversals in the long run. *Journal of Experimental Psychology: Human Perception and Performance, 16,* 429–438.

Wegner, D., Wenzlaff, R., Kerker, R., & Beattie, A. (1981). Incrimination through innuendo: Can media questions become public answers? *Journal of Personality and Social Psychology, 40,* 822–832.

Weisberg, R. (1986). *Creativity: Genius and other myths.* New York: Freeman.

Weisberg, R. (1988). Problem solving and creativity. In R. J. Sternberg (Ed.), *The nature of creativity* (pp. 148–176). Cambridge, England: Cambridge University Press.

Weisberg, R., & Alba, J. (1981). An examination of the alleged role of "fixation" in the solution of several "insight" problems. *Journal of Experimental Psychology: General, 110,* 169–192.

Weisberg, R., DiCamillo, M., & Phillips, D. (1978). Transferring old associations to new problems: A nonautomatic process. *Journal of Verbal Learning and Verbal Behavior, 17,* 219–228.

Weisberg, R., & Suls, J. (1973). An information processing model of Duncker's candle problem. *Cognitive Psychology, 4,* 255–276.

Weiskrantz, L. (1986). *Blindsight: A case study and implications.* New York: Oxford University Press.

Weiskrantz, L. (1997). *Consciousness lost and found.* New York: Oxford University Press.

Wells, G. L., & Bradfield, A. L. (1999). Distortions in eyewitnesses' recollections: Can the postidentification-feedback effect be moderated? *Psychological Science, 10,* 138–144.

Wells, G. L., Lindsay, R. C. L., & Ferguson, T. J. (1979). Accuracy, confidence, and juror perceptions in eyewitness identification. *Journal of Applied Psychology, 64,* 440–448.

Wells, G. L., Luus, C. A. E., & Windschitl, P. (1994). Maximizing the utility of eyewitness identification evidence. *Current Directions in Psychological Science, 3,* 194–197.

Wells, G. L., Olson, E. A., & Charman, S. D. (2002). The confidence of eyewitnesses in their identifications from lineups. *Current Directions in Psychological Science, 11,* 151–154.

Wells, G. L., Olson, E. A., & Charman, S. D. (2003). Distorted retrospective eyewitness reports as functions of feedback and delay. *Journal of Experimental Psychology: Applied, 9,* 42–51.

Wetherick, N. (1989). Psychology and syllogistic reasoning. *Philosophical Psychology, 2,* 111–124.

Wharton, C., Holyoak, K., Downing, P., & Lange, T. (1994). Below the surface: Analogical similarity and retrieval competition in reminding. *Cognitive Psychology, 26,* 64–101.

Wheeler, D. (1970). Processes in word recognition. *Cognitive Psychology, 1,* 59–85.

White, P. (1988). Knowing more than we can tell: "Introspective access" and causal report accuracy 10 years later. *British Journal of Psychology, 79,* 13–45.

Whitney, C. (2001). How the brain encodes the order of letters in a printed word: The SERIOL model and selective literature review. *Psychonomic Bulletin & Review, 8,* 221–243.

Whittlesea, B., Brooks, L., & Westcott, C. (1994). After the learning is over: Factors controlling the selective application of general and particular knowledge. *Journal of Experimental*

Psychology: Learning, Memory and Cognition, 20, 259–274.

Whittlesea, B., Jacoby, L., & Girard, K. (1990). Illusions of immediate memory: Evidence of an attributional basis for feelings of familiarity and perceptual quality. *Journal of Memory and Language, 29,* 716–732.

Whittlesea, B. W. A. (2002). False memory and the discrepancy-attribution hypothesis: The prototype-familiarity illusion. *Journal of Experimental Psychology: General, 131,* 96–115.

Whorf, B. L. (1956). *Language, thought, and reality.* Cambridge, England: Technology Press.

Wilkins, M. (1928). The effect of changed material on ability to do formal syllogistic reasoning. *Archives of Psychology, 16,* 83.

Wilson, T., & Brekke, N. (1994). Mental contamination and mental correction: Unwanted influences on judgments and evaluations. *Psychological Bulletin, 116,* 117–142.

Wilson, T. D. (2002). *Strangers to ourselves: Discovering the adaptive unconscious.* Cambridge, MA: Harvard University Press.

Wilson, T. D., & Dunn, E. W. (2004). Self-knowledge: Its limits, value, and potential for improvement. *Annual Review of Psychology, 55,* 493–518.

Wilson, T. D., Wheatley, T., Meyers, J. M., Gilbert, D., & Axsom, D. (2000). Focalism: A source of durability bias in affective forecasting. *Journal of Personality and Social Psychology, 78,* 821–836.

Winkielman, P., & Schwarz, N. (2001). How pleasant was your childhood? Beliefs about memory shape inferences from experienced difficulty of recall. *Psychological Science, 12,* 176–179.

Winnick, W., & Daniel, S. (1970). Two kinds of response priming in tachistoscopic recognition. *Journal of Experimental Psychology, 84,* 74–81.

Winograd, E., & Neisser, U. (Eds.). (1993). *Affect and accuracy in recall: Studies of "flashbulb" memories.* New York: Cambridge University Press.

Winograd, E., Peluso, J. P., & Glover, T. A. (1998). Individual differences in susceptibility to memory illusions. *Applied Cognitive Psychology, 12,* S5–S28.

Wiseman, S., & Neisser, U. (1974). Perceptual organization as a determinant of visual recognition memory. *American Journal of Psychology, 87,* 675–681.

Wisniewski, E., & Medin, D. (1994). On the interaction of theory and data in concept learning. *Cognitive Science, 18,* 221–282.

Wittgenstein, L. (1953). *Philosophical investigations* (G. E. M. Anscombe, Trans.). Oxford, England: Blackwell.

Wixted, J. (1991). Conditions and consequences of maintenance rehearsal. *Journal of Experimental Psychology: Learning, Memory and Cognition, 17,* 963–973.

Wixted, J. T. (2004). The psychology and neuroscience of forgetting. *Annual Review of Psychology, 55,* 235–269.

Wolfe, J. M. (1999). Inattentional amnesia. In V. Coltheart (Ed.), *Fleeting memories: Cognition of brief visual stimuli* (MIT Press/Bradford Books Series in Cognitive Psychology) (pp. 71–94). Cambridge, MA: MIT Press.

Wolfe, J. M. (2003). Moving towards solutions to some enduring controversies in visual search. *Trends in Cognitive Sciences, 7,* 70–76.

Wollen, K. A., Weber, A., & Lowry, D. (1972). Bizarreness versus interaction of mental images as determinants of learning. *Cognitive Psychology, 3,* 518–523.

Womelsdorf, T., Schoffelen, J.-M., Oostenveld, R., Singer, W., Desimone, R., Engel, A., & Fries, P. (2007). Modulation of neuronal interactions through neuronal synchronization. *Science, 316,* 1609–1612.

Wood, N., & Cowan, N. (1995). The cocktail party phenomenon revisited: How frequent are attention shifts to one's name in an irrelevant auditory channel? *Journal of Experimental Psychology: Learning, Memory and Cognition, 21,* 255–260.

Woodworth, R., & Sells, S. (1935). An atmosphere effect in formal syllogistic reasoning. *Journal of Experimental Psychology, 18,* 451–460.

Wright, D., & Skagerberg, E. (2007). Postidentification feedback affects real eyewitnesses. *Psychological Science, 18,* 172–177.

Wright, D. B., & Davies, G. M. (1999). Eyewitness testimony. In F. T. Davies, R. S. Nickerson, R. W. Schwaneveldt, S. T. Dumais, D. S. Lindsay, & M. T. H. Chi (Eds.), *Handbook of applied cognition* (pp. 789–818). New York: Wiley.

Wright, R. D., & Ward, L. M. (2008). *Orienting of attention.* New York: Oxford University Press.

Yantis, S. (2008). The neural basis of selective attention: Cortical sources and targets of attentional modulation. *Current Directions in Psychological Science, 17,* 86–90.

Yarmey, A. (1973). I recognize your face but I can't remember your name: Further evidence on the tip-of-the-tongue phenomenon. *Memory & Cognition, 1,* 287–290.

Yates, F. A. (1966). *The art of memory.* London: Routledge and Kegan Paul.

Yeni-Komshian, G. (1993). Speech perception. In J. B. Gleason & N. B. Ratner (Eds.), *Psycholinguistics* (pp. 90–133). New York: Harcourt Brace Jovanovich.

Yin, R. (1969). Looking at upside-down faces. *Journal of Experimental Psychology, 81,* 141–145.

Yuille, J. (Ed.). (1983). *Imagery, memory, and cognition.* Hillsdale, NJ: Erlbaum.

Yuille, J., & Cutshall, J. L. (1986). A case study of eyewitness memory of a crime. *Journal of Applied Psychology, 71,* 291–301.

Yuille, J., & Kim, C. (1987). A field study of the forensic use of hypnosis. *Canadian Journal of Behavioral Sciences Review, 19,* 418–429.

Zajonc, R. B. (1980). Feeling and thinking. *American Psychologist, 35,* 151–175.

Zaragoza, M. S., & Mitchell, K. J. (1996). Repeated exposure to suggestion and the creation of false memories. *Psychological Science, 7,* 294–300.

Zaragoza, M. S., Payment, K. E., Ackil, J. K., Drivdahl, S. B., & Beck, M. (2001). Interviewing witnesses: Forced confabulation and confirmatory feedback increases false memories. *Psychological Science, 12,* 473–477.

Zihl, J., Von Cramon, D., & Mai, N. (1983). Selective disturbance of movement vision after bilateral brain damage. *Brain, 106,* 313–340.

Zimler, J., & Keenan, J. M. (1983). Imagery in the congenitally blind: How visual are visual images? *Journal of Experimental Psychology: Learning, Memory and Cognition, 9,* 269–282.

Credits

Photographs

p. 20: AP Photo; **p. 28:** Mark Harmel/Alamy; **p. 31 A:** Courtesy Warren Museum, Harvard Medical School; **p. 31 B:** Damasio, H., Grabowski, T., Frank, R., Galaburda, A. M., and Damasio, A. R. (1994). The return of Phineas Gage: Clues about the brain from the skull of a famous patient. *Science*, *264*, 1102–05; courtesy Hanna Damasio; **p. 90, Figure 3.16:** Thompson, Peter. (1980). Margaret Thatcher: A new illusion. *Perception*, 9, 483–84; **p. 99, Figure 4.1:** Simons, D. J., and Chabris, C. F. (1999). Gorillas in our midst: Sustained inattentional blindness for dynamic events. *Perception*, 28, 1059–74. Photo courtesy of Daniel J. Simons; **p. 102:** Superstock; **p. 112** Al Tielemans/*Sports Illustrated*/Getty Images; **p. 117:** Bridgeman Art Library/Getty Images; **p. 119:** Dave and Les Jacobs/Blend Images/Corbis; **p. 123:** Galina Barskaya/Dreamstime; **p. 145:** AP Photo; **p. 157:** Justpeachy/Dreamstime; **p. 159:** Courtesy of Sidney Harris, ScienceCartoonsPlus.com; **p. 176 (top row, bottom L, bottom center):** AP Photo; **p. 176 (bottom R):** Stephen Shugerman/Getty Images; **p. 201, Figure 7.1:** Photograph from Role of schemata in memory for places, by W. F. Brewer and J. C. Treyens. *Cognitive Psychology*, 13, 207–30; **p. 209:** Kathy Burns-Millyard/Dreamstime; **p. 215:** Bubbles Photolibrary/Alamy; **p. 219:** Richard T. Nowitz/Corbis; **p. 223:** AP Photo; **p. 241:** Photofest; **p. 248 (L):** Tom Schierlitz/Getty Images; **p. 248 (R):** Janpietruszka/Dreamstime; **p. 264:** Elpis Ioannidis/Dreamstime; **p. 271:** Copyright © The New Yorker Collection, 1977, Jeff Kaufman from cartoonbank.com. All Rights Reserved; **p. 275 (top L):** Thomas Lozinski/Dreamstime; **p. 275 (top R):** Jeffrey L. Rotman/Corbis; **p. 275 (bottom R):** Crezalyn Nerona Uratsuji/Getty Images; **p. 277:** Superstock; **p. 278:** Newscom; **p. 282:** © Jim Henson Productions/Courtesy Everett Collection; **p. 286:** Vladimir Mucibabic/Dreamstime; **p. 291:** Bettmann/Corbis; **p. 305:** Maurie Hill/Dreamstime; **p. 312:** Gaetano/Corbis; **p. 315:** Granger Collection; **p. 318:** © Paramount Pictures/Courtesy: Everett Collection; **p. 328:** Image Source/Getty Images; **p. 332:** Courtesy Rebecca Homiski; **p. 345, Figure 11.3A–C:** Shepard, R. N., and Metzler, J. Mental rotation of three dimensional objects. *Science*, 171, 701–3. Copyright © 1971 by the American Association for the Advancement of Science. Reprinted by permission; **p. 353:** Illustration by Marjorie Torrey; from Lewis Carroll's *Alice in Wonderland*, illustrated by Marjorie Torrey. Copyright © 1955 by Random House, Inc. Reprinted by permission of Random House, Inc.; **p. 359:** Oriontrail/Dreamstime; **p. 364:** Alamy; **p. 369, Figure 11.11:** Intraub, H., and Richardson, M. "Boundary extension in picture memory," *Journal of Experimental Psychology*, 15, 179–87. Reprinted by permission; **p. 379:** Daniel Grizelj/Getty Images; **p. 380:** Newscom; **p. 381:** AP Photo; **p. 386:** Hulton Archive/Getty Images; **p. 392:** Jean Louis Atlan/Sygma/Corbis; **p. 396:** AP Photo; **p. 411:** Syracuse Cultural Workers "Tools for Change" catalog is 40 color pages of feminist, progressive, multicultural resources to help change the world and sustain activism. The Peace Calendar, Women Artists Datebook, over 100 posters on social, cultural and political themes, holiday cards for Solstice, Christmas, Chanukah, plus buttons, stickers, T-shirts, note cards, postcards, and books. Great fundraising products. Box 6367, Syracuse, NY 13217 800.949.5139; Fax 800.396.1449. 24-hour ordering Visa/MC; email: scw@syracuseculturalworkers.com; **p. 415:** ScienceCartoonsPlus.com; **p. 417:** ScienceCartoonsPlus.com; **p. 438:** Paul Wicks, PhD. www.PatientsLikeMe.com; **p. 440:** AP Photo; **p. 468:** Christie's Images/Corbis; **p. 484:** Newscom; **p. 486:** © John Caldwell; **p. 489:** Olivia Barr/Getty Images; **p. 494:** Justin Guariglia/Corbis; **p. 496:** Granger Collection.

Figures

p. 68, Figure 3.6: Selfridge, Oliver, "Context influences perception (pattern recognition)" from *Proceedings of the Western Computer Conference*. Copyright © 1955 by IEEE; **p. 83, Figure 3.12:** From Rumelhat and McClelland, "An interactive model of context effects in letter perception," *Psychological Review* 88.5: 375–407. Copyright © 1981 by the American Psychological Association; **p. 86, Figure 3.14:** Reprinted from *Computer Vision, Graphics and Image Processing* 32: 29–73, Irving Biederman, "Human image understanding: Recent research and a theory," Copyright © 1985, Published by Elsevier Inc., with permission from Elsevier; **p. 147, Figure 5.6A–C:** Kimberg, D'Esposito, & Farah, Fig. 1 from "Cognitive Functions in the Prefrontal Cortex—Working Memory and Executive Control," *Current Directions in Psychological Science*, Vol. 6, No. 6 (Dec. 1997), p. 186. Copyright © 1998 American Psychological Society. Reprinted by permission of Blackwell Publishing Ltd.; **p. 163, Figure 5.9:** Wiseman, S., and Neisser, U. (1974). Perceptual organization as a determinant of visual recognition memory. *American Journal of Psychology*, 87:4 (Dec. 1974). Copyright 1974 by the Board of Trustees of the University of Illinois. Used with permission of the authors and the University of Illinois Press; **p. 180: (A, D, F):** From Leeper, Robert. (1935). A study of a neglected portion of the field of learning: The development of sensory organization. *Journal of Genetic Psychology*, 46, 41–75; **p. 180: (B, C, E):** From R. F. Street, *A Gestalt Completion Test*,1931. Bureau of Publication, Teachers College, Columbia University, New York; **p. 193:** From *Fundamentals of Human Neuropsychology*, 2nd ed., by B. Kolb and I. Q. Whishaw, Fig. 20–5, p. 485, San Francisco: W. H. Freeman and Company; **p. 270:** Courtesy Sharon Armstrong; **p. 345, Figure 11.3:** From Shepard and Metzler, "Mental rotation of three-dimensional objects," *Science* 171: 701–03 (1971). Copyright © 1971, The American Association for the Advancement of Science. Reprinted with permission from AAAS. http://www.sciencemag.org/cgi/content/abstract/171/3972/701?ijkey=dc8422bafd676c8c0a72bc baeae34676c570feee&keytype2=tf_ipsecsha Ebook readers may view, browse, and/or download material for temporary copying purposes only, provided these uses are for noncommercial personal purposes. Except as provided by law, this material may not be further reproduced, distributed, transmitted, modified, adapted, performed, displayed, published, or sold in whole or in part, without prior written permission from the publisher; **p. 430, Figure 13.7:** Tversky, A., and Kahneman, D. From "Rational choice and the framing of decisions," *Journal of Business*, 59:4, Part 2. Copyright © 1986 by the University of Chicago Press. Reprinted by permission; **p. 459, Figure 14.11A–C:** R. Bootzen, *Psychology Today: An Introduction*. Copyright the McGraw-Hill Companies. Reproduced with permission of the McGraw-Hill Companies.

Color Insert

Figure 1 (R): Children's Hospital and Medical Center/Corbis; **Figure 3:** Dr. M. Phelps and Dr. J. Mazziotta et al./Neurology/Photo Researchers, Inc.; **Figure 4 (L):** James Cavallini/Photo Researchers, Inc.; **(center):** G. Tompkinson/Photo Researchers, Inc.; **(R):** Scott Camazine/Photo Researchers, Inc.; **Figure 5A–C:** Courtesy of Tong, F., Kakayma, K., Vaughen, J. T., and Kanwisher, N. Binocular rivalry and visual awareness in human extrastriate cortex. *Neuron*, 21, 735–59; **Figure 6 A–C:** From Coren, Porac, and Ward, *Sensation and Perception*, 3rd Edition (1989). Reprinted with permission of John Wiley and Sons., Inc.; **Figure 7B:** SPL/Photo Researchers, Inc.; **Figure 7C:** CNRI/SPL/Photo Researchers, Inc.; **Figure 7D:** Guigoz/Dr. A Privat/Petit Format/Science Source/Photo Researchers, Inc.; **Figure 8A:** Photograph by Jeffery Grosscup; **Figure 9:** Courtesy of Think Fun; **Figure 10 (top):** Galina Barskaya/Dreamstime; **(center):** Titania1980/Dreamstime; **(bottom):** Ivan Hafizov/Dreamstime; **Figure 11: (beans)** Py2000/Dreamstime; **(face):** Jay M. Schulz/Dreamstime; **Figure 12:** Rykoff Collection/Corbis; **Figure 14:** Ranganath, C., Yonelinas, A. P., Cohen, M. X., Dy, C. J., Tom, S., and D'Esposito, M. (2003). Dissociable correlates for familiarity and recollection in the medial temporal lobes. *Neuropsychologia*, 42, 2–13; **Figure 15 (all):** Courtesy of Daniel Reisberg; **Figure 16 (L):** Sean Adair/Reuters/Corbis; **(R):** Bettmann/Corbis; **Figure 17 (top L):** Getty Images; **(all others):** Eric Isselée/Dreamstime.

Author Index

De Neys, W., 398, 400
Dennett, D., 495, 498
De Pauw, K. W., 26
De Renzi, E., 89
Derr, R. F., 190
Desimone, R., 53, 105
Desmond, J., 150
D'Esposito, M., 146
Dess, N. K., 469
Detre, G., 36
Dewey, G. I., 294
Dexter, H. R., 217
DeYoe, E. A., 49
Dhaliwal, H., 114
Diamond, R., 91
Diana, R. A., 176, 177
DiCamillo, M., 455
Dickinson, C. A., 368
Diener, E., 436
Dinges, D., 216
Do, A., 436
Dobbins, I, 177
Dobbins, I. G., 177, 178
Dodds, R., 472
Doherty, M. E., 391, 411, 412
Dolan, P. O., 177
Dolan, R., 438
Donnelly, C., 453
Dooling, D. J., 162
Dougherty, T., 368
Douglas, C., 412
Douglass, A. B., 218
Downing, P., 455
Downs, J., 433
Draguhn, A., 53
Drain, M., 91
Drews, F. A., 118
Drivadahl, S. B., 209
Driver, J., 99, 103, 115
Drummey, A. B., 189
Duara, R., 26
Duchaine, B. C., 91
Dudai, Y., 224
Dueck, A., 162
Dufau, S., 75
Dufresne, R., 458
Dumit, J., 36
Dunbar, K., 456
Dunbar, S., 282
Duncan, J., 119, 122, 147
Duncker, K., 462
Dunkle, M., 462
Dunn, E. W., 482
Dunning, D., 184, 219, 433
Durgin, F. H., 127

Eagleman, D. M., 355
East, R., 223
Easterbrook, J. A., 224
Eberhard, K. M., 326
Ebert, J. E. J., 439
Eckstein, M., 105
Eddy, D. M., 395

Edelstyn, N. M. J., 27
Egan, D., 460
Egeth, H., 102, 103
Egly, R., 115
Egner, T., 122
Eich, J. E., 169
Einhorn, H., 395
Einstein, G. O., 365
Eisenberg, P., 351
Elliot, M. A., 53
Ellis, A., 89
Ellis, H. D., 26, 27, 28, 173
Elstein, A., 378
Emslie, H., 122
Engel, A. K., 492
Engelkamp, J., 352
Engle, R., 120, 121, 122, 127, 141, 144, 147,
    400, 498
Epley, N., 384, 405
Ericsson, K., 461
Ericsson, K. A., 142, 460, 461
Ernest, C., 354
Ernst, G., 454
Ervin-Tripp, S., 328
Estes, Z., 287
Evans, J. S. B. T., 391, 398, 402, 411, 415,
    416, 418, 420, 425, 427
Eylon, B., 460
Eyre, R. N., 405
Eysenck, M. W., 119

Faglioni, P., 89
Farah, M. J., 50, 91, 92, 146, 348, 349, 353
Farinacci, S., 181
Fay, D., 182
Feeney, A., 296, 416
Feldman, H., 331, 400, 498
Feltovich, P., 458
Feng, C., 451
Fenske, M. J., 100
Ferguson, C., 321
Ferguson, T. J., 217
Ferreira, M. B., 398, 400, 406
Fiedler, K., 182, 402
Finke, R., 346, 347, 351, 355, 357, 451
Finucane, M. L., 400, 436, 437
Fischer, I., 383
Fischhoff, B., 378, 381, 437
Fisher, R., 171, 212, 216
Fisher, S. E., 331
Fleck, J., 471
Fleischman, D., 194
Flynn, M., 217
Fodor, J., 263
Foerde, K., 188
Foley, H., 177
Fong, G., 405
Ford, M., 427
Forgas, J., 223
Forstmeier, S., 264
Fox, C., 225
Fox, N. A., 189
Frackowiak, R. S. J., 330

Franklin, S., 490, 492
Franks, J. J., 162
Frederick, S., 437
Fredrickson, B., 436
Freedman, J., 322
French, R. M., 264, 456
Frey, D., 411
Freyd, J. J., 226
Fried, L. S., 281
Friedman, A., 364, 367, 368
Friedman-Hill, S. R., 53, 70
Fries, P., 53
Fromkin, V., 319, 327
Frost, P., 219
Fthenaki, K., 189
Fukui, M., 106
Fulero, S., 411
Fusella, V., 348

Gabbay, P., 211
Gable, P. A., 224
Gabrieli, J., 150
Gabrieli, J. D. E., 194
Gaeth, G., 433
Gage, P., 30, 31
Gaissmaier, W., 406
Galanter, E., 13
Gallistel, C. R., 335
Gallo, D. A., 204
Galton, F., 340, 341, 354
Gandhi, M., 385
Garcia-Marques, L., 398
Garcia-Marques, T, 182
Gardiner, J. M., 177
Garnham, A., 415
Garry, M., 211, 218
Gathercole, S., 22, 144, 219
Gaudreau, D., 185
Gauthier, I., 91
Gazzaniga, M. S., 50, 53, 485, 492
Geiselman, R. E., 212
Gelade, G., 53, 69
Gelman, S., 287
Gentner, D., 289, 293, 453, 456, 457
Geraerts, E., 209, 226, 227
German, T., 287, 463
Ghetti, S., 227
Gibson, E., 72
Gick, M., 453, 454, 456
Giesbrecht, T., 227
Giesler, R. B., 384
Gigerenzer, G., 402, 403, 406, 421
Gilbert, D., 441
Gilbert, D. T., 400, 439
Gilbert, S. J., 147
Gilhooly, K. J., 415, 416, 447
Gilovich, T., 384, 391, 395, 396, 411, 412,
    437
Girard, K., 188
Girotto, V., 402, 420, 423, 427
Gisquet-Verrier, P., 189
Glanzer, M., 136, 137, 139
Glaser, R., 458

Subject Index

Note: Italicized page locators indicate figures; notes and tables are denoted with n and t.

verbal coding of, 362–64, *363*, *364*
vividness of, 354–55
image-scanning experiments, map of fictional island used in, 343, *343*
image-scanning procedure, 343
implicit memory, 178–84, 196–97
  attribution to wrong source, 184
  attribution to wrong stimulus, 183–84
  cognitive unconscious and, 481
  consciousness and, 499
  explicit memory and, 193–94
  false fame test and, 180–81
  familiarity and, 187–89, *188*
  hypothesis about, 185–86, 186n
  illusion of truth and, 181–82, *183*
  theoretical treatments of, 184–89
  without awareness, 178–80, *180*, 185
inattentional blindness, 101–2, *102*
incidental learning, 152, 152t
incubation, creativity and, 469, 472–73
indirect memory tests, 179–80
induction, 375, 407
inferences based on theories, 295–96
inference to best explanation, 12
information processing
  memory acquisition and, 135, 165
  modal model of, 135–36
  view of memory, 134–35, *135*
inhibitory connections, 82, *83*
initial state, 445
inner ear, 17, 18, 19, 21
inner speech, 21
inner voice, 17, 18, 19, 21
input nodes, 249, 250
insight problems
  self-assessments and, *471*
  studies of, *470*
integrative agnosia, 70
intentional behavior, consciousness and, 494
intentional learning, 152t, 153–54
interactive models, 93–94
interference and forgetting, 213, 214, *214*, 221
interpolated activity, recency effect and, *139*
interpret-as-you-go tendency, 324
introspection, 8, 9, 23, 340–41, 482–85, *484*
intrusion errors, 202, 204, 369
intuition, reasoning and, 399
invalid syllogisms, 414

jealous husbands problem, 454–55, *455*, 456
judgment, 375–408
  anchoring and adjustment in, 384–85
  assessment of, 395–407
    background knowledge and, 404–5
    circumstances and, 399–400
    codable data and, 402–4
    data format in, 400–402, *401*
    dual-process models and, 398–99
    evidence and, 406–7

more sophisticated strategies in, *396*, 396–98
statistical training and, 405–6
covariation and, 385–95, 407–8
  base-rate neglect in, 392, 394–95, 401
  base rates in, 392–93, 393n, 401, *401*, 404
  illusory, *386*, 386–88, 391–92, 392
  theory- and data-driven detection, 388–91, *389*, *390*
heuristics, 376–84, 403
  affect, 437
  attribute substitution, 377, *381*
  availability, 377–81, *379*, *380*, *381*
  reasoning from single case to entire population and, 383–84
  reasoning from the population to an instance and, 382–83
  representativeness, 377, 378, 381–82, 395, 397, 407, 435–36
justification for action, consciousness and, 494–94, *496*

Kantian logic, 13, 17
Kennedy assassination, 224
knowledge, 267
  about animals, *244*
  background, 5–6, 294, 296, 297–98, 404–5
  distributed, 80–81
  diversity of, 370
  generic, 205, 221
  locally represented, 80
  past, *see* past knowledge
  schematic, 204–6, *205*
    evidence for, 206–7
    reliance on, 220
  scientific study of, 4
  self, 498–99
  spatial, 364
  visual, 339–72, 371
Korsakoff's syndrome, 190, 191, 192–93, 486

labiodental sounds, 306
language, 301–37
  biological roots of, 329–34, 337
    aphasias, 329–30, *330*
    learning, 330–34, *332*
  competence vs. performance, 319
  generativity of, 314, 315
  hierarchical structure of, *303*
  organization of, 302–3, *303*
  phonology, 304–12
    categorical perception, 309–10, *311*
    complexity of speech perception, 306–7, *307*
    phoneme combinations, 310, 312, *312*
    production of speech, *304*, 304–6, *305*
    speech perception aids, 308–9
  prescriptive rules, 317–18
  sentence parsing, 322–29, *327*, *328*
  syntax, *see* syntax

thought and, 334–36, 337
universals in, 321–22
use of, 326–29, *328*
words and, *313*, 313–15
larynx, 304, *304*
lateral fissure, 32
lateral geniculate nucleus (LGN), 42, 48, *48*, *49*, 50
lateral inhibition, 42–44, *43*, 63
late selection hypothesis, 105
law of large numbers, 382–83
learning
  in connectionism, 261–62
  from images, 357–60, *358*, *359*
  incidental, 152, 152t
  intentional, 152t, 153–54
  language, 330–34, *332*
  optimal, 167, 194–95
  source memory and, 177
  state-dependent, *169*, 169–71, *170*, 196, *241*
  see also memory acquisition
learning algorithms, 262
learning history, record of, 9
learning theory, 10
lemons and counterfeits, 285–89, *286*
lens, of eye, 41, *41*
lesions, 33, 39–40, 50
letter combinations, 75, 249
letter detectors, 75, 249
letter span, 14
lexical-decision task, 178, 179, 242–43
LGN, *see* lateral geniculate nucleus (LGN)
L. H. (brain damage case), 353
limbic system, 32
limited-capacity system, 110
linguistic relativity, 334
linguistic rules, *303*, 317–19, *318*
linguistic units, hierarchy of, *303*
linguistic universals, 321–22
listening, selective, 98–116, *99*
list presentation, serial-position effect and rate of, *140*
lobes
  occipital, 32, *37*, 38, 42, *48*, 194
  parietal, 32, *37*, 39–40, 70
  temporal, 27, 32, *37*
localization of function, 36
locally represented knowledge, 80
local representations, 259
logic, 414–25
  conditional statements and, 416–18, *417*, *418*
  deductive, 424–25
  detecting cheaters via, 420–21
  errors in, *415*, 415–16
  four-card task in, 418–20, *419*, *420*
  Kantian, 13, 17
  necessity and sufficiency in, 423
  of perception, 65–67, *66*
  pragmatic reasoning schemata, 421–22, *422*, 442
  problem content and, 420

priming (cont.)
    stimulus-based, 109–10
    types of, 107–9, 108t
Princess Diana's death, 224, 225
problem content, effects of, 419–20
problem-solving, 444–77
    creativity and, 467–77
        case studies of, 467–69, *468*
        incubation in, 469, 472–73
        moment of illumination in, 469–71,
            470, 471
        nature of, 473–76, *474, 475*
    defining the problem in, 461–67
        Einstellung, 463–65, *465*
        functional fixedness, 462–63, *463, 464*
        ill-defined and well-defined problems,
            461–62
        outside the box, *466*, 466–67
    general methods of, 445–53
        heuristics, 448, *449*, 450–51, *451*, 476
        mental models and mental images,
            451, *451, 452*
        pictures and diagrams in, 452–53
        search process, 445–48, *446, 447*
    goal state in, 445
    initial state in, 445
    operators in, 445
    past knowledge in, *see* past knowledge
    path constraints in, 445
    protocols, 448
    sets, 463–64, 467, 469, 476–77, 485, 488
    working backwards in, 450
problem space, 445–46, *446, 447*
processing fluency, 185–86, 186n, 187, 196
process/product distinction, 480–81
production task, 273
propositional networks and ACT, 251–53,
    252, 253
prosody, 327, 334
prosopagnosia, 89, 90, 91–92
prototypes, 271–78, 292, 299, 300
    counterfeits and, 286, *286*
    exemplars and, 280–83, *282*
    fuzzy boundaries and graded member-
        ship of, 272–73
    resemblance via, 283–90
    testing notion of, 273–76, 274t, *275, 276*
psychology, cognitive, *see* cognitive
    psychology

questions
    framing of, *432*, 432–33
    normative, 410

rating task, 274
reason-based choice, 433, 435–36
reasoning, 409–43
    about conditional statements, 416–18,
        417, 418
    about syllogisms, 414–15, *415*
    cognitive unconscious and, 481
    confirmation and disconfirmation and,
        410–14, *411*

belief perseverance in, 412–14
confirmation bias, *411*, 411–12
memory for disconfirming evidence,
    412
in decision-making, 427–42
    emotional factors in, 436–39, *438*
    framing of
        outcomes in, 429–32, *430, 431*
        questions and evidence in, *432*,
            432–33
        maximizing utility vs. seeing reasons,
            433–35, *434*
    normative theories of, 440–42
    predicting our own values, 439–40,
        440
    reason-based choice and, 435–36
    utility theory in, 427–29
evolutionary perspective on, 420–21
exemplar-based, 279
intuition and, 399
logic and, 414–25
    deductive, 424–25
    detecting cheaters via, 420–21
    errors in, *415*, 415–16
    four-card task and, 418–20, *419, 420*
    necessity and sufficiency in, 423
    pragmatic reasoning schemata,
        421–22, *422*, 442
    problem content and, 419–20
    mental models in, 425–27, *426*
    non-spatial, 363–64, *364*
    from the population to an instance,
        382–83
    from single case to entire population,
        383–84
recall
    cued, 175
    free, 136
recency effect, 136, *139*
receptive fields, 45–47, *46, 47*
recognition
    by components, 84–85, *85, 86*
    of degraded pictures, *86*
    errors, 78–80, *79*, 95
    of faces, 27, 29–30, 89, *89*–92, *90*
    memory tests and, 175
    object, *see* object recognition
    pattern, 91, 95
    via multiple views, 87–88
    viewpoint-dependent, 85, 87
    viewpoint-independent, 85
    visual perception in, 59, 60–67
    word, *see* word recognition
reconstruction, after-the-fact, 483–85
recovered memories, 227
recovery from confusion, 75–76, *77*
reference frame, *359*
regret, decision-making and, 437, 439
rehearsal
    articulatory, 22
    elaborative (relational), 148–49
    memory and, 137–38, 148–50, 165, 229
    types of, 148–50

rehearsal loop, 15–16, *16*, 17, 19, 145, *145*
relational (or elaborative) rehearsal, 148–49
remembering, long, long-term, 227–30, *228*
repetition priming, 71, 74, 88, 93, 178–79
representativeness, 443
representativeness heuristic, 377, 378,
    381–82, 395, 397, 407, 435–36
repressed memories, 226–27
research, in cognitive psychology: an
    example, 13–22
research psychology, field of, 7
resemblance, categorization via, 283–90,
    291, 291–92
response selector, 120, 124
response threshold, 73, 238
response times, 107, *344*
retention intervals, 212–15, *214*
retina, 41, *41*, 42
retrieval, *see* memory retrieval
retrieval blocks, 254–55, 258
retrieval failure, 213, 214, 216
retrieval paths, 157, 168, 172–74, *174*, 196,
    202, 220
retrograde amnesia, 189
right prefrontal cortex, 27
risk-aversion, 431
risk-seeking, 431
rods, of eye, 41
Rorschach tests, 386, *386*, 387
rule-driven thought, 399

sample bias, 391
sample size, 382–83, 397, 398, 406
San Francisco earthquake (1989), 225
schemata, 205–6, 369, 421–22, *422*
schematic knowledge, 204–6, *205*
    evidence for, 206–7
    reliance on, 220
schizophrenia, 28
scientific study of knowledge, 4
segmentation, speech, 307
selection task, 418
selective attention, 110
selective listening, 98–116, *99*
selective priming, 106–7
self, memory and, 222–23
self-knowledge, 498–99
self-reference effect, 222
self-report data, 340–41
self-schema, 222
semantic bootstrapping, 334
semantic facts, time needed in confirming
    of, *245*
semantics in parsing, 325–26
sensory effects in imagery, 350–51
sentences, 302–3, *303*, 315
    active, 324
    d-structure of, 320–21
    in extralinguistic context, 326, *327*
    garden-path, 323–24, *326*
    parsing of, 322–29, *327, 328*
    passive, 324
    s-structure of, 316–17

syntax of, 315–22, 337
  linguistic rules and competence, 317–19, *318*
  linguistic universals, 321–22
  phrase structure of, 316–17, *317*, 319–20, *320*
sentence verification, 243–46, *244*, *245*, 273
sentience, 498
serial-position curve, 137, *137*, 138
serial-position effect, rate of list presentation and, *140*
serial processing, 48
sets, problem-solving, 463–64, 467, 469, 476–77, 485, 488
shadowing, 98
shallow processing, 152–53, 152t, 165–66
short-term memory, 135
similarity, complexity of, 288–90
simultaneous multiple constraint satisfaction, 259–60, *260*
single-cell recording, single neurons and, 44–45, 55
sleep, 493–94, *494*
SLI (specific language impairment), 331
solving problems, *see* problem-solving
somatic markers, 438, *439*
somatosensory projection area, *37*, 38
sounds
  alveolar, 306
  bilabial, 306
  categorization of, 309
  labiodental, 306
  memory acquisition and, 171–72, 172t
  phonology, *see* phonology
source confusion, 184, 481
source memory, familiarity vs., 175, *176*, 176–78, 196, 370
source monitoring, 213
space-based vs. object-based, *112*, 112–15, *114*
span test, 14, 17–18, 22
spatial attention, chronometric studies and, 110–11
spatial images, 351–53, 360, 371
spatial knowledge, 364
spatial position, 52, 53
specificity of resources, 117–18
specific language impairment (SLI), 331
speech, 336
  aids to perception of, 308–9
  categorical perception of, 309–10, *311*
  coarticulation of, 307
  complex perception of, 306–7, *307*
  inner, 21
  performance errors in, 319
  phonemes and, 310, 312, *312*
  production of, *304*, 304–6, *305*
speech segmentation, 307
split-brain patients, *34*
split infinitives, 318
spontaneous behavior, consciousness and, 494

spreading activation, 237–39, *238*, 242–43, 255–56, 472
s-structure, 316–17
state-dependent learning, 169–71, 196, *241*
  and change in physical circumstances, *170*
  experiment design, *169*
statistics, training in, 405–6
stereotypes, illusory covariation and, 393
stimulus-based priming, 109–10
striate cortex, damage to, 487
Stroop interference, 126–27, *127*
subcortical structures of the brain, 32–33
subgoals, in problem-solving, 458–60, *459*
subproblems, 450
subthreshold activation, 238, 242
subvocalization, 16–17, *18*, 20
sufficient condition, 423
summation, 238
superordinate labeling, 277
syllogisms
  categorical, 414, *415*
  invalid, 414
  reasoning about, 414–15, *415*
  valid, 414
symbolic memory, 367
synapse, 44
syntax, 315–22, 337
  as guide to parsing, 324–25
  linguistic rules and competence, 317–19, *318*
  linguistic universals, 321–22
  phrase structure, 316–17, *317*
  D-structure, 320–21
  function of, 319–20, *320*
System 1 thinking, 399, 400, 401, 404, 406, 408
System 2 thinking, 399–401, 404–5, 406, 407, 408

tachistoscope, 70, 95, 179, 180
task-general resources, 119
task-specific resources, 118
temporal lobes, 27, 32, *37*
thalamus, 32
theories
  categorization and, 294–95
  concepts as, 290–99
  inferences based on, 295–96
theory-driven covariation, 388–91, *389*, *390*
thought, language and, 334–36, 337
threshold, 44
tip-of-the-tongue (TOT) phenomenon, 255, 472
TMS (transcranial magnetic stimulation), 36, 70, 350
tobacco industry, 484
token nodes, 252, *253*
top-down processing, 93, 95
TOT (tip-of-the-tongue) phenomenon, 255, 472

Tower of Hanoi problem, 448, *449*
training, in use of statistics, 405–6
transcendental method, 12
transcranial magnetic stimulation (TMS), 36, 70, 350
traumatic memories, 225–27
triangle forms, *69*
tumor problem, 453, 454, *454*, 456
two-point acuity, 351, 355
two-string problem, 463, *464*
type nodes, 252, *253*
typicality, 299
  bias, 283
  category membership and, 283, 286
  concepts influenced by, 290, 296
  exemplars and, *278*, 278–80
  in families, *270*
typicality ratings, 284t
typicality studies, 273–76, 274t, *275*, *276*

unattended channel, 98
unattended inputs, 99–100, 129
unconscious, cognitive, *see* cognitive unconscious
unconscious perception, 102–3, *103*
unconscious thought, *see* cognitive unconscious
understanding
  memory acquisition and, 160–62, 166
  memory errors and, 202–3, 203t
unilateral neglect syndrome, 113
upside-down faces, recognition of, *89*, 89–90, *90*
U-serial position curve, *137*
utility maximization, 429
utility theory, 427–29, 433, 442–43

valid syllogisms, 414
variability, exemplars and, 280–81
vase/profiles figure, 62, 63, *63*
ventriloquism, 60
verbal coding of visual materials, 362–64, *363*, *364*
verb phrase, 317, *317*, 320
verification and creativity, 469
viewpoint-dependent recognition, 85, 87
viewpoint-independent recognition, 85
visual acuity, 350
visual agnosia, 39
visual imagery, 340–60, 371–72
  chronometric studies of, 341–44, *343*, *344*
  demand character and, 347
  individual differences in, 353, 353–55
  introspections about, 340–41
  mental rotation and, *345*, 345–46, *346*
  sensory effects in, 350–51
  spatial imagery and, 351–53
  see also images
visual inputs, 97, 98–99
visual knowledge, 339–72, 371
  see also images; long-term visual memory; visual imagery

visual maps, and firing synchrony, 52–54, 55
visual perception, 59, 60–67, 94, 349, 491
visual processing pathways, 48, *49*
visual search tasks, 69
visual shapes, memory span and, 18–19
visual system, 40–55
    lateral inhibition, 42–44, *43*, 63
    optic nerve, 42, 49–50
    parallel processing in, *48*, 48–51, *49*, *51*
    photoreceptors, 40–42, *41*
    receptive fields, 45–47, *46*, *47*
    single neurons and single-cell recording, 44–45
    visual maps and firing synchrony, 52–54
visuospatial buffer, 145
vivid imagery, 354–55
vocal folds (vocal cords), 304, 305–6, 312
voicing, 304

water-jar problem, 464–65, *465*
water-lilies problem, 450, *451*
well-defined problems, 461–62
well-formedness
    feature nets and, 75
    in word recognition, 72

Wernicke's area, 329, *330*
what system, 50, *51*, 55
where system, 50, *51*, 55
winner-takes-all system, 257–58, 257n
WMC, *see* working-memory capacity (WMC)
word detectors, 83
word recognition, 70–73, 95
    errors in, 72–73, 78–80, *79*, 95
    factors in, 70–74
    feature nets and, 73–81
    McClelland and Rumelhart model of, 82–84, *83*, 93–94
    repetition priming in, 71, 74, 88, 93
    well-formedness in, 72
    word-superiority effect in, 71, 72, 78, *88*, 95
words, *303*, 313
    building, 314–15
    linguistic rules and, *303*
    meaning and, *313*, 313–14
word-stem completion, 179
word-superiority effect, 71, 72, 78, *88*, 95
working backward, in problem-solving, 450
working memory, 14–23, 135–36, 140–48, 165

active nature of, 143–44, *144*
brain damage and, 146–47, *147*
in broader context, 22
function of, 141
holding capacity of, 141–43
initial observations on, 14
long-term memory vs., 136–40, *137*, *139*, *140*
nature of, 19–22, 147–48
neuronal workspace and, 493
proposal in, 15–17
short-term memory as, 135
span test of, 14, 17–18, 22
working-memory capacity (WMC), 121, 124, 144, 400, 408
working-memory system, 15, 144–45, *145*
    central executive in, 15, 16–17, *18*, 23, 120–22, 144–47, *147*, 165
    evidence for, 17–22, 23
    low-level assistants in, 15, *16*, 23
    phonological buffer in, 17
    rehearsal loop in, 17, 19, 145, *145*
    visuospatial buffer in, 145
World Trade Center attack (2001), 224

Great Minds Think Alike.

Freud	LeDoux
Nisbett	Horney
Stack Sullivan	Caccioppo
Gazzaniga	Schore
Erikson	Eichenbaum
Gilovich	Skinner
Lacan	Mangun
Gross	Keltner
Pinker	Siegel
Heatherton	Heine
Gleitman	Bruner
Bradbury	Marcus
Reisberg	Kohler
Halpern	Karney
Jung	Seligman
Funder	Watson
Ekman	Winnicott
Mangun	Morling
Rollo May	Whybrow
Kandel	Deacon

Since 1923, many of the world's greatest psychological thinkers have chosen W. W. Norton to be their publishing home.

We are proud to be their choice.

At W. W. Norton, we are passionate about publishing books that contribute significantly to the study of psychology. Our textbooks are authored by dedicated researchers and teachers who excel at making this remarkable science relevant and accessible for students.

We would be honored to be your choice, too.

INDEPENDENCE IS A VIRTUE.

W. W. Norton & Company
Independent and Employee-owned Since 1923
WWNORTON.COM/COLLEGE/PSYCH